Instructor's Edition
Invitation

French for Communication and Cultural Awareness

SECOND EDITION

Gilbert A. Jarvis
The Ohio State University

Thérèse M. Bonin
The Ohio State University

Donald E. Corbin
James Madison University

Diane W. Birckbichler
The Ohio State University

Holt, Rinehart and Winston
New York   Chicago   San Francisco   Philadelphia
Montreal   Toronto   London   Sydney
Tokyo   Mexico City   Rio de Janeiro   Madrid

Publisher Rita Pérez
Acquisitions Editor Vincent Duggan
Developmental Editor Ernst Schrader
Special Projects Editor Pamela Forcey
Production Manager Lula Als
Design Supervisor Renée Davis
Text Design and Layout Caliber Design Planning
Drawings Ed Malsberg

Composition and camera work Precision Typographers, Inc.
Printing and binding Von Hoffmann Press, Inc.

Reproduced on the cover:
Henri Matisse. *Jazz (2). The Circus*. 1947.
Copyright © Museum of Modern Art, New York, 1962.

Photographic credits appear at the end of the book.

Library of Congress Cataloging in Publication Data

Main entry under title:

Invitation : French for communication and cultural awareness.

   English and French.
   Includes index.
   1. French language—Grammar—1950- . 2. French
language—Text-books for foreign speakers—English.
I. Jarvis, Gilbert A.
PC2112.I5 1984   448.2'421   84-4578

ISBN 0-03-069272-5 Instructor's Edition

Student Edition: ISBN 0-03-069271-7

CBS COLLEGE PUBLISHING
Holt, Rinehart and Winston
The Dryden Press
Saunders College Publishing

Introduction to the Instructor's Edition

Invitation: French for Communication and Cultural Awareness and its supplements, *Invitation à écouter et à parler*, the laboratory manual and tape program, and *Invitation à écrire*, the workbook, are a complete beginning college French program. As the title indicates, the book invites students from the first moments to communicate meaningfully in French and at the same time to understand better the daily life and attitudes of French-speaking people. *Invitation* is designed to accommodate diverse instructional needs rather than to impose a single methodology: its flexible format can be easily adapted to different teaching styles, student preferences, and course objectives and to varying amounts of instructional time. Although equal emphasis is given to the four language skills, this flexibility allows instructors who so desire to emphasize a particular skill or group of skills.

This second edition of *Invitation* is a true revision. More than half of the readings and conversations have been changed or modified; there is an increased emphasis on culture throughout the book; a new thematic vocabulary section with accompanying communication activities has been added to each chapter; changes in the sequencing and presentation of grammar have been made where appropriate; all grammar exercises have been contextualized; and communication activities have been added or modified with a particular emphasis on increasing the student's ability to ask as well as answer questions. True proficiency is the goal of this book.

The goal of communication

The primary goal of *Invitation* is to help students to acquire communication skills within culturally significant contexts. *Communication* refers not only to the ability to express ideas orally or in writing but also to the capacity to comprehend linguistic and cultural meaning while reading or listening to French. To achieve these communication aims with the greatest possible flexibility, *Invitation* includes the following features as an integral part of its organization.

1. *Communication activities accompany all grammar presentations.*
   Varied activities provide for immediate meaningful practice of every new grammar structure. Communication therefore takes place at once rather than at some unspecified time in the future.

2. *Considerable cognate vocabulary is used to provide maximum communication potential with minimal learning loads.*
   The book capitalizes, especially in early chapters, on the large number of French

words that resemble English words. Drills are included to accommodate the special pronunciation problems of cognate vocabulary.

3. *Presentation of each grammar topic is sequenced for greatest efficiency.*
   Each grammar structure is presented comprehensively with ample examples, practiced in carefully structured drills and preparation activities, and then applied meaningfully in communication activities.

4. *Chapters are thematically organized.*
   Readings and grammar are related to a broad chapter theme to maximize communicative potential and facilitate learning. Attitudes, values, and concerns of people from all parts of the French-speaking world are reflected in the reading passages and cultural notes. In addition, each introductory passage is followed by a special communication section that provides vocabulary and expressions related to the chapter theme.

5. *Chapter sequencing encourages successful communication at the earliest possible time.*
   Because topics and structures are sequenced in terms of learning difficulty and usefulness in communication, early chapters allow students to acquire quickly a genuine feeling of being able to speak French.

6. *Grammar coverage is comprehensive.*
   The most common structures and patterns of French are included in the book, although all need not be covered. Flexibility in the coverage of topics is therefore possible.

7. *Vocabulary is presented in context.*
   Principal noncognate vocabulary is presented in the reading passages, which are followed by communication sections that immediately illustrate its use in an appropriate context. Important vocabulary words are listed at the end of each chapter.

8. *Cultural insights are presented throughout the book.*
   Cultural content is not limited to scattered cultural notes but is integrated into various activities throughout the book: in culturally authentic dialogues and reading passages; in contextualized activities that have a cultural context; in many notes in the Instructor's Edition explaining cultural allusions in the text or presenting additional cultural information; and in various communication activities.

9. *Readings are authentic.*
   Rather than contrived readings that fit grammatical structures, the majority of readings in *Invitation* have been taken from French magazines and simplified so that they can be read and understood by beginning language students.

10. *Options are presented throughout the book.*
    Abundant drills and activities are provided so that instructors and students can select those that are best suited to their purposes. Others can be omitted with no resulting confusion. In addition, the organization of the book itself is flexible, and each section can be used in a variety of ways.

⚜ Organization of the book

Invitation is divided into twenty-two chapters. It also contains a preliminary chapter, a final chapter that focuses on the *passé simple (Invitation à la lecture)*, and appendixes. All twenty-two chapters include the following sections:

1. *Introduction*: These introductory texts of varying subject matter and format (e.g., dialogues, interviews, newscasts, monologues) provide diverse contexts for devel-

opment of reading ability and acquisition of cultural insights. New noncognate vocabulary is glossed in the margin to ensure immediate comprehension of unfamiliar words.

Compréhension: This section evaluates the student's understanding of the *Introduction*.

Notes culturelles: Aspects of the introductory reading are elaborated upon in brief descriptions of culture, attitudes, or life in French-speaking countries. The *Notes culturelles* are given in English in the first ten chapters of the book and in French thereafter.

Et vous?: This section introduces new vocabulary centered around a topic that is related to the chapter theme. Varied communication activities involve the student in the active use of this newly presented vocabulary before studying the grammar of the chapter.

2. *Grammaire*: Each grammar topic is presented and practiced in three phases:
Présentation: The grammar structure and examples are presented. Accompanying it are simple pattern drills that appear only in the Instructor's Edition. These drills help students learn to pronounce the new forms and to manipulate them in a simple, controlled way.

Préparation: The grammar topic is practiced in structured, lifelike situations. Many exercises are set in cultural contexts, thereby reinforcing the authenticity of the language used and its value for real-life communication while also providing insights into *Francophone* cultures.

Communication: Varied formats invite the student to use the language to send and receive information that is personally meaningful. These activities give students the opportunity to use the language in situations where such communication takes precedence over grammatical accuracy.

3. *Synthèse*: The *Synthèse* recombines and integrates the grammar and vocabulary used in the chapter and provides cultural insights. It provides further reading practice and introduces new vocabulary in context. The *Synthèse* is followed by *Compréhension* questions and related *Notes culturelles*. In addition, *Communication* activities further integrate the chapter's grammar and/or thematic content while giving students additional opportunities for personal expression.

4. *Vocabulaire*: Each chapter is followed by a list of vocabulary words intended for active use in that chapter and in subsequent chapters. The lists contain the most important noncognate and cognate words used in the lesson or page references for them. Where appropriate, the vocabulary lists are organized in thematic clusters (e.g., sports, foods, etc.).

5. *Prononciation*: The most significant features of spoken French are described in each of the first ten chapters. Practice of both individual sounds and longer sentences containing critical sounds is included.

6. *Appendix*: The appendix contains a key to the phonetic alphabet, a glossary of grammar terminology, verb charts for regular, irregular, and spelling-changing verbs, vocabularies (French–English and English–French), and a grammar index. Because students are not always aware of appendix material, it may be a good idea to point out the different components. The glossary of grammar terms may be particularly helpful to students who lack a knowledge of such terminology and therefore have difficulty understanding some of the explanations in the book.

⚜ The supplementary materials

Tape program and laboratory manual

The tape program and laboratory manual have been designed to provide students with the opportunity to practice their oral skills outside class. Each chapter in *Invitation* has an accompanying tape divided into two twenty- to thirty-minute segments.

Each tape includes: (1) readings of the *Introduction* and *Synthèse* passages; (2) two or three activities for each grammar topic; (3) a listening comprehension passage related to the chapter theme and integrating its vocabulary and grammar. In addition, a pronunciation section (Chapters 1–10) and a short thematic dictation are included at the end of each tape program. When material also appears in the textbook, appropriate page references are given.

The laboratory manual, *Invitation à écouter et à parler*, is the student guide to the tape program. It includes directions and model sentences for all grammar exercises. Space is provided for students to complete various listening tasks, write out dictation sentences, and answer the comprehension questions on the listening passage. Selected parts of the pronunciation sections have also been included so that the laboratory manual can be used as a self-contained instructional unit.

The student workbook

Invitation à écrire, the student workbook, has been designed to expand the student's ability to communicate in writing. Each chapter of *Invitation* has accompanying exercises in the student workbook. A series of exercises and communication activities ranging from the simple to the more complex is coordinated with each grammar topic. This sequencing allows the instructor to assign all or part of the exercises, depending upon the needs of the the class or individual students. Workbook assignments can be made on a daily basis, used for end-of-chapter review, or given to students experiencing difficulty with a specific topic.

The instructor's edition

In addition to the more general introduction, the Instructor's Edition contains the complete Student Edition of *Invitation* accompanied by marginal notes. The marginal notes are not intended to be prescriptive or all-inclusive but are simply suggestions for ways in which various sections, exercises, and activities in the text can be used, modified, or elaborated upon. Implementation of these suggestions will depend to a large degree upon individual instructional preferences and teaching style, students' interests, course objectives, and the amount of class time available. In many cases, however, they may function as a time-saver for the instructor. Where appropriate, the marginal notes offer cultural information.

 # Using each section of *Invitation*

Except for its emphasis on encouraging the meaningful use of language, *Invitation* imposes few constraints and can be used in many ways. It is not intended that every section be used *throughout* or that all exercises and activities always be completed; rather, it is assumed that each instructor will choose sections or activities that best suit his or her purposes. The extent to which a given section of a chapter is emphasized and utilized will depend upon course goals, the amount of instructional time available, teacher preferences, and the needs and interests of the class or individual students. Although specific suggestions and options for using individual activities are given in the marginal notes of the Instructor's Edition, varied ways to use the different sections of the book can be delineated.

Chapitre préliminaire

The purpose of the *Chapitre préliminaire* is to give general language-learning strategies, to introduce the student to useful classroom expressions and everyday conversational phrases, to present useful classroom objects, and to give a brief overview of the *Francophone* countries. Although designed to be completed before beginning *Invitation*, the content of this chapter can be spread across the first several days of instruction.

Introduction

Because the *Introduction* is intended as a vehicle for the presentation of the chapter's theme and of new vocabulary and cultural information rather than the systematic presentation of new grammar structures, it can be used as the first assignment in a lesson or assigned at a later point. As the first assignment, the *Introduction* and the *Compréhension* can be used as a basis for class discussion. The *Introduction* can also serve as an out-of-class reading assignment with the *Compréhension* prepared in writing. Various techniques can be used to enhance student comprehension of the *Introduction:*

- Students can be asked to look at the title and try to guess what the passage is about.
- The photographs and the illustrations that accompany the passages can be used to elicit comments about what students think the passage is about and for discussing the cultural differences and similarities evoked by the *Introduction*.
- A brief introduction in French or in English can help "set the scene."
- The content of the *Introduction* can be related to students' lives. For example, Chapter 6 deals with the theme of television. Students might be asked in this instance: **Avez-vous une télé?** or **Qu'est-ce que vous aimez regarder?**
- Students may be asked to anticipate content by looking over the *Compréhension* before reading or listening to a passage.
- Present new vocabulary through visuals, gestures, French synonyms or paraphrases, and English translations. The marginal glosses can serve as a reference point if students do not remember the meanings of the new words.
- Put the *Introduction* without glosses on duplicating masters and see if students can understand the general meaning of the passage. Then have them guess the meaning of new vocabulary words. Students will not only learn the new vocabulary but will also gain valuable skill in contextual guessing.
- If the passage is assigned as homework, students can be told to study the marginal glosses before beginning and to make sure they think about the meaning as they study it.

After learning the new vocabulary and having an idea about the content of the introductory passage, students will be better able to read and understand the entire passage. Depending on student abilities and available time, the *Introduction* can be presented in one day or spread out across several days. The presentation and practice of the *Introduction* can take several forms. Instructors can present visuals and transparencies that illustrate the passage before students see it in writing. Students can listen to the taped version of the passage before seeing it. The passage can be assigned as homework and gone over in class the next day. Although it is not necessary that students memorize these passages, it is important that they be given the opportunity to say the lines either in class and/or in the language laboratory.

Compréhension

Although individual or whole-class repetition of a dialogue or reading helps pronunciation of new vocabulary and structures, it does not ensure comprehension of content. The *Compréhension* can be used to determine whether or not students have understood meaning. In addition to assigning the *Compréhension* as homework or asking the questions orally in class, instructors might use these questions for guided comprehension practice by asking students to read or listen to the conversation in order to find just one piece of information or the answer to a single comprehension question. They can subsequently be asked to find other bits of information. Although time-consuming, this focused comprehension allows students gradually to make sense of a passage and reduces frustration, especially in early stages of language learning. Responsibility for finding the answers to questions and reporting back to the class may be assigned to individual students or to small groups of students. Other comprehension techniques require students to use the content of the passage in slightly new ways:

- Having students make up a new title for the reading (in English in early chapters and later in French) or choose a title from among several offered by the teacher.
- Having students create a new beginning or end of the passage.
- Having students rewrite the material relating it to their lives or from a different perspective.
- Having students summarize the passage in French or in English.
- Providing students with a résumé of the passage with misinformation and then having them choose only those sentences that summarize it accurately.
- Having students play the role of a character or characters in a conversation and having other students ask them questions.
- Having students choose adjectives that describe the people in conversations or readings, verb phrases that indicate their activities and occupations, particular words that reveal their moods and preoccupations, and phrases that indicate the particular viewpoint of the author.

Notes culturelles

The *Notes culturelles*, which appear in both *Introduction* and *Synthèse* sections, can be assigned as out-of-class supplementary reading or used for discussion in class with the instructor illustrating them with additional information or personal anecdotes, depending upon his or her experience or course objectives. The notes can also be illustrated or enhanced by drawing attention to the photographs and realia in the book or by using slides, songs, and other such materials. In addition, each cultural topic can be elaborated upon by assigning supplementary readings, research projects, or *exposés*. Suggestions for specific activities and discussions appear in the Instructor's Edition.

Et vous?

The *Et vous?* section that follows the *Introduction* not only presents through visuals and interesting contexts vocabulary related to the chapter theme but also provides a variety of communication activities for immediate practice with these words. Using visuals, gestures, synonyms, or English equivalents can help students master this vocabulary; it may also be assigned as homework. Possible ways to complete these activities are described in the *Encouraging communication* section on pp. 9–13.

Grammaire

The three phases of the grammar presentation can be used in a variety of ways:

Présentation   Each *Présentation* is given in English and is basically a deductive grammar explanation; that is, it is based on information the student already knows in

English or in French and proceeds to new material. This type of presentation does not preclude, however, discussing the grammar topic in French should the instructor or the class so desire. In addition, many grammar topics easily lend themselves to inductive presentations in which the instructor leads the students to discover the pattern and rules through judicious comparisons of examples and asking of appropriate questions. If an inductive approach is used, students can use the explanation in the book to check their understanding. Because the grammar patterns are thoroughly illustrated with abundant examples, the instructor can also assign the *Présentation* as homework, thereby preserving valuable class time for oral, especially communication, practice. Each explanation is divided into subsections, thus allowing all or part of a topic to be assigned, depending on the amount of coverage desired. The *Présentations* can also be used for review or remedial work.

Préparation   The mechanical drills provided in the Instructor's Edition are intended to give students initial practice in manipulating grammar structures and making rapid responses to controlled language stimuli. The number of drills used will depend upon student needs, class and laboratory time available, the complexity of the grammar topic, and instructional preferences. A given exercise may be used entirely, or partially, or not at all. If students learn a particular structure rapidly, few exercises will be necessary, and students can move on to *Communication* activities.

The *Préparation* exercises are intended as a bridge between simple manipulative practice, where the establishment of structural patterns and grammatical accuracy is the goal, and free communication, where the transmission or understanding of ideas is emphasized. They provide a realistic context for the structure but do not yet engage the student personally in that context. It is possible to use these realistic transitional exercises instead of manipulative exercises, moving back to drills if students seem to be experiencing difficulty with a structure. On the other hand, if the instructor is satisfied with the understanding and fluency that students have demonstrated in the Instructor's Edition drills, the *Préparation* activity can be omitted. Because these exercises range from easy to more complicated, instructors may choose to complete selected exercises rather than the entire section in class. The selection of exercises depends upon student abilities, class time, the difficulty of the grammar topic, and the extent of student comprehension of the particular grammar topic. In some cases, it may be possible to skip both drills and *Préparation* sections and move directly to *Communication* sections, reserving the omitted exercises for remedial work.

Various approaches can be used with the *Préparation* exercises: instructors can give cues and have students respond individually or as a class; students can be divided into small groups, each with a leader who has the correct answers and the teacher circulating to help each group; students can role-play certain activities, especially those where two individuals are engaged in a simulated conversation. Additional suggestions for use of the *Préparations* are found in the Instructor's Edition.

Although most *Préparation* activities can be completed with books closed, instructors may ask students to keep their books open until they are familiar with the pattern. These activities can then be repeated with books closed. It is important that instructors use the contexts provided so that students associate responses with the situation. Attention should be drawn to model sentences so that students clearly understand their tasks.

Préparation exercises are generally designed to prepare students better for oral communication tasks. This does not, however, preclude their being assigned as written homework should class time be limited or should students need additional practice. Some of these exercises can be completed orally in class without prior preparation; others require advance written work.

Communication   The *Communication* section follows the sequenced series of exercises designed to prepare students for communication tasks. It is not intended that each activity be used or that each question or item be fully discussed but rather that instructors and students choose *Communication* activities that best suit their needs and interests.

Because students, especially in early stages of language learning, can be frustrated by totally unstructured communication tasks, many activities are designed to provide both a framework of language structures and a set of ideas from which the student can draw. Thus, to successfully communicate an idea, less able or secure students may choose ideas from those provided. A question mark invites and encourages others to venture beyond the suggestions provided and to create their own responses. Should an instructor wish, many of these structured tasks can be made more open-ended by having students complete the activity with their books closed. In addition to the guided communication activities, many are less structured and require the student to produce both the necessary language and ideas. Ways of encouraging communication and explanations of how to use the communication activities in *Invitation* are outlined on pp. 9–13 of this introduction.

Synthèse

The *Synthèse* is intended to reinforce and integrate the content of a given chapter and to develop the student's reading skill. Some new cognate and noncognate vocabulary is also introduced. The *Synthèse* can be given as a regularly scheduled class assignment to be used as a basis for oral or written discussion, or it can be assigned as supplementary reading. If instruction time is limited, the *Synthèse* can be omitted, provided that students are held responsible for the end-of-chapter vocabulary lists.

The *Communication* section following the reading passage can be used after reading the *Synthèse*, although many activities can be used to supplement communication practice of previous grammar topics. Although the entire final *Communication* section or some of its activities could be omitted, this section allows students to apply their cumulative knowledge of grammar and vocabulary while exploring their reactions to a wide variety of topics and situations.

Prononciation

The main purpose of the pronunciation section is to provide a systematic presentation of important aspects of French pronunciation. These end-of-chapter pronunciation sections can be used in several ways. They can be completed (1) before beginning a chapter, (2) spread throughout a chapter, or (3) in their entirety at the end of a chapter. The drills provided in these sections can be used for brief but intensive pronunciation practice in class, or they may be completed in the laboratory outside class. The instructor plays an important role, however, in explaining how to form these sounds, in modeling correct pronunciation, and in giving feedback to students.

Invitation à la lecture

The final chapter in *Invitation* has been designed to introduce the forms of the *passé simple* so that students can begin to enjoy literary and historical material that uses the *passé simple*. In addition to presenting the forms of the *passé simple* for recognition purposes, the chapter also contains activities and illustrative readings. This chapter can be done after completing the core chapters in *Invitation*—or taken up earlier should instructors wish to add supplementary reading materials that use the *passé simple* to their course content.

⚜ Encouraging communication

Error correction

Both students and instructors contribute to the creation of an atmosphere in which communication is likely to occur. In a communicative classroom, the student becomes an active participant in the communication process rather than a passive recipient of information about language or a rote manipulator of grammatical forms. If the student's role is defined so that he or she feels comfortable in expressing an idea, then communication is likely to occur. This implies not only that students should be encouraged to express their thoughts but also that what they communicate should be valued and respected. When students feel comfortable, they are more likely to take the necessary risks to express their ideas.

The amount of error correction an instructor undertakes during communication activities will vary. Because no definitive research exists to guide in the correction of student errors, instructors must rely instead on their experience, common sense, intuition, and knowledge of the individuals in the class. Some believe that students generally need not be corrected during communication and prefer to make corrections only during manipulative practice. Still others point out only errors that impede communication or that might be offensive to a native speaker. This does not imply, however, that structure and guidance are not necessary. It implies, rather, that a delicate balance be maintained, allowing students to speak freely and take risks in using French while at the same time having standards that will develop students' language abilities to the fullest.

Errors can often be pointed out to students in discreet and unobtrusive ways. The student's statement **Je suis dix-huit** can be rephrased **Ah, vous avez dix-huit ans**, or the instructor can react to the student's statement by using a variation of the correct structure—**C'est vrai? Moi, je n'ai pas dix-huit ans**. In addition, frequently recurring mistakes can be pointed out to the entire class. Whatever strategies are used, the learning environment should encourage students to take risks, be willing to make errors, and test their limits of self-expression in the second language.

Small-group work

Small-group work is also useful in encouraging communication and cooperation for the following reasons: (1) communication is more lifelike in small groups because real-life communication usually takes place among a small group of people; (2) students are more at ease in small groups; (3) the amount of communication increases because each student talks more frequently; and (4) the teacher, in addition to providing vocabulary or help when needed, can participate in conversations rather than merely direct them.

The instructor is very important if small-group work is to be effective. First, the students' tasks should be clear so that they know exactly what they are to do. Second, the time allotted should be clearly indicated. Third, students should be responsible for the information found out during the activity. If they are to ask other students questions, they can report back to the class what they learned about the student(s) interviewed. They can also write a short report of their interview to submit to the instructor.

Types of communication activities

Below are some of the typical communication activities in *Invitation* and possible ways to use them as whole-class or small-group activities.

Questions/Interview   This consists of a series of questions that students answer or use to interview another student (see Chapter 4, p. 85).

1. Où est-ce que tu aimes aller en vacances?
2. Est-ce que tu préfères voyager en été ou en hiver?
3. Quels pays est-ce que tu désires visiter?
4. Est-ce que tu désires visiter la France un jour?
5. Quelles villes françaises est-ce que tu désires visiter?
   etc.

Students can prepare questions for homework so that they are better able to answer in class. If the questions are used for small-group interviews, various follow-up activities encourage students to be responsible for the information they learned. Students can share with the class information they learned from their partner (e.g., **Michel désire visiter la France un jour**); they can take brief notes on their partner's answers and submit them as an informal composition; or instructors can ask for information that students learned in their small-group interviews (e.g., **Est-ce que Caroline préfère voyager en été ou en hiver?**). This format can also be used for guided composition practice.

Interviews   This activity type consists of a series of cues that students transform into questions that they will then use to interview other students. Though similar to **Questions/Interview**, this format requires the student to formulate and ask questions (see Chapter 4, p. 75).

Exemple   aller à la bibliothèque → **Est-ce que tu vas aller à la bibliothèque le week-end prochain?**

1. aller au concert
2. manger dans un bon restaurant
3. aller à la campagne
4. parler avec des amis
5. aller au cinéma
6. étudier pour un examen
   etc.

Students can use the phrases to ask each other questions in small- or large-group activities, or they can interview another student about the items listed. Interview sheets can be given to students to record the results of their interviews. These interview sheets, which contain the cues and a place for students to mark their partner's answers, can be put on dittos and distributed to students. They can therefore more easily remember their partner's responses for follow-up, whole-class discussions. The cues can also be transformed into questions asked by the instructor (**Est-ce que vous allez à la bibliothèque le week-end prochain?**) or directed dialogues (**Demandez à Michelle si elle va à la bibliothèque le week-end prochain**) and used as a whole-class activity.

Students can also be asked to role-play interviews in both structured activities where cues are provided or in free-response role-plays. In the activity below (see Chapter 11, p. 227), students are asked to role-play a conversation between a patient and his or her doctor, who diagnoses the illness and prescribes a remedy.

1. s'il/elle va bien
2. s'il/elle dort bien
3. s'il/elle a bon appétit
4. s'il/elle est souvent fatigué(e)
5. s'il/elle a mal à la tête

Students can prepare their answers as homework or in class. They can then role-play the situation in small groups, taking first the role of the patient and then the doctor. Selected groups can then present their conversations to the class, which can diagnose the problem and prescribe appropriate remedies. A variation would entail a three-person group where two students role-play the situation while a third student listens and takes notes so that he or she can report to the class the patient's symptoms and the doctor's prescription. If videotaping equipment is available, these role-plays can be recorded and played back to the class.

Surveys   Students are asked to answer survey questions in an activity or a reading (see example 1 from Chapter 17, p. 329) or are asked to prepare their own survey questions to ask other students (see example 2 from Chapter 6, p. 110).

(1) Et vous, aimez-vous le cinéma? Répondez vous-même aux questions du sondage présenté dans la Synthèse. Ensuite, comparez vos réponses à celles d'autres étudiants ou bien à celles des Français.

(2) Make up questions that you would include on a survey of television viewing habits and preferences. Then use these questions to interview another student or group of students.

These questions can be asked by the instructor in a whole-class activity with a student tallying the results. Students can also work in pairs and take turns asking each other the questions or work in groups of five or six where one student asks the questions and tabulates the responses of his or her group. In both cases, the results are reported back to the rest of the class. In addition, student interviewers can be given responsibility for one or two questions. After they have interviewed as many students as possible within a given time frame, each reports his or her findings to the whole class. Students can also respond to the survey questions as a homework assignment, then turn in their answers to be tabulated by the instructor (or a volunteer student) so that the results can be used for subsequent reading practice (by putting the results on a ditto) or for listening-comprehension practice. Survey activities such as those illustrated in the first example provide an excellent way to have students compare their culture with *Francophone* cultures.

Agree/Disagree   Students respond to a series of statements by indicating whether or not the sentences are true for them. The example below (see Chapter 20, p. 400) asks students to use various expressions to begin their sentences (e.g., **je crois, je suis sûr(e), je doute**).

Exemple   Les femmes sont aussi violentes que les hommes. →
          Je crois que les femmes sont aussi violentes que les hommes.
          Je ne crois pas que les femmes soient aussi violentes que les hommes.

1. Les jeunes savent exactement ce qu'ils veulent dans la vie.
2. Les syndicats ouvriers ont trop d'influence.
3. Les jeunes sont bien préparés pour la vie.
4. Les ouvriers font grève trop souvent.
5. Nous entrons dans une période de grande prospérité économique.
   etc.

Agree/Disagree activities can be used in a variety of ways. The statement can be transformed by the teacher or by the student into direct questions (**À votre avis, est-ce que les femmes sont aussi violentes que les hommes?**) and used for whole-class or small-group activities. Students can prepare the activity for homework and be asked to explain their answers.

Completions   Students complete sentences in ways that are personally meaningful. **Que feriez-vous?** (see Chapter 17, p. 331) asks students to tell what they would do in various situations.

1. S'il n'y avait pas de cours aujourd'hui . . .
2. Si je voulais devenir peintre . . .
3. Si j'avais besoin d'une nouvelle voiture . . .
4. Si je pouvais être une autre personne . . .
5. Si j'avais soixante ans . . .
    etc.

Students can complete the statements as homework or in class; in either case, prior preparation is helpful. Students can offer their reactions in response to teacher questions (e.g., **S'il n'y avait pas de cours aujourd'hui, que feriez-vous?**) or in small-group activities where the students elicit information from each other. Depending on the abilities of individual students or the class in general, completion of items can be used for making short statements or as the basis for longer sentences with explanations and elaborations.

Sentence Builders   Students combine items from different columns to make complete sentences that describe their opinions on various topics or typical activities (see Chapter 6, p. 117).

Exemple   Hier j'ai invité des amis à dîner.

		envoyer une lettre à
hier		mes parents
lundi		dîner chez mes amis
mardi		manger au restaurant
mercredi	j'ai	avoir un examen difficile
jeudi	mes amis ont	étudier le français
vendredi	mes amis et moi, nous avons	inviter des amis à dîner
samedi	?	regarder un film à la télé
dimanche		écouter de la musique
la semaine dernière		préparer le dîner [etc.]
		?

Instructors can ask students to volunteer statements about their activities or can elicit responses by using one of the columns given (**Qu'est-ce que vous avez fait mercredi?** or **Est-ce que vous avez regardé un film à la télé vendredi? Et vos amis, qu'est-ce qu'ils ont fait?**) After students have volunteered their statements (or the teacher has asked questions), class members can be asked to remember who did various activities (e.g., **Qui a invité des amis à dîner dimanche?**).

Using Scales   Students use a scale or a continuum to indicate the degree to which they like something or agree with an idea or opinion (see Chapter 8, p. 148).

1 = très important
2 = assez important
3 = pas très important
4 = sans importance

Exemple   La sécurité de l'emploi est assez importante pour moi.

1. _____la sécurité de l'emploi
2. _____un salaire assez élevé
3. _____de bonnes conditions de travail
4. _____des horaires souples
5. _____la liberté et la place à l'initiative personnelle
    etc.

Students can give their preference orally and ask for the opinion of another student in small-group or whole-class situations (**Un salaire assez élevé est très important pour moi. Et pour toi? Est-ce que c'est important aussi?**). In addition, instructors can solicit student opinions by transforming these items into direct questions (e.g., **La sécurité de l'emploi, est-ce important pour vous?**). This activity can also be transformed into a ranking activity where students are asked to rank a list of items in the order of their preference. They can then compare and contrast their choices with those of other students (**Mon premier choix est la liberté et la place à l'initiative personnelle. Quel est ton premier choix?**). Note that as soon as comparatives and superlatives have been presented, they can be used instead of ordinal numbers.

⚜ Planning a course syllabus

As already indicated, *Invitation* consists of twenty-two chapters plus a *Chapitre préliminaire* and a final chapter called *Invitation à la lecture*. In some semester programs, the content of *Invitation* can be divided equally so that twelve chapters are covered each semester. In a quarter system, eight chapters can be assigned for each quarter. Because of the way the chapters are designed, however, coverage can be organized and altered in many ways. In a quarter system, for example, one may elect to teach ten chapters the first quarter, eight the second, and six the third so that supplementary readers may be added in the second and third quarters. In order to achieve more in-depth mastery or to include additional cultural or reading material, the content can also be spread over a greater number of terms in both semester and quarter programs. It is also possible to omit one or more of the last chapters of the book or to skip sections of the later chapters. A large number of structures have been included; those of lesser importance have, however, been placed in the later chapters so that their omission from the curriculum will not create serious problems.

⚜ Sample lesson plans

The sample lesson plans in this section suggest ways in which the material in specific chapters of *Invitation* can be organized and presented. Ultimately, of course, lesson planning, like other aspects of classroom organization, will depend upon the individual needs of the instructor and the class.

Whether lesson plans are prepared in great detail or consist simply of a list of activities and exercises to be covered, it will be important to keep in mind certain guidelines:

1. Plan specific objectives for each class period.
2. Plan activities that relate to course objectives. If the course emphasizes conversation, a correspondingly large portion of class activities should be geared toward developing speaking skill.
3. Plan a variety of activities that sustain students' interest and that give them the opportunity to develop the skills emphasized in the course.
4. Involve students as much as possible. Teaching a skill course implies that students should use that skill rather than talk—or be told—about it.

The sample lesson plans that follow are prepared for a four-skill course that meets four times a week. They do not include specific suggestions for use of the supplementary course materials. The first set of plans includes the preliminary chapter and Chapter 1 and covers six days of instruction. The second set of plans deals with Chapter 12, which occurs approximately halfway through the book and is the second all-French chapter. The third set of plans is for Chapter 20, chosen because students are more sophisticated linguistically at this point and capable of more open-ended and creative classroom activities. The textbook assignments have been kept relatively short in the third set of plans to allow for supplementary cultural or literary readings.

For classes that meet three days a week or five days a week, the division of course material will obviously be different. Suggestions for emphasizing or deemphasizing given sections according to class needs have been discussed in the preceding section. General guidelines—for those who have to condense the course material and for those who, contrariwise, have more time—follow the sample lesson plans.

Chapitre Préliminaire

First day

1. Explain course goals, evaluation procedures, organization of the book (including appendix material), course syllabus, and other administrative matters.
2. Call roll, having students respond **présent** or **présente**.
3. Greet a student by saying **Bonjour, monsieur** or **mademoiselle** and shaking hands. Have the student greet you in turn. Greet several students in this manner and then have them greet each other.
4. Help students get to know each other by giving your name and asking a student his or her name (**Je m'appelle . . . Et vous?**). After students are familiar with this pattern, go around the class until each student has given his or her name. Include a "remembering responses" phase. Give your name and point to another student (**Je m'appelle . . . Et mademoiselle?**), having other members of the class provide the name.
5. Begin teaching the words for classroom objects in the *Dans la salle de classe* section of the *Chapitre préliminaire*. Point out various objects and have students repeat each word. If students catch on rapidly, ask **Qu'est-ce que c'est?** and see if they can provide the appropriate classroom object.
6. Assign the *Chapitre préliminaire* for the next class meeting.

Second day

1. As a warm-up activity, greet students and have them greet each other by using the informal **ça va** pattern.
2. Have students ask each other in turn what their names are and how they are. Go around the class until each student has volunteered this information. Then ask students if they can remember how each person is (**Je vais bien. Et Jean?**). Students will respond **Ça va** or **Ça ne va pas.**
3. Briefly review the types of accents in French and have students find examples in the preliminary activities. Contrast, for example, the **e** in **très** and **répétez** and the **c** in **ça va** and **comment**.
4. Have students identify various classroom objects by asking **Qu'est-ce que c'est?**
5. Have students repeat the useful classroom expressions and then ask if there are any other words or phrases that they might like to know. Have them elicit these expressions by using the phase **Comment dit-on . . . en français?**
6. Have students refer to the map of the French-speaking world and note the different countries where French is spoken, perhaps asking if anyone has lived or traveled in these countries.
7. Ask students to give the gist of the newspaper headlines presented in *Faites le premier pas*. Point out the usefulness of cognates and contextual guessing as well as the need to avoid word-for-word translations. Then tell students that they can also make use of cognates and contextual guessing as they listen to the passage that they

have for the next class meeting. Read them the passage and then have students volunteer what they have understood about the conversation.
8. Assign the *Introduction*, *Compréhension*, and *Et vous?* sections of Chapter 1 for the next class meeting.

Chapitre 1 — Préférences

First day

1. As a warm-up activity, greet several students and have them greet each other and ask how they are. (An alternate warm-up would be a quick review of classroom objects, perhaps having students point at various objects, asking other students to identify them.)
2. To begin the *Introduction*, ask the *Compréhension* questions orally, having students respond **C'est vrai** or **C'est faux** and correct the sentence if it is false. Then have students repeat the sentences in the conversation chorally and then individually so that they become familiar with the vocabulary and structures used. (Optional: Dictate several sentences from the *Introduction*, having students check their work in class.)
3. Review the vocabulary presented in *Et vous, A (Moi, je . . .)* by having students repeat the words and asking for English equivalents from time to time to ensure meaningful processing. (Optional: Read statements to students such as **J'adore la musique** or **Je déteste les sports** and have them indicate by a show of hands whether the statement applies to them or not.) Then have students volunteer statements about their own preferences.
4. Review the vocabulary in *Et vous, B (Activités)* and then give a verb phrase and have students indicate whether or not they like or dislike the activity (**écouter la radio? → Moi, j'adore écouter la radio.**) Then have students work in small groups and ask each other **Qu'est-ce que vous aimez?** and **Qu'est-ce que vous détestez?**
5. Have students work in small groups and rewrite the *Introduction* by using words from the *Et vous* section. (Optional: Encourage students to ask for other words that they might like to use in rewriting the conversation.) If time permits, have one or two groups present their written conversations. Ask students to hand in their work so that it can be checked informally.
6. Begin the pronunciation section by having students repeat the first five vowel sounds and their accompanying words. If time permits, have students find examples of these sounds in the *Introduction*.
7. Present definite articles and nouns inductively or deductively, using *Préparation A* to introduce the forms. Assign the *Présentation* of the definite article as well as the *Préparation* and *Communication* sections for the next class meeting.

Second day

1. As a warm-up activity, read one or several of the students' rewritten conversations for listening practice, adding several comprehension questions.
2. Begin the definite article section by asking students what the definite articles are and how they are used in French. Then complete the Instructor's Edition drills and *Préparation A (Curiosité)* as class activities with books closed. After that, go over *Préparation B (Opinions)* as a class activity, assigning the roles of Véronique and Gérard. Give the the first word and have Véronique respond affirmatively while Gérard takes the opposite point of view. (Optional: Prepare copies of correct answers and divide students into groups of three. The group leader is given the correct answers and helps the students who are playing the roles of Véronique and Gérard.)

3. Complete *Communication A (Réactions)* as a class activity with books closed. Give a word and have students offer their opinions by using one of the verb forms suggested. Then do *Communication B (Questions)* by having students first create the questions as a class and then ask each other these questions in groups of two and record their partner's answers on interview sheets.

4. Include personalized writing practice by having students (individually or in small groups) complete *Communication C (Slogans)*. Encourage them to use the ? and add ideas of their own. If time permits, have students create slogans for famous people or for different groups of people (e.g., politicians, professors, students). Students can work at the board or in their seats.

5. Go over the next five sounds in the pronunciation section, using the same procedures as the preceding day.

6. Briefly present first conjugation verbs, subject pronouns, and negation. Assign both sections for the next class meeting. Have students write out *Préparation C (Variétés)* in the **-er** verb section.

Third day

1. As a warm-up activity, give statements about your own interests and ask students to give their preferences (for example, **Moi, j'aime les sports. Et vous?**)

2. Begin by asking students if they have any questions on how to conjugate **-er** verbs. If not, complete the Instructor's Edition drills very rapidly and then ask students to write the forms from memory. Complete *Préparations A* and *B* with books closed. Then go over *Préparation C (Variétés)*, which students have prepared in writing. Give the answers orally, on the board, or using an overhead projector.

3. Start working with the negative by first completing the Instructor's Edition drills as a closed-book class activity and then the *Préparation (Contradictions)*. If time permits, give a short listening-comprehension test. Read sentences from *Contradictions* (or others)—putting some in the negative, others in the affirmative—and have students indicate whether the sentence is affirmative or negative.

4. Give a short transformational dictation. Have students write the sentence and then make the indicated changes.
   a. **Je voyage beaucoup.** (Change the subject to **nous** and then put the sentence in the negative.)
   b. **Vous aimez la télévision.** (Change the subject to **je** and then put the sentence in the negative. If desired, ask students to change this statement so that it applies to them personally.)
   c. **Paul déteste faire la cuisine.** (Change the subject to **tu** and then put the sentence in the negative.)

5. Complete the *Communication (Préférences)* for first conjugation verbs by having students offer their opinions about the suggestions given or by adding items of their own. Encourage students to use the negative in giving their ideas. Then ask students to volunteer information they remember about the likes and dislikes of members of the class.

6. Complete the pronunciation section.

7. Briefly introduce the interrogative and, if time permits, go over *Préparation A (N'est-ce pas?)*. If desired, introduce the new vocabulary from the *Synthèse* and read it aloud to students. Assign the interrogative section and have students write *Préparation B (Faisons connaissance)*. Also assign the *Synthèse* and have them do the *Compréhension* and *Communication A (Faisons connaissance)* in writing.

Fourth day

1. As a warm-up activity, ask personal questions integrating grammar previously studied.

2. Begin the interrogative by quickly completing the Instructor's Edition drills. Then go over *Préparations A* and *B* as closed-book activities. Then complete *Communication A (Interview)* as a whole-class activity by giving a cue (**aimer danser?**) and having students make up questions to ask another student (e.g., **Michel, est-ce que tu aimes danser?**). If time permits, ask students if they can remember the responses of other students (e.g., **Est-ce que Michel aime danser?**) or complete *Communication B (Oui ou non?)*.

3. Ask the *Compréhension* questions on the *Synthèse* and then discuss briefly the *Notes culturelles* (showing slides of Paris if possible). Dictate several sentences from the *Synthèse* and have students verify their work.

4. Then have several students introduce themselves to the class, using their homework (*Communication A, Faisons connaissance*) as a guide. If time permits, have students introduce themselves to each other in small groups.

5. Do *Communication B (Interview)* by giving students several minutes to prepare questions that they would like to ask another student. Circulate around the class and help students formulate their questions. Then have students interview each other in groups of three, using the questions they have prepared. Using *Communication C (Comparaisons)* as a basis, have them report back the results of their conversations to the class.

6. Allow time for chapter review if it seems necessary or appropriate.

Chapitre 12 — L'apparence

First day

1. Review the clothing and color vocabulary presented in the *Et vous?* section by having students identify articles of clothing and their colors worn by students in the class. After going over the completion items in *A (Vos vêtements)*, have students complete *B (Vos couleurs préférées)*.

2. To discuss the *Introduction*, ask the questions in the survey and have the students compare their answers with those of the French women surveyed. (Optional: Complete *Communication B, Les hommes et leur image*, in the *Synthèse*.)

3. Then briefly discuss the *Notes culturelles*, having students give the names of French and American fashion designers. If time permits, have students look through current French magazines for ads of various fashion products of well-known designers.

4. If students have no questions on the placement of adjectives, complete the Instructor's Edition drills and *Préparation* section, using as many exercises as necessary for student mastery. (Optional: Show pictures from French magazines and have students comment on them, or have students use adjectives to write answers to several personal questions (e.g., **Quelle sorte de voiture préférez-vous? Quelle sorte de restaurant aimez-vous?**).

5. Have students complete the *Communication (Choix)* by working in small groups and asking each other questions. Have students report back some of the preferences of the person they interviewed.

6. Introduce inductively or deductively the comparative and assign the comparative and **mettre** verbs sections for the next class meeting.

Second Day

1. As a warm-up, give a series of statements and have students tell whether the person has made the right choice of clothing or not (e.g., **Marie-Louise va faire du camping ce week-end; elle va porter une robe rose**).

2. Begin working with **mettre** verbs by completing the Instructor's Edition drills and *Préparation A (Qu'est-ce qu'on va mettre?)* with books closed. Then use the sen-

tences in *Préparation B (Promesses)* for a short dictation. Students can then work in small groups to make lists of five things that they would permit their students to do and five that they would not allow them to do (*Communication A, On change de rôle*). Sentences can be shared orally or placed on the board as a follow-up activity.

3. If students have no questions on the comparative, have them complete *Préparations A (Paris et la province)* and *B (Le nouveau prof)* and then work in small groups to go over *Préparation C (Évian ou Vittel?)*. A student leader is given the correct answers to *Préparation C* so that student responses can be checked for accuracy.

4. Have students interview each other in small groups by using the questions in *Communication A (Questions/interview)* and taking notes on their partner's answers for a brief exchange of information after the interviews are completed.

5. With books open, have students create sentences comparing the different items in *Communication B (Comparaisons)*. Cue words could also be given orally or placed on the board with student books closed. If time permits, ask students to give items that they would like to compare and have the class make up sentences.

6. Introduce the superlative and assign this section for the next class meeting, having students prepare both *Communication* activities as homework.

Third day

1. As a warm-up, give comparative sentences and ask students to agree or disagree with the statements (e.g., **Le français est plus facile que les maths**).

2. Give a short dictation on the superlative, using the sentences from *Préparation A (Vendeur aux Galeries Lafayette)*: e.g., **Nous avons de bons prix. Nous avons les meilleurs prix.** Then complete *Préparations B (Paris)* and *C (Le chou-chou du prof)* orally with books closed.

3. Have students complete *Communication A (À votre avis)* in small groups, with instructions to note their partner's answers on interview sheets so that a class tally of answers can be made as a follow-up activity. Use the answers to encourage students to discuss the merits of various choices: e.g., **Mais non! New York n'est pas aussi beau que San Francisco. San Francisco est la plus belle ville des États-Unis.**

4. Use *Communication B (Le plus et le moins)* as a whole-class activity, again encouraging students to explain and discuss their responses.

5. Have students work together to begin making a list of "**les meilleurs aspects de la vie universitaire**" that they might give to a new student. If time permits, have students share their ideas.

6. Assign the *Synthèse* section for the next class meeting. Ask students to prepare a comprehension question to ask about the *Synthèse* reading and to write out *Communication A (Vendeur de tee-shirts)* and *C (Portraits)*.

Last day

1. Have students share the items on their "**les meilleurs aspects de la vie universitaire**" list.

2. To evaluate comprehension of the *Synthèse* reading, have students ask each other the comprehension questions they have prepared. If necessary, go over the questions in the book. Dictate several sentences from the *Synthèse* reading and have students check their work.

3. Have students volunteer the slogans they have prepared for *Communication A (Vendeur de tee-shirts)* and have the class choose the five best slogans.

4. Present briefly the information in the *Notes culturelles* and then ask students to think of compliments they might give in various situations (e.g., a friend has just found a new job, someone has prepared a delicious dinner, a friend is wearing a

nice shirt). If time permits, have them practice complimenting each other in French.

5. With books closed, have students indicate whether they agree or disagree with the statements in *Communication D (Vérité ou chauvinisme)*, encouraging students to explain their answers.

6. Have personalized writing practice by giving a topic (e.g., **la musique**) and having students make up a comparative or superlative statement about the topic.

Chapitre 20 – L'individu face à la société moderne

First day

1. Begin discussing the *Introduction* by asking the comprehension questions. Then have students compare and contrast the situation in France with that in the United States by comparing their answers to the questions in the *Et vous?* section (*Vous sentez-vous en sécurité?*) with those of the original survey. Bring in information from the *Notes culturelles* as appropriate.

2. Read several sentences from the *Introduction* as dictation practice and have students verify their sentences in class.

3. Begin working with **plaire** and **manquer** by making sentences from the *Préparation* section to use as listening-comprehension practice. Read the sentences and have students jot down what Patrick likes and what he misses. After completing the *Préparation* exercises orally, have students ask each other the questions in *Communication A (Interview)* and write a brief paragraph summarizing their partner's answers to submit to the instructor for informal evaluation. If time permits, complete *Communication C (Les rêves ne coûtent pas cher)* as a whole-class activity.

4. Review the formation of regular and irregular subjunctives (Chapter 19), using selected *Préparation* and *Communication* activities.

5. Then present the use of the subjunctive with verbs of volition, emotion, and doubt in as much detail as is necessary for class understanding. To familiarize students with the concept, complete the Instructor's Edition drills or adapt a *Préparation* activity for listening comprehension. Assign this grammar section for the next class meeting.

Second day

1. Use *Communication B (Votre vie à l'université)* as a warm-up and as a review of **plaire** and **manquer**.

2. Begin working with the subjunctive section by completing the Instructor's Edition drills and *Préparations A (Opinions)* and *B (Est-ce que vous vous sentez en sécurité?)*. Then have students work on *Préparation C (Différences d'opinion)* in small groups; give the correct answers orally, on the board, or on an overhead projector. Use this preparation exercise to lead into *Communication A (Et vous?)*.

3. Give orally the statements from *Communication B (Êtes-vous d'accord?)* and have students agree or disagree with each statement. If desired, this activity could also be used for personalized writing practice. Then use the questions in *Communication C (Questions/interview)* for large- or small-group discussion.

4. Present briefly the next grammar section, the passive voice. Have students prepare this section, writing out *Préparation B (Titres de journaux)* and *Communication A (Vos débuts dans le journalisme)*.

Third day

1. As a warm-up activity, read the first paragraph from *Communication C (Que faire?)* in the *Synthèse* for listening practice and have students suggest solutions to the problem described.

2. Use the sentences in the Instructor's Edition drill for a short transformational dictation to introduce the passive voice. Then complete *Préparations A (Au poste de police)* and *B (Titres de journaux)* as a class activity with books closed.

3. Have students present the newspaper headlines prepared for *Communication A* orally to the class, and then have them create additional headlines for other sections of a newspaper or for a French version of the campus newspaper. Complete *Communication B (Testez vos connaissances)* as a whole-class activity. If appropriate, students can create a French newspaper as a class project, using examples of *Francophone* newspapers as guides.

4. Present inductively or deductively other uses of the subjunctive and assign this section and the *Synthèse* for the next class meeting, having students write out *Communication B (Vivent les différences!)* in the *Synthèse*.

5. Introduce the new vocabulary in the *Synthèse* reading and read one or two of the descriptions of the people described in *Ceux qui ont dit non.* Have students listen carefully, taking notes if necessary, so that they can give an oral summary of what they have heard.

Last day

1. Begin class by having students compare and contrast their responses to *Synthèse Communication B (Vivent les différences!).*

2. Then use the Instructor's Edition drills to give a transformational dictation employing other uses of the subjunctive. Have students complete *Préparation A (Projets)* and *Préparation B (Opinions)* orally and then place them in groups of two or three to complete the sentences in the *Communication (Nuances).* Results can be shared orally or placed on the board or on an overhead projector.

3. To discuss the *Synthèse*, use the comprehension questions and the first question in *Communication A (Choix et décisions).* (Optional: Have students take the roles of the persons described and answer questions asked by other members of the class.) Then discuss the remaining questions in *Communication A*, using the last question to bring in the information contained in the *Notes culturelles.*

4. As a class or in small groups, have students find solutions to the problems described in *Communication C (Que faire?).* If time permits, have students prepare similar problems that they present to the class for possible solutions.

5. Use the remaining class time for chapter review.

Classes Meeting Three Times a Week

Because *Invitation* is a book of options, its organization allows instructors to delete or deemphasize sections, exercises, and activities without harming the logic of the instructional process. In a four-skill course meeting three times a week, it may be necessary, for example, to spend less time discussing the *Introduction* and *Synthèse* readings and to assign them instead for out-of-class reading. Instructors will, on the other hand, need to devote proportionally more class time to working with the grammar concepts.

If laboratory facilities are available, much of the manipulative practice of each grammar topic can be completed outside class, allowing more class time to develop the student's ability to communicate. If not, instructors may wish to make a judicious selection of *Préparation* and *Communication* activities to be prepared as homework. In addition, it is possible to delete all or portions of the later chapters in the book, thus allowing students to progress through the remaining material at a more leisurely pace.

Classes Meeting Five Days a Week

Under such a system, a more in-depth coverage of the different sections of the book will be possible. Many of the optional activities and follow-up suggestions given in the marginal notes of the *Instructor's Edition* can be implemented. In addition, the instructor can provide more opportunities to develop listening, reading, writing, and speaking skills as well as to discuss in greater detail the *Notes culturelles*.

 # Sample tests

The sample tests that follow are not intended to prescribe test formats but rather to show a variety of ways in which assimilation of course content can be measured. The first test covers the preliminary chapter and the first two chapters of the book, giving equal weight to listening, reading, and writing. The second test (Chapters 11 and 12) is still relatively structured, whereas the third test (Chapters 19 and 20) contains more open-ended formats that require more language production and creativity on the part of the student. In addition, each test contains a cultural component. The tests are designed to be completed in approximately forty to fifty minutes. If speaking is given equal emphasis as a course goal, ideally it should be evaluated in each testing situation. Available instructor time, however, often precludes frequent formal testing of oral skills. Therefore, a separate section on evaluating speaking skills follows the sample tests.

Sample Test: Preliminary Chapter, Chapters 1 and 2

Listening

A. **C'est combien?** Imagine that you are in a store and have asked the prices of various items. As you hear the prices read aloud, write down in numerals the cost of each item. Each will be read twice. (10 points)
  *1. [10] francs
  2. [5] francs
  3. [3] francs
  4. [8] francs
  5. [4] francs

B. **Oui ou non?** You will hear a statement or a question followed by an answer. Circle **oui** if the answer is an appropriate response to the question or circle **non** if it is not. (10 points)
  1. [Salut! Ça va?
     Je m'appelle Jean, et toi?]
  2. [Est-ce que vous me comprenez?
     Non. Répétez, s'il vous plaît.]
  3. [Tu aimes beaucoup le français, n'est-ce pas?
     Oui, c'est assez facile.]
  4. [Marc adore voyager, n'est-ce pas?
     Oui, il aime bien travailler.]
  5. [Comment vous appelez-vous, monsieur?
     Jean Dufour, et vous?]

C. **Description.** You will hear a passage that describes the life of André and Hélène Lévêque. Based on the information given, answer the questions below in English. The passage will be read twice, followed by pauses during which you may write. (10 points)

---

*Information in brackets is to be read aloud by the instructor and does not appear on the student copy.

[Passage to be read: André et moi, nous sommes canadiens et nous habitons à Montréal. Nous aimons beaucoup Montréal parce que la vie dans les villes est très intéressante. Nous sommes étudiants à l'université. Nous étudions beaucoup parce qu'André désire être professeur de mathématiques et moi, je voudrais être médecin. En général, nous sommes patients, modestes et assez réservés. Nous aimons beaucoup les sports, les vacances à la montagne et le camping. Je préfère le cinéma, mais André aime mieux regarder la télévision. André prépare souvent le dîner parce que je déteste faire la cuisine.]

1. How do André and Hélène feel about living in Montreal?
2. Why do they have to study a lot?
3. Give two adjectives that describe André and Hélène.
4. Give two interests that they share.
5. Which of the two generally prepares dinner and why?

Writing

A. **Quelle est la question?** Listed below are a series of statements that Jean-Luc made in an interview. His statements refer to himself, his sister Marie-Ange, and his brother Antoine. For each statement he made, write in French a question that the interviewer might have asked him. Pay particular attention to the pronoun used by the interviewer so that you know whom the question refers to. (10 points)

1. Le reporter: _____.
   Jean-Luc: Non, il déteste étudier.
2. Le reporter: _____.
   Jean-Luc: Non, je ne parle pas anglais.
3. Le reporter: _____.
   Jean-Luc: Elle préfère la plage.
4. Le reporter: _____.
   Jean-Luc: Oui, nous aimons beaucoup le camping.
5. Le reporter: _____.
   Jean-Luc: Je suis assez content à l'université.

B. **Et vous?** Write a complete sentence in French that expresses your ideas about each of the following topics. Supply the appropriate definite article and be sure to use a different verb in each sentence. For example, given the word **mathématiques**, you might write **Je déteste les mathématiques.** (10 points)

1. vacances à la plage _____
2. cuisine _____
3. camping _____
4. télévision _____
5. français _____

C. **Opinions.** Complete the following sentences so that they express your opinions. Provide the correct form of the verb **être** and at least two adjectives that describe your viewpoint. (10 points)

1. Les étudiants _____.
2. Le professeur idéal _____.
3. Nous, les Américains, nous _____.
4. Je _____.
5. La femme idéale _____.

Reading

A. **C'est logique.** After each of the following statements describing various people, you will find two sentences. Choose the sentence that means most nearly the same thing or that would most logically follow the original statement. Indicate your answer by circling the corresponding letter. (10 points)

1. Henri n'étudie pas beaucoup.
   a. Il est irrésistible.
   b. Il aime mieux regarder la télévision.
2. Jacqueline adore la difficulté et le danger.
   a. Elle est très courageuse.
   b. Elle est souvent assez timide.
3. Jeanne est très honnête.
   a. Elle déteste l'hypocrisie.
   b. Elle n'apprécie pas la sincérité.
4. Jacqueline n'est pas très sérieuse.
   a. Elle étudie beaucoup.
   b. Elle ne travaille pas assez.
5. Marthe est assez heureuse à l'université.
   a. Elle aime les classes et les professeurs.
   b. Elle a toujours des problèmes.

B. **Une lettre de Sylviane.** Sylviane is looking for an American family with whom she can spend the summer. In a letter to a friend, she gives some information about herself. In the space provided, give the English equivalents of the underlined words. (10 points)

Je voudrais (1) visiter les États-Unis parce que (2) j'espère (3) être professeur d'anglais. Maintenant (4) je suis étudiante (5) à Strasbourg où (6) j'étudie l'anglais. Je ne suis pas parfaite, mais je suis polie (7) et je ne suis pas paresseuse (8). Je suis sérieuse et je travaille (9) beaucoup (10).

1. _____   6. _____
2. _____   7. _____
3. _____   8. _____
4. _____   9. _____
5. _____   10. _____

C. **Nous ne sommes pas contents.** Read the following paragraph about Paul and Anne Rocher. Then, based on the information given, answer the questions below in English. (10 points)

Nous sommes parisiens mais nous ne sommes pas très heureux d'habiter à Paris. Nous n'aimons pas la vie compliquée et impersonnelle de la ville. Nous travaillons beaucoup parce que nous désirons voyager. Nous aimons beaucoup la musique—Paul aime la musique classique et moi, j'apprécie beaucoup le jazz américain. Nous ne regardons pas souvent la télévision parce que nous aimons mieux le cinéma et les livres. Moi, j'adore faire la cuisine et Paul aime manger. C'est parfait, n'est-ce pas?

1. How do Paul and Anne feel about living in the city?
2. Why do they work a lot?
3. What types of music do they like?
4. Do they watch a lot of television? Why or why not?
5. Why do Anne and Paul get along in regard to cooking and eating?

Culture
Briefly answer the following questions about culture in the French-speaking world. (10 points)
1. Name at least two French-speaking countries other than France.
2. In what situations is it appropriate to use the **tu** form of the verb?
3. Many Americans think of Paris as being all of France. Do French people agree? Explain your answer.
4. What is the general attitude of French young people toward religion?
5. Name two things that are representative of French-Canadian cultural heritage.

Sample test: Chapters 11 and 12

Listening

A. **Suggestions.** Some patients are talking to a doctor about various health problems. Jot down brief but complete notes in English about the advice you hear the doctor give each person. (10 pts—1 pt per suggestion)

1. a.[1. Vous vous sentez toujours fatigué? Eh bien, couchez-vous plus tôt le soir.
   b. Faites des exercices aérobiques trois fois par semaine. Et n'oubliez pas de
   c. manger plus de légumes verts et de fruits. Non, vous n'avez pas besoin de
   d. prendre des vitamines si vous choisissez mieux ce que vous mangez.]
2. a.[2. Si vous avez mal aux yeux, ça peut venir de plusieurs choses. Vous avez peut-
   b. être besoin d'acheter de nouvelles lunettes, des lunettes plus fortes, mais
   c. pour ça, il faut aller chez un spécialiste. Vos yeux sont peut-être fatigués si
3. a. vous passez de longues heures à étudier. Dans ce cas, vous pouvez aussi es-
   b. sayer de vous reposer plus souvent quand vous étudiez. Mais la meilleure so-
   c. lution est de dormir assez. Les muscles de vos yeux peuvent aussi avoir som-
      meil!]

   [3. Oui, c'est vrai, vous êtes trop souvent malade! Il faut vous préoccuper davantage de votre santé! Voici quelques petites choses qui peuvent vous aider: D'abord, habillez-vous mieux quand vous sortez. Par exemple, mettez un pull chaud quand il fait froid. Prenez de l'aspirine si vous avez mal à la gorge. Et voilà la chose la plus importante: si vous n'êtes pas complètement remis de votre maladie, restez à la maison et reposez-vous.]

B. **Différences d'opinion.** Marie and Jean are talking about the way men dress. In the space provided, write down what each says. You will hear each sentence twice with pauses and a third time without pauses so that you may check what you've written. (17 pts—34 words, ½ pt each)

Marie: [Les hommes ne se préoccupent pas assez de leur apparence.]	10
Jean: [Ce n'est pas vrai; nous nous habillons très bien.]	9
Marie: [Vous mettez toujours la même chose!]	6
Jean: [Arrête-toi! Tu me donnes mal à la tête!]	9

Reading

A. **C'est logique.** For each item below, circle the letter of the sentence that logically follows the underlined sentence. (10 pts—2 pts each)
   1. Pauline a mal aux jambes.
      a. Elle va mettre la table.
      b. Elle a besoin de se reposer.
   2. Daniel est un ancien professeur d'informatique.
      a. Il a choisi une nouvelle profession.
      b. Il a plus de soixante-dix ans.
   3. Les enfants ont mis leur maillot de bain.
      a. Ils vont bientôt se coucher.
      b. Ils vont aller à la piscine avec leurs amis.
   4. Anne porte un corsage noir.
      a. Elle préfère porter des couleurs foncées.
      b. Elle a un jardin avec des fleurs exotiques.
   5. Nous sommes en train de nous préparer pour une surprise-partie.
      a. Nous faisons la cuisine ensemble.
      b. Nous nous lavons et nous nous habillons.

B. **Lettre de Paris.** John, who is visiting Paris for the first time, has just written to his family. Read the following paragraph and circle the word that best completes the meaning of each sentence. (8 pts—1 pt per word)

Paris est une ville sensationnelle et je réussis à (me peigner / me dépêcher / me débrouiller) très bien en français; eh bien, je parle (mieux / meilleur / le meilleur) que toi, papa! J'ai remarqué que de plus en plus de jeunes Français (portent / tiennent / attirent) des blue-jeans. J'ai déjà visité tous les (vieux / anciens / chers) monuments de la ville et j'ai l'impression de commencer à (cacher / couper / connaître) Paris. Mais il y a encore beaucoup (plus / autant / moins) de choses que je voudrais faire ici. C'est pourquoi j'ai (fait / pris / compris) la décision de (me reposer / rester / me remettre) à Paris deux semaines de plus.

Writing

A. **L'université.** Choose five of the following items and, using the superlative, write statements that you think are true about your university. Your sentences will be evaluated on the richness of their content (variety of vocabulary and structures) as well as on their grammatical accuracy. (15 pts—3 pts each)

Exemple les résidences universitaires
J'habite dans la résidence la mieux située mais où on mange le plus mal.

l'équipe de football
la bibliothèque
les professeurs
les étudiants
les cours

les résidences universitaires
les bâtiments
le restaurant universitaire
le campus
les examens

1.
2.
3.
4.
5.

B. **Et vous?** The following questions are addressed to you personally. Answer each, using appropriate, complete French sentences. Your answers will be evaluated on the richness of their content as well as on their grammatical accuracy. (20 pts—5 pts each)
   1. Qu'est-ce que vous avez fait pendant le week-end? (Utilisez au moins quatre des verbes suivants dans votre réponse: se réveiller, se lever, s'occuper, se retrouver, s'amuser, se reposer, se coucher.)
   2. Est-ce que vous vous mettez souvent en colère? Dans quelles circonstances?
   3. Faites une description de vous-même: De quelle couleur sont vos yeux? Et vos cheveux? Quels vêtements préférez-vous porter pour aller à l'université? Pourquoi? Dans quelles situations est-ce que vous vous habillez différemment?
   4. En général, est-ce que les étudiants de votre université se préoccupent assez de leur santé? Et de leur apparence? Expliquez vos réponses.

C. **Préférences.** Using the adjectives listed below, create sentences that describe your preferences. Use each adjective only once and make sure that the adjective you use is appropriately placed and agrees with the noun it modifies. (10 pts—2 pts each)

Exemple avoir / amie
J'ai une très bonne amie qui s'appelle Carole.

Adjectifs: petit, joli, gros, élégant, beau, long, intéressant, français, américain

1. posséder / voiture
2. acheter / vêtements
3. visiter / ville

4. habiter / appartement
5. faire / voyage

Culture

Indicate by circling the appropriate word whether the following statements are **vrai** or **faux**. (10 pts—2 pts each)

1. vrai   faux   Les tee-shirts qui portent des inscriptions amusantes sont une mode qui a ses origines en France.
2. vrai   faux   Selon le sondage sur la beauté féminine organisé par l'IFOP, les Français préfèrent les femmes qui sont à la fois belles et intelligentes.
3. vrai   faux   On a développé la cuisine minceur pour les gens qui aiment la bonne cuisine, mais qui s'intéressent aussi à leur forme.
4. vrai   faux   Quand il se rencontrent, les Français s'embrassent sur les deux joues.
5. vrai   faux   Cacharel et Sonia Rykiel sont des couturiers du «prêt-à-porter».

Sample test: Chapters 19 and 20

Listening

Et vous? The following questions are addressed to you personally. Answer each, using an appropriate, complete French statement. (12 pts—3 pts each)

1. [Qu'est-ce qui vous plaît et qu'est-ce qui ne vous plaît pas dans cette ville?]
2. [Qu'est-ce qu'un nouvel étudiant devrait faire pour réussir dans ses études?]
3. [Si vous voyagiez en France, quels aspects de la vie américaine vous manqueraient le plus?]
4. [Qu'est-ce qu'il faut que vous fassiez cette semaine?]

Reading

Attitudes. Some people are discussing the cities where they live. Indicate by circling the appropriate word whether each person's attitude is **optimiste** or **pessimiste**. (15 pts—3 pts each)

1. optimiste   pessimiste   [Il ne passe pas une journée sans qu'il y ait un vol ou un accident. J'ai peur de sortir seule. Quand j'ai besoin de sortir le soir, je téléphone toujours à mon fils pour qu'il vienne me chercher.]

2. optimiste   pessimiste   [Moi, je dois dire que je n'ai jamais connu de gens aussi sympa que la famille qui habite en face de chez moi; ils sont toujours prêts à m'aider! Ma vie ici me plaît beaucoup.]

3. optimiste   pessimiste   [Récemment ma famille et moi, nous avons passé une journée dans le parc qui est près de chez nous. Il y avait des musiciens qui jouaient, et des gens qui parlaient ensemble. Ça montre bien l'esprit d'amitié de notre ville!]

4. optimiste   pessimiste   [Il y a eu encore un enlèvement cette semaine dans mon quartier. La police donne l'impression de ne vouloir rien faire. Et il n'y a rien que les gens puissent faire pour se protéger. C'est vraiment inquiétant.]

5. optimiste   pessimiste   [J'ai vu des gens à la télé qui disaient que l'eau que nous buvons est polluée, bien que le gouvernement nous dise qu'il n'y a pas de danger. Je ne sais pas qui croire, mais je ne sais pas non plus si je devrais boire cette eau!]

Writing

A. **Notre société.** Complete the following sentences so that they express your thoughts and opinions about problems in today's society. (15 pts—3 pts each)
 1. J'ai peur que . . .
 2. Je ne crois pas que . . .
 3. Je voudrais que . . .
 4. La technologie peut nous aider à mieux vivre à condition que . . .
 5. Nous continuerons à avoir des problèmes à moins que . . .

B. **Le journal.** Imagine that you work for *Le Devoir*, a French-Canadian newspaper. Create five headlines (real or imaginary), using the passive construction in each one. (15 pts—3 pts each)
 Exemple: François Lejeune a été nommé ambassadeur en Irlande.
 1.
 2.
 3.
 4.
 5.

C. **Interprète.** One of your friends who doesn't speak much French wants to talk to the Swiss exchange students living with you. Tell your friend how to say the following in French. (15 pts—3 pts each)
 1. Do you think it will rain?
 2. You must have been a little sad when you arrived.
 3. Do you miss your family a lot?
 4. I'd like you to go to the museum with us.
 5. Are you afraid your plane won't leave on time?

D. **Et vous?** The following questions are addressed to you personally. Answer each, using an appropriate, complete French sentence. Your answers will be evaluated on the richness of their content (vocabulary and structures) as well as on their grammatical accuracy. (20 pts—5 pts each)
 1. Imaginez que vous avez décidé de tourner le dos à la ville pour aller vivre à la campagne. Essayez de persuader vos parents et vos amis que c'est une bonne décision.
 2. Vous sentez-vous en sécurité? Pourquoi ou pourquoi pas? Que pourrait-on faire pour que nous soyons plus en sécurité?
 3. Est-ce que vous préférez habiter dans le centre d'une ville ou en banlieue? Expliquez votre réponse.
 4. Vous assistez à une réunion pour une candidate qui va se présenter aux prochaines élections. Dites-lui ce que vous voulez qu'elle fasse pour améliorer la situation dans le pays.

Culture

Answer each of the following questions about France. Your responses will be evaluated only on the accuracy of the information you give. (8 pts—2 pts each)
1. Selon une commission gouvernementale, la violence est un problème sérieux en France. Indiquez au moins trois choses qui confirment ce point de vue.
2. En quoi le système des partis politiques français est-il différent de celui des États-Unis?
3. Il y a en France des gens qui rêvent de s'acheter une petite maison à la campagne pour aller y passer les week-ends et d'autres pour qui la ville exerce une attraction considérable. Comment pouvez-vous expliquer ces tendances contradictoires?
4. Nommez au moins deux personnages historiques français qui ont dit «non». Qu'est-ce qu'ils ont fait?

⚜ Evaluating speaking

The ability to express oneself orally in French is frequently recognized as an important outcome of learning French; yet often this skill is not evaluated. If speaking French is a course goal, it should be tested either formally or informally, or both, in order to reduce the discrepancy between what we *say* is important and what is actually tested. It is possible, for example, to give students an oral communication grade for their oral work in class, perhaps on a daily or weekly basis. The oral grade can be based on criteria such as the amount of communication the student engages in, the quality of his or her utterances, and the improvement the student shows throughout the grading period. Although this type of evaluation tends to be subjective and qualitative, it does provide a means of evaluating students' oral performance on a regular basis.

Because formal oral testing is time-consuming, many instructors choose to give only a midterm and a final speaking examination. There are many ways to evaluate speaking skill. Students can, for instance, describe visuals or photographs, engage in impromptu role-playing, or speak extemporaneously on a topic or topics covered during the course. The sample speaking test (covering Chapters 11 and 12) is somewhat more structured and is easy to evaluate. It is easily administered and can take as little as ten to fifteen minutes. Students are examined on their ability to both answer and ask questions.

Sample Speaking Test: Chapters 11 and 12

Part A—Answering questions
In this section of the test, students will be asked to answer five questions. Try to put the student at ease and create a relaxed atmosphere. Tell the student that you will ask him or her a series of questions that are to be answered in complete French sentences. Each question will be read twice.

Choose five questions from the following list:
1. À votre avis, jusqu'à quel âge une femme (un homme) peut-elle (il) être belle (beau)?
2. Quel type de beauté féminine (ou masculine) préférez-vous et pourquoi?
3. Beaucoup de gens possèdent de grosses voitures. Et vous, quelle sorte de voiture préférez-vous posséder? Pourquoi?
4. À quelle heure est-ce que vous vous levez (vous vous couchez) d'habitude?
5. Est-ce que vous avez l'intention de vous reposer pendant le week-end?
6. Est-ce que vous vous êtes dépêché(e) pour venir en classe aujourd'hui? Pourquoi ou pourquoi pas?
7. Qu'est-ce que vous faites quand vous avez mal à la tête (à l'estomac, à la gorge)?
8. Qu'est-ce que vous portez pour venir en classe (pour faire du camping, etc.)?
9. Quelle est votre classe la plus facile (difficile, intéressante) ce trimestre?
10. Est-ce que vos cours sont plus faciles ce trimestre que le trimestre dernier?
11. ?

Part B—Asking questions
In this section of the test, students will ask questions to elicit information and will be evaluated on their ability to both ask the question and understand the answer. Have students ask you questions in French that will elicit the information given on their test copy. Give an appropriate answer to the five questions the student will ask. Add additional information where appropriate, keeping in mind the limits of the student's linguistic ability. You might want to keep track of your answers so that you don't forget them. Remind students to jot down answers in English or in French on their copy of the test.

Student Copy of Speaking Test: Chapters 11 and 12

Part A—Answering questions

Your instructor will ask you five questions. Answer in your best French and use complete sentences. Each question will be read twice. You will be evaluated on the appropriateness and the correctness of your responses. (20 pts—4 pts each)

Part B—Asking questions

Ask your instructor questions in French that will elicit the information given below. Take short but complete notes in English or in French about the answers you receive. You will be evaluated on how well you ask the questions and how well you understand your instructor's answers. (30 pts—6 pts each)

Ask your instructor:
1. if he or she prefers big or small schools.
2. what is, in his or her opinion, the best restaurant in town.
3. if French cooking is better than American cooking.
4. if he or she is interested in sports.
5. when he or she has a headache.

Scoring Information for Sample Speaking Test: Chapters 11 and 12

Part A—Answering questions

Use the scale below to evaluate each response (or question). Do not hesitate to assign scores such as 2½ or 1½ if this seems appropriate.

4 points: Excellent—The student's response or question is appropriate, grammatically correct, and delivered with acceptable pronunciation and fluency.

3 points: Good—The student's response or question is appropriate and comprehensible but contains minor errors in pronunciation and/or grammar.

2 points: Fair—The student's response or question contains faulty grammar and poor pronunciation but is still comprehensible.

1 point: Poor—The student attempts a response or question but it is incomprehensible or inappropriate.

0 points: Failing—No response is given.

Part B—Asking questions

Use the scale given for Part A to evaluate the questions asked by the student. Use the scale below to evaluate the written notes recorded by the student.

2 points: The notes contain complete information.

1 point: The notes contain only partial information.

0 points: The notes are incorrect, or no response is given.

Grade Sheet

Nom _____

Partie A—Réponses aux questions (20 pts—4 pts each)

Questions   Commentaires
1. _____
2. _____
3. _____
4. _____
5. _____

Total—Partie A: _____

Partie B—Formulation et compréhension des questions (30 pts—6 pts each)

Questions	Réponses	Commentaires
1. _____	1. _____	
2. _____	2. _____	
3. _____	3. _____	
4. _____	4. _____	
5. _____	5. _____	

Total—Partie B: _____

Note finale: _____

If preferred, the rating scale described in this section can be used to assign an overall rating to the student's answers and questions rather than rating each individual sentence. In addition, the ACTFL (American Council on the Teaching of Foreign Languages) Proficiency Guidelines provide useful scales for global ratings of the student's oral performance.

Invitation

Invitation

French
for Communication
and Cultural
Awareness

SECOND EDITION

Gilbert A. Jarvis
The Ohio State University

Thérèse M. Bonin
The Ohio State University

Donald E. Corbin
James Madison University

Diane W. Birckbichler
The Ohio State University

Holt, Rinehart and Winston
New York   Chicago   San Francisco   Philadelphia
Montreal   Toronto   London   Sydney
Tokyo   Mexico City   Rio de Janeiro   Madrid

Publisher Rita Pérez
Acquisitions Editor Vincent Duggan
Developmental Editor Ernst Schrader
Special Projects Editor Pamela Forcey
Production Manager Lula Als
Design Supervisor Renée Davis
Text Design and Layout Caliber Design Planning
Drawings Ed Malsberg

Composition and camera work Precision Typographers, Inc.
Printing and binding Von Hoffmann Press, Inc.

Reproduced on the cover:
Henri Matisse. *Jazz (2). The Circus.* 1947.
Copyright © Museum of Modern Art, New York, 1962.

Photographic credits appear at the end of the book.

Library of Congress Cataloging in Publication Data

Main entry under title:

Invitation : French for communication and cultural awareness.

  English and French.
  Includes index.
  1. French language—Grammar—1950- . 2. French
language—Text-books for foreign speakers—English.
I. Jarvis, Gilbert A.
PC2112.I5 1984   448.2'421   84-4578

ISBN 0-03-069271-7 Student Edition
                    Instructor's Edition: ISBN 0-03-069272-5

Address correspondence to:
383 Madison Avenue
New York, NY 10017

4 5 6 7 8   032 9 8 7 6 5 4 3 2 1

CBS COLLEGE PUBLISHING
Holt, Rinehart and Winston
The Dryden Press
Saunders College Publishing

Preface

Invitation: French for Communication and Cultural Awareness is a basic French textbook that blends opportunity for the development of genuine proficiency in French with a comprehensive description of the language. The second edition continues the successful approach of the first edition while taking into account recent developments in our understanding of language learning and the suggestions of students and instructors who have used the first edition. Concern for student attitudes, an emphasis on proficiency, and the humanistic value of language study guided the revision.

Invitation presents the basic structures of French and more than 2000 of its most useful words. The program is designed for use in two-year and four-year colleges and universities and is suitable for both semester and quarter systems. Accompanying the student textbook are an Instructor's Edition of the text, a complete laboratory tape program and manual *(Invitation à écouter et à parler)*, and a workbook *(Invitation à écrire)*.

This second edition of *Invitation* is a true revision. More than half of the readings and conversations have been changed or modified; there is an increased emphasis on culture throughout the book; a new thematic vocabulary section with accompanying communication activities has been added to each chapter; changes in the sequencing and presentation of grammar have been made where appropriate; all grammar exercises have been contextualized; and communication activities have been added or modified with a particular emphasis on increasing the student's ability to ask as well as answer questions.

Philosophy

Invitation is unique in that it provides, for every grammar concept, a sequence of practice that leads the student from simple manipulative drills through practice within authentic contexts to meaningful and communicative use of the concept. The meaningful use of French is not relegated to end-of-chapter personalized questions or to drills disguised as communication, but is present on every page. Instead of promising students that they will be able to communicate someday, the book with its activities creates the opportunity to communicate immediately.

Invitation also offers insights into French-speaking cultures and an understanding and appreciation of differences and similarities among individuals and cultures in a pluralistic, interdependent world. Cultural content is not limited to a few cultural notes but is integrated throughout the text.

Flexibility

Each student enrolls in a French class with his or her own purposes, goals, and interests. Each instructor likewise has instructional goals that, within the context of a particular course and school, mean "learning French." *Invitation* has been carefully engineered to accommodate this diversty. It is a

comprehensive book offering a maximum number of options. Particular activities, selections, and even some sections of grammar may be omitted
without disruption of the program.

Organization of the book

Invitation has a preliminary chaper, twenty-two regular chapters, a final
chapter that focuses on the *passé simple (Invitation à la lecture)*, and appendixes. Each of the twenty-two chapters includes the following sections:

1. *Introduction:* These introductory passages of varying subject matter and
   format provide diverse contexts for the development of oral ability and
   acquisition of cultural insights. New noncognate vocabulary is glossed in
   the margin to ensure immediate comprehension of unfamiliar words.
   Compréhension: This section evaluates the student's understanding of the
   introductory passage.
   Et vous? This section, new in the second edition, introduces vocabulary
   centered around a topic that is related to the chapter theme. Varied
   communication activities involve the student in the active use of the vocabulary presented.
2. *Grammaire:* Each grammar topic is presented and practiced in the following phases:
   Présentation: The grammar topic is described and examples of its use are
   presented. Accompanying the *Présentation* are simple pattern drills that
   appear only in the Instructor's Edition.
   Préparation: All grammar concepts are practiced in structured, lifelike
   situations, many of which are placed in authentic cultural contexts.
   Communication: Varied formats invite the student to use the language
   to send and receive messages that are personally meaningful to him or
   her. Each and every pattern is therefore immediately practiced in communicative situations and contexts similar to those in which native speakers would use the structure.
3. *Synthèse:* The *Synthèse* passage, designed primarily to develop reading
   skill, recombines and integrates grammar and vocabulary used in the
   chapter and provides additional cultural insights and the opportunity to
   work with new vocabulary in context. The *Synthèse* is also followed by
   Compréhension questions. In addition, a final sequence of *Communication* activities is provided to integrate the chapter's grammar, vocabulary,
   and thematic content.
4. *Notes culturelles:* The cultural notes elaborate on ideas alluded to in both
   the *Introduction* and the *Synthèse.* They provide insights into the daily
   life and attitudes of people in French-speaking countries.
5. *Prononciation:* The most significant features of spoken French are described in each of the first ten chapters. Drills to practice both individual
   sounds and longer sentences containing critical sounds are also included.
6. *Vocabulaire:* Each chapter is followed by a comprehensive list of vocabulary words intended for active use in the chapter and in subsequent
   chapters. The lists, organized thematically wherever possible, contain the
   most important noncognate and cognate words used in the chapter.

Supplementary materials

Accompanying *Invitation* are the following supplementary materials:

1. The Instructor's Edition of *Invitation:* The Instructor's Edition contains the complete Student Edition of *Invitation* accompanied by marginal notes suggesting ways in which the sections, exercises, and activities can be used, modified, or elaborated upon. The Instructor's Edition also includes an introduction with more general suggestions for using the various sections of the book, as well as sample lesson plans and sample tests.
2. The tape program and the laboratory manual, *Invitation à écouter et à parler:* These provide students with the opportunity to practice oral skills outside of class. Each chapter in *Invitation* has an accompanying tape divided into two twenty-minute segments. Each tape includes the reading of the *Introduction* and *Synthèse* passages, oral drills and a listening comprehension activity for each grammar topic, a listening comprehension passage, a short thematic dictation, personal questions related to the chapter theme, and for Chapters 1–10, pronunciation drills. *Invitation á écouter et à parler* is the student guide to the tape program.
3. The workbook, *Invitation à écrire:* The workbook has been designed to expand students' ability to communicate in writing. Each chapter of *Invitation* has accompanying exercises and activities in the workbook.

Acknowledgments

Special thanks are owed to the students, instructors, and teaching assistants at The Ohio State University who have used the first edition of *Invitation* and whose reactions and comments have been helpful in this revision. Additional thanks are owed to the native speakers of French who were consulted on various language and cultural matters—in particular, Professor Micheline Besnard and Danielle Fréchou, The Ohio State University. Professor Élise André, Berea College, has also provided many valuable comments and suggestions.

We would also like to thank the following reviewers, whose comments helped to shape this revision of *Invitation*: Betsy Barnes, University of Minnesota; Lillian Bulwa, Northeastern University; Walter Gershuny, Northeastern University; Madeleine Hague, University of Maryland; Mary Byrd Kelly, University of North Carolina, Chapel Hill; Norma Jane Murphy, University of Texas, Austin; Judy Shrum, Virginia Polytechnic and State University; Jaqueline Simon, University of California, Santa Barbara; Claire Tufts, University of North Carolina, Chapel Hill; Joel Walz, University of Georgia.

Carl Morse carefully edited the manuscript.

G.A.J.
T.M.B.
D.E.C.
D.W.B.

Table des matières

Invitation

CHAPITRE PRÉLIMINAIRE

Invitation is, quite literally, an invitation to communicate meaningfully in French from the early moments of your exposure to the language. *Invitation* enhances your potential for such communication by capitalizing on some distinct advantages you have as you begin French study. You have, for example, the advantage of dealing not only with a familiar alphabet but also with many words whose spelling and meaning are identical or similar in the two languages. You will immediately recognize such words as **possible, opinion, intelligent,** and **automobile.** And you will easily recognize such words as **université, appartement, problème,** and **musique.** There are also certain aspects of French sentence structure and grammar that are similar to English. Most of the time you will not even notice these similarities because they are so readily understood. There is no need, for example, to emphasize the normal French sentence order of subject, verb, and object because this order is the same as in English.

The French language differs, of course, from English in other fundamental ways. Before beginning Chapter 1, you will want to become familiar with certain preliminary concepts relating to the spoken and written language.

THE SPOKEN AND WRITTEN LANGUAGE

A. Learning to speak French requires modification of some long-established habits. It is especially important to understand three aspects of French pronunciation from the beginning:

1. The stress pattern of French is different from that of English. All the syllables of a French word or group of words receive equal stress, or emphasis, except the last one, which is more heavily emphasized. Compare the consistent pattern in French words with the variable pattern in similar English words:

French	fes ti **val**	po ssi bi li **té**	in te lli **gence**
English	*fes ti val*	*pos si **bil** i ty*	*in **tel** li gence*

2. Certain sounds of spoken French have no counterpart in spoken English. For example, the French nasal vowels are new to speakers of English. These are present in such words as **non, impossible,** and **parent.**

3. Words or groups of letters familiar in English have a different pronunciation in French. The English pronunciation, for example, of such words as **sports, nature,** or **chocolat** would probably not be comprehensible to a French speaker.

B. The pronunciation of unfamiliar sounds, such as the nasal vowels, and of familiar words or groups of letters must be learned primarily by imitation. You will be assisted, however, by the suggestions provided in the pronunciation sections of *Invitation* and by use of the International Phonetic Alphabet when appropriate. The International Phonetic Alphabet is also used to compare written and spoken French. As in English, the various vowel and consonant sounds of the spoken language may have several different spellings in the written language. But in the International Phonetic Alphabet, each sound, whatever the spelling, is designated by one symbol. For example, the French words **mer** (*sea*), **mère** (*mother*), and **maire** (*mayor*) are spelled differently but are pronounced the same. Hence, the same International Phonetic Alphabet symbols designate the sounds of each word: [mɛr]. The International Phonetic Alphabet symbols, which always appear between brackets, are given in the Appendix.

At this point you might want to teach the alphabet. Students can practice by completing activities such as (1) spelling their names, (2) spelling common French first and/or last names, (3) spelling the names of French-speaking countries.

C. Written French includes certain accent marks that should be considered a part of spelling. They often affect the pronunciation of the letter with which they appear.

The **accent aigu** (´) appears over the vowel **e**:

détester, préférence

The **accent grave** (`) appears over the vowels **e** and **a** and on the word **où**:

à, discrète, où

The **accent circonflexe** (ˆ) appears over the vowels **a, e, i, o,** and **u**:

hôtel, honnêtes

The **cédille** (¸) appears under the letter **c**:

français, garçon

The **tréma** (¨) appears over the second of two vowels to indicate that both are pronounced:

Noël, naïf

THE FRENCH-SPEAKING WORLD

French is spoken in many parts of the world. The main language of 130 million people, it is widely spoken in north and west Africa, southeast Asia, and the Caribbean. It is also an official language of Belgium, Switzerland, Luxembourg, and Canada. In the Quebec area of Canada alone, there are more than five million French speakers. And in the United States there are two and one-half million French speakers living especially in the Northeast and in Louisiana.

French was the language of diplomacy for centuries. Today it is an official language of the United Nations and of many other international organizations. Also, French is the first language of the European Common Market.

Aspects du monde francophone

À Paris

Dans la
République
Malgache

En Algérie

En France

Le Français dans le monde

1. l'Algérie
2. les Antilles
   (la Guadeloupe,
   la Martinique,
   Saint-Martin)
3. la Belgique
4. le Cameroun
5. le Canada (le Québec)

6. le Congo
7. la Corse
8. la Côte-d'Ivoire
9. le Bénin
10. les États-Unis
    (la Louisiane,
    la Nouvelle-Angleterre)

11. la France
12. le Gabon
13. la Guinée
14. la Guyane
15. Haïti
16. la Haute-Volta

Give number of country and have
student give name in French.

ACTIVITÉS PRÉLIMINAIRES

Petites conversations

A. Présentez-vous. (*Introduce yourself.*)

1. Greet and introduce yourself to the person next to you in class. Then ask his or her name:

   Salut. Je m'appelle _____ .   *Hi. My name is _____ .*
   Comment vous appelez-vous?   *What is your name?*

2. Greet your professor and introduce yourself:

   Bonjour (Monsieur *or* Madame,   *Hello (said to a man, married*
      or Mademoiselle).   *woman, or unmarried woman).*
   Je m'appelle _____   *My name is _____ .*

   Note that the informal **salut** is not necessarily followed by a person's name. On the other hand, **bonjour** (and **bonsoir,** meaning *good evening*) is almost always followed by **monsieur, madame,** or **mademoiselle,** or by a person's first name.

B. Ça va? (*How are things?*)

1. Ask another student how he or she is. The student may, in turn, ask how you are:

   Ça va?   *How are things?*
   Ça va bien, merci. Et vous?   *Fine, thank you. And you?*
   Ça ne va pas très bien.   *Things aren't going very well.*

2. Ask your professor how he or she is:

   Comment allez-vous?   *How are you?*
   Je vais bien, merci.   *I'm fine, thank you.*

C. Au revoir. (*Good-bye.*)

1. Say good-bye to another student and say that you will see him or her later.

   Au revoir.   *Good-bye.*
   À tout à l'heure.   *See you later.*

2. Say good-bye to your professor and say that you will see him or her tomorrow.

   Au revoir, Monsieur (Madame, Mademoiselle).   *Good-bye.*
   À demain.   *See you tomorrow.*

D. Faisons connaissance. (*Let's get acquainted.*) You may want to recombine the expressions you have learned in A and B to get acquainted with other students. For example, you might want to ask another person what his or her name is and how he or she is. Or, you could greet someone you already know and ask how things are.

Dans la salle de classe *(In the classroom)*

A. Qu'est-ce que c'est? *(What is it?)* The following illustration shows objects typically found in a classroom. See if you can name them when your professor or another student asks you what they are.

Exemple   Qu'est-ce que c'est?   →   **C'est une chaise.**

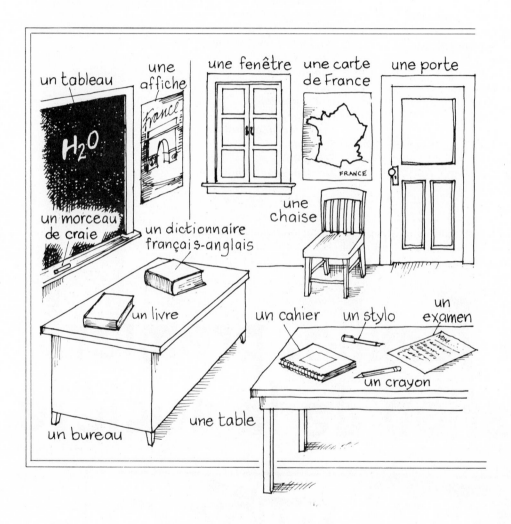

B. Quelques expressions utiles. *(Some useful expressions.)* The following are typical expressions that you or your professor will need to use in class to communicate with each other.

Qu'est-ce que ça veut dire?	*What does that mean?*
Ça veut dire . . .	*That means . . .*
Comment dit-on . . . en français?	*How does one say . . . in French?*
On dit . . .	*One says . . .*
Est-ce que vous comprenez?	*Do you understand?*
Oui, je comprends.	*Yes, I understand.*
Non, je ne comprends pas.	*No, I don't understand.*
Je ne sais pas.	*I don't know.*
Répétez, s'il vous plaît.	*Repeat, please.*
Allez au tableau.	*Go to the board.*
Ouvrez votre livre.	*Open your book.*
Fermez vos livres.	*Close your books.*
Écoutez bien.	*Listen well (carefully).*
Asseyez-vous.	*Sit down.*
Levez-vous.	*Stand up.*
Remettez vos devoirs.	*Hand in your homework.*

Check student comprehension by having students follow directions or give French equivalents for expressions. Students might also give these commands to you or to other students.

Faites le premier pas. *(Take the first step.)*

Students could look through French magazines and newspapers to find other items that they recognize.

What you know about English and about various aspects of daily life can help you as you begin to read in French. See if you can get the general idea of the following items taken from a French-Canadian newspaper.

La famille, premier bastion de la société

$1000 À GAGNER   LOTO BINGO

Petite histoire d'un grand festival

EDITORIAL

La longue marche du Parti libéral du Québec

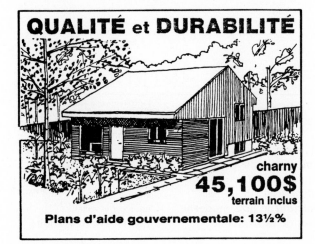

QUALITÉ et DURABILITÉ

charny
45,100$
terrain inclus

Plans d'aide gouvernementale: 13½%

Restauration de la résidence du Gouverneur général

carrières et professions

Préférences
1

Jazz has always been popular in France; many French students know a lot about American jazz.

INTRODUCTION

J'adore, je déteste

La musique, le jazz moderne: Point out that although **le, la, les** usually mean *the,* no article is used here in English.

Jacqueline and Jean-Luc, students at the University of Strasbourg, are talking about some of the things that they like and dislike.

JACQUELINE	*Moi,* j'adore la musique. *Et vous?*	I (with emphasis) / And you?
JEAN-LUC	*Moi aussi,* j'adore la musique, *surtout* le jazz moderne.	me too / especially
JACQUELINE	Ah *oui?* Moi, j'*aime mieux* le jazz de la *Nouvelle Orléans.*	yes / prefer / New Orleans
JEAN-LUC	Vous *aimez voyager?*	like / to travel
JACQUELINE	Oui, j'aime *beaucoup* voyager, *mais* je déteste les voyages *en* groupe. Et vous?	a lot / but in
JEAN-LUC	*Pas moi!* Moi, j'*aime bien* voyager en groupe. Je *trouve* *ça* intéressant.	Not me! / enjoy / find that

Étudiants à Paris

Étudiants en province

Compréhension   Selon les renseignements donnés, est-ce que les phrases suivantes sont vraies ou fausses? *(According to the information given, are the following statements true or false?)*

1. Jacqueline adore la musique.
2. Jean-Luc aime la musique.
3. Jean-Luc aime surtout le jazz de la Nouvelle Orléans.
4. Jacqueline aime mieux le jazz moderne.
5. Jacqueline aime beaucoup voyager.
6. Jacqueline déteste voyager en groupe.
7. Jean-Luc aussi déteste voyager en groupe.

NOTES CULTURELLES

Les jeunes Français

Recent polls indicate that the attitudes of French young people reflect both traditional and nontraditional values. For example, the majority are in favor of marriage, but most believe strongly in retaining independence and avoiding possessiveness in marriage. More than half indicate that they believe in God, but few actively practice their religion. The majority believe that they have a good relationship with their parents, but a significant minority reject their families and traditional family values. Although the majority of young French are less interested in politics and less patriotic than the previous generation, there is a strongly militant and politically active minority. Many French young people are, for example, campaigning

Have students compare attitudes of young Americans on the topics discussed in the **Notes culturelles.**

Une manifestation anti-nucléaire

12

against the use of nuclear power and the establishment of nuclear power plants in France. Occupations such as medicine, architecture, business, and the arts are especially appealing to many. French young people believe in saving the money they earn—at least until they have enough to buy what they want. And if they had the money, the most desirable purchase would be a car.

Et vous?

Use the following words in sentences that tell what you like and what you dislike.

You may find it helpful to follow these guidelines for using the **Et Vous?** section. (1) Have students repeat the words. (2) Have them practice the example sentences. (3) Have them make up their own sentences using the words provided.

A. Moi, je . . .

> **Exemples** J'adore la nature, mais je déteste le camping.
> Je déteste les examens, et j'adore les week-ends.

J'adore   Je déteste

la musique
le cinéma
la solitude
le snobisme
le tennis
le rugby
les professeurs
les sports
la nature   les week-ends   les examens
l'hypocrisie
la politique
le chocolat
la liberté
les voyages
le football

This exercise may also be done with **J'aime bien, J'aime mieux,** and **J'aime beaucoup.**

Point out that **le football** means soccer.

B. Activités. Tell whether you like or dislike each of the following activities.

> **Exemple** parler français
> J'adore parler français!
> Je déteste parler français!

Option: Have students offer an opinion and ask another student what he or she likes to do (e.g., **J'adore parler français. Et vous?**)

1. écouter la radio *to listen to the radio*
2. chanter *to sing*
3. travailler *to work*
4. étudier *to study*
5. parler français *to speak French*
6. manger *to eat*
7. regarder la télé *to watch TV*
8. nager *to swim*
9. marcher *to walk*
10. danser *to dance*

C. Préférences. Ask other students what they like *(Qu'est-ce que vous ai-mez?)* and what they dislike *(Qu'est-ce que vous détestez?).*

Exemple   Qu'est-ce que vous aimez?
              J'aime la musique et les sports.

L'article défini et le nom

Présentation

The French definite article corresponds to *the* in English. In French, the definite article (the) has several forms because it reflects both gender (masculine or feminine) and number (singular or plural). All French nouns—even names of things—are either masculine or feminine. It is important to learn the gender along with the meaning of all nouns because the forms of related words, such as adjectives and articles, often depend upon the gender of the noun they describe.

A. The forms of the definite article are:

Les articles définis	Singular	Plural
Masculine before a consonant	le professeur	les professeurs
Feminine before a consonant	la classe	les classes
Before a vowel or vowel sound	l'examen	les examens

When a masculine or feminine noun begins with a vowel or a vowel sound (e.g., with a mute **h** as in **histoire**), the plural article **les** is pronounced [lez]. For example, one says **les hôtels** and **les examens**. This linking is called liaison. To remind you that liaison takes place, the symbol will be used in the presentations of the first chapters.

B. You already know some nouns related to campus life (**les professeurs, l'examen, la musique, les sports**). Some additional school-related terms are:

Point out that **parler français (anglais)** is an idiom that drops the definite article before the noun.

le cours (*class*)
le livre (*book*)
le restaurant universitaire
le campus
la bibliothèque (*library*)
la leçon (*lesson*)
la résidence universitaire (*dorm*)
l'université (f)
l'étudiant (m) (*student*)
l'étudiante (f) (*student*)
les vacances (f) (*vacation*)

le français (*French*)
la philosophie
la littérature
la géographie
l'anglais (m) (*English*)
l'éducation physique (f)
l'histoire (f)
les sciences (f. pl)
les mathématiques (les maths) (f. pl)
le trimestre (*quarter*)
les explications (f) (*explanations*)

The plural of a noun is usually formed by adding an -s: **le livre → les livres; l'université → les universités; la bibliothèque → les bibliothèques**. The plural ending -s is not added to singular nouns that end in -s, -x, or -z: **le cours → les cours**. The final -s is not pronounced. In spoken language, the article indicates whether a noun is singular or plural.

C. The definite article has two common uses:

1. It corresponds to *the* in English: **le professeur** = *the teacher*, **l'examen** = *the test*, **les étudiants** = *the students*.

Je regarde **le** livre.
J'aime écouter **la** radio.

2. The definite article also precedes nouns used in a general sense and abstract nouns. In these cases, the article is used in French but not in English.

J'aime **les** sports.   *I like sports.*
Je déteste **la** solitude.   *I hate solitude.*

Répétition: Have students repeat the nouns in part B of the **Présentation. Substitution:** Give the noun without the definite article, and have students provide the noun and article (e.g., **livre → le livre**). Then give the singular noun and article and have the students provide the plural (e.g., **le livre → les livres**).

Préparation

A. Curiosité. Robert and Liliane are beginning their studies at the University of Poitiers. Robert wants to know what subjects Liliane likes. What does he ask?

During the **premier cycle** (first two years), university students take courses in several related areas (e.g., **sciences humaines—philosophie, histoire, sciences sociales**). After passing the **D.E.U.G. (Diplôme d'Études Universitaires Générales)**, they choose an area of specialization.

Modèle   histoire → **Vous aimez l'histoire?**

1. maths
2. anglais
3. littérature
4. philosophie
5. sciences
6. géographie
7. éducation physique
8. musique
9. histoire

B. Opinions. Véronique and Gérard, students at the Saint-Martin d'Hères campus of the University of Grenoble, disagree about various aspects of university life. Tell what each says.

Modèle   campus → VÉRONIQUE **J'aime le campus.**
              GÉRARD **Moi, je déteste le campus.**

1. université
2. professeurs
3. bibliothèque
4. résidences
5. examens
6. étudiants
7. restaurant universitaire
8. cours

Although French universities have traditionally been located in the center of town, many have also built new campuses on the outskirts of town to accommodate increasing numbers of students.

Un campus moderne

Communication

A. Réactions. Words often evoke positive, negative, or neutral feelings. Using the scale, indicate your attitudes toward each of the following words.

Exemples   J'aime bien le cinéma.
               J'adore les vacances.

Suggestion: Teacher or student gives words, students give opinions. Written preparation may be helpful.

Je déteste   J'aime bien   J'aime beaucoup   J'adore

1. _____ le football.
2. _____ le cinéma.
3. _____ le chocolat.
4. _____ la nature.
5. _____ la musique.
6. _____ les sports.
7. _____ les vacances.
8. _____ la politique.
9. _____ la télévision.
10. _____ la solitude.

Option: Using the list of courses presented in the **Présentation** on the definite article, have students tell whether they like or dislike the courses given (e.g., **J'aime bien les maths et j'adore la littérature**).

B. Questions. Use the following words to make questions asking other students if they like or dislike various aspects of campus life.

Exemple   université → **Vous aimez l'université?**

1. université
2. campus
3. professeurs
4. littérature
5. sciences
6. étudiants
7. restaurant universitaire
8. cours
9. vacances

C. Slogans. Create slogans that tell whether you are for (**vive** = *long live)* or against (**à bas** = *down with*) the following things. The question mark following the list of suggestions is an invitation to add or substitute any items you wish.

Vive . . .   *Suggestions:* la politique / les mathématiques / le football
À bas . . .   / la liberté / les professeurs / les examens / l'hypocrisie /
                    les vacances / ?

A question mark **?** signals free response. Encourage students to use known words and/or add other words.

Exemples: Vive la liberté!
                 À bas l'hypocrisie!

⚜ Les verbes de la première conjugaison et les pronoms sujets

Présentation

In English, verb forms sometimes change endings according to the subject of the verb. We say, for example, *I like* but *he likes, we wish* but *Mary wishes.* In French, there is a specific verb ending for each subject.

A. One large group of French verbs, called the first conjugation (**la première conjugaison**), has infinitives that end in **-er.** The present tense of a first-conjugation verb is formed by dropping the **-er** from the infinitive (**aimer, étudier, parler, travailler**) and adding the ending that corresponds to the subject.

travailler			
je travaille	*I work*	**nous travaillons**	*we work*
tu travailles	*you work*	**vous travaillez**	*you work*
il/elle/on travaille	*he/she/one works*	**ils/elles travaillent**	*they work*

Je parle français.
Nous étudions beaucoup.
Ils travaillent en groupe.

The present tense in French is used to express a variety of meanings.

Je travaille.   *I work.*
                 I am working.
                 I do work.

1. In spoken French, there are only three distinguishable **-er** verb forms. All singular forms and the **ils/elles** form (in the darker shaded area) have the same pronunciation. These endings add no sound at all, as indicated by the crossed-out letters.

    When the verb begins with a vowel sound, **je** shortens to **j'**, and **nous, vous, ils, elles** all link to the verb with a [z] sound, as shown:

aimer	
j'aimé	nous aimons
tu aimés	vous aimez
il/elle/on aimé	ils/elles aimént

2. **Voyager** and **manger** (and other verbs ending in **-ger**) follow the same pattern as other first-conjugation verbs, except that in the **nous** form, an e is added before the **-ons** ending to indicate the soft sound of the g.

    Nous mangeons beaucoup.
    Nous voyageons en France.

Despite their spelling irregularities (which need not be overemphasized at this point), **voyager** and **manger** are very useful in communication.

3. You already know the adverbs **bien** and **beaucoup**. Other common adverbs used to modify verbs are:

rarement *rarely*	Ils étudient **rarement**.
quelquefois *sometimes*	Nous écoutons **quelquefois** la radio.
souvent *often*	Vous regardez **souvent** la télévision.
tout le temps *all the time*	Tu travailles **tout le temps**.
toujours *always*	Ils voyagent **toujours** en groupe.

B. The French subject pronouns are shown on the verb charts: **je, tu, il, elle, on, nous, vous, ils, elles.** A subject pronoun can be used to replace a noun that is the subject of a sentence.

1. Two French pronouns correspond to the English pronoun *you*. To address another person directly, a choice must be made between **tu**, which is the familiar form, and **vous**, the more formal form. **Tu** is used only with close friends, relatives, children, and pets; otherwise **vous** is used. Note that **vous** is also used when speaking to more than one person.

    Tu danses bien, Pierre!
    Paul et Nicole, **vous** travaillez beaucoup!
    Vous parlez anglais, Madame?

2. **On** is an impersonal pronoun like English *one, we, they,* or *people*.

    On aime mieux écouter la radio.   *We prefer to listen to the radio.*
    On parle français en Belgique.   *They speak French in Belgium.*

Répétition: Have students repeat the conjugations of **travailler, aimer, étudier.** **Substitution:** (1) Je regarde la télévision. vous / tu / nous / Marie / Gérard et Robert. (2) On parle français. je / Marc / vous / tu / nous / les étudiants. (3) Alain et Michel adorent voyager. nous / tu / Sylvie et Anne / je / vous.

3. In the third person, **il** or **ils** is used when the replaced noun is masculine, **elle** or **elles** when it is feminine. When a mixed group of masculine and feminine nouns is replaced by a subject pronoun, **ils** is used.

    Alain et Patrick aiment la musique. →   **Ils** aiment la musique.
    Monique et Françoise adorent le camping. →   **Elles** adorent le camping.
    Henri et Julie détestent les mathématiques. → **Ils** détestent les mathématiques.

A. Autoportrait. Geneviève is talking about some of the things she does. What does she say?

> **Modèle** nager rarement → **Je nage rarement.**

Repeat with **elle**. (Elle nage rarement.)

1. travailler beaucoup
2. voyager souvent
3. regarder quelquefois la télé
4. étudier tout le temps
5. nager bien
6. danser rarement
7. écouter souvent la radio
8. chanter bien

Point out that **la télé** is the short form for **la télévision**.

B. Curiosité. Alain wants to know what his friends do or like to do. Give his friends' answers.

> **Modèle** Vous travaillez beaucoup? → **Oui, nous travaillons beaucoup.**

Repeat with **ils**. (Ils travaillent beaucoup.)

1. Vous écoutez souvent la radio?
2. Vous regardez quelquefois la télé?
3. Vous aimez danser?
4. Vous dansez bien?
5. Vous voyagez beaucoup?
6. Vous aimez marcher?
7. Vous parlez toujours français?
8. Vous nagez bien?

C. Variété. Solange is telling what several people are doing now. What does she say?

> **Modèle** nous / étudier le français → **Nous étudions le français.**

1. Michel / nager
2. je / travailler
3. Paul et Luc / écouter la radio
4. vous / parler anglais
5. tu / étudier les maths
6. nous / regarder la télé
7. on / écouter les explications
8. vous / chanter
9. nous / manger
10. vous / nager

A. Préférences. Using verbs like **adorer, aimer, aimer bien, détester,** make sentences expressing your likes and dislikes, those of other students, and those of Americans in general.

Options: (1) Written. (2) Oral—Student gives preferences or teacher gives word, student gives preference.

> **Exemple** Moi, j'aime bien le cinéma.

Moi, je . . .
En général, les Américains . . .
Nous, les étudiants, nous . . .

Suggestions: les sports / la musique / le camping / la politique / les mathématiques / le cinéma / le chocolat / l'hypocrisie / les vacances / voyager / travailler / étudier / danser / manger / parler français / ?

B. Rarement ou souvent? Using the scale, tell how often you do each activity.

Exemple   Je parle souvent français.

rarement   quelquefois   souvent

1. étudier
2. danser
3. écouter la radio
4. regarder la télé

5. travailler
6. nager
7. parler français
8. marcher

Option: Have students compliment each other (e.g., **Tu danses bien. Tu parles bien français.**).

C. Interview. Using the list of activities that you prepared in *Communication B*, tell another student what you do and ask if he or she does the same thing.

Exemple   J'étudie souvent. Et vous?
              Moi aussi, j'étudie souvent.
    or   Pas moi! J'étudie rarement.

Have students report back the results of their interviews.

⚜ La forme négative

Présentation

A. In French, **ne . . . pas** is used to make a sentence negative. **Ne** precedes the conjugated verb and **pas** follows it.

Vous parlez beaucoup.	*You talk a lot.*
Vous **ne** parlez **pas** beaucoup.	*You don't talk a lot.*
Nous nageons souvent.	*We swim often.*
Nous **ne** nageons **pas** souvent.	*We don't swim often.*

1. When a verb begins with a vowel sound, **ne** becomes **n'**.

   Je **n'**aime **pas** danser.
   Vous **n'**écoutez **pas**.

2. When an infinitive follows a conjugated verb, **ne . . . pas** surrounds the conjugated form of the verb.

   Nous aimons voyager.   Nous **n'**aimons **pas** voyager.

B. In order to say that something *never* takes place, **ne . . . jamais** is used. It functions in the same ways as **ne . . . pas**.

Tu **n'**écoutes **jamais**.	*You never listen.*
Gilbert **ne** parle **jamais** anglais.	*Gilbert never speaks English.*

Préparation

Have students conjugate the following in the negative: **Je ne travaille pas beaucoup. Je n'aime pas voyager. Je ne regarde jamais la télé.**

Contradictions. Each time that Monique makes a statement, Serge disagrees with her. Tell what Serge says.

Modèle   Nous aimons parler anglais. → **Non, nous n'aimons pas parler anglais.**

1. Nous regardons la télé.
2. Les étudiants travaillent beaucoup.
3. Nous aimons les professeurs.
4. Ils voyagent beaucoup.
5. On aime danser.
6. Hélène travaille beaucoup.
7. On parle anglais en classe.
8. Richard déteste la politique.

Communication

A. Oui ou non? Do you agree or disagree with the following statements? If you disagree, make the statement negative by using **ne . . . pas** or **ne . . . jamais**.

Exemple   Vous voyagez beaucoup.
             Non, je ne voyage pas beaucoup.
    or   Non, je ne voyage jamais.

1. Vous travaillez tout le temps.
2. Vous aimez étudier.
3. Les étudiants adorent les examens.
4. Vous détestez les week-ends.
5. Les Américains détestent les sports.
6. Vous parlez bien français.
7. Vous chantez bien.
8. Vous aimez beaucoup les maths.
9. Les étudiants écoutent toujours en classe.
10. Vous nagez souvent.

B. Pas moi! Using vocabulary you know, make a list of things you don't do or never do.

Exemples   Je ne regarde jamais la télé.
Je n'aime pas chanter.

La forme interrogative

Présentation

The most common way to find out information is by asking questions.

A. You have already asked questions by raising the pitch of your voice at the end of a sentence.

Vous aimez la musique?
Tu parles anglais?

Remind students of the difference between a statement where the voice goes down at the end of the sentence and a question where the voice goes up slightly.

B. Another common way of asking a question is to precede a statement with the phrase **est-ce que** without changing the word order of the sentence. As in all questions that can be answered by yes or no, the voice goes up slightly at the end of the sentence.

Est-ce que vous parlez anglais?
Est-ce que Chantal aime le cinéma?

*Point out that the voice rises mostly on **est-ce que** and only slightly on the last word.*

When **est-ce que** precedes a noun or a pronoun beginning with a vowel sound, it becomes **est-ce qu'**.

Est-ce qu'il aime danser?
Est-ce qu'Hélène regarde la télévision?

*In colloquial language, **n'est-ce pas** is often replaced by **hein**.*

C. Another kind of question is the confirmation question. In English one asks, *You're tired, aren't you?* or *He doesn't speak French, does he?* To express this idea in French, the expression **n'est-ce pas** is added to the end of a statement.

Vous marchez beaucoup, **n'est-ce pas?**
Jacques n'étudie pas beaucoup, **n'est-ce pas?**

*Have students change the following to questions with **est-ce que**: (1) Chantal étudie beaucoup. (2) Vous aimez le cinéma. (3) Georges et Jean détestent nager. (4) Irène parle anglais. (5) Tu aimes la solitude. Have students change the following to questions with **n'est-ce pas**: (1) Vous voyagez beaucoup. (2) Chantal aime la musique. (3) Vous étudiez le français. (4) Brigitte ne mange pas beaucoup. (5) Ils aiment mieux le tennis.*

Préparation

A. N'est-ce pas? Marie-Claude is fairly sure what classes her friends are taking, but, to be certain, she asks them. Give her questions.

Modèle   Michel / la philosophie → **Michel étudie la philosophie, n'est-ce pas?**

1. tu / la littérature
2. vous / les maths
3. Véronique / l'anglais
4. Michel et Roger / les sciences
5. tu / la géographie
6. vous / l'histoire

B. **Faisons connaissance.** Pauline is talking with Marc and wants to find out about him and his roommate Georges. What questions would she ask to obtain the following information?

Modèle   if he enjoys soccer → **Est-ce tu aimes bien le football?**

1. if he works a lot
2. if they like the student restaurants
3. if Georges is studying science
4. if they like the teachers
5. if they like camping
6. if they watch television often
7. if Georges speaks English
8. if they travel a lot

Option: Have students use vocabulary they know to make up questions that they might ask a prospective roommate.

Communication

A. **Interview.** Using the words provided, make up questions to ask another student. Begin your questions with **est-ce que.**

Exemple   écouter souvent la radio
Est-ce que tu écoutes souvent la radio?
Non, je n'écoute pas souvent la radio.

1. aimer danser
2. étudier tout le temps
3. voyager souvent
4. étudier la philosophie
5. écouter quelquefois la radio
6. aimer les sports
7. aimer étudier en groupe
8. aimer le campus

B. **Oui ou non?** Based on what you know about other students in your class, see if you can identify some of their activities or interests. Use **n'est-ce pas.** They will confirm whether you are right or not.

Exemple   Tu aimes beaucoup les sports, n'est-ce pas?
Oui, j'aime beaucoup les sports.
or   Non, je n'aime pas beaucoup les sports.

SYNTHÈSE

Faisons connaissance

Several students from different French-speaking countries are getting acquainted at a neighborhood *café* in Paris.

TAHAR (de *Tunis*):
Je m'appelle Tahar. J'étudie la médecine *ici* à Paris. J'aime beaucoup Paris, surtout le Quartier latin. Mais je déteste le climat. Je ne regarde jamais la télévision, mais j'écoute souvent la radio. J'aime beaucoup la musique classique.

The café is still an important meeting place for French people. Many students, for example, like to sit in their favorite café to study or talk with friends.

from

here / at, in

ANNE-MARIE DUCLERC *(de Lausanne):*

Moi, je m'appelle Anne-Marie Duclerc. J'adore Paris. Je travaille ici *comme* secrétaire-bilingue. La *vie* à Paris—les films, les *expositions*, les concerts, les *musées*—je trouve ça *formidable.*

as / life / exhibits
museums / great

MONIQUE ET ANDRÉ DUCHEMIN *(de Québec):*

Nous *habitons maintenant* à Paris. André étudie *l'informatique* et moi, j'étudie le *droit* et les sciences politiques. Nous aimons bien Paris, mais nous préférons* la vie à Québec.

live / now / computer science
law

CATHERINE SIMON *(de Saint-Étienne):*

Est-ce que je préfère Paris *ou* Saint-Étienne? Paris, *bien sûr!* J'adore marcher *dans* les *rues*, regarder les *gens* et les *magasins.* Mais je déteste le *métro.*

or / of course
in / streets / people / shops
subway

Compréhension Selon les renseignements donnés, répondez aux questions suivantes. *(According to the information given, answer the following questions.)*

1. Qu'est-ce que Tahar étudie?
2. Est-ce qu'il aime Paris?
3. Est-ce qu'il regarde souvent la télévision?
4. Est-ce qu'Anne-Marie aime beaucoup Paris?
5. Est-ce qu'elle travaille comme professeur à Paris?
6. Qu'est-ce que les Duchemin étudient?
7. Est-ce qu'ils préfèrent Paris ou Québec?
8. Est-ce que Catherine préfère Paris ou Saint-Étienne?
9. Est-ce que Catherine aime marcher dans les rues de Paris?

À la terrasse d'un café

*Préférer** is a regular -er verb, except that, in writing, the second accent changes in all singular forms and in the ils/elles form: **je préfère, tu préfères, il/elle/on préfère, ils/elles préfèrent;** but **nous préférons, vous préférez.**

Footnotes are used to deal with aspects of grammar that do not require systematic full-length presentations.

NOTES CULTURELLES

Paris et le reste de la France

The richness of Parisian history and the diversity of its cultural and intellectual life have always attracted visitors, students, and artists from all over the world. Among the well-known attractions of Paris are its famous museums (le Louvre, le Jeu de Paume, le Centre Pompidou); its landmarks (la Tour Eiffel, Notre Dame, l'Arc de Triomphe); its prestigious schools (la Sorbonne, l'École Polytechnique); its world-renowned restaurants (la Tour d'Argent, Chez Maxime); and its interesting areas (le Quartier latin, Montmartre). This same diversity exists in its population, which is comprised not only of native Parisians and *provinciaux* who have moved to Paris from the provinces but also of a varied international community. Sizable groups of Indochinese, North Africans, and black Africans are among the most recent ethnic groups to establish themselves in Paris.

Despite considerable effort in recent years to decentralize economic, political, and cultural affairs in France, Paris still remains the hub of most aspects of French life. Although there are a number of urban centers throughout France—thirty-two cities have a population of more than 100,000—many French people and foreigners still tend to think of areas outside Paris as *en province* and to equate Parisian culture with French civilization itself.

Paris is not really representative of all of France, however. The country is geographically varied, including high mountains in the south (the Pyrenees form a natural boundary with Spain) and in the east (the Jura and the Alps form the boundary with Switzerland and Italy). Mont Blanc, the highest mountain in Europe (4810 meters), is located in the French Alps, just south of the Swiss city of Geneva.

Les Champs Élysées le soir du 14 juillet

Un village français

Communication

A. Faisons connaissance. Using vocabulary you know, introduce yourself to another student in the class. Use the *Synthèse* as a guide.

B. Interview. Use the suggested words and phrases to formulate questions, or create questions of your own to ask other students.

Exemple   voyager beaucoup → **Est-ce que vous voyagez beaucoup?**

1. aimer la musique (l'éducation physique / la nature / les sports / le camping / le jazz / la solitude / le cinéma / ?)
2. aimer voyager (travailler / étudier / manger / chanter / parler français / regarder la télévision / ?)
3. détester l'hypocrisie (la violence / l'autorité / la politique / le snobisme / ?)
4. travailler beaucoup (étudier les mathématiques / regarder la télévision / parler français / voyager / ?)

C. Comparaisons. Using what you have found out about other students in the preceding activity, tell what you and other students like and dislike.

Exemple   Marc et moi, nous aimons travailler, mais Michelle aime manger.

Options: (1) Written. (2) Oral. (3) Elicit information through direct questions.

PRONONCIATION

The French vowel system *differs* from the English system in significant ways. In French, you will be learning a new pronunciation for some familiar vowels and encountering vowel sounds that do not exist in English. It will be important to remember also that French vowels are pronounced with greater tenseness than English vowels, and that they are never glided or diphthongized. Compare the pronunciation, for example, of the French and English words **qui** and *key*, **mes** and *may*, **sot** and *so*.

A. To become familiar with French vowel sounds and their most common spellings, repeat the words below.

[i]   philosophie, politique, liberté

[e]   aimer, étudier, autorité, général, les, et

[ɛ]   liberté, intellectuel, détester, secrétaire

[a]   adorer, chocolat, mathématiques

[y]   solitude, musique, nature, étudier

[ø]   mieux

[ə]   je, le, regarder

[œ]   professeur

[u]   beaucoup, vous

[o]   radio, beaucoup, faux

[ɔ]   sport, Paul

[ɛ̃]   Américain, magasin, maintenant

[ã]   français, anglais, violence, préférence, science, gens

[o]   opinion, nous aimons, télévision

B. Repeat the following sentences, paying special attention to the vowel sounds and making sure that your voice goes down at the end of each statement and up at the end of each question.

1. Tu étudies beaucoup?
2. Elle aime mieux regarder la télévision.
3. Le professeur adore la musique classique.
4. Est-ce que vous aimez la nature?

VOCABULAIRE

noms

la vie universitaire (voir p. 14)

les activités
° le camping*
° le café
° le cinéma
° le concert
  la cuisine *cooking*
  l'exposition (f) *exhibit*
° le film
  le football *soccer*
° le jazz
  le magasin *store*
  le musée *museum*
° la politique
° la radio
° le restaurant
° le rugby
° le sport
° la télévision
° le tennis
  les vacances (f) *vacation*
° le voyage
° le week-end

d'autres noms
  le chocolat
  le climat
  le droit *law (profession)*
  les gens (m,f) *people*
° l'hypocrisie (f)
° la liberté
  la médecine *medicine (profession)*
  le métro *subway*
° la nature
  la rue *street*
  le secrétaire, la secrétaire *secretary*
  la vie *life*

verbes
° adorer
  aimer *to like*
  chanter *to sing*
° danser
° détester
  écouter *to listen*
  étudier *to study*
  habiter *to live*

  manger *to eat*
  marcher *to walk*
  nager *to swim*
  parler *to speak*
° préférer
  regarder *to watch*
  travailler *to work*
  trouver *to find*
° voyager

adjectifs

bilingue *bilingual*
formidable *great*
intéressant(e) *interesting*
universitaire *university*

adverbes

aussi *also*
beaucoup *a lot*
bien *well*
maintenant *now*
mieux *better*
ne . . . jamais *never*
ne . . . pas *not*
quelquefois *sometimes*
rarement *rarely*
souvent *often*
surtout *especially*
toujours *always*
tout le temps *all the time*

divers

à *at, in*
bien sûr *of course*
ça *that*
comme *as, like*
dans *in*
de *from, of*
en *in*
et *and*
ici *here*
mais *but*
moi *me*
n'est-ce pas? *right? isn't it (he, she, you, etc.)?*
non *no*
ou *or*
oui *yes*
qu'est-ce que *what*

* The degree signs in the chapter vocabularies indicate words whose spelling and meaning are identical or similar in French and English.

CHAPITRE DEUX

Identité 2

Une interview avec Serge Lambert

A reporter is trying to interview an uncooperative participant in the *Tour de France*, France's most famous bicycle race.

LE REPORTER	Bonjour, Monsieur. Vous *êtes* Serge Lambert, n'est-ce pas?	are
SERGE	Oui, *c'est* moi.	it's
LE REPORTER	Vous êtes *français?*	French
SERGE	Non, je *suis belge.*	am / Belgian
LE REPORTER	Vous êtes *de* Bruxelles?	from
SERGE	Non, je suis d'Anvers.	
LE REPORTER	Vous *espérez* gagner* le Tour?	hope / to win
SERGE	*Pourquoi* pas?	why
LE REPORTER	*Quelles* qualités est-ce qu'*il faut posséder pour* gagner?	what / one must have / to
SERGE	Il faut *être très* patient—surtout avec les journalistes!	to be / very

Il faut + **infinitif** is introduced early because of its communicative value. Its opposite is **Il n'est pas necessaire de.**

---

* **Espérer** and **posséder** are conjugated like **préférer** and have the same accent changes: j'espère, tu espères, il/elle/on espère, nous espérons, vous espérez, ils/elles espèrent; je possède, tu possèdes, il/elle/on possède, nous possédons, vous possédez, ils/elles possèdent.

Le Tour de France

Compréhension   Selon les renseignements donnés, est-ce que les phrases suivantes sont vraies ou fausses? Corrigez le sens de la phrase s'il est faux. *(According to the information given, are the following statements true or false? If a statement is false, reword it to make it true.)*

1. Serge Lambert est français.
2. Il habite à Paris.
3. Il est journaliste.
4. Il espère gagner le Tour de France.
5. Il n'aime pas beaucoup les journalistes.

NOTES CULTURELLES

La Belgique

After centuries of being governed by other powers (Rome, France, Spain, Holland, Austria), Belgium gained its independence in 1830 and since then has been governed by a constitutional monarchy. Surrounded by Holland, Germany, France, Luxembourg, and the North Sea, it is a small country (11,781 square miles). Nonetheless, it has one

Bruxelles: Le marché aux fleurs sur la Grand'Place

of the world's most highly developed economies (chemicals, glass, textiles, grains, sugar beets). Belgium is a member of the European Common Market and the North Atlantic Treaty Alliance, whose headquarters is located in Brussels. The vast majority of Belgium's ten million inhabitants are Roman Catholic.

Well-known Belgians include writers such as the nineteenth-century symbolist Maeterlinck and, more recently, Georges Simenon, author of the immensely popular Maigret detective stories, and painters such as Van Eyck, Bosch, Bruegel, and Rubens. Eddie Merckx, multiple winner of the Tour de France, is a well-known name to European bicycle enthusiasts. Jacques Brel, a famous contemporary singer-composer, was also Belgian.

There are two major languages spoken in Belgium. According to recent statistics, the 44 percent of Belgians who speak French (**wallon**) live primarily in the southern part of the country. Belgians who live in the north speak Flemish (**flamand**), which is similar to Dutch. Although the capital city of Brussels is officially bilingual, the linguistic, economic, and social dominance of the Walloons has long been a major source of irritation for the Flemish and has caused serious social and political unrest.

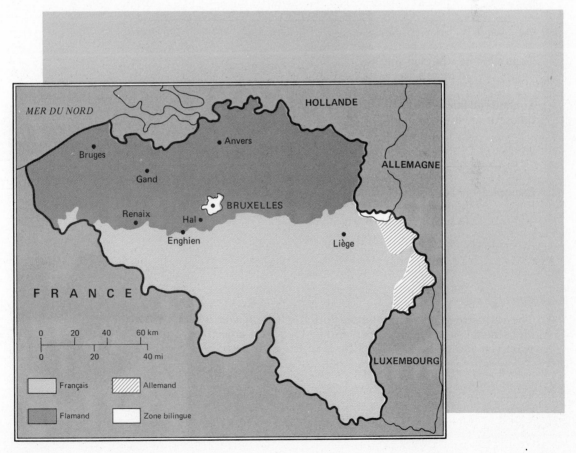

La Belgique linguistique

Et vous?

A. Quelles qualités est-ce que vous possédez? Tell whether each adjective describes you or not.

Exemple   Je ne suis pas riche mais je suis optimiste.

Je suis . . .
Je ne suis pas . . .

optimiste	riche	dynamique
pessimiste	pauvre *(poor)*	sympathique *(nice)*
modeste	honnête *(honest)*	romantique
timide	sincère	formidable *(great)*
conformiste	triste *(sad)*	irrésistible

B. Nuances. Using the scale, tell to what extent the adjectives given in Activity A describe your personality.

pas assez	assez	très	trop
not enough	*fairly*	*very*	*too much*

Exemples   Je suis trop sincère.
Je ne suis pas assez modeste.

C. Toujours ou jamais? Using the scale, tell whether you never, rarely, sometimes, or always have the qualities or feelings given in Activity A.

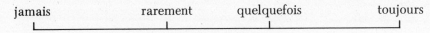

jamais   rarement   quelquefois   toujours

Exemples   Je suis toujours optimiste.
Je ne suis jamais triste.
Je suis quelquefois trop honnête.

⚜ Le verbe *être* et l'utilisation des adjectifs

Présentation

A. The verb **être** *(to be)* can be used to tell who you are, where you are, and where you are from. It can also be used with adjectives to describe what you and others are like. **Être** is an irregular verb.

être	
je **suis**	nous **sommes**
tu **es**	vous **êtes**
il/elle/on **est**	ils/elles **sont**

Est-ce que **vous êtes** étudiant?
Non, **je suis** professeur.

Ils sont à la bibliothèque?
Non, **ils** ne **sont** pas à la bibliothèque.

Vous êtes de Paris?
Non, **nous sommes** de Grenoble.

Elle est sympathique.
Tu es formidable!

Note that liaison is necessary in **vous êtes**. Liaison also frequently occurs when a form of **être** is followed by a word beginning with a vowel sound.

Ils sont à Paris.

Il est irrésistible.

C'est intéressant.

B. In French, adjectives agree in number and gender with the nouns they modify. The adjectives that you have already learned (such as **modeste, sincère, riche**) are part of a large group of French adjectives that end in **-e**. These adjectives have one singular form for both masculine and feminine nouns or pronouns. Their plural is formed by adding -s.

Je suis optimiste.	Nous sommes optimistes.
Tu es optimiste.	Vous êtes optimiste(s).
Il/elle/on est optimiste.	Ils/elles sont optimistes.

Other useful adjectives in this category are:

agréable *(pleasant)*	juste *(fair)*
bête *(stupid, silly)*	impossible
célèbre *(famous)*	possible
difficile *(difficult)*	moderne
facile *(easy)*	simple
injuste *(unfair)*	sévère

C. An adjective usually follows the nouns it modifies.

Il n'aime pas les examens **faciles**.
Nous préférons la musique **moderne**.

D. Adjectives can also be used to refer to a general idea or situation when used with **c'est,** the impersonal form of **être**. In this case, there is no agreement because there is no specific noun that the adjective refers to.

C'est facile.
Ce n'est pas possible.
C'est trop difficile.

Répétition: Have students repeat these sentences. (1) Je suis sincère, tu es sincère, etc. (2) Je ne suis pas célèbre, tu n'es pas célèbre, etc. **Substitution:** (1) Il est sympathique. tu / je / Monsieur Junot / vous / Mademoiselle Rochefort / nous. (2) Je ne suis pas de Paris. vous / tu / Chantal / nous / Roger et Hélène.

Préparation

A. Nous ne sommes pas modestes! Some friends are very satisfied with themselves. Tell what they say.

Modèle sincères → **Nous sommes sincères.**

1. honnêtes
2. optimistes
3. dynamiques
4. sympathiques
5. formidables
6. irrésistibles

*Repeat with **ils.***

B. Personnalité. Raymond is telling some friends what their zodiac signs say about their personalities. Tell what he says.

Modèle honnête et sincère → **Tu es honnête et sincère.**

1. timide et modeste
2. triste et pessimiste
3. sympathique et agréable
4. romantique et irrésistible
5. riche et célèbre
6. honnête et sympathique

*Repeat with **tu** and in the negative.*

C. À la résidence universitaire. Students at Laval University are telling where some of their friends are from. What do they say?

Modèle Geneviève / Trois-Rivières → **Geneviève est de Trois-Rivières.**

1. je / Québec
2. nous / St.-Jean
3. tu / Jonquières
4. Pierre / Montréal
5. nous / Beauport
6. Catherine / Toronto
7. vous / Victoriaville
8. Jacques et Michelle / Sherbrooke

Communication

A. Origines. Find out what city or town other students in your class are from.

Exemple Est-ce que tu es de Chicago?
Non, je ne suis pas de Chicago.

B. En France. With another student, pretend that you are from one of the French cities on the map. Other students will then try to guess which city the two of you are from.

Exemple Est-ce que vous êtes de Dijon?
Oui, nous sommes de Dijon.

C. Opinions. Using the cues provided, ask other students their opinions about various aspects of campus life.

Exemple professeurs / sympathiques →
Est-ce que les profs sont sympathiques?
Oui, les profs sont sympathiques.

1. français / facile
2. étudiants / sympathiques
3. cours / difficiles
4. profs / sévères
5. examens / difficiles
6. campus / agréable

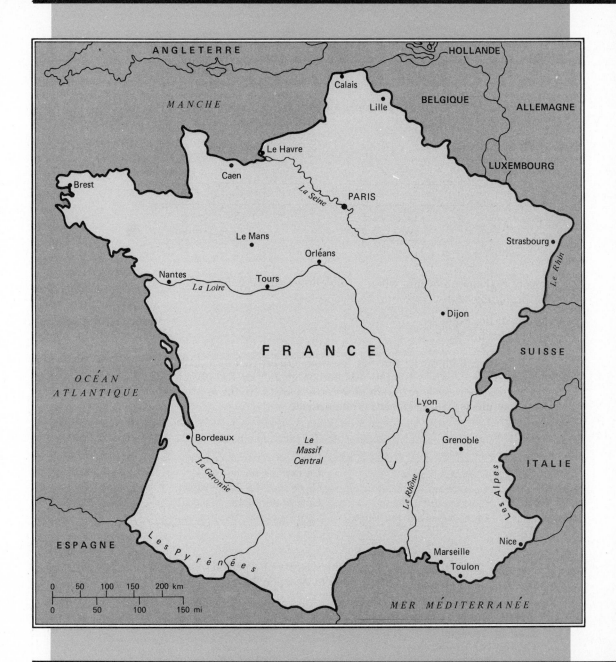

⚜ Les articles indéfinis

Présentation

A. The French indefinite articles **un, une,** and **des** correspond to *a*, *an*, and *some* in English.

Les articles indéfinis		
	Singular	*Plural*
Masculine	**un** concert	**des** concerts
Feminine	**une** exposition	**des** expositions

Note that liaison occurs when an indefinite article is followed by a noun beginning with a vowel or a vowel sound:

un examen, des examens
un hôtel, des hôtels

B. To ask what something is, use the question **Qu'est-ce que c'est?** This question does not vary with the number or gender of the object. To answer, however, use **c'est** *(it is)* or **ce sont** *(they are)* with the appropriate singular or plural form of the indéfinite article.

	Singular	*Plural*
Masculine	**C'est un** magasin.	**Ce sont des** magasins.
	Ce n'est pas un musée.	**Ce ne sont pas des** musées.
Feminine	**C'est une** bibliothèque.	**Ce sont des** bibliothèques.
	Ce n'est pas une résidence.	**Ce ne sont pas des** résidences.

C. The question **Qui est-ce?** is used to ask the identity of a person or a group of persons. **C'est** or **ce sont** is used in the answer.

Qui est-ce?
    C'est Jacques.
    C'est un étudiant.
    Ce sont des professeurs.

D. To identify people or to talk about their professions, the following vocabulary is useful.

un homme *(man)*   **un** enfant *(child)*
une femme *(woman)*   **un** avocat *(lawyer)*
un garçon *(boy)*   **une** avocate
une fille *(girl)*   **un** médecin *(doctor)*

un/une écrivain *(writer)*	**une** ouvrière
un/une dentiste	**un** commerçant *(shopkeeper)*
un ingénieur *(engineer)*	**une** commerçante
un/une architecte	**un** employé
un/une journaliste	**une** employée
un ouvrier *(worker)*	

E. When talking about people's professions, nationalities, and religions, the indefinite article must be used with **c'est** and **ce sont,** and when the profession is modified by an adjective.

C'est **une** journaliste.
C'est **une** journaliste formidable.
Catherine est **une** journaliste formidable.

However, the indefinite article is *not* used when the name of the profession follows a noun (or pronoun) and the verb **être**.

Catherine est journaliste.
Elle est journaliste.

Préparation

A. Curiosité. Little Madeleine wants to know what various things around the house are. Give her questions and her parents' responses.

Modèle

Qu'est-ce que c'est? → C'est un livre.

1.

2.

3.

4.

5.

6.

7.

8.

Have students repeat the following nouns, replacing the definite article with the appropriate form of the indefinite article: le professeur, le livre, le cahier, le crayon, le médecin, le stylo, la résidence, l'université, la bibliothèque, l'étudiante, le journaliste, la classe, les restaurants, les cinémas, les examens, les étudiants, les cours, les ouvriers, la commerçante.

B. Professions. What is the profession of each person?

Modèle

C'est une ouvrière.

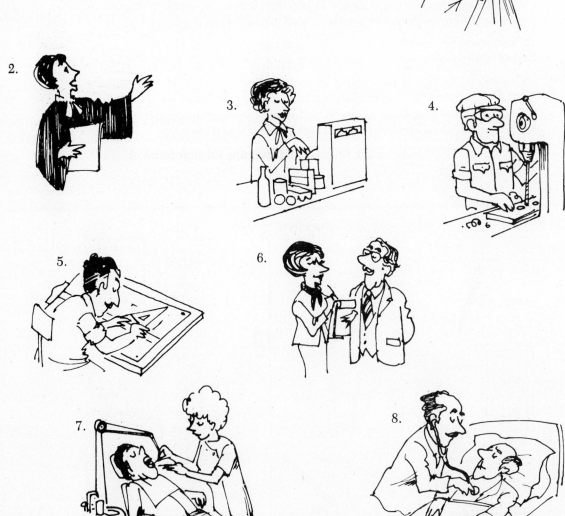

Communication

A. Dans la classe de français. Point to an object in the classroom and ask another student to tell you what it is.

> **Exemple**   Qu'est-ce que c'est?
> C'est une affiche.

B. Un objet ou une personne? Think of an object or a person. Other students will ask you yes-or-no questions until they guess who or what it is.

> **Exemple**   Est-ce que c'est une personne?
> Non, ce n'est pas une personne.

C. Célébrités. Make a list of people who are well known in the following categories. As you name them, other students will identify their professions.

Catégories: professeur, médecin, dentiste, ingénieur, journaliste, avocat, architecte, écrivain

> **Exemple**   Gloria Steinem → **C'est une journaliste.**

 # Les adjectifs

Présentation

As you already know, the masculine singular and feminine singular forms of French adjectives that end in **-e** are the same. To make them plural, add **-s.**

	Singular	Plural
Masculine	pauvre	pauvres
Feminine	pauvre	pauvres

Most other adjectives change their forms to agree in gender and number with the noun or pronoun they describe. Add **-e** to the masculine singular to make the feminine singular; add **-s** to make these singular forms plural.

	Singular	Plural
Masculine	patient	patients
Feminine	patiente	patientes

Adjectives fall into two categories: (1) those with changes that are evident only in written language, and (2) those with changes that are evident in both written and spoken language.

A. When the masculine singular form of an adjective ends in a pronounced vowel, its masculine and feminine forms are pronounced alike even though they are spelled differently.

Paul est fatigué; Jeanne est fatiguée.
Vous détestez les questions compliquées.

Useful adjectives in this category are:

compliqué(e)   fatigué(e) *(tired)*   poli(e) *(polite)*   vrai(e) *(true)*

B. When the masculine singular form of an adjective ends in an unpronounced consonant, its corresponding feminine form ends in a pronounced consonant. In this case, the change in gender is reflected in both spelling and pronunciation.

Marc est patient, mais Monique n'est pas patiente.
Les étudiants aiment les professeurs compétents.
C'est une femme très intéressante.

Useful adjectives in this category are:

amusant(e)	fascinant(e)	intelligent(e)
compétent(e)	français(e)	intéressant(e)
content(e)	impatient(e)	parfait(e)
excellent(e)	indépendant(e)	prudent(e)
embêtant(e) *(annoying)*	passionnant(e) *(exciting)*	violent(e)

When the masculine singular form of an adjective already ends in **-s** or **-x**, its singular and plural forms are identical. No additional s is added.

Est-ce qu'il est français?
Est-ce qu'ils sont français?

C. Some adjectives do not fit into the previous categories but do follow specific patterns.

1.

	Singular	Plural
Masculine	impulsif	impulsifs
Feminine	impulsive	impulsives

actif, active
naïf, naïve
sportif, sportive *(athletic)*
compréhensif, compréhensive
   (understanding)

	Singular	Plural
Masculine	sérieux	sérieux
Feminine	sérieuse	sérieuses

ambitieux, ambitieuse
courageux, courageuse
heureux, heureuse *(happy)*
paresseux, paresseuse *(lazy)*

3.

	Singular	*Plural*
Masculine	parisien	parisiens
Feminine	parisienne	parisiennes

ancien, ancienne *(old)*
canadien, canadienne
italien, italienne

4.

	Singular	*Plural*
Masculine	naturel	naturels
Feminine	naturelle	naturelles

exceptionnel, exceptionnelle
intellectuel, intellectuelle
personnel, personnelle
quel, quelle *(what* or *which)*
sensationnel, sensationnelle

Have students repeat the following adjectives and then put them in the masculine: **contente, parfaite, française, ambitieuse, courageuse, active, impulsive, parisienne, canadienne, paresseuse, intellectuelle.** Then have them repeat these adjectives and then give the feminine form: **compliqué, heureux, naïf, intéressant, modeste, violent, italien, compréhensif, ancien, sincère, amusant, exceptionel.**

D. An adjective used to describe two or more masculine nouns is masculine plural. An adjective used to describe two or more feminine nouns is feminine plural. An adjective used to describe a mixture of masculine and feminine nouns is always in the masculine plural.

Bruno et Alain sont prudents.
Brigitte et Denise sont sportives.
Jean-Luc, Anne et Yvonne sont intelligents.

Préparation

A. Égalité. Hubert is convinced that men are superior to women; Diane doesn't agree at all. Tell what she says.

Modèle   Les hommes sont ambitieux. → **Les femmes aussi sont ambitieuses!**

In French a male chauvinist is a **phallocrate.** Explain that chauvinist comes from **Chauvin,** an extreme patriot.

1. Les hommes sont sérieux.
2. Les hommes sont sportifs.
3. Les hommes sont intelligents.
4. Les hommes sont courageux.
5. Les hommes sont indépendants.
6. Les hommes sont prudents.

B. Curiosité. Hélène has just started her first year at the University of Strasbourg. A friend wants to know how she is getting along. Give her friend's questions.

Modèle   les professeurs / sévère → **Est-ce que les professeurs sont sévères?**

1. les examens / difficile
2. les professeurs / sympathique
3. les cours / intéressant
4. les étudiants / amusant
5. la bibliothèque / excellent
6. les professeurs / compréhensif
7. tu / content
8. tu / fatigué

C. Qualités et défauts. Alain and Janine are talking about their friends. Tell what they say.

Modèle   Hélène / modeste / honnête → **Hélène n'est pas très modeste, mais elle est honnête.**

1. Chantal / intellectuel / compétent
2. Marc / patient / courageux
3. Georges / intelligent / sympathique
4. Antoine / ambitieux / content
5. Catherine / naïf / sincère
6. Claudine / sérieux / amusant
7. Robert / compliqué / heureux

Communication

A. Préférences. What kinds of teachers, classes, books, etc., do you like? Using adjectives you know, give your preferences for each of the following.

Exemple   la musique → **Je préfère la musique classique.**

1. les professeurs
2. les hommes
3. les femmes
4. la musique
5. les cours
6. les films
7. les livres
8. les examens

B. Autoportrait. Prepare a self-portrait using adjectives you know. You may also want to use words like **en général, rarement, souvent, assez, trop.**

Exemple   En général, je ne suis pas très modeste, mais je suis honnête.

Students can also describe someone they know or a famous person.

C. Interview. Ask questions to find out if other students think that the following adjectives describe their personalities. Be sure to make your adjectives agree with the person you are talking with.

Exemple   ambitieux → **Est-ce que tu es très ambitieux?**

1. ambitieux
2. prudent
3. exceptionnel
4. impatient
5. sportif
6. impulsif
7. paresseux
8. indépendant

Option: Give each student a card containing one or several adjectives. Their task is to circulate asking other students if they possess this characteristic (e. g., **Roger, est-ce que tu es sportif?**). If yes, the student's name is recorded on the card. At the end of the established time limit, students report back the results of their interviews (e.g., **Roger et Caroline sont sportifs**).

Les nombres de 1 à 59

Présentation

A. The numbers from one to twenty in French are:

1	un	11	onze
2	deux	12	douze
3	trois	13	treize
4	quatre	14	quatorze
5	cinq	15	quinze
6	six	16	seize
7	sept	17	dix-sept
8	huit	18	dix-huit
9	neuf	19	dix-neuf
10	dix	20	vingt

When certain numbers are followed by nouns, their pronunciation varies. For example, the *q* in **cinq** is silent before a consonant (**cinq professeurs**) but pronounced when followed by a vowel or vowel sound (**cinq étudiants**). The linking sound between **deux** and **dix** and a vowel or vowel sound is [z]: **deux étudiants, dix étudiants.**

B. The numbers from twenty to fifty-nine are:

20	vingt	28	vingt-huit	42	quarante-deux
21	vingt et un	29	vingt-neuf		. . .
22	vingt-deux	30	trente	50	cinquante
23	vingt-trois	31	trente et un	51	cinquante et un
24	vingt-quatre	32	trente-deux	52	cinquante-deux
25	vingt-cinq		. . .		. . .
26	vingt-six	40	quarante	59	cinquante-neuf
27	vingt-sept	41	quarante et un		

C. To ask how much something costs, use the question **Combien est-ce que ça coûte?** or the more colloquial **Combien est-ce que ça fait?** *(How much does that make?)*, **Ça fait combien?** or **C'est combien?**

Combien est-ce que ça coûte?
Ca coûte douze francs.

Combien est-ce que ça fait?
Ça fait huit francs.

> Although **combien** can be combined with **coûter** to ask prices (**Combien coûte cette affiche?**), the questions given in the text are more typical of everyday speech.

D. When doing basic math problems, **plus** is used for *plus*, **moins** for *minus*, **fois** for *times*, and **divisé par** for *divided by*. **Ça fait** *(that makes)* is used to express the result.

Neuf plus cinq? Combien est-ce que ça fait?
Ça fait quatorze.

Dix-huit moins huit? Ça fait combien?
Ça fait dix.

> (1) Have students count 1–20 and then 20–59. (2) Write numbers on the board and have students read them aloud. (3) Call out a number and have students write it down. (4) Have students write down the numbers from 1–20. Read aloud in random order all the numbers except one. Students check all numbers except the one that was omitted. Repeat (1) through (3), with the numbers 20–59.

Préparation

A. Le Tour de France. The results of the Tour de France are being announced on French television. What would the sportscaster say?

Modèle   Numéro un, Schulz

Numéro 1	Schulz	Numéro	6	Steen
Numéro 2	Vigo	Numéro	7	García
Numéro 3	Lafayette	Numéro	8	Belmondi
Numéro 4	Dingelhoffer	Numéro	9	Maréchal
Numéro 5	Lemartin	Numéro	10	Schmidt

Although the Tour de France takes place in France, participants come from all over Europe, as indicated by the names of the different riders.

B. À la librairie. Some students are asking the prices at a bookstore near Laval University. Give the salesperson's response.

Modèle   un livre de maths / 15 dollars → **Un livre de maths?**
                                                          Quinze dollars.

1. cinq crayons / $1
2. deux cahiers / $4
3. un stylo / $2
4. six affiches / $41
5. un livre de français / $16
6. un dictionnaire / $39
7. une radio / $55
8. un livre de maths / $22

C. Mais non! A salesclerk at Les Galeries Lafayette in Paris is not doing a good job making change. Tell what he says and what his customers say to correct him.

Modèle $20 - 3 = 15$ → **Vingt moins trois, ça fait quinze.**
                Mais non! Ça fait dix-sept.

1. $15 - 1 = 3$
2. $10 - 5 = 4$
3. $37 + 2 = 38$
4. $20 - 4 = 14$
5. $12 + 3 = 16$
6. $50 - 6 = 43$
7. $13 + 7 = 17$
8. $39 + 8 = 48$

Point out that Galeries Lafayette, Le Printemps, and La Samaritaine are some of the main Parisian department stores. One can also find discount stores such as Monoprix and Prisunic.

Give a list of scores of recent sports events and have students give the scores in French. Students could also report on the scores of games played recently.

Communication

A. Petits problèmes. Working with another student or a group of students, take turns giving each other addition and subtraction problems to solve.

Exemple   vingt plus huit? Ça fait combien?
                Ça fait vingt-huit.

B. Sondage d'opinion. Take an opinion poll to find out the favorite singers, writers, actors, actresses, school subjects, etc., of students in your class. Write a possible list of candidates on the board and then count in French the number of votes for each candidate.

Exemple   Combien préfèrent le français?
                un, deux, trois, . . .

C. Qualités. Ask other students questions to find out if they have the following qualities. Find out how many students fit in each category.

1. Les pessimistes
2. Les conformistes
3. Les honnêtes
4. Les modestes
5. Les irrésistibles

SYNTHÈSE

Identité

For possible further discussion: See the questions and answers within the song.

The song below was written by Claude Gauthier, a French-Canadian singer. Its words evoke with great simplicity what it is like to be a French-Canadian. It also reveals the need that many French-Canadians feel to find their own identity and cultural heritage apart from the rest of Canada.

Je suis de lacs et de rivières.
— I come from, I am made up of

Q: Are there many lakes and rivers in Quebec? Which are the main ones? A: Yes. Lake Ontario, St. Lawrence River, Lake Winnepeg.

Je suis de *gibier,* de *poissons.*
— wild game / fish

Q: Is there much hunting and fishing in Quebec? Why? A: Yes, because of numerous waterways and untamed land.

Je ne suis pas de *grandes moissons.*
— large harvests

Q: Are large amounts of wheat produced in Quebec or on the plains of Alberta and Saskatchewan? A: On the plains of Alberta and Saskatchewan.

Je suis de *sucre* et d'*eau d'érable,*
— sugar / maple sap

Q: In what season is the maple sap collected? A: Late winter, when the sap runs.

de *pater noster,* de *credo.*
— Roman Catholic prayers

Q: What is the main religion in Quebec and why? A: Catholic, because of French ancestors.

Je suis de dix enfants à table.

Q: Why have French-Canadians tended to have large families? A: Because of Catholic traditions.

Je suis de *janvier sous* zéro.
— January / under, below

Q: What are winters like in Quebec? A: Cold, snowy.

Je suis d'Amérique et de France.

Q: In what ways is Quebec a blend of French and American cultures? A: The "Québecois" have carefully guarded their French traditions, but close proximity to the U. S. has affected their culture—e.g., K-Marts, Kentucky Fried Chicken, American TV.

Je suis de *chômage* et d'exil.
— unemployment

Q: When were the Acadians exiled from Canada? A: In the early 18th century after the Treaty of Utrecht (1713) when Acadia was ceded to the British.

Je suis d'octobre et *d'espérance.*
— hope

Q: Are French-Canadians generally happy with their relationship with the rest of Canada? Why do many favor greater independence? A: It depends. The "Québecois" voted down the resolution for a separatist Quebec but still seek more cultural autonomy.

Je suis l'énergie qui *s'empile* d'Ungava à Manicouagan.
— piles up

Q: Why is Canada so rich in hydroelectric energy? A: Many waterways—i.e., natural resources for electricity.

Je suis Québec *mort* ou *vivant.*
— dead / alive

«Je suis de lacs et de rivières.»

«Je suis . . . de pater noster, de credo.»

«Je suis d'Amérique et de France.»

Compréhension Tell whether the statements are true or false based on Claude Gauthier's song and what you know about Quebec.

1. Quebec is a land of many lakes and rivers.
2. Wild game is still plentiful in Quebec.
3. There are large grain harvests in Quebec.
4. Making maple sugar is a traditional activity in Quebec.
5. Quebec is noted for its mild winters.
6. The Catholic religion has had little influence on the life of French-Canadians.
8. Quebec is a blend of French and American cultures.
9. French-Canadians are torn between a sense of futility and hope for the future.
10. The production of electricity is an important aspect of Quebec's economy.

Using Gauthier's song as a guide, have students (alone or in small groups) compose a similar poem about the United States.

«Je suis Québec mort ou vivant.»

JE ME SOUVIENS

NOTES CULTURELLES

L'histoire du Canada français en bref

These important historical and political events have shaped the current situation in Quebec.

1497 John Cabot discovers Canada.

1535 Jacques Cartier discovers the St. Lawrence River and goes as far as present-day Montreal.

1608 Samuel de Champlain builds the first French settlements in Quebec and creates alliances with Indian tribes.

1630 Cardinal Richelieu sends Jesuit missionaries to convert the Indians.

1663 Louis XIV proclaims "La Nouvelle France" to be a French province.

1759 The French are defeated by the English in the Battle of the Plains of Abraham at Quebec City and give up their lands to the English.

1960 The FLQ (**Front pour la libération du Québec**) is formed, leading to increased separatist activity.

1970 The Canadian government officially declares Canada a bilingual country. French and English are the two official languages.

1974 The province of Quebec establishes French as its sole official language.

1979 The Canadian Parliament defeats a bill to grant Quebec its independence.

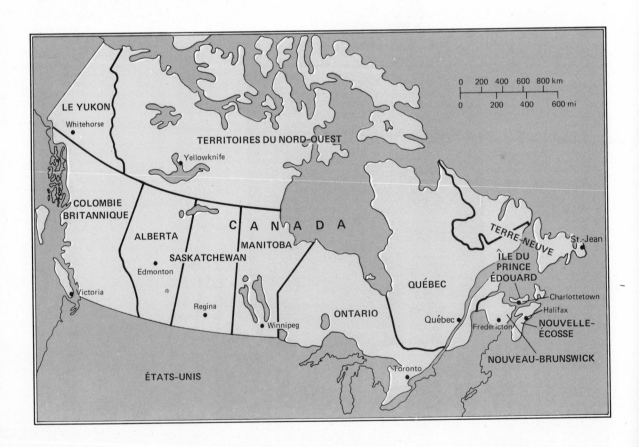

Communication

A. Qu'est-ce que c'est? The following names are familiar to French-Canadians. Can you identify them and match them with the appropriate description from the list of possibilities below?

Exemple   Trois-Rivières → **C'est une ville.**

1. le Saint-Laurent
2. le Québec
3. Québec
4. Saint-Jean
5. Chicoutimi
6. Champlain
7. le pater noster
8. Maria Chapdeleine
9. le Château Frontenac
10. Laval
11. Pierre Trudeau

Possibilités:

un lac	une région
une rivière	une ville
une prière catholique	un livre
une tribu indienne	
un homme politique	
une université	
un film	
une province	
un explorateur	
un monument historique	

The new cognates introduced in this activity are not part of this chapter's active vocabulary.

B. Les Américains. Prepare a description of what you think Americans are like and share it with the class.

Exemple   Les Américains sont courageux et optimistes, mais ils sont trop conformistes.

Other possible categories: les étudiants, les professeurs, les hommes, les femmes.

C. Opinions. Using adjectives you know, ask another student his or her opinions about the following aspects of campus life.

Exemple   le campus
              Est-ce que le campus est très moderne?

1. les cours	5. les professeurs
2. les résidences	6. les étudiants
3. les restaurants universitaires	7. l'université
4. la classe de français	8. la bibliothèque

D. Qualités et défauts. Choose one or several public figures and describe their good and bad points. (Remember that you can use words like **très, trop, assez,** etc.) Compare your opinions with those of other students.

PRONONCIATION

A. Liaison may occur when a word that ends in a silent consonant is followed by a word that begins with a vowel sound. In such cases, the consonant is sounded and linked to the vowel sound that follows it. Liaison occurs between an article, subject pronoun, adjective, or adverb ending with an **-s** or **-x** and a following word beginning with a vowel sound. It also occurs after words ending with **-t** or **-n** (huit_étudiants, un_hôtel).

Repeat the following:

Articles	Subject pronouns	Adjectives and adverbs	Numbers
les_Américains	nous_aimons	très_ambitieux	deux_enfants
les_ouvriers	vous_habitez	très_impulsif	trois_enfants
les_étudiants	vous_êtes	moins_amusant	six_enfants
les_hommes	ils_espèrent	quels_employés	dix_enfants

B. When the following combinations of letters occur at the end of a word or before a consonant other than **n** or **m**, they are pronounced as nasal vowel sounds:

in, im, ain, (i)en, yn = [$\tilde{\varepsilon}$]
an, am, en, ean = [$\tilde{a}$]
on, om = [$\tilde{o}$]

Listen and compare:

English	French
dentist	dentiste
content	content
engineer	ingénieur
impatient	impatient

Repeat the following words:

[$\tilde{\varepsilon}$]	[$\tilde{a}$]	[$\tilde{o}$]
intéressant	anglais	bonjour
Américain	ambitieux	région
parisien	amusant	montagne
impression	employée	conformiste
bien	excellent	content

When the above letter combinations are followed by **n**, **m**, or a vowel, they are not pronounced as nasals and the **n** or **m** is sounded.

Compare the following words:

parisien—parisienne   Jean—Jeanne   bon—bonne

C. Except for the letters **c, f, l,** and **r,** a consonant that is the final letter of a word is usually not pronounced. A word may end in a consonant sound, however, when its final letter is a silent **-e.** This difference is especially evident in the contrast between the masculine and feminine forms of adjectives.

Repeat the following pairs of words:

content—contente   parfait—parfaite
intelligent—intelligente   sérieux—sérieuse
amusant—amusante   paresseux—paresseuse
patient—patiente   français—française

D. Repeat the following sentences, paying special attention to the sounds you have been practicing.

1. Les deux enfants sont très intelligents.
2. Vous avez une profession intéressante.
3. Jeanne est contente, mais Jean n'est pas content.

VOCABULAIRE

noms

les gens/les professions

°   l'architecte (m, f)
    l'avocat (m), l'avocate (f) *lawyer*
le, la commerçant (e) *shopkeeper*
°le, la dentiste
°   l'employé (m), l'employée (f)
    l'enfant (m, f) *child*
    la femme *woman*
    la fille *girl*
    le garçon *boy*
    l'homme (m) *man*
    l'ingénieur (m, f) *engineer*
°le, la journaliste
    le médecin *doctor*
    l'ouvrier (m), l'ouvrière (f) *worker*
°   la personne
°le, la reporter

d'autres noms

°   l'Amérique (f)
    le chômage *unemployment*
°   l'énergie (f)
    le lac *lake*
°   le monument
°   la province
°   la question
°   la qualité
°   la région
    la rivière *river*
    la ville *city*

verbes

ça fait *that makes*
c'est *it is*
coûter *to cost*
espérer *to hope*
être *to be*
il faut *it is necessary*
gagner *to win*
posséder *to own*

adjectifs (voir pp. 32, 33 et 40-41)

belge *Belgian*
grand(e) *large*
mort(e) *dead*
quel, quelle *what, which*
vivant(e) *living*

adverbes

assez *fairly*
très *very*
trop *too much*

les nombres (voir p. 43)

divers

avec *with*
combien *how much*
divisé par *divided by (math)*
fois *times, multiplied by (math)*
non *no*
plus *plus*
pour *in order to*
pourquoi *why*
qui *that, which*
sous *under, below*

CHAPITRE TROIS

Possessions 3

Monologue

Patrick is reflecting on the good things in his life.

J'*ai* des livres et des *disques.*	have / records
J'ai une *chaîne-stéréo.*	stereo set
J'ai une guitare.	
J'ai un *vélomoteur qui marche bien*	moped / that / runs well
et un *magnétophone* qui ne marche pas!	tape recorder
J'ai dix-neuf *ans.*	years
J'ai un *frère* et une *sœur.*	brother / sister
J'ai des parents qui sont formidables.	
J'ai des cours intéressants et des profs assez *sympas.*	short for *sympathiques*
J'ai des *amis.*	friends
J'ai deux *camarades de chambre.*	roommates
J'ai un bon *travail.*	job, work
Je suis en *bonne santé.*	good / health
J'ai quelquefois des problèmes—comme *tout le monde.*	everyone
Mais, *c'est la vie,* n'est-ce pas?	that's life

«J'ai un vélomoteur qui marche bien.»

Compréhension   Selon les renseignements donnés, est-ce que les phrases suivantes sont vraies ou fausses? Corrigez le sens de la phrase s'il est faux. *(According to the information given, are the following statements true or false? If a statement is false, reword it to make it true.)*

1. Patrick possède une chaîne-stéréo.
2. Patrick aime la musique.
3. Le vélomoteur de Patrick ne marche pas bien.
4. Les parents de Patrick sont très sympas.
5. Patrick est professeur.
6. Patrick est assez heureux.

Have students tell which sentences in the **Introduction** apply to them (e.g., **J'ai aussi un frère et une sœur**).

NOTES CULTURELLES

Les étudiants français

Like their American counterparts, many French students have stereos and enjoy listening to various types of music. Although they prefer **la musique pop** and **le rock**—and are very familiar with American singers and musicians—many also enjoy traditional ballads.

The typical French student usually does not have very much money. Relatively few students have part-time jobs. Most depend upon modest but readily available government scholarships. Annual tuition ranges from the equivalent of fifty to sixty dollars and also entitles students to complete medical coverage. Moreover, they can eat inexpensive meals costing about eight to ten francs (about a dollar and a half) in student restaurants and live in modestly priced university housing. Because only limited space is available in university housing, large numbers of students live in rooms in town or in small apartments that they share with friends. Off-campus housing tends to be quite expensive and consumes a large portion of a student's budget. Other students live at home with their parents and commute daily from surrounding suburbs or small towns.

Many French students have **vélomoteurs,** or **motos** (*motorcycles*). Others walk or ride city buses. A smaller but growing number have cars, often an inexpensive and economical 2 CV (**Deux-chevaux**).

Vive la musique!

Et vous?

Possessions. Tell which of the following you have (**J'ai . . .**) and which you would like to have (**Je voudrais avoir . . .**).

Exemple

1.   J'ai une chaîne-stéréo. Je voudrais avoir un piano.

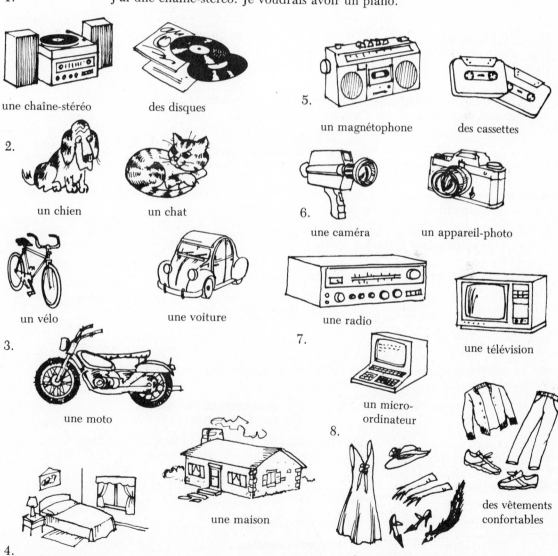

une chaîne-stéréo   des disques

5.
un magnétophone   des cassettes

2.
un chien   un chat

6.
une caméra   un appareil-photo

un vélo   une voiture

une radio

3.
7.
une télévision

une moto

un micro-
ordinateur

8.

une maison

des vêtements
confortables

4.
une chambre

des vêtements
élégants

Le verbe *avoir*

Présentation

Avoir *(to have)* is an irregular verb.

avoir	
j'ai	nous avons
tu as	vous avez
il/elle/on a	ils/elles ont

Est-ce que tu as un frère?
Nous avons trois chats.
Ils ont un appartement en ville.

A. When the verb **avoir** is used in the negative, the indefinite articles **un,
une,** and **des** change to **de** or **d'.**

Il a une moto.	Elle n'a pas **de** moto.	Point out that the same rule
J'ai des disques.	Tu n'as pas **de** disques.	applies for **posséder** and other
Nous avons un appartement.	Vous n'avez pas **d'**appartement.	verbs that indicate possession or consumption.

B. **Avoir** is used in many common expressions. One of the most useful is **il
y a**, meaning *there is* or *there are.*

Il y a dix-huit étudiants dans la classe.
Il n'y a pas de métro à Québec.

Have students conjugate the verb **avoir** in these sentences: **Répétition:** (1) J'ai un vélo, tu as un vélo, etc. (2) Je n'ai pas d'appartement, tu n'as pas d'appartement, etc. **Substitution:** J'ai un frère. tu / nous / Serge / vous / Robert et Solange. (2) Est-ce que tu as un stylo? Marc / le professeur / vous / Cécile et Patrick.

C. **Avoir** is also used to tell somebody's age.

Quel âge est-ce que vous avez?   *How old are you?*
J'ai vingt ans.   *I'm twenty years old.*

Préparation

A. **La vie n'est pas parfaite.** Richard is talking about some of the things that
he has and doesn't have. Tell what he says.

Modèle   magnétophone / cassettes → **J'ai un magnétophone mais je**   Repeat with il.
n'ai pas de cassettes.

1. cahier / crayon   3. chaîne-stéréo / disques   5. cours de français / livre
2. table / chaise   4. cassettes / magnétophone   6. frère / sœur

B. **Une partie sympathique.** Some friends are planning a party. Tell what
each says he or she can contribute.

Une surboum (boum) is a more colloquial word for party.

Modèle   je / chaîne-stéréo → **J'ai une chaîne-stéréo.**

Repeat in the negative.

1. nous / appartement   4. Alice / cassettes   7. vous / radio
2. Michel et Hélène / voiture 5. André / magnétophone   8. nous / amis
3. tu / une guitare   6. je / disques

C. Une salle de classe impossible! Geneviève is taking an English course this year but is not pleased with her overcrowded, sparsely furnished classroom. Tell what she says.

Modèles   tableau (non) → **Il n'y a pas de tableau.**
porte (oui) → **Il y a une porte.**

1. fenêtre (non)
2. porte (oui)
3. affiches (non)
4. carte (non)
5. magnétophone (non)
6. table (oui)
7. chaises (oui)
8. tableau (non)

D. Possessions. Pierre Sanlesous is telling what his family has and does not have. Tell what he says.

Modèles   voiture (non) → **Nous n'avons pas de voiture.**
amis (oui) → **Nous avons des amis.**

1. chien (oui)
2. chat (non)
3. maison (non)
4. appartement (oui)
5. amis (oui)
6. livres (oui)
7. chaîne-stéréo (non)
8. problèmes (non)

Communication

A. Interview. Find out if other students have the following things. Report the results of your interview to the class.

Exemple   un chien ou un chat → **Est-ce que tu as un chien ou un chat?**

1. un chien ou un chat
2. une radio ou une télévision
3. un vélo ou une voiture
4. une chambre dans une résidence ou un appartement
5. des disques ou des cassettes
6. une guitare ou un piano
7. un frère ou une sœur
8. un appareil-photo ou une caméra

Using the cues provided, have students formulate questions with **il y a.**

Point out that very few French university students begin studying language at the university level. Many arrive with several years of a language. Common languages taught are English, German, Italian, Spanish, some Russian, and Latin and Greek.

Using known vocabulary, have students ask each other about their possessions until they find at least five things that they have in common. Students can consult the vocabulary list on p. 69 or a list of suggestions can be put on the board.

B. **Les étudiants américains.** Tell a French friend about some of the things that American students generally have.

Exemple En général, les étudiants américains ont une chambre dans une résidence ou un appartement.

 ## Les nombres de 60 à 1000

Point out that only **quatre-vingts** and round hundreds (**deux cents**, etc.) end in **-s**.

Présentation

The numbers from 60 to 1000 are given below. Notice that a pattern of twenties appears from 60 to 100.

Have students count from 60 to 100. Have students count by 10's to 100 and then by 5's to 100. Have students give the numbers that come after each of the following: 55, 59, 62, 69, 70, 76, 78, 80, 89, 90, 95, 99, 100.

60	soixante	80	quatre-vingts	100	cent
61	soixante et un	81	quatre-vingt-un	101	cent un
62	soixante-deux	82	quatre-vingt-deux	102	cent deux
	. . .		. . .		. . .
69	soixante-neuf	89	quatre-vingt-neuf	200	deux cents
70	soixante-dix	90	quatre-vingt-dix	201	deux cent un
71	soixante et onze	91	quatre-vingt-onze	202	deux cent deux
72	soixante-douze	92	quatre-vingt-douze		. . .
	. . .		. . .	1000	mille
79	soixante-dix-neuf	99	quatre-vingt-dix-neuf		

In Switzerland and Belgium, seventy is **septante** and ninety is **nonante.**

Have students count by 100's to 1000. Write random numbers from 100 to 1000 on the board. Have students say the numbers.

Préparation

A. **Distances.** A group of French students who commute each day to the university are comparing the distances they have to travel. Tell what they say.

Many French students who live close to a university town commute by train from surrounding suburbs and small towns.

Modèle 25 → J'habite à vingt-cinq kilomètres de l'université.

Option: Have students tell how far they live from campus.

1. 100	5. 86	8. 75
2. 61	6. 71	9. 82
3. 126	7. 93	10. 72
4. 69		

Although it is less difficult than in the past for French people to have a phone installed in their homes, they still have to wait a long time. Those without phones can use pay phones or go to the bureau des **P.T. (Postes, Télécommunications).**

B. **Le téléphone.** Assume that you are a telephone operator working at the information switchboard. Give your customers the numbers they are requesting. Note that French phone numbers are said as three pairs of numbers, except in Paris and its suburbs where phone numbers now have seven digits.

Listening: Read additional phone numbers, and have students write them out. Have students give their own phone numbers.

Modèle Madame Martin (43.32.15) → **C'est le quarante-trois, trente-deux, quinze.**

1. Monsieur Humbert (82.53.46)
2. Mademoiselle Lacoste (96.75.84)
3. Madame Seurat (49.13.97)
4. Monsieur Picot (45.41.99)
5. Mademoiselle Granville (69.71.17)
6. Madame Arnaud (51.81.85)

C. Entre deux villes. A travel agent in Montreal is answering questions about the distances of various cities from Montreal. Tell what she says.

Modèle   Boston 546 → **La distance entre Boston et Montréal est de cinq cent quarante-six kilomètres.**

1. Ottawa 190
2. Trois-Rivières 138
3. Québec 270
4. New York 613
5. Philadelphie 745
6. Washington 932
7. Détroit 908
8. Toronto 539

Communication

A. C'est combien? With another student, play the roles of a salesperson and a customer who is comparison shopping. The salesperson gives the price, and the customer writes it down. Then compare your prices to verify your comprehension.

Ask students the cost of classroom objects.

Exemple   *Salesperson says:*   *Customer writes:*
—trente-neuf francs cinquante   39F50
—vingt-deux francs trente   22F30

C'est combien?

B. Vente aux enchères. Conduct an auction *(vente aux enchères)* with your class. Auction off items in the classroom, personal items, services, etc., to the highest bidder. Note the language used in an auction.

> **Exemple**   1er ÉTUDIANT   Combien pour un livre de français en excellente condition?
>   2e ÉTUDIANT   quarante-cinq francs
>   3e ÉTUDIANT   cinquante-cinq francs
>   1er ÉTUDIANT   cinquante-cinq francs, une fois *(once)*, deux fois, trois fois. Adjugé, vendu! *(Sold!)*

⚜ Les adjectifs possessifs

Présentation

In French, ownership is commonly indicated with a possessive adjective (corresponding to English *my, your, their . . .*) or a phrase with **de: le livre de David** *(David's book)*, **le frère de Suzanne** *(Susan's brother)*.

A. A possessive adjective, like any other French adjective, agrees in gender and number with the noun it modifies.

	Singular		Plural
	Masculine	*Feminine*	*Masculine and Feminine*
my	mon frère	ma sœur	mes parents
your	ton frère	ta sœur	tes parents
his/her/its/one's	son frère	sa sœur	ses parents
our	notre frère	notre sœur	nos parents
your	votre frère	votre sœur	vos parents
their	leur frère	leur sœur	leurs parents

B. Mon, ton, and **son** are used with both masculine and feminine singular nouns that begin with a vowel or vowel sound. Note that the linking sound is [n].

Est-ce que tu aimes mon‿affiche?
Ton‿amie Françoise est très sympathique.
Son‿appartement est très moderne.

C. In French, the possessive adjectives agree with the noun modified rather than with the possessor. This difference is especially important with **son, sa,** and **ses**—each of which can mean *his, her, its,* or *one's.*

Robert travaille avec son frère et
   sa sœur.

Robert works with his brother and
   his sister.

Annick travaille avec son frère et
   sa sœur.

Annick works with her brother
   and her sister.

D. The preposition **de** may also be used to express possession. The owned
object is followed by **de** and the name of the possessor. For example,
Robert's car would be **la voiture de Robert.**

le professeur de Robert   la voiture du médecin

la voiture de ma sœur   le bureau du professeur

le cahier de l'étudiant   les livres des étudiants

> Note that **de** + **le** becomes **du**
> and **de** + **les** becomes **des.**

Préparation

A. En voyage. André Dunin, a correspondent for the newspaper *Le Monde*,
is getting ready for a trip abroad. A friend wants to make sure he hasn't
forgotten anything. Give his friend's questions and André's answers.

Modèle   une caméra   →   **Est-ce que tu as ta caméra?**
                                    Oui, j'ai ma caméra.

1. un dictionnaire   5. un stylo
2. un magnétophone   6. des crayons
3. une caméra   7. des vêtements
4. un appareil-photo   8. des cassettes

B. Album de photos. Joëlle and Brigitte are looking at Joëlle's photo album.
Give Joëlle's answers to Brigitte's questions.

Modèle   C'est la maison de tes parents?   →   **Oui, c'est leur maison.**

1. Ce sont tes parents?   5. C'est le vélomoteur de ton frère?
2. C'est ton frère?   6. C'est votre chat?
3. C'est l'appartement de ta sœur?   7. Ce sont les amis de tes parents?
4. C'est la voiture de tes parents?   8. C'est ta chambre?

Communication

A. C'est ma vie! Comment on the following aspects of your own or someone
else's life.

Exemple   vos cours   →   **Mes cours sont très intéressants mais ils sont**
                                assez difficiles.

1. votre appartement (maison, chambre)   5. vos amis (camarades de chambre)
2. votre université   6. votre voiture (vélo, moto, vélomoteur)
3. vos professeurs   7. vos disques (cassettes)
4. vos cours   8. vos parents (frères, sœurs)

B. On n'est pas content! Alone or with another student, make up a list of typical student complaints about university life.

> **Exemples**   Notre cours de maths est trop difficile.
> Nos chambres ne sont pas assez modernes.

Survey the class to find the most common complaints.

⚜ Quelques adjectifs prénominaux

Présentation

A. In addition to the adjectives you already know, the adjectives **grand** *(large, tall)*, **petit** *(small)*, **joli** *(pretty)*, **beau** *(handsome, beautiful)*, **bon** *(good)*, **nouveau** *(new)*, and **vieux** *(old)* are very useful in descriptions. These adjectives are usually placed before the noun rather than after it. Note how these adjectives change form or pronunciation in the feminine or before a vowel sound.

Masculine	Masculine before a vowel sound	Feminine
un **petit** magasin	un **petit** appartement	une **petite** maison
un **grand** magasin	un **grand** appartement	une **grande** maison
un **joli** magasin	un **joli** appartement	une **jolie** maison
un **beau** magasin	un **bel** appartement	une **belle** maison
un **bon** magasin	un **bon** appartement	une **bonne** maison
un **nouveau** magasin	un **nouvel** appartement	une **nouvelle** maison
un **vieux** magasin	un **vieil** appartement	une **vieille** maison

The liaison sound of **grand** is [t], and **bon** followed by a vowel sound is pronounced the same as **bonne**.

Substitution: (1) C'est un bon ami. appartement / livre / film / vélo. (2) Ils ont une grande cuisine. garage / salle à manger / bureau / salle de séjour. (3) C'est un vieux monsieur. femme / homme / musée / appartement / magasin

B. In conversational French, when one of these adjectives precedes a plural noun, the indefinite article **des** is often used: **des bons magasins, des vieilles maisons.** In careful and formal French, the indefinite article **des** becomes **de: de bons magasins, de vieilles maisons.**

C. These adjectives and others you already know are useful in describing the parts of a home or an apartment.

> **Exemples**   C'est une belle maison de sept pièces. *(rooms)*
> La salle de séjour est très jolie.

You may wish to note two common ways of asking for the bathroom: **Où sont les W.-C.?** and **Où sont les toilettes?**

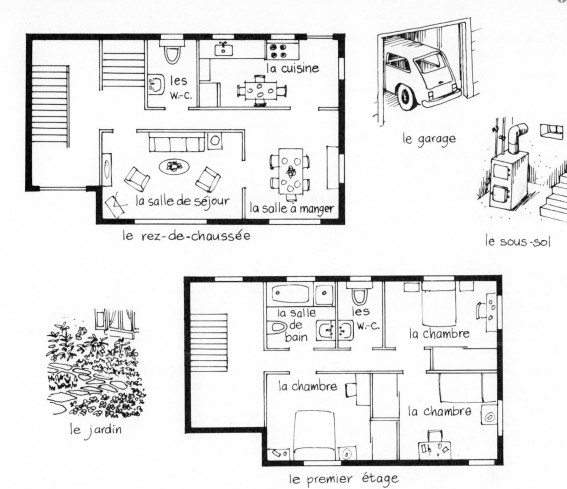

la cuisine

les w.-c.

le garage

le sous-sol

le jardin

la salle de séjour

la salle à manger

le rez-de-chaussée

la salle de bain

les w.-c.

la chambre

la chambre

la chambre

le premier étage

Préparation

A. Un agent immobilier. A real estate agent is showing some clients through a home and comments on various rooms of the house. Tell what the clients say.

Modèle   La cuisine est très grande. → **Oui, c'est une très grande cuisine.**

1. La salle de séjour est très jolie.
2. Le bureau est assez petit.
3. La salle à manger est belle.
4. Le jardin est joli.
5. La chambre est assez petite.
6. La maison est assez vieille.
7. Le garage est nouveau.
8. Le sous-sol est assez grand.

B. Possessions. Anne-Marie is describing some of the things and people in her life. What does she say?

Modèles   une chaîne-stéréo (bon) → **J'ai une bonne chaîne-stéréo.**
des professeurs (compétent) → **J'ai des professeurs compétents.**

1. des livres (intéressant)
2. une voiture (vieux)
3. des amis (sympathique)
4. un appartement (beau)
5. une chambre (grand)
6. des disques (américain)
7. un chat (joli)
8. un magnétophone (nouveau)
9. un travail (bon)
10. une camarade de chambre (amusant)
11. un professeur (italien)
12. une vie (intéressante)

Communication

A. Vos possessions. List and describe some of the things that you have or people that you know have.

Exemples   J'ai de bons amis.
J'ai un vieux vélo.

Students can also ask other students questions: **Est-ce que tu as un joli appartement? Est-ce que tu as des disques français?**

B. Votre maison. Describe your apartment, home, or the home that you would like to live in some day. Be sure to include adjectives in your description.

SYNTHÈSE

La vie de Louis Duvivier

Il **dort** is used for recognition only.

Sa vie? Il travaille, il *dort*, il mange. Il habite un petit appartement dans un *H.L.M.* à Paris. Il est marié et il a trois *enfants*—Michel, dix ans, Anne-Marie, sept ans, et Paulette, deux ans. Duvivier, qui a trente-quatre ans, travaille dans une *usine* d'automobiles. Sa vie est simple et tranquille. Il est assez content.

sleeps
low-cost government housing / children
factory

Sa *femme* ne travaille pas maintenant; elle *reste* à la maison *avec* les enfants. Elle aussi est assez contente. «Nous ne sommes pas riches, c'est vrai, mais nous ne sommes pas pauvres. Nous avons trois enfants qui sont adorables et un appartement qui est modeste mais confortable.»

wife / stays / with

Les Duvivier possèdent l'essentiel: une auto, un réfrigérateur, une *machine à laver* et une télévision. Ils aiment regarder la télévision et inviter des amis à dîner. En général, ils n'aiment pas beaucoup les livres et le cinéma.

washing machine

Introduce **le frigo** as the short form of **le réfrigérateur.**

Oui, ils ont une vie confortable. Oui, ils sont assez satisfaits, mais
ils sont aussi résignés à la monotonie de leur vie. «Je suis trop fatigué
pour être ambitieux», *explique* Duvivier.   explains

Leur *rêve?* Posséder une petite maison *à la campagne.*   dream / in the country

Extrait et adapté d'un article de *L'Express.*

Compréhension   Répondez aux questions suivantes selon les renseignements
donnés dans le texte. *(Answer the following questions according to the information given in the text.)*

Option: Have students prepare
questions on reading to ask each
other.

1. Où est-ce que Louis Duvivier habite?
2. Est-ce qu'il a des enfants?
3. Quel âge ont-ils?
4. Où est-ce qu'il travaille?
5. Est-ce que sa femme travaille aussi?
6. Est-ce que les Duvivier sont riches?
7. Qu'est-ce que les Duvivier possèdent?
8. Est-ce qu'ils sont satisfaits de leur vie?
9. Quel est leur rêve?

NOTES CULTURELLES

La classe ouvrière

The expression **métro, boulot, dodo** (*subway, work, sleep*) is often used to symbolize the working-class person's frustration with the predictable routine of daily life.

The standard of living of French working-class and lower-middle-class families has steadily improved since the end of World War II. For a long time, housing was expensive and in short supply, but many of these families are now able to live in **cités ouvrières** (*housing developments*) or in H.L.M.'s (**habitations à loyer modéré**). The H.L.M.'s are government-sponsored, moderate-rent apartment buildings that have been built on the outskirts of French cities during the past thirty years. Individual apartments are small—averaging three rooms per family—but even in the most modest, a refrigerator and a washing machine are now considered necessities rather than luxuries, as they once were. Statistics show, moreover, that ownership of television sets and other home appliances is nearly universal.

Many French employees belong to labor unions. The three major unions are highly politicized, based on political belief rather than on craft or industry. One is communist led; another is moderately socialist in outlook; a third is militantly socialist. Some major firms, however, including leading automobile manufacturers, have nonpolitical "house" unions.

Communication

A. Êtes-vous poète? With the **Introduction: Monologue** as a guide, use the vocabulary you know to write a French poem about yourself, someone you know, or an imaginary person.

B. Les ouvriers américains. Do you think that the life of an American worker is very different from that of Louis Duvivier? In French, try to describe an American worker's life and typical possessions.

C. Vrai ou faux? Make up true or false statements about the number of people or objects found in places like your classroom, your university, your town, etc. Other students will agree or disagree with your statements. Use vocabulary and numbers that you know.

> **Exemples**   Il y a quarante étudiants dans notre classe.
> Il y a dix-huit cinémas dans notre ville.

D. Petites annonces. People often advertise items in the **petites annonces** *(classified)* section of the newspaper. Using vocabulary you know and the terms **à vendre** *(to sell)* and **à louer** *(to rent)*, make up ads to sell or rent items that you have (or could have).

> **Exemples**   Vieux livres de français à vendre.
> À louer: petite maison avec joli jardin.

Additional useful vocabulary: cher / chère, en solde, très bon marché.

PRONONCIATION

A. French vowels (other than nasals) can be differentiated in terms of three articulatory factors: (1) the position of the tongue, which may be placed toward the front or back of the mouth; (2) the shape of the lips, which may be spread or rounded; (3) the degree of openness of the mouth.

1. Some vowels are pronounced with the tongue to the front and the lips spread. They are, in order of increasing openness:

[i] as in am**is**   [e] as in id**ée**   [ɛ] as in fr**ère**   [ɑ] as in t**a**lent

Repeat the following groups of words:

[i]	[e]	[ɛ]	[ɑ]
si	ses	cette	ça
lis	les	l'air	la
dis	des	dette	date

2. Some vowels are pronounced with the tongue back and the lips rounded.
    They are, in order of increasing openness:

[u] as in v**ou**s   [o] as in ph**o**to   [ɔ] as in sp**o**rt

> Repeat the following words:

[u]	[o]	[ɔ]
nous	nos	notre
vous	vos	votre
sous	sot	sotte

3. Some vowels are pronounced with the tongue to the front and the lips
    rounded. They are, in order of increasing openness:

[y] as in d**u***   [ø] as in d**eu**x   [œ] as in s**œu**r

> Repeat the following words:

[y]	[ø]	[œ]
su	ceux	sœur
pu	peu	peur
bu	bœufs	beurre

B. The vowel sounds [i], [y], and [u] are equally closed. They differ, how-
    ever, in the position of the tongue and the shape of the lips. Notice that
    the written forms of these vowel sounds are always **i**, **u**, and **ou**, respec-
    tively.

1. Repeat and contrast the following words:

    si—su—sous
    dit—du—doux
    lis—lu—loup
    fit—fut—fou
    ni—nu—nous

2. Repeat the following words:

[i]	[y]	[u]
idée	tu	nous
aussi	une	toujours
riche	usine	courageux
timide	naturel	douze
italien	amusant	beaucoup

C. Repeat the following sentences, paying special attention to the sounds
    you have been practicing.

    1. Henri a une très bonne idée.
    2. Tu as un peu peur.
    3. Paul a beaucoup de difficultés.
    4. Les adultes n'ont pas toujours
        une vie amusante.
    5. As-tu dix ans ou douze ans?

* A way to learn to produce the [y] sound is by saying [i] with the lips rounded.

VOCABULAIRE

noms

les possessions

l'appareil-photo (m)   *camera*
la **caméra**   *movie camera*
° la **cassette**
la **chaîne-stéréo**   *stereo*
le **chat**   *cat*
le **chien**   *dog*
le **disque**   *record*
° la **guitare**
le **magnétophone**   *tape recorder*
la **moto**   *motorbike*
le **micro-ordinateur**   *microcomputer*
° le **piano**
la **santé**   *health*
le **vélo**   *bicycle*
le **vélomoteur**   *moped*
les **vêtements** (m)   *clothing*
la **voiture**   *car*

la maison et l'appartement (voir pp. 62–63)

d'autres noms

l'**ami** (m), l'**amie** (f)   *friend*
l'**an** (m)   *year*
le **camarade de chambre**
la **camarade de chambre**   *roommate*
la **campagne**   *country*
° le **kilomètre**
la **machine à laver**   *washing machine*
° le **problème**
qui   *which, who, that*
° le **réfrigérateur**
le **rêve**   *dream*
le **travail**   *work*
l'**usine** (f)   *factory*

verbes

avoir   *to have*
dîner   *to eat dinner*
expliquer   *to explain*
je voudrais   *I would like*
il y a   *there is, there are*
°**inviter**
marcher   *to work*
rester   *to stay*

adjectifs

beau, bel, belle   *handsome, beautiful*
bon, bonne *good*
°**confortable**
°**élégant(e)**
grand(e) *large, tall*
joli(e) *pretty*
°**marié(e)**
nouveau, nouvel, nouvelle *new*
petit(e) *small*
satisfait(e) *satisfied*
°**simple**
vieux, vieil, vieille *old*
votre, vos *your*

adjectifs possessifs (voir p. 60)

les nombres *(voir p. 58)*

divers

c'est la vie *that's life*
comme *like, as*
en général *in general*
tout le monde *everyone*

CHAPITRE QUATRE

En vacances

INTRODUCTION

Bonnes vacances!

Note that the abbreviation for **monsieur** takes a period, and those for **madame** and **mademoiselle** do not.

Paris, le 31 *juillet*. Un reporter *pose* des questions aux automobilistes qui *quittent* la *ville*.

<table>
<tr><td></td><td></td><td>July / asks</td></tr>
<tr><td></td><td></td><td>are leaving / town</td></tr>
<tr><td>LE REPORTER</td><td>Bonjour, Monsieur. Bonjour, Madame. Où *est-ce que vous allez* en vacances *cette année?*</td><td>are you going
this / year</td></tr>
<tr><td>M. BLANC</td><td>Nous *allons* à Antibes, *sur* la *Côte d'Azur.*</td><td>are going / on / Riviera</td></tr>
<tr><td>LE REPORTER</td><td>Est-ce que c'est la *première fois que* vous allez à Antibes?</td><td>first / time / that</td></tr>
<tr><td>MME BLANC</td><td>Oui. *D'habitude*, nous *passons* nos vacances dans un petit village de Bretagne *parce que* nous avons des cousins *là-bas.*</td><td>usually / spend
because
there, in that area</td></tr>
<tr><td>LE REPORTER</td><td>*Eh bien, bonnes vacances!*</td><td>Well then, have a good vacation!</td></tr>
<tr><td>LE REPORTER</td><td>Bonjour, Madame. Bonjour, Monsieur. Vous allez en vacances?</td><td>Use **partir** only in the infinitive.</td></tr>
<tr><td>MME ARLAND</td><td>Non, *pas aujourd'hui.* Nous allons passer le week-end à la campagne. Mais nous allons *partir* en vacances dans quinze *jours.*</td><td>not / today
in the country / to leave
days</td></tr>
<tr><td>LE REPORTER</td><td>Est-ce que vous allez passer vos vacances en France ou dans un *pays étranger?*</td><td>country / foreign</td></tr>
<tr><td>MME ARLAND</td><td>Dans un pays étranger. Cette année, nous allons au Portugal et l'année *prochaine*, nous allons visiter la Grèce et la Yougoslavie.</td><td>next</td></tr>
<tr><td>LE REPORTER</td><td>*Alors*, bon voyage!</td><td>well then</td></tr>
</table>

Compréhension   Selon les renseignements donnés, est-ce que les phrases suivantes sont vraies ou fausses? Corrigez le sens de la phrase s'il est faux.

1. D'habitude, Monsieur et Madame Blanc passent leurs vacances sur la Côte d'Azur.
2. Ils ne passent jamais leurs vacances en Bretagne.
3. Ils ont des cousins qui habitent en Bretagne.
4. Monsieur et Madame Arland passent le week-end à la campagne.
5. Ils partent en vacances aujourd'hui.
6. Cette année, Monsieur et Madame Arland visitent la Grèce et la Yougoslavie.
7. D'habitude, ils passent leurs vacances dans un pays étranger.

Option: Have students make up additional titles for the **Introduction** reading.

FERMETURE ANNUELLE du 1er au 31 Août

NOTES CULTURELLES

Les vacances

Vacations are sacred for most French people. Every employee is guaranteed by law a minimum of five weeks' paid vacation. Unlike many Americans, who often tend to work overtime, the French prefer to have time away from their usual occupations. Although more people are spending all or part of their vacations at winter sports resorts, most take their vacations during the summer, especially in August. (It has been said that in August, the only people in Paris are tourists.) Camping, renting old houses in the many villages that dot the countryside, staying in small hotels, or **pensions de famille,** and visiting relatives are all popular vacation choices. For children and teenagers, a variety of summer camps, called **colonies de vacances,** are available. These are sponsored and subsidized by government agencies, industries, cities, and religious or social groups. College students often work during the summer as camp instructors. Or they may attend camps sponsored by the **Ministère de la Jeunesse et des Sports,** where they participate in such activities as sailing, mountain climbing, scuba diving, and spelunking.

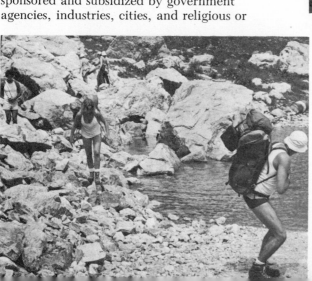

Et vous?

En vacances! Use the questions below to tell about your vacation preferences.

1. Où est-ce que vous préférez passer vos vacances?

à la montagne   à la campagne   à la plage

2. Comment est-ce que vous préférez voyager?

en voiture   en train   en avion   en moto   en vélo   à pied

3. Avec qui est-ce que vous préférez voyager?

seul(e)   avec vos amis   avec votre famille

4. Où est-ce que vous préférez voyager?

dans votre région   dans votre pays   dans un pays étranger

5. Qu'est-ce que vous allez emporter?

votre passeport   votre carte d'identité   votre permis de conduire
une valise   un sac à dos

6. Quand vous visitez une ville, qu'est-ce que vous aimez faire?

aller au concert ou au théâtre   visiter des musées et des monuments   manger au restaurant
marcher dans les rues   parler avec les gens   acheter des souvenirs

7. Qu'est-ce que vous préférez faire?

aller à l'hôtel   rester chez des amis   faire du camping

Vocabulaire

où *where*	**seul(e)** *alone*
la montagne *mountain*	**emporter** *to take along*
la plage *beach*	**le permis de conduire** *driver's license*
en *in, on, at, by*	**la valise** *suitcase*
en avion *by plane*	**le sac à dos** *backpack*
à pied *on foot*	**acheter** *to buy*
chez *at the home of*	**faire du camping** *to go camping*

 ## Le verbe *aller*

Présentation

The verb **aller** *(to go)* can be used to indicate movement or travel to a place, or to express future plans or intentions. **Aller** is an irregular verb.

aller	
je **vais**	nous **allons**
tu **vas**	vous **allez**
il/elle/on **va**	ils/elles **vont**

A. When used to express future plans or intentions, a conjugated form of **aller** is followed by an infinitive.

Nous allons voyager en train.
Il va étudier à Strasbourg.
Je vais acheter un micro-ordinateur.

Some useful expressions in talking about future plans or intentions are:

aujourd'hui *today*	**la semaine prochaine**
demain *tomorrow*	*next week*
pendant les vacances (f) *during vacation*	**le week-end prochain**
	next weekend

B. To indicate travel or movement to a place, **aller** is often used with the preposition **à** *(at, to).* **À** + **le** contract to **au.** **À** + **les** contract to **aux.** Compare the following sentences.

Nous allons **à la** plage.   Nous allons **au** cinéma.
Il va **à l'**hôtel.   Il va **aux** concerts.

Note that the preposition **à** can also be used with other verbs.

Elle parle **à** son ami.   Ils sont **à la** plage.

Préparation

A. Projets. Danielle's friends all have plans for this weekend. Tell where they are going.

Modèle   Catherine / concert → **Catherine va au concert.**

1. Rémi / la plage
2. Bernard / le restaurant
3. Christiane / la bibliothèque
4. Frédéric / le cinéma
5. Julie / le théâtre
6. Martine / les musées
7. Robert / l'exposition
8. Serge / la campagne

On va à l'exposition

B. Où est-ce qu'on va? Some friends are on vacation in Nice and are trying to decide what to do. What do they say?

Modèle café → **On va au café?**

1. plage
2. concert
3. restaurant
4. théâtre

5. expositions
6. musée
7. montagne
8. cinéma

C. On fait le pont. Students have a four-day weekend because Labor Day (May 1st) falls on a Tuesday. What are the following people going to do?

Modèle Serge / rester à la maison → **Serge va rester à la maison.**

Point out that **faire le pont** refers to an extended weekend when a holiday occurs on a Thursday or Tuesday.

1. nous / faire du camping
2. Claudine / aller à la plage
3. mes amis / aller au théâtre
4. vous / regarder la télé
5. je / acheter des vêtements
6. tu / aller chez tes parents
7. mon frère / aller à la montagne

Communication

A. **Vacances à Paris.** Imagine that you are spending a few days in Paris. Tell where you are going to go.

Exemple   Je vais aller au cinéma.

B. **Le week-end prochain.** Ask other students if they plan to do these things next weekend.

Exemple   aller à la bibliothèque → **Est-ce que tu vas aller à la bibliothèque?**

1. aller au concert
2. manger dans un bon restaurant
3. aller à la campagne
4. parler avec des amis
5. aller au cinéma
6. étudier pour un examen
7. écouter des disques
8. voyager en voiture
9. visiter les grands magasins
10. rester à la maison

MAISON DES ARTS·CRETEIL

jeudi 31 décembre

la nuit du jazz

un réveillon pas comme les autres
de 22 h à 4 h du matin

**Barney Willen & les Mokos
Le Quintet Philippe Briand
avec le saxophoniste Pete King
Trovesi Trio
Portal/Trovesi
le Onz' tet Caratini Fosset (Endeka)
Boto-Novos Tempos
Solal/Portal**

prix unique 60 F
brasserie-restaurant dans le hall

Place Salvador Allende tel. 899 94 50
M° Créteil Préfecture

   # Les prépositions et les noms de lieux

Présentation

In French, the preposition used to indicate a location or destination depends on the kind of place that is named.

A. Prepositions are used as follows:

chez + *person's name*	**chez** Madame Ménard
+ *person*	**chez** des amis
+ *pronoun*	**chez** moi
+ *person's profession or business*	**chez** le dentiste
à + *city*	**à** Paris
	à la Nouvelle Orléans
en + *feminine country*	**en** France
	en Belgique
au + *masculine country*	**au** Canada
	aux États-Unis

B. All countries ending in **e** are feminine except **le Mexique** and **le Zaïre**. All others are masculine singular except **les États-Unis** *(the United States)*, which is masculine plural.

Quelques pays féminins

l'Algérie	la Hollande
l'Allemagne *(Germany)*	l'Inde
l'Angleterre *(England)*	l'Irlande
l'Australie	l'Italie
l'Autriche *(Austria)*	la Norvège
la Belgique	la Pologne *(Poland)*
la Chine	la Russie ou l'U.R.S.S.
l'Égypte	la Suède *(Sweden)*
l'Espagne *(Spain)*	la Suisse
la France	la Tunisie
la Grèce	la Yougoslavie

Quelques pays masculins

le Brésil
le Canada
le Danemark
les États-Unis
le Japon
le Maroc
le Mexique
le Portugal
le Sénégal
le Zaïre

Point out that the definite article is used with **visiter**. (**Je vais visiter le Canada.**)

Although **Israël** is masculine, it does not take an article (**Je vais visiter Israël**), and one says **en Israël**.

C. **En** is also used with continents, which are feminine: **l'Afrique, l'Amérique du Nord, l'Amérique du Sud, l'Antarctique, l'Asie, l'Australie, l'Europe.**

Substitution: (1) Nous allons à Paris. Madrid / Genève / Montréal / Dakar. (2) Ils habitent en France. Belgique / Allemagne / Suède / Chine / Australie / Espagne. (3) Je voudrais voyager au Portugal. Mexique / Maroc / Japon / Canada / États-Unis.

Préparation

A. Quel pays visiter? Agnès is talking about the countries she would like to visit. What does she say?

Modèle   Italie → **Je voudrais visiter l'Italie.**

This exercise can be repeated using **aller** (e.g., **Je voudrais aller en Italie**). Students can be asked to tell whether or not they would like to go to the countries given in this exercise.

1. Portugal
2. Grèce
3. Mexique
4. Japon
5. Chine
6. Norvège
7. Canada
8. Tunisie
9. Russie
10. Sénégal
11. Égypte
12. États-Unis

B. En vacances. A group of students have met in an **auberge de jeunesse** *(youth hostel)*. Tell how each introduces himself or herself and says where he or she is from.

Modèle   Brigitte / Nice / France → **Je m'appelle Brigitte et j'habite à Nice en France.**

1. Pablo / Séville / Espagne
2. María / Lisbonne / Portugal
3. Juanita / Acapulco / Mexique
4. Karl / Vienne / Autriche
5. Théo / Athènes / Grèce
6. Erik / Oslo / Norvège
7. Djenat / Alexandrie / Égypte
8. Bob / Philadelphie / États-Unis
9. Miko / Tokyo / Japon
10. Amadou / Dakar / Sénégal

Communication

A. Je voudrais aller . . . Make a list of the countries you would like to visit. Then find out if another student would like to visit those countries too.

Exemple   Je voudrais aller en Grèce. Et vous?
Pas moi. Moi, je voudrais aller en Suède.

B. Il faut aller . . . Tell where one has to go to see the following sites.

Options: (1) Written. (2) Oral. Ask or have students ask each other Où désirez-vous aller et pourquoi?

> **Exemple**   la Tour Eiffel → **Il faut aller en France (ou à Paris) pour visiter la Tour Eiffel.**

Monuments et sites à visiter: la Tour Eiffel / les pyramides / le Vatican / le Parthénon / le Louvre / les Alpes / le Kremlin / la Casbah / ?

Pays et villes: Sénégal / Canada / Italie / Suède / Japon / Algérie / Hollande / Grèce / Mexique / Chine / France / Égypte / Russie / Paris / Moscou / Stockholm / Montréal / Amsterdam / Acapulco / ?

C. Villes et pays. Give the name of a city and see if other students can give the name of the country where it is located.

Option: Give the names of cities and have students tell where they are located.

> **Exemple**   Où est Dakar?
> C'est au Sénégal.

Les jours, les mois et les saisons

Présentation

Here are the French words for the days of the week and the months of the year. All are masculine. They are not capitalized.

Les jours de la semaine	**Les mois de l'année**		**Les saisons**
lundi	janvier	juillet	l'automne
mardi	février	août	l'hiver
mercredi	mars	septembre	le printemps
jeudi	avril	octobre	l'été
vendredi	mai	novembre	
samedi	juin	décembre	
dimanche			

Point out that **août** is pronounced [u] or [ut].

A. To indicate that an event occurs on a particular day, one uses the day without any preposition or article.

Il y a un match de football **samedi.**   There is a soccer game **(on) Saturday.**

B. To indicate that an event occurs repeatedly or habitually on a certain day, the definite article and the singular form of the noun are used.

J'ai une classe de français **le mardi.**   I have French class **(on) Tuesdays.**

C. To ask what day it is, one says:

Quel jour est-ce aujourd'hui?	*What day is it today?*
C'est lundi.	*It's Monday.*
C'est aujourd'hui lundi.	*Today is Monday.*

D. To ask what the date is, one says:

Quelle est la date aujourd'hui?
C'est le 11 février.
C'est aujourd'hui le premier mai.

   Note that dates are expressed by **le** plus a number. An exception is the first day of the month, for which **le premier (le 1ᵉʳ)** is used. Note also that the day precedes the month in French. Thus, 6/1/85 refers to January 6, 1985.

E. To indicate that an event occurs in a given month or season, **en** plus the month or season is used, except for **le printemps**, with which **au** is used.

Son anniversaire est en novembre.   *His birthday is in November.*
Je n'aime pas voyager en hiver.   *I don't like to travel in winter.*
Nous avons dix jours de vacances   *We have ten days of vacation*
   au printemps.   *in the spring.*

Préparation

Have students repeat and then give the days of the week (**C'est aujourd'hui dimanche,** etc.) and the months of the year (**C'est le 1ᵉʳ janvier,** etc.)

A. Une semaine à Dakar. Solange and some friends are visiting Dakar, the capital of Sénégal, and are planning their week's activities. Tell what they are going to do each day.

Modèle   Dimanche? (aller à la cathédrale) → **Dimanche, nous allons à la cathédrale.**

1. Dimanche? (marcher dans les rues de la ville)
2. Lundi? (manger au restaurant)
3. Mardi? (visiter l'université)
4. Mercredi? (visiter le musée)
5. Jeudi? (acheter des souvenirs)
6. Vendredi? (aller au théâtre)
7. Samedi? (aller à la plage)

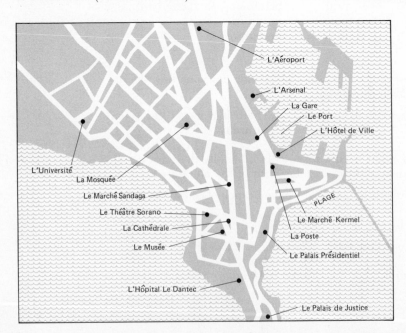

Dakar

B. C'est quand ta fête? Many French people celebrate their saint's day (la fête) as well as their birthday. Tell when the following have their fête.

Modèle   Didier   23 / 5   →   **La fête de Didier est le vingt-trois mai.**

1. Gilles   1 / 9
2. Germaine   15 / 6
3. Jacqueline   8 / 2
4. Vincent   22 / 1
5. Albert   15 / 11
6. Valérie   28 / 4
7. Dominique   8 / 8
8. Colette   6 / 3
9. David   30 / 12
10. Serge   7 / 10
11. Olivier   12 / 7
12. Yves   19 / 5

C. Les jours fériés. Ann, an American student, wants to know on which holidays the French do not work. What does her French friend tell her?

Modèle   25 décembre / Noël   →   **On ne travaille pas le 25 décembre parce que c'est Noël.**

1. 1er janvier / le Jour de l'An
2. 1er mai / la Fête du Travail
3. 14 juillet / la Fête Nationale
4. 15 août / une fête religieuse
5. 1er novembre / la Toussaint
6. 11 novembre / l'Armistice

Le 14 juillet à Paris

Communication

A. Les fêtes américaines. Tell a French student on which holidays people in the United States do not work.

Exemple   On ne travaille pas le quatre juillet parce que c'est la Fête Nationale.

B. Bon anniversaire. Ask yes-no questions to try to find out the birthday of another student.

Exemples   Est-ce que ton anniversaire est en mars?
             Est-ce que ton anniversaire est le sept octobre?

C. Questions/Interview. Answer the following questions or use them to interview another student.

1. Quel jour est-ce aujourd'hui?
2. Quel jour de la semaine est-ce que tu préfères? Pourquoi?
3. Quand est ton prochain examen de français?
4. En quel mois est ton anniversaire?
5. Quand est-ce que tu as des vacances?
6. Est-ce que tu restes ici en juin?
7. Quelle saison de l'année est-ce que tu préfères?
8. Quel mois de l'année est-ce que tu préfères?

⚜ Les nationalités

Présentation

A. Nouns and adjectives of nationality are formed by using the following general patterns.

1. la France → les Français/les Françaises

   l'Angleterre → les Anglais; l'Irlande → les Irlandais; la Hollande → les Hollandais; le Japon → les Japonais; le Portugal → les Portugais; le Sénégal → les Sénégalais

2. le Canada → les Canadiens/les Canadiennes

   la Tunisie → les Tunisiens; l'Égypte → les Égyptiens; l'Italie → les Italiens; le Brésil → les Brésiliens; l'Autriche → les Autrichiens; l'Inde → les Indiens; l'Australie → les Australiens; la Norvège → les Norvégiens

3. le Mexique → les Mexicains/les Mexicaines

   l'Amérique → les Américains; le Maroc → les Marocains

4. la Chine → les Chinois/les Chinoises

   la Suède → les Suédois; le Danemark → les Danois; le Zaïre → les Zaïrois

5. l'Allemagne → les Allemands/les Allemandes

la Russie → les Russes; la Belgique → les Belges; la Suisse → les Suisses; l'Espagne → les Espagnols; la Grèce → les Grecs/les Grècques

B. Two patterns can be used to indicate someone's nationality:

C'est + indefinite article + capitalized noun	Noun or pronoun + **être** + adjective (not capitalized)
C'est un Français.	Il est français.
C'est une Italienne.	Elle est italienne.
Ce sont des Belges.	Ils sont belges.

(1) Have students repeat, giving the masculine form of the nationality. Elle est française → Il est français. Elle est canadienne. Elle est belge. Elle est mexicaine. Elle est japonaise. Elle est russe. Elle est anglaise. Elle est égyptienne. Elle est sénégalaise. (2) Have students repeat, giving the feminine form. Il est américain. → Elle est américaine. Il est suisse. Il est danois. Il est tunisien. Il est marocain. Il est espagnol. Il est américain.

Préparation

A. À la résidence internationale. The staff of the **résidence internationale** is counting the number of students from different countries who live there. Tell what they say based on the following information.

Modèle   Angleterre (3) → **Il y a trois Anglais.**

1. Belgique (9)	7. Autriche (1)
2. Espagne (4)	8. Maroc (8)
3. Sénégal (6)	9. Japon (5)
4. Zaïre (7)	10. Allemagne (10)
5. États-Unis (14)	11. Russie (2)
6. Norvège (3)	12. Hollande (11)

B. À l'auberge de jeunesse. Yves and Gisèle are talking about where different people staying at the youth hostel are from. What do they say?

Modèle   Il est anglais? → **Oui, c'est un Anglais.**

1. Elle est suédoise?	6. Il est brésilien?
2. Ils sont algériens?	7. Elles sont canadiennes?
3. Il est allemand?	8. Il est portugais?
4. Elle est italienne?	9. Elle est hollandaise?
5. Ils sont japonais?	10. Ils sont américains?

Communication

Contacts internationaux. Using the following categories, tell about people from other countries with whom you have some contact.

Exemple   dans votre université → **Dans mon université, il y a des Français, des Allemands, des Italiens, et des Japonais.**

1. dans votre université	4. dans votre région
2. dans votre famille	5. dans votre pays
3. dans votre ville	

Vacances d'hiver

Vacances d'été ou vacances d'hiver?

Les vacances d'été, surtout en juillet et en août, restent sacrées pour les Français. *Séjours* à la plage, à la campagne, ou à la montagne; es *à l'étranger;* vacances tranquilles, exotiques ou aventureuses— une formule pour *tous** les *goûts* et tous les budgets. Mais maintenant les vacances d'hiver *commencent* à *concurrencer* les vacances d'été. Leur popularité *augmente chaque* année. Un Français *sur quatre* va en vacances en hiver et pour une ou deux semaines. La *neige* et les sports d'hiver restent leur objectif *numéro* un. Mais chaque hiver, il y a aussi deux millions de Français qui vont à l'étranger. Qu'est-ce qu'ils *cherchent?* Le *soleil*, la plage, la *détente*, mais aussi la *découverte* et l'aventure.

Où est-ce qu'ils vont? *Partout:* du Maroc à l'Inde, de la Guadeloupe à l'Égypte, de l'Afrique du Sud aux Îles Galapagos, du Népal au Brésil.

Voici quelques exemples de séjours proposés par différentes agences de voyages.

stays	
abroad	
all / tastes	
begin / compete with	
increases / each, every / out of four / snow	
number	
look for / sun / relaxation / discovery	
everywhere	
here are / several, some	

Plages

Sénégal	8 jours au Sénégal; 3 765 F. Bungalows. Tennis, vélos, sports nautiques.	
Guadeloupe	9 jours à la Guadeloupe; de 3 860 à 5 620 F. *Bord de mer* ou campagne.	seashore
Martinique	8 jours à la Martinique; de 4 625 à 6 505 F. Voiture (kilométrage illimité), tennis, sports nautiques.	

* **Tout** is an irregular adjective whose forms are **tout, toute, tous, toutes.**

La Guadeloupe

Sports		
Maroc	8 jours au Maroc; de 3 495 à 4210 F. Hacienda ranch à 6 km de la mer. *Promenades à cheval.*	horseback riding
Gambie	15 jours en Gambie; 4 750 F. *Croisière en voilier le long des côtes* du Sénégal et sur les rivières Saloum, Gambie et Casamance.	sailboat cruise along / coast
Espagne	8 jours en Espagne; 4 960 à 5 110 F. 12 courts de tennis *dessinés par* Borg et 5 *terrains* de golf.	designed / by / courses

Aventure		
Thaïlande	15 jours en Thaïlande; 6 990 F. À pied et *à dos* d'éléphant dans la jungle thaïlandaise. Campement et logement dans les villages.	on the back
Sénégal	12 jours au Sénégal. 5 880 F. Circuit le long de la Casamance, expédition dans la *brousse* en *pirogue*, en land rover. Campement ou logement dans les villages.	brush/canoe
Népal	17 jours au Népal; 9 200 F. Trekking dans l'Himalaya, rafting sur la rivière Trisuli, avec chef d'expédition népalais. Campement ou logement dans les villages.	

Culture		
Égypte	10 jours en Égypte; 5 180 F. Le Caire et les grands sites de la vallée du Nil en autocar.	
Mexique	22 jours au Mexique; 9 690 F. Mexique colonial indien, maya et mer des Caraïbes. Fêtes religieuses ou carnaval du Yucatan.	
Brésil	14 jours au Brésil; 14 100 F. Spécial carnaval du 8 au 19 février en hôtels de luxe.	

Extrait et adapté d'un article de l'*Express*.

Compréhension   Répondez aux questions suivantes selon les renseignements
donnés dans le texte.
1. Est-ce que les vacances d'été sont très importantes pour les Français?
2. Où est-ce qu'ils aiment passer leurs vacances?
3. Est-ce que les vacances d'hiver sont très populaires?
4. Quel est l'objectif principal des gens qui préfèrent les vacances d'hiver?
5. Combien de Français vont passer leurs vacances d'hiver à l'étranger?
6. Qu'est-ce qu'ils cherchent?
7. Où est-ce qu'ils vont?
8. Dans quels pays sont les séjours proposés?
9. Quelles sont les activités proposées?

NOTES CULTURELLES

Faire la France

Despite the continuing popularity of travel
abroad (an average of six million French
people vacation abroad each year), more and
more French people are rediscovering their
own country. The reasons for vacationing in
France rather than abroad are partly
economic (the cost of air travel, inflation in
some of the most popular countries, the
increased value of the dollar) and partly
sentimental. **Faire la France** is fashionable
once again. The French see it as a means of
getting back in touch with their roots and
memories as well as an expression of national
pride. Although seaside vacations and
camping are immensely popular (eight
million French people camp each year in
addition to two million foreigners), more and
more people are rediscovering the joys of the
countryside. Hiking, biking, and staying on
farms set up to receive guests are quite
popular. In addition, touring the countryside
on horseback or in horsedrawn carriages and
gliding along the quiet rivers and canals of
France in a houseboat attract those looking
for more original or challenging forms of
vacations.

Ask students what itinerary they
would suggest for a French-
speaking visitor coming to the
United States for the first time.

Communication

A. Où aller? Which of the vacations described in the *Synthèse* do you prefer
and why (activities, cost, environment, etc.)?

   Exemple   Je voudrais aller au Sénégal parce que j'aime l'aventure et je
                voudrais voyager en pirogue sur une rivière africaine.

B. Activités. Imagine that a group of French-speaking students are going to
visit your city. Plan a week's activities for them.

   Exemple   Lundi, nous allons visiter le campus et manger dans un
                restaurant universitaire.

C. Questions/Interview. Answer the following questions or use them to interview another student.

1. Où est-ce que tu aimes aller en vacances?
2. Est-ce que tu préfères voyager en été ou en hiver?
3. Quels pays est-ce que tu désires visiter?
4. Est-ce que tu désires visiter la France un jour?
5. Quelles villes françaises est-ce que tu désires visiter?
6. Quels monuments de Paris est-ce que tu désires visiter?
7. Quel est le voyage de tes rêves?
8. ?

Options: (1) Written. Directed composition. (2) Small-group interview. Have students write summary of partner's answers.

PRONONCIATION

A. In French, the letter **a** is always pronounced [a]. Compare the pronunciation of the following cognates:

English	French
village	village
parent	parent
theater	théâtre
special	spécial
garage	garage

Repeat the following words:

1. village	2. journal	3. impatient
éducation	spécial	adorable
voyage	garage	salade
théâtre	nature	magasin

B. The French consonant sounds [p], [t], and [k] are not "exploded," or released with the same force as they are in English. The French pronunciation of these sounds is similar to their pronunciation in English when they follow an **s.** (Compare **p**air—s**p**are, **t**op—s**t**op, **k**it—s**k**it.)
Repeat the following words:

1. patient	2. télévision	3. confortable
police	talent	colonie
petit	téléphone	compétent
pays	travailler	capitale

C. Repeat the following sentences, paying special attention to the sounds you have been practicing.

1. C'est un tout petit garage.
2. Elle travaille dans la capitale.
3. Il y a un téléphone sur la place du village.
4. Il faut être plus patient avec tes parents.
5. Ma machine à laver ne marche pas.

VOCABULAIRE

noms

les pays (voir p. 76)
les jours de la semaine (voir p. 77)
les mois de l'année (voir p. 77)
les saisons (voir p. 77)
les nationalités (voir pp. 80–81)

les voyages

l'agence de voyages (f)   *travel agency*
l'autocar (m)   *bus*
° l'automobiliste (m,f)   *driver*
l'avion (m)   *airplane*
le bord de la mer   *seashore*
°la carte d'identité
la côte   *coast*
le logement   *lodging*
la mer   *sea*
la montagne   *mountain*
°le passeport
le pays   *country*
le permis de conduire   *driver's license*
la plage   *beach*
le sac à dos   *backpack*
°le souvenir
°le train
la valise   *suitcase*

d'autres noms

l'année (f)   *year*
° l'aventure (f)
°le budget
le chef   *leader*
°le cousin
la découverte   *discovery*
la détente   *relaxation*
la fois   *time, instance*
le goût   *taste*
le jour   *day*
°le million
le mois   *month*
la neige   *snow*
le numéro   *number*
° l'objectif (m)
le pied   *foot*
°la popularité
que   *that*
la saison   *season*
le soleil   *sun*

verbes

acheter   *to buy*
aller   *to go*
augmenter   *to increase*
chercher   *to look for*
°commencer
emporter   *to take along*
faire du camping   *to go camping*
partir   *to leave*
passer   *to spend (vacation)*
poser une question   *to ask a question*
quitter   *to leave*
°visiter

adjectifs

°aventureux, aventureuse
chaque   *each*
dessiné(e)   *designed*
°différent(e)
étranger, étrangère   *foreign*
premier, première   *first*
prochain(e)   *next*
quelques   *several, some*
°religieux, religieuse
seul(e)   *alone*
tout(e), tous   *all*

adverbes

pas aujourd'hui   *not today*

divers

à   *to, at, in*
à cheval   *on horseback*
à l'étranger   *abroad*
alors   *well then*
à pied   *on foot*
Bonnes vacances!   *Have a good vacation!*
chez   *at (to) the home (business) of*
d'habitude   *usually*
eh bien   *well, well then*
en   *to, at, in, by*
là-bas   *there, over there*
le long de   *along*
où   *where*
par   *by*
parce que   *because*
partout   *everywhere*
pour   *for*
Quel jour est-ce?   *What day is it?*
Quelle est la date?   *What is the date?*
sur   *on*
voici   *here is, are*

CHAPITRE CINQ

La vie quotidienne: nourriture, logement et activités

INTRODUCTION

À midi

Suzanne et Monique travaillent dans un bureau qui *ferme* à *midi*. Elles ont deux *heures* pour *déjeuner* en ville ou pour *rentrer* manger à la maison. En général elles déjeunent dans un restaurant ou dans un snack-bar du *quartier* parce qu'elles habitent dans la *banlieue* de la ville.

closes / noon

hours / to eat lunch / return

neighborhood / suburb

MONIQUE   Tu ne déjeunes pas avec nous? On va manger au restaurant du *coin*.

corner

SUZANNE   Non, pas aujourd'hui. *Cet après-midi* j'ai des *courses à faire* dans les magasins.

this afternoon / errands to run
If desired, point out that **différents** when used as a prenominal adjective means *various*.

MONIQUE   Qu'est-ce que tu vas acheter?

SUZANNE   Euh, *rien de spécial*. Les enfants *ont besoin* de différentes *choses* pour l'*école*. *Après ça*, je voudrais aller à la *poste* pour acheter des *timbres*.

nothing special / need
things / school / after that / post office / stamps

MONIQUE   Moi aussi, j'ai besoin d'aller à la poste. J'ai des *tas* de lettres à *envoyer*. La poste n'est pas *fermée* à midi?

a lot, stacks
send / closed

SUZANNE   Non, le bureau de la *rue* Saint-Vincent reste *ouvert toute la journée*.

street / open / all day long

MONIQUE   C'est *loin d'ici*?

far from here

SUZANNE   Non, c'est *tout près d'ici*. Tu vas *jusqu'à* l'avenue Pasteur et tu tournes *à droite*. La poste est au coin.

very near here / as far as
right

Nous avons des courses à faire

Compréhension   Répondez aux questions suivantes selon les renseignements donnés dans l'Introduction.

1. Est-ce que le bureau où Suzanne travaille reste ouvert toute la journée?
2. Où est-ce que Monique va déjeuner?
3. Pourquoi est-ce que Suzanne ne déjeune pas avec Monique aujourd'hui?
4. Qu'est-ce qu'elle va acheter?
5. Pourquoi est-ce qu'elle a besoin d'aller à la poste?
6. Et Monique, pourquoi est-ce qu'elle a besoin d'aller à la poste?
7. Est-ce qu'il y a un bureau de poste qui est ouvert à midi?
8. Est-ce que la poste est loin du bureau où Monique et Suzanne travaillent?

Option: Using vocabulary they know, have students rewrite the **Introduction** imagining that they are talking with a friend.

NOTES CULTURELLES

La ville française

A tourist visiting a French city is likely to be
struck by certain contrasts with most
American cities. For example, French cities
are not always clearly divided into
downtown business districts and residential
areas. The downtown area (**centre-ville**)
usually remains a highly desirable place to
live. In general, streets are lined with
buildings three to six stories high, with small
shops on the street level and apartments of
various sizes on the upper levels. Some
apartments are rented, others are owned by
their occupants. As a result, within each
neighborhood there may be considerable
intermingling of diverse socio-economic
groups. The many small shops where people
do their daily shopping also facilitate
personal contact. Despite the existence of
supermarkets, the French still like to buy
their meat, bread, and produce fresh daily
from their neighborhood stores.

Et vous?

Votre quartier. Use the suggested words to answer the questions about
the neighborhood where you live.

1. Est-ce que votre quartier est près de . . . ?

la gare (*railway station*)   l'aéroport   l'autoroute (*highway*)

2. Est-ce que vous habitez près de(d') . . . ?

un arrêt autobus (*bus stop*)   une station de métro   un parc
une école (*school*)

3. Dans votre quartier est-ce qu'il y a . . . ?

une banque   une bibliothèque   un restaurant
une poste   un bureau de tabac (*tobacco shop*)   une pharmacie
une librairie   une église (*church*)   un cinéma

4. Est-ce qu'il y a aussi . . . ?

un supermarché
une boulangerie (*bakery*)
une boucherie (*butcher shop*)
une épicerie (*grocery store*)
une pâtisserie (*pastry shop*)

⚜   Le verbe *faire*

Présentation

Faire (*to do*, *to make*) is an irregular verb.

faire	
je **fais**	nous **faisons**
tu **fais**	vous **faites**
il/elle/on **fait**	ils/elles **font**

Je **fais** mon travail
Qu'est-ce que tu **fais** dimanche?
Qu'est-ce qu'on va **faire** demain?

    Faire is used in the following idiomatic expressions.

faire du sport	*to play sports*
faire du ski	*to go skiing*
faire le ménage	*to do the housework*
faire la vaisselle	*to do the dishes*
faire ses devoirs	*to do one's homework*
faire la cuisine	*to cook, to do the cooking*
faire le marché	*to go shopping*
faire les courses	*to run errands*
faire un voyage	*to take a trip*
faire une promenade	*to go for a walk*

Point out that all the singular forms of **faire** have the same pronunciation [fɛ], but that **nous faisons** is pronounced [fəzõ].

Préparation

Répétition: (1) Je fais du sport, tu fais du sport, etc. (2) Je ne fais pas le marché, tu ne fais pas le marché, etc. **Substitution:** (1) Nous faisons souvent du ski. tu / je / Gilbert / vous / mes amis. (2) Qu'est-ce que tu fais aujourd'hui? nous / vous / vos amis / Luc / je / tu

A. Activités. Some friends are talking about what they are doing this afternoon. What do they say?

    Modèle   Sylvie / faire le marché → **Sylvie fait le marché.**

1. nous / faire du ski
2. je / faire mes devoirs
3. tu / faire une promenade
4. Monique et Simon / faire le ménage
5. vous / faire des courses
6. Micheline / faire la vaisselle
7. nous / faire du sport

B. Questions. Jean-Jacques is asking his friends about their plans. Give his questions.

    Modèle   Fabien / samedi après-midi → **Qu'est-ce que Fabien fait samedi après-midi?**

1. tu / maintenant
2. Jacques / l'année prochaine
3. Pierre et Sylvie / l'été prochain
4. les enfants / en juin
5. vous / dimanche
6. nous / demain après-midi
7. Véronique / lundi soir
8. le professeur / pendant les vacances

Nous faisons du sport

Communication

Have students ask each other questions about their activities (e.g., **Est-ce que tu fais souvent le ménage?**).

A. Activités. Tell how often you do the following activities.

Exemple faire le ménage → **Je fais rarement le ménage.**

ne . . . jamais   rarement   quelquefois   souvent

1. faire le ménage
2. faire une promenade
3. faire du sport
4. faire du camping
5. faire mes devoirs
6. faire la cuisine
7. faire un voyage
8. faire la vaisselle
9. faire des courses
10. faire du ski

B. Interview. Make up questions to ask other students about what they generally do or are going to do at various times. If someone asks you a question that you think is indiscreet or too personal, you can respond: **C'est une question trop indiscrète,** or simply, **Je ne sais pas.**

Exemples Qu'est-ce que tu fais mercredi après-midi?
Qu'est-ce tu vas faire après la classe?

91

C. Questions. Imagine that some French friends are asking about typical activities of Americans. How would you answer their questions?

1. Est-ce que les hommes font souvent la cuisine dans les familles américaines?
2. Est-ce que les Américains font souvent du camping?
3. Est-ce que les Américains aiment faire des promenades en voiture le dimanche après-midi?
4. Est-ce qu'ils font souvent leur marché dans les petits magasins du quartier?
5. Est-ce que les Américains font souvent du sport?
6. En général, est-ce que ce sont les femmes, les hommes ou les enfants qui font la vaisselle?
7. Est-ce que les enfants américains ont des devoirs à faire chaque soir?
8. Est-ce que les enfants américains font le ménage dans leur chambre?
9. Est-ce que les Américains aiment faire des promenades à pied pendant le week-end?

⚜ Les prépositions

Présentation

Prepositions are useful in indicating the location of a person, object, or place. The most common prepositions in French are listed below.

A. Certain prepositions directly precede the noun.

dans *in*	Ils sont **dans** la maison.
sur *on*	Ses livres sont **sur** votre chaise.
sous *under*	Le chien est **sous** la table.
devant *in front of*	Votre voiture est **devant** l'épicerie.
derrière *behind*	La pharmacie est **derrière** la poste.
entre *between*	Trois-Rivières est **entre** Québec et Montréal.

B. Other prepositions contain **à** or **de** and contract with **le** or **les**.

jusqu'à *as far as, up to*	Il faut aller **jusqu'au** café.
au milieu de *in the middle of*	L'université est **au milieu de** la ville.
loin de *far from*	La banque est **loin de** l'hôtel.
près de *near*	L'hôtel est **près de** la gare.
à côté de *beside, next to*	La boulangerie est **à côté du** cinéma.
en face de *facing, across from*	La librairie est **en face du** musée.

C. The following expressions are also useful when telling where something is.

Traversez la rue.	*Cross the street.*
Allez jusqu'à la pâtisserie.	*Go as far as the pastry shop.*
Allez tout droit.	*Go straight ahead.*
Tournez à gauche.	*Turn left.*
Tournez à droite.	*Turn right.*
Prenez la rue Carnot.	*Take Carnot Street.*

Préparation

A. Mais non! Eric doesn't know his way around his new neighborhood yet. Thérèse is telling him where various places are. What does she say?

Modèle   Ton appartement est à côté de l'église? (en face) → **Non, il est en face de l'église.**

1. L'arrêt d'autobus est devant le cinéma? (en face)
2. Le restaurant universitaire est près d'ici? (loin)
3. Tes amis habitent en face de la poste? (à côté)
4. La station de métro est devant la boucherie? (derrière)
5. Tu habites loin du bureau de poste? (près)
6. Le musée est à côté du parc? (au milieu)

B. C'est où, s'il vous plaît? A tourist has asked Monique how to get to various places in Paris. Give Monique's answers.

Options: Written/oral role-play.

Modèle   Où est la rue de Londres? (behind the Gare Saint-Lazare) → **Elle est derrière la Gare Saint-Lazare.**

1. Est-ce que le Sacré-Cœur est près du Louvre? (very far from the Louvre)
2. Où est le Panthéon? (near the Sorbonne)
3. Où est la place de l'Opéra? (in front of the Opéra)
4. Où est la tombe de Napoléon? (at the Invalides)
5. Où est l'Obélisque? (in the middle of the place de la Concorde)
6. Où est le Louvre? (between the Seine and the rue de Rivoli)
7. Où est l'Île Saint-Louis? (next to the Île de la Cité)

Le Sacré-Coeur de Montmartre

Communication

A. Vrai ou faux? Indicate whether the following statements based on the map of Paris are true or false. If a statement is false, reword it to make it true.

Option: Exercises A and B can be modified using city or campus maps.

1. Les Tuileries sont à côté de la Tour Eiffel.
2. Le Grand Palais est à côté du Petit Palais.
3. La Cité Universitaire est près de la Sorbonne.
4. La Bibliothèque Nationale est sur le boulevard Saint-Germain.
5. La Gare de l'Est est loin de la Gare de Lyon.
6. L'Église de la Madeleine est près de l'Opéra.
7. Le Palais de Chaillot est en face de la Tour Eiffel.

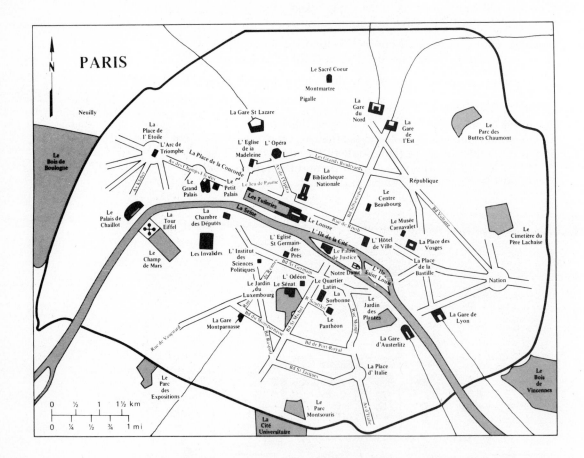

B. Où est . . . ? Imagine that someone asks you for directions in Paris. Based on the map, what would your answers be?

Option: One student chooses where he or she is on map; others ask questions to find the location.

1. Où est l'Opéra? Et le Sénat? Et la Gare du Nord?
2. Et la Tour Eiffel? Et le Jardin du Luxembourg? Et le Sacré-Coeur?

C. Renseignements. Imagine that you are a new French-speaking student on campus and are asking how to get to various locations. Another student will give you directions.

Exemple   Je voudrais aller à la bibliothèque.
Prenez la rue Marconi, tournez à droite, allez jusqu'à la rue Smith. C'est là.

⚜ La nourriture et les repas

Présentation   Point out that there is no liaison with **haricots**.   Contrast the pronounciation of **un œuf** [oenoef] and **des œufs** [dezø].

Basic food items are:

les **légumes** (m)   *vegetables*
les artichauts (m)   *artichokes*
les carottes (f)   *carrots*
les épinards (m)   *spinach*
les haricots verts (m)   *green beans*
les oignons (m)   *onions*
les petits pois (m)   *peas*
les pommes de terre (f)   *potatoes*
les tomates (f)   *tomatoes*

les **fruits** (m)   *fruit*
les bananes (f)   *bananas*
les cerises (f)   *cherries*
les pêches (f)   *peaches*
les poires (f)   *pears*
les pommes (f)   *apples*
les raisins (m)   *grapes*

les **viandes** (f)   *meats*
le bœuf   *beef*
le jambon   *ham*
le poisson   *fish*
le porc   *pork*
le poulet   *chicken*
le veau   *veal*

les **boissons** (f)   *beverages*
la bière   *beer*
le café   *coffee*
l'eau (f)   *water*
le jus d'orange   *orange juice*
le lait   *milk*
le thé   *tea*
le vin   *wine*

quelques autres aliments (m) *some other foods*
le beurre   *butter*
la confiture   *jam*
les frites (f)   *French fries*
le fromage   *cheese*
le gâteau   *cake*
la glace   *ice cream*
les œufs (m)   *eggs*
le pain   *bread*
le poivre   *pepper*
la salade
le sel   *salt*
la soupe
le sucre   *sugar*

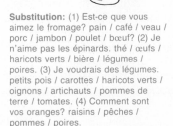

Suggestion: Introduce other food or beverage items (**le Coca-Cola, la limonade,** etc.).

Substitution: (1) Est-ce que vous aimez le fromage? pain / café / veau / porc / jambon / poulet / bœuf? (2) Je n'aime pas les épinards. thé / œufs / haricots verts / bière / légumes / poires. (3) Je voudrais des légumes. petits pois / carottes / haricots verts / oignons / artichauts / pommes de terre / tomates. (4) Comment sont vos oranges? raisins / pêches / pommes / poires.

les **repas** (m)   *meals*
le petit déjeuner   *breakfast*
le déjeuner   *lunch*
le dîner   *dinner*

Préparation

A. Au supermarché. Monsieur and Madame Legrand are doing their shopping at Carrefour and are asking where various items are. Give their questions.

Carrefour is one of the largest chains of **hypermarchés**.

Modèle   pain → **Où est le pain, s'il vous plaît?**

1. sucre
2. fromage
3. œufs
4. café
5. eau minérale
6. légumes
7. fruits
8. viande

B. Au restaurant. Janine and Henri are eating in a neighborhood restaurant and commenting on their food. Tell what they say.

Modèles   salade / excellente → **La salade est excellente.**
              légumes / pas très bon → **Les légumes ne sont pas très bons.**

1. poisson / très bon
2. veau / excellent
3. haricots verts / assez bons
4. carottes / pas très bonnes
5. pommes de terre / très bonnes
6. fromage / exceptionnel
7. gâteau / pas formidable
8. vin / excellent

Communication

A. Préférences. Use the scale to describe your preferences in foods.

Suggestion: Have students share their preferences with class or in small groups.

Je déteste   Je n'aime pas   J'aime assez   J'aime beaucoup   J'adore

Les légumes:	*La viande:*	*Les boissons:*	*Les fruits:*
les carottes	le jambon	le lait	les poires
les petits pois	le veau	le café	les pommes
les épinards	le poisson	la bière	les oranges
?	?	?	?

B. Questions/Interview. Answer the following questions or use them to interview another student.

1. Quels sont tes légumes préférés?
2. Quels sont tes fruits préférés?
3. Quelles boissons est-ce que tu aimes?
4. Quels sont tes desserts préférés?
5. Qu'est-ce que tu aimes préparer quand tu invites des amis à dîner?
6. Qu'est-ce que tu manges d'habitude pour le petit déjeuner? Le déjeuner? Le dîner?
7. Qu'est-ce que tu aimes manger quand tu vas au restaurant?
8. En général, où est-ce que tu fais ton marché?
9. Est-ce que tu aimes les fromages français? Et les vins français?
10. Est-ce qu'il y a des restaurants français dans votre ville? Où?

⚜ Le partitif

Présentation

Some items (such as coffee, sugar, patience) cannot be counted. In English, we often use the words *some*, *no*, or *any*, or no article at all with such items. One says, for example, *I would like some coffee; we don't have any time; he has no patience; we have money.* In French, the partitive article conveys these meanings, but it cannot be omitted.

Les articles partitifs			
	Before a masculine noun	*Before a feminine noun*	*Before a noun beginning with a vowel sound*
Affirmative	du café	de la salade	de l'eau minérale
Negative	pas de café	pas de salade	pas d'eau minérale

Note that the partitive articles, like the indefinite articles, change to **de** or **d'** in the negative.

Elle ne mange jamais **de** viande.
Je voudrais **de** l'eau, s'il vous plaît.
Nous avons **du** travail à faire, mais nous n'avons pas **d'**énergie.
Il n'a pas **d'**autorité.

A. It is important to know when to use the definite article and when to use the partitive. As you have learned, the definite article is used to refer to general categories, as when talking about likes and dislikes. The partitive is used to indicate an undetermined amount of a noncountable item.

Compare:
J'aime **le** poisson.   Je mange **du** poisson.
Je préfère **la** viande.   Je vais acheter **de la** viande.
J'adore **la** glace.   Je voudrais **de la** glace.
Je n'aime pas **la** bière.   Il n'y a pas **de** bière dans mon frigo.

Have students repeat the following nouns, replacing the definite article with the partitive article: le pain, le fromage, le vin, le thé, le lait, la viande, la soupe, la salade, la glace, la bière.

B. Especially when talking about buying and eating food, one has to decide whether to use the partitive or an indefinite article. When food items cannot be counted or come in bulk, or when one talks about buying or eating an undetermined amount of a food item, the partitive is used.

Je mange souvent **de la** viande.
Je voudrais **du** lait, s'il vout plaît.
Nous allons acheter **du** beurre.

But when food items are counted as separate items (an artichoke, an orange) or used in the plural (some green beans, some fruits), the indefinite article is used.

Je voudrais **une** glace et **une** poire.
Nous allons manger **des** petits pois et **des** tomates.

Préparation

A. On fait le marché. Monique and Alain are shopping in the various stores in their neighborhood. Tell what they are going to buy.

Modèle   poisson → **On va acheter du poisson.**

1. poulet
2. bœuf
3. fromage
4. pâin

5. vin rouge
6. bière
7. glace

8. sucre
9. lait
10. eau minérale

B. Qu'est-ce qu'il y a au menu? Several students are talking about the foods served in the student restaurant. Tell what they say.

Modèle   soupe (souvent) → **Il y a souvent de la soupe.**

1. viande (souvent)
2. poisson (rarement)
3. glace (quelquefois)
4. salade (souvent)
5. pain (toujours)

6. eau minérale (toujours)
7. vin (toujours)
8. fromage (souvent)
9. légumes (toujours)
10. fruits (rarement)

C. À la bonne soupe. Fabienne and Céline are eating in a small neighborhood café with a limited menu. Give the waiter's answers to their questions.

Modèle   Est-ce que vous avez de la soupe aujourd'hui? (non) → **Non, nous n'avons pas de soupe.**

1. Est-ce que vous avez du porc? (oui)
2. Est-ce que vous avez du poisson? (non)
3. Est-ce que vous avez des haricots verts? (oui)
4. Est-ce que vous avez de la salade? (non)
5. Est-ce que vous avez du fromage? (oui)
6. Est-ce que vous avez de la glace? (non)

Communication

A. Préférences et habitudes. Tell how well you like and how often you eat the following foods.

Exemple   la glace → **J'aime beaucoup la glace et je mange souvent de la glace.**

1. le poisson
2. le pain français
3. le fromage français
4. la soupe

5. la viande
6. la glace
7. la salade
8. le dessert

B. Contrastes. The pictures on the next page illustrate three typical French meals. Describe what is served at each meal and then tell if Americans have the same eating habits.

Exemples   Pour le petit déjeuner, les Français mangent . . .
               Pour le petit déjeuner, nous mangeons . . .

SYNTHÈSE

Où habiter: banlieue ou centre-ville?

Est-ce qu'on est heureux quand on habite en banlieue? *Selon* un récent sondage d'opinion, deux Français sur trois *pensent* que oui. Les *autres* sont *sceptiques*. La réalité est que pour certains, c'est un paradis mais pour d'autres, c'est un *cauchemar*.

according to
think / others
skeptical
nightmare

Banlieue = cauchemar
Myriam Lebeau, qui habite dans un *ensemble* d'H.L.M., trouve la banlieue *ennuyeuse* et *laide*. Mère de trois enfants, elle ne travaille pas. Elle n'a pas de voiture et l'arrêt d'autobus est trop loin. Résultat: elle est prisonnière.

cluster, group
boring / ugly

   René Pannier est ouvrier. Il faut une heure pour aller de son appartement à l'usine où il travaille. Résultat: deux heures d'autobus à *ajouter* à la fatigue du travail.

add

Banlieue = paradis
Hervé et Marie-Louise Jacolot habitent une petite maison beige au milieu de *milliers* d'autres petites maisons beiges. *Chaque* maison a son petit jardin et sa *pelouse*. En comparaison avec l'H.L.M., c'est un rêve.

thousands / each
lawn

   Pierre et Catherine habitent une jolie maison au milieu des *arbres* à 20 kilomètres du Vieux Port de Marseille. On *respire* le parfum des *fleurs* et des herbes de Provence. Le tennis et la *piscine* ne sont pas loin.

trees
breathe
flowers / swimming pool

   Brigitte et Jean-Claude possèdent une grande maison dans un vieux village près de Lille. Il y a des fleurs partout. Ils sont *ravis*.

delighted

   Les résultats du sondage confirment que pour les Français les principaux avantages de la banlieue sont le calme et la possibilité d'avoir un jardin, mais le principal *inconvénient* est le temps qu'il faut pour aller à son travail.

disadvantage

Extrait et adapté d'un article de *l'Express*

Un H.L.M.

Une petite maison
beige . . .

Une vieille ferme

Compréhension   Répondez aux questions selon les renseignements donnés
dans le texte.

1. Est-ce que tous les Français pensent que la vie en banlieue est idéale?
2. Est-ce que Myriam trouve la vie en banlieue amusante? Pourquoi?
3. Et pour René Pannier, est-ce que la banlieue est un cauchemar ou un paradis? Pourquoi?
4. Où est-ce qu'Hervé et Marie-Louise Jacolot habitent?
5. Comment sont les maisons dans leur quartier?
6. Est-ce que Pierre et Catherine aiment leur maison? Pourquoi?
7. Près de quelle grande ville est-ce qu'ils habitent?
8. Est-ce que Brigitte et Jean-Claude sont contents de leur maison? Pourquoi?
9. Quel est le principal avantage de la vie en banlieue?
10. Quel est son principal inconvénient?

NOTES CULTURELLES

La banlieue

Critical housing shortages in France, particularly after World War II, during which more than 450,000 dwellings were destroyed, necessitated extensive construction of new homes and apartments. Expansion was concentrated on the outskirts of French towns and cities. One typically finds two kinds of housing in French suburbs: high-rise apartments and individual homes. The large clusters of H.L.M. apartments have been widely criticized for their sterility, crowded conditions (one such cluster contains 1,800 apartments in two blocks), and inadequate shopping and recreational facilities. These conditions have led in some cases to serious problems of juvenile delinquency. Other high-rise apartments in the suburbs have attracted the more affluent middle class. Many sections of French suburbs contain individual homes, or **villas,** for middle-class French families and more modest homes in areas known as **cités ouvrières.** Like their American counterparts, these suburbanites (**banlieusards**) especially enjoy the opportunities to have a yard and garden, live closer to the countryside, and enjoy cleaner air.

Communication

A. Où habiter? Tell which of the following types of housing you prefer and why. Then tell why the other choices are less appealing.

Exemple Moi, je voudrais avoir un appartement en ville parce que j'aime faire des courses dans les magasins et aller souvent au théâtre ou au cinéma.

1. un appartement en ville
2. une maison dans la banlieue
3. une maison à la campagne
4. un H.L.M.

Chez Mimi

Menu à 38 francs

Salade de tomates   ou Soupe à l'oignon
Rôti de porc   ou Boeuf bourguignon
Carottes Vichy   ou Tomates provençales
Glace au chocolat ou Fruits
Vin rouge   ou Vin blanc

B. Au restaurant. Imagine that you are in a small family restaurant and are going to order your dinner from the menu above. What would you select? One student can play the role of the waiter, **le garçon** or **la serveuse,** and ask you, the **client(e),** what you would like.

Exemple GARÇON: Est-ce que vous désirez de la salade de tomates ou de la soupe à l'oignon?
CLIENT(E): Je voudrais de la salade de tomates.

Option: Have students make up their own restaurant menus, including both the name of the restaurant and the list of foods served.

C. Interview. Make up questions to ask other students about what they usually do or plan to do at various times.

Exemples   Qu'est-ce que tu fais dimanche après-midi?
Qu'est-ce que tu vas faire aujourd'hui après la classe?

PRONONCIATION

A. The French [r] is very different from the *r* sound in English. It is pronounced at the back of the mouth—almost in the throat. It is similar to the sound produced when one says the name of the German composer Bach, pronounced with a guttural **-ch.** To learn the pronunciation of the French **r,** one can (1) always come back to a familiar sound, as in Bach, or (2) start with words in which the sound that precedes or follows the **r** is also pronounced toward the back of the mouth—[a], as in **garage,** or [k], as in **parc.**

Repeat the following words:

1. bar	2. derrière	3. faire	4. rare	5. frère	6. quatre
car	haricot	épinard	rester	traverser	être
gare	arrêt	poire	région	fruit	chambre
Marc	carottes	bonjour	regarder	grand	livre
parc	toujours	confiture	radio	train	votre

B. To pronounce the French [l] the tip of the tongue is placed against the upper front teeth rather than on the bony ridge behind the teeth as it is in English.

Repeat the following words:

1. le	2. valise	3. ville
la	milieu	tranquille
loin	village	salle
liberté	soleil	hôtel
livre	aller	quelle

C. Repeat the following sentences, paying special attention to the sounds you have been practicing.

1. Bonjour et au revoir!
2. Le garage est derrière la gare.
3. Je voudrais quatre chambres sur la rue.
4. L'arrêt d'autobus est près de l'Opéra.
5. En général, il est très difficile de trouver un hôtel à Paris.

VOCABULAIRE

noms

la nourriture et les repas (voir p. 95)

les bâtiments et les lieux

° l'aéroport (m)
  l'arrêt d'autobus (m)
  l'autoroute (f)   *major highway*
  la banlieue   *suburb*
° la banque
  la bibliothèque   *library*
  la boucherie   *butcher shop*
  la boulangerie   *bakery*
  le bureau   *office*
  le bureau de tabac   *tobacco shop*
  le coin   *corner*
  l'école (f)   *school*
  l'église (f)   *church*
  l'épicerie (f)   *grocery store*
  la gare   *train station*
° le parc
  la pâtisserie   *pastry shop*
° la pharmacie
  la piscine   *swimming pool*
  la poste   *post office*
  le quartier   *neighborhood*
  la station de métro   *subway stop*
° le supermarché

d'autres noms

  l'arbre (m)   *tree*
° l'avantage (m)
° le calme
  le cauchemar   *nightmare*
  la chose   *thing*
° la fatigue
  la fleur   *flower*
  l'heure (f)   *hour*
  l'inconvénient (m)   *disadvantage*
  la journée   *day*
  midi   *noon*
  le millier   *(about) a thousand*
° le paradis
  le parfum   *scent*
  la pelouse   *lawn*
° la possibilité
° la réalité
° le résultat
  le sondage   *poll*
  le timbre   *stamp*

verbes

expressions idiomatiques avec le verbe faire
   (voir p. 90)

  ajouter   *to add*
  avoir besoin de   *to need*
  avoir des courses à faire   *to have errands to run*
° confirmer
  déjeuner   *to eat lunch*
  envoyer   *to send*
  faire   *to do, to make*
  fermer   *to close*
  penser   *to think*
  rentrer   *to return*
° tourner
  traverser   *to cross*

adjectifs

° beige
  ennuyeux, eunuyeuse   *boring*
  laid(e)   *ugly*
  ouvert(e)   *open*
° principal(e), principaux
  ravi(e)   *delighted*
° récent(e)

divers

  à côté de   *beside, next to*
  à droite   *to the right*
  à gauche   *to the left*
  après ça   *after that*
  au milieu de   *in the middle of*
  certain(e)(s)   *certain (ones)*
  dans   *in*
  d'autres   *others*
  derrière   *behind*
  devant   *in front of*
° en comparaison avec
  en face de   *facing, across from*
  entre   *between*
  ici   *here*
  jusqu'à   *up to, as far as*
  loin de   *far from*
  prenez   *take*
  près de   *near*
  qui   *that*
  rien de spécial   *nothing special*
  selon   *according to*
  sous   *under*
  sur   *on*
  tout droit   *straight ahead*
  un tas de   *a lot of*

CHAPITRE SIX

Le temps passe

6

The following **Introduction,** based on a section of *l'Express,* outlines the best television programs for the week and does not therefore include the range of programs generally seen on French television.

INTRODUCTION

Télévision: Les sélections de la semaine

Quelles *émissions* de télévision est-ce que vous allez regarder cette semaine? . . . Voici notre sélection des *meilleurs* programmes du *soir*
qu'on va *montrer* cette semaine sur les différentes *chaînes.*

programs

best / evening

show / channels

VENDREDI SOIR	**Sur TF1:** Un concert avec Charles Aznavour, Julien Clerc et Anne Dufresne.
	Sur FR3: *Contes* et légendes des provinces françaises. «Pierrot le *loup*» de Denis Bonan.
	Sur A2: «Apostrophes: Culture et Politique», avec des personalités du *monde* politique et culturel.
SAMEDI SOIR	**Sur FR3:** «De la Démocratie en Amérique.» Deuxième partie d'un *reportage* spécial sur la vie politique aux États-Unis.
	Sur A2: *Carnets* de l'aventure. «Aventures en Himalaya.» L'ascension de l'Annapurna par une *équipe* d'*alpinistes* allemands.
LUNDI SOIR	**Sur FR3:** Musiclub. Émission spéciale sur Beethoven, sa vie et son *oeuvre.*
MARDI SOIR	Rien de spécial (excepté la *coupe* d'Europe de football sur TF1. Pour les *passionnés* de football).
MERCREDI SOIR	**Sur A2:** «Venise en hiver.» Première partie d'un téléfilm en deux parties, basé sur un *roman* d'Emmanuel Roblès.
JEUDI SOIR	**Sur A2:** L'histoire en question. Alain Decaux évoque le *mur* de Berlin.
	Sur TF1: *Histoire* de la vie: Le phénomène de la reproduction.

stories, tales
wolf

world

documentary

team / mountain climbers

work

cup
fans

novel

wall
story, history

Extrait et adapté de *l'Express.*

104

Compréhension   Indiquez quelles sont les différentes émissions susceptibles d'intéresser les personnes suivantes. (Indicate which programs might be of interest to the following people.)

1. Jean-Louis aime seulement les émissions culturelles et les débats politiques.
2. Michel aime mieux les émissions amusantes et les sports.
3. Catherine n'a pas le temps de regarder la télévision pendant la semaine, mais elle aime bien rester à la maison et regarder la télé le samedi soir.
4. Stéphanie a seulement onze ans, mais elle rêve d'être un jour une grande alpiniste.
5. Alain et Marie-Claire ne vont pas souvent au concert, mais ils adorent la musique classique.
6. Sylvie pense qu'on ne montre pas assez de bonnes émissions scientifiques.
7. Chantal et Pierre sont contents quand il y a un bon film à la télé.
8. François passe une bonne partie de son temps à écouter ses disques favoris. Julien Clerc est son chanteur préféré.

NOTES CULTURELLES

La télévision française

There are three French television channels that broadcast throughout much of the day on weekdays and all day long on weekends: **TF1—Télévision française 1, A2—Antenne 2, and FR3—France Régions 3.** Luxembourg and Monte Carlo have independent stations that can be seen throughout most of French-speaking Europe. **Eurovision,** a new form of television programming, broadcasts special programs simultaneously via satellite in multiple countries—each with its own sound track in the appropriate language.

The government-controlled **R.T.F. (Radio-Télévision France)** is financed by special taxes paid by owners of radios and television sets. Consequently, **R.T.F.** enjoys financial autonomy and is relatively free of commercials. Advertising never interrupts programs but occurs between them. French television can thus offer a greater variety of programs and appeal to a wider range of interests than can American commercial stations. On the other hand, the top officials of **R.T.F.** are appointed by the **Conseil des Ministres,** which is similar to the American president's Cabinet, and these close ties with the government have led to charges of biased programming that favors the official point of view.

Une journaliste pose des questions à des manifestants

SAMEDI 2 JANVIER

TELEVISION FRANÇAISE I

12h10 : Magazine de l'aventure. — 13h : 12h40 : Cultivons notre jardin. — 13h : Journal. — 13h30 : Le monde de l'accordéon. — 13h50 : Fugues à Fugain. — 18h05 : Trente millions d'amis. 18h45 : Magazine auto, moto. — 19h20 : Actualités régionales. — 19h45 : Bonsoir Fernand. — 20h : Journal. — 20h30 : Droit de réponse. — 22h : Dallas, série. — 22h50 : Glenn Gould joue Bach. — 23h40 : Un Noël, une vie : Leopold Sédar Senghor. — 23h55 : Journal.

ANTENNE II

10h30 : A.2. Antiope. — 11h40 : Journal des sourds et des malentendants. — 12h : La vérité est au fond de la marmite. — 12h30 : Prochainement — 13h : l'A.2. — 12h45 : Journal. — 14h : Des animaux et des hommes. — 18h : Salut les dessins animés. — 18h : trophées sports d'antenne 2. — Journal. — 20h35 : « Le voyageur imprudent », d'après le roman de Barjavel, avec Thierry Lhermitte, Caudry, Jean-Marc Thibault, Lily Baron, Jean Bouise. — 22h05 : Requiem de Berlioz. — 23h30 : Journal.

FRANCE REGIONS

15h : F.R.3. Jeunesse. — 19h10 : 19h20 : Actualités régionales. 19h40 : La télévision régionale. 19h55 : Dessin animé. — 20h : petits papiers de Noël. — 20h35 : chartreuse de Parme » (2e époque). 21h35 : Gershwin en fête. — Soir 3. — 23h25 : Mes meilleurs...

Et vous?

A. Vos programmes préférés. Listed below are some typical kinds of programs shown on French television. Use the scale to tell how well you like each kind.

je déteste	je n'aime pas beaucoup	j'aime	j'aime beaucoup	j'adore

1. les reportages sportifs (*sports reports*)
2. les émissions scientifiques ou culturelles
3. les feuilletons (m) (*soap operas*)
4. le bulletin météorologique (*weather report*)
5. les spectacles (m) de variétés (*variety shows*)
6. les matchs télévisés et les reportages sportifs (*games, sports, athletic events*)
7. les documentaires (m)
8. les films et les téléfilms
9. les dessins animés (*cartoons*)
10. les causeries (f) et les débats télévisés (*talk shows*)
11. les jeux télévisés (*game shows*)
12. la publicité (*advertising*)
13. les actualités (f) / le journal télévisé (*news*)
14. les comédies (f)
15. les pièces (f) de théâtre (*plays*)
16. les séries (f)

20.35 Dallas : « L'enquête »
Nouvel épisode de la série américaine, réalisée par Irving J. Moore.

18.45 L'écho des bananes
Une émission rock, produite et présentée par Vincent Lamy. Spécial Nina Hagen à Berlin ; Didier Makaga ; Vidéo : Rainbow

16.00 Dessin animé, Capitaine Flam
« LE SECRET DE WRACHAS »

20.35 A la recherche du temps présent
Une émission de Pierre Sabbagh et Robert Clarke.
CE SOIR : L'homme et les insectes.
INVITÉ : Le professeur Jacques Carayon, directeur du laboratoire d'entomologie au Muséum national d'histoire naturelle.

23.10 Sports dimanche
Une émission du service des Sports, présentée par François Janin.
Au programme :
VOILE : La Baule-Dakar, avec sur le plateau Philippe Pallu de la Barrière, le skipper de « Charente-Maritime » qui recevra le trophée TF1, et des sujets sur le rugby, l'automobile, l'équitation, le football et la natation synchronisée.

B. Opinions. Make a list of popular American television shows. Then use the following scale from the magazine *l'Express* and rate the quality of these programs.

À mon avis (*in my opinion*) . . .

*** C'est une émission à ne pas manquer.
 (*It's a program that shouldn't be missed.*)
** C'est une émission à regarder si vous êtes chez vous.
 (*It's a program to watch if you're at home.*)
* C'est un navet.
 (*It's a loser [turnip].*)

Exemple À mon avis, «Nova» est une émission à ne pas manquer.

Have class make à list of programs. Small groups can rate the programs and then compare the results in a whole-class activity.

C. Les vedettes de la télévision. What television stars and celebrities come to mind in each of the following categories? Use one or more adjectives to describe each star.

Exemple   Lily Tomlin est une comédienne amusante.

1. un héros ou une héroïne de dessins animés
2. un acteur ou une actrice
3. un présentateur ou une présentatrice du journal télévisé *(anchorperson)*
4. un animateur ou une animatrice de causeries *(host)*
5. un chanteur ou une chanteuse *(singer)*
6. un comédien ou une comédienne

 ## Les questions par inversion

Présentation

In Chapter 1, you learned to ask questions by using intonation, **est-ce que,** and **n'est-ce pas.** A fourth way of asking questions is to invert (reverse) the subject pronoun and verb and link them with a hyphen. Questions by inversion are commonly used in written and formal language, but less often in conversation. Inversion is not normally used with **je.** Inversion may occur:

A. when the subject of a sentence is a pronoun. In the third-person singular, **-t-** is added when the verb does not already end in a **t** or **d.**

Vous regardez souvent la télévision.	**Regardez-vous** souvent la télévision?
Ils ont la télévision.	**Ont-ils** la télévision?
C'est une actrice américaine.	**Est-ce** une actrice américaine?
Ils préfèrent les dessins animés.	**Préfèrent-ils** les dessins animés?
On montre souvent des films étrangers.	**Montre-t-on** souvent des films étrangers?
Il y a un bon film à la télé.	**Y a-t-il** un bon film à la télé?

You may wish to note that the parts of the negative do not change position in inversion, e.g., **Ne montre-t-on pas des films étrangers?**

B. when the subject of the sentence is a noun. The noun subject is not inverted, but a subject pronoun of the same number and gender is added for inversion.

Diane Dufresne est-elle française?
Charles Aznavour et Julien Clerc sont-ils de bons chanteurs?
Votre télévision marche-t-elle bien?

C. after question words such as the following:

qui *(who, whom)*	**Avec qui** allez-vous au cinéma demain soir?
que *(what)*	**Que** faites-vous lundi soir?
où *(where)*	**Où** vont-ils?
quand *(when)*	**Quand** regardez-vous la télévision?
comment *(how)*	**Comment** trouvez-vous le film?
pourquoi *(why)*	**Pourquoi** détestent-elles les jeux télévisés?
combien de *(how many)*	**Combien** de chaînes y a-t-il?
combien *(how much)*	**Combien** gagnez-vous?

All of these question words, except **que,** can also be used with **est-ce que. (Que** becomes **qu'est-ce que.)**

Préparation

A. Pardon, Madame? The host of a television talk show is having a hard time interviewing her guest because of technical difficulties. Rephrase her questions by using inversion.

Modèle   Où est-ce que vous travaillez maintenant? → **Où travaillez-vous maintenant?**

Substitution: (1) Aimez-vous les feuilletons? tu / elles / nous / il / vous / ils / elle. (2) Vos amis regardent-ils souvent la télé? Vos parents / Sa sœur / Ton professeur / Leurs amis.
Transformation: Have students put the following sentences in the interrogative. Il y a une banque prés d'ici. → Y a-t-il une banque prés d'ici? (1) C'est une grande vendette. (2) Tu vas à Paris. (3) Elles sont ici. (4) Vous écoutez souvent la radio. (5) Elle aime les westerns. (6) Il y a un documentaire intéressant.

1. Est-ce que vous travaillez dans un bureau?
2. Est-ce que vous êtes content?
3. Est-ce que votre travail est difficile?
4. Est-ce que c'est loin de chez vous?
5. Combien de temps est-ce qu'il faut pour aller à votre travail?
6. Est-ce que les autres employés sont sympathiques?
7. Est-ce que le bureau ferme à midi?
8. Combien est-ce que vous gagnez par mois?

B. Au téléphone. Monsieur Lebrun is answering a telephone survey about his family's television-viewing habits. Using Monsieur Lebrun's answers, give the interviewer's questions.

Modèle   Oui, nous possédons une télévision.
              Possédez-vous une télévision?

1. Oui, notre télévision marche bien.
2. Oui, nous avons des enfants.
3. Non, les enfants n'ont pas de télé dans leur chambre.
4. Oui, en général, nous regardons la télé tous les jours.
5. Non, nous ne regardons pas la télé pendant le dîner.
6. Non, ma femme ne regarde pas la télé pendant la journée.
7. Non, elle n'aime pas les feuilletons télévisés.

C. Préférences. Catherine is asking a friend about her television and movie preferences. Using the cues provided, give her questions.

Modèle   quelle chaîne elle préfère regarder → **Quelle chaîne préfères-tu regarder?**

1. quelles émissions elle préfère
2. quand elle regarde la télé
3. combien de temps elle passe à regarder la télé chaque soir
4. comment elle trouve les émissions sur FR3
5. pourquoi elle n'aime pas les films américains
6. combien de cinémas il y a dans sa ville
7. avec qui elle va généralement au cinéma

Communication

A. Et les Français? You are going to interview some visitors from France about the television-viewing habits of French people. Use the items below to prepare a list of questions using inversion.

> **Exemple**   si les Français regardent beaucoup la télévision → **Les Français regardent-ils beaucoup la télévision?**

1. si tout le monde a la télévision
2. s'il y a souvent des documentaires intéressants
3. s'il y a des publicités pendant les films
4. si les gens regardent la télévision pendant les repas
5. si on montre souvent des films ou des feuilletons américains
6. si les Français aiment les westerns
7. si les Français aiment les reportages sportifs et les matches télévisés
8. si les enfants français regardent des dessins animés le samedi matin

B. Sondage. Using various question words with inversion, make up questions that you would include on a survey of television-viewing habits and preferences. Then use these questions to interview another student or group of students.

> **Exemples**   Combien de temps passez-vous à regarder la télévision chaque semaine?
> Quelles émissions aimez-vous regarder pendant le week-end?

C. Interview. Using inversion, make up questions that you would like to ask another student in your class.

> **Exemples**   Aimes-tu aller au cinéma?
> D'habitude, quand vas-tu à la bibliothèque?
> Que fais-tu le samedi?

You might want to pick a specific topic (e.g., daily activities with **faire,** foods) that students can base their questions on.

⚜ L'heure

Présentation

To ask what time it is in French the following questions are used: **Quelle heure est-il?** *(What time is it?)* or, more informally, **Vous avez l'heure, s'il vous plaît?** *(Do you have the time, please?)* To answer these questions the following patterns are used:

A. On the hour:

Il est une heure.   Il est quatre heures.   Il est sept heures.   Il est midi. *(noon)*
Il est minuit. *(midnight)*

B. On the quarter or half hour:

Il est trois heures
et demie.

Il est midi et demi.

Il est deux heures
et quart.

Il est huit heures
moins le quart.

> Point out that there is no **e** when
> **demi** is used with **minuit** and
> **midi** and that one says **et quart**
> but **moins le quart**.

C. Minutes after or before the hour:

Il est une heure dix.

Il est neuf heures cinq.

Il est midi vingt.

Il est six heures vingt-
deux.

Il est deux heures
moins cinq.

Il est quatre heures
moins dix.

Il est neuf heures
moins vingt.

Il est minuit moins
vingt-six.

> Because of digital watches, one
> increasingly hears **huit heures**
> **quarante-cinq** instead of **neuf**
> **heures moins le quart**.

D. To ask or indicate at what time an event takes place, the following patterns are used:

À quelle heure le téléfilm commence-t-il?
Il commence **à dix heures.**

Notice that **heure**(s) is never omitted in French, whereas in English
we often omit the word *o'clock.*

E. The French system does not use A.M. and P.M. In conversation, **du matin,**
(in the morning), **de l'après-midi,** and **du soir** are used instead.

Il est onze heures **du matin.**
Je vais partir à quatre heures **de l'après-midi.**
Nous dînons à sept heures et demie **du soir.**

F. In official time schedules (for example, schedules for planes, trains, buses, radio, or television programs), the twenty-four-hour system is used. Time is stated precisely in terms of twenty-four hours, beginning at midnight.

Official time	Conventional time
zero heure trente (0 h 30)	minuit et demi
trois heures cinq (3 h 05)	trois heures et demie
douze heures (12 h)	midi
quinze heures quinze (15 h 15)	trois heures et quart
vingt-trois heures cinquante-cinq (23 h 55)	minuit moins cinq

G. Additional expressions used in discussing time are:

arriver à l'heure   *to arrive on time*   Il est tôt.   *It's early.*
être en retard   *to be late*   Il est tard.   *It's late.*
être en avance   *to be early*

(1) Beginning with one o'clock, have students give the time at hour intervals until they reach noon. (2) Beginning with two o'clock, have students give the time at fifteen-minute intervals until they reach five o'clock. (3) Beginning with six o'clock, have students give the time at five-minute intervals until they reach seven o'clock.

Préparation

A. Quelle heure est-il? The announcers on radio give the time at various intervals. Using the watches below, tell what they say.

1.  2.  3.  4.

5.  6.  7.

8.  9.  10.

B. À l'aéroport. At Charles de Gaulle Airport in Paris, flights are being announced using the twenty-four-hour system. Use the more common twelve-hour system to tell when each flight leaves.

Modèle   22 h 45   →   onze heures moins le quart

1. 8 h 30   3. 16 h 20   5. 3 h 15   7. 12 h 05   9. 5 h 25
2. 20 h 35   4. 13 h 50   6. 17 h 35   8. 23 h 55   10. 0 h 15

À l'aéroport Charles de Gaulle

C. À quelle heure? Jane is asking Jean-Pierre at what time the French usually do various things. Using the cues, give Jean-Pierre's answers.

Modèle   À quelle heure les dessins animés commencent-ils? (4 h 30)
→ **Les dessins animés commencent à quatre heures et demie de l'après-midi.**

1. À quelle heure est-ce qu'on va au théâtre le soir? (8 h 30)
2. À quelle heure les enfants vont-ils en classe le matin? (8 h 30)
3. À quelle heure est-ce qu'ils quittent l'école? (4 h)
4. À quelle heure est-ce qu'on dîne dans les restaurants? (entre 7 h et 10 h)
5. À quelle heure les ouvriers commencent-ils à travailler dans les usines? (8 h)
6. À qeulle heure est-ce qu'ils quittent l'usine? (6 h)
7. Combien de temps les Français ont-ils pour manger à midi? (entre 1 heure et 2 heures)

Communication

A. Questions/Interview. Answer the following questions or use them to interview another student.

1. À quelle heure quittes-tu la maison le matin?
2. À quelle heure as-tu ton cours de français? Est-ce que tu arrives toujours à l'heure?
3. Est-ce que tu es souvent en retard? En avance?
4. À quelle heure quittes-tu le campus?
5. À quelle heure dînes-tu? Est-ce que tu préfères dîner tôt ou tard?
6. Écoutes-tu les actualités régionales? À quelle heure?
7. À quelle heure est ton programme de télévision favori?

Suggestion: Ask questions and keep track of answers. Then ask students if they remember other students' answers—**À quelle heure est-ce que Lynne quitte la maison?**, etc.

TÉLÉVISION

TÉLÉVISION FRANÇAISE **1**

12.25 AU NOM DE LA LOI
« Qui est cet homme ? », avec Steve Mac Queen (Josh Randall).

13.00 TF1 ACTUALITÉS

13.35 CHAPEAU MELON ET BOTTES DE CUIR
MEUTRE AU PROGRAMME. Avec Patrick Mac Nee et Linda Thorson.

14.25 HISTOIRE DU CINÉMA FRANÇAIS PAR CEUX QUI L'ONT FAIT.
L'IMAGINATION, ET LE FRONT POPULAIRE AU POUVOIR (1935–1936).

15.15 L'ÉTÉ EN PLUS
15.15 VARIÉTÉS: Adamo chante: « Parlons-en du bonheur ».
15.20 NICOLAS LE JARDINIER : La liane Hoya : la cellule végétale.
15.35 LA CUISINE LÉGÈRE : Le Pithiviers.
15.55 VARIÉTÉS : Maxime Le Forestier chante « Le Silence » ; Kim Carnes, « Bette Davis eyes ».
16.00 LES LOISIRS DE L'ESPRIT : « Les mots croisés », avec Guy Hachette.
16.15 L'INVITÉ DE LA SEMAINE : Lucien Bodard parle de Saigon (1948–1953).
16.30 VARIÉTÉS : Adamo chante « Je m'en vais ».

16.45 CROQUE VACANCES
Émission proposée et présentée par Claude Pierrard.

17.50 GÉNÉRATION UNE
« Et si l'on vivait » (évocation de Patrick Pons).

18.00 FLASH TF1

18.05 CAMÉRA AU POING
Émission de Christian Zuber:
LA VIE INTIME DES TARENTULES (N° 1).

18.20 TRÉSOR DES CINÉMATHÈQUES

19.20 ACTUALITÉS RÉGIONALES

19.45 SUSPENSE
L'AUTO-STOP.

19.50 TIRAGE LOTO

20.00 TF1 ACTUALITÉS

20.30 LE RENARD ET LE LOUBARD
Téléfilm réalisé par Jean-Pierre Gallo. Scénario et dialogues : Louis Rognoni.

ANTENNE **2**

12.30 LES GAIETÉS DE LA CORRECTIONNELLE
L'AMOUREUX OPINIÂTRE.

12.45 JOURNAL
SPÉCIAL ANDRZEL WADJA. — Le réalisateur polonais est l'invité de cette édition du journal, quelques jours avant la sortie sur les écrans français de son dernier film : « L'Homme de fer », palme d'or au récent festival de Cannes.

13.35 POIGNE DE FER ET SÉDUCTION
Série britannique.
ZEKE.

14.00 AUJOURD'HUI MADAME
HISTOIRE DE LA CHANSON FRANÇAISE (2). Pierre Saka, Jean-François Kahn, André Horner, entourés de Patachou, Jean Constantin, Laurent Voulzy, racontent un demi-siècle de chansons, de 1930 à nos jours. Évocation (en images) de Ray Ventura, Charles Trenet, Édith Piaf, Yves Montand, Jacques Brel, Honny Hallyday, Sylvie Vartan, Eddy Mitchell.

15.05 RACINES
Cinquième épisode.

16.00 SPORTS D'ÉTÉ
PELOTE BASQUE
Commentaires : Jo Choupin et J.-P. Aren. Réalisation : Henri Carrier.
HANDISPORTS
Commentaire : Dominique Le Glou et Christine Paris. Il s'agit d'un film-montage sur l'approche et la pratique sportive par les handicapés.

18.00 RÉCRÉ A2
L'U.R.S.S. (3). — PINOCCHIO : L'orgue de Barbarie volé.

18.30 C'EST LA VIE... SUR L'EAU
Tour de France à la voile.

18.50 DES CHIFFRES ET DES LETTRES

19.20 ACTUALITÉS RÉGIONALES

19.45 LA COMMODE

20.00 JOURNAL

20.35 GALA DE L'UNION DES ARTISTES
Réalisation : Claude Barrois.

22.00 ON N'A PAS TOUS LES JOURS VINGT ANS :
GUY BEDOS
Émission d'Anne Sinclair. Réalisation : Gilles Daude.

23.00 UN HOMME, UN CHÂTEAU : CHAMBORD
Émission de François Gall. Réalisation : Raoul Ruiz.

23.30 JOURNAL

FRANCE – RÉGIONS **3**

19.10 SOIR 3

19.20 ACTUALITÉS RÉGIONALES

19.40 POUR LA JEUNESSE
OUM LE DAUPHIN.
LE PASSE-CARTE, sorte de réussite télévisée, qui se joue avec 32 cartes : La dame de pique.

20.00 LES JEUX DE 20 H
À Mulhouse. Avec : Pierre Desproges, Christine Fabrega et Maurice Biraud.

20.30 QUENTIN DURWARD
Film américain de Richard Thorpe (1955), en version française.

22.10 SOIR 3

22.30 PRÉLUDE À LA NUIT

t.m.c. Monte-Carlo

18.30 DESSINS ANIMÉS
Tom et Jerry, Une Souris à Manhattan, Les Surprises de l'amour.

18.45 LE CLUB DES CINQ
Feuilleton.
LES CINQ ET LES SALTIMBANQUES (Première partie).

19.20 NOUVELLES DE LA CÔTE
Présentées par Pierre Cazenave.

19.20 TEISSI-BAR
Une émission de José Sacré, présentée par Jacques Bal.

19.45 MÉTÉO

19.50 SUPER JAIMIE
SOSIE BIONIQUE (Première partie).

20.50 L'ITINÉRAIRE MYSTÉRIEUX
Jeu de l'été de José Sacré, présenté par Carole Chabrier en liaison avec le podium Télé Monte-Carlo–« Nice-Matin » à Cannes-la-Bocca.

21.00 LES SIX FEMMES D'HENRI VIII
Série de la B.B.C. (Troisième épisode).
JANE SEYMOUR.
Réalisation de John Glenister.

22.30 DERNIÈRES NOUVELLES RÉGIONALES
HOROSCOPE.

Although students will not understand every word in the television schedule, it will give the opportunity to examine an authentic television schedule and enable them to answer the questions in **B**. If desired, new words can be used to give students practice in guessing from context.

B. Qu'est ce qu'il y a à la télé? The television schedule opposite is taken from *Nice Matin*, a French newspaper. Answer the questions based on the information in the schedule.

1. À quelle heure commencent les émissions sur TF1? Et sur FR3? Et sur Télé Monte Carlo?
2. À quelle heure et sur quelle chaîne passe le film américain «Quentin Durward»?
3. À quelle heure sont les actualités sur TF1?
4. Combien de films y a-t-il à la télé ce soir? Sur quelles chaînes et à quelle heure?
5. Quelle est la première émission de la journée sur Télé Monte Carlo?
6. À quelle heure y a-t-il un reportage sportif sur A2?
7. Est-ce qu'il y a un programme sur A2 pour les gens qui aiment la musique? À quelle heure? Et sur TF1?

Have students decide which programs they would like to watch during the evening. Then have them get together with another student or group of students and negotiate what they will watch.

Le passé composé avec l'auxiliaire *avoir*

Présentation

To indicate that an event occurred in the past, the **passé composé** is used. It can express the same meaning as three different English constructions: *I traveled, I have traveled, I did travel.*

A. The **passé composé** of most verbs is formed by using the present tense of **avoir** plus a past participle. The past participle of **-er** verbs is formed by dropping the **er** ending of the infinitive and replacing it with **é: parler → parlé, étudier → étudié.** The form of **avoir** must correspond to the subject.

Le passé composé avec *avoir*	
j'**ai regardé**	nous **avons regardé**
tu **as regardé**	vous **avez regardé**
il/elle/on **a regardé**	ils/elles **ont regardé**

Elle a travaillé toute la journée.   *She's worked all day long.*
Nous avons regardé un match télévisé.   *We watched a televised game.*
Ils n'ont pas voyagé à l'étranger.   *They didn't travel abroad.*

B. Avoir, être, and **faire** have irregular past participles: **avoir — eu, être — été, faire — fait.**

Nous avons eu des difficultés.
Vous avez été trop imprudent.
Est-ce que **tu as fait** tes devoirs?

C. In the negative, **ne** precedes and **pas** (or **jamais**) follows the form of **avoir.** In the interrogative by inversion, only the form of **avoir** and the pronoun are inverted.

Elle **n'**as **pas** trouvé de travail.
Ils **n'**ont **jamais** visité la Belgique.
Avez-vous fait une promenade?
A-t-il aimé les dessins animés?

D. Useful expressions for referring to past events are:

hier	*yesterday*
la semaine passée, la semaine dernière	*last week*
samedi passé, samedi dernier	*last Saturday*
hier soir	*yesterday evening, last night*
hier matin	*yesterday morning*
l'année passée, l'année dernière	*last year*
déjà	*already*
pas encore	*not yet*

Répétition: (1) J'ai dîné au restaurant, tu as dîné au restaurant, etc. (2) Je n'ai pas regardé la télé, tu n'as pas regardé la télé, etc. **Substitution:** (1) Il a déjà visité l'Italie. vous / je / Claudine / nous / Nicole et Henri. (2) Nous n'avons pas encore voyagé au Mexique. tu / vous / ses amis / Anne / je. (3) Chantal a-t-elle aimé le téléfilm? vos amis / les autres / ton frère / Jean-Luc. **Substitution:** Hier, j'ai fait une promenade. lundi soir / samedi matin / hier soir / la semaine dernière.

Préparation

A. Activités et occupations. Sylviane is talking about some of the things she has done on her day off. Using the cues, describe her activities.

Modèle   10 h / téléphoner à Suzanne → **À dix heures, j'ai téléphoné à Suzanne.**

1. 9 h / commencer à travailler
2. 11 h 30 / envoyer une lettre à mes parents
3. 12 h 15 / quitter la maison pour aller en ville
4. 12 h 30 / manger au restaurant avec des amis
5. 3 h / faire des courses
6. 4 h / acheter des timbres
7. 4 h 45 / avoir la visite de Raymonde
8. 5 h 15 / acheter les provisions pour le dîner
9. 7 h 45 / regarder les actualités

Options: (1) Written. (2) Oral. (3) Repeat with **nous, elle,** etc. (4) Listening: Read account of Sylviane's day and ask questions.

Have students note that **Apostrophes** is a high-quality television talk show that features interviews with prominent people on topics of social, artistic, and political interest. **Mammouth** is a chain of supermarkets. **Carrefour** is another important chain.

B. Différences culturelles. Some French students are talking about things that are part of their daily lives but that people from other countries might find different. Tell what they say.

Modèle   regarder «Apostrophes» → **Ils n'ont jamais regardé «Apostrophes».**

1. écouter Johnny Halliday
2. faire leur marché à Mammouth
3. faire ses devoirs dans un café
4. habiter dans un H.L.M.
5. acheter *Télé 7 Jours*
6. passer leurs vacances sur la Côte d'Azur
7. visiter le musée du Louvre
8. faire du camping dans les Alpes

C. Encore et toujours des excuses! Some students are talking about why they aren't prepared for class today. Tell what they say.

Modèle   Micheline / étudier   →   **Micheline n'a pas étudié.**

1. nous / acheter les livres pour le cours
2. Michelle et Juliette / écouter en classe
3. tu / être sérieux
4. je / trouver mon cahier
5. Catherine / travailler pendant le week-end
6. vous / avoir le temps d'étudier
7. Pierre / faire ses devoirs

Communication

A. Vous et la télé. Tell what television programs you watched last week. Indicate the day, the hour, the program, and your opinion of the program.

Exemple   Dimanche à sept heures, j'ai regardé «Soixante Minutes».
À mon avis, c'est une émission à ne pas manquer.

B. La semaine dernière. Create sentences expressing what you did last week by combining one element from each column.

Exemple   Hier, j'ai invité des amis à dîner.

		envoyer une lettre à mes parents
		dîner chez des amis
		manger au restaurant
		avoir un examen difficile
		étudier le français
		inviter des amis à dîner
hier		regarder un film à la télé
lundi		écouter de la musique
mardi	j'ai	préparer le dîner
mercredi	mes amis ont	avoir la visite d'un(e) ami(e)
jeudi	mes amis et moi, nous avons	être en retard pour mon cours de
vendredi	?	français
samedi		nager
dimanche		faire une promenade
la semaine dernière		faire le ménage
		passer l'après-midi à la biblio-
		thèque
		faire des courses
		acheter des provisions
		?

C. Et hier? Using the suggestions provided in *Communication B*, ask questions to find out what other people in your class did yesterday.

Exemples   Est-ce que tu as fait des courses?
Qu'est-ce que tu as acheté?

⚜ Le passé composé avec l'auxiliaire *être*

Présentation

Some French verbs use **être** instead of **avoir** as their auxiliary verb. They are usually verbs of motion or transition. Only four of these verbs have been presented thus far: **aller, rester, rentrer,** and **arriver.**

When **être** is used as the auxiliary, the past participle agrees with the subject in gender and number, just as adjectives agree with nouns.

Le passé composé avec être	
je suis allé(e)	nous sommes allé(e)(s)
tu es allé(e)	vous êtes allé(e)(s)
il/on est allé	ils sont allés
elle est allée	elles sont allées

Other verbs conjugated with **être** are presented in chapter 10, p. 199.

Je suis allé au cinéma hier soir.
Marie est allée à Paris en juin.
Est-ce que vous êtes allé en Europe?
Nous ne sommes pas restés à la maison.
Sont-elles déjà **allées** à Genève?
À quelle heure **êtes-vous arrivés?**
Ils ne sont pas encore **rentrés.**

Répétition: (1) Je suis allé en vacances, tu es allé en vacances, etc. (2) Je ne suis pas resté à l'hôtel, tu n'es pas resté à l'hôtel, etc. **Substitution:** (1) Ils sont restés à la maison. je / tu / mon frère / Monique et Jean / nous. (2) Nous ne sommes pas allés à la plage. tu / mes amis / on / ma sœur / je. (3) Chantal est-elle allée chez le médecin? ton ami / sa sœur / ses amis.

Préparation

A. Pendant le week-end. Some students are telling where they went last weekend. Use the cues to tell what they say.

Repeat in negative.

Exemple   Robert / café → **Robert est allé au café.**

1. tu / restaurant
2. Micheline / théâtre
3. Raoul et Marie / concert
4. nous / cinéma
5. vous / match de football
6. Henri / piscine
7. Roger et Jean-Marc / supermarché
8. Viviane et Louise / plage

B. Où aller? Monsieur and Madame Lafleur want to take a different vacation this year, so they're trying to find out where their friends have already been. Using the cues provided, give their questions.

Modèle   les Monet / Grèce → **Est-ce que les Monet sont déjà allés en Grèce?**

1. Marie-Claire / Guadeloupe
2. tes amis / Mexique
3. tu / Brésil
4. Monsieur Lemaître / États-Unis
5. tes voisins / Canada
6. les parents de Monique / Tunisie
7. vous / Norvège

C. **Occupations d'une étudiante française.** Here are some activities of Juliette Cordier, a French political science student. Tell what she did yesterday, making sure to use the correct form of **avoir** or **être.**

Modèles   étudier à la maison   →   **Elle a étudié à la maison.**
rester à la maison jusqu'à 9 h   →   **Elle est restée à la maison jusqu'à neuf heures.**

1. arriver à l'université à 10 h
2. manger au restaurant universitaire
3. aller au café avec des amis
4. avoir son cours d'histoire
5. écouter les explications du professeur
6. rester à la bibliothèque jusqu'à 6 h
7. quitter l'université à 6 h 30
8. acheter ses provisions
9. rentrer à la maison
10. faire la cuisine
11. manger un bon repas
12. regarder la télé

Communication

Options: Have students give sentences or questions that elicit information. See **Synthèse**, exercise B, for another variation.

A. **Où êtes-vous allé(e)(s)?** Create sentences describing where you and your friends have gone. Begin your sentences with expressions like **hier, pendant le week-end, la semaine dernière, l'été passé, l'année dernière.**

Exemples   Hier je suis allé(e) à la campagne; mon ami Jean est allé à la plage.
L'été dernier, je suis allé(e) en Allemagne et au Danemark.
Pendant les vacances, mes amis sont allés au Japon.
Pendant le week-end, mes amis et moi, nous sommes allés chez les Monets.

Suggestions: à la montagne / au Canada / à New York / en Californie / en Europe / au concert / au restaurant / chez mes parents / à un match de football / chez le médecin / au théâtre / à la bibliothèque / ?

B. **Trouvez un(e) étudiant(e)** . . . Ask questions to find out who in your class has gone to the following places. Either ask questions of individual students, **Jean, est-ce que tu es allé à la plage?** or address the whole class, **Qui est allé au cinéma?**

Trouvez un(e) étudiant(e):

1. qui est allé(e) à la montagne en hiver
2. qui est allé(e) au bord de la mer l'été passé
3. qui est allé(e) en Floride pendant les vacances de printemps
4. qui est allé(e) au théâtre la semaine dernière
5. qui est allé(e) chez ses parents samedi dernier
6. qui est allé(e) dans un pays où on parle français
7. qui est allé(e) en Amérique du Sud
8. qui est allé(e) en Russie

Options: Elicit information through questions or directed dialogue—**Demandez à Marc s'il est allé à la montagne en hiver.**

C. Déjà ou pas encore? Tell whether you have already done or not yet done the following things.

> Exemples: aller à la bibliothèque → **Je suis déjà allé(e) à la bibliothèque aujourd'hui.**
>
> avoir le temps d'étudier aujourd'hui → **Je n'ai pas encore eu le temps d'étudier aujourd'hui.**

1. faire vos devoirs pour demain
2. étudier pour l'examen
3. écouter les cassettes qui vont avec la leçon six
4. faire les exercices sur le passé composé
5. aller à la bibliothèque aujourd'hui
6. acheter un dictionnaire anglais-français
7. parler avec des Français
8. manger dans un restaurant français
9. voyager dans un pays où on parle français

SYNTHÈSE

Huit heures dans la vie d'un agent de police

Un agent de police fait son *rapport* à *la fin* de sa journée de travail.	report / end
18 h 05 Pendant notre inspection du quartier, nous avons trouvé un *jeune* homme en pyjama, *sans* adresse et sans papiers d'identité. Un *amnésique* probablement. Nous avons *emmené* le jeune homme à l'hôpital psychiatrique.	young / without amnesia victim took
20 h 15 Accident de *moto*, rue de Sèvres. Nous avons transporté la victime, une jeune *fille* de dix-huit ans, à l'hôpital.	motorcycle girl
21 h 00 Dans un restaurant de la rue d'Alger, un client *ivre* a refusé de payer l'*addition*. Le *patron* a téléphoné à la police. *Quand* nous avons interrogé le client, il a commencé à *raconter* ses exploits en Indochine. Nous avons emmené l'homme au *poste de police*.	drunk bill / owner when tell police station
22 h 10 Des *cambrioleurs* ont *volé l'argent* d'une *dame* de soixante-quinze ans. Nous avons montré des photos des suspects à la victime. Elle a identifié les cambrioleurs.	burglars / stole / money / lady
23 h 45 Le patron d'un bar a téléphoné pour *signaler* une *bagarre*. Nous avons séparé les adversaires et nous avons emmenés les victimes à l'hôpital.	to report / brawl
0 h 45 Un monsieur de la rue des Arcades a téléphoné pour signaler une *surprise-partie* trop *bruyante*. Nous avons *demandé* aux participants d'être moins bruyants.	party / noisy ask
1 h 30 Nous avons trouvé un homme *à genoux* au milieu de la rue. Nous avons interrogé l'homme. Il a expliqué: «Je parle avec la *Vierge Marie*». Nous avons persuadé l'homme de continuer la conversation sur le *trottoir*.	on his knees Virgin Mary sidewalk

Extrait et adapté d'un article de *Paris Match*.

Compréhension   Selon les renseignements donnés, est-ce que les phrases suivantes sont vraies ou fausses? Corrigez le sens de la phrase s'il est faux.

1. A 18 h 05 les agents de police ont trouvé un homme ivre dans la rue.
2. A 21 h 15 un jeune homme a eu un accident de moto rue des Arcades.
3. Les agents ont transporté la victime chez ses parents.
4. Le patron du restaurant de la rue d'Alger a téléphoné à la police parce qu'un client a volé son argent.
5. La dame de soixante-quinze ans a identifié les cambrioleurs qui ont volé son argent.
6. A 23 h 45 le patron d'un bar a téléphoné pour signaler une surprise-partie trop bruyante.
7. Les agents de police ont participé à la bagarre.
8. A 0 h 45 un monsieur de la rue d'Alger a téléphoné pour inviter les agents de police à une surprise-partie.
9. Les agents ont persuadé les participants de continuer leur surprise-partie.
10. À 1 h 30 les agents ont trouvé un homme à genoux au milieu de la rue.

Follow-up: Have students describe eight hours in the life of a campus police officer, professor, etc.

NOTES CULTURELLES

Les agents de police

A typical eight-hour shift of the blue-uniformed French **agents de police** who patrol city streets and direct traffic is similar to that of their American counterparts. But while most American police patrol their areas in cars, French police generally cover their beat on foot. They are always armed with a revolver and a white nightstick. In France, as in most Western countries, the crime rate has risen dramatically in recent years, making the police officer's job more difficult today than in the past. Given the French love for independence and individualism, the **flics**, as police are called, have traditionally been an easy target for jokes and a certain amount of resentment.

Gendarmes, who wear tan uniforms, are responsible for maintaining order in rural communities. **Motards**, dressed in blue motorcycle uniforms and helmets, patrol France's highways.

Un gendarme et son cyclomoteur

Un agent de police à Paris

Communication

Suggested for written homework.

A. **Huit heures dans la vie d'un(e) étudiant(e).** Tell what you did yesterday, using the following questions as a guide: À quelle heure est-ce que vous êtes allé(e) à l'université? À quelles classes est-ce que vous êtes allé(e) et à quelle heure? Avez-vous étudié à la bibliothèque? Où avez-vous mangé et avec qui? À quelle heure avez-vous quitté le campus? Avez-vous regardé la télévision? Quand avez-vous fait vos devoirs? À quelle heure avez-vous commencé à étudier?, etc.

B. **Qu'est-ce que vous avez fait?** Create sentences describing what you did during your vacation last year, last weekend, or last night by choosing from the suggestions below or by adding your own. You may also want to tell what your parents or friends did.

Options: (1) Written. (2) Oral. Elicit information through questions or directed dialogue—**Demandez à Jean s'il a fait un voyage l'année dernière.**

    Exemples   Pendant les vacances l'année dernière, je suis allé(e) au bord de la mer.
                  Pendant le week-end, mes amis ont fait une promenade en moto.
                  Hier soir, nous sommes allé(e)s au concert.

1. Pendant les vacances d'été . . .
   faire un voyage / visiter un pays étranger / aller au bord de la mer / passer un mois à la campagne / passer l'été avec ma famille / travailler dans un restaurant / ?
2. Pendant le week-end . . .
   rester à la maison / manger au restaurant / acheter des vêtements / aller à une surprise-partie / regarder la télévision / écouter de la musique / téléphoner à des amis / étudier / aller au cinéma / ?
3. Hier soir . . .
   aller à un concert / inviter des amis à dîner / emmener mon ami(e) au cinéma / faire la cuisine / regarder un film à la télévision / étudier / faire une promenade / raconter des histoires amusantes / ?

C. **Questions/Interview.** Use the following questions to interview another student. If the answer to the numbered question is affirmative, proceed with the lettered questions. If the answer is negative, move on to the next numbered question. Each main question has a series of related questions to help you gain skill in sustaining a conversation in French.

This is an important skill to emphasize and encourage in other conversational situations.

1. Est-ce que tu as regardé la télévision hier soir?
   a. Est-ce que tu as regardé les actualités?
   b. Est-ce que tu as regardé un film policier?
   c. Est-ce que tu as écouté le bulletin météorologique?
   d. ?
2. Est-ce que tu as écouté des disques hier soir?
   a. Est-ce que tu as écouté des disques de musique classique?
   b. Où est-ce que tu as écouté des disques et avec qui?
   c. Quel est ton chanteur préféré?
   d. ?

3. Est-ce que tu as mangé à la maison hier soir?
   a. Est-ce que tu as fait la cuisine?
   b. Qu'est-ce que tu as préparé?
   c. Est-ce que tu as invité des amis?
   d. À quelle heure est-ce que tu as mangé?
   e. ?
4. Est-ce que tu as mangé au restaurant la semaine passée?
   a. À quel restaurant est-ce que tu es allé(e)?
   b. Est-ce que tu as aimé la cuisine?
   c. Qu'est-ce que tu as mangé?
   d. À quelle heure est-ce que tu es rentré(e) à la maison?
   e. ?
e. Est-ce que tu as fait un voyage pendant les vacances d'été ou de prin-temps?
   a. Où est-ce que tu es allé(e)?
   b. Avec qui est-ce que tu as voyagé?
   c. Est-ce que tu es resté(e) à l'hôtel ou chez des amis?
   d. ?
6. Est-ce que tu es déjà allé(e) en Europe?
   a. Dans quels pays est-ce que tu es allé(e)?
   b. Est-ce que tu as visité des villes intéressantes?
   c. ?

PRONONCIATION

Certain French vowels—[e], [ɛ]; [ø], [œ]; and [o], [ɔ]—can be pronounced with the mouth more, or less, open. The closed vowels are [e], as in **mes**; [ø], as in **deux**; and [o], as in **beau**. The open vowels are [ɛ], as in **frère**; [œ], as in **heure**; and [ɔ], as in **bord**. Note that the closed vowels generally occur in an open syllable, that is, in a syllable ending in a vowel sound. Open vowels generally occur in a closed syllable, that is, in a syllable ending in a consonant sound.

1. Repeat and contrast the following words:

[e]	[ɛ]
ouvrier	ouvrière
dernier	dernière
premier	première
étranger	étrangère

2. Repeat the following words containing the sound [e]. Note the various spellings associated with the sound.

marié	travailler	mes
métro	regarder	et
année	allez	chez
été	écoutez	j'ai

3. Repeat the following words containing the sound [ɛ]. Note the various spellings associated with the sound.

j'espère	j'aime	rester	sept
frère	faire	sélection	quel
problème	satisfaite	accepter	n'est-ce pas
rêve	prochaine	personne	elle

4. Repeat the following sentences, paying close attention to the sounds you have been practicing.

1. J'aime regarder les ouvriers et les ouvrières.
2. J'espère qu'elle va rester chez son frère.
3. Vous pouvez aller au café pour regarder la télé.
4. Cette année il fait très beau au bord de la mer.
5. J'ai peur de faire des rêves.

VOCABULAIRE

noms

la télévision (voir p. 107)

d'autres noms

l'addition (f)   *bill*
° l'adresse (f)
l'agent de police (m,f)   *police officer*
l'alpiniste (m,f)   *mountain climber*
l'après-midi, (m)   *afternoon*
la bagarre   *brawl*
le cambrioleur   *burglar*
le carnet   *notebook*
le chanteur, la chanteuse   *singer*
le conte   *story, tale*
le client, la cliente   *customer*
° la conversation
la coupe   *cup*
l'équipe (f)   *team*
le héros, l'héroïne
l'histoire (f)   *story*
° l'hôpital (m)
° l'inspection (f)
le match   *game (sports)*
le matin   *morning*
   minuit   *midnight*
le monde   *world*
le mur   *wall*
l'œuvre (m)   *work*
° les papiers d'identité
° le participant
la partie   *part*
le patron, la patronne   *owner, boss*
° la photo
le poste de police   *police station*

le rapport   *report*
le rêve   *dream*
le roman   *novel*
la semaine   *week*
le soir   *evening*
la surprise-partie   *party*
° le suspect
° la victime

verbes

°continuer
demander   *to ask*
emmener   *to take (away)*
expliquer   *to explain*
°identifier
interroger   *to question*
manquer   *to miss*
montrer   *to show*
°payer
°persuader
raconter   *to tell*
°refuser
°téléphoner
°transporter
voler   *to steal*

adjectifs

animé(e)   *animated, lively*
°basé(e)
bruyant(e)   *noisy*
°culturel, culturelle
demi(e)   *half*

dernier, dernière *last*
deuxième *second*
jeune *young*
meilleur(e) *best*
°**passé(e)**
°**psychiatrique**
°**scientifique**
°**spécial(e)**
°**télévisé(e)**

adverbes

déjà *already*
hier *yesterday*
pas encore *not yet*

divers

à l'heure *on time*
à quelle heure *at what time*
combien *how much, how many*
comment *how*
en avance *early (before appointed time)*
en retard *late (after appointed time)*
excepté *except*
quand *when*
que *what*
Quelle heure est-il? *What time is it?*
qui *who, whom*
sans *without*
tard *late*
tôt *early*

CHAPITRE SEPT

La pluie et le beau temps

7

You might want to point out the difference between **jour,** which refers to a specific day **(Quel jour allez-vous partir?)** and **journée,** which refers to a length of time **(J'ai passé toute la journée à la bibliothèque).**

INTRODUCTION

Bulletin météorologique du vendredi 22 février

NUAGES DANS LE *NORD*, *SOLEIL* DANS LE RESTE DE LA FRANCE

clouds / North / sun

    —En France aujourd'hui—

    Aujourd'hui, une zone de *mauvais temps* va progresser de l'*Ouest* à l'*Est.* Dans le Nord et le Centre, le *ciel* va *devenir nuageux* ou très nuageux. Dans le *Midi* il va continuer *à faire beau.*

bad / weather / West
East / sky / become / cloudy
southern France / to be fair

    Les *vents, faibles* et variables le matin, vont devenir modérés dans le nord du pays.

winds / light, weak

    Dans le Nord, les températures assez *froides* le matin vont *monter* jusqu'à dix degrés pendant la *journée.* Dans le reste de la France, les températures vont rester stables.

cold / climb, go up
day

    —Demain—

    Demain, il va faire beau dans le *Sud-ouest* de la France. Dans le reste du pays, le temps va rester variable. Possibilité de *pluie* et de *neige* dans les Alpes.

Southwest
rain / snow

126

Possibilité de pluie . . .

. . . et de neige

Compréhension   Répondez aux questions suivantes selon les renseignements donnés dans le texte.

1. Est-ce que le mauvais temps va progresser de l'Est à l'Ouest ou de l'Ouest à l'Est?
2. Est-ce que le ciel va être nuageux ou est-ce qu'il va faire beau dans le Nord?
3. Est-ce que les vents vont devenir modérés ou violents pendant la journée?
4. Dans le Nord, est-ce que les températures vont rester stables ou est-ce qu'elles vont monter?
5. Demain, est-ce qu'il va faire beau ou mauvais dans le Sud-ouest de la France?
6. Est-ce qu'il y a des possibilités de pluie et de neige dans le Sud-ouest du pays ou dans les Alpes?

NOTES CULTURELLES

Le climat des pays francophones

The climate of France is generally mild and varied. The warm and sunny climate of southern France is particularly appealing to French people and tourists from all of Europe. The Côte d'Azur has especially pleasant weather all year round because the Alps protect it from the Mistral, a powerful wind that sweeps through the Rhone River Valley. In winter months its powerful gusts are sometimes strong enough to blow over cars and cause considerable property damage. Houses are often protected by a windbreak of cypress trees.

Although the French-speaking countries in Europe (Belgium, Luxembourg, and Switzerland) have climates similar to that of France, weather conditions in other French-speaking countries vary considerably. For example, the harsh French-Canadian winters contrast with the year-round tropical climates of Guadeloupe, Martinique, and Haiti in the Caribbean and Madagascar in the Indian Ocean. Francophone countries such as Algeria, Mali, and Chad in Africa tend to have climates that are hot and arid.

L'oasis de Kerzas, dans le Sahara

Et vous?

A. Les jours de pluie. Qu'est-ce que vous aimez faire les jours de pluie? Est-ce que vous aimez . . .

1. rester à la maison?
2. passer la journée au coin du feu *(fireside)*?
3. marcher sous la pluie?
4. lire* *(read)* un bon livre?
5. regarder des revues *(magazines)*?
6. jouer aux cartes *(play cards)*?
7. dormir *(sleep)* toute la journée?
8. écrire *(write)* des lettres?
9. ranger *(clean)* votre chambre?
10. téléphoner à vos amis?
11. jouer à des jeux *(games)* électroniques?
12. regarder des vidéocassettes?
13. aller au café ou au cinéma?
14. travailler sur votre micro-ordinateur?

Option: Use as small-group activity where students ask each other which activities they like (e.g., **Est-ce que tu préfères rester à la maison?,** etc.) Take a class survey to find out the preferred activities of students in the class.

B. Quand il fait beau. Et quand il fait beau, est-ce que vous aimez . . .

1. sortir *(go out)*?
2. aller à la pêche *(go fishing)*?
3. aller à la piscine?
4. prendre un bain de soleil *(take a sunbath)*?
5. faire du sport?
6. travailler dans le jardin?
7. faire une promenade?
8. prendre des photos?
9. promener le chien *(take the dog for a walk)*?
10. faire un pique-nique?

⚜ Le temps

Présentation

Many French weather expressions use the impersonal subject pronoun **il** (it) and the verb **faire.** Useful expressions are:

Quel temps fait-il?	*How is the weather?*
Il fait beau.	*It's nice. (The weather is nice.)*
Il fait chaud.	*It's warm.*
Il fait froid.	*It's cold.*
Il fait frais.	*It's cool.*
Il fait mauvais.	*The weather is bad.*
Il fait du vent.	*It's windy.*
Il fait du soleil.	*It's sunny.*
Il va pleuvoir.	*It's going to rain.*
Il pleut.	*It's raining.*
Il a plu.	*It rained.*
Il va neiger.	*It's going to snow.*
Il neige.	*It's snowing.*
Le ciel est couvert.	*It's cloudy.*
Il y a un orage.	*There is a storm.*
La température est de 15°C.	*The temperature is 15 degrees Centigrade.*

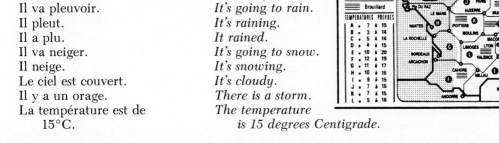

Le temps prévu dimanche

* The verbs **dormir, écrire, lire, prendre,** and **sortir** are used in this chapter in the infinitive only. Their conjugated forms will be presented in subsequent chapters.

Substitution: (1) Il fait beau maintenant. mauvais / froid / trop chaud / très frais / du soleil / du vent. (2) Il pleut aujourd'hui. il neige / il y a des orages / le ciel est couvert. (3) Est-ce qu'il a plu pendant le week-end? neigé / fait froid / fait du vent. **Transformation:** Have students put these sentences first in the past and then in the near future. (*Modèle:* Il neige aujourd'hui. Il a neigé hier. Il va neiger demain.) (1) Il fait beau aujourd'hui. (2) Il pleut aujourd'hui. (3) Il ne fait pas mauvais aujourd'hui. (4) Il fait du soleil aujourd'hui. (5) Il fait du vent aujourd'hui. (6) Quel temps fait-il aujourd'hui?

Préparation

A. Quel temps fait-il? A Paris newspaper reported the following temperatures and weather conditions in various cities around the world. Describe the weather in each city.

Local newspaper listings of temperatures may also be used and converted to Celsius. C = 5/9 (F − 32).

Modèle   Berlin 10°C PV → **À Berlin la température est de dix degrés centigrade. Il pleut et il fait du vent.**

Températures et conditions météorologiques			
N = neige *P = pluie* *V = vent* *S = soleil* *C = couvert* *O = orage*			
Paris	10°C VP	Melbourne	25°C OV
Madrid	14°C S	Oslo	7°C S
New York	2°C N	Berlin	10°C PV
Londres	8°C C	Rome	13°C SV

B. Quel temps de chien! Last week's weather was terrible. Using the cues provided, tell what the weather was like each day.

Modèle   dimanche / faire très frais → **Dimanche, il a fait très frais.**

1. lundi / pleuvoir
2. mardi / faire du vent
3. mercredi / avoir un orage
4. jeudi / faire mauvais
5. vendredi / neiger
6. samedi / faire froid

C. Interprète. Robert Degagne is preparing a bilingual edition of a weather report for a Canadian radio station. How would he put these sentences into French?

Modèle   It is very cold in Quebec City. → **Il fait très froid à Québec.**

1. It is also cold in Winnepeg.
2. The sky is cloudy in Montreal.
3. It's not very hot in Vancouver.
4. It's going to snow tomorrow in Calgary.
5. It was very nice yesterday in Toronto.
6. It's sunny today in Ottawa.
7. There was a storm yesterday near Quebec.
8. It's cool and windy in Sept-Îles.

Point out to students that one refers to Quebec City as **à Québec** and the province of Quebec as **au Québec.**

Communication

A. Ça dépend du temps. Referring to your own experience, complete the following sentences with an appropriate weather expression.

Suggested for written homework.

1. Je ne quitte pas la maison quand . . .
2. Je n'aime pas voyager quand . . .
3. En général, on ne va pas à la plage quand . . .
4. J'aime faire des promenades quand . . .
5. Je fais du sport quand . . .
6. Les étudiants n'aiment pas aller en classe quand . . .
7. Il y a souvent des accidents quand . . .
8. Je n'aime pas faire du camping quand . . .

Option: Have students complete **Synthèse A (Le Bulletin météorologique).**

B. Questions/Interview. Answer the following questions or use them to interview another student.

1. Quel temps fait-il aujourd'hui?
2. Quel temps va-t-il faire demain?
3. Quel temps a-t-il fait hier?
4. Quel temps fait-il en février dans ta ville? Et au mois d'août?
5. Quel temps fait-il dans ta région au printemps?
6. Est-ce qu'il pleut beaucoup dans ta région?
7. Quelle saison préfères-tu? Pourquoi?
8. Qu'est-ce que tu aimes faire quand il fait beau? Et quand il fait mauvais?

 ## Les adjectifs démonstratifs

Présentation

Demonstrative adjectives (in English, *this* and *that*, *these* and *those*) are used to point out objects or people. The forms used in French are determined by the number and gender of the noun modified.

Les adjectifs démonstratifs		Singular	Plural
Masculine	Before a consonant	**ce** vent	**ces** vents
	Before a vowel sound	**cet** orage	**ces** orages
Feminine		**cette** pluie	**ces** pluies

Ce soir, je vais chez Alain.	*This evening I'm going to Alain's house.*
Cet été, il va faire frais.	*This summer it's going to be cool.*
Est-ce que **cette** pluie va continuer?	*Is this rain going to continue?*
Ces revues ne sont pas intéressantes.	*These (those) magazines are not interesting.*

French speakers do not normally make the distinction between *this* and *that*, or *these* and *those*. When it is necessary to do so, the suffixes **-ci** and **-là** are added to the noun. The suffix **-ci** conveys a meaning similar to *this* and *these*; **-là** is similar to *that* and *those*.

Sur la photo, cet homme**-ci** est la victime et cet homme**-là** est le cambrioleur.	*In the photo, this man is the victim and that man is the burglar.*
Est-ce que tu préfères ces vêtements**-ci** ou ces vêtements**-là**?	*Do you prefer these clothes or those clothes?*

You may wish to point out that **-ci** generally indicates proximity ("here") and **-là** distance ("there").

Transformation: Donnez la forme appropriée de l'adjectif démonstratif. (la maison → cette maison). (1) le professeur (2) la rue (3) le matin (4) la pluie (5) l'année (6) l'hiver (7) les étudiants (8) les classes (9) les enfants (10) le café (11) le soir (12) l'église (13) les vacances (14) l'université.
Transformation: Mettez les phrases suivantes au singulier. (1) ces montagnes (2) ces maisons (3) ces livres (4) ces hôtels (5) ces usines (6) ces femmes (7) ces professeurs (8) ces photos.

Préparation

A. Curiosité. Jean-Pierre is asking some friends what they are going to be doing at various times. What does he ask?

Modèle　Claude / soir → **Qu'est-ce que Claude fait ce soir?**

1. tu / matin
2. vous / après-midi
3. nous / week-end
4. le prof de français / semaine
5. Richard et Brigitte / été
6. Danielle / samedi

B. Au café. Several friends are spending a rainy afternoon in a café watching people go by. Tell what they say.

Modèle　femme / élégante → **Cette femme est élégante.**

1. homme / beau
2. voiture / sensationnelle
3. pluie / désagréable
4. temps / impossible
5. enfants / pas polis
6. vin / excellent
7. glaces / délicieuses
8. sandwichs / pas bons

C. Indécision. Phillipe and Solange are taking a vacation on l'Île Maurice and are having a hard time deciding what to do. Using the cues provided, tell what they say.

Modèle　le restaurant où ils vont manger → **Est-ce qu'on va manger dans ce restaurant-ci ou ce restaurant-là?**

1. l'hôtel où ils vont rester
2. les souvenirs qu'ils vont acheter
3. l'exposition qu'ils vont visiter
4. la carte qu'ils vont acheter
5. les disques qu'ils vont écouter
6. le musée qu'ils vont visiter

Communication

A. Observations. Listed below are some aspects of your daily life. Using the examples as a guide, make comments about each of them.

Exemples　le soir → Ce soir, je vais étudier pour mon examen de français.

la classe / le professeur / les étudiants / l'université / la ville / l'année / l'après-midi / l'hiver / l'été / le temps

B. Compliments et commentaires. Imagine that you are in the following situations and want to compliment your French-speaking friends about various things. What would you say? Try to come up with several reactions.

Exemple　Vous faites une promenade dans le quartier où habitent vos amis.
　　　　　Ce quartier est très joli!
　　　　　J'aime beaucoup cette maison.

1. Vous visitez leur ville.
2. Vos amis ont préparé un bon dîner.

3. Vous mangez dans un bon restaurant avec vos amis.
4. Vous regardez un film.
5. Vous écoutez un concert à la radio.
6. Vous regardez un programme de variétés à la télé.
7. Vous allez au marché avec vos amis.
8. Vous faites une promenade en voiture dans la campagne.

⚜ Les expressions idiomatiques avec *avoir*

Présentation

The verb **avoir** occurs in many idiomatic expressions used to indicate various reactions, feelings, needs, and intentions. The most useful of these are:

A. Reactions and feelings

avoir froid *to be cold*	Nous avons froid.
avoir chaud *to be hot*	J'ai trop chaud.
avoir faim *to be hungry*	Est-ce que tu as faim?
avoir soif *to be thirsty*	Nous avons très soif.
avoir sommeil *to be sleepy*	Il est tard et ils ont sommeil.
avoir peur *to be afraid*	Elle n'a pas peur des chiens.
avoir honte *to be ashamed*	Moi, je n'ai pas honte.
avoir mal *to hurt*	J'ai mal partout.

B. Opinions

avoir raison *to be right*	Tu as raison d'être très prudent.
avoir tort *to be wrong*	J'ai eu tort de faire ça.
avoir l'air *to appear, look*	Il n'a pas l'air content.
avoir de la chance *to be lucky*	Tu as eu de la chance!

You may want to have students notice the differences between sentences like **je voudrais du pain** and **j'ai besoin de pain.**

C. Intentions and needs

avoir l'intention de *to intend to*	J'ai l'intention de rester à la maison.
avoir envie de *to want, to feel like*	Est-ce que tu as envie de lire ce livre?
avoir besoin de *to need*	J'ai besoin de prendre des vacances.
avoir l'occasion de *to have the chance (the opportunity)*	As-tu déjà eu l'occasion de voyager à l'étranger?

D. Avoir also occurs in such idiomatic expressions as **avoir lieu** (to take place) and **avoir . . . ans** (to be . . . years old).

Le concert a eu lieu dimanche après-midi.
Ce garçon a dix-sept ans.

E. Note that **avoir envie de** and **avoir besoin de** can be followed by an infinitive (**j'ai besoin de travailler**), by a noun (**il a besoin d'argent**), or by an article (**elle a besoin de la voiture ce soir**).

Substitution: (1) Est-ce que tu as faim? chaud / froid / peur / sommeil / soif. (2) Ils ont besoin de travailler. l'intention / envie / l'air / raison / tort.

Préparation

A. Mères poules et papas poules! Nadine's parents seem to be overly solici-tious about the comfort of her friends who are visiting for the weekend. What do they ask?

Modèle   Robert / soif? → **Est-ce que Robert a soif?**

1. Marie-Claire / trop chaud?
2. tu / besoin de dormir?
3. vous / froid?
4. tes amis / faim?
5. ils / sommeil?
6. Micheline / envie de manger quelque chose?
7. tu / soif?
8. vous / intention de sortir ce soir?

B. Suivez le guide, s'il vous plaît! Serge, who is studying English, works during the summer as an assistant tour guide for English-speaking tourists in Paris. He has to report some of their complaints and comments to the tour director. What does he say?

Modèle   We are hungry. → **Nous avons faim.**

1. Mrs. White needs to go to the bank.
2. We are cold and hungry!
3. When does this concert take place?
4. Mr. Collins does not feel like visiting Versailles.
5. Mr. Wolf is afraid to go shopping alone.
6. The others are very sleepy.
7. I am thirsty.
8. You look very tired.
9. You are lucky to live in Paris!

Communication

A. Options. Complete the following sentences by using one or more of the options provided or by creating one of your own.

1. Ce week-end j'ai l'intention de . . .
   rester à la maison / aller chez le coiffeur / aller au cinéma / inviter des amis à dîner / ?
2. Quand il pleut, j'ai souvent envie de . . .
   dormir jusqu'à midi / regarder des dessins animés à la télévision / faire une promenade sous la pluie / ?
3. Moi, j'ai besoin de . . .
   sommeil / vacances / argent / voiture / ?
4. Pendant l'été, j'ai l'intention de . . .
   rester à l'université / travailler pour gagner de l'argent / voyager en France / ?
5. Je suis courageux(euse); je n'ai pas peur de . . .
   orages / examens / cambrioleurs / professeurs / ?
6. Le vendredi après-midi, les étudiants n'ont pas envie de . . .
   travailler / aller en classe / écouter les explications du professeur / rester à la maison / faire leurs devoirs / ?

B. Petits dialogues. Complete each of the following dialogues with an appropriate **avoir** expression.

Options: (1) Written. (2) Oral. (3) Have students prepare additional **petits dialogues.**

Modèle   MARC: On va au café?

PIERRE: Oui, je . . .

Oui, j'ai soif.

1. LA MÈRE: Il faut manger ton dîner, mon petit!
   L'ENFANT: Mais Maman, je . . .
2. L'ÉTUDIANT: New York est la capitale des États-Unis.
   LE PROFESSEUR: Mais non, vous . . .
3. M. DUPONT: Où est-ce que vous allez en vacances cette année?
   MME LECLERC: Je ne suis pas sûre, mais nous . . . aller sur la Côte d'Azur.
4. JEAN-LUC: Je voyage toujours en avion—c'est très rapide.
   CLAUDE: Pas moi! Je n'aime pas les avions; je . . . d'avoir un accident.
5. PAUL: Est-ce qu'on va danser ce soir?
   CHANTAL: Non, pas ce soir. J'ai travaillé jusqu'à minuit hier soir et je . . .
6. LE PROFESSEUR: Vous n'avez pas encore fait vos devoirs?
   L'ÉTUDIANT: Non, Monsieur. Mais je . . . travailler aujourd'hui.

C. Questions/Interview. Answer the following questions or use them to interview another student.

Option: Have students practice giving related questions to use in small-group interviews. (See Chapter 6, **Synthèse A.**)

1. Qu'est-ce que tu as l'intention de faire demain?
2. Et samedi, qu'est-ce que tu as l'intention de faire?
3. Quand tu as très faim, qu'est-ce que tu aimes manger?
4. Est-ce que tu as souvent sommeil en classe?
5. Qu'est-ce que tu as envie de faire ce soir?
6. Est-ce que tu as déjà eu l'occasion de voyager dans un pays étranger?
7. Est-ce que tu as envie d'habiter dans un pays étranger?
8. Quelle région des États-Unis est-ce que tu as envie de visiter?
9. Quel âge as-tu?
10. Est-ce que tu as besoin d'étudier ce soir?

Les verbes *vouloir* et *pouvoir*

Présentation

The verbs **pouvoir** (to be able, can, may) and **vouloir** (to want, to wish) have similar irregularities of form.

Contrast [ø] of **peux/veux** vs. [œ] of **peuvent, veulent.**

pouvoir		vouloir	
je **peux**	nous **pouvons**	je **veux**	nous **voulons**
tu **peux**	vous **pouvez**	tu **veux**	vous **voulez**
il/elle/on **peut**	ils/elles **peuvent**	il/elle/on **veut**	ils/elles **veulent**
passé composé:	j'ai **pu**	**passé composé:**	j'ai **voulu**

Est-ce que je peux sortir?	*May I go out?*
On peut acheter des légumes à l'épicerie.	*One can buy vegetables at the grocery store.*
Elles ne veulent pas rester ici.	*They don't want to stay here.*
Je veux mon petit déjeuner!	*I want my breakfast!*

A. Pouvoir and **vouloir** are often used to make requests. In the present tense, these requests are very direct, almost blunt:

Pouvez-vous . . . ?	*Can you . . . ?*
Voulez-vous . . . ?	*Do you want . . . ?*
Je veux . . .	*I want . . .*

Point out that in formal style **puis-je** may replace **est-ce que je peux?**

To be less direct and more polite, the following forms are used:

Pourrais-tu . . . ?	
Pourriez-vous . . . ?	*Could you . . . ?*
Voudrais-tu . . . ?	
Voudriez-vous . . . ?	*Would you . . . ?*
Je voudrais . . .	*I would like . . .*
Je pourrais . . .	*I could . . .*

You may wish to point out that **pourrais**, etc., are forms of the conditional tense, which will be covered fully on p. 316.

A polite way to accept an offer or agree to a request is:

Oui, je veux bien . . .	*Yes, I'm willing (I accept) . . .*

B. The **passé composé** of **pouvoir** and **vouloir** conveys various special meanings.

Remind students that they already know **Qu'est-ce que ça veut dire?**

Elle n'a pas voulu ranger sa chambre.	*She refused to clean her room.*
Ils n'ont pas pu aller à la piscine.	*They were not able to go to the pool.*
Elle a pu identifier les cambrioleurs.	*She succeeded in identifying the thieves.*

Préparation

A. Une surboum. Solange and her friends are planning a **surboum** (party). Her friends offer to help or to bring something. Indicate what each can do.

> **Modèle** je / apporter du vin → **Je peux apporter du vin.**

Follow-up: Have students plan a hypothetical **surboum**.

1. nous / ranger l'appartement
2. Jean-Luc / aider Solange à faire la cuisine
3. Claude et moi, nous / aller au supermarché
4. je / faire un gâteau
5. tu / apporter des disques
6. vous / téléphoner aux copains

B. Il ne fait pas beau! It's a rainy day and Dominique and her friends are telling some of the things they want and don't want to do. What do they say?

> **Modèle** Micheline / écrire des lettres (non) → **Micheline ne veut pas écrire des lettres.**

1. moi / jouer aux cartes (oui)
2. Robert / lire un bon livre (oui)
3. nous / marcher sous la pluie (non)
4. toi / dormir toute la journée (oui)
5. Anne et Gabrielle / rester à la maison (non)
6. vous / ranger votre chambre (non)

Communication

A. Vouloir, c'est pouvoir. Using the suggestions below or adding ideas of your own, create sentences to describe what is really important to you in life.

Follow-up: Have students contrast their own priorities with those of other students.

> **Exemple**   Je veux avoir une profession intéressante, mais je veux pas habiter dans une grande ville.

Suggestions: avoir des enfants / être heureux(euse) / voyager dans des pays étrangers / avoir une maison au bord de la mer / avoir une vie simple et tranquille / participer à la vie politique / être indépendant(e) / aider les autres / habiter à la campagne / rester dans cette ville / continuer mes études / **?**

B. Trouvez un(e) étudiant(e) . . . Ask questions to find out who in your class can or wants to do the following things.

Options: Use as questions or directed dialogue—**Demandez à Alice si elle peut parler italien,** etc.

Trouvez un(e) étudiant(e) . . .
1. qui peut parler italien
2. qui veut aller dans un pays étranger
3. qui veut être journaliste
4. qui veut être célèbre
5. qui peut raconter des histoires amusantes
6. qui peut persuader le professeur de changer la date de l'examen
7. qui peut préparer un bon dîner
8. **?**

⚜ Les nombres supérieurs à 1000 et les nombres ordinaux

Présentation

A. Numbers above 1000 (**mille**) are expressed in the following ways:

Point out that three-digit groups may be separated by spaces *or* by periods, and that the French use a comma to indicate a decimal point.

Remind students that **cent** takes an *s* in the plural only when it is *not* followed by another number.

1351	mille trois cent cinquante et un
3000	trois mille
4445	quatre mille quatre cent quarante-cinq
19 300	dix-neuf mille trois cents
541 000	cinq cent quarante et un mille
2 000 000	deux millions

Note that **mille** is never spelled with an **-s**, while **million** has an **-s** in the plural.

These numbers are also used to give dates, which can be expressed in two ways. For example, to say that an event took place in 1789, the following patterns can be used:

en mille sept cent quatre-vingt-neuf
en dix-neuf cent quatre-vingt-neuf

B. Ordinal numbers (first, second, third, etc.) are given below.
Premier(-ière) agrees with the noun modified; other ordinal numbers always end in **-ième.**

premier (1er)	sixième	onzième	seizième	vingt et unième
première (1ère)	septième	douzième	dix-septième	vingt-deuxième
deuxième (2e)	huitième	treizième	dix-huitième	etc.
troisième (3e)	neuvième	quatorzième	dix-neuvième	dernier/dernière *(last)*
quatrième	dixième	quinzième	vingtième	
cinquième				

Point out that **second(e)** *is also used.*

C'est le premier jour de l'année.
C'est la première maison à droite.

C. Fois *(time)* is used in the following types of expressions.

la première fois *(the first time)*   deux fois par semaine *(twice a week)*
la dernière fois *(the last time)*   trois fois par an *(three times a year)*
une fois par jour *(once a day)*   à la fois *(at the same time)*

D. Other useful terms related to numbers are:

pourcentage	*percentage*
pour cent (%)	*percent*
la moitié	*half*
le tiers	*third*
le quart	*quarter*
environ	*about, around*

Point out to students that percentages carried to one or more decimal places are written with a comma in French: **Les étrangers qui travaillent en France représentent 7,7% (sept virgule sept pour cent) de la population totale.**

Read numbers in French and have students write them.

Répétition: 1. 10, 100, 1000, 10 000, 100 000, 1 000 000. 2. 3 000, 15 000, 55 000, 106 000, 3 700 000. 3. 1 200, 9 110, 69 821, 238 402, 248 669 329. 4. la 1ère visite, le1^{er} jour, la 3e auto, la 7e leçon, la 10e fois. 5. 10%, 100%, 37%, 75%, 91%. Have students give the following dates in French: 1291, 1412, 1789, 1822, 1900, 1943, 1951, 1986, 2000.

Préparation

A. Arrondissements. Different people in Paris are telling which district they are from. Tell what they say.

Modèle   19e → **Nous habitons dans le dix-neuvième.**

1. 3^e	6. 4^e
2. 6^e	7. 20^e
3. 14^e	8. 16^e
4. 18^e	9. 2^e
5. 1er	10. 15^e

Paris is divided into twenty administrative districts called **arrondissements.**

B. Populations. Students from various cities in France are telling how large their home towns are. What do they say?

Modèle   Lyon (1 083 000h) → **Lyon est une ville d'un million quatre-vingt-trois mille habitants.**

1. Marseille (964 412h)	6. Nancy (127 826h)
2. Lille (881 271h)	7. Brest (159 857h)
3. Bordeaux (471 540h)	8. Strasbourg (334 668h)
4. Nice (325 400h)	9. Montpellier (167 211h)
5. Nantes (393 731h)	10. Grenoble (332 423h)

Read numbers in French and have students write them.

These figures are for "agglomérations," which include the city and its suburbs.

Communication

A. Le budget des Français. Using the table below, tell what percentage of their budget French people spend on the following categories. Then estimate what percentage you spend on each of these categories.

Exemple nourriture 27 % → **La nourriture représente vingt-sept pour cent de leur budget. Pour moi, ça représente environ vingt pour cent de mon budget.**

Catégorie	Pourcentage
1. nourriture	27 %
2. vêtements	9 %
3. maison ou appartement	22 %
4. santé et hygiène	13 %
5. transports et téléphone	11 %
6. cinéma, théâtre, concerts, etc.	9 %
7. hôtels, restaurants, cafés, etc.	9 %

B. C'est combien? A French friend wants to know how much various items cost. What would you tell them about the following?

Exemple une bonne chaîne-stéréo → **Une bonne chaîne-stéréo coûte environ douze cents dollars.**

1. une radio
2. un vélomoteur
3. une voiture
4. un téléviseur
5. une moto
6. une caméra
7. un appareil-photo
8. un ordinateur

C. Quelques statistiques. Using the following graph, give the number of students (**élèves**) in both public and private nursery schools (**écoles maternelles**), elementary schools, special programs such as adult education, and secondary schools in France.

Exemple Il y a 336 704 élèves dans les écoles maternelles privées.

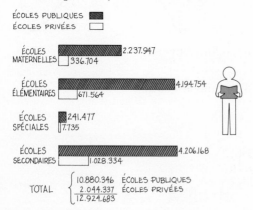

ÉCOLES PUBLIQUES
ÉCOLES PRIVÉES

ÉCOLES MATERNELLES: 2.237.947 / 336.704

ÉCOLES ÉLÉMENTAIRES: 4.194.754 / 671.564

ÉCOLES SPÉCIALES: 241.477 / 7.735

ÉCOLES SECONDAIRES: 4.206.168 / 1.028.334

TOTAL: 10.880.346 ÉCOLES PUBLIQUES / 2.044.337 ÉCOLES PRIVÉES / 12.924.683

SYNTHÈSE

Un pays où il fait toujours beau

Est-ce que vous *rêvez* d'un pays où il fait toujours beau, . . . un pays
sans usine et sans pollution et où les touristes sont rares, . . . un pays
qui est à la fois l'Inde, le Pakistan, la Chine, l'Afrique, et la France?

dream

    Ce pays, c'est l'Île Maurice, au milieu de l'océan Indien. Dans cette
île, il y a 550 000 Hindous, 250 000 Chinois, 250 000 Créoles et 3000
ou 4000 Français. L'Île Maurice a été sous le contrôle de l'Angleterre
pendant deux cents ans. La *langue* officielle est l'anglais, mais *tout le
monde* continue à parler français: l'agent de police hindou, le garagiste
pakistanais, le chauffeur de taxi chinois, le *garçon* de café créole.

language / everyone

waiter

    L'architecture de l'île est très variée; sa cuisine aussi. Il y a des
restaurants chinois qui sont à la fois chinois et hindous, des restaurants
hindous qui ont des spécialités chinoises et des restaurants français qui
ne sont pas *vraiment* français.

really

    Le *paysage* est très varié aussi. Il y a des montagnes volcaniques,
une mer vraiment *bleue* et calme (excepté pendant la saison des cyclones), des plages magnifiques *protégées* par des *récifs de corail*, et une
végétation tropicale. À l'intérieur du pays, il y a des *forêts* sur les montagnes et des plantations de *canne à sucre* dans les plaines. *Partout* les
gens sont *accueillants*.

landscape
blue
protected / coral reefs
forests
sugar cane / everywhere
hospitable

Extrait et adapté d'un article de *Paris Match*.

L'Île Maurice: un marché
en plein air

Compréhension Selon les renseignements donnés, est-ce que les phrases suivantes sont vraies ou fausses? Si le sens de la phrase est faux, corrigez-le.

1. L'Île Maurice est située dans l'océan Pacifique.
2. C'est un pays très industrialisé.
3. La population de l'île est très variée.
4. L'Île Maurice a été sous le contrôle de la France pendant deux cents ans.
5. La langue officielle du pays est l'anglais.
6. À l'Île Maurice, tout le monde parle chinois.
7. À l'Île Maurice, il y a des restaurants français mais il n'y a pas de restaurants chinois.
8. La mer est très calme pendant la saison des cyclones.
9. On trouve des forêts dans les plaines et des plantations de canne à sucre sur les montagnes.
10. L'Île Maurice a un climat très froid.

Follow-up: Have students prepare short travel slogans to entice visitors to l'**Île Maurice**.

NOTES CULTURELLES

L'Île Maurice

Mauritius, located in the Indian Ocean east of Madagascar, was under French control from 1715 until 1814, when it became part of the British Empire. In 1968 Mauritius became an independent state of the British Commonwealth. Despite the island's close ties with Britain, French influence remains strong there even today. In addition to French and English, several Indian languages, two Chinese dialects, and Creole are spoken on the island. The island's distinctive international character and beautiful countryside are appealing not only to French tourists but to visitors from many countries.

Other French-speaking places in the Indian Ocean with official or unofficial ties with France are l'Île de la Réunion, a French overseas department off the east coast of Africa; les Séychelles, a group of islands northeast of Madagascar; and Madagascar, the fourth largest island in the world, which was a French protectorate until receiving its independence in 1960.

Communication

A. **Bulletin métérologique.** Using the **bulletin métérologique** in the *Introduction* as a model, prepare your own weather forecast for tomorrow. Your forecast might be for your own town, for a city or town in the French-speaking world, or for a country where the climate is either ideal or miserable.

Suggested for written homework.

B. **Vouloir, c'est pouvoir.** Where there's a will, there's a way. What would you do in each of the following situations? Compare your solutions with those of other students.

1. Vous avez l'occasion de visiter l'Île Maurice. Qu'est-ce que vous pouvez faire pendant votre séjour sur cette île?
2. Vos amis ont l'intention de faire un pique-nique au bord de la rivière. Mais selon la météo, il va pleuvoir. Qu'est-ce qu'ils peuvent faire?

3. Vous avez des amis français qui visitent votre ville pour la première fois. Il pleut tous les jours pendant leur visite. Qu'est-ce que vous pouvez faire?

4. Vos amis et vous, vous avez envie de passer l'été dans un pays où on parle français. Mais vous êtes étudiants et vous n'êtes pas très riches. Que pouvez-vous faire?

5. Vous avez des amis français qui veulent visiter les États-Unis. Qu'est-ce qu'ils peuvent faire?

6. Il a fait très beau ce week-end. Et maintenant, c'est dimanche soir et vous avez oublié que vous avez un examen demain matin à neuf heures! Que pouvez-vous faire?

7. Vous avez un(e) ami(e) qui a de la difficulté dans son cours de français. Qu'est-ce qu'il/elle peut faire?

8. Vous avez besoin de travailler pour payer vos études. Qu'est-ce que vous pouvez faire pour gagner de l'argent?

C. Vrai ou faux? Based on what you know about different French-speaking countries, tell whether the following statements are true or false. If possible, correct those statements that are false.

Exemple   Québec est une ville de deux millions d'habitants. → **C'est faux. Il y a 551 000 habitants à Québec.**

1. La moitié des Français habitent à la campagne.
2. Les francophones représentent 28% de la population du Canada.
3. Montréal est une ville de 2 800 000 habitants.
4. Quatre-vingts pour cent de la population du Canada est au Québec, en Ontario, en Alberta, et en Colombie Britannique.
5. Les trois-quarts des Français ont la télévision.
6. Seulement un tiers des Français ont un réfrigérateur.
7. Il y a cent millions d'habitants en France.
8. Trente-neuf pour cent des Français travaillent dans l'industrie.
9. En France, les femmes représentent 35% des gens qui travaillent.
10. Madagascar a environ 10 millions d'habitants.

1.-non; seulement 30%
2.-vrai
3.-vrai
4.-vrai
5.-vrai 79%
6.-faux; 87% en ont un.
7.-faux; 50 millions
8.-vrai
9.-vrai
10.-faux; 6 millions

L'Île Maurice

PRONONCIATION

A. The vowel sound [œ] always occurs in a closed syllable. The vowel sound [ø] occurs in open syllables and in syllables closed by a [z] sound. Compare:

[ø]	[œ]
il peut	ils peuvent
il veut	ils veulent
danseuse	danseur

1. Repeat the following words containing the sound [ø]:

   deux   il pleut   heureux   paresseux   heureuse   paresseuse

2. Repeat the following words containing the sound [œ]:

   heure   neuf   peur   sœur   ordinateur   vélomoteur

B. The vowel sound [ɔ] generally occurs in a closed syllable. The vowel sound [o] occurs in open syllables, in syllables closed by a [z] sound, and when the spelling is **au, eau,** or **ô.** Compare:

[o]	[ɔ]
beau	bord
vos	votre
cause	poste

1. Repeat the following words containing the sound [o]:

   numéro   rose   aussi   chaud   animaux   photo

2. Repeat the following words containing the sound [ɔ]:

   tort   sport   Europe   Paul   octobre   sommeil

C. The spelling **oi** is pronounced [wa]. Repeat the following words:

   moi   voici   soir   trois   pourquoi   froid   soif   pleuvoir

D. Repeat the following sentences, paying special attention to the sounds you have been practicing.

1. **V**oici les **deux jeu**nes **pro**fesseurs.
2. Vous avez **tort** de **sor**tir **seul** le **soir.**
3. Quel est le **nu**méro de **vo**tre **voi**ture?
4. **R**ose est un peu **pa**resseuse, mais elle est **heu**reuse.
5. Les **dan**seurs et les **dan**seuses vont **sor**tir à **deux heu**res.

VOCABULAIRE

noms

le temps et la météo (voir p. 129)

activités et loisir (voir p. 129)

d'autres noms
le **chauffeur** (m,f)   *driver*
°l'**est**   *east*
°la **forêt**
°le **garagiste**, la **garagiste**
le **garçon de café**   *waiter*
l'**île** (f)   *island*
° l'**intérieur** (m)
la **langue**   *language*
la **moitié**   *half*
la **neige**   *snow*
le **nord**   *north*
le **nuage**   *cloud*
l'**ouest**   *west*
le **pays**   *country*
le **paysage**   *landscape*
°le **pique-nique**
la **pluie**   *rain*
°le **pourcentage**
°le **reste**
la **revue**   *magazine*
le **sud**   *south*
le **tiers**   *third*
°le **touriste**, la **touriste**

verbes

expressions avec le verbe **avoir** (voir p. 133)
aller à la pêche   *to go fishing*
devenir   *to become*
monter   *to go up, climb*
neiger   *to snow*
pleuvoir   *to rain*
pouvoir   *to be able to*
promener   *to walk (dog, etc.)*
vouloir   *to want to*

adjectifs

nombres ordinaux (voir p. 139)
accueillant(e)   *hospitable*
bleu(e)   *blue*
chaud(e)   *warm*
faible   *weak*
frais, fraîche   *cool*
froid(e)   *cold*
mauvais(e)   *bad*
mille   *thousand*
nuageux, nuageuse   *cloudy*
°**rare**

adverbes
vraiment   *really*

divers
à la fois   *at the same time*
environ   *about, around*
par   *by*
°**pour cent**
une fois par jour   *once a day*

Choix et décisions

INTRODUCTION

Qu'est-ce que vous faites dans la vie?

Une *société* de sondages d'opinion a organisé une *enquête* pour *savoir* si les Français sont satisfaits de leur travail et pour faire «un classement des *métiers* heureux». Des *enquêteurs* parlent avec des gens de différentes professions.

company / survey / to know

professions, trades / pollsters

Monsieur Panneau, *plombier* à Lyon   *plumber*

L'ENQUÊTRICE	Quel est votre métier, monsieur?
M. PANNEAU	Je suis plombier.
L'ENQUÊTRICE	Vous êtes content de votre métier?
M. PANNEAU	Oui, j'aime *ce que* je fais et je gagne bien ma vie. Je suis mon *propre patron*. J'aime ça.
L'ENQUÊTRICE	Vous travaillez beaucoup?
M. PANNEAU	Oui, il faut être là à toutes les heures du jour et de la *nuit*. Mais j'ai de la chance, le *chômage* est le dernier de mes *soucis*!

what

own / boss

night / unemployment
worries

Madame Aubourg, médecin à Strasbourg

L'ENQUÊTEUR	Vous aimez votre travail?
MME AUBOURG	Oui, c'est un travail *passionnant*. Il faut faire de longues *études* pour être médecin, mais *ça en vaut la peine.*
L'ENQUÊTEUR	*Qu'est-ce qui compte le plus* pour vous?
MME AUBOURG	Le contact humain, le *sentiment* d'aider les autres.
L'ENQUÊTEUR	Quels sont les inconvénients de votre métier?
MME AUBOURG	Les longues heures de travail. Souvent je travaille dix et même douze heures *par jour* et quand je suis *de garde*, c'est vingt-quatre heures sur vingt-quatre. Ça ne *laisse* pas beaucoup de temps pour la famille et les *loisirs*.

exciting

studies / it's worth the trouble

what / counts / the most
feeling

a day / on duty

leave
leisure-time activities

146

Compréhension   Répondez aux questions suivantes selon les renseignements donnés dans le texte.

1. Quel est le métier de Monsieur Panneau?
2. Est-il satisfait de son travail? Pourquoi?
3. Est-ce qu'il travaille beaucoup? Quel est le principal inconvénient de son métier?
4. Pourquoi pense-t-il qu'il a de la chance?
5. Et Madame Aubourg, qu'est-ce qu'elle fait dans la vie?
6. Pourquoi aime-t-elle son travail?
7. Quels sont les aspects de son travail qui comptent le plus pour elle?
8. Quels sont les inconvénients de son métier?

NOTES CULTURELLES

Choix d'un métier

A recent survey conducted by the **Centre d'études de l'emploi** asked French young people what they looked for in the choice of a future profession. As the table indicates, the responses of French young men and women were somewhat different.

	Garçons	*Filles*
Salaire	71,7 %	57,7 %
Temps *consacré* à la famille	56,3	65,6
Stabilité de l'emploi	56,0	56,8
Contacts humains	24,7	40,9
Activités de loisirs	28,9	26,7
Avantages sociaux	26,9	16,2
Intérêt des *tâches*	17,2	22,6
Possibilité de promotion	10,3	4,8
Prestige social	1,8	1,6

devoted

benefits
tasks, duties

Female respondents placed time for family in first place whereas males indicated that salary would be the most important consideration. This difference in perspective reflects perhaps the need that women have to combine career and family along with the knowledge that family responsibilities, despite changing roles and attitudes, are still largely the domain of the female. Human contacts were also more important for young women than for their male counterparts.

This difference may be related to general trends in job choices. Although women are increasingly choosing nontraditional careers, they still tend to be more numerous in areas such as teaching, nursing, and social services where human relations play an important role. Men, on the other hand, tend to prefer careers in industry, technology, and the sciences. The survey also showed that women indicate a greater willingness to accept responsibility than do men.

Et vous?

A. Choix et décisions. Using the scale, tell how important each of the following is to you in the choice of a profession.

1 = très important
2 = assez important
3 = pas très important
4 = sans importance

The first eleven items on the list in **A** were given as important job qualities by 2500 French people in a recent survey. The items are given in the order of their importance and percentages accorded to each are indicated. Students might want to compare their own rankings with those given in the survey. They could also make up a comparative ordering for Americans.

Exemple La sécurité de l'emploi est assez importante pour moi.

1. 34% la sécurité de l'emploi *(job)*
2. 29% un salaire *(salary)* assez élevé *(high)*
3. 24% de bonnes conditions de travail
4. 24% des horaires *(schedule)* souples *(flexible)*
5. 24% la liberté et la place à *(room for)* l'initiative personnelle
6. 24% un travail intéressant
7. 20% le prestige social
8. 10% le contact humain
9. 8% la possibilité de participer aux décisions
10. 6% un emploi facile
11. 5% la possibilité de promotion
12. ___ un travail qui laisse du temps libre *(free)* pour la famille et les loisirs
13. ___ la possibilité de voyager

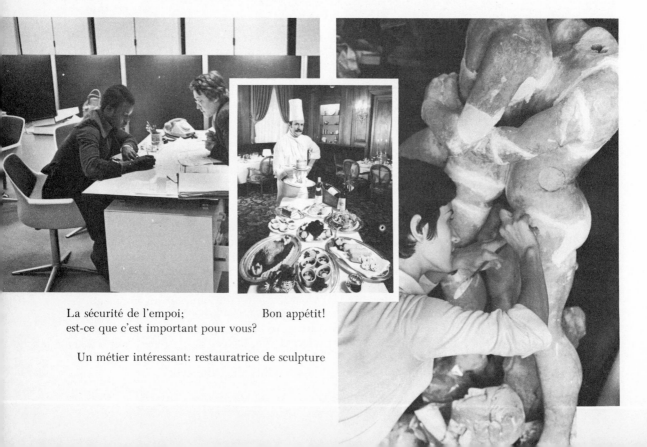

La sécurité de l'empoi;   Bon appétit!
est-ce que c'est important pour vous?

Un métier intéressant: restauratrice de sculpture

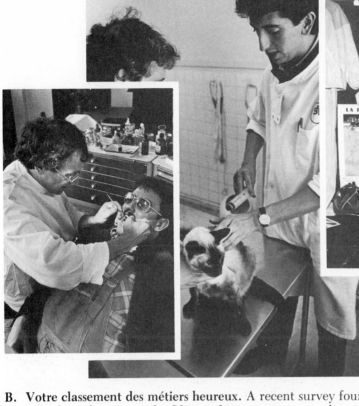

Vendeuse dans une boutique

B. Votre classement des métiers heureux. A recent survey found the following jobs to be among the fifty professions most appealing to French people. Indicate whether or not you would be interested in these jobs.

Exemples Je voudrais être vétérinaire parce que j'aime les animaux.
Je ne voudrais pas être comptable parce que je trouve les maths difficiles.

chirurgien/ne *(surgeon)*
professeur d'université (m)
dentiste (m,f)
avocat(e)
médecin (m)
comptable (m,f) *(accountant)*
vétérinaire (m,f)
publicitaire (m,f) *(advertising agent)*
chercheur scientifique (m) *(scientific researcher)*
psychologue (m,f) *(psychologist)*
directeur/trice d'entreprise *(head of a business)*
informaticien/ne *(computer programmer)*

cadre commercial (m) *(business executive)*
ingénieur (m)
instituteur/trice *(elementary school teacher)*
commerçant(e)
mécanicien/ne
artisan(e)
chauffeur de taxi (m) *(taxi driver)*
secrétaire (m,f)

Although the fifty professions are not all listed, those included here are given in the order in which they were chosen.

⚜ Les verbes de la deuxième conjugaison

Présentation

A group of French verbs has infinitives that end in **-ir.** These verbs are especially useful when talking about decisions and accomplishments. The present tense of many of these verbs is formed by dropping the **-ir** from the infinitive and adding the endings shown. The past participle is formed by dropping the **-r** from the infinitive.

choisir	
je choisis	nous choisissons
tu choisis	vous choisissez
il/elle/on choisit	ils/elles choisissent
passé composé: j'ai choisi	

Other useful verbs conjugated like **choisir** are:

accomplir *to accomplish*	Qu'est-ce que vous avez accompli?
obéir (à) *to obey*	Il n'a pas obéi à son patron.
désobéir (à) *to disobey*	Cet enfant désobéit toujours à ses parents.
enrichir *to enrich*	Vous avez besoin d'enrichir votre vocabulaire.
établir *to establish, set up*	As-tu établi ton programme?
finir *to finish*	Tu n'as pas fini ton dessert!
grandir *to grow up, to expand*	Elle a grandi au Maroc.
punir *to punish*	Punissez-vous vos enfants quand ils désobéissent?
réfléchir (à) *to reflect, to consider, to think about*	Vous ne réfléchissez pas assez.
réussir *to succeed, to pass (a test)*	Elles réussissent bien dans leurs études.
rougir *to blush, to get red*	Pourquoi rougissez-vous?

Répétition: (1) Je finis à cinq heures, tu finis à cinq heures, etc. (2) Qu'est-ce que je choisis, Qu'est-ce que tu choisis?, etc. **Substitution:** (1) Qu'est-ce que tu choisis? vous / je / Vincent / nous / les enfants. (2) Est-ce que vous obéissez à vos parents? Claudine / nous / Luc / les enfants / tu. (3) Elle n'a pas réfléchi au problème. je / les étudiants / nous / Pierre / vous.

Préparation

A. Comparaisons. Several students are talking about which courses they generally do well in. What do they say?

Modèle   Paul / maths → **Paul réussit bien en maths.**

1. nous / français
2. Geneviève / sciences
3. tu / histoire
4. vous / psychologie
5. je / littérature
6. Jean et Annette / anglais

B. Retravailler. In France an organization called «Retravailler» has been created to help women re-enter the work force after raising a family. Re-create some of the comments made at one of their meetings.

Modèle le nombre de femmes qui travaillent / grandir chaque jour → **Le nombre de femmes qui travaillent grandit chaque jour.**

1. ma journée de travail / finir à dix heures du soir
2. notre travail / enrichir les autres
3. vous / obéir sans réfléchir
4. nous / punir nos filles et encourager nos garçons
5. il faut / établir ton programme
6. je / choisir de retravailler

C. Petits et grands succès. The Monots are talking about some of the things that various family members have accomplished recently. What do they say?

Modèle Roger / finir ses études → **Roger a fini ses études.**

1. vous / réfléchir à ce que vous voulez faire dans la vie
2. Madeleine / réussir à tous ses examens
3. tu / choisir un métier intéressant
4. nous / accomplir des choses importantes
5. je / établir mon programme d'études pour l'an prochain
6. mes amis / réussir à trouver du travail
7. Caroline / choisir un joli appartement près d'ici
8. les enfants / ne pas désobéir trop souvent

Communication

Questions/Interview. Answer the following questions or use them to interview another student.

Explain **lycée** and the three-semester system.

1. Où est-ce que tu as grandi?
2. Quand est-ce que tu as fini tes études au lycée?
3. Est-ce que tu as déjà choisi tes cours pour le trimestre prochain?
4. Quels sont les cours où tu réussis bien?
5. Est-ce que tu as beaucoup enrichi ton vocabulaire en français?
6. Est-ce que tu as déjà établi ton programme d'études pour l'an prochain?
7. Quand est-ce que tu vas finir tes études?
8. Est-ce que tu as déjà choisi ta future profession?
9. Est-ce que tu penses qu'il faut punir les enfants quand ils désobéissent?

⚜ L'impératif

Présentation

Imperative verb forms are used to give orders and advice, to make requests, or to explain how to do something. They are identical to the **tu, vous,** and **nous** forms of the present indicative, with one exception: the final **-s** is dropped from the **tu** form of **-er** verbs, including **aller.** They are used without subject pronouns.

L'impératif	
-er verbs	**-ir** verbs
écoute	réfléchis
écoutez	réfléchissez
écoutons	réfléchissons

Note that the negative of the imperative is regular; **ne** precedes the verb and **pas** follows it.

Finis tes études.	*Finish your studies.*
Ne travaille pas trop.	*Don't work too hard.*
Va chez le médecin ce matin.	*Go to the doctor's this morning.*
Téléphonez à la patronne.	*Call the boss.*
Ne choisissez pas ce métier.	*Don't choose this profession.*

A. The **nous** form of the imperative is used for the *let's . . .* form of command.

Finissons notre travail.	*Let's finish our work.*
Expliquons le problème à cet agent.	*Let's explain the problem to that police officer.*
N'allons pas au match dimanche.	*Let's not go to the game Sunday.*

The **nous** form of the imperative is not as commonly used as the present tense (**on va, on fait,** etc.) or the imperfect with **si** (**si on allait au cinema,** etc.). Although students should be able to recognize this form, it does not need to be emphasized in speaking or writing.

B. The verbs **être** and **avoir** have irregular imperatives.

être	avoir
sois	aie
soyez	ayez
soyons	ayons

Sois calme!	*Be calm.*
Soyons prudents.	*Let's be careful*
N'ayez pas peur.	*Don't be afraid.*

Préparation

A. Un homme difficile à satisfaire. Lucette is thinking about things she might want to do. Antoine, who is in a rather contrary mood, objects to each of her statements. Give his responses.

Modèle Je vais rester à la maison. → **Ne reste pas à la maison.**

1. Je vais étudier ce matin.
2. Je vais réfléchir.
3. Je vais faire la cuisine.
4. Je vais aller à la boulangerie.
5. Je vais regarder cette émission.
6. Je vais être en retard.
7. Je vais punir les enfants.
8. Je vais finir mon travail maintenant.

B. Faites le premier pas. Andrée is having some difficulty adjusting to her new job. An experienced co-worker is encouraging her to take the first step (**faire le premier pas**). What advice does she give?

Modèle ne pas avoir peur → **N'ayez pas peur.**

1. ne pas rester seule dans votre coin
2. faire un effort
3. aller manger avec les autres employées
4. participer aux conversations
5. ne pas rougir tout le temps
6. ne pas être découragée
7. faire bien votre travail
8. être gentille avec tout le monde
9. ne pas être si sérieuse
10. oublier vos soucis personnels

N'aie pas peur de faire le premier pas . . .

Communication

A. Conseils. Indicate whether new students at your university should or should not do the following things in order to succeed. Then give them your own "experienced" advice.

Exemple   habiter dans une résidence universitaire → **N'habitez pas dans une résidence universitaire.** *or* **Habitez dans un appartement.**

1. avoir peur de poser des questions
2. choisir des cours faciles
3. passer tout votre temps à étudier
4. habiter près de l'université
5. aller quelquefois au concert
6. manger au restaurant universitaire
7. passer votre temps dans les cafés
8. oublier de faire vos devoirs
9. écouter en classe
10. ?

B. Et encore des conseils! What advice would you give to the following groups of people?

Exemple   aux professeurs → **Ne donnez pas d'examens le lundi ou le vendredi.**

1. aux professeurs
2. aux futurs parents
3. aux enfants
4. aux touristes français aux États-Unis
5. à un(e) étudiant(e) qui ne réussit pas bien en français
6. à une(e) ami(e) qui cherche du travail
7. aux journalistes
8. au président de votre université

⚜ Les pronoms compléments d'objets directs

Présentation

In French, direct object pronouns have the same forms as the definite article (**le**—*him, it;* **la**—*her, it;* and **les,** *them*). They agree in gender and number with the nouns they replace.

Les pronoms compléments d'objets directs		
Elle fait **le ménage.**	Elle **le** fait.	*(masculine singular)*
Elle fait **la vaisselle.**	Elle **la** fait.	*(feminine singular)*
Elle fait **les courses.**	Elle **les** fait.	*(masculine or feminine plural)*

A. Direct object pronouns are placed immediately before the verb not only in affirmative sentences (as shown above) but also in negative and interrogative sentences. When the verb begins with a vowel or vowel sound, however, **le** and **la** change to **l'**.

Est-ce qu'il aime **la cuisine française?**	Est-ce qu'il **l'**aime?
Il aime **le chocolat.**	Il **l'**aime.
Il n'aime pas **les légumes.**	Il ne **les** aime pas.

Note that direct-object pronouns can also replace proper nouns or nouns introduced by possessive or demonstrative adjectives.

Nous trouvons **Alice** intéressante.	Nous **la** trouvons intéressante.
Préférez-vous **cet appartement?**	**Le** préférez-vous?
Mon frère n'aime pas **son travail.**	Il ne **l'**aime pas.
Elles font bien **leur travail.**	Elles **le** font bien.

B. With compound tenses such as the **passé composé**, direct object pronouns precede the auxiliary verb. Past participles agree in number and gender with a preceding direct object; thus, they always agree with direct-object pronouns.

Est-ce qu'elle a fait **ses études** en France?	Est-ce qu'elle **les** a **faites** en France?
Ils n'ont pas invité **leurs amis?**	Ils ne **les** ont pas invité**s**?
Avez-vous fini **vos devoirs?**	**Les** avez-vous fini**s**?

C. When an infinitive has a direct object, the direct-object pronoun immediately precedes the infinitive.

Je vais acheter **ce livre.**	Je vais **l'**acheter.
Il n'a pas envie de finir **son dîner.**	Il n'a pas envie de **le** finir.

D. In an affirmative command, the direct-object pronoun follows the verb, and a hyphen links them. In a negative command, the direct-object pronoun remains in its usual place before the verb. Compare:

Fais-**le.**	Ne **le** fais pas.
Regardez-**les.**	Ne **les** regardez pas.
Achetez-**la.**	Ne **l'**achetez pas.
Finissons-**les.**	Ne **les** finissons pas.

E. Direct-object pronouns can also be used with **voici** *(here is)* and **voilà** *(there is).*

Voici **Paul.**	**Le** voici.
Voilà **vos livres.**	**Les** voilà.
Voilà **Anne et Jean.**	**Les** voilà.

Transformation I: Je fais mon travail. → Je le fais. (1) Je fais mes études à Paris. (2) Il finit ses devoirs. (3) Nous regardons le match. (4) Tu achètes tes provisions. (5) Vous regardez ces photos. (6) Ils font la vaisselle. **II:** Repeat in the negative. Je ne fais pas mon travail. → Je ne le fais pas. **III:** Repeat in the **passé composé.** J'ai fait mon travail. → Je ne l'ai pas fait. **IV:** Repeat in the negative **passé composé.** Je n'ai pas fait mon travail. → Je ne l'ai pas fait. **V:** Repeat in the near future. Je vais faire mon travail. → Je vais le faire.

Préparation

A. Compatibilité. Anne-Marie is deciding whether or not she and Monique would get along as roommates. Using the cues provided, give Monique's answers to her questions.

> **Modèle**   Est-ce que tu aimes la musique classique? (oui) → **Oui, je l'aime.**

1. Est-ce que tu écoutes souvent la radio? (oui)
2. Est-ce que tu écoutes souvent tes disques? (oui)
3. Est-ce que tu regardes la télé tous les soirs? (non)
4. Est-ce que tu achètes tes provisions au supermarché? (non)
5. Est-ce que tu fais le ménage toutes les semaines? (oui)
6. Est-ce que tu fais souvent la cuisine? (non)
7. Est-ce que tu invites souvent tes amis? (non)
8. Est-ce que tu trouves cet appartement agréable? (oui)

B. Pense-bête. Richard is checking off the various items on his reminder list (**pense-bête**). Using the cues provided, tell whether or not he has already done them.

> **Modèles**   faire le ménage (oui) → **Je l'ai déjà fait.**
> écouter les informations (non) → **Je ne les ai pas encore écoutées.**

1. acheter les provisions (oui)	5. préparer les légumes (non)
2. ranger ma chambre (oui)	6. faire mes devoirs (non)
3. fermer les fenêtres (oui)	7. préparer le dîner (non)
4. faire la vaisselle (oui)	8. finir tout ce travail (non)

C. C'est samedi. Véronique and Armand are trying to decide what they are going to do this Saturday. Using the cues provided, tell what they say.

> **Modèle**   Est-ce que tu préfères passer le week-end à la maison?
> (oui) → **Oui, je préfère le passer à la maison.**

1. Est-ce qu'on a besoin de faire le ménage? (oui)
2. Est-ce qu'on va faire le marché ensemble? (oui)
3. Est-ce qu'on va acheter nos provisions à l'épicerie? (non)
4. Est-ce que tu veux inviter Claude et Michelle à dîner? (oui)
5. Est-ce que je peux faire la cuisine ce soir? (oui)
6. Est-ce que tu veux faire la vaisselle après le dîner? (non)
7. Est-ce qu'on peut faire la vaisselle ensemble? (oui)

D. En classe d'anglais. Georges has missed a week of his English class and is asking Monsieur Bacquet how to catch up with his work. Using the cues provided, tell what his teacher suggests.

> **Modèle**   Il faut étudier les verbes? (oui) → **Oui, étudiez-les.**

1. Est-ce qu'il faut étudier cette leçon? (oui)
2. Est-ce qu'il faut acheter ces livres? (oui)
3. Est-ce qu'il faut acheter les cassettes? (non)

4. Est-ce qu'il faut écouter les cassettes? (oui)
5. Est-ce qu'il faut faire cet exercice? (non)
6. Est-ce qu'il faut finir cette leçon aujourd'hui? (non)

Communication

A. Responsabilités. Tell how often you do the following activities.

Exemples   faire la cuisine? → **Je la fais tous les jours.**
Je la fais une fois par semaine.

1. faire la cuisine?
2. faire le ménage?
3. acheter les provisions?
4. ranger votre chambre?
5. faire la vaisselle?
6. écouter vos disques préférés?
7. regarder les dessins animés?
8. faire vos devoirs?

Have students review different
time expressions (e.g., **une fois
par semaine, tous les jours, ne
. . . jamais**).

Have students compare their
answers with those of other
students: **Regarder la télé?
Robert et moi, nous la
regardons chaque soir, mais
Susan ne la regarde jamais.**

B. Questions/Interview. Answer the following questions or use them to interview another student.

1. Est-ce que tu aimes le café? Et le vin? Et la bière?
2. Est-ce que tu écoutes souvent la radio?
3. Est-ce que tu regardes les matchs de football à la télévision?
4. Est-ce que tu as fait tes devoirs pour aujourd'hui?
5. Est-ce que tu aimes les sciences? Et les maths? Et les langues?
6. Est-ce que tu fais souvent la cuisine?
7. Est-ce que tu invites souvent tes amis à dîner?
8. Est-ce que tu as choisi ta future profession?
9. Est-ce que tu as déjà visité l'Europe?

C. Aidez-les! Some first-year students seem to be puzzled in the areas mentioned. What advice would you give them?

Exemple   nos devoirs / les faire maintenant ou plus tard → **Faites-les
maintenant.**

1. nos leçons / les étudier chaque jour ou le jour avant l'examen
2. nos provisions / les acheter dans les petits magasins ou au supermarché
3. la télévision / la regarder tout le temps ou seulement quand il y a des émissions exceptionelles
4. le ménage / le faire chaque semaine ou seulement une fois par mois
5. la vaisselle / la faire tous les jours ou seulement quand c'est nécessaire
6. nos amis / les inviter tout le temps ou seulement pendant le week-end
7. nos devoirs / les faire le matin ou le soir
8. nos vêtements / les ranger ou les laisser sur toutes les chaises

Les pronoms compléments d'objets directs: *me, te, nous, vous*

Présentation

The first- and second-person direct-object pronouns are used only to refer to people.

Les pronoms compléments d'objets directs			
Singular		*Plural*	
me (m')	Ils m'écoutent	**nous**	Ils **nous** écoutent
te (t')	Ils t'écoutent	**vous**	Ils **vous** écoutent

A. Like **le, la,** and **les,** these pronouns are placed directly before the conjugated verb or the infinitive of which they are the object. And as you have already learned, the past participle of a verb in a compound tense like the **passé composé** agrees with the direct-object pronoun.

Elle **te** cherche.   Il ne **m'**a pas regardé(e).
Elle va **nous** emmener chez le médecin.   Paul ne **vous** a-t-il pas aidé(e)(s)?

B. Imperatives follow the same pattern as imperatives with **le, la,** and **les.** But note that in affirmative commands, **me** and **te** become **moi** and **toi.**

Regardez-**moi**!   Ne **me** regardez pas!
Écoute-**moi**!   Ne **m'**écoute pas!
Aidez-**nous**!   Ne **nous** aidez pas!

Point out that **chercher** and **écouter** take a direct object in French.

C. Some useful verbs that are often used with these direct-object pronouns are:

accepter   embêter *(to annoy)*
admirer   insulter
apprécier   intéresser
critiquer   respecter

Substitution: (1) On te demande au téléphone. vous / nous / le / les / me. (2) Ils vous ont invités samedi. nous / te / me / les / le. (3) Ne nous oubliez pas. me / les / la / nous. (4) Ils ne nous ont pas écoutés. me / te / la / vous. (5) Est-ce qu'ils vont nous quitter? me / la / vous / te. (6) Aide-moi. nous / le / les / la. (7) Ne m'embête pas! nous / le / la / les.

Préparation

A. **Est-ce que tu m'aimes?** Danielle's boyfriend is very insecure and needs a lot of reassurance. Give Danielle's answers to his questions.

Modèle   Est-ce que tu m'aimes? → **Mais oui, je t'aime.**

1. Est-ce que tu m'aimes beaucoup?
2. Est-ce que tu m'admires un peu?
3. Est-ce que tu me respectes?

Have students give negative answers: **Est-ce que tu m'aimes?** → **Non, je ne t'aime pas.**

4. Est-ce que tu me trouves amusant?
5. Est-ce que tu vas m'inviter chez tes parents ce week-end?
6. Est-ce que tu vas m'oublier un jour?

B. Les bons amis. Violette is talking about what she and her friends do for each other. Complete her statements.

Modèle   Je les écoute → **et ils m'écoutent.**

1. Je les respecte
2. Je les aide
3. Je les aime bien
4. Je les trouve intéressants
5. Je les laisse tranquilles
6. Je ne les oublie pas
7. Je ne les critique pas
8. Je ne les embête pas

C. Et les autres. Christophe and Michel are not happy with the way their friends are treating them. Complete their statements.

Modèle   Nous les aimons bien → **mais ils ne nous aiment pas.**

1. Nous les respectons
2. Nous les apprécions
3. Nous les écoutons
4. Nous les aidons
5. Nous les trouvons intéressants
6. Nous les admirons

D. L'amitié. Georges has made a list of what he expects from his friends. What would he say to them?

Modèle   m'accepter comme je suis → **Acceptez-moi comme je suis.**
ne pas me critiquer tout le temps → **Ne me critiquez pas tout le temps.**

1. me respecter
2. m'aider de temps en temps
3. m'accepter comme je suis
4. m'inviter quelquefois
5. ne pas m'embêter
6. ne pas me critiquer tout le temps
7. ne pas m'insulter
8. ne pas m'oublier

Communication

A. Questions/Interview. Answer the following questions or use them to interview another student.

1. Est-ce que tes amis t'invitent souvent à aller au cinéma? Et toi, est-ce que tu les invites?
2. Est-ce qu'ils t'aident quand tu as des problèmes? Et toi, est-ce que tu les aides?
3. Est-ce que tes amis te trouvent sympathique?
4. Est-ce que tes professeurs t'apprécient assez?
5. Est-ce qu'ils t'aident quand tu as des problèmes?
6. Est-ce qu'ils t'écoutent quand tu parles? Et toi, est-ce que tu les écoutes?
7. Est-ce qu'ils te critiquent trop souvent? Et toi, est-ce que tu les critiques souvent?

B. Décisions. Indicate whether the following suggestions for summer plans interest you or not.

Exemple   travailler dans un restaurant → **Oui, ça m'intéresse beaucoup.**
                                                            Non, ça ne m'intéresse pas.

1. passer l'été dans un pays où on parle français
2. rester à l'université
3. passer l'été à la plage
4. rester à la maison
5. travailler dans une usine
6. faire du camping
7. étudier dans un pays étranger
8. travailler dans un hôpital

Students could also find out the preferences of other students (**Est-ce que ça vous intéresse de travailler dans un restaurant?**) and report results to the class (**Ça l'intéresse beaucoup**). They could also work in small groups and find common interests (**Travailler dans un restaurant? Ça ne nous intéresse pas beaucoup.**).

C. Avez-vous de l'autorité? What commands would you give to the people in the following situations?

Exemple   Vous faites vos devoirs et votre petit frère vous embête tout
                      le temps. Demandez à votre petit frère de ne pas vous
                      embêter. → **Ne m'embête pas!**

1. Vous ne pouvez pas faire vos devoirs parce qu'ils sont trop difficiles. Demandez à votre camarade de chambre de vous aider.
2. Votre petit(e) ami(e) va partir en vacances. Demandez à votre petit(e) ami(e) de ne pas vous oublier.
3. Vous êtes au café. On vous regarde tout le temps. Demandez à ces gens de ne pas vous regarder.
4. Vous parlez et vos amis ne vous écoutent pas. Demandez à vos amis de vous écouter.
5. Vous avez besoin d'aller à la gare et votre voiture ne marche pas. Demandez à un(e) ami(e) de vous emmener à la gare.

SYNTHÈSE

L'autre solution: Inventer son métier

Si votre *formation* ne vous offre pas les *débouchés* que vous désirez ou si le travail que vous faites ne vous satisfait pas, la solution est *peut-être* d'inventer votre emploi comme l'ont fait ces jeunes Français.

training / job openings

perhaps

Sophie de Menthon
Sophie est fatiguée d'*enseigner* l'anglais à des étudiants qui n'ont pas très envie d'*apprendre*. *Au lieu de* continuer à enseigner, elle choisit de travailler comme enquêtrice dans une agence de publicité. Mais elle n'aime pas beaucoup marcher *non plus*. Elle préfère poser ses questions par téléphone. Ça réussit. Alors, elle a l'idée de *créer* sa propre entreprise de marketing téléphonique. Ses *affaires* marchent si bien que maintenant elle a trente-trois employées qui, comme elle, préfèrent travailler à la maison.

teach

learn / instead of

either
form, create
business

Jean-Luc Garnier

Passer des journées entières sur un *bateau*, c'est un rêve de vacances. | boat
Mais Jean-Luc a réussi à *concilier* son *amour* de la mer et la nécessité | reconcile / love
de gagner sa vie: pendant l'été, il emmène les bateaux *là* où leurs *pro-* | there / owners
priétaires vont passer leurs vacances. Les autres mois de l'année, il
travaille pour des constructeurs de bateaux ou pour des organisateurs
de *courses*. | races

Arnaud de Villars

Arnaud grandit dans un milieu *aisé*. Quand il finit ses études de math- | well-to-do
ématiques supérieures, il entre dans *la marine* comme officier. Mais ce | navy
travail l'*ennuie*. Il accepte un *poste* de mécanicien sur Boeing 707. Un | bores / job, position
jour, il achète un *ballon Montgolfier*. Très vite, il décide de quitter son | hot-air balloon
poste de mécanicien et de créer une école de pilotage de montgolfières.
Les *débuts* ont été difficiles et ses *revenus* continuent à être irréguliers | beginnings / income
mais maintenant il est son propre patron et il n'a pas besoin d'obéir à
des horaires rigides.

Gérard Bayle

Gérard est *diplômé* d'une école supérieure de commerce. Il travaille | graduate
d'abord comme cadre commercial dans une entreprise, mais ce travail | first (of all)
ne le satisfait pas vraiment. Il réfléchit. Il veut gagner de l'argent, c'est
vrai, mais il ne veut pas sacrifier son indépendance. Il *finit par avoir* | ends up having
une idée: créer un centre où les gens peuvent *apporter* les choses qu'ils | bring
veulent *vendre* et où d'autres personnes peuvent les acheter. | sell

Jean-Luc Lefebvre

Jean-Luc est *cuisinier*. Il est employé comme *conseiller technique* pour | cook / technical advisor
l'utilisation du froid dans la conservation des *aliments*. Il veut prouver | food products
que le *surgelé* est un bon système *même* pour les plats difficiles à pré- | quick-freezing / even
parer. Il choisit le soufflé, ce cauchemar des cuisinières. Et il réussit.
Maintenant, il est directeur de sa propre entreprise, La Maison du
Soufflé, qui fabrique 7 000 soufflés surgelés par jour.

Option: Have students play the roles of those mentioned in the **Synthèse**; other students will ask them questions based on the readings.

Extrait et adapté d'un article de *l'Express*.

Compréhension   Indiquez si les phrases suivantes sont vraies ou fausses. Si
le sens de la phrase est faux, corrigez-le.

1. Sophie enseigne l'anglais et elle est très satisfaite de son travail.
2. Elle a créé une entreprise de marketing téléphonique qui marche très bien.
3. Pour gagner sa vie, Jean-Luc travaille dans une usine de construction de bateaux.
4. Arnaud a grandi dans une famille pauvre.
5. Il est content de son nouveau travail parce qu'il n'a pas besoin d'obéir à des horaires rigides.
6. Il préfère être son propre patron.
7. Gérard a fait ses études dans une école de commerce.
8. Il a quitté son poste du cadre commercial parce qu'il ne veut pas sacrifier son indépendance.
9. Jean-Luc Lefebvre est ouvrier dans une usine où on fabrique des soufflés.

NOTES CULTURELLES

Les qualités humaines recherchées par les entreprises

In a recent study, 1500 French businesses were asked what personal qualities they were currently looking for in their new recruits from French universities and what they thought they would be looking for in five years. The results show a remarkable consistency: the ability to communicate was viewed as the most essential quality in both lists. Another related quality, the ability to negotiate and make compromises, moved from fifth to third place.

LE HIT-PARADE DES QUALITÉS

Maintenant		Dans cinq ans	
1ᵉʳ Sens de la communication		Sens de la communication	1ᵉʳ — ability to communicate
2ᵉ Organisation et méthode		Organisation et méthode	2ᵉ
3ᵉ Implication dans l'entreprise		Capacité de négociation	3ᵉ — involvement
4ᵉ Esprit d'innovation		Implication dens l'entreprise	4ᵉ
5ᵉ Capacité de négociation		Esprit d'innovation	5ᵉ
6ᵉ Aptitude au commandement		Aptitude au commandement	6ᵉ — leadership
7ᵉ Capacité à anticiper		Capacité à anticiper	7ᵉ
8ᵉ Étendue de la culture générale		Étendue de la culture générale	8ᵉ — extent, range
9ᵉ Sens de la discipline		Sens de la discipline	9ᵉ

Communication

A. Inventez votre emploi! Alone or with other students, create a job based on your individual or combined talents. Use the guidelines below to assess your possibilities.

Vos qualités:	*Vos aptitudes:*	*Vos préférences:*	*Solution:*
Nous sommes très indépendants, etc.	Nous pouvons parler français, etc.	Le prestige social ne compte pas beaucoup pour nous, mais nous avons besoin d'horaires souples, etc.	Nous pouvons enseigner le français aux enfants le samedi matin.

B. Aidez-les! What suggestions would you give to friends who are in the following situations?

Exemple   à un(e) ami(e) qui n'a pas envie de finir ses études → **Finis d'abord tes études et cherche un métier après.**

1. à un(e) ami(e) qui va bientôt finir ses études
2. à un(e) ami(e) qui veut travailler cet été
3. à un(e) ami(e) qui va rencontrer son futur patron pour la première fois
4. à un(e) ami(e) qui n'est pas satisfait(e) de son emploi présent
5. à un(e) ami(e) qui a de la difficulté à choisir son futur métier

The situation described in this letter is confirmed by recent statistics that predict there will be approximately 4000 jobs for the almost 30,000 graduates from **lettres, droit, et sciences humaines** in France.

C. Courrier du cœur. The following letter was sent to Marcelle Ségal, a well-known French advice columnist. How would you respond?

J'ai vingt-deux ans. Je vais finir mes études l'an prochain. Je vais passer mes examens en juin. Mais je suis pessimiste quand je pense à mon avenir. Quelle profession peut-on trouver avec une formation littéraire? C'est trop tard pour choisir un autre programme et je n'ai pas envie de recommencer mes études. Mes parents possèdent un magasin de vêtements mais le commerce ne m'intéresse pas. Qu'est-ce que je peux faire?

Option: Have students make up letters to Marcelle Ségal, which other students will answer. Suggested for small-group work.

PRONONCIATION

Cognates are easy to recognize in writing, but it is often difficult to recognize them when you hear them and to pronounce them correctly. The following patterns of correspondence between French and English account for a large number of cognates.

A. Many nouns ending in **-é** or **-ie** in French correspond to nouns ending with *-y* in English. These nouns are always feminine. Compare:

sécurité	*security*
liberté	*liberty*
hypocrisie	*hypocrisy*

Repeat the following words:

possibilité   nécessité   autorité   personnalité   partie   écologie

B. French nouns ending in **-isme** correspond to English nouns ending in *-ism*. These nouns are always masculine. Compare:

optimisme	*optimism*
communisme	*communism*

Repeat the following words:

optimisme   pessimisme   racisme   sexisme   féminisme   capitalisme

C. French nouns ending in **-tion** or **-ssion** have counterparts in English with the same endings. In French, however, the endings are pronounced [sjõ], and the nouns are always feminine. Compare:

solution	*solution*
profession	*profession*

Repeat the following words:

promotion   condition   situation   profession   impression   possession

D. Many English nouns identifying professions and ending in *-or* or *-er* have French counterparts that end in **-eur** in the masculine form and **-euse** or **-trice** in the feminine form.
Repeat the following pairs of words:

directeur—directrice   acteur—actrice   danseur—danseuse

E. English nouns ending in *-arian* or *-ary* and adjectives ending in *-ary* or *-ar* often have French counterparts ending in **-aire.**
Repeat the following words:

secrétaire   vétérinaire   salaire   nécessaire   contraire   populaire

F. English adjectives ending in *-al* often have counterparts in French that end in **-el** or **-al.**
Repeat the following words:

personnel   professionnel   essentiel   commercial   régional   social

G. Repeat the following sentences, paying special attention to the sounds
you have been practicing.

1. Il faut respecter les libertés individuelles.
2. Choisissez une profession où il y a de bonnes possibilités de promotion.
3. Ce sont des acteurs et des actrices du Théâtre Populaire.
4. La solution, c'est d'augmenter le salaire de votre secrétaire!

VOCABULAIRE

noms

les professions (voir p. 149)

le travail et d'autres professions

les **affaires** (f) *business*
le **chômage** *unemployment*
le **commerce** *business*
le **cuisinier** *cook*
l'**emploi** (m) *job*
l'**enquêteur** (m), l'**enquêtrice** (f) *pollster*
l'**entreprise** (f) *business*
la **marine** *navy*
le **métier** *profession, trade*
° le **pilote**
le **plombier** *plumber*
le **poste** *job, position*
° la **promotion**
le, la **propriétaire** *owner*
° le **salaire**

d'autres noms

l'**aliment** (m) *food product*
l'**amour** (m) *love*
le **bateau** *boat*
la **course** *race*
le **début** *beginning*
l'**enquête** (f) *survey*
l'**étude** (f) *study*
la **formation** *training*
l'**horaire** (m) *schedule*
° l'**indépendance** (f)
° l'**initiative** (f)
les **loisirs** *leisure activities*
le **milieu** *surroundings*
le **plat** *dish*
° le **prestige**
le **souci** *worry*
° le **système**
° l'**utilisation** (f)

verbes

les verbes de la deuxième conjugaison (voir p. 150)

d'autres verbes

°**accepter**
°**admirer**
aider *to help*
apporter *to bring*
°**apprécier**
apprendre *to learn*

compter *to count*
créer *to create*
critiquer *to criticize*
embêter *to annoy*
ennuyer *to bore*
enseigner *to teach*
gagner *to earn*
°**insulter**
°**intéresser**
°**inventer**
laisser *to leave*
°**organiser**
°**participer**
°**respecter**
satisfaire *to satisfy*
savoir *to know*
vendre *to sell*

adjectifs

°**commercial(e)**
élévé(e) *high*
entier, entière *entire*
humain(e) *human*
libre *free*
°**long, longue**
passionnant(e) *exciting*
°**personnel, personnelle**
propre *own*
°**rigide**
°**social(e)**
souple *flexible*

adverbes

beaucoup *much, a lot*
même *even*
le plus *the most*

divers

alors *so*
au lieu de *instead of*
ça en vaut la peine *it's worth the trouble*
ce que *what*
d'abord *first of all*
là *there*
non plus *not . . . either, neither*
peut-être *perhaps*
qu'est-ce qui *what*
voilà *there is, there are*

CHAPITRE NEUF

9

Français! Achetez et consommez!

Qu'est-ce que tu as acheté?

Jean, je suis très occupée aujourd'hui.
Est-ce que tu peux faire le marché?
Achète :   une baguette
            un kilo de pommes de terre
            trois boîtes de petits pois
            une douzaine d'œufs
            une livre de café
            deux tranches de jambon
            une bouteille d'eau minérale

busy

long, thin loaf of French bread

2.2 pounds (1000 grams)

cans

dozen

pound

slices / ham

bottle

Have students create additional titles for the **Introduction**.

JEAN	Michelle! Michelle! Tu es là?
MICHELLE	Oui. Je suis *en train de* finir mon article pour le *journal*.
JEAN	Regarde. J'ai acheté les provisions pour ce soir.
MICHELLE	Merci, tu es *gentil*! Je vais commencer à préparer le dîner *tout de suite*. Où sont les provisions?
JEAN	Ici, sur la table.
MICHELLE	Tu as acheté du pain?

in the process of / newspaper

nice
immediately

166

JEAN	*Zut!* J'ai oublié d'aller à la boulangerie.	Shoot!
MICHELLE	*Ça ne fait rien.* La boulangerie de la rue Vendôme est ouverte jusqu'à huit heures.	That doesn't matter.
JEAN	Je suis allé à la *charcuterie*.	shop that sells pork products
MICHELLE	Chez qui est-ce que tu es allé?	
JEAN	Chez Saclier, rue Voltaire.	
MICHELLE	Bon. Tu as acheté du jambon?	
JEAN	Non, j'ai acheté un rôti de porc. Le porc est *bon marché* en ce moment.	cheap
MICHELLE	*Voyons*, Jean, un rôti de porc à huit heures du soir, mais tu es *fou!* C'est trop *lourd* à digérer et c'est bien trop long à préparer. Et tu oublies que j'ai *encore* cet article à finir pour demain.	come on crazy / heavy still
JEAN	*Ne t'en fais pas.* Toi, tu finis ton article et moi, je vais préparer une omelette.	Don't worry.

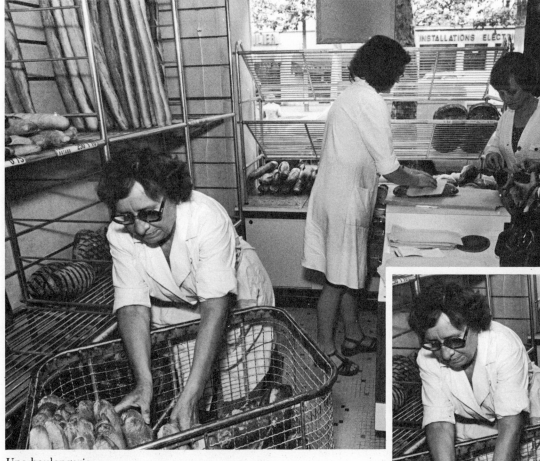

Une boulangerie

Compréhension   Répondez aux questions suivantes selon les renseignements donnés dans le texte.

1. Pourquoi est-ce que Michelle a demandé à Jean de faire le marché aujourd'hui?
2. Qu'est-ce qu'elle a demandé à Jean d'acheter?
3. Qu'est-ce que Michelle est en train de faire?
4. Qu'est-ce que Jean a acheté?
5. Est-ce que Jean a acheté du pain?
6. Pourquoi est-ce qu'il n'a pas acheté de jambon?
7. Pourquoi est-ce Michelle n'est pas contente?
8. Quelle est la profession de Michelle?
9. Est-ce que Michelle travaille beaucoup?
10. Qu'est-ce qu'ils vont manger ce soir?

Have students compare and contrast stores and shopping habits of French and Americans.

NOTES CULTURELLES

Les petits commerçants

In the last twenty-five years, shopping habits in France have undergone many changes. For example, supermarkets have forced many small neighborhood grocery stores out of business, and shopping centers modeled on those in the United States have opened throughout France, especially in large urban areas. Nevertheless, predictions that the small shopkeeper, long an important part of French daily life, would become a relic of the past fortunately have not been confirmed. Instead, recent statistics indicate an increase in the number of small shops (notably those specializing in fresh fruits and vegetables or in clothing) and a return to more traditional habits of daily shopping in the small shops in one's neighborhood. In a recent survey, French people indicated that these small shops, even if higher-priced, had an appeal and charm that was important to them. Economists also believe that unemployment, a desire for greater independence, and improved marketing techniques have also contributed to the renewed strength of the **petit commerçant**.

In addition to small shops and supermarkets, most cities have an outdoor market once or twice a week for the sale of fresh produce, meat, fish, and cheese. Larger

Un marché en plein air

Dans un supermarché

cities have permanent markets (**halles**) where both individuals and restaurants can purchase daily supplies. These markets are generally open from five in the morning until noon. Because these markets and many small neighborhood stores do not provide shopping bags, shoppers have their own mesh shopping bags (**filets**) that can easily be kept in a pocket or purse for use when needed.

Et Vous?

Marchandise et magasins. Tell where you would go to buy the items mentioned.

Exemple   On peut acheter des vêtements dans une boutique de mode, dans un magasin de vêtements, ou dans un grand magasin.

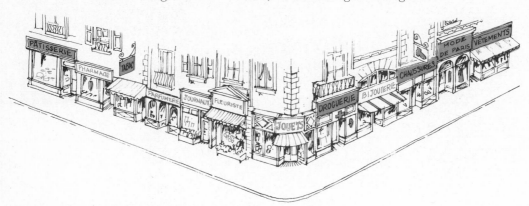

Pour acheter ce que vous voulez, vous pouvez aller . . .

dans une pâtisserie
dans une pharmacie
dans un bureau de tabac
dans une parfumerie
chez un marchand de journaux
chez un fleuriste

dans un magasin de jouets (*toy store*)
dans une droguerie
dans une bijouterie
dans un magasin de chaussures (*shoe store*)
dans une boutique de mode
dans un magasin de vêtements

Et si vous avez de la difficulté à trouver ces magasins, vous pouvez toujours aller dans un grand magasin (*department store*) où on peut acheter toutes sortes de choses.

Les choses que vous pouvez acheter:

des bijoux (m)

des revues (f) et des journaux (m)

des médicaments (m)

des jouets (m)

du dentifrice, du shampooing, du déodorisant et d'autres produits pour l'hygiène personnelle

des fleurs (f)

des vêtements (m)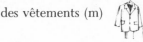

des chaussures (f)

des cigarettes (m)

du parfum

des bonbons (m) et des gâteaux (m)

See note at bottom of opposite page.

Vendre et les autres verbes de la troisième conjugaison

Présentation

Vendre *(to sell)* belongs to a group of French verbs that have infinitives ending in **-re**. The present tense of these verbs is formed by dropping the **-re** from the infinitive and adding the endings shown. The past participle is formed by dropping the **-re** from the infinitive and adding **-u**.

vendre	
je vends	nous vend**ons**
tu vends	vous vend**ez**
il/elle/on vend	ils/elles vend**ent**
passé composé: j'ai vendu	

Remind students that only **-er** verbs drop the **-s** to form the second person singular imperative.

Qu'est-ce qu'on vend dans une droguerie?
Janine a vendu son vieux vélo.
Ne vends pas ta voiture maintenant.

Note that the **-d** is not pronounced in the singular (**il vend**) but is pronounced in the plural (**ils vendent**). In the third person singular inversion, **vend-il**, the liaison sound is [t].

Other **-re** verbs that follow this pattern are:

attendre *to wait for, expect*	Georges attend Alice devant la bijouterie.
entendre *to hear*	Répétez, s'il vous plaît. Je n'ai pas bien entendu.
perdre *to lose*	Ne perdez pas votre temps.
répondre *to answer*	Qu'est-ce que tu as répondu?
rendre + noun *to hand back, to return*	Est-ce que le prof a rendu les examens?
rendre + noun + adjective *to make*	L'argent ne rend pas les gens heureux.
rendre visite à *to visit (a person)*	Ils ont rendu visite à leurs amis canadiens.

Répétition: Je n'entends pas bien, tu n'entends pas bien, etc. **Substitution:** (1) J'attends un taxi. mes parents / mon frère / tu / vous / nous. (2) Nous avons répondu à la question. les étudiants / je / tu / Charles / vous. (3) Est-ce qu'elle perd souvent patience? tu / les professeurs / nous / Maurice.

Possible follow-up: Name a store and have student give items that might be purchased there. Have students indicate that they need a particular item (**J'ai besoin d'acheter du dentifrice.**); another student will indicate where the item can be purchased (**Il faut aller à la droguerie.**). You may also want to point out the difference between the **pharmacie** (which sells drugs and personal hygiene items only) and the **droguerie** (home maintenance and personal hygiene products but no drugs of any kind). Other stores of interest: **une rôtisserie** or **un traiteur** for ready-to-serve foods; **une maroquinerie** (for leather goods and items such as **sacs, valises, parapluies, portefeuilles**); the **kiosque à journaux;** and the **confiserie,** which sells candy only.

Au marché aux puces

Préparation

A. Au marché aux puces. Some merchants at the flea market in Paris are talking about some of the items that they are selling. Tell what they say.

Modèle   Annette / livres → **Annette vend des livres.**

1. les Leclerc / affiches
2. je / vêtements
3. tu / revues
4. Marcel / bijoux
5. nous / chaussures
6. vous / jouets

Point out that both the French and tourists enjoy rummaging through the many and varied items (e.g., old books, furniture, clothing, jewelry) in the **marché aux puces** in Paris and other cities in the hope of finding a bargain or a valuable antique.

B. Où est-ce qu'ils ont attendu? André had planned to go shopping with some friends but forgot to tell them where he would meet them. Using the cues provided, tell where his friends waited.

Modèle   Monique / devant le magasin de vêtements → **Monique a attendu devant le magasin de vêtements.**

1. je / près de la pharmacie
2. nous / devant la charcuterie
3. vous / devant le grand magasin
4. Robert / près du bureau de tabac
5. tu / à côté de la parfumerie
6. les autres / près de la droguerie

Communication

A. Questions/interview. Answer the following questions or use them to interview another student.

1. Est-ce que tu perds souvent patience?
2. Qu'est-ce que tu aimes faire quand tu as du temps à perdre?
3. Est-ce que tu réponds toujours aux lettres de tes amis ou de tes parents?
4. Est-ce que tu attends une lettre aujourd'hui? De qui?
5. Est-ce que tu aimes attendre?
6. Est-ce que l'argent rend les gens heureux?
7. Qu'est-ce que les étudiants peuvent faire pour rendre les professeurs heureux?
8. Qu'est-ce que les professeurs peuvent faire pour rendre les étudiants heureux?
9. Est-ce que tu vas rendre visite à des amis pendant les vacances?

B. Des produits internationaux. Using vocabulary you know, tell what foreign products (e.g., **chaussures, journaux, voitures**) are sold in your city and in what shops.

Exemple   On vend des fromages français et des fromages suisses dans plusieurs supermarchés.

Before completing this activity, it might be helpful to have students first make a list of foreign products that might be sold in American stores.

 Les expressions de quantité

Présentation

A. Most expressions of quantity are followed by **de (d')** alone, rather than by the full partitive article (**de l', de la, du, des**). The most useful of these expressions are:

Option: Introduce the adjectival expressions of quantity **quelques, certain(e)(s), plusieurs.**

Adverbs of quantity
assez de   *enough*
autant de   *as much, as many*
beaucoup de   *much, many, a lot*
combien de   *how much, how many*
moins de   *less, fewer*
peu de   *little, few*
plus de   *more*
tant de   *so much, so many*
trop de   *too much, too many*

Measures of quantity
un verre de   *a glass of*
une livre de   *a pound of*
un kilo de   *a kilo of*
une boîte de   *a box of, a can of*
un litre de   *a liter of*
une bouteille de   *a bottle of*
un peu de   *a little, some*
une tasse de   *a cup of*

Suggestion: Point out that **un peu** is used with mass nouns, **quelques** with count nouns.

Nous n'avons pas assez d'argent.
Il y a beaucoup de magasins dans cette rue.
Combien d'argent as-tu gagné?
Ils ont très peu de légumes aujourd'hui.
Nous n'avons pas autant de travail cette semaine.

B. To indicate that there is no more (not any more) of an item, **ne . . . plus de** is used.

Il n'y a plus de pain.
Non merci, je ne veux plus de vin.

Point out that the **s** in **plus de** is not pronounced when it means *no more*, but can be pronounced when it means *more*.

C. The partitive article is retained in the expressions **la plupart de** (*most, the majority*) and **bien de** (*many*).

La plupart des gens sont satisfaits.
Bien des Français font leur marché tous les jours.

Substitution: (1) J'ai des devoirs à faire. beaucoup / trop / peu / moins / assez. (2) Il y a des haricots verts dans la salade. beaucoup / trop / tant / assez / peu. (3) Je voudrais un verre de vin. une bouteille / deux litres / un peu / cinq bouteilles. (4) J'ai acheté du pain. assez / deux kilos / un peu / beaucoup.

Préparation

A. Inventaire. Before going shopping, Jean and Michelle check to see what items they may need. What do they say?

Modèle   pas beaucoup / café → **Nous n'avons pas beaucoup de café.**

1. assez / pommes de terre
2. un peu / fromage
3. un kilo / pommes
4. pas assez / beurre
5. trois bouteilles / vin
6. beaucoup / légumes
7. pas trop / lait
8. trois boîtes / petits pois

B. Au supermarché. Lynne is now working part-time in a supermarket and wants to tell a French friend about her job. How would she say these sentences in French?

1. I have a lot of work.
2. I have less free time now.
3. I'm drinking too much coffee.
4. I have so many responsibilities.
5. I don't have enough free time.
6. I do not have as many new clothes this year.
7. Most of the time I'm very tired.

Communication

A. La vie universitaire. Using an expression of quantity, make up questions to ask other students about the following topics. Then choose a partner and ask him or her the questions.

Exemples   travail → **Est-ce que tu as beaucoup de travail cette semaine?**
Est-ce que tu as moins de travail cette semaine?

1. devoirs
2. bons professeurs
3. amis sympathiques
4. temps libre
5. examens
6. classes intéressantes
7. travail
8. soucis

B. Votre ville. Using expressions of quantity, describe the following aspects of your town or region.

Exemple   parcs → **Il n'y a pas assez de parcs dans notre ville.**

1. théâtres
2. piscines
3. cinémas
4. bons restaurants
5. cafés
6. choses intéressantes à faire
7. supermarchés
8. musées intéressants

C. Vos achats. Using vocabulary you know and various expressions of quantity, make up a real (or imaginary) shopping list.

Exemple   J'ai besoin d'acheter une bouteille de lait, un kilo de sucre, et une livre de beurre.

Option: Have students create lists for someone with extravagant tastes (**Je vais acheter vingt bouteilles de champagne.**) or a list for a famous person.

 # Le verbe *boire*

Présentation

The verb **boire** *(to drink)* is irregular.

boire	
je **bois**	nous **buvons**
tu **bois**	vous **buvez**
il/elle/on **boit**	ils/elles **boivent**
passé composé: j'ai bu	

Qu'est-ce que vous buvez?
J'aime boire du café le matin.
Nous avons bu une bouteille de champagne.
Bois un peu de lait.

In addition to vocabulary already presented, the following expressions and names of beverages are useful in a French café or restaurant.

Boissons
un apéritif   *before-dinner drink*
un café au lait   *coffee with milk (usually served in the morning)*
un café crème   *coffee with cream*
un café noir   *black coffee*
une carafe de vin   *a carafe of wine*

un chocolat chaud   *hot chocolate*
un citron pressé   *fresh lemonade*
un demi   *mug of draft beer*
un digestif   *after-dinner drink*
une eau minerale   *mineral water*
un expresso   *espresso coffee*

Expressions
On va boire (prendre) un pot (un verre, un coup)?
Apportez-moi un café, s'il vous plaît.
L'addition, s'il vous plaît.
À votre santé!

Let's go have a drink. Shall we have a drink?
Bring me a coffee, please.
The bill (check), please.
Cheers! (To your health!)

Some typical **apéritifs** are Pernod, Cinzano, St. Raphaël, and Martini. Cognac, Benedictine, Chartreuse, and Grand Marnier are popular **digestifs.** Vittel, Vichy, and Perrier are popular **eaux minerales.**

Chez le marchand de vins

Répétition: Je bois du thé, tu bois du thé, etc.
Substitution: (1) Tu bois trop de café. il / nous / je / vous / mes parents / Robert. (2) Nous avons bu du bon vin. je / tu / Claudine et Roger / vous / nous.

Préparation

A. Les pays et leurs boissons. Some international students are talking about typical drinks in their countries. What do they say?

Modèle   En France nous / du vin → **En France nous buvons du vin.**

1. Les Anglais / du thé
2. Au Japon / nous / du saki
3. Aux États-Unis / on / du Coca-Cola
4. En Allemagne / vous / de la bière, n'est-ce pas?
5. Et chez toi en Russie / tu / de la vodka
6. Quand je suis en Italie / je / du vin

B. À la foire des vins. Some French friends have gone to the wine festival in Mâcon and are talking about some of the good wines from different wine-growing regions that they tasted. What do they say?

Modèle   je / un bon Pouilly Fuissé → **J'ai bu un bon Pouilly Fuissé.**

1. mes amis / un bon Côte du Rhône
2. nous / un beaujolais de première classe
3. vous / un rosé de Provence excellent
4. je / un vin d'Alsace formidable
5. Micheline / un bon bourgogne
6. tu / un rosé d'Anjou exceptionnel

You may want to mention the **"routes des vins,"** i.e., wine-tasting circuits during which people are invited to stop in different towns and villages to sample the particular wines of the region.

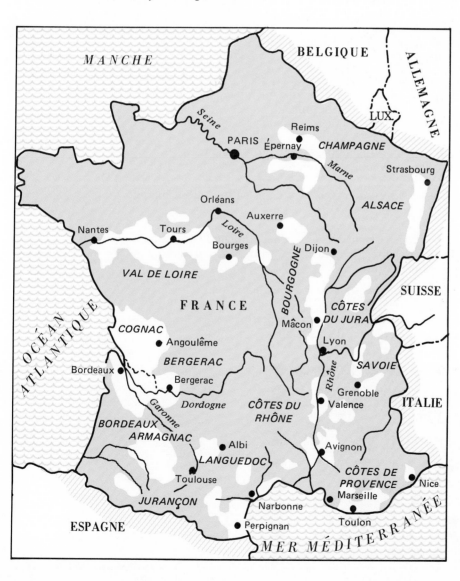

Communication

A. Préférences. Using the scale below, tell how much of the following beverages you generally drink.

Exemple   Je bois trop de café.

pas	peu	assez	beaucoup	trop

1. le café
2. le vin
3. le Coca-Cola
4. le lait
5. l'eau
6. l'eau minérale
7. les jus de fruits
8. la bière

B. Questions/interview. Answer the following questions or use them to interview another student.

1. En général, qu'est-ce que tu bois avec tes repas?
2. Qu'est-ce que tu bois quand tu as très soif? Et quand tu es obligé(e) de passer la nuit à étudier pour un examen?
3. Qu'est-ce que tu bois quand il fait très chaud? Et quand il fait très froid?
4. Est-ce que tu as déjà bu du champagne? Et du vin français?
5. À ton avis, quelle est la boisson préférée des Américains? Et des Français?
6. À ton avis, est-ce que les étudiants boivent trop? Et les Américains en général?

C. Au café français. Get together with several other students. One student will play the role of the waiter (**le garçon**) or waitress (**la serveuse**) and ask you what you want to drink.

Exemple   LE GARÇON: Qu'est-ce que vous buvez aujourd'hui?
           VOUS: Je voudrais un café.
           LE GARÇON: Un café crème ou un expresso?
           VOUS: Un café crème, s'il vous plaît.

Upon completion, have students verify the accuracy of the order taken by the waiter or waitress.

Point out to students that to attract the waiter's attention it is more polite to say **monsieur, s'il vous plaît** than **garçon.**

EAU MINERALE NATURELLE GAZEUSE
DECANTEE ET REGAZEIFIEE AVEC SON PROPRE GAZ
Société Commerciale d'Eaux Minérales du
bassin de Vichy
Saint ~ Yorre
NOUVEAU bouchon à vis

Les pronoms compléments d'objets indirects

The object of a verb can either be direct (**Nous avons vendu** *notre voiture*) or indirect (**Nous avons vendu notre voiture** *à M. Gérard*). Indirect objects are introduced by the preposition **à**: **Je donne les livres à Pierre; Elle parle aux étudiants.** The following indirect object pronouns can replace **à** + a noun:

Les pronoms compléments d'objets indirects	
Singular	*Plural*
me (m')	nous
te (t')	vous
lui	leur

Note that only the third person indirect object pronouns differ from direct object pronouns. **Lui** means either *to him* or *to her;* **leur** means *to them.*

Je parle **à Anne.**	Je **lui** parle.
Je donne le livre **à Paul.**	Je **lui** donne le livre.
Je téléphone **à mes amis.**	Je **leur** téléphone.

A. Indirect object pronouns, like direct object pronouns, are placed directly before the verb of which they are the object.

Il te répond.	Il t'a répondu.	Il va te répondre.
Il ne te répond pas.	Il ne t'a pas répondu.	Il ne va pas te répondre.
Te répond-il?	T'a-t-il répondu?	Va-t-il te répondre?

B. In affirmative commands the indirect object pronoun follows the verb, and **moi** and **toi** replace **me** and **te**. In negative commands, the indirect object pronoun remains in its usual place before the verb, and its form does not change.

Apportez-**moi** votre livre.	Ne **m'**apportez pas votre livre.
Expliquez-**lui** vos problèmes.	Ne **lui** expliquez pas vos problèmes.
Donnez-**leur** votre argent.	Ne **leur** donnez pas votre argent.

Remind students that in the **passé composé**, only when a direct-object pronoun precedes the verb does the past participle agree with it. The past participle never agrees with an indirect-object pronoun (e.g., **Je vous ai parlé, mademoiselle, et je vous ai invitée à danser.**).

Substitution: (1) Jeannette me téléphone le samedi. te / lui / vous / leur. (2) Il ne me parle pas. lui / nous / leur / vous / te. (3) Il m'a apporté une glace. lui / nous / leur / te / vous. (4) Donnez-lui votre adresse. nous / moi / leur / lui. (5) Elle va lui parler. leur / vous / me / te / nous. **Transformation:** Le professeur explique la leçon aux étudiants. → Le professeur leur explique la leçon. (1) Marc téléphone à Suzanne. (2) Nous rendons visite à nos amis anglais. (3) Je parle souvent à mon voisin. (4) Mon frère a vendu sa moto à Georges. (5) Elle a donné de l'argent à Danielle et Richard. (6) Elle a loué son appartement à des Anglais. (7) Téléphone à Henri. (8) Donnez du lait aux enfants. (9) Ne parlez pas aux autres. (9) Michel va expliquer le problème à son patron. (10) Je voudrais donner quelque chose à mes parents.

*C. When both direct and indirect object pronouns occur in the same sentence, they are placed in the following order in all uses except affirmative commands.

me te nous vous	before	le la l' les	before	lui leur

Il me l'a montré.
Je la leur ai expliquée.
Nous ne les lui avons pas vendus.
Ne nous les apporte pas maintenant.

Double-object pronouns are introduced here for the sake of completeness. However, owing to the complexity of the topic and to the fact that use of double-object pronouns can often be circumvented without impeding communication, they are introduced for recognition only.

*D. In affirmative commands the pronouns are separated by hyphens and are placed in the following order:

le la les	before	moi lui nous leur

Expliquez-le-moi.   Ne me l'expliquez pas.
Apportez-les-nous.   Ne nous les apportez pas.
Rendez-le-lui.   Ne le lui rendez pas.
Montrez-les-leur.   Ne les leur montrez pas.

Préparation

A. Générosité. Monsieur Robert, a businessman, has bought presents for his family and employees. Tell what he gave them.

Modèle   à ses parents / un appareil-photo → **Il leur a donné un appareil-photo.**

1. à sa femme / des bijoux
2. à sa fille / des jouets
3. à ses amis / des fleurs
4. à son frère / des disques
5. à ses clients / du vin
6. à ses employés / des chocolats
7. à sa secrétaire / du parfum
8. aux enfants du quartier / des bonbons

B. Conversation. At the end of the day, Jean is asking Michelle about her day. Using the cues provided, give Michelle's answers to Jean's questions.

Modèle   Est-ce que tu as téléphoné à tes parents? (non) → **Non, je ne leur ai pas téléphoné.**

1. Est-ce que tu as montré ton article à ton patron? (oui)
2. Est-ce que mon client suisse m'a téléphoné? (oui)
3. Est-ce qu'il t'a parlé de ses problèmes? (non)
4. Est-ce qu'il va me téléphoner demain? (oui)
5. Est-ce que tes parents vont nous rendre visite dimanche? (non)
6. Est-ce que Paul nous a rendu nos disques? (non)
7. Est-ce que je t'ai rendu ton argent? (oui)
8. Est-ce que Bruno veut nous louer son appartement pour l'été? (oui)

* For recognition only.

C. **Il y a des gens qui changent d'avis comme de chemise.** Jean-Luc is a person who changes his mind frequently. Just after he tells someone to do something, he decides he wants something else. What does he say?

Modèle Apportez-moi un sandwich. → **Ne m'apportez pas de sandwich.**

1. Téléphone-nous ce soir.
2. Achetez-leur un jouet.
3. Parle-moi de tes voyages.
4. Montre-lui tes revues.
5. Donnez-moi ton opinion.
6. Demandez-lui pourquoi elle est triste.
7. Répondez-moi.
8. Vendez-leur votre appareil-photo.

Communication

A. **Interview.** Using the words and phrases provided, make up questions that you will ask another student.

Exemple tes parents / te rendre quelquefois visite à l'université → **Est-ce que tes parents te rendent quelquefois visite à l'université?**

1. tes amis / te téléphoner souvent
2. ta famille / te rendre souvent visite
3. tes amis / te parler de leurs problèmes
4. tes professeurs / te poser des questions difficiles
5. tes amis / t'acheter quelque chose pour ton anniversaire
6. tes amis / te donner quelquefois des conseils

Suggestion: Have students work in small groups and report back their partners' answers.

B. **J'ai une autre suggestion.** A friend has made the following suggestions. Indicate whether you would accept the idea or if you would suggest something else.

Modèle Est-ce que je peux te parler de mes voyages? → **Oui, parle-moi de tes voyages.**
Non, ne me parle pas de tes voyages! Parle-moi de ton travail.

1. Est-ce que je peux te téléphoner ce soir?
2. Est-ce que je peux te montrer mes photos de voyage?
3. Est-ce que je peux te donner mon numéro de téléphone?
4. Est-ce que je peux t'apporter un sandwich?
5. Est-ce que je peux te rendre visite pendant l'été?
6. Est-ce que je peux t'acheter des fleurs?

Il faut profiter de l'occasion

La publicité

Pour vendre, il faut de la publicité. Les produits varient mais le message
final reste toujours le même: achetez et consommez!

    La publicité vous encourage à *dépenser* votre argent et elle vous   spend
donne toujours de bonnes raisons de ne pas attendre.

Soldes de fin d'année!

Profitez de l'occasion!

Prix réduits!

sales / end / take advantage
of / reduced

Quelquefois, elle vous encourage même à *économiser*:   save

Ne laissez pas dormir votre argent. Placez-le.

invest

Si vous n'avez pas l'argent nécessaire pour acheter ce que vous voulez, *empruntez*-le. Les banques sont là pour vous *prêter* tout l'argent que vous voulez.

borrow / lend

loan

Si vous n'avez pas assez d'argent pour acheter une voiture *neuve*, vous pouvez acheter une voiture *d'occasion*.

new
used

Et *si* vous trouvez que c'est trop *cher*, vous pouvez toujours *essayer de marchander*!

if / expensive / try
bargain

La publicité est partout: le long des routes, sur les *murs* des maisons, et dans les journaux et revues:

walls

saucisson *salami*
suivi *followed*
recette *recipe*

Saucisson Loste:
nous avons suivi la recette des charcutiers.

LOSTE

allez vivre à la montagne!..
ou buvez beaucoup d'eau d'evian!

vivre *to live*

Kleenex* Extra Fort.
Le grand mouchoir qui résiste
aux gros rhumes.

fort *strong*
mouchoir *handkerchief*
gros *big*
rhumes *colds*

Pour
les vrais gourmands,
du vrai
chocolat velouté :
Menier au lait

gourmands *people who like to eat*
velouté *velvety*

Compréhension Quel produit est-ce que chacun des slogans suivants décrit
le mieux? (*Which product does each of the following slogans best describe?*)

1. Préparé avec de la viande de porc de première qualité.
2. Pour rester jeune, buvez un grand verre d'eau chaque matin.
3. Un mouchoir qui résiste au rhume, c'est un mouchoir irrésistible.
4. Vous n'avez pas besoin d'avoir soif pour apprécier notre bière.
5. Essayez notre chocolat. Il a un goût riche et délicat qui encourage la
   gourmandise.

Follow-up: Have students prepare
additional slogans for the same
products.

Have students find ads for the
same product in both French and
in English and compare and
contrast the approach used in
each.

NOTES CULTURELLES

La publicité

In magazines and newspapers, on buses and subways, at the movies, on the radio, and even on television, the French, like Americans, are increasingly subject to a constant stream of advertising. Statistics indicate that there is more advertising for household products and for beauty and personal-hygiene products than for other products. Surprisingly, a relatively small percentage of advertising is for alcoholic beverages, food, tobacco, cars, and leisure or travel activities.

Advertising in France tends to be more descriptive or intellectually oriented than in the United States. Advertisers for certain goods such as wines and beer often focus on the long history and tradition or the superior quality of their products rather than on the social benefits or attractiveness that they bestow.

Although consumer protection agencies are not as common in France as in the United States, false advertising is prohibited by law and severe penalties are imposed on guilty parties.

Communication

A. **Soyez persusasif(-ive).** Using words and phrases from the *Synthèse* and other vocabulary that you know, create individually or in small groups short advertisements for real or imaginary products.

B. **Au marché.** Make a shopping list and then role-play a trip to the market with another student or group of students. One student will play the role of a difficult customer; another student will play the role of a person trying very hard to sell the merchandise. Useful sentences include:

Client(e)
Je voudrais une bouteille de ___.
J'ai besoin de trois kilos de ___.
C'est combien?
Qu'est-ce que c'est?
Est-ce que les _____ sont bon marché?
Je voudrais des _____ .
?

Marchand(e)
Que désirez-vous?
Les _____ coûtent _____ le kilo.
Le _____ coûte _____ le litre.
Nous n'avons pas de _____ mais nous avons _____ .
Nous n'avons pas beaucoup de _____ aujourd'hui mais ils (elles) vont arriver demain.
Avez-vous besoin de _____ ?
Avez-vous assez de _____ ?
?

C. **Cherchez!** Using the suggestions provided, make up questions to find out who in your class does the following things.

Exemple   vendre ses livres à la fin de l'année → **Est-ce que tu vends tes livres à la fin de l'année?**

1. préférer acheter des livres d'occasion
2. préférer acheter des livres neufs
3. prêter sa voiture à ses amis
4. boire plus de cinq verres de lait par jour
5. boire du thé avec son petit déjeuner
6. avoir assez de temps libre
7. faire presque tout son marché dans les petits magasins de son quartier
8. dépenser trop d'argent pendant le week-end
9. essayer toujours de rendre ses devoirs à temps
10. rendre les choses qu'on lui prête
11. emprunter souvent les livres des autres
12. avoir beaucoup de choses intéressantes à faire cette semaine

Option: Prepare a ditto on which you put a grid that includes each of the items in Activity C. After setting a time limit, have students circulate and ask each other questions until they have one or several names in each box. Students can also report back their findings.

PRONONCIATION

The letter **e** (without accent marks) is usually pronounced [ə], as in the following words:

le, de, me, ce, je, demain, regarder

The mute [ə] is not always pronounced, however. Whether it is pronounced or not depends upon its position in a word or group of words and upon its "phonetic environment." The patterns are:

A. The mute [ə] is not pronounced:

1. At the end of a word:

   ouverté   chancé   voituré   anglaisé

2. When it is preceded by only one consonant sound:

   samédi   tout dé suite   seulément

   Listen and repeat:

achéter	chez lé marchand
boulangérie	ça né fait rien
épicérie	en cé moment
heureusément	un kilo dé pain
tout lé monde	je n'ai pas lé temps

B. The mute [ə] is pronounced:

1. When it is preceded by two consonant sounds and followed by a third:
vendredi   quelque chose   mon propre patron

> Listen and repeat:

mercredi	pour demain
quelquefois	ça marche bien
premier	faire le marché
votre livre	pomme de terre
notre voiture	une autre personne

2. When it is at the beginning of a word or an utterance:

demain   regardez   le marché   ce journal

C. In fast speech, the mute [ə] may be dropped even at the beginning of an utterance. This is especially true of the pronoun **je**. Listen and compare:

Careful speech	**Fast speech**
je mange [ʒəmãʒ]	jé mange [ʒmãʒ]
je réponds [ʒərepõ]	jé réponds [ʒrepõ]
je suis [ʒəsyi]	jé suis [ʃsyi]*
je pense [ʒəpãs]	jé pense [ʃpãs]*

> In fast, informal speech the **ne** of the negative may even be omitted entirely.

Careful Speech	**Fast, Informal Speech**
ça né fait rien	ça fait rien
je n'ai pas lé temps	j'ai pas lé temps
ce n'est pas possible	c'est pas possible
il n'a pas oublié	il a pas oublié
je né sais pas	j(e) sais pas

D. Repeat the following sentences, paying special attention to the mute e's.

  1. Est-cé que ça marche bien en cé moment?
  2. Je né sais pas cé que jé vais fairé samédi.
  3. Jé vais achéter quelque chosé à la bouchérie ou à l'épicérie.
  4. Heureusément, il reste du rôti dé veau et un kilo dé pain.
  5. Tout lé monde fait lé marché lé vendredi ou le samédi.

---

* Before an unvoiced consonant [ʒ] becomes [ʃ].

VOCABULAIRE

noms

l'alimentation

l'**apéritif** (m)   *before-dinner drink*
la **baguette**   *long, thin loaf of French bread*
la **boîte**   *can*
le **bonbon**   *candy*
le **café au lait**   *coffee with milk*
le **café crème**   *coffee with cream*
le **café noir**   *black coffee*
° la **carafe**
le **demi**   *mug of draft beer*
le **digestif**   *after-dinner drink*
° l'**expresso** (m)
le **goût**   *taste*
le **jambon**   *ham*
° l'**omelette** (f)
les **provisions** (f)   *groceries*
la **recette**   *recipe*
le **saucisson**   *salami*

les magasins (m) (voir p. 170)

d'autres noms

l'**addition** (f)   *bill*
l'**article** (m)
le **bijou**   *jewel*
la **charcuterie**   *shop that sells pork products*
la **chaussure**   *shoe*
le **dentifrice**   *toothpaste*
le **déodorisant**   *deodorant*
la **douzaine**   *dozen*
° l'**hygiène** (f)
le **jouet**   *toy*
le **journal**   *newspaper*
la **livre**   *pound*
le **médicament**   *medicine*
° le **message**
le **mouchoir**   *handkerchief*
le **mur**   *wall*
le **parfum**   *perfume*
le **prix**   *price*
le **produit**   *product*
le **rhume**   *cold*
la **solde**   *sale*
° le **shampooing**
la **table**
le **vêtement**   *article of clothing*
° la **vitamine**

verbes

verbes de la troisième conjugaison (voir p. 171)

d'autres verbes

boire   *to drink*
dépenser   *to spend (money)*
économiser   *to save*
emprunter   *to borrow*
essayer   *to try*
marchander   *to bargain*
prêter   *to lend*
profiter de   *to take advantage of*
vivre   *to live*

adjectifs

bon marché   *cheap*
cher, chère   *expensive*
° **final(e)**
fort(e)   *strong*
fou, folle   *crazy*
gazeux, gazeuse   *effervescent, carbonated*
gentil, gentille   *nice*
gros, grosse   *big*
lourd(e)   *heavy*
neuf, neuve   *new*
occupé(e)   *busy*
prêt(e)   *ready*
réduit(e)   *reduced*

divers

les expressions de quantité (voir p. 173)

d'autres expressions

À votre santé   *Cheers! (To your health!)*
d'occasion   *used*
encore   *still*
en train de   *in the process of*
Ne t'en fais pas.   *Don't worry.*
tout de suite   *right away*
Voyons!   *Come on!*
Zut!   *Shoot!*

CHAPITRE DIX

La vie n'est pas toujours facile

10

INTRODUCTION

Mohammed Alimi

Il y a un grand nombre de Nord-Africains (Algériens, Tunisiens et Marocains) qui travaillent en France. Certains ont fait des études, ont de bons emplois et sont bien intégrés à la vie française. D'autres n'ont jamais appris un métier et sont obligés d'accepter *n'importe quel* travail (surtout dans la construction et les *travaux publics*). Dans ce cas, leur vie n'est pas toujours facile. Ici, Mohammed Alimi, un jeune Algérien, parle avec un reporter.

any (i.e., anything they can find) / public works

LE REPORTER   Pourquoi avez-vous quitté l'Algérie?

MOHAMMED   J'ai quitté mon pays pour *venir* travailler en France. Mon *père est mort* en 1967, cinq ans après l'indépendance de l'Algérie. J'ai été obligé de travailler pour nourrir toute la famille. J'ai travaillé comme

to come
father / died

Dans le métro parisien

	manœuvre dans le port d'Alger pendant *plusieurs* années. Mais j'ai eu un accident et je suis resté *quelques* mois à l'hôpital.	laborer / several a few
LE REPORTER	Qu'est-ce que vous avez fait quand vous *êtes sorti* de l'hôpital?	left
MOHAMMED	J'ai cherché du travail, mais sans succès. Alors, j'ai décidé de partir en France. Je suis arrivé à Marseille en 1975.	
LE REPORTER	Est-ce que vous avez eu beaucoup de difficulté à trouver du travail?	
MOHAMMED	Oui, j'ai été obligé d'attendre plusieurs mois. *Finalement*, j'ai trouvé du travail dans les travaux publics, comme manœuvre.	finally
LE REPORTER	Vous n'avez pas pu trouver un travail plus facile?	
MOHAMMED	Non, parce que je n'ai pas d'*instruction*. J'ai commencé à *apprendre* à lire et à écrire seulement après mon arrivée en France. Ce n'est pas facile à mon âge, surtout quand on travaille du matin au soir. Mais maintenant je peux lire le journal sans trop de difficulté.	education to learn

LE REPORTER Est-ce que vous êtes satisfait de votre vie ici?

MOHAMMED Oui et non. *À mon avis*, pour avoir un travail décent, il faut avoir de l'instruction. Je suis fatigué de faire le travail que les autres ne veulent pas faire. Mais avec tout le *chômage* qu'il y a, j'ai *quand même* de la chance d'avoir du *boulot*.

in my opinion

unemployment / all the same
work (slang)

LE REPORTER Est-ce que vous regrettez votre décision de venir en France?

MOHAMMED Non, mais je ne veux pas rester manœuvre toute ma vie. J'*envoie* une partie de mon salaire à ma famille en Algérie et j'économise le reste pour pouvoir apprendre un vrai métier.

send

Have students write a short description of Mohammed Alimi.

Compréhension   Selon les renseignements donnés, est-ce que les phrases suivantes sont vraies ou fausses? Corrigez le sens de la phrase s'il est faux.

1. Mohammed Alimi a quitté son pays parce qu'il aime voyager.
2. Après la mort de son père, il a été obligé de travailler pour nourrir toute sa famille.
3. Quand il est sorti de l'hôpital, il a trouvé du travail sans difficulté.
4. Mohammed est arrivé à Marseille le jour de l'indépendance de l'Algérie.
5. Après son arrivée en France, Mohammed a eu beaucoup de difficulté à trouver du travail.
6. Mohammed a finalement trouvé du travail dans une banque.
7. C'est difficile pour Mohammed de trouver un bon travail parce qu'il n'a pas d'instruction.
8. C'est seulement après son arrivée en France qu'il a commencé à apprendre à lire.
9. Mohammed n'a pas envie de rester manœuvre toute sa vie.
10. Mohammed envoie tout son argent à sa famille.

Carrières & Emplois

---

* **Envoyer** is an irregular verb whose present tense forms are: **j'envoie, tu envoies, il/elle/on envoie; nous envoyons; vous envoyez; ils/elles envoient. Renvoyer** *(to send back;* also, *to fire somebody)*, **essayer**, and **payer** follow this same pattern.

NOTES CULTURELLES

L'Algérie

Algeria, along with two other countries in
North Africa (Morocco and Tunisia), was
French territory during French colonial days.
The country remained under French control
until 1954 when Algerian nationalists began
fighting for independence. After a long and
difficult war, which bitterly divided French
public opinion, President Charles de Gaulle
granted Algeria its independence in 1962.
The peace accords gave Algerians the option
of retaining French citizenship and provided
for continued economic cooperation between
France and Algeria. The majority of the
1,500,000 European settlers, nicknamed
pieds noirs by the Arabs because they wore
black shoes instead of sandals, elected to
return to Europe. Since 1962, large numbers
of Algerians have also emigrated to France.
Although many are engaged in various
professions, a large number work as unskilled
laborers, especially in large urban areas. It is
not uncommon for them to send part of their
income back to North Africa to support their
families. In addition to their contributions to
the French work force, the presence of North
Africans is evidenced in other ways. Because
most Arabs are devout Moslems, many
French cities now have mosques. Arab
restaurants and grocery stores are also
common in large cities, especially in Paris.
The feelings of the French toward North
Africans living in France are a mixture of
guilt, because of the economic exploitation

Un village algérien

undergone by the North Africans, and
mistrust because of their different life-style
and high crime rate.

Une boucherie musulmane à Paris

Additional family members that can be introduced are: **beau-père, belle-mère** (father-in-law, mother-in-law), **arrière grands-parents** (great grandparents), etc. The addition of **beau** and its variations to family names can also indicate step relationships. Some familiar forms used for family members are: **pépé (grand-père), mémé (grand-mère), tonton (oncle),** and **tatan (tante).**

Et vous?

A. La famille de Mohammed Alimi. After looking at the pictures and the descriptions of Mohammed's family, answer the questions according to the information given.

Son grand-père paternel. Il est encore *en vie* et habite à Ténès.

Sa grand-mère paternelle. Elle est morte cette année.

Ses grands-parents maternels. Ils habitent dans un petit village près d'Alger.

alive

Son père qui est mort en 1967.

Sa mère avec ses trois frères et sa sœur. Deux de ses frères travaillent en France; l'autre fait son service militaire. Il a aussi un *neveu* et une *nièce* qui ne sont pas sur la photo.

nephew / niece

Son *oncle* Saïd. Il a émigré en France en 1963. Maintenant il est marié à une Française et ils ont deux enfants.

Son oncle Nasra et sa *tante* Nabila. Son oncle est artisan et il a une boutique dans la Casbah. Son cousin Tahar est encore au lycée et sa cousine Djenat fait des études de droit à l'université.

Fatima, sa fiancée. Il l'a *rencontrée* pendant sa dernière visite en Algérie.

uncle / aunt
met

Questions:

1. Est-ce que ses grands-parents paternels sont encore en vie?
2. Où habitent ses grands-parents maternels?
3. Combien de frères et de sœurs est-ce qu'il a?
4. Que font ses frères?
5. Combien de nièces et de neveux est-ce qu'il a?
6. Où habite son oncle Saïd?
7. Que fait son oncle Nasra?
8. Qu'est-ce que sa cousine Djenat étudie?
9. Quel est le nom de sa fiancée?
10. Quand est-ce que Mohammed l'a rencontrée?

B. Votre famille. Describe your family including information such as age, profession, appearance, personality, etc. You might also want to describe a typical French family, an imaginary family, or the family of a well-known person.

     ## Les adverbes

Présentation

A. Most French adverbs are formed by adding **-ment** to an adjective. This process is similar to the addition of *-ly* to many English adjectives to form adverbs. Most adverbs are formed according to the following rules:

1. Add **-ment** to the masculine singular form of any adjective that ends in a vowel.

facile	→ facilement	vrai	→ vraiment
sincère	→ sincèrement	poli	→ poliment

2. Add **-ment** to the feminine singular form of any adjective whose masculine singular form ends in a consonant.

parfait, parfaite → parfaitement
impulsif, impulsive → impulsivement
heureux, heureuse → heureusement
traditionnel, traditionnelle → traditionnellement
premier, première → premièrement
franc, franche → franchement *(frankly)*

3. If the masculine singular form of an adjective ends in **-ent** or **-ant**, replace the **-ent** with **-emment**, or the **-ant** with **-amment**, to form the corresponding adverb. In both cases the pronunciation of the adverb ending is the same: [amã].

patient → patiemment
intelligent → intelligemment
constant → constamment

B. There are certain common adverbs, a number of which you already know, that are not formed from adjectives:

aujourd'hui	souvent	vite *(quickly)*	très
demain	toujours	bien	peu
hier	assez	mal *(badly)*	partout
déjà	beaucoup	aussi	là-bas *(over there)*
quelquefois	dur *(hard)*	pas encore *(not yet)*	

C. Adverbs can be used in several positions within a sentence:

1. Adverbs usually follow immediately a verb in a simple tense, such as the present tense.

Michel parle constamment.
Jacqueline attend patiemment la fin de la classe.
Est-ce que le professeur parle trop vite?

2. Short adverbs usually come between the auxiliary verb and the past participle of a verb in a compound tense, such as the **passé composé.** Adverbs that end in **-ment,** however, often follow the past participle.

> Il a déjà fini son devoir.
> Nous n'avons pas bien étudié la leçon.
> Marc a répondu impulsivement.
> Mohammed a finalement trouvé du travail.

3. Adverbs of time and place usually are placed at the beginning or end of a sentence.

> Habib ne travaille pas aujourd'hui.
> Hier, un des manœuvres a eu un accident.

Transformation: Donnez l'adverbe qui correspond à chacun des adjectifs suivants. 1. difficile 2. final 3. modeste 4. courageux 5. actif 6. impulsif 7. intelligent 8. patient 9. constant 10. traditionel 11. exceptionnel 12. vrai

Préparation

Conversation. Mohammed Alimi is talking with a reporter. Give his answers to the reporter's questions.

Modèle   Vous êtes content de votre travail? (oui . . . assez) → **Oui, je suis assez content de mon travail.**

1. Vous parlez français? (oui . . . bien)
2. Vous êtes fatigué ce soir? (oui . . . vraiment)
3. Vous avez trouvé du travail? (oui . . . finalement)
4. Vous retournez en Algérie? (oui . . . quelquefois)
5. Vous allez en Algérie cet été? (oui . . . probablement)
6. Vous envoyez de l'argent à votre famille? (oui . . . souvent)
7. Vous êtes marié? (non . . . pas encore)
8. Vous aimez votre appartement? (non . . . pas vraiment)
9. Vous rêvez de retourner en Algérie? (oui . . . constamment)
10. Vous avez envie d'apprendre un métier? (oui . . . sérieusement)

Communication

A. Opinions. To express your opinions choose one of the adverbs provided and, if necessary, make the sentence negative.

Options: Use as direct questions or adapt for directed dialogue (**Demandez à David s'il téléphone souvent à ses amis,** etc.).

1. Mon professeur de français parle . . .
   bien / vite / tout le temps
2. Mes amis et moi, nous parlons français . . .
   rarement / souvent / tout le temps
3. Je suis . . . fatigué(e).
   constamment / assez / très / rarement / un peu
4. J'ai tendance à parler trop . . .
   impulsivement / franchement / vite / souvent
5. L'année dernière, j'ai . . . travaillé.
   beaucoup / bien / mal / trop
6. Je téléphone . . . à mes amis.
   souvent / rarement / quelquefois / tous les soirs

B. La vie d'un(e) étudiant(e). The life of a student is not always easy. Make up sentences describing the problems that students face. Use an adverb in each of your sentences.

Exemples   Mes camarades de chambre parlent constamment au téléphone. Les professeurs sont quelquefois sévères.

Suggested for individual or small-group writing. Have students share their sentences. Students can also use adverbs to describe the life of Mohammed Alimi.

 ## Les verbes conjugués comme *dormir*

Présentation

The present tense forms of several **-ir** verbs like **partir** *(to leave)* and **dormir** *(to sleep)* do not follow the regular pattern of second conjugation verbs like **choisir**:

Option: Contrast verbs like **dormir** with those like **finir**.

dormir	
je dors	nous dormons
tu dors	vous dormez
il/elle/on dort	ils/elles dorment
passé composé: j'ai dormi	

Ne dormez pas en classe.
Est-ce que tu as bien dormi?

Other verbs that follow this pattern are:

partir* *to leave (opposite of* arriver)   Nous partons en vacances jeudi.
sortir* *to go out, to leave (opposite of* entrer)   Est-ce que tu sors avec des amis ce soir?
sentir *to smell, to feel*   Ça sent bon.
servir *to serve*   À quelle heure est-ce qu'on sert le dîner?

Substitution: (1) Elle ne dort pas très bien. je/vous/Jeanne/mon mari/nous (2) Nous avons servi du gâteau. Suzanne / je / leurs amis / vous. **Transformation:** Tu dors bien. → Vous dormez bien. (1) Tu pars demain. (2) Il part pour la France. (3) Tu sers le dessert. (4) Pourquoi est-ce qu'elle part demain? (5) Je ne sors pas ce soir. (6) Ce fromage sent bon.

Préparation

Il y a des gens qui ont de la chance! André, a well-to-do and rather arrogant bachelor, is comparing his life-style with that of his married friends Josette and François. Using the cues given, formulate their answers to his statements.

Modèle   Moi, le dimanche, je dors jusqu'à midi. Et vous? (seulement jusqu'à neuf heures) → **Nous, nous dormons seulement jusqu'à neuf heures.**

1. Le matin, je pars à mon travail à dix heures. Et vous? (à sept heures et demie)
2. Moi, je sors chaque fois que j'ai envie de sortir. Et vous? (seulement une ou deux fois par mois)
3. La semaine prochaine, je vais sortir tous les soirs. Et vous? (samedi soir)
4. Quand j'invite mes amis, je sers du champagne. Et vous? (du vin rouge)

* **Partir** and **sortir** are verbs of motion conjugated with **être** in the **passé composé** (see p. 199).

5. Chaque année, je pars en vacances avec mes amis. Et vous? (avec nos enfants)
6. Je dors souvent jusqu'à dix ou onze heures du matin. Et vous? (rarement)

Communication

Questions/interview. Answer the following questions or use them to interview another student.

Options: (1) Written. (2) Oral— Ask questions or adapt for directed dialogue. (3) Have students work in small groups and report back their partners' responses.

1. Est-ce que tu dors jusqu'à midi le samedi ou le dimanche?
2. Est-ce que tu dors bien ou mal quand tu vas avoir un examen?
3. Est-ce que tu as bien dormi hier soir? Pendant combien de temps as-tu dormi?
4. Est-ce que tu sors souvent le vendredi soir? Et pendant la semaine?
5. Le matin, à quelle heure est-ce que tu pars pour l'université?
6. Est-ce que tu vas partir en vacances cette année? Si oui, où est-ce que tu vas aller?
7. Est-ce qu'on sert souvent des choses que tu aimes au restaurant universitaire?
8. Quand tu invites des amis à dîner, qu'est-ce que tu sers comme boisson? Comme entrée? Comme dessert?

 # Les verbes conjugués comme *venir*

Présentation

The verb **venir** *(to come)* is irregular:

venir	
je **viens**	nous **venons**
tu **viens**	vous **venez**
il/elle/on **vient**	ils/elles **viennent**
passe composé: je suis venu(e)*	

Il vient d'Alger.
Venez ici.
Je suis venu en France pour travailler.

A. Other verbs similar to **venir** are:

appartenir à   *to be a member of, to belong to*   Nous appartenons au club franco-américain.

devenir*   *to become*   Les conditions de vie deviennent difficiles.

obtenir   *to obtain, to get*   Il a finalement obtenu son diplôme.

prévenir   *to announce, to warn*   Prévenez-moi si vous ne pouvez pas venir ce soir.

retenir   *to hold back, to reserve (a seat, a room)*   J'ai retenu deux places dans l'avion Paris-Alger.

revenir*   *to come back, to return*   Revenez plus tard. Il n'y a pas de travail maintenant.

tenir à   *to really want to, to insist, to really care for*   Est-ce que tu tiens à apprendre un métier?
          Elle tient beaucoup à sa famille.

Introduce idiomatic **tiens/tenez** *(say, hey).*

* **Venir**, **revenir**, and **devenir** are conjugated with **être** in the **passé composé** (see p. 199).

B. Venir de, when followed by an infinitive, means *to have just done* something.

Je viens de trouver du travail.   *I just found a job.*
Nous venons d'arriver d'Algérie.   *We just arrived from Algeria.*

You have now seen three ways to express actions that relate closely to present time: (1) **aller** + infinitive is used to express an action that is about to take place: **Je vais servir le dîner**; (2) **être en train de** + infinitive is used to express an action in the process of taking place: **Je suis en train de servir le dîner**; (3) **venir de** + infinitive is used to express an action that has just taken place: **Je viens de servir le dîner**.

Substitution: (1) Marcel vient d'arriver. vous/je/Monsieur et Madame Dupont/nous. (2) Quand reviennent-ils de vacances? tu/vous/vos amis/Chantal. (3) Ils ont obtenu des résultats intéressants. nous/je/le médecin/tu.
Transformation: Mettez les formes des verbes au pluriel. À quelle heure reviens-tu? → À quelle heure revenez-vous? (1) Elle vient de Toulouse. (2) Je reviens de mon cours de français. (3) Tu deviens paresseux. (4) Est-ce qu'il appartient à votre groupe de discussion? (5) Je ne tiens pas particulièrement à ce disque. (6) Préviens la police.

Préparation

A. Tu es d'où? Some North African students are talking about where they are from. What do they say?

Modèle   Habib / Carthage en Tunisie → **Habib vient de Carthage en Tunisie.**

1. je / Casablanca au Maroc
2. Nasra / Oran en Algérie
3. vous / Sousse en Tunisie
4. tu / Fez au Maroc
5. nous / Marrakech au Maroc
6. Saïd et Mohammed / Ténès en Algérie

B. Vous êtes prêts? Some friends are getting ready for a trip to Tunisia and Morocco. Using the model as a guide, tell what they say.

Modèle   Est-ce que Michel a retrouvé son passeport? → **Oui, il vient de retrouver son passeport.**

1. Est-ce que tu as retenu nos chambres d'hôtel?
2. Est-ce que vous avez fait vos valises?
3. Est-ce que Georges est allé à la banque?
4. Est-ce que vous avez acheté vos billets d'avion?
5. Est-ce que Caroline a retrouvé son appareil-photo?
6. Est-ce que tu as obtenu ton passeport?

C. À l'agence de voyages. Souad works at a travel agency in Casablanca and is translating what an English-speaking tour guide tells her boss. What does she say?

1. My secretary came back yesterday.
2. She's in the process of reserving some hotel rooms.
3. She's also going to call the restaurant.
4. I just talked with our office in Paris.
5. The weather is becoming impossible.

Communication

A. Questions/interview. Answer the following questions or use them to interview another student.

Suggestion: Have students work in small groups and write summary of partners' answers.

1. De quelle ville est-ce que tu viens?
2. De quel pays ta famille vient-elle?
3. À ton avis, est-ce que la vie à l'université devient plus facile après la première année?
4. Est-ce que tes études deviennent plus faciles ou plus difficiles?
5. Est-ce que tu vas revenir à cette université l'an prochain?
6. Quand est-ce que tu vas obtenir ton diplôme?
7. À quels clubs ou groupes est-ce que tu appartiens?
8. Est-ce que tu tiens beaucoup à ton indépendance?
9. Quels sont les projets que tu tiens à accomplir dans ta vie?

B. Points communs. Interview other students in your class in order to find students who fit the following descriptions.

Suggested as whole-class activity.

Trouvez des étudiants:
1. qui viennent de la même ville
2. qui appartiennent au même club ou groupe
3. qui tiennent à devenir célèbres ou riches
4. qui viennent de passer un examen
5. qui vont obtenir leur diplôme cette année

 ## Les verbes conjugués avec l'auxiliaire *être*

Présentation

Like **aller** and **rester**, certain verbs indicating motion or transition are conjugated with **être** in the **passé composé**.

Option: Introduce acronym "Dr. Mrs. Vandertrampp" as device to help students remember **être** verbs.

aller *to go*	venir *to come*
arriver *to arrive*	partir *to leave*
entrer (dans) *to enter*	sortir *to go out, to leave*
monter *to go up*	descendre *to go down*
naître *to be born*	mourir *to die*

rester *to stay*
rentrer *to return home*
revenir *to come back*
retourner *to go back*
tomber *to fall*
tomber malade *to get sick*
devenir *to become*
passer *to come by, to go by*

Substitution: (1) Nous sommes rentrés à midi. partis / venus / arrivés / descendus / sortis / entrés / passés / revenus. (2) Elles ne sont pas encore parties. arrivées / revenues / sorties / rentrées / venues. (3) En quel mois est-ce que ta sœur est née? tu / vous / ta mère / Monique. (4) Pourquoi es-tu retourné à Alger? vous / tes amis / nous / ton père.

Transformation: Je viens à huit heures. → Je suis venu(e) à huit heures. (1) Nous retournons en Europe. (2) Il part à six heures. (3) Est-ce que vous entrez? (4) Pourquoi ne viens-tu pas? (5) À quelle heure arrivent-elles? (6) Où est-ce que nous descendons? (7) Il tombe malade.

A. Like **aller** and **rester**, the past participles of verbs conjugated with **être** agree in number and gender with their subjects. All past participles of these verbs are regular except **naître** → **né; devenir** → **devenu; revenir** → **revenu; venir** → **venu; mourir** → **mort**

Elle est entrée dans une casbah.
Les enfants sont déjà montés dans leur chambre.
Albert Camus est né en Algérie.
Elle est morte l'année dernière.
Pierre et Jacqueline sont rentrés à quatre heures du matin.
Je suis tombé malade.
Ton père n'est pas encore revenu de Tunis?

B. Note that the verbs conjugated with **être** are intransitive: they do not have direct objects. Several of these verbs can also be transitive. They are then conjugated with **avoir** and take on a slightly different meaning.

Nous sommes passés par Marseille.   *We passed through Marseilles.*
Nous avons passé trois mois à Marseille.   *We spent three months in Marseilles.*

Il est monté dans sa chambre.   *He went up to his room.*
Il a monté ses valises.   *He took his suitcases upstairs.*

Elle est sortie de la maison.   *She left the house.*
Elle a sorti sa voiture du garage.   *She took her car out of the garage.*

Je suis descendu de l'autobus.   *I got off the bus.*
J'ai descendu l'avenue.   *I went down the street.*

Un souk à Fez, au Maroc

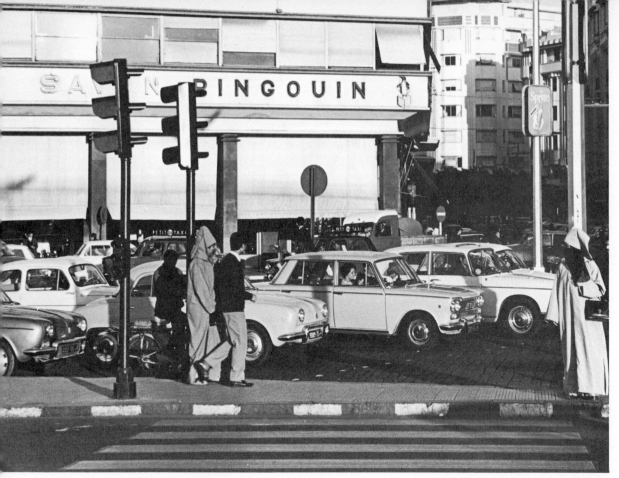

Une rue de Casablanca, au Maroc

Préparation

A. Il y a des gens qui travaillent . . . The driver of a sightseeing bus in Casablanca is reporting what happened today. Using the cues provided, tell what he says.

Modèle   je / arriver à l'hôtel à midi → **Je suis arrivé à l'hôtel à midi.**

1. les touristes / sortir de l'hôtel
2. ils / monter dans le bus
3. nous / partir immédiatement
4. nous / passer devant le souk
5. nous / arriver à la médina à deux heures
6. les touristes / descendre de l'autobus
7. ils / entrer dans une casbah
8. je / revenir à la gare
9. je / rester là pendant deux heures
10. je / retourner chercher les touristes
11. nous / rentrer à l'hôtel
12. finalement, je / rentrer chez moi

Follow-up: Form complete sentences and read as listening comprehension practice.

Point out to students that a **souk** is an outdoor market, a **casbah** is the palace of an Arab chieftan, and the **médina** is the Arab section of Casablanca.

B. Et d'autres qui voyagent. Jean-Luc and his brother Alain took a trip to Morocco last summer. Using the cues provided, create sentences describing their trip. Be sure to use the right auxiliary verb (**avoir** or **être**) in each sentence.

Modèles   partir de Paris le 1er août → **Nous sommes partis de Paris le 1er août.**
quitter Paris très tôt le matin → **Nous avons quitté Paris très tôt le matin.**

1. arriver à dix heures à Casablanca
2. déjeuner à l'aéroport
3. aller à l'hôtel
4. monter dans notre chambre
5. téléphoner à des amis marocains
6. dormir un peu
7. sortir pour visiter la ville
8. entrer dans la médina
9. rencontrer d'autres Français
10. manger du couscous
11. rentrer à l'hôtel
12. passer une bonne journée

Repeat with **ils** (e.g., **Ils sont partis de Paris le 1er août.**)

Point out that couscous is a typical North African dish made with crushed wheat, usually steamed with lamb, chicken, etc.

Communication

A. Expériences communes. Interview other students in your class in order to find one or several students who have done the following things. Then report your findings to the class.

Trouvez un ou plusieurs étudiants . . .

Ask as questions or adapt for directed dialogue.

1. qui sont sortis tous les soirs cette semaine
2. qui sont restés deux jours sans dormir
3. qui sont nés le même jour
4. qui ne sont jamais montés dans un avion
5. qui sont arrivés à l'université à sept heures et demie ce matin
6. qui sont venus en classe tous les jours
7. qui sont rentrés à la maison à deux heures du matin la nuit dernière
8. qui sont revenus récemment d'un pays étranger
9. qui sont déjà allés au Maroc, en Algérie, ou en Tunisie

B. Votre emploi du temps. Using verbs you know, describe what you did yesterday or on a day when you were particularly busy.

Exemple   Je suis sorti(e) de chez moi à sept heures et demie. J'ai rencontré quelques amis à l'arrêt d'autobus, etc.

Encourage students to use time expressions or words like **ensuite, après ça,** etc.

SYNTHÈSE

Les tensions de la vie moderne

Certains *événements* de notre vie peuvent être une cause considérable de tension nerveuse. Dans certains cas, nous risquons même de tomber malades *à cause de* ce stress. Les psychologues ont attribué une valeur numérique à chaque événement capable de provoquer ce stress. Vos chances de *maladies* sont proportionnelles au total des points accumulés.

events

because of

illnesses

Heurté par deux trains

140 000 emplois perdus dans l'industrie française depuis un an

80 Parisiens bloqués dans les ascenseurs par une panne

Vendredi matin la coupure d'électricité a touché 1 million de personnes

Une lanceuse de tomate inculpée

Une étudiante en lettres de dix-sept ans qui avait lancé une tomate en direction du président de la République, jeudi à Poitiers, a été inculpée vendredi d'outrage à magistrat.

La jeune fille n'avait pas atteint le président qui visitait à ce moment-là le secteur sauvegardé de Poitiers.

100	mort d'une personne très aimée	
73	divorce ou séparation	
53	maladie ou accident sérieux	
50	mariage	
47	*perte* de votre *emploi*	loss / job
39	*naissance* d'un enfant	birth
37	*déception* ou *échec* dans votre vie personnelle	disappointment / failure
36	conflits fréquents avec vos *proches*	those close to you
28	grand succès personnel	
26	début ou fin des études	
20	*déménagement*	moving
19	changement de *distractions*	leisure activities
17	départ ou retour de vacances	
11	petites difficultés avec la police	

Explosion de gaz à Nîmes : 18 blessés

Certains de ces facteurs de stress peuvent être *évités*, d'autres sont *hors de* notre contrôle. *Ce qui* est important, c'est d'essayer de minimiser le stress. Voici quelques conseils contre le stress.

           avoided / outside of

           that which, what

1. Aimez ce que vous faites. Choisissez bien vos *buts* et vos objectifs et utilisez vos *forces* judicieusement.   goals / strength
2. Faites l'inventaire de vos facteurs de stress. Essayez d'éliminer les frustrations *inutiles.*   useless
3. N'essayez pas de *faire plaisir* à tout le monde. C'est un but impossible.   please
4. Soyez *vous-même.* Si vous essayez d'être ce que vous n'êtes pas, vous allez dépenser inutilement votre précieuse énergie.   yourself
5. N'ayez pas peur de *dire* ce que vous pensez, ce que vous vous sentez. Ne le gardez pas pour vous-même.   say
6. *Faites face* à vos problèmes; ne les *cachez* pas sous le *tapis.*   face / hide / carpet
7. Évitez d'avoir trop de changements en même temps.
8. Réservez chaque jour quelques périodes de temps libre dans votre *emploi du temps* et faites au moins deux pauses de relaxation.   schedule
9. Faites du sport au moins trois fois par semaine et pendant une demi-heure chaque fois.
10. Laissez votre voiture au garage ou au parking et marchez.
11. Ne sacrifiez pas le temps réservé aux distractions.
12. Évitez les substances et les aliments qui favorisent le stress: le tabac, l'alcool, les sucres, les charcuteries, le café, etc.

Extrait et adapté d'un article de *l'Express.*

Compréhension   Selon les renseignements donnés dans le texte, attribuez une valeur numérique à chacun des événements suivants et donnez un conseil approprié à chaque personne. (Using the information given in the text, assign stress points to each of the following situations and give appropriate advice to each person.)

1. G. Dupot vient de gagner 100 000 francs à la Loterie Nationale.
2. Ilad Laveine va aller passer quinze jours de vacances au bord de la mer.
3. Les Bontemps viennent d'avoir un enfant.
4. Mlle C. Dommage est tombée malade et a passé trois semaines à l'hôpital.
5. Jean Némard est très triste parce que son amie l'a quitté.
6. Hélène Gémonbaque vient de finir ses études et elle va commencer à travailler la semaine prochaine.
7. Ella Letrac vient d'être arrêtée par la police.
8. C. Padraule vient de perdre son emploi.

Ask students what changes they would make, if any, in the assignment of stress points given to the situations described in the **Synthèse** reading.

NOTES CULTURELLES

Les tensions de la vie moderne

J'en ai marre!
J'en ai assez!   *I've had it!*
J'en ai ras le bol!

Laissez-moi tranquille!
Fichez-moi la paix!   *Leave me alone!*

Quelle barbe! *What a bore!*

Like most industrial societies, France is experiencing such tensions of modern life as pollution, a rising crime rate, and changing life-styles. This is especially true in large urban centers where the pace of life is becoming increasingly hectic.

   Whether owing to the increasing pressures of modern society, or to a long-

Espèce d'imbécile! *You jerk!*

honored tradition of speaking their mind, the French tend to let off steam rather than keep problems or dissatisfaction to themselves. This outspokenness often may manifest itself in a certain gruffness in dealing with others, and visitors to France sometimes think that the French seem blunt or curt. Yet their comments and complaints are often simply a good-natured way of expressing irritation with things in general.

Communication

A. Évaluez la situation. Using the information given in *Les tensions de la vie moderne*, how many stress points would you assign to the people described below?

Follow-up: Have students compare and discuss the stress points given to each situation.

1. Bertrand Lasalle vient de perdre son emploi. Il décide de continuer ses études à l'université Laval à Québec. Mais pour cela, il est obligé de quitter sa petite ville et sa famille et de trouver un appartement près de l'université.
2. Antoine Lazare et sa femme Hélène viennent d'avoir un enfant. Le jour où Hélène est rentrée à la maison, Antoine a eu un accident et il a été obligé de passer une semaine à l'hôpital.
3. Arlette Santerre et ses parents ont des opinions différentes sur l'éducation, sur la politique, sur les distractions, sur tout. Elle a décidé de quitter sa famille et de vivre avec trois autres jeunes filles de son âge. Elles ont trouvé un petit appartement, mais malheureusement elles ont des personnalités très différentes et il y a des conflits fréquents.

B. Encore et toujours des problèmes! Create descriptions of other problem situations. Present your descriptions to other students and see if they can agree on how many stress points should be assigned.

Written preparation may be helpful.

C. Les tensions de la vie universitaire. What about the tensions that are specific to student life? Give a numerical value (from 0 to 100) to each of the following events or conditions according to how stressful you judge them to be. You may want to compare and discuss your reactions with those of other students.

Follow-up: Keep class tally to find most stressful situations.

1. _____ conflits fréquents avec votre camarade de chambre ou avec vos professeurs
2. _____ début ou fin du trimestre ou du semestre
3. _____ semaine des examens
4. _____ problèmes d'argent
5. _____ visite des parents
6. _____ problèmes avec votre voiture
7. _____ cours qui ne sont pas intéressants ou qui sont une perte de temps
8. _____ trop de distractions
9. _____ perte de vos notes de classe
10. _____ ?

D. **La vie n'est pas facile.** Alone or with a group of students describe a day
   in the life of a student where anything that could go wrong did go wrong.

   Exemple   Je suis arrivé une demi-heure en retard pour ma classe de   Have students share their
                  français. Pendant la classe on a volé mon vélo, etc.   descriptions. Class might also
                                                                                vote on the "best" description.

PRONONCIATION

A. When the letters **i, u,** and **ou** are followed by another vowel, their pronunciation changes and they become semi-vowels:

   [i] + vowel → [j] as in métier
   [y] + vowel → [ɥ] as in lui
   [ou] + vowel → [w] as in Louis

   Repeat the following words:

[j]	[ɥ]	[w]
je viens	puis	oui
tension	huit	besoin
voyage	juillet	droite
viande	ensuite	voici
mieux	je suis	choisir

B. When the letter **s** occurs between two vowels, it is pronounced [z] as in
   poison. When two s's occur together, the sound is always [s] as in **poisson.**
   The sound [s] also corresponds to the following spellings: **ç, c** followed
   by **i** or **e, t** in the **-tion** ending (**ça, ceci, nation**).

1. Listen and repeat:

[z]	[s]
ils ont	ils sont
poison	poisson
désert	dessert
nous avons	nous savons
deux heures	deux sœurs

2. Repeat the following words:

cuisine	usine	musée	français	glace
maison	valise	impression	cinéma	intuition

C. Repeat the following sentences, paying special attention to the sounds
   you have been practicing.

   1. Ils sont **bien** contents de leur métier.
   2. **Voici** de la **vian**de et du poisson.
   3. Les **fru**its sont bons en **c**ette saison.
   4. La **cu**isine française a une excellente réputa**tion**.
   5. **Lou**is aime **mi**eux **vo**yager en Suisse en juillet.

VOCABULAIRE

noms

les membres de la famille (voir p. 193)

les événements et les difficultés de la vie

l'alcool (m)
le conflit *conflict*
la déception *disappointment*
le déménagement *moving*
les distractions (f) *leisure-time activities*
° le divorce
l'échec (m) *failure*
l'événement (m) *event*
° la frustration
la maladie *illness*
la naissance *birth*
la perte *loss*
° le stress
° la tension

d'autres noms

le boulot *(slang)* *job*
° la boutique
le but *goal*
le cas *case*
le conseil *advice*
la demi-heure *half hour*
° la difficulté
l'emploi du temps (m) *schedule*
la fin *end*
la force *strength*
l'instruction (f) *education*
le lycée *high school*
le manœuvre *laborer*
le retour *return*

verbes

les verbes conjugués comme dormir (voir p. 196)

les verbes conjugués comme venir (voir p. 197)

d'autres verbes
apprendre *to learn*

°arriver
cacher *to hide*
descendre *to go down*
dire *to say*
entrer *to enter*
envoyer *to send*
éviter *to avoid*
faire face à *to face*
faire plaisir à *to please*
garder *to keep*
monter *to go up*
mourir *to die*
naître *to be born*
passer *to come by, go by*
provoquer *provoke*
quitter *to leave*
°regretter
rencontrer *to meet by chance*
retourner *to go back*
tomber *to fall*
tomber malade *to get sick*

adjectifs
inutile *useless*
°militaire

adverbes
demain *tomorrow*
dur *hard*
franchement *frankly*
°judicieusement
mal *badly*
vite *quickly*

divers
à mon avis *in my opinion*
ce qui *that which, what*
hors de *outside*
n'importe quel *any*
plusieurs *several*
quand même *all the same*

CHAPITRE ONZE

11

Santé et habitudes personnelles

INTRODUCTION

La nouvelle culture, c'est la culture physique

Confessions d'un nouvel *adepte*

    J'ai résisté longtemps. Mais c'est fini, j'abandonne. Les conseils de mes amis, les messages *étalés* partout sur les pages des magazines et sur les *écrans* de télévision, les titres de livres dans les *vitrines* des librairies, la *vue* de mes voisins qui, chaque matin, font quinze fois le tour de notre *pâté* de maisons, tout cela a fini par me persuader.

    Je suis maintenant membre d'un club de gymnastique. Je suis *parmi* les millions de Français qui veulent *«se sentir bien dans leur peau»*.

    Me voilà donc parti à la conquête de mon corps. La route n'est pas facile. Je fais des «*développé-couché*» pour mes muscles pectoraux, des «*squatts*» pour mes *cuisses*, des abdominaux pour mon *ventre*. Je *soulève des poids* pour développer mes biceps. Je fais du jogging pour mes *poumons*, mon *cœur* et mes artères. J'*avale* des vitamines, je bois du ginseng et je mange de la cuisine diététique. Mon médecin m'assure que c'est bon pour ma santé, alors . . . je *sue*. Je sue *donc* je suis.

Inspiré d'un article de *l'Express*.

(glosses:)

fan, enthusiast

displayed
screens / store windows
sight
block
among
feel good about themselves (la
  peau = skin)
push-ups
thighs / belly / lift weights

lungs / heart / swallow

sweat / therefore

''**Le courrier du corps**''
is a play on words based
on ''**le courrier du
cœur**,'' a magazine
advice column.

vieillir *to age,
   grow old*
courrier *mail*

forme *shape*
corps *body*
adieu *goodbye, farewell*
vive *long live*
santé *health*

Les secrets de la forme

Adieu le sport-compétition!

Le corps retrouvé

Vive le sport-santé!

C'est beau le muscle!

Dialoguez avec votre corps

Les leçons du corps

Réhabilitez votre corps!

Mon corps, c'est mon capital

Ask students which activities they would prefer doing if they were to visit a health spa. They could also be asked (1) to rank these activities in order of preference (2) to make up additional health-related slogans.

CLUB DE GYMNASTIQUE

cours de gymnastique	massages	
leçons de yoga	sauna	
séances de gymnastique collective	exercices de respiration et de relaxation	sessions / breathing
dance aérobique	solarium	
relaxation	bains remous	whirlpool
jazz dance	cure d'amaigrissement	weight-loss program

Compréhension Répondez aux questions suivantes selon les renseignements donnés dans le texte.

1. Est-ce que l'auteur a toujours été un adepte de la culture physique?
2. Qu'est-ce qui l'a persuadé de changer son style de vie?
3. Qu'est-ce que ses voisins font chaque matin?
4. Quels sont les titres de certains livres étalés dans les vitrines des librairies?
5. À quel club est-ce qu'il appartient maintenant?
6. Selon l'auteur, est-ce que c'est facile de retrouver sa forme une fois qu'on l'a perdue?
7. Qu'est-ce qu'il fait pour être en forme et pour développer ses muscles?
8. Qu'est-ce que son médecin pense de tout ça?

209

Dans un club de gymnastique

NOTES CULTURELLES

Encore un petit effort

Santé et forme

Est-ce vrai qu'en France la nouvelle culture,
c'est la culture physique? C'est peut-être un
peu exagéré mais ce qui est évident c'est que
les Français, traditionnellement assez peu
sportifs et grands amateurs de bonne cuisine,
s'intéressent de plus en plus à leur santé et à
leur forme. Par exemple, de récentes statistiques indiquent qu'en ville 21% des habitants et 10% à la campagne pratiquent régulièrement le jogging. Chaque année, de
nouveaux clubs gymnastiques ouvrent° leur
porte et de nombreux livres sur la santé, la
forme, les régimes° et la cuisine minceur°

Ask students to compare and
contrast the importance of
''santé et forme'' in France
and in the United States.

font leur apparition° à la vitrine des librairies. Les stations thermales,° populaires depuis longtemps en France, continuent à attirer° un grand nombre de gens qui viennent là pour soigner° leur foie,° leurs reins,° leurs bronches° ou leurs rhumatismes. Chaque jour, ils boivent leur ration d'eau, prennent des bains ou des douches° d'eau ou de vapeur thermale et suivent° un régime spécial. À cela, on ajoute° maintenant tout un programme d'activités physiques et il n'y pas seulement les gens qui ont des problèmes de santé qui viennent dans ces stations thermales. On peut faire «une cure d'amaigrissement» ou un stage de «redécouverte° de son corps et de la forme». Même le Club Méditerranée offre à ses clients des minicures de huit jours dans une station thermale pour les aider à lutter contre° le stress et à retrouver leur forme.

Une future championne . . . peut-être

ouvrent *open* régimes *diets* minceur *low-calorie*
apparation *appearance* stations thermales *spas*
attirer *attract* soigner *take care of* foie *liver*

reins *kidneys* bronches *respiratory system*
douches *showers* suivent *follow* ajoute *add*
redécouverte *rediscovery* lutter *fight* contre *against*

Et vous?

A. Les parties du corps. Quand vous avez un accident ou des problèmes de santé, il faut aller chez le médecin. Pour vous préparer à cette visite, apprenez le nom des différentes parties du corps.

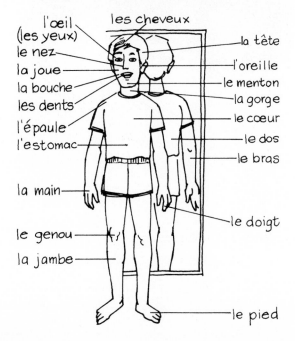

You may wish to mention additional vocabulary here, e.g., **la cheville, le cou, la cuisse, la figure, les hanches, les lèvres, les orteils, le poignet, la pouce, les sourcils.** In French, **estomac** refers to the area above the waist and **ventre** below the waist.

B. Où ont-ils mal? Quel est le problème des gens qui sont dans la salle d'attente du médecin?

Exemples   Il a mal aux pieds.
Elle a mal à l'estomac.
Il a mal à la gorge.

«Au suivant, s'il vous plaît—»

C. C'est votre tour. Maintenant, c'est votre tour. Essayez d'expliquer au médecin où vous avez mal.

Exemple   J'ai très mal à la tête aujourd'hui.

⚜ Le présent des verbes réfléchis

Présentation

In both French and English an action can be performed on an object or on another person.

Je lave la voiture. *I wash the car.*

When the action is performed on oneself—that is, when the object of the verb is the same as the subject—French uses a reflexive construction.

Je me lave. *I wash myself.*
Je m'habille. *I'm getting dressed.*

Reflexive verbs are conjugated with reflexive pronouns:

se laver *(to wash oneself)*		s'habiller *(to get dressed, to dress oneself)*	
je **me** lave	nous **nous** lavons	je m'habille	nous **nous** habillons
tu **te** laves	vous **vous** lavez	tu t'habilles	vous **vous** habillez
il/elle/on **se** lave	ils/elles **se** lavent	il/elle/on s'habille	ils/elles s'habillent

Note that the **e** of the reflexive pronouns **me**, **te**, and **se** is dropped before a vowel sound.

A. Reflexive verbs fall into three main categories.

1. Certain reflexive verbs, such as **se laver** and **s'habiller**, indicate that the subject performs the action on himself or herself.

s'arrêter *to stop*	Vous vous arrêtez à la boulangerie chaque matin?
se coucher *to go to bed*	Elle se couche à onze heures.
se détendre *to relax*	Nous nous détendons un peu pendant le week-end.
se lever* *to get up*	Je me lève à sept heures.
se peigner *to comb one's hair*	Il se peigne plusieurs fois par jour.
se préparer à *to get ready*	Nous nous préparons à partir.
se reposer *to rest*	Mon père se repose un peu chaque après-midi.
se réveiller *to wake up*	À quelle heure est-ce que tu te réveilles d'habitude?

2. Many verbs can be used as reflexive verbs to indicate a reciprocal action.

s'aimer *to like, to love each other*	Pierre et Hélène s'aiment beaucoup.
s'embrasser *to kiss*	On ne s'embrasse pas en public!
se rencontrer *to meet (by accident)*	Nous nous rencontrons chaque matin.
se retrouver *to meet (by prior arrangement)*	Après la classe, nous nous retrouvons au café.

*se lever is a regular -er verb except for the spelling changes in its stem. It is conjugated like acheter: je me lève, tu te lèves, il/elles/on se lève, nous levons, vous vous levez, ils/elles se levent.

3. Certain reflexive verbs have an idiomatic meaning.

s'amuser *to have a good time*	On s'amuse bien au club de gymnastique.
s'appeler* *to be named*	Comment vous appelez-vous?
se débrouiller *to manage, to get along*	Est-ce que tu te débrouilles bien en français?
se dépêcher *to hurry*	Nous nous dépêchons de finir notre travail.
s'entendre (avec) *to get along (with)*	Henri ne s'entend pas très bien avec son frère.
s'intéresser à *to be interested in*	Est-ce que vous vous intéressez à la culture physique?
se marier (avec) *to get married (to)*	Ils se marient samedi.
s'occuper de *to be busy with, to take care of*	Qui s'occupe des enfants?
se préoccuper de *to be concerned with*	Il se préoccupe trop de l'opinion des autres.
se souvenir de *to remember*	Je ne me souviens pas de son adresse.
se sentir *to feel*	Monique ne se sent pas bien aujourd'hui.

B. To form the negative of reflexive verbs, the **ne** is placed before the reflexive pronoun and the **pas** after the verb.

Je me lève très tôt.	Je ne me lève pas très tôt.
Il se débrouille bien.	Il ne se débrouille pas bien.
Nous nous entendons bien.	Nous ne nous entendons pas bien.

C. As with all other verbs, questions can be asked with reflexives by adding **est-ce que** (**Est-ce que tu te souviens de son adresse?**) or **n'est-ce pas** to the sentence (**Tu t'intéresses à la littérature, n'est-ce pas?**) or by intonation (**Tu te lèves à six heures demain?**). To form questions by inversion, the positions of the subject pronoun and the verb are reversed, and the reflexive pronoun remains.

Anne se marie la semaine prochaine.	Anne se marie-t-elle la semaine prochaine?
Ils s'entendent bien avec Georges.	S'entendent-ils bien avec Georges?
Vous vous arrêtez ici.	Vous arrêtez-vous ici?

The information on the use of questions by inversion is presented for recognition only and will not be practiced in subsequent exercises because of the general tendency in conversational French to avoid using inversion.

D. Certain reflexive verbs can also be used with parts of the body: **se laver les mains, les cheveux,** etc.; **se brosser** *(to brush)* **les dents, les cheveux; se couper** *(to cut)* **le doigt; se casser** *(to break)* **la jambe, le bras,** etc.

Elle se lave les mains.
Nous nous brossons les dents trois fois par jour.

*****s'appeler** also has spelling changes: **je m'appelle, tu t'appelles, il/elle/on s'appelle, nous nous appelons, vous vous appelez, ils/elles s'appellent.**

Préparation

Substitution: (1) Je m'amuse bien. on / nous / tu / vous / tes amis. (2) Elle se marie cette semaine. vous / Jean / tu / nous / Martine et Joseph. (3) Je ne me souviens pas de son nom. Michelle / nous / vous / tu / les professeurs.

A. C'est l'heure! À quelle heure est-ce que ces étudiants se lèvent d'habitude pour aller à l'université?

Modèle   Paul / 6 h 30   →   **Paul se lève à six heures et demie.**

1. nous / 6 h
2. Catherine / 9 h 15
3. vous / 5 h
4. tu / 7 h 30
5. Roger et Serge / 8 h 45
6. je / 9 h

Have students repeat in negative (e.g., **Paul ne se lève pas à six heures et demie.**).

B. Tout va mal. Pierre ne va pas très bien et décide d'aller chez le médecin. Donnez ses réponses aux questions du médecin.

Modèle   Est-ce que vous vous sentez bien aujourd'hui? (non . . . pas très bien)   →   **Non, je ne me sens pas très bien.**

1. Est-ce que vous vous reposez assez? (non)
2. Est-ce que vous vous couchez assez tôt? (non)
3. Est-ce que vous vous intéressez à votre travail? (non . . . pas vraiment)
4. Est-ce que vos enfants se débrouillent bien à l'école? (non . . . pas très bien)
5. Est-ce qu'ils se couchent assez tôt? (non)
6. Est-ce que vous vous entendez pas bien avec vos voisins? (non . . . pas très bien)
7. Est-ce que vos amis et vous, vous vous retrouvez quelquefois pour parler ensemble? (non . . . jamais)
8. Est-ce que vous vous amusez bien quand vous sortez avec vos amis? (non)

Repeat using il.

C. Un étudiant à ne pas imiter. Georges est loin d'être l'étudiant idéal. Au cours d'une discussion avec son conseiller, il révèle une attitude assez blasée. Donnez ses réponses aux questions du conseiller.

Follow-up: Have students answer as "perfect" students.

Modèle   À quelle heure est-ce que vous vous réveillez? (midi)   →   **Je me réveille à midi.**

1. À quelle heure est-ce que vous vous levez? (deux heures de l'après-midi)
2. À quelle heure est-ce que vous vous couchez d'habitude? (trop tard)
3. Est-ce que vous vous entendez bien avec vos professeurs? (pas toujours)
4. Est-ce que vous vous débrouillez bien dans vos cours? (pas très bien)
5. Est-ce que vous vous intéressez à vos cours? (pas vraiment)
6. Est-ce que vous vous arrêtez quelquefois à la bibliothèque? (non)
7. Est-ce que vous vous amusez bien pendant le week-end? (oui . . . bien sûr)
8. Est-ce que vous vous détendez après le travail? (toujours)

Communication

A. Êtes-vous d'accord? Si vous n'êtes pas d'accord avec l'opinion exprimée, modifiez la phrase.

Options: (1) Written. (2) Oral— Read statements or ask as questions. Encourage students to explain their answers.

1. Les médecins ne s'occupent pas assez de leurs clients.
2. Les Américains s'habillent très bien.
3. Tous les vendredis soirs les étudiants américains se retrouvent à la bibliothèque.
4. On se sent bien quand on fait des exercices de relaxation.
5. Les jeunes s'entendent bien avec leurs parents.
6. On se marie trop jeune aux États-Unis.
7. Les Américains ne s'intéressent pas assez à la politique.
8. Les parents d'aujourd'hui ne s'occupent pas assez de leurs enfants.
9. Les étudiants américains ne se préoccupent pas assez de leur santé.

B. Questions/interview. Répondez aux questions suivantes ou utilisez-les pour interviewer un(e) autre étudiant(e).

Options: (1) Written. (2) Oral— Ask questions or adapt for directed dialogue. (3) Have students work in small groups and report back their partners' responses.

1. Est-ce que tu te lèves tard d'habitude? Et le dimanche?
2. Est-ce que tu te souviens toujours de l'anniversaire de tes amis?
3. En général, à quelle heure est-ce que tu te couches?
4. Est-ce que tu te dépêches souvent pour arriver à l'heure en classe?
5. Est-ce que tu t'amuses bien pendant les week-ends?
6. Est-ce que tu t'intéresses à la politique? Et au sport? Et à la musique?
7. Est-ce que tu te débrouilles bien en français? Et en mathématiques? Et en sciences?
8. Est-ce que tu t'entends bien avec tes professeurs? Et avec tes camarades de chambre?

C. Votre routine matinale. Décrivez ce que vous faites généralement chaque matin. Utilisez autant de verbes réfléchis que possible.

Exemple   Je me lève à sept heures et je déjeune immédiatement, etc.

L'infinitif et l'impératif des verbes réfléchis

Présentation

Like all verbs, reflexives can also be used in the infinitive and in the imperative.

A. When used in the infinitive, the reflexive pronoun is always in the same person and number as the subject and precedes the infinitive.

Je vais **me** reposer.	**Nous** allons **nous** reposer.
Tu vas **te** reposer.	**Vous** allez **vous** reposer.
Elle va **se** reposer.	**Elles** vont **se** reposer.
Il va **se** reposer.	**Ils** vont **se** reposer.

*Point out that certain expressions that students already know lead to the use of the infinitive (**aller, vouloir, pouvoir, avoir envie de, avoir besoin de, avoir l'intention de, avoir l'air de, avoir l'occasion de,** etc.). Another useful expression when talking about daily activities is **avoir l'habitude de** (to be in the habit of, to usually do something): **J'ai l'habitude de me coucher assez tôt.***

Je suis obligé de me dépêcher.
Tu n'as pas l'air de te sentir bien.
On va bien s'amuser.
Les enfants ne veulent pas se laver les mains.

B. In the affirmative imperative, the reflexive pronoun follows the verb. In the negative imperative, it precedes the verb.

Dépêchez-vous!	Ne vous dépêchez pas!
Mariez-vous!	Ne vous mariez pas!
Brossez-vous les dents!	Ne vous brossez pas les dents!

The reflexive pronoun **te** changes to **toi** in the affirmative imperative.

Lève-toi!	Ne te lève pas!
Amuse-toi!	Ne t'amuse pas!
Coupe-toi les cheveux.	Ne te coupe pas les cheveux!

Substitution: (1) Est-ce que tu vas te laver? nous / je / Jean-Claude / les enfants / vous. (2) J'ai besoin de me détendre. Odile / ses parents / tu / vous / nous.
Transformation: Modèle: Dépêche-toi! → Ne te dépêche pas! (1) Rase-toi. (2) Repose-toi. (3) Couche-toi. (4) Lavez-vous. (5) Levez-vous. (6) Amusez-vous.
Transformation: Modèle: Ne te réveille pas. → Réveille-toi. (1) Ne t'arrête pas de travailler. (2) Ne te lève pas. (3) Ne t'amuse pas. (4) Ne vous dépêchez pas. (5) Ne vous coupez pas les cheveux. (6) Ne vous peignez pas.

Préparation

A. Différences. Il y a des gens qui aiment se coucher tôt et d'autres qui n'aiment pas ça. Utilisez les suggestions suivantes pour donner l'opinion de chaque personne.

> **Modèle**   se coucher tôt? Marc n'aime pas . . . → **Marc n'aime pas se coucher tôt.**

1. Thérèse préfère . . .
2. Tu as besoin de . . .
3. Nous ne voulons pas . . .
4. Je voudrais . . .
5. Ils ont l'intention de . . .
6. Vous n'avez pas envie de . . .

B. Conseils. Gilbert va partir en vacances parce qu'il a envie de se reposer. Il parle avec ses amis qui lui donnent toutes sortes de conseils.

> **Modèle**   Je vais me réveiller tôt. (mais non) → **Mais non, ne te réveille pas tôt.**
> Je vais bien m'amuser. (oui) → **Oui! Amuse-toi bien.**

Repeat with formal imperative (Mais non, ne vous réveillez pas tôt.).

1. Je vais bien me reposer. (oui)
2. Je vais m'occuper un peu de mon jardin. (mais non)
3. Je vais me préparer à partir. (oui)
4. Je vais me dépêcher de revenir. (mais non)
5. Je vais me coucher tard. (mais non)
6. Je vais m'arrêter de travailler. (oui)
7. Je vais me détendre. (oui)
8. Je vais me lever tôt. (mais non)

C. Chez le médecin. Jean-Luc ne se sent pas bien. Quels conseils est-ce que le médecin lui donne?

> **Modèles**   se coucher tôt   →   **Couchez-vous tôt.**
> manger trois repas par jour   →   **Mangez trois repas par jour.**

1. se détendre un peu
2. faire un peu de sport
3. ne pas boire trop de vin
4. ne pas avoir peur de dire ce que vous pensez
5. ne pas se dépêcher tout le temps
6. sortir plus souvent
7. se reposer quand vous vous sentez fatigué
8. se débrouiller pour avoir du temps libre
9. oublier vos soucis de temps en temps

*This exercise reviews both reflexive and nonreflexive verbs in the negative and affirmative. Repeat in the **tu** form as **conseils d'un ami.***

Communication

A. Habitudes et santé. Nos habitudes de vie ne sont pas toujours très bonnes pour notre santé. Utilisez des verbes réfléchis pour décrire votre situation, vos habitudes et vos obligations d'une part et d'autre part ce que vous pouvez faire pour éviter de «brûler la chandelle par les deux bouts» *(burn the candle at both ends).*

> **Exemple**   Je suis obligé(e) de me lever tôt parce que j'ai un cours à huit heures. J'ai besoin de me reposer un peu.
>
> *Suggestions:* J'ai l'habitude de, je n'ai pas l'habitude de, je voudrais, j'ai besoin de, j'ai envie de, je n'ai pas envie de, j'aime

*Have students compare and contrast answers. They can also give each other advice (**Repose-toi un peu pendant le week-end.**).*

B. Avez-vous de l'autorité? Est-ce que vous aimez donner des ordres? Si oui, profitez de l'occasion et donnez des ordres à un(e) autre étudiant(e). Utilisez autant de verbes réfléchis que possible. L'autre étudiant(e) va décider s'il ou elle va accepter ou refuser ces ordres.

> **Exemple**   Étudiant(e) n° 1: Lève-toi à cinq heures du matin.
> Étudiant(e) n° 2: Non, je refuse de me lever à cinq heures du matin. *ou* Oui, c'est une bonne idée. Je vais me lever à cinq heures du matin.

Suggested for oral work. Written preparation may be helpful.

piscines

L'ÉTOILE, 32, rue de Tilsitt (M° Etoile), 380.50.99. Lundi 8 h à 14 h et 20 h à 22 h. Mardi, 7 h à 8 h 30 et 9 h 30 à 20 h. Mercredi, 7 h à 20 h. Jeudi, 7 h à 19 h 30 et 20 h 30 à 22 h. Vendredi 7 h à 20 h. Samedi 8 h à 20 h. Dimanche 8 h à 18 h. Entrée 8 F. Enfants 6 F (Fermeture lundi)

patinoires

LE STADIUM (Voir Centre de Loisirs)
PALAIS DE GLACE, Rond-Point des Champs-Elysées (M° Franklin-Roosevelt), 359.46.72. Tous les jours, de 10 h 30 à 14 h (sauf mercredi, de 10 h 30 à 13 h et dimanche de 10 h à 12 h 30). Tous les jours, de 14 h 30 à 18 h. Du mardi au samedi, de 21 h à 23 h 30. Entrée 9.50 F. Moins de 16 ans : 8 F. Location de patins 6 F

⚜ Le passé composé des verbes réfléchis

Présentation

The auxiliary verb **être** is used to form the **passé composé** of reflexive verbs. The past participle agrees in gender and in number with the preceding direct object, i.e., the reflexive pronoun.

Le passé composé de *se laver*	
je me suis lavé(e)	nous **nous sommes** lavé(e)s
tu t'es lavé(e)	vous **vous êtes** lavé(e)(s)
il s'est lavé	ils **se sont** lavés
elle s'est lavée	elles **se sont** lavées

Ils se sont mariés l'été dernier.
Nous nous sommes bien amusés.
Elle s'est bien débrouillée à l'examen.

A. The negative is formed by placing the **ne** before the reflexive pronoun and **pas** after the auxiliary verb.

Je ne me suis pas souvenu de son anniversaire.
Nous ne nous sommes pas réveillés assez tôt.
Claude ne s'est pas bien reposé.

B. As with other verbs, questions with reflexives can be formed through intonation, by using **est-ce que,** and by using inversion. To use questions by inversion, the subject pronoun is placed after the verb and the reflexive verb stays before the auxiliary verb.

S'est-elle bien débrouillée en maths?
Où vous êtes-vous rencontrés?
T'es-tu arrêté à la boulangerie ce matin?

*C. In some cases, the reflexive pronoun is not a direct but an indirect object. In this case, there is no agreement.

Ils se sont téléphoné.   (i.e., on téléphone à quelqu'un)
Ils se sont parlé.   (i.e., on parle à quelqu'un)

This is a complex grammar topic that need not be taught actively at this point.

Similarly, there is no agreement when the reflexive verb is followed by a direct object. Compare:

Elle s'est coupé le doigt.   (**le doigt** is the direct object)
Elle s'est coup**ée.**   (the reflexive pronoun **se** is the direct object)

This rule of no agreement applies in particular to expressions indicating that an action is performed on a part of the body:

Ils se sont brossé les dents.
Elle s'est cassé la jambe.

*Point out to students that reflexives are not used when the action is performed with a part of the body: **Elle a tourné le dos; Levez la main.***

*For recognition only.

Préparation

A. Un matin comme les autres. Ce que Marie-José a fait ce matin n'est pas différent de ce qu'elle fait tous les matins. Qu'est-ce qu'elle a fait?

Modèle   se réveiller à six heures → **Je me suis réveillée à six heures.**

1. se lever
2. se préparer
3. se laver
4. se brosser les dents
5. se peigner
6. s'occuper du chat
7. se dépêcher de partir
8. s'arrêter à la boulangerie

Repeat using **elle, nous, on.** Give new context **(un matin pas comme les autres)** and repeat in the negative.

B. On va faire une cure à Vichy. Il y a beaucoup de choses à faire quand on part en voyage. Indiquez ce que chaque membre de la famille Bertrand a fait le matin de leur départ à Vichy.

Modèle   nous / se réveiller à 5 heures → **Nous nous sommes réveillés à cinq heures.**

1. je / se lever immédiatement
2. nous / se dépêcher de se préparer
3. Solange / s'occuper des enfants
4. elle / bien se débrouiller
5. les enfants / s'habiller tout seuls
6. Pierre et Gilles / se brosser les dents
7. tu / se souvenir de fermer les fenêtres
8. vous / s'occuper des valises

Point out that many French people go to places like Vichy, Vittel, and Évian, where there are mineral waters that are reputed to have therapeutic effects for the liver, kidneys, arthritis, etc.

Substitution: (1) Je me suis bien débrouillé(e) à l'examen. nous / vous / tu / Marcel / Monique et Sylvie. (2) Ils ne se sont pas rasés ce matin. tu / je / vous / mon frère / nous. (3) À quelle heure est-ce qu'elle s'est couchée? Pierre / vos parents / tu / vous / Jeanne.

C. On s'est débrouillé comme on a pu. Madame Augeron a été obligée de partir pendant quelques jours. Elle demande à son mari et à ses enfants comment ils se sont débrouillés pendant son absence. Qu'est-ce qu'ils répondent?

Modèle   Est-ce que vous vous êtes bien débrouillés? (oui . . . assez bien) → **Oui, nous nous sommes assez bien débrouillés.**

1. À quelle heure est-ce que vous vous êtes couchés? (assez tard)
2. Qui s'est occupé des enfants? (ta mère)
3. Est-ce que tu t'es souvenu de ton rendez-vous? (non)
4. Paul, est-ce que tu t'es brossé les dents chaque soir? (non, maman)
5. À quelle heure est-ce que les enfants se sont réveillés? (7 heures)
6. Et toi, à quelle heure est-ce que tu t'es réveillé? (5 heures)
7. Est-ce que les enfants se sont habillés seuls? (oui . . . la plupart du temps)
8. Est-ce que les enfants se sont dépêchés pour aller à l'école? (oui)
9. Est-ce que tu t'es bien reposé? (non)
10. Est-ce que vous vous êtes bien amusés? (oui)

D. Au club de gymnastique. Isabelle travaille dans un club de gymnastique. Elle parle de ce qu'elle a fait hier.

Modèle   se lever très tôt → **Je me suis levée très tôt.**

1. arriver au club à dix heures
2. faire des exercices de respiration
3. aider Monique à enseigner sa classe
4. aller déjeuner au restaurant diététique
5. s'occuper de mes clients
6. soulever des poids
7. se détendre dans le sauna
8. quitter le club à six heures et demie
9. s'arrêter chez des amis
10. rentrer chez moi à dix heures
11. boire un verre d'eau minérale
12. se coucher avant onze heures

*This exercises reviews the **passé composé** of reflexive verbs as well as those conjugated with **avoir** and **être.***

Communication

A. Interview. Utilisez les phrases suivantes pour formuler des questions à poser à un(e) autre étudiant(e) de votre classe.

Exemple   bien s'amuser hier → **Est-ce que tu t'es bien amusé(e) hier?**

1. bien s'amuser hier
2. se réveiller tôt
3. se lever tout de suite
4. se dépêcher
5. se reposer un peu pendant la journée
6. s'arrêter chez des amis après les cours
7. se détendre un peu après le dîner
8. se coucher avant minuit

*Have students try to guess the exact time that another student went to bed (or got up): **Est-ce que tu t'es couché à onze heures et quart?**, etc.*

*Students might also complete Activity B (**Synthèse**).*

B. Est-ce vrai? Avec un(e) autre étudiant(e) ou un groupe d'étudiants, décidez si les phrases suivantes s'appliquent à tous les membres de votre groupe. Sinon *(if not)*, faites les changements nécessaires.

Options: (1) Have students report back to class. (2) Adapt for directed dialogue.

Exemple   Nous nous sommes levés à huit heures. → **Oui, c'est vrai. Nous nous sommes levés à huit heures.** ou Non, Jean et moi nous nous sommes levés à huit heures, mais Michel s'est levé à six heures.

1. Nous nous sommes couchés à trois heures du matin.
2. Ce matin, nous nous sommes dépêchés pour venir en classe.
3. Nous nous sommes arrêtés pour manger un sandwich.
4. Nous nous sommes retrouvés au cinéma hier soir.
5. Nous nous sommes rencontrés pour la première fois en classe de français.
6. Samedi dernier nous nous sommes réveillés à midi.

Les verbes conjugués comme *prendre*

Présentation

Prendre is an irregular verb. Its basic meaning is *to take*, but it has many idiomatic uses.

prendre	
je **prends**	nous **prenons**
tu **prends**	vous **prenez**
il/elle/on **prend**	ils/elles **prennent**
passé composé: j'ai pris	

There is a contrast between the pronunciation of the singular forms, [prɑ̃], and third person plural, [prɛn]. The **nous** and **vous** forms are [prənõ] and [prəne], respectively. In the third person singular inversion (**prend-il**), the liaison sound is [t] rather than [d].

Je prends des vitamines.
Qu'est-ce que vous allez prendre comme dessert?
Prends tes médicaments.
Quand as-tu pris cette décision?

Note that the French equivalent of *to make a decision* is **prendre une décision.**

The verbs **apprendre** *(to learn)* and **comprendre** *(to understand)* are conjugated like **prendre.**

Nous apprenons à faire du ski.
Ils ne comprennent pas ma question.
Je n'ai pas compris ses explications.

Note that **à** must follow **apprendre** when used with an infinitive. Compare:

Annick apprend le français.   Annick apprend à parler français.

Substitution: (1) Je prends des vitamines. tu prends / elle prend / nous prenons / vous prenez / ils prennent. (2) Madeleine apprend le français. nous / vous / Marie et Thérèse / je / on. (3) Est-ce que vous comprenez la question? Caroline / tu / Jacques et son frère / nous / les étudiants. (4) J'ai appris à danser. nous / Anne / Annette et Françoise / tu / vous. Option: Give pronouns; have students provide verb forms.

Préparation

A. Quand on a la santé, on a tout . . . Serge et ses amis parlent de ce qu'ils font pour rester en bonne santé.

Modèle   Annette / des vitamines → **Annette prend des vitamines.**

1. je / un bon petit déjeuner
2. Pierre / des médicaments
3. nous / trois repas par jour
4. vous / le temps de vous amuser
5. mes amis / des vacances
6. tu / le temps de faire du sport

B. Il faut prendre le temps de vivre! Quelques amis ont décidé de consacrer plus de temps à leurs loisirs. Ils parlent de ce qu'ils ont appris à faire.

Modèle Marc / nager → **Marc a appris à nager.**

1. nous / faire la cuisine
2. je / prendre des photos
3. Yvonne / parler espagnol
4. tu / danser
5. mes amis / utiliser un ordinateur
6. vous / jouer aux cartes

Communication

Questions/interview. Répondez aux questions suivantes ou utilisez-les pour interviewer un(e) autre étudiant(e).

1. Quand tu voyages, est-ce que tu prends le train, l'avion, ou ta voiture?
2. Est-ce que tu as pris ton vélo, ta voiture, ou l'autobus pour venir en classe ce matin?
3. Est-ce que tu prends de l'aspirine quand tu as mal à la tête?
4. Est-ce que tu aimes prendre des photos?
5. Est-ce que tu prends beaucoup de photos quand tu es en vacances?
6. Est-ce que les parents comprennent toujours leurs enfants? Est-ce que les enfants comprennent toujours leurs parents?
7. Est-ce que tu comprends la littérature moderne? Et l'art moderne?
8. Est-ce que tu comprends l'italien? Et l'allemand?
9. Est-ce que tu as envie d'apprendre à faire du ski? À faire la cuisine? À parler russe?
10. À quel âge as-tu appris à parler? Et à lire?

Options: (1) Written. (2) Oral—Ask questions or adapt for directed dialogue. (3) Have students work in small groups and report back their partners' responses.

PRENEZ LA ROUTE DU BON CÔTÉ

SYNTHÈSE

Attention à vos gestes

Chaque pays possède son propre répertoire de *gestes* qui viennent de sa culture et de ses traditions. Il faut les *connaître* pour éviter les *malentendus*. Voici quelques exemples de gestes qui peuvent avoir une interprétation différente.

gestures

to know, to be acquainted with / misunderstandings

Oui ou non?

En France, pour dire oui, on *remue* la tête verticalement. Mais en Grèce, c'est le contraire. On la remue horizontalement pour dire oui, et verticalement pour dire non. En Iran, pour dire oui, on tourne le menton à gauche. À Tahiti, on *hausse les sourcils*.

moves

raises one's eyebrows

À la table

En France, il faut *garder* les deux mains sur la table pendant le repas. Mais dans tous les pays anglo-saxons, il faut garder la main gauche sous la table. On peut *tenir* la *fourchette* dans la main gauche seulement quand on coupe sa viande; après il faut la repasser dans la main droite.

to keep

hold / fork

Dans certains pays arabes, on n'utilise pas de *couteau* ou de fourchette—on mange avec les trois doigts de la main droite. Mais *il ne faut pas* utiliser la main gauche qui est considérée comme impure.

knife

one must not

Chez les Arabes et chez les Esquimaux, il faut *roter* pour manifester sa satisfaction après un bon repas.

to burp

En Allemagne, évitez de couper les pommes de terre avec votre couteau; utilisez seulement votre fourchette. En Italie, ne coupez pas les spaghetti avec votre couteau; débrouillez-vous avec votre fourchette.

Un dîner en famille

Salutations et contacts physiques

Quand les Français rencontrent des *parents* ou des amis, ils adorent les gros *baisers* sur les joues. Les Esquimaux *se frottent* le nez; les Russes s'embrassent sur la bouche. Et au Tibet, on *tire la langue* pour dire bonjour.

relatives
kisses / rub
sticks out one's tongue

Dans les pays arabes, les hommes se tiennent par le petit doigt quand ils marchent dans la rue. Mais les hommes et les femmes ne se touchent pas en public.

Au Japon, si vous êtes invité dans une famille, quittez vos *chaussures avant* d'entrer et placez-les devant la porte. *Inclinez-vous* pour dire bonjour, ne regardez pas les gens dans les yeux et surtout, ne *vous mouchez* pas en public!

shoes
before / bow
blow your nose

Extrait et adapté d'un article de *Paris Match.*

Compréhension   Complétez les phrases suivantes selon les renseignements donnés.

Follow-up: Discuss other typical French gestures and compare with American gestures.

1. En Iran, pour dire oui . . .
2. En France, quand on mange, il faut . . .
3. En Allemagne, il ne faut pas couper . . .
4. Dans certains pays arabes, on mange . . .
5. Quand ils rencontrent des amis ou des parents, les Russes . . .
6. Quand ils marchent dans la rue, les hommes arabes . . .
7. Si vous êtes invité chez des Japonais, il faut . . .

NOTES CULTURELLES

Les expressions figuratives

Un des aspects les plus fascinants du langage humain est l'utilisation de certains mots et expressions dans un sens figuré.° Cette tendance se manifeste dans la langue de tous les jours aussi bien que° dans le langage poétique. Les images et expressions figuratives qui sont passées dans la langue de tous les jours constituent une forme de poésie, d'humour et de sagesse° populaire. Leur utilisation est particulièrement fréquente dans la conversation familière. Voici, par exemple, quelques expressions qui se réfèrent au corps humain.

figuré *figurative*   aussi bien que *as well as*   sagesse
wisdom

Tu me casses les pieds.
You're bothering me.

Ne vous cassez pas la tête.
Don't worry.

Il a mis les pieds dans le plat.
He put his foot in his mouth.

Ça saute aux yeux.
That's evident.

Suggestion: Introduce other expressions (**faire du pied, se casser la figure, avoir une dent contre quelqu'un, manger sur le pouce, avoir mal aux cheveux,** etc.).

Il a le bras long.
He has influence (connections).

C'est un casse-cou.
He's a daredevil.

Tu es tombé sur la tête.
You're crazy.

Communication

A. Chez le médecin. Imaginez que vous êtes chez le médecin. L'étudiant(e) qui joue le rôle du médecin va poser les questions suivantes au client. Le client répond à chaque question. Ensuite le médecin va donner son diagnostic et suggérer les remèdes (par exemple: **Reposez-vous et mangez beaucoup d'épinards,** etc.).

Follow-up: Have patient report diagnosis and have doctor tell the remedy and reasons.

Le médecin va demander au client si . . .

1. il/elle va bien
2. il/elle dort bien
3. il/elle a bon appétit
4. il/elle est souvent fatigué(e)
5. il/elle a mal à la tête
6. il/elle a souvent mal à l'estomac
7. il/elle a quelquefois mal au dos
8. il/elle a déjà eu un accident
9. il/elle s'est déjà cassé la jambe ou le bras
10. ?

B. Hier. Racontez votre journée d'hier. Utilisez autant de verbes réfléchis que possible dans votre description. Par exemple, vous pouvez commencer, «Je me suis réveillé (e) à sept heures. Après ça . . . »

Suggested for written homework.

C. Apprenez à vous débrouiller. Comment allez-vous vous débrouiller si vous vous trouvez dans les situations suivantes? Si vous n'avez pas encore appris le vocabulaire nécessaire, utilisez d'autres mots et même quelques gestes si c'est nécessaire.

1. You have a bad cold and need to buy some cough medicine.
2. You broke a filling and need to have it replaced.
3. You have to explain to the doctor that you have just been bitten by a dog.
4. You have a splinter in your thumb and need help to get it out.
5. You have a prescription for airsickness pills that you need to have refilled.
6. You lost a contact lens and need a replacement.

Bring in additional photos (or have students bring them in) and write captions for them.

D. Les photos parlent. Imaginez ce que les personnes sur les photos suivantes sont en train de dire . . . ou de penser.

Les photos parlent

VOCABULAIRE

noms

les parties du corps humain (voir p. 211)

le corps et la santé
le cœur   *heart*
le corps   *body*
le dévéloppé-couché   *push-up*
° l'exercice (m)
la forme   *shape*
° la gymnastique
° le muscle
la peau   *skin*
le poumon   *lung*
° la relaxation
la respiration   *breathing*
la santé   *health*
° le sauna
le ventre   *abdomen, belly*
° le yoga

d'autres noms
le baiser   *kiss*
° le club
le contraire   *opposite*
le courrier   *mail*
le couteau   *knife*
° la culture
la fourchette   *fork*
le geste   *gesture*
° l'interprétation (f)
la langue   *tongue*
la leçon   *lesson*
la librairie   *bookstore*
° le magazine
le malentendu   *misunderstanding*
° le membre
° le message
° les parents   *relatives*
la porte   *door*
la raison   *reason*
° la route
° la satisfaction
le titre   *title*
° la tradition
la vitrine   *store window*
le voisin (m), la voisine (f)   *neighbor*

verbes

les verbes réfléchis (voir pp. 213–214)

d'autres verbes
abandonner   *to give up*
apprendre   *to learn*
°**assurer**
avaler   *to swallow*
avoir mal à   *to have an ache or pain*
comprendre   *to understand*
connaître   *to know, to be acquainted with*
couper   *to cut*
°**développer**
il ne faut pas   *one must not*
manifester   *to show*
se moucher   *to blow one's nose*
°**persuader**
prendre   *to take*
se sentir bien   *to feel good*
soulever des poids   *to lift weights*
tenir   *to hold*
toucher   *to touch*
utiliser   *to use*
vieillir   *to grow old*

adjectifs

°**aérobique**
°**considéré(e)**
°**diététique**
droit(e)   *right*
étalé(e)   *displayed*
gauche   *left*

adverbes

°**horizontalement**
seulement   *only*
°**verticalement**

divers

adieu   *good-bye, farewell*
avant de (+ *infinitive*)   *before*
donc   *therefore*
parmi   *among*
vive . . . !   *long live . . . !*

CHAPITRE DOUZE

L'apparence

12

INTRODUCTION

Les Françaises et leur image

La femme française a *longtemps* été considérée comme le symbole de la beauté et de l'élégance. Mais en réalité, quelle importance la beauté a-t-elle pour les Françaises? Pour trouver la réponse, *Marie-Claire*, un *journal de mode*, et le Comité français de produits de beauté ont demandé à l'**IFOP** (Institut français d'opinion publique) d'organiser un sondage d'opinion. Voici les résultats.

long (a long time)

fashion magazine

229

1. À votre avis, jusqu'à quel âge une femme peut-elle être belle?

30 ans	2%
40 ans	11
50 ans	13
60 ans	6
Pas de limite	66
Sans opinion	2

2. À votre avis, *qu'est-ce qui* est préférable pour une femme?   what

a. Être belle . . .	3%	d. Être belle . . .	15%
Ou être intelligente	94	Ou avoir de la chance	80
Sans opinion	3	Sans opinion	5
b. Être belle . . .	5%	e. Être belle . . .	59%
Ou avoir de la personnalité	93	Ou être célèbre	33
Sans opinion	2	Sans opinion	8
c. Être belle . . .	59%		
Ou être riche	33		
Sans opinion	8		

3. Personnellement, quel type de beauté préférez-vous posséder? Et votre *mari*, quel type de beauté féminine préfère-t-il?   husband

	Vous	*Votre mari*
Naturelle	65%	63%
Raffinée	20	12
Sportive	8	6
Modeste et réservée	4	5
Sexy	1	10
Sans opinion	1	4

4. Il y a *de moins en moins* de différence entre les hommes et les femmes.   less and less
À votre avis, est-ce que cela signifie que . . .

Les femmes vont se préoccuper de moins en moins de leur beauté.	14%
Les hommes vont se préoccuper *de plus en plus* de leur beauté.	53	more and more
Sans opinion	33

La question de la beauté est une question difficile pour les femmes. Si elles sont belles et se préoccupent de leur beauté, on les accuse de frivolité et de vanité. Si elles ne sont pas belles ou ne se préoccupent pas de leur beauté, on les accuse de *manquer* de féminité.   lacking (to lack, to miss)

Mais heureusement pour les Françaises, aujourd'hui, ces contradictions sont en train de *disparaître*. Il n'y a pas, pour elles, de contradiction entre beauté et intelligence. Elles pensent que si la beauté est désirable pour les femmes, elle est désirable aussi pour les hommes. Une société qui emprisonne les femmes dans l'obligation d'être belles—et les hommes dans l'obligation d'être forts et virils—est une société qui refuse aux hommes et aux femmes la possibilité de réaliser *pleinement* leur individualité.   disappearing (to disappear)   fully

Extrait et adapté d'un article de *Marie-Claire*.

Compréhension   Selon les renseignements donnés, est-ce que les phrases suivantes sont vraies ou fausses? Corrigez le sens de la phrase s'il est faux.

Option: Ask as questions. Have students respond to survey questions and compare their answers with the results of the original survey.

1. Ce sondage a été organisé par un groupe de professeurs.
2. Les Françaises préfèrent les femmes qui sont à la fois belles, intelligentes et capables.
3. Si elles ont le choix entre l'intelligence et la beauté, la majorité des Françaises préfèrent la beauté.
4. Si elles ont le choix entre être belles et avoir de la personnalité, les Françaises préfèrent avoir de la personnalité.
5. Les Françaises pensent qu'à l'avenir les hommes vont se préoccuper de plus en plus de leur beauté.
6. Pour les Françaises la beauté et l'intelligence sont des qualités incompatibles.
7. Les Françaises pensent que si la beauté est importante pour les femmes, elle est importante aussi pour les hommes.
8. Elles pensent que c'est injuste de demander aux hommes d'être toujours forts et aux femmes d'être toujours belles.

NOTES CULTURELLES

La mode

La France est depuis longtemps la capitale de la haute couture° et les noms des grands couturiers et couturières français sont connus° partout dans le monde. Courrèges, Chanel, Givenchy, Saint-Laurent, Cardin évoquent l'image de vêtements élégants et chers. Chaque saison, ces maisons de couture lancent° la mode et on attend avec impatience leurs présentations. Ce qui se montre à Paris inspire beaucoup de couturiers étrangers.

Mais la mode française est en train d'évoluer. Le fait° que la haute couture coûte très cher et n'est pas à la portée° de tout le monde explique le développement du «prêt-à-porter».° Mais le prêt-à-porter a aussi ses couturiers—Cacharel, Hechter, Sonia Rykiel, par exemple—qui maintiennent la qualité et l'esthétique de leurs créations.

Depuis les années 60, les blue-jeans, les tee-shirts et les sweat-shirts (beaucoup portent le nom d'une université américaine) font partie de la garde-robe° des jeunes Français. Le blue-jean et le tee-shirt sont des vêtements démocratiques: ils cachent les différences sociales tandis que° la haute couture les met en évidence. Mais pour les Français, même un tee-shirt se porte° avec style, et le chic et l'élégance traditionnels des Français n'ont pas disparu.°

haute couture *high fashion*   connus *known*
lancent *launch*   fait *fact*   à la portée *within reach*
prêt-à-porter *ready to wear*   garde-robe *wardrobe*
tandis que *whereas*   se porter *be worn*
disparu *disappeared*

A. Vos vêtements. Qu'est-ce que vous portez généralement dans les situations suivantes?

Exemple   Pour venir en classe, je porte un pantalon et un chemisier.

1. Pour venir en classe . . .
2. Pour aller à la plage . . .
3. Pour aller à un concert . . .
4. Pour faire du camping . . .
5. Pour aller dîner dans un restaurant élégant . . .
6. Pour passer une soirée tranquille à la maison . . .

des jeans

un pull-over

des souliers

un pantalon

un corsage

des bottes

une jupe

une veste

des chaussures de tennis

une robe

un complet

des sandales

une chemise

un tailleur

un short

un tee-shirt

un manteau

un maillot de bain

des lunettes

un chapeau

une cravate

Bien entendu, vous portez des *chaussettes* ou des *bas* et aussi des sous-vêtements (un *soutien-gorge*, un *slip* et un *jupon* pour les filles et un slip et un *maillot de corps* pour les garçons). La nuit vous portez probablement un pyjama ou une *chemise de nuit*.

socks / hose
bra / underpants / slip
undershirt
nightgown

B. Vos couleurs préférées. De quelle couleur sont les vêtements que vous portez ou que vous possédez?

Des bas is a general term for hosiery. **Des collants** refers to pantyhose.

Exemples   J'ai un pantalon bleu et une chemise blanche.
Je porte une veste grise.

Les couleurs: **blanc/blanche** *white;* **gris/grise** *gray;* **noir/noire** *black;* **bleu/bleue** *blue;* **rouge** *red;* **jaune** *yellow;* **marron** *brown;* **rose; mauve; bleu clair** *light blue;* **bleu foncé** *dark blue.*

Point out that **marron** is an invariable adjective.

C. Votre apparence physique. Comment êtes-vous physiquement?

1. Est-ce que vous avez les yeux . . . ?

bleus   verts   noirs   marrons

In order to avoid sensitive areas of weight and height, such questions have been omitted. If students feel comfortable about it, they could also describe these aspects.

2. Est-ce que vous avez les cheveux . . . ?

blonds   bruns *(dark)*   châtains *(brown)*   roux *(red)*   gris

2. Est-ce que vous avez les cheveux longs ou courts?

Other useful vocabulary for describing clothing might be introduced: à **carreaux** *(checked);* à **rayures** *(striped);* à **fleurs** *(floral);* **imprimé** *(print);* à **manches** *(sleeves);* **longues/courtes; en laine** *(wool);* **en coton; en nylon; en soie** *(silk);* **en tergal** *(polyester)*

 # Le placement des adjectifs

You may wish to refer students to the table of forms for **beau, nouveau, vieux,** etc., in Chapter 3.

Présentation

A. Although most descriptive adjectives in French come after the noun (**une chemise bleue, une femme sportive, un homme sympathique**), there are several frequently used adjectives that are usually placed before the noun:

Masculine	Feminine	Meaning
un **bon** dîner	une **bonne** boulangerie	*good*
un **beau** pull	une **belle** chemise	*beautiful*
un **grand** verre	une **grande** maison	*large, tall, big*
un **gros** livre	une **grosse** voiture	*big, large, fat*
un **jeune** homme	une **jeune** femme	*young*
un **joli** tailleur	une **jolie** couleur	*pretty*
un **long** voyage	une **longue** vie	*long*
un **mauvais** film	une **mauvaise** journée	*bad*
un **nouveau** magasin	une **nouvelle** boutique	*new*
un **petit** café	une **petite** maison	*little*
un **vieux** manteau	une **vieille** robe	*old*
un **vrai** Français	une **vraie** amie	*real, true*

1. As has already been noted, **beau, nouveau,** and **vieux** change before a masculine singular noun that begins with a vowel: **un nouvel appartement; un vieil ami; un bel homme.** The plural of these adjectives is formed by adding an s or an x.

2. When a prenominal adjective precedes a plural noun, the indefinite article **des** becomes **de**:

    des tomates → **de** grosses tomates
    des amis   → **de** bons amis
    des hôtels   → **de** nouveaux hôtels

B. The meaning of certain adjectives varies depending on whether they precede or follow the noun:

ancien (ancienne)	mon ancien professeur	*my former teacher*
	un livre ancien	*an old book*
cher (chère)	chers amis	*dear friends*
	un livre cher	*an expensive book*
grand	un grand homme	*a great man*
	un homme grand	*a tall man*
même	la même personne	*the same person*
	ce soir même	*this very evening*
pauvre	un pauvre homme	*a poor, unfortunate man*
	un homme pauvre	*a man who is poor*
propre	ma propre chemise	*my own shirt*
	une chemise propre	*a clean shirt*

Point out that **une grande personne** is ''an adult'' and **une personne grande** is ''a tall person.''

Substitution: (1) C'est un bon ami. hôtel / livre / vie / voiture / film. (2) Regardez ce vieux monsieur. café / femme / homme / musée / hôtel. (3) Ce sont de belles voitures. garçons / montagnes / enfants / restaurants / pommes / livres. (4) C'est un gros pull. joli / italien / noir / beau / vieux / confortable. (5) C'est une petite boutique. nouvelle / élégante / grande / américaine / jolie.

Préparation

A. **Extravagance.** Corinne, qui est mannequin à Paris, est allée faire des achats dans des boutiques de mode. Elle parle des jolis vêtements qu'elle vient d'acheter.

   Modèles   un pantalon (nouveau)   → **Je viens d'acheter un nouveau pantalon.**

   des chaussures (italiennes)   → **Je viens d'acheter des chaussures italiennes.**

   1. un pull (gros)
   2. une chemise de nuit (jolie)
   3. des chaussures (confortables)
   4. une robe (belle)
   5. un maillot de bain (nouveau)
   6. des sous-vêtements (élégants)
   7. une veste (petite)
   8. des jeans (américains)
   9. un tailleur (gris)
   10. un corsage (rose)

B. **Impressions.** Robert, un Américain, regarde *Paris Match* avec son ami
français Jean-Marie. Il veut vérifier ses impressions au sujet de différentes
choses qu'il remarque dans cette revue. Formulez les réponses de Jean-
Marie.

Options: Oral/written.

Modèle   Cette voiture est économique, n'est-ce pas? (la
Renault) → **Oui, la Renault est une voiture économique.**

1. Ce film est intéressant, n'est-ce pas? (*Le Monde selon Garp*)
2. Ces vins sont bons, n'est-ce pas? (le beaujolais et le bordeaux)
3. Ce restaurant est excellent, n'est-ce pas? (la Tour d'Argent)
4. Ces fromages sont bons, n'est-ce pas? (le camembert et le brie)
5. Ce musée est nouveau, n'est-ce pas? (le Centre Georges Pompidou)
6. Cet hôtel est cher, n'est-ce pas? (l'hôtel Georges V)
7. Cet avion est très rapide, n'est-ce pas? (le Concorde)
8. Cette église est très belle, n'est-ce pas? (la cathédrale de Chartres)

Communication

Choix. Indiquez ce que vous préférez dans chacune des situations suivantes.

Qu'est-ce que vous préférez?

Options: Ask as questions or
have students interview each
other and report back the
preferences of their partner.

1. Manger un bon dîner ou lire un bon livre?
2. Habiter dans une grande maison ou dans un petit appartement?
3. Faire un long voyage ou passer un mois à la plage?
4. Manger dans un bon restaurant ou dormir dans un bon hôtel?
5. Posséder une petite voiture ou une grosse voiture?
6. Étudier dans une grande université ou dans une petite université?
7. Avoir un bon salaire ou un travail agréable?
8. Avoir des vêtements confortables ou des vêtements élégants?

 ## Les verbes conjugués comme *mettre*

Présentation

The verb **mettre** (*to place, to put, to put on*) is irregular:

mettre	
je **mets**	nous **mettons**
tu **mets**	vous **mettez**
il/elle/on **met**	ils/elles **mettent**
passé composé: j'ai **mis**	

Qu'est-ce que tu vas mettre pour sortir?
Mets ton joli complet gris.
Je ne mets pas de sucre dans mon café.
Où est-ce que tu as mis mon stylo?

A. Mettre has several idiomatic uses:

mettre la table *to set the table*   Est-ce que tu as mis la table?
se mettre à *to start to*   Il se met à pleuvoir.
se mettre à table *to sit down to eat*   Nous allons nous mettre à table.
se mettre en colère *to get angry*   Il se met facilement en colère.

B. Other verbs conjugated like **mettre** are:

permettre à *to allow, to permit*   Elle ne permet pas à Jean de sortir
                                          seul.
promettre à *to promise*   J'ai promis à mes parents de dîner
                                          avec eux ce soir.
admettre *to allow, to admit*   J'admets que j'ai eu tort.
remettre *to hand in, to postpone*   Remettez-moi vos devoirs.
                                       Ne remettez pas à demain ce que
                                          vous pouvez faire aujourd'hui.

Note that both **permettre** and **promettre** take indirect object pronouns in French: **permettre à quelqu'un de faire quelque chose; promettre à quelqu'un de faire quelque chose.**

Substitution: (1) Je mets la table. Pierre et Marc / tu / Janine / vous / nous. (2) Qu'est-ce que tu mets pour sortir? vous / Jean-Luc / Roger et Martine / tu / je. (3) Où est-ce que j'ai mis la lettre? nous / vous / on / Jeannette / mon frère. (4) Il a promis à Sylvie de préparer le repas. je / nous / tu / vous / Monique.

Préparation

A. Qu'est-ce qu'on va mettre? Véronique veut savoir ce que ces amis vont mettre pour aller au concert ce soir. Donnez leurs réponses.

Modèle   Henri / pantalon gris → **Henri met un pantalon gris.**   Repeat in passé composé
                                                                               (Henri a mis un pantalon gris.).

1. vous / jupe
2. Roger / chemise blanche
3. Suzanne / robe noire
4. nous / cravate
5. je / corsage rose
6. tu / complet bleu

B. Promesses. Il n'est jamais trop tard pour prendre de bonnes résolutions. Voici ce que différentes personnes ont promis.

Modèle   Pierre / sa mère / écrire plus souvent → **Pierre a promis à sa mère d'écrire plus souvent.**

1. je / ma petite sœur / réparer son vélo
2. nous / le professeur / faire nos devoirs
3. tu / ton patron / arriver à l'heure
4. les enfants / leurs parents / ranger leur chambre
5. Catherine / son fiancé / prendre une décision
6. vous / votre mère / aider un peu à la maison

Have students repeat using
indirect object pronouns in their
answers (e.g., **Pierre lui a
promis d'écrire plus souvent.**).

C. Est-ce que tout va bien? Julien vient de commencer ses études à l'université de Grenoble. C'est la première fois qu'il est loin de sa famille. Son père lui téléphone pour s'assurer que tout va bien. Voici les questions posées par le père. Donnez les réponses de Julien.

Modèle Est-ce que tu as promis à Maman de revenir à la maison pour Noël? (oui) → **Oui, j'ai promis à Maman de revenir à la maison pour Noël.**

1. Est-ce que tu as mis ton argent à la banque? (non, pas encore)
2. Est-ce qu'on te permet d'avoir des visites dans ta chambre? (non)
3. Est-ce qu'on t'a permis de choisir tes propres cours? (oui)
4. Est-ce que tu me promets de bien travailler? (mais oui, Papa)
5. Est-ce que tu mets le pull-over que ta mère t'a donné? (oui, tous les jours)
6. Est-ce que tu permets à tes amis d'utiliser ta voiture? (non)
7. Est-ce que tu vas te mettre à travailler sérieusement? (oui)
8. Est-ce que tu nous promets de nous envoyer une lettre chaque semaine? (oui)

Options: Written/oral/role play.

You may want students to answer using direct and indirect object pronouns when possible.

Communication

A. On change de rôle. Imaginez que vous êtes le professeur. Qu'est-ce que vous allez permettre et ne pas permettre à vos étudiants? Par exemple, est-ce que vous allez leur permettre de dormir en classe? De ne pas remettre leurs devoirs? D'être souvent en retard?

Students might also share their New Year's resolutions.

B. Les bonnes résolutions. Le début du trimestre est le temps des bonnes résolutions. Qu'est-ce que vous avez promis de faire ou de ne pas faire ce trimestre?

Exemple J'ai promis de mieux écouter en classe et de ne pas remettre mon travail jusqu'à la dernière minute.

C. Futurs parents. Vous allez peut-être avoir des enfants un jour. Est-ce que vous allez leur permettre de sortir seuls? De rentrer après minuit? D'avoir leur propre téléphone? De choisir leurs vêtements? De ne pas faire leur travail? Est-ce qu'il y a d'autres choses que vous allez leur permettre ou ne pas leur permettre?

HENRI GARCIN · ALEXANDRA GONIN

LES PARENTS NE SONT PAS SIMPLES CETTE ANNEE!

⚜ Le comparatif

Présentation

Comparative constructions are used to compare two things, individuals, or actions. In English, comparatives are formed by adding the suffix *-er* (fast*er*, long*er*) or by using the adverbs *more* or *less* (*more* quickly, *less* intelligent).

A. In French, comparisons of adjectives can take three forms:

aussi . . . que *as . . . as*	Il est aussi grand que sa sœur.
plus . . . que *more (-er) . . . than*	Il est plus grand que son frère.
moins . . . que *less (-er) . . . than*	Il est moins grand que son père.

Mets cette veste. Elle est beaucoup plus chaude que ton pull.
Ces souliers sont moins confortables que ces bottes.
Est-ce que la beauté est aussi importante pour les hommes que pour les femmes?

     The same constructions are used to compare adverbs:

aussi . . . que	Je marche aussi vite que Robert.
plus . . . que	Je marche plus vite que Michel.
moins . . . que	Je marche moins vite que Monique.

Est-ce que les vêtements coûtent aussi cher en France qu'aux États-Unis?
Mes enfants ne travaillent pas aussi sérieusement que leurs cousins.
Elle apprend plus facilement que son frère.
Vous vous levez beaucoup plus tôt que moi.

Point out that **cher** functions as an invariable adverb in the verb phrase **coûter cher.**

B. The following expressions of quantity are combined with **que** to compare amounts of things.

autant de + *noun* + que *as much (many) . . . as*	Tu as autant d'argent que Jean.
plus de + *noun* + que *more . . . than*	Tu as plus d'argent que Suzanne.
moins de + *noun* + que *less . . . than*	Tu as moins d'argent que Mireille.

Est-ce que la beauté a autant d'importance pour les hommes que pour les femmes?
Il y a plus de choix dans ce magasin que dans l'autre.
Nous avons moins de temps libre que le trimestre passé.

    Autant, plus, and **moins** are also used in adverbial expressions to compare how much or how little one does something.

Nous travaillons autant que Paul.
Nous travaillons plus que Serge.
Nous travaillons moins que Sophie.

C. Bon has an irregular comparative form, which is equivalent to *better* in English.

	Singulier	*Pluriel*
Masculin	meilleur	meilleurs
Féminin	meilleure	meilleures

Cette boutique de mode est meilleure que l'autre.
Les vêtements sont meilleurs ici.

The adverb **bien** also has an irregular form, **mieux**, which means *better*.

Est-ce vrai que les Français s'habillent mieux que les Américains?
On travaille mieux quand on a bien dormi.
Tu chantes de mieux en mieux!

Substitution: (1) Je ne suis pas aussi grand que lui. tu / vous / nous / Jeannette. (2) Marie est plus patiente que Philippe. Jean-Claude et Lucien / nous / tu / je. (3) Ce livre est moins intéressant que les autres. ces films / cette histoire / ce programme / ces classes. (4) Ce programme est meilleur que les autres. ce livre / ces restaurants / cet hôtel / cette classe / cet étudiant / ces étudiants. (5) Jean travaille mieux que ses frères. chante / parle / travaille / étudie / comprend.

Préparation

A. Paris et la province. Madame Chanet, une Marseillaise qui vient de faire un séjour dans la capitale, a décidé qu'elle préfère la vie en province. Comment compare-t-elle les deux?

Modèle les gens / moins heureux → **Les gens sont moins heureux que chez nous.**

1. la vie / moins agréable
2. les prix / plus élévés
3. les vêtements / aussi chers
4. les restaurants / moins bons
5. les vendeuses / moins patientes
6. les magasins / moins intéressants
7. les gens / plus froids
8. le climat / beaucoup plus froid
9. le poisson / moins bon
10. les maisons / moins jolies

B. Le nouveau prof. Véronique est assez contente de Mademoiselle Villiers, son nouveau professeur d'anglais, surtout en comparaison avec son ancien prof.

Modèles Elle est dynamique → **Elle est plus dynamique que mon ancien prof.**

Elle explique bien. → **Elle explique mieux que mon ancien prof.**

Repeat with **aussi . . . que** and **moins . . . que.**

1. Elle est gentille.
2. Elle s'habille bien.
3. Elle parle vite.
4. Elle est sympathique.
5. Elle explique bien.
6. Elle est facile à comprendre.
7. Elle enseigne bien.
8. Elle est jeune.
9. Elle est patiente.
10. Elle est amusante.

C. Évian ou Vittel? Monsieur Achard fait chaque année une cure à Vittel. Madame Simon préfère aller à Évian. Pourquoi?

Modèles   On mange bien à Vittel. → **On mange mieux à Évian.**
Il y a beaucoup de piscines à Vittel. → **Il y a plus de piscines à Évian.**

Point out that Vittel is a spa in the Vosges and that Évian is on Lake Geneva, near Switzerland.

1. Les hôtels sont bons à Vittel.
2. L'eau de Vittel est très bonne pour la santé.
3. La vie est très agréable à Vittel.
4. On se repose bien à Vittel.
5. On s'amuse bien à Vittel.
6. Les gens sont très gentils à Vittel.
7. Il y a beaucoup de nouveaux hôtels à Vittel.
8. Il y a beaucoup de choses intéressantes à faire à Vittel.
9. Il y a beaucoup de jolis parcs à Vittel.
10. Il y a beaucoup de gens qui vont à Vittel.

Communication

A. Questions/interview. Répondez aux questions suivantes ou utilisez-les pour interviewer un(e) autre étudiant(e).

1. Est-ce que tu as l'impression que le français est plus facile ou plus difficile que l'anglais?
2. Est-ce que ton cours de français est plus facile ou plus difficile que tes autres cours?
3. Pour toi, est-ce que les maths sont plus faciles que les langues?
4. Est-ce que tu as autant de travail qu'à la fin du trimestre?
5. Est-ce que tu penses que tes cours à l'université sont plus faciles ou plus difficiles que tes cours au lycée?
6. Est-ce que tu trouves que les programmes à la télé sont meilleurs cette année que l'année dernière?
7. Est-ce que tu penses que les vêtements sont plus jolis cette année que l'année dernière?
8. Est-ce que tes profs ce trimestre sont plus sévères ou moins sévères que le trimestre passé?

B. Comparaisons. Utilisez les adjectifs ou les expressions suggérés pour exprimer votre opinion sur les sujets suivants. Notez les différentes possibilités dans l'exemple suivant.

Exemple   l'avion ↔ le train
rapide / dangereux / confortable / pratique / cher / bon marché / ?
Le train est moins rapide que l'avion.
Le train n'est pas aussi dangereux que l'avion.
Le train est meilleur marché que l'avion.

Options: (1) Written. (2) Oral— Have students share sentences with class and exchange opinions.

1. la cuisine américaine ↔ la cuisine française
variée / bonne / raffinée / mauvaise / simple / de bonne qualité / ?

2. Les Américains ↔ les Européens
   cultivés / conformistes / grands / naïfs / optimistes / ?
3. les voitures étrangères ↔ les voitures américaines
   économiques / chères / confortables / pratiques / de bonne qualité /
   rapides / ?
4. le football américain ↔ le football européen
   intéressant / violent / populaire / difficile / brutal / ?
5. les hommes ↔ les femmes
   courageux / capables / sportifs / ambitieux / indépendants /
   intelligents / ?

⚜ Le superlatif

Présentation

Superlatives are used to express the idea of *the most*, *the least*, *the best* and
to distinguish or set off individuals, people, or things from a group. In French,
the superlative adjectives and adverbs are formed according to the following
patterns:

A. Superlatives of adjectives are formed by using the appropriate definite
article with **plus** or **moins** before the adjective.

le plus
le moins   joli magasin

la plus
la moins   jolie voiture

les plus
les moins   jolis vêtements

C'est le plus grand hôtel de Paris.   *It's the biggest hotel in Paris.*
Voici la plus vieille maison de la   *Here is the oldest house in town.*
   ville.
C'est le restaurant le moins cher   *It's the cheapest restaurant in the*
   du quartier.   *neighborhood.*

   Note in the above examples that **de** after the superlative corresponds
to the English *in*. Note also that the group or category can be omitted:
C'est toi qui portes la plus jolie robe.
   Adjectives in the superlative follow their normal pattern in following
or preceding the noun they modify.

C'est une ville intéressante.   C'est la ville la plus intéressante de la région.
C'est une petite ville.   C'est la plus petite ville de la région.

B. Superlatives can be followed by nouns:

le plus de   *the most*   C'est Jean qui a le plus de talent.
le moins de   *the least*   C'est le magasin où il y a le moins de choix.

C. When an adverb is used in the superlative, the definite article is always **le** because adverbs do not have gender or number.

C'est la robe que j'aime le moins.
Voici les vêtements que je porte le plus souvent.

D. To form the superlative for **bon**, simply place the appropriate definite article before the irregular comparative forms you learned in the preceding *Présentation:* **le meilleur; la meilleure; les meilleurs; les meilleures.**

C'est le meilleur magasin de la ville.
Andrée est la meilleure étudiante de la classe et Jacques est le plus mauvais.

The superlative of **mauvais** can be **le plus mauvais** or **le pire.**

Le mieux is the superlative of **bien.**

Quand est-ce que vous vous sentez le mieux?
C'est ici qu'on mange le mieux.

Substitution: (1) C'est le plus beau monument de la ville. église / musée / quartier / rue / parc. (2) Nous avons les plus beaux vêtements. jolis / chers / élégants / confortables. (3) C'est Geneviève qui chante le mieux. Paul / moi / mon père / ma sœur / mon ami. (4) C'est Frédéric qui travaille le mieux. chante / étudie / parle / comprend.

Préparation

A. **Vendeur aux Galeries Lafayette.** Olivier est très content de travailler aux Galeries Lafayette, un des grands magasins de Paris. Qu'est-ce qu'il dit?

Modèle   un grand choix → **Nous avons le plus grand choix.**

1. de bons prix
2. un magasin moderne
3. une jolie vitrine
4. des vêtements élégants
5. des employés sérieux
6. des clients distingués
7. une bonne publicité
8. un patron sympathique

B. **Paris.** Monsieur Lefort pense que Paris est la plus belle ville du monde. Qu'est-ce qu'il dit?

Modèles   des gens intéressants → **C'est à Paris qu'on trouve les gens les plus interessants.**
des clubs où on s'amuse bien → **C'est à Paris qu'on trouve les clubs où on s'amuse le mieux.**

1. des femmes élégantes
2. de beaux quartiers
3. des restaurants où on mange bien
4. de jolis parcs
5. de beaux vêtements
6. de bonnes écoles
7. des clubs où on s'amuse bien
8. des musées exceptionnels
9. des acteurs qui jouent bien
10. des choses intéressantes à faire
11. des chanteuses qui chantent bien
12. des monuments anciens

C. Le chou-chou du prof. Clarisse fait un stage de formation *(workshop)*   **Chou-chou**=teacher's pet.
pour devenir mannequin de mode. Son professeur de danse pense que
Clarisse est une de ses meilleures étudiantes. Qu'est-ce qu'elle pense de
Clarisse?

Modèles   Elle est gentille. → **C'est elle qui est la plus gentille.**
               Elle travaille bien. → **C'est elle qui travaille le mieux.**
               Elle a de l'ambition. → **Cest elle qui a le plus d'ambition.**

1. Elle est intelligente.
2. Elle a du talent.
3. Elle danse bien.
4. Elle comprend vite.
5. Elle apprend facilement.
6. Elle est sérieuse.
7. Elle a du courage.
8. Elle fait bien son travail.
9. Elle est raffinée.
10. Elle réussit bien.

Communication

A. À votre avis. Utilisez les suggestions suivantes pour formuler des questions
que vous allez poser à un(e) autre étudiant(e).

Exemple   la plus belle région des États-Unis → **À votre avis, quelle
est la plus belle région des États-Unis?**

1. le meilleur chanteur ou la meilleure chanteuse
2. le meilleur acteur ou la meilleure actrice
3. le groupe le plus populaire en ce moment
4. la plus belle ville des États-Unis
5. le meilleur restaurant de la ville
6. le plus mauvais restaurant de la ville
7. le cours le plus difficile
8. le cours le plus facile
9. le film le plus amusant
10. le plus beau pays du monde

    Encourage students to come up
    with other questions.

B. Le plus et le moins. Donnez votre réponse à chacune des questions suivantes ou posez-les à un(e) autre étudiant(e).

Exemple   le dessert que vous aimez le mieux? → **Quel est le dessert
que vous aimez le mieux?
Le dessert que j'aime le mieux est la glace.**

1. la personne que vous admirez le plus?
2. le fruit que vous aimez le mieux?
3. le cours où vous travaillez le plus?
4. le légume que vous aimez le moins?
5. le programme de télé que vous regardez le plus souvent?
6. le disque que vous aimez le plus?
7. le cours où vous réussissez le mieux?
8. le moment de la journée où vous vous sentez le mieux?
9. le mois de l'année que vous aimez le moins?
10. le pays que vous avez la plus envie de visiter?

    You may want to encourage
    students to explain their answers
    whenever appropriate.

L'aventure du tee-shirt

Oui, les pantalons, les robes, les complets, les cravates existent encore. Mais, de Rome à Tokyo, de Paris à San Francisco, le vêtement le plus *porté semble* être le tee-shirt et le blue-jean. Quelles sont les raisons de cette popularité? Est-ce que c'est parce que le tee-shirt est plus pratique et meilleur marché? Parce qu'on peut le porter en été aussi bien qu'en hiver? Ou bien, est-ce à cause de sa fonction de *panneau d'affichage*?

 Le tee-shirt *attire* les inscriptions et les graffiti comme un *mur* ou une page blanche. Les vêtements ont toujours été un moyen d'expression, mais le tee-shirt va plus loin. Le message est ouvertement exprimé. *Grâce au* tee-shirt, on peut rendre public son signe du zodiaque, son université, sa bière préférée, ses vedettes favorites ou même ses idées sur l'amour, la politique et la vie en général.

 Le tee-shirt, comme le blue-jean, est une mode venue des États-Unis. Il a traversé l'Atlantique pour la première fois en 1945, comme sous-vêtement porté par les soldats américains. Plus récemment, il est revenu sur le dos des étudiants et il est très vite devenu populaire parmi les jeunes Français. Même les grands *couturiers* l'ont adopté, et *apparemment*, il n'y a pas beaucoup de différence entre un tee-shirt de Monoprix et un tee-shirt de Pierre Cardin, excepté le prix, bien entendu. Maintenant, les tee-shirts traversent *de nouveau* l'Atlantique mais dans l'autre *sens* et avec l'*étiquette* «Made in France». On peut voir sur les campus américains des tee-shirts qui portent des inscriptions en français. «Faites l'amour, pas la guerre», proclament certaines. «Voulez-vous jouer avec moi?» suggèrent d'autres. D'autres encore, plus philosophes, se contentent de dire «C'est la vie!».

worn / seems

bulletin board

attracts / wall

thanks to

Suggestion: Point out that Monoprix is a chain of inexpensive French department stores.

designers / apparently

again
direction / label

Options: (1) Have students create additional titles for the **Synthèse**. (2) Do **Synthèse Communication**, exercise A.

Compréhension Selon les renseignements donnés, est-ce que les phrases suivantes sont vraies ou fausses? Corrigez le sens de la phrase s'il est faux.

1. Les vêtements préférés des jeunes sont les tee-shirts et les blue-jeans.
2. C'est à cause de son élégance que le tee-shirt est particulièrement populaire.
3. Les tee-shirts sont généralement bon marché.
4. Les tee-shirts sont pratiques, mais on peut les porter seulement en hiver.
5. Les vêtements sont un moyen d'expression de la personnalité.
6. La mode des tee-shirts est venue du Japon.
7. Le tee-shirt est venu en France pour la première fois en 1975.
8. La différence principale entre un tee-shirt de Monoprix et un tee-shirt d'un grand couturier, c'est le prix.
9. On trouve maintenant en Amérique des tee-shirts qui portent des inscriptions en français.

NOTES CULTURELLES

Les compliments

Have students practice giving and receiving compliments in French.

Quand on fait un compliment à un Américain, sa réponse habituelle est de sourire° et de remercier°. Un Français, par contre°, a tendance à minimiser le compliment et à dénigrer ses possessions. Si on lui dit°, par exemple, «J'aime bien ta veste. Elle est très jolie», il va répondre quelque chose comme «Oh, tu trouves? Je l'ai achetée en solde l'année dernière.»

En France, comme aux États-Unis, il est aussi très important de savoir faire un compliment ou d'exprimer° son appréciation quand cela est nécessaire. Après un bon dîner, on peut remercier l'hôte et l'hôtesse en disant° «mes compliments au chef» ou plus simplement «merci infiniment» ou «merci mille fois». On peut dire «chapeau»° pour exprimer son admiration d'une manière plus familière, aussi bien que° «sensationnel», «chic alors», «chouette» et «formidable».

sourire *smile* remercier *thank* par contre *on the other hand* dit *says* exprimer *express* en disant *by saying* chapeau *hats off* aussi bien que *as well as*

Il est mignon, ton petit chapeau

Communication

A. Vendeur de tee-shirts. Imaginez que vous travaillez dans une boutique où on vend des tee-shirts et des blue-jeans. Votre patron veut mettre des inscriptions différentes sur les tee-shirts qu'il vend. C'est à vous de suggérer toutes sortes d'inscriptions différentes. Quelles inscriptions françaises allez-vous lui proposer?

Have class choose five best slogans.

B. Les hommes et leur image. Est-ce que la beauté a la même importance pour les hommes que pour les femmes? Pour le savoir, vous pouvez faire un petit sondage dans votre classe. Voici quelques questions pour vous aider.

1. Est-ce que la beauté est importante pour les hommes?
2. À votre avis, jusqu'à quel âge un homme peut-il être beau?
3. Quel type de beauté masculine préférez-vous? (Un homme sexy? Un homme sportif? Un homme élégant et distingué? Un homme fort et viril?)
4. À votre avis, qu'est-ce qui est préférable pour un homme? Être beau ou être intelligent? Être beau ou avoir de la personnalité? Être beau ou être riche? Être beau ou avoir de la chance? Être beau ou être célèbre?
5. Est-ce que les hommes se préoccupent assez de leur apparence?

C. Portraits. Utilisez les suggestions suivantes (ou ajoutez vos propres idées) et faites le portrait (1) d'une personne que vous connaissez, (2) d'un personnage célèbre ou (3) de la femme idéale ou de l'homme idéal.

Suggested for written homework. If students describe famous people, have other students guess identity.

L'apparence physique: être petit, grand, gros / avoir les cheveux blonds, bruns / avoir les yeux bleus, verts / s'habiller bien, mal / avoir l'air gentil / ?

La personnalité: individualiste / généreux / timide / impulsif / cynique / sérieux / amusant / ?

D. Vérité ou chauvinisme? Jean Chauvin est un Français qui a des opinions bien définies sur toutes sortes de sujets. Êtes-vous d'accord avec lui?

Options: (1) Written. (2) Oral— Read statements or ask as questions. Encourage students to explain their answers.

1. C'est en France qu'on boit les meilleurs vins du monde.
2. Les Françaises sont les plus belles femmes du monde.
3. Pour être heureux, il faut travailler le moins possible et s'amuser le plus possible.
4. Les hommes sont plus intelligents et plus capables que les femmes.
5. La cuisine française est la meilleure du monde.
6. Paris est la plus belle ville du monde.
7. Les femmes sont moins courageuses et moins ambitieuses que les hommes.
8. Les Français s'habillent mieux que les Américains.
9. La beauté a plus d'importance pour les femmes que pour les hommes.
10. Les gens les plus intéressants sont aussi les plus modestes (comme moi)!

VOCABULAIRE

noms

les vêtements (voir pp. 232–233)

d'autres noms
°la **beauté**
le **couturier**, la **couturière** *designer*
° l'**élégance** (f)
 l'**étiquette** (f) *label*
la **guerre** *war*
° l'**importance** (f)
° l'**individualité** (f)
le **journal de mode** *fashion magazine*
°le **mari** *husband*
°la **mode** *fashion*
°le **moyen** *means*
le **mur** *wall*
° l'**obligation** (f)
la **réponse** *answer*
le **sens** *direction*
le **soldat** *soldier*
°la **vanité**

verbes

les verbes conjugués comme **mettre** (voir pp. 235–236)

d'autres verbes
attirer *to attract*
se contenter de *to be satisfied with*
disparaître *to disappear*
°**emprisonner**
°**exister**
manquer *to lack, to miss*
°**organiser**
°**proclamer**
°**réaliser**
°**refuser**
sembler *to seem*

adjectifs

les couleurs (voir p. 233)

les adjectifs prénominaux (voir p. 233)
d'autres adjectifs
fort(e) *strong*
meilleur(e) *better;* le, la, les **meilleur(e)(s)** *best*
pratique *practical*
raffiné(e) *refined*
°**sexy**
°**viril(e)**

adverbes

apparemment *apparently*
longtemps *long, a long time*
mieux *better;* le **mieux** *best*
ouvertement *openly*
récemment *recently*

divers

aussi bien que *as well as*
bien entendu *of course*
bon marché *inexpensive*
de moins en moins *less and less*
de nouveau *once again*
de plus en plus *more and more*
encore *still, yet*
grâce à *thanks to*

CHAPITRE TREIZE

Le passé et les souvenirs

13

Jacques Prévert

Jacques Prévert (1900-1977) a été le poète de la vie de tous les jours, des choses simples et familières, de la solidarité humaine. Il prend le temps d'écouter, de regarder, de sentir les gens et les choses vivre *autour de lui*. Et ensuite il les *exprime* avec des *mots* de tous les jours, dans un style simple et spontané, mais *plein de* fantasie et de tendresse.

    Dans ses poèmes, Prévert *décrit* les choses qu'il aime, les choses qui *chantent* la vie, la tendresse et la liberté, et il se révolte contre toute forme d'injustice, de servitude ou d'hypocrisie. Il est aussi le *témoin* discret des drames de la vie: la séparation, le *chagrin*, la solitude comme, par exemple, dans le poème suivant.

Suggestion: Point out difference between **le petit déjeuner** (also called **le déjeuner**) **le déjeuner, le dîner,** and **le souper** as well as corresponding verbs.

around
him / expresses / words
full of
describes
celebrate (sing)
witness
sorrow

248

Le déjeuner du matin

Il a mis le café
Dans la tasse
Il a mis le lait
Dans la tasse de café
Il a mis le sucre
Dans le café au lait
Avec la petite *cuiller*   spoon
Il a tourné
Il a bu le café au lait
Et il a *reposé* la tasse   put back down
Sans me parler
Il a *allumé*   lighted
Une cigarette
Il a fait des *ronds*   circles, rings
Avec la *fumée*   smoke
Il a mis les *cendres*   ashes
Dans le *cendrier*   ashtray
Sans me parler
Sans me regarder
Il s'est levé
Il a mis
Son chapeau sur sa tête
Il a mis
Son manteau de pluie
Parce qu'il *pleuvait*   it was raining
Et il est parti
Sous la pluie
Sans une *parole*   word
Sans me regarder
Et moi j'ai pris
Ma tête dans ma main
Et j'ai *pleuré*   cried

Jacques Prévert

Jacques Prévert, "Le déjeuner du matin" extrait de *Paroles* © Éditions Gallimard.

Compréhension Répondez aux questions suivantes selon les renseignements donnes dans le texte.

1. Où et quand ce drame de la vie a-t-il lieu?
2. À votre avis, qui sont les deux personnages du poème?
3. Quelles sont les actions principales de l'homme?
4. Est-ce que ces actions sont des actions ordinaires et habituelles ou des actions inhabituelles? Donnez des exemples.
5. À votre avis, quelle attitude est-ce que ces gestes et ces actions révèlent?
6. Quelle est la réaction de l'autre personne?
7. À votre avis, quel est le problème principal entre ces deux personnages?
8. Quelle est votre réaction personnelle devant l'attitude de chaque personnage du poème?
9. Est-ce que vous pouvez suggérer une solution à leur problème?
10. Imaginez les événements ou les discussions qui ont précédé la situation décrite dans le poème.

NOTES CULTURELLES

Leçon de catéchisme, avant la première communion

Rites et coutumes

En France, comme dans la plupart des autres cultures, les étapes° et les événements importants de la vie sont marqués par des rites particuliers. La France étant° un pays de tradition catholique, la plupart de ces

cérémonies ont une origine religieuse. Les enfants, par exemple, sont généralement baptisés dans les quelques mois qui suivent° leur naissance. Jusqu'à une époque récente, l'Église exigeait° même° qu'on donne aux enfants des noms de saints, tels que° Jean, Paul, Thérèse ou Marie. Ainsi° en France, on célèbre non seulement° l'anniversaire mais aussi la fête° d'une personne. Le baptême° est suivi d'un° dîner qui réunit toute la famille et le parrain° et la marraine.° Il y a également° une cérémonie religieuse suivie d'un dîner de famille quand l'enfant fait sa première communion, généralement à l'âge de onze ou douze ans. Selon les statistiques, la plupart des Français se marient entre l'âge de vingt et un et vingt-trois ans. Pour être marié légalement, il faut se marier à la mairie° mais un grand nombre de couples choisissent également d'avoir une cérémonie religieuse. Le mariage, surtout à la campagne, reste souvent une occasion de faire un grand dîner qui peut durer de midi jusqu'au soir.

étapes *stages* étant *being* suivent *follow*
exigeait *required* même *even* tels que *such as*
ainsi *thus* seulement *only* fête *patron saint's day*
baptême *baptism* suivi d'un *followed by a*
parrain *godfather* marraine *godmother*
également *also* mairie *city hall*

Have students describe for a French person different **rites et coutumes** of American life in general and/or college life in particular.

Le mariage civil, à la mairie

Et vous?

A. **Les sentiments.** À votre avis, quels sentiments la personne qui parle dans le poème de Jacques Prévert éprouve-t-elle?
Est-ce qu'elle éprouve . . .

1. de la joie?
2. du plaisir?
3. du bonheur (*happiness*)?
4. de la tristesse?
5. du chagrin?
6. de l'inquiétude (*worry, anxiety*)?
7. du regret?
8. du désespoir (*despair*)?
9. de la fierté (*pride*)?
10. de la jalousie (*jealousy*)?
11. de la haine (*hatred*)?
12. de l'amour (*love*)?
13. de l'amertume (*bitterness*)?
14. de la peine (*sorrow*)?
15. de l'amitié (*friendship*)?
16. de l'affection?

—Et l'autre personne, l'homme, qui part sans dire un mot, qu'est-ce qu'il éprouve, à votre avis?
—Quels sentiments semblent être absents de leur vie?

B. **Les étapes de la vie et les événements importants.** Notre vie est marquée par toutes sortes d'événements et elle est divisée en plusieurs grandes étapes.

Les étapes de la vie	Les événements
la naissance (*birth*)	le baptême
l'enfance (*childhood*)	
l'adolescence	
la jeunesse	le mariage
l'âge adulte	le divorce
la vieillesse (aussi appelée le troisième âge)	la retraite (*retirement*)
la mort	l'enterrement (*burial*)

—À votre avis, quelle étape de la vie est la plus heureuse? Et la plus difficile?
—À votre avis, quel est l'événement le plus important dans la vie d'une personne?

C. **La poésie et la vie.** Inspirez-vous du poème de Jacques Prévert pour écrire un poème au sujet d'un moment de la journée, d'une étape de la vie ou d'un événement particulier.

Option: You might also want students to create a "calligramme," using Apollinaire's calligrammes as models.

⚜ L'imparfait

Présentation

The imperfect tense (**l'imparfait**) provides another way of talking about past events. It is formed by dropping the **-ons** ending from the **nous** form of the present tense and adding the endings shown below.

nous **parl**ons → parl- + *imperfect endings*
nous **av**ons → av- + *imperfect endings*
nous **finiss**ons → finiss- + *imperfect endings*

The only exception is **être**, whose imperfect stem is **ét-**.

L'imparfait de *parler*		L'imparfait d'*être*	
je parl**ais**	nous parl**ions**	j'**étais**	nous ét**ions**
tu parl**ais**	vous parl**iez**	tu ét**ais**	vous ét**iez**
il/elle/on parl**ait**	ils/elles parl**aient**	il/elle/on ét**ait**	ils/elles ét**aient**

    All the singular forms and the **ils/elles** form are pronounced the same: [parlɛ] and [etɛ].
    Depending on the context used, the imperfect has several translations in English:

j'habitais   *I was living*
               I used to live
               I lived

Point out that "would" is often used to express the idea of "used to" in English.

A. There are two main uses of the imperfect:

1. To indicate an habitual past action:
Nous allions en Bretagne tous les étés.
Chaque matin je me levais à huit heures.
Ma mère m'emmenait au marché aux poissons.

2. To describe a situation or condition that existed in the past:

Quand il était petit, il était souvent malade.
J'étudiais quand ils sont rentrés.
Ils avaient une petite maison à la campagne.
Il portait un complet gris.

B. Certain time expressions are often used with the imperfect:

à cette époque-là   *at that time, in those days*
autrefois   *in the past, long ago*
d'habitude   *generally, usually*
chaque année, mois, etc.   *every year, month, etc.*
tous les jours   *every day*

Substitutions: (1) D'habitude, je finissais à huit heures. tes amis / tu / nous / Marc / vous / je. (2) Autrefois, tu perdais souvent patience. nous / vous / mon professeur / les étudiants. (3) Je n'étais pas fatigué après l'examen. nos amis / vous / nous / tu / Henriette.

Préparation

A. De bons souvenirs. Voici ce que Michel et Raymonde ont mis sur la carte postale qu'ils ont envoyée à leurs amis pendant leurs vacances à Antibes. D'après leurs commentaires, comment étaient leurs vacances?

Modèle Il fait du soleil. → **Il faisait du soleil.**

1. Il fait beau.
2. La mer est bonne.
3. Les gens sont sympathiques.
4. L'hôtel se trouve près de la mer.
5. Nous avons une grande chambre.
6. Notre chambre donne sur la mer.
7. La cuisine est excellente.
8. Nous dormons jusqu'à dix heures.
9. Chaque matin nous faisons une petite promenade.
10. L'après-midi nous allons à la plage.

B. C'était impossible. Catherine voulait inviter ses amis à dîner mais tout le monde était occupé. Pourquoi ne pouvaient-ils pas venir?

Modèle Serge/ avoir mal à la tête → **Serge avait mal à la tête.**

1. tu / être malade
2. vous / ne pas être libres
3. Pierre / attendre la visite de sa mère
4. nous / avoir du travail à faire
5. Hélène / avoir besoin de se reposer
6. je / vouloir regarder une émission spéciale à la télé
7. Bruno / faire le ménage
8. Roger et Claudine / être en voyage

Can be used for listening comprehension by completing the sentences and reading as a paragraph.

C. Souvenirs d'enfance. Au cours d'une visite dans le quartier du vieux Lyon où il a grandi, Monsieur Berger évoque quelques souvenirs de son enfance.

Modele je / jouer souvent dans cette rue avec mes amis → **Je jouais souvent dans cette rue avec mes amis.**

1. mes parents / habiter dans ce quartier
2. ma mère / faire son marché chaque matin
3. elle / m'emmener avec elle
4. nous / s'arrêter dans chaque magasin
5. elle / prendre le temps de parler avec les marchands
6. ils / parler de la pluie et du beau temps
7. nous / passer ensuite devant le garage de Monsieur Giraud
8. je / vouloir être mécanicien comme lui
9. il / répondre à toutes mes questions
10. ma mère / attendre patiemment

Dans le vieux Lyon

Communication

A. Questions/interview. Répondez aux questions suivantes ou utilisez-les pour interviewer un(e) autre étudiant(e).

1. Où habitait ta famille quand tu étais petit(e)?
2. Quel était ton programme de télévision favori?
3. Quelle était ta classe préférée?
4. Quelles étaient tes distractions favorites?
5. Quels étaient tes disques et tes livres préférés?
6. Qu'est-ce que tu voulais devenir?
7. Est-ce que tu avais un chien ou un chat?
8. Où est-ce que tu allais en vacances?
9. Qu'est-ce que tu faisais pendant tes vacances?
10. Qu'est-ce que tu faisais après tes classes?

Suggestion: Have students work in small groups and write a summary of partners' answers.

B. Le monde de votre enfance. Faites une description d'un ou plusieurs aspects du monde de votre enfance.

1. Un quartier ou une ville où vous avez habité (ou que vous avez visité) autrefois. Comment était ce quartier ou cette ville?
2. La maison où vous avez grandi. Comment était-elle?
3. Un(e) ami(e) d'enfance. Comment était cette personne?
4. Le lycée où vous avez fait vos études. Comment étaient les étudiants, les professeurs, les cours?
5. Les dimanches de votre enfance. Que faisiez-vous d'habitude?

Suggested for writing. If used for oral work in class, written preparation would be helpful.

 ## Le verbe *dire*

Présentation

Dire (*to say* or *to tell*) is an irregular verb.

Suggestion: Point out that dire can take both direct and indirect objects.

dire	
je **dis**	nous **disons**
tu **dis**	vous **dites**
il/elle/on **dit**	ils/elles **disent**
passé composé: j'ai dit	

Qu'est-ce que vous dites?	*What are you saying?*
Elle nous a dit de venir ce soir.	*She told us to come this evening.*
Est-ce que vous disiez la vérité?	*Were you telling the truth?*
Dis à Yvonne d'attendre devant la pharmacie.	*Tell Yvonne to wait in front of the pharmacy.*

A. **Dire** is also used in several expressions:

dire la vérité	*to tell the truth*
dire un mensonge	*to tell a lie*
dire des mots doux	*to whisper sweet nothings*
Qu'est-ce que ça veut dire?	*What does that mean?*
Qu'est-ce que vous voulez dire?	*What do you mean?*
C'est-à-dire . . .	*That is (to say) . . .*
Dis, qu'est-ce que tu vas faire?	*Hey, what are you going to do?*
Dites donc, vous!	*Hey you!*
Comment dit-on . . . ?	*How do you say . . . ?*

B. **Dire** can be followed by an infinitive verb phrase introduced by **de:**

Dites à Claudine de se dépêcher.
Nous leur avons dit de ne pas nous attendre.

Substitutions: (1) Qu'est-ce que tu dis? je / vous / ton frère / vos amis / nous. (2) Je leur ai dit de s'arrêter. nous / Marc / nos amis / vous / tu. (3) Il ne disait pas la vérité. son frère / nous / vous / ses amis / Jeanne / je.

Préparation

A. **On dit ce qu'on pense.** Certaines personnes disent toujours ce qu'elles pensent; d'autres, non.

Modèle   Claude (jamais)   → **Claude ne dit jamais ce qu'il pense.**

1. je (toujours)
2. Anne (quelquefois)
3. vous (jamais)
4. mes amis (toujours)
5. tu (rarement)
6. nous (tout le temps)

Suggestion: Explain the role of a **concierge**.

B. **Les observations de Madame Forestier.** Madame Forestier, la concierge d'un immeuble, raconte à son mari ce qu'elle a entendu pendant la journée.

Modèle   les Dupont / à leurs enfants / ne pas jouer dans la rue → **Les Dupont ont dit à leurs enfants de ne pas jouer dans la rue.**

1. l'agent / à Monsieur Durant / venir au poste de police
2. Madame Rosier / à son mari / ne pas perdre son temps
3. Jean-Luc / à Madeleine / arriver avant neuf heures
4. je / à notre fille / ne pas sortir ce soir
5. Madame Leroi / à son fils / travailler plus sérieusement
6. je / à Madame Blanc / ne pas écouter les conversations des clients
7. je / à monsieur Poirier / ne pas oublier de me payer

Have students repeat using indirect object pronouns. **Les Dupont leur ont dit de ne pas jouer dans la rue.**

Communication

A. Qu'est-ce que vous dites? Répondez aux questions suivantes.

1. Est-ce que vous dites toujours la vérité?
2. Est-ce que vous dites toujours ce que vous pensez?
3. Est-ce que vous disiez quelquefois des mensonges quand vous étiez petit(e)?
4. Comment dit-on bonjour en espagnol? Et en italien? Et dans d'autres langues?
5. Qu'est-ce que vous dites au professeur quand vous ne comprenez pas? Et quand vous n'avez pas fait vos devoirs?
6. Quel est le premier mot que vous avez dit?

B. Qui a dit . . . ? Quel personnage historique a dit chacune des phrases suivantes?

1. Qui a dit: «Après moi, le déluge»?
   a. Noé b. Louis XV c. Napoléon
2. Qui a dit: «Vive le Québec libre!»?
   a. De Gaulle b. Jeanne d'Arc c. Lafayette
3. Qui a dit: «L'état, c'est moi»?
   a. Charlemagne b. César c. Louis XIV
4. Qui a dit: «Il faut cultiver notre jardin»?
   a. Léonard de Vinci b. Voltaire c. Renoir
5. Qui a dit: «Je pense, donc je suis»?
   a. Descartes b. Hamlet c. Sartre
6. Qui a dit qu'il aimait mieux une tête bien faite qu'une tête bien pleine?
   a. Rousseau b. Montaigne c. Rabelais

Follow-up: Have students prepare phrases that famous people have said or might have said.

Réponses: 1. Louis XV 2. De Gaulle 3. Louis XIV 4. Voltaire 5. Descartes 6. Montaigne

Les pronoms disjonctifs

Présentation

The disjunctive, or stress, pronouns are:

Les pronoms disjonctifs	
moi *I, me*	nous *we, us*
toi *you*	vous *you*
lui *he, him, it*	eux *they, them (m)*
elle *she, her, it*	elles *they, them (f)*
soi *one*	

These pronouns are used:

A. After prepositions:

Est-ce que tu parles de moi?
Voulez-vous venir avec nous?
Ils sont restés chez eux.

B. After **c'est** or **ce sont.**

Point out that the verb agrees
with the antecedent of **qui**.

Qui a fait cela? C'est moi.	*Who did that? **I** did.*
Est-ce que c'était Jacques? Oui, c'était lui.	*Was it Jacques? Yes, it was **he** (him).*
C'est moi qui ai fait cela.	*I did it. (I am the one who did it.)*
Ce sont elles qui ont identifié le cambrioleur.	*They identified the thief. (They are the ones who identified the thief.)*

C. Alone or in short phrases where there is no verb:

Qui veut une tasse de café? —Moi.
Hélène est fatiguée. —Nous aussi.

D. To put emphasis on the subject of the verb:

Eux, ils ont bu du thé, mais nous, nous avons bu du café.
Moi, je suis français. Lui, il est suisse.

E. With **-même**(s) to talk about oneself or others (myself, yourself, etc.):

Tu l'as fait toi-même, n'est-ce pas?	*You did it yourself, didn't you?*
Ils font leur cuisine eux-mêmes.	*They do their cooking themselves.*
On ne peut pas tout faire soi-même.	*You can't do everything yourself.*

F. In compound subjects where a pronoun is used for at least one of the persons or items:

Philippe et moi, nous avons faim.
Elle et toi, vous êtes de bonnes amies.

G. To indicate possession following **être à:**

Ce livre n'est pas à moi; il est à eux.   *This book isn't mine; it's theirs.*

H. In comparisons after **que,** where **que** means *than* or *as*:

Paul est plus grand que toi.   *Paul is taller than you.*

Substitution: (1) Ce livre est à moi. toi / lui / elle / nous / vous / eux / elles. (2) Je l'ai fait moi-même. tu / Marc / mes frères / vous / nous / je. (3) Moi, j'ai très faim. il / tu / vous / nous / elle / elles.

Préparation

A. On joue en peu. Un groupe d'amis jouent à un jeu qui consiste à deviner qui est la personne qu'on a choisie. C'est le tour de Sylvie. Donnez les réponses des autres à ses questions.

> **Modèle**   Est-ce que cette personne est près de moi?   →   **Non, elle n'est pas près de toi.**

1. Est-ce qu'elle est à côté de Suzanne?
2. Est-ce qu'elle est devant Pierre?
3. Est-ce qu'elle est derrière moi?
4. Est-ce qu'elle est avec Georges et Denise?
5. Est-ce qu'elle est en face de Colette?
6. Est-ce qu'elle est près de toi, Robert?
7. Est-ce que cette personne est parmi nous?

If appropriate for your students, this game can be used in the classroom.

B. Quel désordre! Henri et ses camarades de chambre ont décidé de ranger leur appartement. À qui appartiennent ces différentes choses?

> **Modèle**   Jérôme, il est à toi ce vieux pull? (non)   →   **Non, il n'est pas à moi.**

1. Ce livre de maths, il est à toi, Alain? (non)
2. Il est à ta fiancée? (oui . . . peut-être)
3. Cette boîte de chocolats est à vous? (oui)
4. Et ces souliers, ils sont à toi, Michel? (non)
5. Et ces sous-vêtements, est-ce qu'ils sont à moi? (oui . . . probablement)
6. Elle est à nous, cette affiche? (non)
7. Ces photos sont à Alain? (oui)
8. Et ces jolies revues, elles sont à tes parents? (oui)

C. Qui a fait ça? La vie de famille a ses hauts et ses bas. Aujourd'hui Madame Savabarder n'est pas contente du tout. Donnez les réponses de ses enfants à ses questions.

> **Modèle**   C'est toi qui as laissé tes vêtements dans la salle de bain? (non)   →   **Non, maman, ce n'est pas moi.**

1. C'est toi qui as utilisé toute l'eau ce matin? (non)
2. Alors, c'est ta sœur? (oui)
3. C'est toi qui as oublié de sortir le chien? (non)
4. C'est vous, les enfants, qui avez mangé toute la glace? (non)
5. C'est moi qui ai laissé la porte du frigo ouverte? (oui)
6. Ce sont tes amis qui t'ont enseigné ce mot-là? (oui)
7. C'est toi qui as cassé ce verre? (non)
8. Alors, c'est ton petit frère? (oui)

*Have students complete this **Préparation** in groups of three or four. Give a student leader the correct responses so that he or she can monitor the responses of other group members. Instructor can circulate and listen to different groups.*

D. Une famille indépendante. Les Thomas sont des gens qui tiennent à tout faire eux-mêmes. Dites ce qu'ils font.

> **Modèle**   Nous faisons notre pain.   →   **Nous faisons notre pain nous-mêmes.**

1. Nous lavons notre voiture.
2. Je fais ma cuisine.
3. Jean choisit ses vêtements.
4. Ma femme répare tout.
5. Les enfants préparent leur petit déjeuner.
6. Je fais mon jardin.
7. Nous allons vendre notre maison.
8. Hélène se coupe les cheveux.

Communication

A. Moi, je . . . Répondez aux questions suivantes en utilisant des pronoms disjonctifs.

Exemple   Beaucoup d'étudiants aiment manger au restaurant. Et vous? → **Moi aussi, j'aime manger au restaurant.** ou **Moi, je n'aime pas manger au restaurant.** ou **Pas moi, je préfère faire ma cuisine moi-même.**

Suggested for oral whole-class activity.

1. La plupart des étudiants détestent les examens. Et vous? Et vos amis?
2. Beaucoup d'étudiants mangent au restaurant universitaire. Et vous?
3. En général, les Français boivent du vin avec leurs repas. Et vous?
4. Beaucoup de gens ne prennent pas de petit déjeuner le matin. Et vous?
5. Peu de gens aiment se lever avant huit heures du matin. Et vous?
6. Certains étudiants se dépêchent pour venir en classe. Et vous? Et vos amis?
7. Il y a des gens qui se mettent facilement en colère. Et vous? Et votre professeur?
8. La plupart des Américains s'intéressent aux sports. Et vous? Et les étudiants de votre université?

B. Questions/interview. Répondez aux questions suivantes ou utilisez-les pour interviewer un(e) autre étudiant(e). N'oubliez pas d'utiliser des pronoms disjonctifs dans vos réponses.

1. Quand tu étais petit(e), est-ce que tu t'entendais bien avec les autres enfants du quartier?
2. Est-ce que tu jouais souvent avec eux?
3. Est-ce que tu réparais tes jouets toi-même?
4. Est-ce que tu mangeais souvent chez toi à midi?
5. Est-ce que le lycée était loin de chez toi?
6. Est-ce que tu parlais souvent au téléphone avec tes ami(e)s?
7. Dans ta famille, est-ce que c'était toujours toi qui faisais la vaisselle?
8. C'était toi qui rangeais ta chambre?

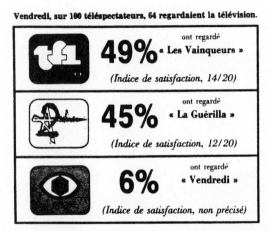

Vendredi, sur 100 téléspectateurs, 64 regardaient la télévision.

tf1 **49%** ont regardé « Les Vainqueurs »
(Indice de satisfaction, 14/20)

45% ont regardé « La Guérilla »
(Indice de satisfaction, 12/20)

6% ont regardé « Vendredi »
(Indice de satisfaction, non précisé)

L'imparfait et le passé composé

Présentation

Although the imperfect and the **passé composé** are both past tenses, they have different purposes. Whether the imperfect or **passé composé** is used depends on the speaker's view or perception of a past action.

Suggestion: Use time line to further contrast **imparfait** and **passé composé**.

Imparfait
Background: The imperfect describes a condition, state, state of mind, or action that was continuing or was in progress. There is no concern for the time when the situation started or ended.

Il finissait ses devoirs.
He was finishing his homework.
Il pleuvait.
It was raining.
À cette époque-là, il travaillait dans une usine d'automobile.
At that time he was working in an automobile factory.
Il était très malheureux.
He was very unhappy.

Passé composé
Event: In contrast, the **passé composé** expresses:
1. An action that is a completed event:
   Il a fini ses devoirs.
   He finished his homework.
2. An event that had a known beginning or end or a specific duration that may vary from a few moments to many years:
   Nous avons travaillé pendant deux heures.
   We worked for two hours.
3. A change in state of mind or a reaction to an event:
   J'ai eu très peur quand le téléphone a sonné.
   I was afraid (became afraid) when the telephone rang.
4. A succession of events; each event moves the story forward:
   Il s'est réveillé, il s'est habillé, il a quitté la maison.

Repeated action: The imperfect describes a habitual action in the past.

Le samedi, mon père faisait la cuisine.
My father used to do the cooking on Saturdays.
Autrefois, j'allais rarement au cinéma.
In the past, I rarely went to the movies.

Specific action: In contrast, the **passé composé** describes what happened or what was done or said at a particular time.
Hier, mon père a fait la cuisine.
Yesterday my father did the cooking.
Je suis allé(e) quatre fois au cinéma la semaine dernière.
I went to the movies four times last week.

One of the most frequent cases where the **passé composé** and the imperfect are contrasted is when a continuing action is interrupted by a specific event.

Nous parlions quand le professeur est entré.
Ils étaient en train de manger quand nous sommes arrivés.
Il faisait froid quand je suis sortie ce matin.

Préparation

A. Dites-moi pourquoi. Bertrand veut toujours savoir pourquoi les gens font ce qu'ils font. Donnez leurs réponses à ses questions.

Modèle   Pourquoi as-tu acheté un sandwich? (avoir faim) → **J'ai acheté un sandwich parce que j'avais faim.**

Transformation: Utilisez les éléments donnés pour former des phrases qui contrastent l'utilisation de l'imparfait et du passé composé.Modèle: Nous écoutons des disques. Pierre arrive → Nous écoutions des disques quand Pierre est arrivé. (1) Paul étudie. Jacques téléphone. (2) Je fais du ski. Je me casse la jambe. (3) Patrick finit ses devoirs. Sa sœur entre. (4) Il fait beau. Nous faisons une promenade. (5) Hélène attend l'autobus. Il commence à pleuvoir. (6) Nous allons à la gare. Nous rencontrons Martine.

1. Pourquoi es-tu allé chez le medecin? (être malade)
2. Pourquoi vous êtes-vous couchés à 9 heures? (être fatigués)
3. Pourquoi t'es-tu levée si tôt? (avoir beaucoup de travail)
4. Pourquoi Janine est-elle allée à la poste? (vouloir envoyer une lettre)
5. Pourquoi avez-vous vendu votre vieille voiture? (ne pas marcher bien)
6. Pourquoi n'as-tu pas travaillé? (avoir mal à la tête)
7. Pourquoi sont-ils restés jusqu'à minuit? (s'amuser bien)
8. Pourquoi Josette s'est-elle dépêchée? (être en retard)

B. Que faisiez-vous? La mort du Président Kennedy est un événement qui a marqué beaucoup de gens, même les Français. Beaucoup se souviennent exactement de ce qu'ils faisaient au moment où ils ont appris la nouvelle.

Modèle   je / être chez des amis → **J'étais chez des amis quand j'ai appris la nouvelle.**

1. nous / être dans un magasin
2. mon père / venir de rentrer à la maison
3. vous / faire la vaisselle
4. je / servir le dîner
5. tu / s'habiller
6. mes amis / finir leur dîner
7. tu / attendre l'autobus
8. vous / écouter la radio

Suggestion: Point out that *Cendrillon* is from *Les Contes de ma Mère l'Oie* by Perrault (as are *Le Petit Chaperon Rouge, Le Petit Poucet, Barbe Bleue*, etc.)

C. L'histoire de Cendrillon. Pour compléter l'histoire, mettez les verbes suggérés à l'imparfait ou au passé composé selon le cas.

Il était une fois une jeune fille qui _____ (s'appeler) Cendrillon. Elle _____ (avoir) deux demi-sœurs qui n' _____ (être) pas gentilles avec elle. C' _____ (être) Cendrillon qui _____ (faire) tout le travail à la maison.

Un jour, le prince _____ (décider) de donner un grand bal. Mais Cendrillon ne _____ (pouvoir) pas aller au bal parce qu'elle n' _____ (avoir) pas de jolis vêtements.

Suggested for individual or small-group writing.

Cendrillon _____ (être) en train de pleurer quand sa marraine (*godmother*) _____ (arriver). Elle _____ (posséder) une baguette magique (*magic wand*). La marraine _____ (toucher) les vêtements de Cendrillon et ils _____ (devenir) très beaux. Centrillon a promis à sa marraine de rentrer avant minuit et elle _____ (partir) au bal.

Le prince _____ (inviter) à danser la mystérieuse jeune fille et ils _____ (danser) pendant tout le bal. Cendrillon _____ (être) si heureuse qu'elle _____ (oublier) l'heure. Quand elle _____ (entendre) minuit sonner (*ring*), elle _____ (partir) si vite qu'elle _____ (perdre) une de ses chaussures.

Le prince, qui _____ (aimer) Cendrillon, _____ (aller) dans toutes les maisons de son pays pour essayer de la retrouver. Finalement, le prince _____ (venir) à la maison où Cendrillon et ses sœurs _____ (habiter). Les deux sœurs _____ (essayer) la chaussure mais elle _____ (être) beaucoup trop petite pour elles. Timidement Cendrillon _____ (demander): «Est-ce que je peux l'essayer?» La chaussure lui allait (*fitted*) parfaitement. Il _____ (être) évident que la belle jeune fille du bal et Cendrillon _____ (être) la même personne. Ils _____ (se marier) et ils _____ (avoir) beaucoup d'enfants.

Communication

A. Cendrillon! Tu viens de loin, ma petite! L'histoire de Cendrillon appartient au folklore international et reflète les valeurs traditionnelles de notre culture. Transformez-la pour la rendre plus moderne, moins sexiste, plus amusante, etc. Vous pouvez changer les personnages, le pays où l'action a lieu, le développement de l'histoire ou sa conclusion. Si vous préférez, inventez une autre histoire. Suggested for individual or small-group writing. Students may share **contes** with class.

B. Vérité ou bluff. Racontez une histoire vraie ou imaginaire. Les autres étudiants peuvent vous poser quelques questions pour clarifier certains points. Ensuite ils vont dire s'ils pensent que vous dites la vérité ou non. N'oubliez pas d'utiliser l'imparfait pour décrire les circonstances (le temps qu'il faisait, quelle heure il était, etc.) et le passé composé pour dire ce que chaque personne a fait.

SYNTHÈSE

Souvenirs d'enfance de Kiwele Shamavu

Dans un petit village zaïrois

Kiwele Shamavu, un Africain né au Zaïre parle de son enfance.

LE REPORTER	Où est-ce que vous avez passé votre enfance?
KIWELE	Je suis né et j'ai grandi dans un petit village du Zaïre. C'était à l'époque où le Congo était encore sous le contrôle de la Belgique.
LE REPORTER	Combien d'habitants y avait-il dans votre village?
KIWELE	C'était un petit village d'environ trois ou quatre cents habitants situé à cinquante kilomètres de Kisangani.

LE REPORTER	Quelle langue parlait-on dans votre village?	
KIWELE	Notre tribu parlait le luba. Mais la langue de communication avec les autres tribus était le swahili, et à l'école on parlait français. J'ai donc trois langues *maternelles*.	native
LE REPORTER	Il y avait une école dans votre village?	
KIWELE	Oui, c'était une école *dirigée* par des missionnaires belges. C'est là que je suis allé à l'école jusqu'à l'âge de douze ans.	directed, run
LE REPORTER	Et après, qu'est-ce que vous avez fait?	
KIWELE	Mon grand-père, qui était le *chef* du village, m'a envoyé en Belgique pour continuer mes études au lycée. Je suis resté en Belgique pendant six ans et en France pendant quatre ans. Je suis retourné au Congo seulement une fois pendant toute cette période. C'était l'année où j'ai commencé mes études universitaires en France. Au début, cette séparation a été très difficile.	chief
LE REPORTER	Vous avez des frères et des sœurs?	
KIWELE	Oui, j'ai cinq frères et trois sœurs, et des multitudes de cousins! Mes parents habitaient dans une grande maison au centre du village. Oncles, tantes, cousins, cousines, nous formions tous une grande famille. Un de mes cousins était *gardien* dans une réserve d'animaux *sauvages*. Quelquefois, il m'emmenait avec lui quand il partait en jeep dans la *brousse*. J'avais toujours grand plaisir à l'accompagner.	guard / wild / bush
LE REPORTER	Est-ce que vous avez été très surpris quand vous êtes arrivé à Bruxelles pour la première fois?	
KIWELE	Oui, c'était en hiver et il y avait de la neige. J'étais absolument *ravi*. J'ai touché la neige. Et puis, j'ai vite *rempli* mes *poches* de neige. La dame qui m'attendait à l'aéroport m'a demandé: «Mais Kiwele, qu'est-ce que tu fais? Pourquoi mets-tu de la neige dans tes poches?» Et j'ai répondu: «C'est pour l'envoyer à maman.»	delighted / filled /pockets

Texte basé sur une interview avec un Africain originaire du Zaïre.

Compréhension   Répondez aux questions suivantes selon les renseignements donnés.

1. Où est-ce que Kiwele a passé son enfance?
2. Est-ce qu'il habitait dans une grande ville?
3. Quelles langues est-ce que Kiwele parle?
4. Où est-ce qu'il allait à l'école?
5. Pourquoi est-ce qu'il est parti en Belgique quand il avait douze ans?
6. Est-ce que Kiwele est resté longtemps sans retourner dans son pays?
7. Est-ce que Kiwele était le seul enfant de sa famille?
8. Est-ce qu'il y avait d'autres membres de la famille qui habitaient dans le même village?
9. Quelle a été sa réaction quand il est arrivé à Bruxelles?
10. Pourquoi a-t-il mis de la neige dans ses poches?

Option: Have students write a description of Kiwele Shamavu using questions as a guide.

NOTES CULTURELLES

Le Zaïre

La République du Zaïre (ancien Congo Belge) avec une population de 28 millions d'habitants est le deuxième pays d'Afrique. Colonie belge pendant quatre-vingts ans, le Zaïre est devenu indépendant en 1960. Quelques années après, le Zaïre était totalement africanisé: on a demandé à tous les Zaïrois d'adopter un nom africain et on a donné des noms africains aux rues et aux villes. Par exemple, la capitale, Léopoldville, est devenue Kinshasa.

La plupart des tribus du Zaïre ont leur propre dialecte et leurs propres coutumes. Il existe encore d'assez fortes° rivalités locales, en particulier, entre le Katanga où se trouvent les riches mines de cuivre° et le reste du pays. Les langues principales de ce pays sont le tshiluba au centre et au sud-est, le kikongo à l'ouest, le lingala au nord-ouest et le swahili à l'est. En raison de° cette diversité linguistique, le lingala est généralement utilisé comme lingua franca (langue de communication) et peut devenir la langue officielle. Le français continue à être la langue officielle.

L'influence de la langue et de la culture françaises est toujours présente au Zaïre de même que° dans les dix-sept pays d'Afrique noire qui sont devenus indépendants pendant les années soixante. La plupart de ces pays sont membres de la Communauté Franco-Africaine et ont une monnaie° commune (le franc C.F.A.).

fortes *strong*   cuivre *copper*   en raison de *because of*
de même que *just as*   monnaie *currency*

Communication

A. **Questions/interview.** Répondez aux questions suivantes ou utilisez-les pour interviewer un(e) autre étudiant(e). Commencez par la première question de chaque série et selon la réponse que vous obtenez, posez les autres questions de la série ou passez à la question suivante.

1. Où es-tu né(e)? En quelle année est-ce que c'était? Où est-ce que ta famille habitait à cette époque-là? Est-ce que tu avais des frères et des sœurs? Dans combien de villes différentes est-ce que tu as habité? ?

2. Est-ce que tu avais un(e) ami(e) que tu aimais beaucoup quand tu étais petit(e)? Comment s'appelait ton ami(e)? Où est-ce qu'il(elle) habitait? Pourquoi est-ce que vous étiez de bon(ne)s ami(e)s? Est-ce que vous alliez à la même école? Est-ce que tu es resté(e) en contact avec cette personne? ?

3. Est-ce que tu te souviens d'une personne de ton enfance avec un plaisir particulier? Qui était cette personne? Pourquoi est-ce que tu te souviens de cette personne? Est-ce que tu l'admirais beaucoup? Quelles qualités possédait cette personne? ?

4. Est-ce que tu te souviens d'un événement de ton enfance avec un plaisir particulier? Quel était cet événement? Quand et où est-ce que cet événement a eu lieu? Que faisais-tu? ?

5. Où est-ce que tu es allé(e) au lycée? Est-ce que tu avais de bons professeurs? Quels étaient tes classes et tes professeurs préférés? Est-ce qu'il y avait des classes ou des professeurs que tu n'aimais pas? Est-ce que tu appartenais à différents clubs? Est-ce que tu travaillais pour gagner ton argent de poche? ?

This is an important skill to emphasize. Encourage students to add other related questions.

Option: Each series of questions can also be used for a guided composition.

B. **Souvenirs d'enfance.** Racontez vos propres souvenirs d'enfance ou les souvenirs d'une autre personne (parents, grands-parents, ami(e), personne imaginaire).

C. **Un événement spécial.** Tout le monde se souvient d'un événement spécial avec un plaisir particulier. Décrivez un de vos souvenirs (fête, anniversaire, occasion spéciale). Qu'est-ce que vous avez fait? Qui était là? Où étiez-vous?, etc.

VOCABULAIRE

noms

les sentiments (voir p. 251)

les étapes de la vie (voir p. 251)

d'autres noms
  le **cendrier** *ashtray*
  le **chagrin** *sorrow*
  la **cuiller** *spoon*
° le **drame**
  la **fumée** *smoke*
  le **gardien** *guard*
° l'**injustice** (f)
  le **mensonge** *lie*
  le **mot** *word*
  la **parole** *(spoken) word*
° la **période**
  le **rond** *circle, ring*
° le **style**
  la **tasse** *cup*
  le **témoin** *witness*
° la **tendresse**
  la **vérité** *truth*

verbes

allumer *to light*
chanter *to celebrate, sing*
dire *to say, tell*
éprouver *to feel*
être à *to belong to*
exprimer *to express*
pleurer *to cry*
remplir *to fill*
reposer *to put back down*

adjectifs

  dirigé(e) *directed, run*
° **discret, discrète**
  maternel, maternelle *native*
  ravi(e) *delighted*
  sauvage *wild*
° **situé(e)**
° **spontané(e)**

divers

les expressions avec le verbe **dire** (voir p. 255)

d'autres expressions
à cette époque-là *at that time, in those days*
autour de *around*
autrefois *in the past, long ago*
contre *against*
d'habitude *generally, usually*
tous les jours *every day*

Face à l'avenir

Une salle de conférences dans une université française

INTRODUCTION

L'avenir, c'est un gros ? . . .

Au cours d'une enquête sur les sentiments des jeunes Françaises au sujet
de leur *avenir*, une journaliste parle avec Christine, une parisienne.   future
Elle est assez pessimiste.

LA JOURNALISTE	À votre avis, est-ce que vos études sont une bonne préparation pour la vie?	
CHRISTINE	Pas particulièrement. Autrefois, on faisait des études et on avait un *boulot* assuré. Maintenant les études *ne mènent* à rien.	job lead / (ne . . . rien = nothing) / goal
LA JOURNALISTE	Est-ce que le *but* principal des études est de préparer une profession?	
CHRISTINE	Pour moi, oui. On nous dit que c'est pour nous donner une bonne culture générale, pour nous préparer à jouer notre rôle dans la société. Tout ça, *c'est bien beau*, mais ça ne va pas m'aider à gagner ma vie. Et sans boulot, quel rôle peut-on jouer?	that's all well and good
LA JOURNALISTE	Est-ce que vous avez l'intention de vous marier un jour?	
CHRISTINE	Peut-être, mais je ne suis pas *pressée*. Le mariage est une chose sérieuse et je ne veux pas *me tromper*. Être mariée, avoir un ou deux *gosses*, oui, *je voudrais bien*, éventuellement. Mais, *de toute façon*, je veux avoir un travail intéressant et raisonnablement bien payé. Je ne veux pas être obligée de *compter sur quelqu'un d'autre*.	in a hurry make a mistake kids (slang) / I'm willing, I'd like that / at any rate count on / someone else
LA JOURNALISTE	Est-ce que vous pensez que les femmes et les hommes ont les mêmes chances de réussir dans la vie?	
CHRISTINE	En théorie, oui. En réalité, non.	
LA JOURNALISTE	Quel sentiment avez-vous quand vous pensez à l'avenir?	
CHRISTINE	Je suis un peu *inquiète*. Avec tous les problèmes qu'il y a dans le monde, c'est difficile de savoir ce qui va *arriver*. L'avenir, c'est un gros *point d'interrogation*.	worried happen / question mark

Compréhension   Répondez aux questions suivantes selon les renseignements donnés dans le texte.   Option: Have students also answer questions in notes for instructor.

1. Est-ce que Christine est assez optimiste quand elle pense à son avenir?   Et vous?
2. Est-ce qu'elle est satisfaite de ses études? Expliquez.   Et vous?
3. Pour elle, quel est le but principal des études?   Et pour vous?
4. Est-ce que tout le monde est d'accord avec elle?
5. Est-ce qu'elle a l'intention de se marier un jour?   Et vous?
6. Pourquoi préfère-t-elle attendre?   Et vous, préférez-vous attendre pour vous marier?
7. Pourquoi tient-elle à travailler?   Et vous, tenez-vous à travailler?
8. Selon elle, est-ce qu'une femme peut réussir aussi facilement qu'un homme?   Et selon vous?
9. Pourquoi est-elle inquiète quand elle pense à l'avenir?   Avez-vous les mêmes sentiments?

NOTES CULTURELLES

Les Français et l'avenir

Les Français, en général, ont une attitude assez prudente et même blasée envers l'avenir. Cette attitude est évidente dans le dicton° «Plus ça change, plus c'est la même chose.»

Contrairement aux Américains, qui ont souvent une foi° absolue dans l'avenir et dans le progrès scientifique et technologique, les Français ont plus tendance à se tourner vers° le passé, vers le bon vieux temps.° Les traditions culturelles et la place accordée à l'histoire dans l'enseignement° donné dans les écoles soulignent° l'importance du passé et de l'héritage national.

Mais cette attitude est maintenant en train de changer et cela est évident dans la vie quotidienne° des Français aussi bien que dans les programmes gouvernementaux.

dicton *proverb*   foi *faith*   vers *toward*   le bon vieux temps *good old days*   l'enseignement *education* soulignent *emphasize*   quotidienne *daily*

Et vous?

Et vous, quel sentiment avez-vous quand vous pensez à l'avenir? Est-ce que vous avez *confiance* en l'avenir ou est-ce que vous avez peur de l'avenir?   confidence

1. Il y a des dangers qui *menacent* sérieusement notre planète. À votre avis, threaten
   est-ce que les dangers suivants sont très sérieux?

   —les guerres entre nations *voisines*   neighboring
   —la possibilité d'une guerre nucléaire
   —la possibilité d'une catastrophe dans une *centrale nucléaire*   nuclear power plant
   —les catastrophes naturelles
   —la pollution de l'atmosphère

2. Il y a aussi des problèmes qui risquent de détruire la qualité de la vie si
   nous ne réussissons pas à les *résoudre*. Quels sont les problèmes qui vous   solve
   préoccupent le plus personnellement?

   —l'inflation
   —la *faim*   hunger
   —le chômage
   —les *grèves*   strikes
   —la violence et les crimes
   —les inégalites sociales
   —le racisme
   —le sexisme
   —la surpopulation
   —le *bruit*   noise
   —l'*espionnage électronique*   electronic surveillance
   —la crise de l'énergie

3. Les progrès de la technologie et de la recherche scientifique vont apporter
   beaucoup de changements dans notre vie. Êtes-vous très enthousiaste,
   modérément enthousiaste, indifférent(e), un peu inquiet (inquiète), ou
   très inquiet (inquiète) quand vous pensez aux progrès possibles dans chacun des domaines suivants?

   —la technologie
   —la recherche médicale
   —l'exploration spatiale
   —l'*informatique*   computer science

4. Personellement, quels aspects de la vie future vous intéressent le plus? Est-ce que vous avez envie de participer un jour à un des projets suivants?

—vivre dans une ville sous la mer
—travailler dans une station spatiale
—établir une colonie humaine sur la *lune* ou sur une autre planète   moon
—devenir astronaute et participer à l'exploration spatiale
—établir un système de communication avec les extra-terrestres
—posséder votre propre robot
—faire un voyage interplanétaire

⚜ La négation

Présentation

In addition to **ne . . . pas** and **ne . . . jamais**, there are several other ways to express negative meanings. All such negative expressions are composed of **ne** and another element:

ne . . . plus *no longer*	ne . . . personne *nobody*
ne . . . pas du tout *not at all*	ne . . . que *only*
ne . . . rien *nothing*	ne . . . aucun(e) *none, not a single*
	ne . . . ni . . . ni *neither . . . nor*

A. **Ne . . . jamais, ne . . . plus,** and **ne . . . pas du tout** function in the same way as **ne . . . pas. Ne** precedes the verb, and the second part of the negative expression follows the verb or the auxiliary in a compound tense. When the partitive follows the negative, its form is **de** or **d'.**

Je ne pense jamais à l'avenir.	Nous n'avons plus d'argent.
Ce projet ne m'intéresse plus.	Il ne se trompe jamais.
Il ne se préoccupe pas du tout de son avenir.	Je n'ai jamais visité Paris.

Jamais without **ne** means *ever:*

Avez-vous jamais visité la Chine?	*Have you ever visited China?*

B. **Personne** and **rien** used with **ne** can be either subjects or objects of the verb and are sometimes objects of prepositions.

Nous n'achetons rien dans ce magasin.	Elle n'a parlé à personne.
Il n'y avait personne en classe vendredi.	La victime ne s'est souvenue de rien.

When **rien** and **personne** are direct object pronouns, the word order differs in a compound tense. **Rien** comes before the past participle and **personne** comes after it.

Je n'ai rien vu.	Il n'a rien entendu.
Je n'ai vu personne.	Il n'a entendu personne.

When **rien** and **personne** are subjects, both come at the beginning of the sentence.

Rien n'est simple.
Personne n'a pensé aux conséquences.

C. With **ne . . . que** and **ne . . . aucun(e)**, the second part of the negative is placed directly before the item modified. Notice that **aucun(e)** is an adjective used only in the singular. Notice also that the partitive article is retained after **ne . . . que**.

Il n'y a qu'un choix possible.   Je n'ai aucune idée.
Je ne mange que des légumes.   Aucun magasin n'est ouvert aujour-
                                                       d'hui.

D. In response to a question, **jamais, personne, rien,** and **aucun(e)** can be used alone.

Quand vas-tu prendre une décision? Jamais!
Qui est pressé? Personne!
Qu'est-ce qui est arrivé? Rien!

Option: Point out that prepositions are also retained—**Il n'est allé ni en Espagne ni au Portugal.**

E. In the expression **ne . . . ni . . . ni**, **ne** is placed before the verb, and **ni** is placed before each item negated. After **ni**, the indefinite and partitive articles are not used, but the definite articles are retained. Compare:

Elle a un frère et deux sœurs.   Elle n'a ni frère ni sœur.
Nous avons acheté des légumes et   Nous n'avons acheté ni légumes ni
   des fruits.   fruits.
Il aime la bière et le vin.   Il n'aime ni la bière ni le vin.
Victor et Alfred ont répondu à   Ni Victor ni Alfred n'a répondu à
   notre invitation.   notre invitation.

F. **Aussi** is used to agree with a positive statement; **non plus** is used to agree with a negative statement.

Christine est inquiète. Moi aussi.
Elle n'est pas optimiste. Nous non plus.

G. To disagree with a negative statement **si** is used instead of **oui**. Compare:

—Tu as fait tes devoirs, n'est-ce pas? —Oui, je les ai faits.
—Tu n'as pas fait tes devoirs, n'est-ce pas? —Si, je les ai faits.

Transformation: Mettez les phrases suivantes au passé composé. Modèle: Nous ne voyons rien. → Nous n'avons rien vu. (1) Il ne voit personne. (2) Elle ne mange que des légumes. (3) Vous ne vous souvenez plus de son nom. (4) Personne ne vient ici. (5) Je ne parle à personne. (6) Nous n'avons aucun problème. (7) Nous n'achetons ni légumes ni fruits.
Transformation: Mettez les phrases suivantes à la forme négative en utilisant les expressions négatives indiquées. Modèle: Nous avons peur de l'avenir. (ne . . . plus) → Nous n'avons plus peur de l'avenir. (1) Il fait du vent au mois de juin. (ne . . . jamais). (2) Hélène sort avec Patrick. (ne . . . plus). (3) Ils boivent du lait. (ne . . . que). (4) Elle aime la cuisine italienne et la cuisine française. (ne . . . ni . . . ni). (5) J'ai une chance de réussir. (ne . . . aucune). (6) Nous comprenons ses idées. (ne . . . pas du tout).

Préparation

A. La vie est cruelle! Jean se sent abandonné et négligé par ses amis. Retrouvez les réponses négatives que Jean a données aux questions qu'on lui a posées.

Options: Oral/written. Point out that **que** in the title means *how* and is used to intensify the sentence.

Modèle   Qui as-tu vu cet après-midi? (personne) → **Je n'ai vu personne cet après-midi.**

1. Qui est venu te voir hier soir? (personne)
2. Est-ce qu'on te téléphone quelquefois? (non . . . jamais)
3. Qu'est-ce qu'on t'a donné pour ton anniversaire? (rien)
4. Est-ce que ton père t'envoie encore de l'argent? (non . . . plus)
5. Qu'est-ce que ta petite amie t'a dit? (rien)
6. Est-ce qu'André et toi, vous avez aimé le film? (non . . . pas du tout)
7. Est-ce que tu as des projets pour le week-end? (non . . . aucun)
8. Est-ce que quelque chose a changé dans ta vie? (non . . . rien)
9. Est-ce que tu as jamais été vraiment heureux? (non . . . jamais)

B. Ça va mieux. Bernard est inquiet au sujet de tout le monde. Mireille le rassure.

Modèle   Tout le monde est malade. → **Mais non, personne n'est malade.**

1. Isabelle a beaucoup de problèmes en ce moment.
2. Quelque chose lui est arrivé.
3. Tu as toujours l'air triste.
4. Tout le monde est inquiet à ton sujet.
5. Pierre est encore à l'hôpital.
6. Il y a eu plusieurs accidents dans notre quartier.
7. Les agents ont emmené tout le monde au poste de police.
8. Les enfants ont tout cassé.
9. Ils sont impatients et fatigués.
10. Colette a peur de tout.

Point out that the negative answer to a question with **encore** is **ne . . . plus.**

Communication

A. Questions/interview. Répondez aux questions suivantes ou utilisez-les pour interviewer un(e) autre étudiant(e). Si votre réponse est négative, utilisez l'expression négative appropriée.

1. Est-ce que tu as encore les jouets que tu avais quand tu étais petit(e)?
2. Est-ce que tu te souviens du nom de ton premier professeur à l'école élémentaire?
3. Est-ce que tu regardes encore les dessins animés pour les enfants?
4. Est-ce que tu as jamais voyagé au Japon ou en Chine?
5. Est-ce que tu as jamais étudié une langue orientale?
6. Est-ce que quelqu'un est venu te voir hier soir?
7. Est-ce que tu te mets souvent en colère?

Options: Ask questions or adapt for directed dialogue. Then ask what students have said (**Est-ce que Jean a jamais voyagé au Japon?**, etc.).

B. Rien ne va plus. Il y a des jours où tout va mal. Imaginez que c'est le cas et faites une liste de toutes les choses qui vont mal. Utilisez autant d'expressions négatives que possible.

> **Exemples**   Personne ne s'est souvenu de mon anniversaire.
> Je n'ai rien fait d'intéressant pendant le week-end.

Suggested for individual or small-group writing. Have students share their sentences with the class.

⚜ Le pronom *y*

Présentation

A. The pronoun *y* is used to replace a prepositional phrase indicating location. Its meaning is often approximated by *there*. Like direct and indirect object pronouns, *y* is placed before the verb except in affirmative commands.

Je vais à Québec la semaine prochaine.	J'y vais la semaine prochaine.
Elle va rester en Belgique tout l'été.	Elle va y rester tout l'été.
Roland n'est jamais entré dans ce musée.	Roland n'y est jamais entré.
N'allez pas chez le dentiste.	N'y allez pas.
Va au cinéma.	Vas-y.

Note that an *s* is added to **va** for the affirmative command with **y** to make it easier to pronounce.

B. Sometimes the preposition **à** is used in constructions where it does not refer to physical location. The pronoun *y* can nevertheless replace the prepositional phrase, as long as the object of the preposition is a *thing*, not a person.

Je pense à mon enfance.	J'y pense.
Il réfléchit au problème.	Il y réfléchit.
As-tu répondu à ma lettre?	Y as-tu répondu?
Ne pensez pas trop à l'avenir.	N'y pensez pas trop.

C. When the object of the preposition is a *person*, disjunctive pronouns are used instead of *y*. This contrast is especially important when using the verb **penser à**, which means *to think about* or *have one's mind on someone or something*. Compare:

Je pense à mon travail.	J'y pense.
Je pense à mes parents.	Je pense à eux.

Transformation: Transformez les phrases suivantes selon le modèle donné. Modèle: Il travaille dans cette banque. → Il y travaille. (1)J'habite à Lyon. (2) Ne répondez pas à ses questions. (3) Je ne suis jamais retourné dans cette ville. (4) Vous passez vos vacances en Suisse? (5) Tu es resté un an au Mexique, n'est-ce pas? (6) Annette et Pierre vont être chez eux à huit heures. (7) Va au marché cet après-midi. (8) Nous avons rencontré Guy au bureau de poste. (9) Les livres sont sur mon bureau.

Préparation

A. Curiosité. Marguerite veut savoir où ses amis vont ce week-end. Donnez leurs réponses à ses questions.

Modèle   Est-ce que Serge va au cinéma? (oùi) → **Oui, il y va.**

1. Est-ce que tu vas au concert? (non)
2. Est ce que Robert et Anne-Marie vont au théâtre? (oui)
3. Est-ce que vous allez à la campagne ce week-end? (oui)
4. Est-ce que nous allons à la plage samedi après-midi? (oui)
5. Est-ce que Bruno va aller à la montagne avec ses amis? (non)
6. Est-ce que Paul et toi, vous allez à la piscine? (oui)

> Have students repeat in the passé composé (**Est-ce que Serge est allé au cinéma? Oui, il y est allé.**).

B. Différences. Charles et Henri sont deux frères qui sont très différents l'un de l'autre. Décrivez-les.

Modèles   leurs anciens amis → **Charles pense souvent à ses anciens amis mais Henri ne pense jamais à eux.**
leur avenir → **Charles pense souvent à son avenir mais Henri n'y pense jamais.**

1. leur travail
2. leurs amis d'enfance
3. leur avenir
4. leurs responsabilités
5. leur grand-mère
6. leurs problèmes
7. leur neveu

Communication

A. Questions/interview. Répondez aux questions suivantes ou utilisez-les pour interviewer un(e) autre étudiant(e).

1. Est-ce que tu vas au cinéma ce soir?
2. Est-ce que tu vas à la bibliothèque cet après-midi?
3. Est-ce que tu as l'intention d'aller à la campagne ce week-end?
4. Est-ce que tu vas à ton cours de français tous les jours?
5. Est-ce que tu aimes aller au restaurant de temps en temps?
6. Est-ce que tu es allé(e) au concert le week-end dernier?
7. Est-ce que tu passes quelquefois les week-ends à la bibliothèque?
8. Quand tu étais au lycée, est-ce que tu allais souvent aux matchs de football? Et maintenant?

B. Habitudés et activités. Utilisez les phrases suivantes pour dire où vous allez ou où vous êtes allé(e). N'oubliez pas d'utiliser y dans vos réponses.

> This activity can be used for whole-class or small-group activity by converting to questions: **Est-ce que tu vas au cinéma ce soir?**

Exemple   au cinéma / ce soir → **Non, je n'y vais pas ce soir.**
Oui, j'y vais ce soir.

1. au concert / ce week-end
2. à la bibliothèque / cet après-midi
3. à la plage / l'été dernier
4. au théâtre / la semaine dernière
5. à la montagne / autrefois
6. à la campagne / pendant les week-ends
7. à ma classe de français / tous les jours
8. au restaurant / de temps en temps

C. On rêve un peu. Dites à un(e) autre étudiant(e) quels pays vous avez envie de visiter et demandez-lui s'il/si elle a envie d'y aller aussi.

Students could also name a city or country that they have visited and ask others if they have gone there: **Moi, je suis allé au Japon. Et toi?**

Exemple   Moi, j'ai envie d'aller au Sénégal un jour? Et toi?
Oui, je voudrais bien y aller un jour.
Non, je n'ai pas envie d'y aller.

⚜ Le pronom *en*

Présentation

A. The pronoun **en** replaces the partitive or any other construction with **de, du, de la, de l'** or **des** plus a noun denoting a thing. Its meaning is usually the equivalent of *some, any, not any, of (about, from) it (them).*

Nous avons acheté du pain.	Nous **en** avons acheté.
Il n'a pas de chance.	Il n'**en** a pas.
Elle va nous parler de ses projets d'avenir.	Elle va nous **en** parler.
Prenez de la salade.	Prenez-**en**.
Il vient de l'épicerie.	Il **en** vient.

B. En is also used to replace a noun modified by a number or by an expression of quantity.

J'ai un disque.	J'**en** ai un.
Il y a dix étudiants.	Il y **en** a dix.
Nous avons beaucoup de travail.	Nous **en** avons beaucoup.
Il n'y a plus de sucre.	Il n'y **en** a plus.

Note that **moi** contracts to **m'** before **en**:

Donnez-moi trois kilos de veau.   Donnez-**m'en** trois kilos.

When the expression of quantity **quelques** is used with the pronoun **en**, it becomes **quelques-unes** when it refers to a feminine noun and **quelques-uns** if it refers to a masculine noun.

Je voudrais quelques timbres.	J'**en** voudrais **quelques-uns**.
Achetez quelques oranges.	Achetez-**en** **quelques-unes**.

C. En is also used with the verb **penser de** (*to have an opinion about*) when the object of the prepositional phrase is a thing or an idea. When it is a person, disjunctive pronouns are used. Compare:

Qu'est-ce que tu penses de cette idée?	Qu'est-ce que tu **en** penses?
Qu'est-ce que tu penses du professeur?	Qu'est-ce que tu penses **de lui**?

Note that **penser de** is used only in the interrogative and that questions using **penser de** are usually answered by **Je pense que** . . . .

Qu'est-ce que tu **penses de** son camarade de chambre?
Je pense qu'il est assez sympa.

*D. Y and **en** can occur in combinations with other object pronouns, though these combinations are not very frequent in spoken French. When they do occur, the normal order of pronouns is:

me								
te		le						
se	before	la	before	lui	before	y	before	**en** before verb
nous		les		leur				
vous								

Nous avons donné de l'argent aux enfants.   Nous **leur en** avons donné.   For passive recognition.
Le marchand nous a vendu dix litres de   Le marchand **nous en** a vendu dix litres.
    vin.
Ne donnez pas de conseils aux autres.   Ne **leur en** donnez pas.
Elle s'intéressait à la politique.   Elle **s'y** intéressait.
Est-ce que tu te souviens de son adresse?   Est-ce que tu **t'en** souviens?

In affirmative commands:

		le		moi (m')				
				toi (t')				
verb before		la	before	lui	before	y	before	**en**
		les		nous				
				vous				
				leur				

Donnez-moi deux bouteilles de vin.   Donnez-**m'en** deux.
Apportez trois cafés à mes amis.   Apportez-**leur-en** trois.
Montrez-nous quelques photos.   Montrez-**nous-en** quelques-unes.

*For recognition only.

Transformation: Transformez les phrases suivantes selon le modèle donné. Modèle: Nous avons acheté des légumes. → Nous en avons acheté. (1) Il prend beaucoup de risques. (2) Elle ne mange jamais de viande. (3) J'ai trop de devoirs. (4) Est-ce que tu vas m'envoyer une lettre? (5) J'ai acheté quatre livres. (6) Apportez-nous des sandwichs. (7) Avez-vous pris quelques photos?

Préparation

A. C'est la vie. La vie de Jean n'est pas parfaite mais ça peut aller. Qu'est-ce qu'il dit?

Modèle   du temps libre (pas assez) → **Je n'en ai pas assez.**

1. de l'argent (pas beaucoup)
2. des devoirs (trop)
3. des amis (quelques-uns)
4. de bons profs (plusieurs)
5. des problèmes (aucun)
6. des disques français (beaucoup)
7. de la chance (un peu)
8. des frères et des sœurs (trois)

B. Curiosité. Colette veut savoir ce que ses amis pensent de sa nouvelle situation. Qu'est-ce qu'elle dit?

Modèles   son nouvel appartement → **Dites-moi ce que vous en pensez.**

            son fiancé → **Dites-moi ce que vous pensez de lui.**

1. les photos qu'elle a prises
2. son nouveau patron
3. la jupe qu'elle vient d'acheter
4. une actrice qu'elle admire beaucoup
5. un ami qu'elle vient de rencontrer
6. les gens avec qui elle travaille
7. les petites boutiques dans son quartier
8. sa nouvelle camarade de chambre

Transformation: Répondez affirmativement et ensuite négativement aux questions suivantes. Utilisez y ou en dans vos réponses. (1) Est-ce que vous allez à Québec cet été? (2) Est-ce qu'ils ont vu quelques films français? (3) Est-ce que vous faites souvent des erreurs? (4) Est-ce que tu t'intéresses à la politique? (5) Est-ce que Lisette a envie de sortir? (6) Est-ce que vous buvez du café? (7) Est-ce que son père va lui envoyer de l'argent? (8) Est-ce que le professeur leur a donné trop de devoirs?

C. Projets de week-end. Des étudiants sont en train de parler de leurs projets pour le week-end. Formulez leurs réponses en utilisant **y** ou **en**.

Modèle   Est-ce que vous allez chez vos parents ce week-end? (non,   Options: Oral/written.
          nous . . .) → **Non, nous n'y allons pas.**

1. Est-ce que vous êtes allé chez vos parents récemment? (non)
2. Est-ce que vous allez chez eux ce week-end? (oui)
3. Est-ce que tu vas aller au cinéma, Henri? (oui)
4. Est-ce que tu as vu des films américains récemment? (oui . . . deux)
5. Est-ce que Jean va nous retrouver au café? (non)
6. Est-ce que Jean était au café hier soir? (non)
7. Est-ce que vous avez envie d'aller à Versailles? (non)
8. Est-ce que tu es déjà allé à Versailles? (non . . . jamais)
9. Est-ce que vous avez beaucoup de travail ce week-end? (oui . . . beaucoup)

Communication

A. Vos habitudes. Utilisez les suggestions suivantes pour indiquer ce que vous faites et ce que vous ne faites pas. Utilisez le pronom **en** dans vos réponses.

Exemples   boire du vin → **Je n'en bois pas souvent.**
            Chez nous, nous en buvons de temps en temps.

Can be used as direct questions or for small-group work (e.g., **boire du vin → Est-ce que tu bois souvent du vin?**).

1. acheter des revues françaises
2. faire du sport
3. avoir du travail
4. manger des légumes
5. prendre des vitamines
6. porter des blue-jeans
7. boire du lait
8. prendre des photos
9. se souvenir de l'anniversaire de vos parents ou de vos amis
10. dire des mensonges

B. Questions/interview. Répondez aux questions suivantes ou utilisez-les pour interviewer un(e) autre étudiant(e). Utilisez **y** ou **en** dans vos réponses.

1. Est-ce que tu achètes quelquefois des journaux français?
2. Est-ce que tu as jamais mangé du fromage français?
3. Est-ce que tu as trop de travail en ce moment?
4. Est-ce que tu as envie d'écouter des disques français?
5. Est-ce que tu as une bicyclette? Une voiture? Une moto?
6. Combien d'habitants est-ce qu'il y a dans la ville d'où tu viens?
7. Est-ce que tu vas souvent aux matchs de football? De basket-ball? De base-ball?
8. Est-ce que tu vas au cinéma plusieurs fois par semaine?
9. Est-ce que tu t'intéresses beaucoup aux sports? À la musique? À la politique?
10. Est-ce que tu tiens à te marier un jour?

Options: (1) Written. (2) Oral— ask questions or adapt for directed dialogue.

⚜   Le futur

Présentation

In French, the future tense is a single word formed by adding endings to a stem. It is used both in writing and in speaking, though **aller** + an infinitive is very commonly used in conversation.

A. Most verbs form the future by adding the endings shown to the infinitive. When the infinitive ends in **-re**, the **-e** is dropped. Note the similarities between the future endings and the present tense forms of **avoir**.

Le futur de *manger*	
je manger**ai**	nous manger**ons**
tu manger**as**	vous manger**ez**
il/elle/on manger**a**	ils/elles manger**ont**

Le futur de *finir*		Le futur d'*attendre*	
je finir**ai**	nous finir**ons**	j'attendr**ai**	nous attendr**ons**
tu finir**as**	vous finir**ez**	tu attendr**as**	vous attendr**ez**
il/elle/on finir**a**	ils/elles finir**ont**	il/elle/on attendr**a**	ils/elles attendr**ont**

Je parlerai à Jacqueline.
Qu'est-ce que vous boirez avec votre dîner?
On ne servira pas le dîner avant sept heures.
Je suis sûr qu'Anne et Paul se débrouilleront.
Dira-t-il la vérité?

B. Although the future endings are the same for all French verbs, certain common verbs have irregular stems.

Verb	Future stem	
aller	ir-	Je n'irai pas en classe demain.
avoir	aur-	Vous n'aurez aucune difficulté.
être	ser-	Nous serons ici à six heures.
envoyer	enverr-	Est-ce que tu lui enverras un télégramme?
faire	fer-	Est-ce que vous ferez du ski cet hiver?
falloir	faudr-	Il faudra partir à huit heures.
pleuvoir	pleuvr-	Pleuvra-t-il demain?
pouvoir	pourr-	Je pourrai vous aider plus tard.
tenir, etc.	tiendr-	Il obtiendra facilement son diplôme.
venir, etc.	viendr-	Quand reviendras-tu?
vouloir	voudr-	Qu'est-ce qu'ils voudront faire?

Préparation

A. J'ai confiance . . . Dominique est assez optimiste quand elle pense à l'a-
venir. Qu'est-ce qu'elle dit?

Modèle   nous / trouver du travail →
    Je suis sûre que nous trouverons du travail.

1. Hélène / réussir bien
2. vous / faire des progrès
3. Sylvie et Bertrand / se marier
4. ils / être heureux
5. tu / aller à l'université
6. je / apprendre beaucoup de choses
7. la vie / devenir plus facile
8. vous / avoir de la chance
9. nous / pouvoir trouver une solution
10. tu / revenir nous rendre visite

Substitution: Substituez les mots suggérés aux mots en italique et faites les changements nécessaires. (1) Nous partirons à onze heures.   tu / vous / je / les étudiants / mon ami. (2) J'attendrai cinq minutes.   tu / nous / les étudiants / vous / le professeur. (3) Est-ce qu'ils iront au cinéma ce soir?   vous / tu / nous / on / Jeannette / tes amis. (4) Tu seras en classe, n'est-ce pas?   les étudiants / le professeur / vous / nous. (5) Elle s'en occupera.   nous / mes amis / tu / je / vous. (6) Un jour, elle aura beaucoup d'argent.   tu / je / mes amis / vous / nous.

B. Plus jamais! Des étudiants sont en train de contraster leur vie présente à
l'université et leur vie future quand ils auront leur diplôme. Retrouvez
les phrases qu'ils ont prononcées à propos de leur avenir.

Modèle   Maintenant nous passons tout notre temps à étudier. →
    Nous ne passerons plus jamais tout notre temps à étudier.

1. Je vais en classe tous les jours.
2. Nous mangeons la délicieuse cuisine du restaurant universitaire.
3. Georges écoute les explications des professeurs.
4. Françoise se lève à cinq heures pour étudier.
5. Je passe tout mon temps à la bibliothèque.
6. Nous avons besoin d'étudier.
7. Je dépense tout mon argent pour acheter des livres.
8. Claude a peur des examens.
9. Nous nous retrouvons au café après la classe.

Follow-up: Have students tell what they will or will not do after they graduate (**Je dormirai jusqu'à midi tous les jours,** etc.)

Communication

A. Projets d'avenir. Voici une liste de projets d'avenir. Choisissez-en cinq que vous avez l'intention d'accomplir au cours de votre vie. Si vous préférez, vous pouvez substituer vos propres projets. Ensuite, discutez vos choix avec d'autres étudiants et essayez d'en expliquer les raisons.

Follow-up: Have students report back the plans of their partner(s).

Exemple   apprendre à parler une autre langue étrangère →
J'apprendrai à parler une autre langue étrangère parce que c'est important pour la profession que j'ai choisie.

1. avoir un métier intéressant
2. faire le tour du monde
3. gagner beaucoup d'argent
4. prendre le temps de s'amuser un peu
5. se marier et avoir des enfants
6. faire du sport régulièrement pour rester en bonne forme physique
7. faire de la recherche scientifique
8. passer plusieurs années de ma vie dans un pays étranger
9. aller habiter à la campagne
10. acheter une maison
11. devenir ingénieur (pilote, etc.)
12. ?

Avez-vous envie de vous marier? . . .

. . . ou de devenir pilote?

B. L'été prochain. Posez des questions aux autres étudiants pour savoir ce qu'ils ont l'intention de faire l'été prochain.

Exemple   Est-ce que tu resteras ici l'été prochain? → **Non, ma famille et moi, nous irons au Canada.**

Options: Use for guided composition or large- or small-group discussion.

C. Imaginez que . . . Que ferez-vous dans les situations suivantes?

1. Imaginez que vous avez la possibilité de faire un grand voyage. Où irez-vous? Que ferez-vous? Avec qui et comment voyagerez-vous? Quels monuments et quelles villes visiterez-vous? Comment gagnerez-vous l'argent pour le voyage?

2. Imaginez que vous êtes le président de votre université. Que ferez-vous? Quelles décisions prendrez-vous? Quelles seront vos priorités?

3. Imaginez que vous êtes le professeur de français. Comment organiserez-vous votre classe? Quelle sorte de devoirs donnerez-vous aux étudiants? Quelle sorte d'examens donnerez-vous?

SYNTHÈSE

La Tour Eiffel va-t-elle mourir?

Suggestion: Point out that the Eiffel Tower is 352 meters high including the TV antenna.

Repairs on the Eiffel Tower are now underway and will be completed for the 1990 World's Fair.

Paris sans la Tour Eiffel? C'est impossible. C'est le monument le plus prestigieux du monde, le pôle d'attraction des touristes de tous les pays, le symbole de Paris. Chaque année elle *attire* plus de visiteurs que la Statue de la Liberté ou même que le Parthénon. Que feront-ils sans elle? Qui inspirera les poètes, les *peintres* et les *cinéastes*? Au cours de l'histoire la tour a eu ses admirateurs et ses critiques, mais belle ou non, elle *fait* maintenant *partie de* Paris comme la Seine ou Notre-Dame.

    Pourtant cette fabuleuse structure de métal construite en 1889 par Gustave Eiffel (à l'occasion de l'*Exposition universelle* et pour célébrer l'anniversaire de la Révolution) est en danger. Peut-être en danger de mort . . .

    Elle est encore parfaitement solide, *bien sûr*, mais pour assurer son avenir, il faudra faire des travaux importants. En particulier, il faudra remplacer l'*escalier de secours*, il faudra reconstruire certaines plates-formes et surtout, il faudra remplacer l'*ascenseur* qui est en service *depuis* 1889.

    Le danger n'est évidemment pas immédiat, et les touristes pourront continuer à la visiter en toute sécurité. Les travaux *d'entretien* sont accomplis très sérieusement et très régulièrement par une équipe de techniciens. Il y en a quarante qui sont responsables de l'entretien de la tour. Chaque matin à sept heures, leur travail commence. Ils descendent *d'abord* dans les pieds de la tour pour vérifier et *graisser* les énormes machines. Ensuite ils montent jusqu'au dernier *étage* pour graisser tous les mécanismes de l'ascenseur.

attracts

painters / filmmakers

is part of

however, yet
World's Fair

of course

emergency staircase
elevator
since

maintenance, upkeep

first / grease
floor

La tour est entièrement *repeinte* tous les sept ans. Pour cela il faut plus de cinquante tonnes de peinture et des ouvriers qui *n'ont pas le vertige*! Périodiquement, des ingénieurs spécialisés et des techniciens examinent aussi toutes les parties de la tour. Les 3 millions de touristes qui visitent annuellement la tour peuvent donc être *rassurés*: l'entretien et la surveillance sont excellents.

repainted

are not afraid of heights

reassured

Le problème, c'est l'avenir de la tour. Les travaux de modernisation coûteront au moins 90 millions de francs. L'ascenseur hydraulique, en particulier, coûtera 35 millions de francs. Il sera remplacé par un ascenseur électrique moderne et rapide. Il pourra monter mille visiteurs à l'heure et fonctionnera en hiver comme en été. Mais qui paiera?

Extrait et adapté d'un article de *l'Express* par Marie Laure de Léotard.

Compréhension   Selon les renseignements donnés, est-ce que les phrases suivantes sont vraies ou fausses? Corrigez le sens de la phrase s'il est faux.

1. La Statue de la Liberté attire beaucoup plus de visiteurs que la Tour Eiffel.
2. La Tour Eiffel a été construite en 1789.

Option: Ask as questions.

3. Si on veut assurer l'avenir de la Tour Eiffel, il faudra faire des travaux importants.
4. La réparation la plus nécessaire est le remplacement de l'ascenseur.
5. Les touristes ne peuvent pas visiter la tour maintenant parce qu'on est en train de faire des réparations.
6. On n'a pas repeint la tour depuis sa construction parce qu'il est impossible de trouver des ouvriers.
7. Il y a 3 millions de touristes qui visitent la tour chaque année.
8. Le nouvel ascenseur fonctionnera en été et en hiver et il pourra monter quarante visiteurs à l'heure.

NOTES CULTURELLES

Le vieux Paris: Montmarte

Le Paris moderne

Paris change. Les nouvelles constructions
d'aujourd'hui soulèvent° autant de
controverse que la Tour Eiffel en a soulevé il
y a un siècle. Ces nouveautés choquent les
uns, enthousiasment les autres, mais tous

finiront par s'y habituer,° tout comme° on
s'est habitué à la Tour Eiffel. Un visiteur qui
n'est pas venu à Paris depuis une vingtaine°
d'années sera frappé° par les changements
qui ont eu lieu. Par exemple, la plupart des
monuments et édifices publics ont été
nettoyés° pour redonner à la pierre° sa
couleur originelle.

   Il y a aussi des bâtiments° modernes.
Parmi les plus controversés, on peut citer la
Tour Maine-Montparnasse et la Maison de la
Radio. Ce sont de belles réussites°
architecturales mais certains pensent qu'elles
détruisent° l'harmonie de leur quartier.

   Un des changements les plus
spectaculaires a été le transfert des Halles à
Rungis dans la banlieue° sud de Paris. Sur le
plateau Beaubourg, situé entre les anciennes
Halles et le quartier du Marais, on a
construit le Centre National d'Art et de
Culture Georges Pompidou. L'organisation
du Centre et son architecture sont basées sur
des concepts ultra-modernes que beaucoup de
gens ont encore de la difficulté à accepter.

soulèvent *arouse*   s'y habituer *get used to it*   tout
comme *just as*   vingtaine *about twenty*   frappé *struck,*
surprised   nettoyé *cleaned*   pierre *stone*
bâtiments *buildings*   réussites *successes*
détruisent *destroy*   banlieue *suburb*

Le Paris moderne: La Maison de la Radio.

Communication

A. Prédictions. Dites ce que vous pensez de chacune des prédictions suivantes. Ensuite, faites vos propres prédictions et demandez aux autres étudiants ce qu'ils en pensent.

Exemple   Les hommes ne seront jamais parfaits. → **C'est vrai, les hommes ne seront probablement jamais parfaits.**

1. On ne pourra jamais éliminer totalement la nécessité de travailler.
2. L'énergie solaire sera notre principale source d'énergie.
3. Dans deux siècles, il n'y aura plus de vie sur cette planète.
4. On pourra habiter sous les mers.
5. Un jour on ne mangera que des aliments artificiels.
6. Personne ne travaillera plus. Ce sont les robots qui feront tout.
7. Personne ne pourra jamais résoudre le problème des inégalités sociales.
9. Il n'y aura plus jamais de guerre.

Options: (1) Written. (2) Oral— read statements or ask as questions. Encourage students to explain their answers. Also encourage students to use **y** and **en** where appropriate.

B. Apprenez à dire «non». Il est important de savoir dire «non» quand c'est nécessaire, mais il est préférable de le dire aussi gentiment que possible. Comment allez-vous refuser si un jour vous vous trouvez dans les situations suivantes?

Option: Can be used for listening practice by reading the problem situation and having students suggest possible refusals without looking at the options provided in the text.

1. Un ami vous invite à dîner chez lui. La dernière fois que vous avez mangé chez lui, vous avez été malade pendant plusieurs jours. Comment allez-vous refuser son invitation?
   a. Non, merci, je n'ai plus d'Alka-Seltzer.
   b. Non, je ne sors jamais pendant la semaine.
   c. Merci, c'est gentil de m'inviter, mais je n'ai pas le temps cette semaine. J'ai trop de travail.
   d. ?
2. Votre voiture ne marche pas bien. Un ami propose de vous aider à la réparer. Vous n'avez pas beaucoup de confiance en ses talents de mécanicien. Comment allez-vous refuser son aide?
   a. Toi? Réparer ma voiture? Je ne te le permettrai jamais!
   b. Je préfère attendre un peu; je n'ai pas besoin de ma voiture maintenant.
   c. Impossible! Ma voiture n'est pas un jouet pour les enfants!
   d. ?
3. Un groupe d'amis vous invite à aller faire du ski. Vos amis ont tendance à être imprudents et vous préférez rester chez vous. Comment allez-vous refuser?
   a. Non, merci, je n'ai aucune envie de me casser une jambe.
   b. J'ai écouté le bulletin météorologique et ils ont dit qu'il risque de faire très mauvais.
   c. Je préfère y aller la semaine prochaine: la neige n'est pas bonne en ce moment.
   d. ?
4. Vous avez envie d'acheter une voiture, mais vous n'avez pas beaucoup d'argent. Vous décidez d'acheter une petite voiture économique. Mais l'employé tient absolument à vous vendre une voiture grand-luxe. Qu'est-ce que vous allez répondre?
   a. Je n'aime vraiment pas la couleur de cette voiture.
   b. Ça! Ce n'est pas une voiture, c'est un tank!
   c. Cette voiture n'est ni économique ni pratique. Ce n'est pas du tout le type de voiture que je veux!
   d. ?

5. Un de vos amis a besoin d'argent. Il vous demande de lui en prêter. Vous êtes sûr(e) qu'il ne vous le rendra pas. Qu'est-ce que vous allez dire pour refuser?
   a. Mais tu ne m'as pas encore rendu l'argent que je t'ai prêté le mois passé.
   b. C'est intéressant! Moi aussi, j'ai besoin d'argent et j'allais t'en demander.
   c. Tu n'as pas de chance. Je viens d'acheter une nouvelle voiture et je n'ai plus d'argent.
   d. ?

C. **Dans dix ans . . .** Essayez d'imaginer comment sera votre vie dans dix ans.

Exemple Je serai probablement plus riche que maintenant.

D. **Qu'en pensez-vous?** Donnez votre opinion personnelle sur les sujets suivants.

   1. Votre université. Qu'est-ce que vous en pensez? Est-elle trop grande ou trop petite? Y a-t-il trop ou pas assez d'étudiants? Est-ce que les professeurs sont bons? Est-ce que les étudiants sont sympathiques? Comment est la cuisine dans les restaurants universitaires? Y a-t-il assez d'activités culturelles et sportives? Quels changements sont nécessaires pour l'avenir? À votre avis, comment seront les universités de demain?
   2. Le président des États-Unis. Qu'est-ce que vous pensez de lui? Est-ce que ses décisions vont aider le pays à résoudre ses problèmes présents et futurs? A-t-il établi de bons rapports avec les autres pays? Êtes-vous d'accord avec les décisions qu'il a prises? Comment imaginez-vous l'avenir de votre pays?

Encourage students to use the comparative in their answers where appropriate. Students can also imagine their lives at other intervals of time (e.g., **dans vingt ans, dans quarante ans**).

Options: Use for guided composition or large- or small-group discussion.

VOCABULAIRE

noms

l'ascenseur (m)   *elevator*
l'avenir (m)   *future*
le boulot   *job*
le bruit   *noise*
le but   *goal*
°la catastrophe
la centrale nucléaire   *nuclear power plant*
la confiance   *trust, confidence*
la crise   *crisis*
l'entretien (m)   *upkeep, maintenance*
l'escalier (m)   *stairway*
l'espionnage électronique (m)   *electronic surveillance*
l'étage (m)   *story, floor*
l'Exposition universelle (f)   *World's Fair*
° l'extra-terrestre (m)
la faim   *hunger*
la grève   *strike*
l'inégalité (f)   *inequality*
le peintre   *painter*
°la planète
le point d'interrogation   *question mark*
°le robot

verbes

arriver   *to happen*
attirer   *to attract*
avoir le vertige   *to be afraid of heights*
compter sur   *to count on*
détruire   *to destroy*
faire partie de   *to be a part of*
°inspirer

menacer   *to threaten*
mener   *to lead*
rassurer   *to reassure*
reconstruire   *to reconstruct*
remplacer   *to replace*
repeindre   *to repaint*
résoudre   *to solve*
se tromper   *to make a mistake*
je voudrais bien   *I'm willing, I'd like that*

adjectifs

inquiet, inquiète   *worried*
°interplanétaire
°médical(e)
°nucléaire
pressé(e)   *in a hurry*
°spatial(e)
voisin(e)   *neighboring*

adverbes

la négation (voir p. 270)

divers

bien sûr   *of course*
d'abord   *first of all*
depuis   *since*
de toute façon   *at any rate*
en   *some, any, not any, of (about, from) it (them)*
pourtant   *however*
quelqu'un d'autre   *someone else*
y   *there*

INTRODUCTION

Portrait des étudiants québécois

Que pensent les étudiants québécois de leurs études universitaires? Quelles sont leurs ambitions? Comment imaginent-ils leur avenir? Que veulent-ils faire dans la vie? Quelles sont leurs relations avec leurs parents? Pourquoi étudient-ils? Sont-ils obligés de travailler? Comment s'habillent-ils? Quelle est leur attitude *au sujet de* l'amour et du mariage? Que pensent-ils de la politique et de la religion?   about

    Pour avoir des réponses à ces questions, un éducateur canadien a organisé un sondage d'opinion. Il a interrogé mille étudiants et étudiantes de seize à vingt-trois ans. Cette étude a *duré* dix ans.   lasted

Leur but dans la vie

    Quand on les a interrogés sur leur idéal dans la vie, la plus grande partie des jeunes (32%) ont choisi la *réussite* personnelle et le *bonheur* (17%) *plutôt que* la réussite financière ou le désir d'être *utile* à la société.   success / happiness   rather than / useful

Leurs qualités et leurs *défauts*   faults

    Quand on leur a présenté une liste de qualités et qu'on leur a demandé d'indiquer la qualité principale qu'ils possédaient, ils ont choisi la sociabilité (14%) et la *franchise* (13%). Ces résultats sont restés constants pendant les dix dernières années. Ils pensent que leur principal défaut est l'*orgueil*.   sincerity, frankness   pride, arrogance

Leur avenir

    Cinquante-neuf pour cent des étudiants québécois sont optimistes au sujet de leur avenir. Peu d'étudiants se sont déclarés pessimistes ou indifférents. Ces réponses n'ont pas changé au cours des années.

Leur orientation professionnelle

    Les professions libérales attirent de plus en plus de jeunes (44%). Un fait intéressant est que la proportion de jeunes qui désirent devenir *agriculteurs augmente* chaque année. Par contre, l'intérêt pour le travail de commerçant diminue chaque année.   farmers / increases

La famille

    Les jeunes ont des relations plus profondes avec leur mère qu'avec leur père. En général aussi, ils s'entendent mieux avec leur mère. Ils

À l'université de Québec

Des étudiants québecois pendant le Carnaval

parlent plus souvent avec elle qu'avec leur père. Quand ils étaient petits, ils *se confiaient* plus facilement à leur mère (43%) qu'à leur père   confided
(11%).

Les études
À la question «Pourquoi continuez-vous vos études?» la majorité
des jeunes (71%) ont répondu que c'est parce qu'ils veulent réussir dans
la vie. La proportion de jeunes qui ont choisi cette réponse a augmenté
d'année en année. Mais 10% disent qu'ils continuent leurs études parce
qu'ils aiment étudier.

Le travail
La majorité des jeunes (50%) disent que leurs parents ne leur
donnent aucune aide financière. Seulement 23% disent qu'ils travaillent pour pouvoir continuer leurs études, et 43% disent qu'ils travaillent
pour avoir de l'argent de poche.

Les vêtements
La majorité des jeunes disent qu'ils s'habillent comme ils veulent.
En fait, *presque* tous les jeunes *portent* des jeans. Est-ce que cela veut   almost / wear
dire qu'ils ont les mêmes goûts ou qu'ils sont conformistes?

L'amour
La plupart des jeunes (69%) pensent que l'amour donne un *sens* à   meaning
la vie; mais pour eux il n'y a pas de *partenaire* prédestiné et l'amour   partner
dure rarement toute la vie.

La politique
En général, les jeunes qui s'intéressent à la politique préfèrent le
Parti québécois.

La religion
Seulement *un tiers* des jeunes pratiquent une religion, mais 81%   one-third
pensent qu'il existe un Être Suprême.

Extrait et adapté d'un article du *Québec en Bref*.

Follow-up: Do **Communication D
(Le portrait de l'étudiant
américain)**, p. 303. Students
might also be asked to compare
French students and French-
Canadian students.

Compréhension Selon les renseignements donnés, est-ce que les phrases suivantes sont vraies ou fausses? Corrigez le sens de la phrase s'il est faux.

1. La réussite financière est moins importante pour les jeunes Québécois que la réussite personnelle et le bonheur. Et pour vous?
2. Selon eux, le principal défaut des jeunes est la franchise. Et selon vous?
3. L'intérêt pour les professions libérales diminue chaque année. Êtes-vous d'accord?
4. Le travail de commerçant intéresse de moins en moins les jeunes Québécois. Et les Américains?
5. Il y a de moins en moins de jeunes qui veulent devenir agriculteurs. Êtes-vous d'accord?
6. En général, les jeunes s'entendent moins bien avec leur père qu'avec leur mère. Êtes-vous d'accord?
7. La majorité des jeunes Québécois continuent leurs études parce qu'ils aiment étudier. Est-ce votre cas?
8. Presque la moitié des jeunes sont obligés de travailler pour gagner leur argent de poche. Et vous?
9. Le parti politique que les jeunes Québécois préfèrent est le Parti libéral. Et aux États-Unis?
10. Plus de deux tiers des jeunes pratiquent une religion. Et aux États-Unis?

Et vous?

A. Le métier d'étudiant. Quelles sont vos principales responsabilités ce trimestre?

—*assister aux* cours et aux *conférences*	attend / lectures
—assister à des *séances de travaux pratiques*	lab sessions
—prendre des notes	
—faire des recherches à la bibliothèque	
—faire des *lectures*	readings
—faire des *expériences* en laboratoire	experiments
—participer aux discussions	
—présenter des *exposés*	oral reports
—écrire des *comptes rendus* ou des compositions	reports, reviews

B. Préférences. Quel type de cours ou d'activités trouvez-vous le plus utile?

—les conférences	
—les séances de travaux pratiques	
—les discussions *dirigées*	directed
—les cours télévisés	
—les cours *programmés*	computerized
—les travaux en groupe	
—les présentations *enregistrées* sur *magnétoscope*	recorded / videotape recorder

C. Vos lectures. Qu'est-ce que vous êtes obligé(e) de lire pour vos cours et qu'est-ce que vous aimez lire pour votre plaisir? Avez-vous un auteur préféré?

—des *livres de classe*	—des revues	textbooks
—des romans	—des *nouvelles*	short stories
—des romans de science-fiction	—des poèmes	
—le journal	—des *pièces de théâtre*	plays
—des *bandes déssinées*		comics

NOTES CULTURELLES

L'enseignement au Québec

Comme l'étudiant français et américain, l'étudiant québécois va d'abord à l'école maternelle° puis° à l'école élémentaire de six à 12 ans. De 12 à 16 ans, les jeunes Québécois vont à l'école polyvalente ainsi° appelée à cause des° diverses options qui sont offertes à l'étudiant. Le tronc° commun à la polyvalente se compose de cours de langue maternelle et de langue secondaire, de cours de mathématiques, d'histoire, de catéchèse,° et d'éducation physique. En ce qui concerne° les autres matières, les étudiants peuvent choisir parmi les différentes options celles° qui les intéressent le plus ou qui semblent les mieux adaptées à leurs talents et capacités.

 Après la polyvalente, les jeunes Québécois peuvent entrer directement dans le marché du travail. Par contre,° si un jeune veut aller à l'université ou recevoir° une formation technique, c'est le moment d'entrer dans un des nombreux CÉGEP (Collège d'enseignement général et professionnel) du Québec. Chaque CÉGEP offre plus de 130 options professionnelles aux étudiants et un choix de deux programmes généraux. D'un côté,° il y a le cours général qui dure deux ans et qui prépare à l'entrée dans une des six universités québécoises. De l'autre côté, il y a le cours professionnel qui dure trois ans et qui prépare l'étudiant à une profession dans un des cinq domaines suivants: techniques biologiques, techniques physiques, techniques humaines, techniques de l'administration, et arts.

école maternelle *nursery school* puis *then* ainsi *thus*
à cause des *because of* tronc *core*
catéchèse *catechism* en ce qui concerne *concerning*
celles *those* par contre *on the other hand*
recevoir *receive* d'un côté *on the one hand*

Les verbes *lire* et *écrire*

Présentation

The verbs **lire** (*to read*) and **écrire** (*to write*) are irregular but resemble each other in several ways.

lire		écrire	
je **lis**	nous **lisons**	j'**écris**	nous **écrivons**
tu **lis**	vous **lisez**	tu **écris**	vous **écrivez**
il/elle/on **lit**	ils/elles **lisent**	il/elle/on **écrit**	ils/elles **écrivent**
passé composé: j'ai **lu**		passé composé: j'ai **écrit**	
futur: je **lirai**		futur: j'**écrirai**	

D'habitude je lis *Montréal-Matin.*
Hier j'ai lu le dernier livre d'Anne Hébert.
À cette époque-là, je lisais *Sélections du Reader's Digest.*
Je lirai le livre que vous m'avez suggéré.

Est-ce que vous lui écrivez tous les jours?
Gilles Vignault a écrit un très beau poème sur le Canada.
Ses enfants lui écrivaient toutes les semaines.
Demain j'écrirai au centre d'orientation professionnelle.

Suggestion: Point out that Anne Hébert, author of *Le Seigneur de Kamouraska,* is a French-Canadian novelist and that Gilles Vignault is a French-Canadian poet and singer.

Another verb like **écrire** is **décrire** (*to describe*).

Décrivez la maison où vous habitez.

Substitutions: (1) J'écris bien. tu écris / elle écrit / nous écrivons / vous écrivez / ils écrivent. (2) Je lis le journal. tu lis / il lit / nous lisons / vous lisez / elles lisent. (3) Je lirai cet article. Monique / nous / vous / tu / les gens. (4) J'écrivais peu mais je lisais beaucoup. tu / vous / on / nous / les enfants. (5) Nous n'avons pas lu cette lettre. je / Colette / le directeur / vos parents / on.

Préparation

A. Sujets de composition. Madame Degagne a demandé à ses étudiants quel sujet de composition ils ont choisi. Qu'est-ce qu'ils disent?

Modèle Jean-Marie / la musique québécoise → **Jean-Marie écrit sa composition sur la musique québécoise.**

1. nous / le problème du chômage au Québec
2. je / l'histoire du Québec
3. vous / le rôle de la religion au Québec
4. Jean et Roger / le roman québécois
5. Madeleine / l'histoire du Parti québécois
6. tu / la chanson québécoise
7. nous / le dernier livre d'Antonine Maillet
8. Armand / le français québécois

B. Au Québec. Deux étudiants québécois parlent de ce qu'ils aiment lire. Formulez leurs réponses selon les indications données.

Modèle   Est-ce que tu lis des journaux? (oui . . . plusieurs)   → **Oui, je lis plusieurs journaux.**

1. Quel journal est-ce que tu lis le matin? (*Montréal-Matin*)
2. Et tes parents, quel journal est-ce qu'ils lisent? (*La Presse*)
3. Quand vous habitiez à Québec, quel journal est-ce que vous lisiez? (*Le Soleil*)
4. Est-ce que tu as lu *Maria Chapdelaine* quand tu étais jeune? (oui)
5. Est-ce que tu lis souvent des revues américaines? (oui . . . de temps en temps)
6. Quelles revues françaises est-ce que tu lis? (*L'Express* et *Le Nouvel Observateur*)
7. Est-ce que ta mère lit une revue féminine? (oui . . . *Châtelaine*)
8. Et les jeunes, qu'est-ce qu'ils lisent? (*Vidéo-Presse*)
9. Est-ce que tu as lu un bon roman récemment? (oui . . . *Pélagie La Charrette*)

Communication

Questions/interview. Répondez aux questions suivantes ou utilisez-les pour interviewer un(e) autre étudiant(e).

1. Est-ce que tu écris bien?
2. Est-ce que tu es obligé(e) d'écrire beaucoup de compositions ce trimestre? Si oui, sur quels sujets?
3. Est-ce que tu écris beaucoup de lettres? À qui?
4. Qui t'écrit des lettres?
5. Aimes-tu écrire des poèmes? As-tu jamais écrit un poème en français?
6. Qu'est-ce que tu aimes lire? Qui est ton auteur préféré?
7. Quels livres as-tu lus cette année?
8. Est-ce que tu lis le journal tous les jours? Est-ce que tu le lis le matin ou le soir?
9. Est-ce que tu lisais beaucoup quand tu étais petit(e)? Qu'est-ce que tu lisais?
10. Est-ce que tu as déjà lu un livre en français? Et dans une autre langue étrangère?

⚜ *Depuis* et autres expressions de temps

Présentation

To indicate that an action or condition that began in the past is still going on in the present, the present tense is used with the expressions **depuis** or **il y a . . . que.**

A. **Depuis** and **il y a . . . que** can be used interchangeably when the condition or action that started in the past has lasted a given amount of time. In this case their meaning corresponds to *for* in English. Note that each expression requires a different word order.

Nous habitons à Toronto depuis
   trois mois.
Il y a trois mois que nous habitons
   à Toronto.
                We've been living in Toronto for
                three months.

Il pleut depuis trois jours.
Il y a trois jours qu'il pleut.
                It has been raining for three days.

J'attends depuis vingt minutes.
Il y a vingt minutes que j'attends.
                I've been waiting for twenty min-
                utes.

B. To indicate that a condition or action started at a particular time in the past, only **depuis** is used; its meaning corresponds in this case to *since* in English.

Suzanne enseigne dans une école
   bilingue depuis l'année dernière.
                Suzanne has been teaching in a
                bilingual school since last
                year.
Le Parti québécois existe depuis
   1968.
                The Québécois party has been in
                existence since 1968.
André sort avec Lucette depuis
   Noël.
                André has been going out with
                Lucette since Christmas.

In conversational French, **depuis quand** (*since when*) and **depuis combien de temps** are often used interchangeably.

Depuis quand as-tu ton diplôme? (depuis le mois de juin, depuis deux mois, etc.)
Depuis combien de temps travailles-tu ici? (depuis six mois, depuis le mois de janvier, etc.)

C. **Il y a** without **que** is the equivalent of the English word *ago*. In this case a past tense is used.

Il a fini ses études il y a deux ans.
Raymonde et Pierre se sont mariés
   il y a six mois.
                He finished school two years ago.
                Raymonde and Pierre got mar-
                ried six months ago.

D. To speak of an action or condition that began and ended in the past, **pendant** (*for, during*) is used with the **passé composé.**

Pendant combien de temps avez-vous habité au Canada?

How long did you live in Canada?

Nous avons habité au Canada pendant deux ans.

We lived in Canada for two years.

Pendant nos vacances nous avons travaillé dans un restaurant.

During our vacation we worked in a restaurant.

Suggestion: Remind students that **pendant** can also be used with the present or the future.

Note the different meanings conveyed by **depuis** and **pendant:**

J'ai étudié à l'université Laval pendant trois ans.

I studied at Laval University for three years.

J'étudie à l'université Laval depuis trois ans.

I've been studying at Laval University for three years.

Transformation: Transformez les phrases suivantes selon les modèles donnés. Modèle: Je suis ici depuis deux mois. → Il y a deux mois que je suis ici. (1) Ils écrivent depuis une heure. (2) Il neige depuis deux jours. (3) Nous sommes en classe depuis un quart d'heure. (4) Elle a une voiture depuis trois ans. (5) Ils sont au Canada depuis longtemps. Modèle: Il y a une heure que nous attendons ici. → Nous attendons ici depuis une heure. (1) Il y a une semaine qu'il pleut. (2) Il y a une heure qu'elle étudie. (3) Il y a vingt minutes que tu lis le journal. (4) Il y a quinze ans que tu habites à Toronto. (5) Il y a deux jours que ma tante est ici.

Préparation

A. Interview. Léon Forestier se présente comme candidat pour un poste dans un service d'administration québécois. On lui pose des questions. Formulez ses réponses selon les indications données.

Follow-up: Using the same questions, have students role-play a job interview.

Modèle   Excusez-moi, Monsieur, est-ce qu'il y a longtemps que vous attendez? (non . . . seulement dix minutes) → **Non, il y a seulement dix minutes que j'attends.**

1. Depuis quand cherchez-vous un nouvel emploi? (janvier)
2. Quand avez-vous fini vos études? (trois ans)
3. Depuis quand habitez-vous à Québec? (deux ans)
4. Pendant combien de temps êtes-vous resté dans votre emploi précédent? (trois mois)
5. Quand avez-vous commencé à travailler pour la première fois? (sept ans)
6. Depuis quand parlez-vous anglais? (l'âge de dix ans)

B. À l'école bilingue. Le professeur a demandé à ses étudiants de traduire les phrases suivantes. Comment faut-il les traduire?

1. How long have you been reading?
2. How long have you been living in Toronto?
3. I've been studying for four hours.
4. I wrote for two hours.
5. We read that book two months ago.
6. She's been working since 1935.
7. We've been waiting since two o'clock.

Communication

A. Questions/interview. Répondez aux questions suivantes ou utilisez-les pour interviewer un(e) autre étudiant(e).

1. Depuis quand es-tu étudiant(e) dans cette université?
2. Depuis combien de temps étudies-tu le français?
3. Pendant combien de temps as-tu regardé la télévision hier?
4. Où habitais-tu il y a dix ans?
5. Où étais-tu il y a deux heures?
6. Quand as-tu voyagé seul(e) pour la première fois?
7. Est-ce que tu as une voiture? Depuis quand?
8. Où est-ce que tu habites maintenant? Y habites-tu depuis longtemps?

Options: (1) Written. (2) Oral—ask questions or adapt for directed dialogue. (3) Have students work in small groups and report back their partners' responses.

B. Points communs . . . Posez des questions aux autres étudiants pour découvrir qui, dans votre classe, se trouve dans les situations suivantes.

Trouvez un(e) étudiant(e):
1. qui est allé(e) au Canada pendant ses vacances
2. qui est marié(e) depuis un an ou plus
3. qui a habité dans la même ville pendant dix ans
4. qui est né(e) il y a vingt et un ans
5. qui est sorti(e) avec la même personne pendant plus de six ans
6. qui parle une langue étrangère depuis son enfance
7. qui a habité dans un pays étranger pendant un an ou plus
8. qui dort en classe depuis le début du trimestre

Options: Ask as questions or adapt for directed dialogue.

⚜ Le futur avec *quand, lorsque, dès que* et *aussitôt que*

The use of **dès que**, etc., is still limited at this point because it is more frequently used with the **futur antérieur** to be introduced in Chapter 22.

Présentation

In French, when a clause begins with **quand** (*when*), **lorsque** (*when*), **dès que** (*as soon as*), or **aussitôt que** (*as soon as*) and future time is implied, the verb is in the future. In English the present tense is used in similar instances.

Faisons une promenade quand il fera beau.	*Let's take a walk when it's nice.*
Lorsque nous irons à Québec, nous visiterons le Château Frontenac.	*When we go to Quebec, we'll visit Frontenac Castle.*
Dès qu'ils arriveront, nous nous mettrons à table.	*As soon as they arrive, we'll sit down to eat.*
J'achèterai une maison aussitôt que j'aurai assez d'argent.	*I'll buy a house as soon as I have enough money.*

Notice that either clause can come first and that the verb in the main clause can be either in the future or in the imperative. Although the meanings of **quand** and **lorsque** and **dès que** and **aussitôt que** are similar, **lorsque** and **dès que** tend to be used in slightly more formal or literary style. Note also that **lorsque** cannot be used to ask a question.

Substitution: (1) Quand j'aurai le temps, je lirai un bon livre. tu / il / nous / vous / elles. (2) Elle partira aussitôt qu'elle pourra. tu / les autres / nous / je / vous.

Québec: la vieille ville et le Château Frontenac

Préparation

A. Quand le ferez-vous? Quelques amis indiquent quand ils vont faire certaines choses cette semaine. Qu'est-ce qu'ils disent?

Have students note that the verbs in the exercise below are states of being, a common type of verb in **dès que,** etc., clauses (e.g., **Je sortirai quand j'aurai le temps, quand il fera beau,** etc.).

> **Modèle** Quand est-ce que tu vas faire le ménage? (quand je me sentirai mieux) → **Je ferai le ménage quand je me sentirai mieux.**

1. Quand est-ce que vous allez vous occuper du jardin? (quand il fera beau)
2. Quand est-ce que Paul va réparer son vélo? (quand il aura le temps)
3. Quand est-ce que tu vas être plus sérieux? (quand je serai vieux)
4. Quand est-ce que je vais faire un promenade? (quand j'en aurai envie)
5. Quand est-ce que Gérard va acheter de nouveaux vêtements? (quand il ira en ville)
6. Quand est-ce que tu liras cet article? (quand je n'aurai rien de mieux à faire)
7. Quand est-ce que Valérie va manger? (quand elle aura faim)
8. Quand est-ce que vous allez vous reposer? (quand nous aurons moins de travail)

B. L'amour n'a pas de frontières. Robert, un Américain, a rencontré une jeune Québécoise qu'il a bien envie de revoir. Malheureusement, il ne parle pas français. Il vous a demandé de traduire *(translate)* ce qu'il veut lui dire.

Written preparation may be helpful.

1. When you come to the United States, you can stay with my family.
2. Write to me as soon as you return home.
3. As soon as you write to me, I'll answer.
4. I'll call you when I am at home.
5. I'll come back as soon as I have enough money.
6. We'll get married as soon as we can.

Communication

Réactions. Complétez les phrases suivantes pour exprimer vos opinions ou vos intentions.

Options: (1) Written. (2) Oral— ask as questions (**Que ferez-vous quand vous aurez trente-cinq ans?**, etc.)

1. Quand j'aurai trente-cinq ans, je . . .
2. Je partirai en vacances dès que . . .
3. Quand j'aurai le temps, je . . .
4. Dès que j'aurai assez d'argent, je . . .
5. Aussitôt que la classe sera terminée, les étudiants . . .
6. Les étudiants seront contents quand . . .
7. Quand j'aurai besoin d'argent, je . . .
8. Quand il fera froid, nous . . .
9. Lorsque nous serons au vingt et unième siècle . . .
10. Je prendrai ma retraite quand . . .

⚜ Le verbe *suivre* et les différents cours qu'on peut suivre

Présentation

Suivre *(to follow)* is an irregular verb. Its most frequent use is in the expression **suivre un cours** *(to take a course)*.

suivre	
je **suis**	nous **suivons**
tu **suis**	vous **suivez**
il/elle/on **suit**	ils/elles **suivent**
passé composé: j'ai suivi	
futur: je suivrai	

Suivez-moi au poste de police.
Étudiez bien l'exemple qui suit.
Je te suivrai n'importe où.
Ses explications sont difficiles à suivre.

Quels cours suiviez-vous à cette époque-là?
J'ai déjà suivi quelques cours d'informatique.

à suivre = to be continued

Suivre can be used with names of courses and subjects. Some of the more common ones that have not yet been introduced are:

les sciences: la biologie, la chimie *(chemistry)*, la physique, la géologie
les sciences politiques, les sciences économiques, la comptabilité *(accounting)*, la gestion et l'administration des entreprises *(business administration)*
les sciences humaines: l'anthropologie, la psychologie, la sociologie
les langues: le chinois, le grec, le latin, etc.
l'agriculture
l'architecture
les arts: la peinture, la photographie, la sculpture, etc.
les arts ménagers
le journalisme
la pédagogie *(education)*

Substitution: (1) Je suis plusieurs cours. tu suis / elle suit / nous suivons / vous suivez / ils suivent. (2) Il l'a suivi jusqu'au restaurant. je / les agents / vous / nous / tu. (3) Elle suivait un cours de biologie. histoire / pédagogie / sociologie / russe / allemand.

Préparation

A. À l'université Laval. Élizabeth, une étudiante américaine, a décidé de passer un an à l'université Laval. Elle explique à son nouveau conseiller pédagogique les cours qu'elle a suivis l'année dernière. Récréez ses explications en utilisant le bulletin scolaire suivant.

Modèle   Pendant le trimestre d'automne, j'ai suivi un cours de français.

Autumn quarter	Grade	Winter quarter	Grade
French	A	Anthropology	B
Biology	B	Physics	A
Political Science	A	Sociology	A
Physical Education	A	History	B

Suggestion: Point out that French-Canadian universities use essentially the same grading system as in the United States, but that the usual French grading system is on a 0-20 scale with 10 as passing.

B. Quels cours suivez-vous? Des étudiants québécois sont en train de parler de leurs programmes d'études. Indiquez leurs réponses aux questions qu'on leur a posées.

Modèle   Quels cours est-ce que vous suivez ce trimestre? (biologie et physique) → **Nous suivons un cours de biologie et un cours de physique.**

1. Est-ce que Laurent suit un cours de chimie? (oui)
2. Et toi, Denise, quel cours est-ce que tu suis? (psychologie)
3. Est-ce que vous suivez un cours de géographie? (oui)
4. Et tes camarades de chambre, est-ce qu'ils suivent beaucoup de cours? (non)
5. Depuis quand suis-tu des cours de français? (trois ans)
6. Quels cours est-ce que vous avez suivis le trimestre passé? (histoire, pédagogie et russe)
7. Et l'an prochain, quels cours suivras-tu? (latin et anthropologie)
8. Est-ce que tu es content des cours que tu suis maintenant? (oui . . assez)

Communication

Questions/interview. Répondez aux questions suivantes ou utilisez-les pour interviewer un(e) autre étudiant(e).

1. Quels cours suis-tu ce trimestre?
2. Quel est le cours le plus intéressant? Et le plus difficile?
3. Quels cours as-tu suivis à l'université jusqu'à présent? Quels étaient les meilleurs cours?
4. Quels cours as-tu suivis au lycée? Quels étaient tes cours préférés?
5. A ton avis, quelles sortes de cours suivront les étudiants dans vingt ans?
6. Est-ce que tu as envie de suivre des cours pendant toute ta vie?
7. Est-ce qu'il y a beaucoup de cours obligatoires dans ton programme? Qu'en penses-tu?
8. Quels cours est-ce que tu recommandes pour un(e) étudiant(e) qui vient d'arriver à l'université?

SYNTHÈSE

Une invitation à visiter Québec

La ville de Québec possède un charme unique en Amérique du Nord. Ce charme vient en grande partie de son atmosphère européenne et de ses traditions françaises. Capitale de la province du même nom, la ville de Québec a été fondée en 1608 par Samuel de Champlain, qui était à la fois soldat, navigateur et explorateur. Elle est située sur une *colline* qui domine le Saint-Laurent.

hill

L'accès de la ville est facile. On peut y arriver par la route, par le train, par l'avion, ou même par bateau. Le port est équipé pour recevoir les plus gros bateaux transatlantiques, et de l'aéroport partent de fréquents *vols* vers Montréal et vers les diverses régions de la province. Québec possède tout ce qu'il faut pour recevoir les visiteurs: d'excellents hôtels, des restaurants réputés, des *boîtes de nuit* et des discothèques, des salles de concert et des musées, et toutes sortes d'activités et de compétitions sportives.

flights

nightclubs

La ville de Québec a une population d'*environ* 575 000 habitants; environ 95 pour cent d'entre eux sont de langue française.

approximately

L'université Laval, fréquentée par plus de 20 000 étudiants, est située à l'ouest de la ville. C'est la plus vieille université de langue française en Amérique du Nord. En été des étudiants de presque tous les pays du monde viennent y suivre des cours de français. C'est à Québec aussi que se trouve le campus principal de l'université du Québec, créée en 1968, et qui est organisée selon les concepts les plus modernes.

Les rivières et les montagnes qui *entourent* la ville en font un *lieu* idéal pour la pratique des sports d'été et d'hiver, mais c'est pendant le Carnaval que l'exubérance générale est à son plus *haut* point. Pendant les jours de festivités populaires qui précèdent le *Carême*, on peut voir

surround / place

high

Lent

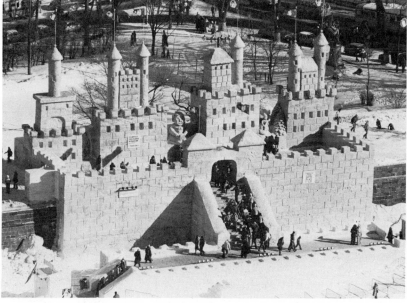

Course de canots sur le
Saint-Laurent pendant le
Carnaval . . .
Le Palais de Neige du
Carnaval de Québec

toutes sortes de *défilés* et de danses dans les rues décorées de monuments de *glace*. On peut aussi assister à la célèbre *course* de *canots* parmi les glaces du Saint-Laurent, à une compétition internationale de hockey pee-wee, à des courses de chiens, et à bien d'autres choses encore.

    Québec est une ville moderne qui est restée *fidèle* à son passé et qui a protégé son riche héritage historique. Toute visite de la ville est un petit voyage dans l'histoire: monuments, architecture traditionnelle, vieilles églises—tout y *rappelle* son passé. Intimement associé à l'histoire du Canada depuis l'arrivée des premiers explorateurs, Québec a conservé une façon de vivre et une ambiance française qui en font une des grandes villes touristiques du monde.

Extrait et adapté d'une publication de *Tourisme Québec*.

parades
ice / race / canoes

faithful

recalls

301

Compréhension   Répondez aux questions suivantes selon les renseignments donnés dans le texte.

1. Quand et par qui la ville de Québec a-t-elle été fondée?
2. Quels sont les différents moyens de transport qu'on peut utiliser pour aller à Québec?
3. Pourquoi est-ce que la ville de Québec est bien équipée pour recevoir des touristes?
4. Quel est le pourcentage de gens qui parlent français à Québec?
5. Quelles sont les caractéristiques respectives de l'université Laval et de l'université du Québec?
6. Dans quelle sorte de région la ville de Québec est-elle située?
7. Quels sont les principaux événements qui ont lieu à Québec pendant le Carnaval?
8. Qu'est-ce qui fait le charme particulier de la ville de Québec?

NOTES CULTURELLES

L'avenir du Québec

«Je me souviens» est la devise° officielle de la province de Québec, et même aujourd'hui beaucoup de Québécois n'ont pas oublié que leur province a longtemps été sous la domination britannique. «Vive le Québec libre» est le cri de ralliement° du mouvement séparatiste. Le but de ce mouvement est de couper les liens° qui unissent le Québec au reste du Canada. Le Parti québécois est le parti politique qui revendique°

l'indépendance de la province. Pour les séparatistes, il est important de préserver et de protéger la culture et l'héritage français. Il y a aussi le problème de la mobilité sociale et de l'accès des francophones aux travaux bien payés qui ont longtemps été réservés aux anglophones. Dans un livre intitulé *Les Nègres blancs d'Amérique*, Pierre Vallières a comparé la situation des Québécois à celle des noirs américains.

devise *motto*   cri de ralliement *rallying cry*
liens *ties*   revendique *demands*

D'autres pensent que le séparatisme conduira° à un isolement° culturel et économique qui peut être dangereux dans un monde de plus en plus interdépendant. Ils pensent que les lois qui ont établi le français comme la seule langue officielle de la province sont responsables du départ de certaines entreprises commerciales et d'un certain nombre d'anglophones.

De toute évidence, la solution ne sera pas facile.

conduira *will lead*   isolement *isolation*

Communication

A. Agence de voyages. Imaginez que vous travaillez pour une agence de voyages canadienne. Vous répondez aux questions des touristes éventuels *(prospective)* et vous leur décrivez les charmes du Québec pour les persuader de venir y passer leurs vacances. Jouez le rôle de l'employé et essayez de décrire le Québec. D'autres étudiant(e)s peuvent être les touristes éventuels.

Suggested as whole-class or small-group activity.

B. Une brochure touristique. Vous êtes chargé(e) de préparer une brochure qui décrit les différentes attractions de la ville où vous habitez pour les touristes francophones qui visiteront cette ville. Quels sont les monuments et les attractions touristiques que vous leur suggérez de visiter? Quels sont les meilleurs restaurants et les meilleurs hôtels de la ville? Y a-t-il des parcs, des théâtres, des concerts, des compétitions sportives, des musées ou des activités folkloriques susceptibles d'intéresser des touristes étrangers?

Suggested for individual or small-group writing.

C. Imaginez que . . . Imaginez que vous êtes dans les situations suivantes. Que ferez-vous?

Option: Have whole class choose five most useful phrases.

1. Vous avez un(e) ami(e) qui part au Québec dans quinze jours. Vous avez très peu de temps pour lui apprendre quelques phrases utiles. Quelles sont, à votre avis, les dix ou quinze phrases les plus utiles pour se débrouiller dans un pays où on parle français?
2. Vous avez un(e) ami(e) québécois(e) qui va passer un an dans votre université. Il(elle) ne parle pas bien l'anglais. Quelles sont les dix ou quinze phrases les plus utiles dans la vie d'un étudiant américain et que vous allez lui apprendre? Bien entendu, il(elle) a besoin de comprendre ces phrases. Comment allez-vous les lui expliquer en français?

Option: Have students compare their choices.

D. Le portrait de l'étudiant américain. Est-ce que les étudiants américains ressemblent aux étudiants québécois? Par exemple, est-ce qu'ils ont les mêmes buts dans la vie? À quelles professions s'intéressent-ils le plus? Sont-ils satisfaits de leurs relations avec leur famille? Etc.

Options: Use for class discussion or written composition.

VOCABULAIRE

noms

les cours (voir p. 299)

d'autres noms

l'**agriculteur** (m)   *farmer*
l'**aide** (f)   *help*
l'**argent de poche** (m)   *pocket money*
° l'**atmosphère** (f)
l'**avenir** (m)   *future*
la **bande dessinée**   *comic strip*
la **boîte de nuit**   *night club*
° le **bonheur**   *happiness*
° le **charme**
le **compte rendu**   *report, review*
la **conférence**   *lecture*
la **course**   *race*
le **défaut**   *fault*
le **défilé**   *parade*
l'**expérience** (f)   *experiment*
l'**exposé** (m)   *oral report*
le **fait**   *fact*
la **franchise**   *sincerity, frankness*
la **glace**   *ice*
° l'**intérêt** (m)
la **lecture**   *reading*
le **lieu**   *place*
le **livre de classe**   *textbook*
le **magnétoscope**   *videotape recorder*
la **nouvelle**   *short story*
le **partenaire**   *partner*
la **réussite**   *success*
la **séance de travaux pratiques**   *lab session*
le **sens**   *meaning* (also *direction*)

verbes

assister à   *to attend*
augmenter   *to increase*
se confier à   *to confide in*
décrire   *to describe*
diminuer   *to lessen*

durer   *to last*
écrire   *to write*
entourer   *to surround*
fonder   *to found*
lire   *to read*
porter   *to wear*
rappeler   *to recall*
suivre   *to follow*
suivre un cours   *to take a course*

adjectifs

dirigé(e)   *directed*
enregistré(e)   *recorded*
fidèle   *faithful*
financier, financière   *financial*
haut(e)   *high*
programmé(e)   *computerized*
québécois(e)   *pertaining to Quebec*
utile   *useful*

divers

depuis *et autres expressions de temps* (voir pp. 294–295)

d'autres expressions
aussitôt que   *as soon as*
au sujet de   *about, concerning*
dès que   *as soon as*
lorsque   *when*
plutôt que   *rather than*
presque   *almost, nearly*

Sports et loisirs

16

INTRODUCTION

Les plaisirs de la marche à pied

Quel est le sport le plus populaire en France? Est-ce que c'est le football? Le ski? Le cyclisme? Peut-être, . . . si on considère seulement les reportages sportifs à la télévision. Mais si on parle du sport que les Français *pratiquent* vraiment, c'est peut-être tout simplement la *marche à pied*. Même les gens qui ne pratiquent aucun sport régulièrement font fréquemment une petite promenade à pied en famille le dimanche après-midi.

play / walking, hiking

De plus en plus, la marche devient un sport. Sa popularité correspond à un désir général de retour à la nature et à la simplicité, et à un besoin d'effort physique. Il y a en France un Comité National des *Sentiers* qui est responsable de l'entretien de 22 000 kilomètres de sentiers. *paths, trails*
Il y a soixante-trois itinéraires qui traversent la France, et parmi les cinq sentiers européens, il y en a trois qui passent par la France.

Le Comité National organise aussi des conférences et des présentations du film «La France et ses sentiers». Il a même organisé un marathon de 4 000 kilomètres qui a duré d'avril à octobre. Chaque équipe de *randonneurs* marchait pendant quinze jours avant *hikers*
d'être remplacée par une autre équipe. À chaque *ville-étape*, il y avait *stopover*
des activités et des jeux organisés par les municipalités locales.

L'*ouverture* de ces sentiers est due non seulement aux services pu- *opening*
blics mais aussi à des initiatives privées. La famille Cabouat, par exemple, a beaucoup contribué à la création de tout un *réseau* de sentiers *network*
dans les Cévennes. Tous les membres de la famille sont des «mordus» *chain of mountains in the south of the Massif Central*
de la marche à pied. Chaque week-end, trois générations de Cabouat
(Jean-Pierre et Daniel, les fils, Françoise et René, la fille et le *gendre*, *son-in-law (**belle-fille** =daughter-in-law)*
Eric et Sophie, les petits enfants) partent avec leurs pots de peinture et
leurs *pancartes* pour préparer de nouveaux sentiers. Cette passion de *signs*
la marche à pied leur a été *léguée* par le patriarche du clan, Paul *given, bequeathed*
Cabouat qui, *bon pied, bon œil malgré* ses 93 ans, continue à montrer *in good health/in spite of*
le *chemin*. *way, road*

Il a découvert les Cévennes juste après la *Grande Guerre* quand il *First World War*
est venu s'installer à Nîmes comme chirurgien. Il est toute de suite
tombé amoureux de ces belles montagnes, mais il n'y avait aucun sen- *fall in love*
tier. Alors, il s'est mis au travail, et pendant des années il a passé tous
ses loisirs à en créer. Aujourd'hui, il continue à *emporter* dans son sac *take along*
à dos les mêmes provisions que du temps de sa jeunesse: une banane et
un paquet de *biscuits*. *Sobriété* de *chameau* et jambes d'*acier*, il fait *crackers, cookies / endurance (here) / camel / steel*
encore facilement ses 30 ou 40 kilomètres dans la journée.

Comme vous *voyez*, pour pratiquer ce sport, on n'a pas besoin *see*
d'avoir beaucoup d'argent ni d'être très jeune. Les jeunes randonneurs
peuvent passer la nuit dans des *auberges de jeunesse* qui sont très bon *youth hostels*
marché. L'équipement n'est ni très cher ni très compliqué non plus.
Une bonne paire de chaussures, des chaussettes, un pantalon, une
chemise, un pull-over, un *anorak*, et un sac à dos suffisent. Mais pour *ski jacket*

être un bon randonneur, *il ne suffit pas* d'être bien équipé, il faut aussi   it is not enough
être très prudent et connaître ses possibilités et ses limites. Et surtout,
il faut respecter la nature. Voici les dix commandements du randonneur:

1. Tu porteras de bonnes chaussures.
2. Tu seras en bonne condition physique.
3. Tu étudieras ton itinéraire sur la *carte*.   map
4. Tu t'informeras sur la nature du terrain.
5. Tu éviteras les *randonnées* qui sont *au-dessus de* tes forces.   trips, hikes / above, beyond
6. Tu ne partiras jamais seul au-dessus de 1500 mètres d'altitude.
7. Tu emporteras des vêtements chauds; les nuits sont froides en toute
   saison dans les montagnes.
8. Tu feras attention aux *vipères*.   poisonous snakes
9. Tu n'oublieras pas que tu es toujours sur la propriété de quelqu'un
   d'autre.
10. Tu respecteras la nature.

Extrait et adapté des articles de *L'Express*.

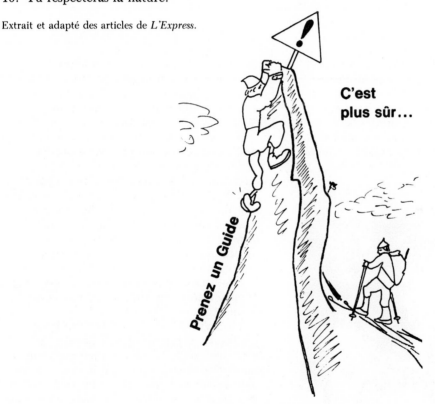

C'est
plus sûr...

Prenez un Guide

Patrice Kohli

Guide

1882 Gryon

Tél. (025) 68 10 20

Compréhension   Répondez aux questions suivantes selon les renseignements donnés dans le texte.

1. Quel est le sport qu'on pratique le plus en France?   Et aux États-Unis?
2. Pourquoi est-ce que les Français marchent beaucoup?   Les Américains marchent-ils autant?
3. Qu'est-ce que beaucoup de Français font le dimanche après-midi?   Et les Américains?
4. Quelles sont les raisons principales de la popularité de la marche à pied en France?   Est-ce la même chose aux États-Unis?
5. Est-ce que la France est bien équipée en sentiers?   Et les États-Unis?
6. Comment est organisé le marathon qui dure d'avril à octobre?
7. Selon les dix commandements du randonneur, quelles sont les choses principales qu'il faut emporter?   Êtes-vous d'accord?
8. Quelles sont les précautions qu'il faut prendre avant de partir?   Êtes-vous d'accord?

NOTES CULTURELLES

Les Français et le sport

Les Français s'intéressent beaucoup aux sports et comme les Américains, ils aiment regarder les compétitions sportives à la télévision ou les écouter à la radio. Le football (ce que nous appelons le soccer aux États-Unis) jouit d'une° grande popularité, et les Français regardent avec intérêt, et même

jouit d'une *enjoys a*

passion, les matchs de leurs équipes favorites. Les équipes des grandes villes comme Saint-Étienne, Clermont-Ferrand et Lille jouent non seulement dans des compétitions régionales mais aussi dans des compétitions nationales et internationales comme la Coupe de France et le Championnat d'Europe.

Le cyclisme est un sport très populaire aussi. Parmi les différentes courses cyclistes, c'est le Tour de France qui est suivi avec le plus de passion par les Français. Le Tour de France, comme son nom l'indique, fait le tour de presque toute la France y compris° les régions montagneuses comme les Alpes ou les Pyrénées. Les Français s'intéressent aussi aux courses automobiles—surtout aux Vingt-Quatre Heures du Mans et au Rallye de Monte Carlo.

En plus de° ces sports internationaux, il y a les sports typiquement français: la pétanque, ou les boules, un jeu qui ressemble un peu au «bowling» et qui se joue° surtout dans le sud de la France, et la pelote basque (ce que nous appelons le jai alai) qui se joue au Pays Basque dans le sud-ouest de la France.

y compris *including*   en plus de *besides*
se joue *is played*

Joueurs de football

Joueurs de pétanque

Un match de rugby

Et vous?

A. Quels sports pratiquez-vous? Utilisez la liste des sports suivants et indiquez si vous les pratiquez régulièrement, de temps en temps, rarement ou jamais.

Exemple   Je joue souvent au tennis, mais je fais rarement du cheval.
Je ne vais jamais à la pêche ou à la chasse.

jouer
au tennis
au football
au base-ball
au basket-ball
au golf
au rugby
à la pétanque
au hockey

Option: Also introduce **faire de la natation, du footing, du ski de randonnée.**

du ski
du ski nautique *(water skiing)*
de l'alpinisme *(mountain climbing)*
du patinage sur glace *(ice skating)*
de la gymnastique *(exercise or gymnastics)*
de l'athlétisme *(track and field)*

faire
de la boxe
de la lutte *(wrestling)*
de la marche à pied
de la course automobile *(racing)*
de la course à pied *(running)*
du cheval *(horseback riding)*
de la bicyclette / du vélo

aller à la chasse *(hunting)*
aller à la pêche *(fishing)*

B. Vous et le sport. Répondez aux questions suivantes ou utilisez-les pour interviewer un(e) autre étudiant(e).

1. Préférez-vous les sports d'équipe ou les sports individuels?
2. Préférez-vous être spectateur(trice) ou participer au jeu?
3. Faites-vous du sport surtout pour la compétition, pour le plaisir ou pour rester en forme?
4. Y a-t-il un(e) athlète ou un(e) champion(ne) que vous admirez particulièrement?
5. À quelles compétitions sportives avez-vous assisté ou participé?

   —un match
   —un championnat
   —une course
   —un marathon

6. Où allez-vous pour faire du sport?

   —au stade
   —dans un club de gymnastique
   —au gymnase de l'université

C. Sports et sportifs. Donnez le nom d'un(e) athlète. Les autres étudiants diront quel sport cette personne pratique (ou pratiquait).

Exemple   Babe Ruth → **Babe Ruth jouait au base-ball.**

Les verbes *voir* and *croire*

Présentation

The verbs **voir** *(to see)* and **croire** *(to believe)* are irregular:

Note that all uses of **croire** are in the affirmative. The use of the negative of **croire** with the subjunctive will be introduced in Chapter 20.

voir		croire	
je **vois**	nous **voyons**	je **crois**	nous **croyons**
tu **vois**	vous **voyez**	tu **crois**	vous **croyez**
il/elle/on **voit**	ils/elles **voient**	il/elle/on **croit**	ils/elles **croient**
passé composé: j'ai vu		passé composé: j'ai cru	
futur: je verrai		futur: je croirai	

Je ne vois pas très bien.
Est-ce que tu as vu le dernier match à la télé?
Vous verrez que c'est facile.

Je crois que tu pourras te débrouiller.
On le croira quand il dira la vérité.
Personne n'a cru cette histoire.

Préparation

Substitution: (1) Je crois que oui. nous / Paul / les autres / tu / vous. (2) Nous ne verrons pas le match. mes amis / Serge / je / vous / tu / je. (3) Je n'ai rien vu. Paul et Serge / tu / Micheline / nous / vous. (4) Je croyais que ce serait facile. nous / les étudiants / le professeur / tu / vous.

A. La coupe du monde de football. Qui va gagner la coupe du monde? Il y a autant d'opinions que de personnes.

> **Modèle**   Pierre / l'équipe du Brésil → **Pierre croit que c'est l'équipe du Brésil qui va gagner.**

1. nous / l'équipe de France
2. moi / les Italiens
3. tu / les Allemands
4. vous / l'équipe d'Angleterre
5. Cécile / les Espagnols
6. mes amis / les Irlandais

Possible follow-up: Have students offer opinions about upcoming sports events: e.g., **Moi, je crois que les Bengals vont gagner le match dimanche.**

B. Sportifs en pantoufles. Il y a des gens qui font du sport et d'autres qui se contentent d'aller voir les matchs ou de les regarder à la télé. Quelles compétitions sportives ont-ils vues?

Point out that **sportif en pantoufles** is similar to an armchair quarterback.

> **Modèle**   Henri / le championnat du monde de hockey sur glace → **Henri a vu le championnat du monde de hockey sur glace.**

1. nous / la coupe du monde de tennis
2. tu / le Rallye de Monte Carlo
3. vous / le Marathon de Boston
4. ma sœur / les 24 heures du Mans
5. moi / le départ du Rallye Paris-Dakar
6. mes amis / les derniers Jeux Olympiques

Possible follow-up: Have students tell the major sports events they have seen or would like to see.

Communication

A. Qui a vu . . . ? Posez des questions aux autres étudiants de votre classe pour découvrir qui a vu les choses suivantes. Trouvez un(e) étudiant(e):

1. qui a vu un film français récemment
2. qui a vu sa famille la semaine dernière
3. qui n'a jamais vu un match de base-ball
4. qui voit son(sa) petit(e) ami(e) tous les jours
5. qui voit très bien de loin
6. qui a vu le Mont Blanc
7. qui a vu le dernier championnat de patinage artistique
8. ?

Option: Have students share interesting things that they have seen recently: **J'ai vu un film de Woody Allen.**

B. Qui est d'accord? Indiquez qui partage les opinions suivantes (vous, vos amis, parents, professeurs, médecins, etc.).

> **Exemple**   Il est important de faire du sport au moins trois fois par semaine.
> Les médecins croient qu'il est important de faire du sport au moins trois fois par semaine. Moi, je crois que c'est important aussi.

1. Les sports compétitifs ne sont pas bons pour les jeunes enfants.
2. Il y a trop de reportages sportifs à la télévision.
3. On se sent mieux quand on fait du sport régulièrement.
4. Les femmes sont aussi sportives que les hommes.

5. Les Américains ne marchent pas assez.
6. Le meilleur sport est la natation.
7. Les athlètes professionels gagnent trop d'argent.
8. Il y a certains sports qui ne sont pas bons pour la santé.
9. Le sport occupe une place trop importante dans les universités américaines.
10. ?

⚜ Les pronoms interrogatifs

Présentation

Since the early chapters of this book you have been forming questions using **qu'est-ce que** and **qui** as interrogative words meaning *what* and *who*. **Qu'est-ce que** and **qui** are part of a larger group of interrogative pronouns that includes:

A. Pronouns referring to persons. These correspond to *who* and *whom* in English. The pronoun **qui** is always used to refer to persons.

1. **Qui** can function as the subject of a sentence. This short form **qui** can be replaced by the longer form **qui est-ce qui.**

   Qui a gagné le Tour de France?   Qui veut aller nager?
   Qui est-ce qui a gagné le Tour de France?   Qui est-ce qui veut aller nager?

2. **Qui** can function as a direct object or as the object of a preposition. It can be used with **est-ce que** or with inversion.

   Qui avez-vous rencontré pendant votre promenade?
   Qui est-ce que vous avez rencontré pendant votre promenade?

   Avec qui as-tu joué au golf?
   Avec qui est-ce que tu as joué au golf?

3. **Qui est-ce** is used to ask the identity of a person.

   Qui est-ce? C'est Jean.

B. Pronouns referring to things. These correspond to *what* in English.

1. **Qu'est-ce qui** is used as the subject of a sentence.

   Qu'est-ce qui est arrivé?
   Qu'est-ce qui te préoccupe?

   A useful expression used with **qu'est-ce qui** is **Qu'est-ce qui se passe?** (*What's going on?*).

2. Either **qu'est-ce que** or **que** is used as the direct object of a sentence. With **que** inversion is required.

   Qu'est-ce que vous faites?   Qu'est-ce qu'elle a vu?
   Que faites-vous?   Qu'a-t-elle vu?

3. **Quoi** *(what)* is used after a preposition when there is not a specific antecedent.

De quoi est-ce qu'il a parlé?   À quoi est-ce que tu penses?
De quoi a-t-il parlé   À quoi penses-tu?

4. **Qu'est-ce que c'est** or **qu'est-ce que c'est que** is used to ask someone to identify or define something.

Qu'est-ce que c'est? C'est un sac à dos.
Qu'est-ce que c'est qu'une 2CV? C'est une petite voiture française.

The following table summarizes the uses of the interrogative pronouns.

Les pronoms interrogatifs

	Subject	Object	Object of a preposition	Definition or identification
Persons	qui qui est-ce qui	qui qui est-ce que	qui	qui est-ce
Things	qu'est-ce qui	que qu'est-ce que	quoi	qu'est-ce que c'est qu'est-ce que c'est que

Transformation: Pour chaque série de phrases, donnez les questions correspondantes. Modèle: Hélène a apporté ses disques. → **Qu'est-ce qu'Hélène a apporté?** (1) Tu m'as envoyé ce livre. (2) Ils ont acheté une carte de la région. (3) Vous avez vu un bon film. (4) Robert attendait l'autobus. (5) Vous avez regardé le match à la télé? Modèle: Hélène a apporté ses disques. → **Qui a apporté ses disques?** (Utilisez les phrases de l'exercice précédent.) Modèle: Tu as vu Claude au match. → **Qui as-tu vu au match?** (1) Nous avons invité les Dupont. (2) Elle a emmené ses enfants à la plage. (3) Jean a retrouvé ses amis en ville. (4) Ils ont rencontré Michelle au cinéma. (5) Nous avons vu Bernard à la gare. Modèle: Tu as vu Claude au match. → **Qui a vu Claude au match?** (Utilisez les phrases de l'exercice précédent.)

Préparation

A. Un vrai fiasco. André était responsable de l'organisation d'une randonnée du club. Malheureusement, le résultat est un vrai fiasco. D'après ses réponses, quelles sont les questions que les autres membres du club lui ont posées?

Modèle   C'est moi qui ai choisi l'itinéraire.
             Qui a choisi l'itinéraire?

1. C'est moi qui ai décidé de partir à quatre heures du matin.   Repeat with **qui est-ce qui**.
2. C'est moi qui ai acheté les provisions.
3. C'est moi qui ai promis d'apporter une carte.
4. C'est moi qui suis responsable de tout ça.
5. C'est moi qui ai choisi cette auberge.

Modèle   Je ne sais pas ce qu'on va faire ce soir.
             Qu'est-ce qu'on va faire ce soir?

1. Je ne sais pas ce qu'on va manger.
2. Je ne sais pas ce qu'on va boire.
3. Je ne sais pas ce qu'on va trouver à l'auberge.
4. Je ne sais pas ce qu'on va faire demain.
5. Je ne sais pas ce qu'il faut faire maintenant.

B. Au Club Alpin. Les employés du bureau du Club Alpin sont obligés de répondre à toutes sortes de questions. Voici quelques-unes de leurs réponses. Quelles sont les questions qu'on leur a posées? Remplacez les mots en italique par l'interrogatif approprié.

Modèle   Vous aurez besoin d'*un anorak.* → **De quoi aurons-nous besoin?**

1. Vous avez besoin d'*une carte.*
2. C'est *le nouveau président de notre club.*
3. Il faudra emporter *des vêtements chauds.*
4. Vous pouvez écrire *au président du club.*
5. C'est *une carte qui indique les principaux sentiers.*
6. *C'est Bertrand qui* organise toutes les randonnées.
7. Nous avons invité *Monsieur Brun* à donner une conférence.
8. *Madame Lambert* veut être membre du club.

C. À l'auberge de jeunesse. Plusieurs randonneurs anglais passent la nuit dans une auberge de jeunesse. Ils désirent parler un peu avec des randonneurs français. Malheureusement les Anglais ne parlent pas français, et les Français ne comprennent pas l'anglais. Pouvez-vous les aider?

1. Where did you buy your ski jacket?
2. Who told you about this youth hostel?
3. What are you going to do tomorrow?
4. What do you need for this trip?
5. What do I do if I see a poisonous snake?
6. What's a **sac à dos**?
7. What happened to the others?
8. Who is that man over there?

Communication

A. Des oreilles indiscrètes. Vous êtes candidat(e) pour un emploi de moniteur (monitrice) de ski dans une station de sports d'hiver. Le directeur de la station est en train d'interviewer un autre candidat. Vous entendez seulement les réponses du candidat. Quelles questions le directeur a-t-il posées?

Le directeur: _____ ?
Le candidat: Je m'appelle Charles Girard.
Le directeur: _____ ?
Le candidat: J'ai vingt-cinq ans.
Le directeur: _____ ?
Le candidat: Un de mes amis m'a parlé de ce travail.
Le directeur: _____ ?
Le candidat: Je veux être professeur de gymnastique.
Le directeur: _____ ?
Le candidat: En ce moment je suis étudiant et je travaille dans un restaurant.
Le directeur: _____ ?
Le candidat: J'ai travaillé dans un club de gymnastique.
Le directeur: _____ ?
Le candidat: Parce que j'aime faire du ski et j'ai besoin d'argent.
Le directeur: _____ ?
Le candidat: Je m'intéresse à tous les sports.

Options: Oral/written.

Follow-up: Have students role-play a job interview.

B. Questions/interview. Préparez une série de questions que vous poserez à un(e) autre étudiant(e) de votre classe. (Essayez d'utiliser autant de pronoms interrogatifs que possible.)

Follow-up: Have students report back their partners' responses.

Exemples   Qu'est-ce que tu aimes faire pour rester en forme?
Avec qui est-ce que tu joues au tennis?

Option: If preferred, have students ask questions related to a particular topic (**les sports**, **les cours**, etc.).

 # Le conditionnel

Présentation

The use of **si** clauses is explained in the next chapter.

In English a conditional verb can always be recognized by the word *would* in the verb phrase: I *would* like a new backpack; he *would* like to go to the Olympic games.

In French the conditional is formed by adding the endings of the imperfect tense to the future stem of a verb. There are no exceptions to this pattern.

Le conditionnel d'*aimer*	
j'aimer**ais**	nous aimer**ions**
tu aimer**ais**	vous aimer**iez**
il/elle/on aimer**ait**	ils/elles aimer**aient**

The conditional is used:

A. To express a wish or a suggestion:

| J'aimerais jouer au tennis ce soir. | *I'd like to play tennis tonight.* |
| Nous voudrions faire une randonnée. | *We'd like to go on a hike.* |

B. When a condition is stated or implied:

À votre place, je ne dirais rien.	*In your place, I wouldn't say anything.*
Dans ce cas-là, tu pourrais venir demain.	*In that case, you could come tomorrow.*
Si j'avais le temps, je ferais du camping plus souvent.	*If I had the time, I'd go camping more often.*

C. The conditional is used to be less direct and more polite in:

1. Making requests or suggestions: **je voudrais** . . . ; **pourriez-vous** . . . ; **voudriez-vous** . . . ; **accepteriez-vous** . . . ; **aimeriez-vous** . . . ; **est-ce que cela vous arrangerait de** *(would it suit you to)* . . . ; **est-ce que cela vous dérangerait si** *(would it bother you if)*; etc.

2. Accepting invitations: **oui, ça me ferait plaisir; je serais ravi(e); ce serait une excellente idée; j'aimerais bien.**

Aimeriez-vous faire une promenade à bicyclette cet après-midi?
Oui, ça me ferait vraiment plaisir.

D. In indirect style, to relate what somebody has said:

Il a dit qu'il parlerait au professeur.	*He said that he would speak to the instructor.*
Ils ont dit qu'ils aimeraient mieux y aller à pied.	*They said that they'd prefer to walk there.*

Remind students that the imperfect, not the conditional, is used to express the idea of *would* in the sense of *used to.*

Préparation

Substitution: (1) J'aimerais sortir. tu / il / nous / vous / elles. (2) Je voudrais regarder la carte. nous / vous / cette personne / tu / les étudiants. (3) Elle a dit qu'elle attendrait. tu / vous / je / mon mari / nos amis. (4) Dans ce cas-là, vous pourriez jouer au tennis. je / on / tu / Marie-Claire / Claude et son ami.

A. Chacun a des responsabilités. Plusieurs amis vont faire une grande randonnée à pied. Voici ce que chaque personne a promis de faire.

> **Modèle** Luc va s'occuper des repas. → **Luc a dit qu'il s'occuperait des repas.**

1. Nous allons choisir l'itinéraire.
2. Tu vas acheter une carte.
3. Je vais retenir des places dans une auberge.
4. Nous allons acheter les provisions.
5. Catherine va apporter sa guitare.
6. Vous allez emporter des médicaments.
7. Mes amis vont me prêter un sac à dos.

B. Je me suis trompée. Monique a mal compris ce que les autres ont dit. Elle est surprise quand on lui dit qu'elle s'est trompée.

> **Modèle** Il viendra demain. (aujourd'hui) → **Ah, oui? Moi, je croyais qu'il viendrait aujourd'hui.**

1. Le match aura lieu vendredi. (samedi)
2. Nous irons au cinéma. (au concert)
3. Nos amis arriveront lundi. (dimanche)
4. On jouera au tennis. (au golf)
5. Tu m'attendras à la piscine. (dans le parc)
6. On sera de retour à huit heures. (à sept heures)

C. Politesse. Monsieur Bourru, un reporter sportif, n'a pas toujours le succès qu'il aimerait avoir parce qu'il est souvent trop direct. Pourriez-vous l'aider à être plus poli?

> **Modèles** Je veux parler avec un autre joueur. → **Je voudrais parler avec un autre joueur.**
> Aidez-moi. → **Pourriez-vous m'aider?**

Options: Have students make polite requests. Also introduce **auriez-vous l'obligeance (la bonté) de; vous serait-il possible de; pourrais-je.**

1. Je veux prendre votre photo.
2. Jeune homme, apportez-moi les résultats du match.
3. Je veux parler avec le médecin de l'équipe.
4. Soyez ici à huit heures pour notre interview.
5. Dites aux autres membres de l'équipe que je veux les voir.
6. Mademoiselle, envoyez cet article au journal.
7. Donnez-moi votre opinion sur les athlètes canadiens.
8. Téléphonez au nouveau champion et dites-lui que je veux lui parler.

A. À votre place, moi, je . . . Que feriez-vous à la place de la personne qui parle?

Option: Read sentences and have students respond.

Exemple   Je vais me coucher à trois heures du matin parce que j'ai un examen demain matin. → **Moi, à votre place, je me coucherais avant minuit.** ou
Moi, à votre place, je ferais la même chose. ou
À votre place, je ne me coucherais pas à trois heures du matin.

1. Je vais aller faire une promenade. J'irai en classe un autre jour.
2. J'ai besoin de rester en forme. Je vais faire de la marche à pied.
3. Je n'ai pas envie d'écrire cette lettre aujourd'hui. Je l'écrirai un autre jour.
4. Je n'ai pas assez d'argent en ce moment. Mais j'ai vraiment envie d'une nouvelle stéréo. Je vais l'acheter à crédit.
5. J'ai déjà bu trois verres de vin mais j'ai encore soif. Je vais en boire un autre.
6. Je vais regarder le match de football à la télévision. Je finirai mes devoirs demain.
7. Je ne permettrai pas à mes enfants de boire de l'alcool avant l'âge de dix-huit ans.

B. Vrai hier, faux aujourd'hui? Avez-vous jamais changé d'avis? Quelles sont les choses que vous avez dites ou pensées et qui ne sont plus vraies maintenant?

Options: Oral/written.

Exemples   J'ai dit que je ne me marierais jamais.
J'ai pensé que ce trimestre serait plus facile que les autres.

C. Invitations. On dit que la façon de donner est aussi importante que ce qu'on donne. La façon de répondre à une invitation est importante aussi. Posez les questions suivantes (ou d'autres questions) à un(e) autre étudiant(e) qui va accepter—ou refuser—aussi gentiment que possible.

Exemple: Demandez-lui si vous pourriez l'emmener à l'aéroport.
Est-ce que je pourrais t'emmener à l'aéroport?
Oui, ce serait gentil de ta part.
Ce serait gentil mais Pierre a déjà dit qu'il m'y emmènerait.

Demandez-lui . . .
1. s'il/si elle voudrait boire quelque chose
2. s'il/si elle aimerait aller au cinéma ce soir
3. si cela lui ferait plaisir de venir au match avec vous
4. s'il/si elle aimerait jouer au tennis cet après-midi
5. s'il/si elle aurait le temps de vous aider à faire vos devoirs
6. s'il/si elle pourrait vous prêter ses notes de classe
7. s'il/si elle aurait envie de faire une petite promenade
8. ?

Le verbe *conduire*

Présentation

The verb **conduire** *(to drive)* is irregular.

conduire	
je **conduis**	nous **conduisons**
tu **conduis**	vous **conduisez**
il/elle/on **conduit**	ils/elles **conduisent**

passé composé: **j'ai conduit**
futur: **je conduirai**

Tu conduis trop vite.
Pourriez-vous me conduire à l'aéroport?

Verbs that are conjugated like **conduire** are:

se conduire	*to behave, to conduct oneself*	Tu t'es conduit comme un idiot.
construire	*to build*	Vous avez construit une belle maison.
détruire	*to destroy*	Ne détruisez pas nos ressources naturelles.
produire	*to produce*	À cette époque-là, on produisait plus de vin.
traduire	*to translate*	Vous traduirez toutes ces phrases en français.

Substitution: (1) Je conduis bien. tu / il / nous / vous / elles. (2) Nous traduisons quelques phrases. tu / je / vous / les etudiants / on. (3) Nous nous sommes bien conduits. je / vous / tu / Paulette / les enfants.

Préparation

Option: Give pronouns; have students provide verb forms.

Clichés. Jean Chauvin parle de ses idées sur les différentes sortes de conducteurs qu'on trouve sur les routes de France. Reconstituez les phrases qu'il a prononcées.

Modèle Moi, je / très bien → **Moi, je conduis très bien.**

Follow-up: Have students give other clichés.

1. les femmes / très mal
2. les jeunes / comme des idiots
3. ma femme / trop vite
4. les vieux / trop lentement
5. nous, les hommes / mieux que les femmes
6. vous, les Américains / trop prudemment

Mouffetard AUTO ÉCOLE

49, Rue Censier, 75005 Paris
SARL CAPITAL 20.000 Frs

Téléphone : 535 55-92
R. C. 76 B 7804

Communication

Êtes-vous d'accord? Indiquez si vous êtes d'accord avec les phrases suivantes. Si vous n'êtes pas d'accord, modifiez la phrase pour exprimer votre opinion personnelle.

Options: (1) Written. (2) Oral—read statements or ask as questions. Encourage students to explain their answers.

1. Je conduis bien.
2. J'aimerais conduire une voiture de sport.
3. Les femmes conduisent mieux que les hommes.
4. Les jeunes conduisent beaucoup plus prudemment que les gens plus âgés.
5. Les Français aiment conduire de grosses voitures.
6. Mon (ma) meilleur(e) ami(e) conduit comme un(e) idiot(e).
7. Il est dangereux de conduire quand on a trop bu.
8. Je conduis une voiture depuis l'âge de seize ans.
9. Quand j'étais plus jeune, je conduisais plus vite que maintenant.
10. Les spectateurs se conduisent toujours très bien quand ils vont à des compétitions sportives.
11. C'est aux États-Unis qu'on produit les meilleures voitures.

SYNTHÈSE

Les Français et l'automobile

Chaque année le prix des automobiles augmente—et le prix de l'*essence* aussi. Pourtant, le nombre de voitures en circulation continue à augmenter d'année en année. Est-ce que les Français pensent que la voiture est devenue un élément indispensable de la vie moderne? Quelle est leur réaction devant l'augmentation des prix et la crise d'énergie? Est-ce qu'ils pourraient *se passer de* leur voiture? Un sondage organisé par *L'Express* vous donne leurs réponses à ces questions.

gasoline

do without

1. Quel effet l'augmentation des prix a-t-elle sur votre *comportement*?

behavior

	Oui	Non
L'augmentation des prix n'a rien changé; j'utilise ma voiture comme avant.	51%	48%
J'essaie d'utiliser ma voiture moins souvent.	47	52
Je voulais remplacer ma voiture *actuelle*, mais je ne l'ai pas fait *à cause de* l'augmentation.	44	55
Je n'ai pas acheté la voiture que je voulais acheter.	42	55
Je fais des économies sur l'entretien de ma voiture.	35	65
J'ai acheté une voiture moins *puissante* que la voiture que je possédais avant.	18	74

present
because of

Suggestion: Contrast **parce que** and **à cause de.**

powerful

2. Combien de kilomètres faites-vous chaque année avec votre voiture?

Moins de 7500 km	27%	Plus de 25 000	14%
De 7500 à 15 000	36	Je ne sais pas	3
De 15 000 à 25 000	20		

virage à droite   virage à gauche interdit   virages dangereux

vitesse limitée à   fin de limitation de vitesse   passage à niveau gardé

stop 150

ralentir travaux   arrêt absolu à 150m   sens interdit

chaussée rétrécie   intersection   route à priorité

chaussée glissante   cassis ou dos d'âne   pente dangereuse

non gardé   attention enfants   passage pour piétons

interdit aux autos et motos   interdiction de dépasser   signaux sonores interdits

sens obligatoire   sens giratoire   parc pour automobiles

3. Accepteriez-vous de payer 5 pour cent de plus quand vous acheterez une nouvelle voiture si elle possédait . . .

	Oui	Non
Un moteur qui consomme moins d'essence	82%	17%
Une meilleure protection en cas d'accident	68	29
Un système qui diminue la pollution	67	30
Un plus grand confort	34	63
Un moteur plus puissant	19	80

4. Pensez-vous que vous pourriez facilement vous passer de votre voiture et utiliser d'autres moyens de transport (taxi, autobus, etc.)?

Non	60%
Oui, mais avec difficulté	23
Oui, facilement	14

5. Seriez-vous content s'il y avait de plus en plus de taxis et de moins en moins de voitures individuelles?

Non	46%
Oui	44
Sans opinion	10

6. Quand vous conduisez, est-ce que vous respectez la limite de *vitesse*?   speed

Toujours	49%
Souvent	29
De temps en temps	18
Jamais	4

7. Pour vous, est-ce que posséder une voiture représente surtout . . .

Une nécessité dans votre vie de tous les jours	53%
La liberté d'aller où vous voulez quand vous voulez	36
Une nécessité pour les week-ends	3
Un moyen de transport plus économique que les autres	3
Une nécessité pour vos vacances	3
Le plaisir de conduire	2

Extrait et adapté d'un article de *L'Express* par Georges Valence et Nicolas Langlois.

Compréhension   Selon les renseignements donnés, est-ce que les phrases suivantes sont vraies ou fausses? Corrigez le sens de la phrase s'il est faux.

1. L'augmentation des prix n'a eu aucun effet sur le comportement de la plupart des Français.
2. La majorité des Français ont acheté des voitures moins puissantes à cause de l'augmentation des prix.
3. Les Français utilisent très peu leur voiture. La majorité d'entre eux conduisent moins de 5000 kilomètres par an.
4. La majorité des Français accepteraient de payer plus cher pour une voiture qui consommerait moins d'essence.
5. La plupart des Français pensent qu'ils se passeraient facilement de leur voiture.
6. Les Français seraient contents s'il y avait plus de taxis et moins de voitures individuelles.
7. Tous les Français disent qu'ils conduisent au-dessus de la limite de vitesse.
8. La plupart des Français possèdent une voiture seulement pour le plaisir de conduire.

NOTES CULTURELLES

Les Français et leur voiture

Le sondage précédent indique que la voiture représente une nécessité plutôt qu'un luxe pour la majorité des Français. La raison n'est pas l'absence ou l'insuffisance des transports publics; il y a dans tout le pays d'excellents réseaux° de lignes d'autobus et de trains et même de lignes de métro à Paris et à Lyon. Mais les Français apprécient la liberté de mouvement que leur donne une voiture. Un autre sondage indique même que la promenade en voiture est la distraction favorite des Français.

Pour les Français, la voiture idéale est une voiture qui est à la fois économique, rapide et maniable.° Parmi les voitures fabriquées en France, il y a les Peugeot, les Renault, les Citroën et les Simca.

Sans vouloir trop généraliser, on peut dire que le Français au volant° a tendance à être assez indépendant, agressif et même impatient. Si un autre conducteur lui semble trop timide, trop prudent ou trop lent, il n'hésitera pas à montrer son impatience: «Espèce d'imbécile! Tu peux pas faire attention, non?»

réseaux *networks*

maniable *easy to drive*   au volant *at the wheel*

Communication

A. Les Américains et leur voiture. Répondez vous-même aux questions du sondage et discutez vos réponses avec les autres étudiants.

B. Qui suis-je?

1. Imaginez que vous êtes un(e) athlète célèbre. Les autres étudiants vont vous poser des questions pour trouver qui vous êtes.

   Written preparation may be helpful.

2. Imaginez que vous êtes un(e) reporter et que vous allez interviewer des athlètes célèbres. Quelles questions allez-vous leur poser? Trouvez un(e) autre étudiant(e) qui jouera le rôle d'un(e) athlète de son choix et interviewez-le(la).

C. Les dix commandements. Prenez les «dix commandements du randonneur» comme modèle et écrivez (1) les dix commandements de l'automobiliste ou (2) les dix commandements pour rester en bonne condition physique.

Students may use either the future or imperatives.

D. Athlètes et performances sportives. Pouvez-vous répondre aux questions suivantes? Pouvez-vous créer d'autres questions sur le même sujet?

1. Quel Américain a gagné de nombreuses compétitions de course à pied aux Jeux Olympiques de 1936? Jesse Owens
2. Qui a gagné le décathlon aux Jeux Olympiques de 1976? Bruce Jenner
3. Quels skieurs américains ont gagné une médaille d'or *(gold medal)* aux Jeux Olympiques d'hiver à Sarajevo en 1984? Bill Johnson et Phil Mahre
4. Qui a gagné la compétition de patinage artistique pour femmes en 1984? Katarina Witt, l'Allemagne de l'est
5. Quel Français a gagné de nombreuses compétitions de ski aux Jeux Olympiques de 1968? Jean-Claude Killy
6. Qui était l'organisateur des Jeux Olympiques modernes? Pierre de Coubertin, en 1896
7. Qui a gagné la compétition de hockey sur glace aux Jeux Olympiques de 1980? l'équipe américaine
8. Quelle équipe de base-ball a gagné le «World Series» l'année dernière? Et le «Super Bowl»?
9. Dans quelles villes les prochains Jeux Olympiques auront-ils lieu?
10. ?

1988: Calgary, Alberta (winter games)—Seoul, South Korea (summer games)

VOCABULAIRE

noms

les sports (voir pp. 310–311)

d'autres noms
l'**acier** (m)   *steel*
la **belle-fille**   *daughter-in-law*
la **carte**   *map*
le **chameau**   *camel*
le **chemin**   *way, road*
le **comportement**   *behavior*
l'**essence** (f)   *gasoline*
le **gendre**   *son-in-law*
la **Grande Guerre**   *First World War*
l'**ouverture** (f)   *opening*
la **pancarte**   *placard, sign*
le **réseau**   *network*
la **vipère**   *poisonous snake*
la **vitesse**   *speed*

verbes

arranger   *to suit, to be agreeable*
conduire   *to drive*
se conduire   *to behave*
construire   *to build*

croire   *to believe*
déranger   *to disturb, to bother*
détruire   *to destroy*
emporter   *to take along*
jouer   *to play*
tombèr amoureux   *to fall in love*
se passer de   *to do without*
pratiquer   *to do, practice, play (sports)*
produire   *to produce*
voir   *to see*

adjectifs

actuel, actuelle   *present*
puissant(e)   *powerful*

divers

les pronoms interrogatifs (voir pp. 313–314)

d'autres expressions
au-dessus   *above, beyond*
à cause de   *because of*
il ne suffit pas   *it is not enough*
malgré   *in spite of*

La vie artistique

Le musée Pompidou

Georges Pompidou was president of France from 1969 to 1974; he died in office. The museum, one of the great centers of modern art in the world, opened in January, 1977.

INTRODUCTION

Un musée pas comme les autres

La plupart des musées d'aujourd'hui ne sont pas des *endroits* gris et tristes qu'on voit *une fois pour toutes* et où on vient pour admirer des *tableaux*. On y vient aussi pour écouter de la musique, pour voir un film, pour écouter un récital de poésie, ou pour *assister à* un *spectacle* vidéo. Les expositions organisées sur des thèmes variés invitent les visiteurs à revenir périodiquement. Les nombreux espaces *libres*, les *fauteuils* où on peut *s'asseoir* pour se reposer, ou pour *bavarder*, permettent aux visiteurs de s'y sentir bien, d'avoir envie d'y revenir. Le musée Georges Pompidou (aussi appelé Beaubourg) est un de ces musées *vivants* et changeants.

places
once and for all
paintings
attend / show

open, free / armchairs
sit / chat

living

Dans le texte suivant, l'auteur nous invite à visiter un musée «pas comme les autres», le Musée international du masque et du carnaval. Ce musée est situé à Binche, une petite ville du sud de la Belgique célèbre depuis longtemps pour son carnaval.

«Si vous voyagez en Belgique, n'hésitez pas à faire un détour pour venir voir ce musée. Vous ne regretterez ni le détour ni le prix du *billet d'entrée*. Vous ne trouverez pas ici les *défilés* de clowns et de personnages de Walt Disney qui trop souvent caractérisent nos carnavals modernes. Mais vous y rencontrerez plusieurs *centaines* de personnages de rêve—ou de cauchemar—venus des quatre coins du monde. Vous ne pourrez pas rester indifférent non plus devant ce spectacle *éblouissant* où les *sorcières* et les *dieux*, la magie et les rites, les masques et les *déguisements* forment une mosaïque fantastique. Vous apprendrez que le masque a existé dans toutes les civilisations et qu'il a toujours un caractère rituel et sacré. Il est utilisé dans les pratiques religieuses ou magiques pour chasser les *mauvais esprits*, les maladies et la famine, pour *fêter* le retour des saisons, pour soliciter les faveurs des dieux ou pour les *remercier* de leur générosité.

«Ce magnifique musée est l'œuvre de Monsieur Glotz. Sa création a demandé de longues années d'études, de nombreuses rencontres avec des spécialistes du monde entier et surtout beaucoup de patience. En effet, l'acquisition de chaque pièce a demandé des négociations souvent longues et difficiles *car* chaque pays tient à *protéger* son propre héritage culturel.»

Extrait et adapté d'un article par Michèle Jean dans *Femmes d'aujourd'hui.*

entrance ticket
parades

hundreds

dazzling
witches / gods
costumes

evil spirits
celebrate
thank

because / protect

MUSÉES NATIONAUX
DROIT d'ENTRÉE
9 F
180589

Un des masques qu'on peut voir au musée de Binche . . . et un des costumes

Compréhension Indiquez si les phrases suivantes sont vraies ou fausses. Si le sens de la phrase est faux, corrigez-le.

1. Les musées d'aujourd'hui sont des endroits gris et tristes où personne ne va.
2. Beaucoup de gens reviennent plusieurs fois parce que le thème des expositions varie d'une saison à l'autre.
3. Il y a beaucoup d'endroits à l'intérieur du musée Georges Pompidou où on peut s'asseoir pour se reposer ou pour bavarder.
4. Le musée de Binche n'est pas un musée français, c'est un musée belge.
5. Si vous vous intéressez à Walt Disney, Binche est un musée qu'il faut absolument visiter.
6. Les masques et les déguisements qu'on peut y voir viennent des quatre coins du monde.
7. L'utilisation de masques et de déguisements est un phénomène assez récent.
8. Autrefois les masques étaient utilisés dans certaines pratiques religieuses.
9. Leur rôle était de chasser les mauvais esprits et de soliciter les faveurs des dieux.
10. Monsieur Glotz, le créateur du musée de Binche, s'intéresse surtout à l'art moderne.
11. Monsieur Glotz a acheté toutes les pièces du musée au cours d'un récent voyage en Amérique du Sud.
12. Son travail a été facile parce que les gens voulaient lui donner ces vieux masques.

NOTES CULTURELLES

L'art

Même si les Français ne s'intéressent pas tous
à l'art, d'une façon générale, on accorde une
assez grande importance à l'art en France.
Ce respect de l'art est évident dans les
institutions mêmes du pays; il existe un
Ministère de la Culture dont le rôle est de
protéger et de développer le patrimoine°
culturel national et d'intéresser le public à
l'art.

 Le gouvernement accorde aussi d'assez
généreuses subventions° aux différentes
entreprises culturelles: théâtres, musées, salles
de concert, expositions, etc. Pour intéresser
les jeunes à la musique, on a créé les
Jeunesses Musicales, séries de concerts
données par des artistes célèbres et auxquels°
on peut assister pour un prix modeste.
Chaque année, on organise des festivals qui
attirent des artistes et des spectateurs du
monde entier: le festival d'art dramatique
d'Avignon, le festival de Cannes (cinéma), le
festival d'Aix (musique), par exemple.

 Pour les Français, l'art est aussi dans la
rue. À Paris on découvre partout de
magnifiques exemples d'architecture
ancienne, des jardins et des places ornés de
statues, des galeries d'art et même des artistes
qui travaillent dans la rue sous les yeux des
curieux. On peut passer quelques minutes (ou
quelques heures) à regarder les gravures° des
bouquinistes° installés sur les quais de la
Seine; on peut aller faire un tour au marché
aux fleurs et si on est fatigué, on peut se
reposer tranquillement à l'ombre° de Notre-
Dame, dans le jardin des Tuileries ou sur les
bancs° des places et des parcs publics. Le
soir, l'illumination des monuments et des
fontaines offre au regard un spectacle de
choix,° et tout cela, gratuitement.

Au festival d'Avignon

patrimoine *heritage* subvention *subsidy*
auxquels *which* gravure *print, sketch*
bouquiniste *outdoor bookseller* ombre *shade*
banc *bench* de choix *choice*

Les bouquinistes sur le quai de la Seine

Et vous?

Les arts et vous. Allez-vous quelquefois au musée? D'une façon générale, vous intéressez-vous à l'art?

1. Est-ce que vous préférez l'art classique ou l'art d'avant-garde? Aimez-vous les impressionnistes? Les cubistes? Les fauves?
2. Est-ce que vous aimez . . .

   peindre?   paint
   dessiner?   draw
   sculpter?
   chanter?
   prendre des photos?
   Si non, est-ce que vous aimeriez apprendre à peindre ou à sculpter?
3. Comment est décoré votre appartement ou votre chambre? Est-ce que vous avez . . .

   des reproductions de tableaux?
   des *peintures* originales?   paintings
   des gravures?
   des affiches?
   des dessins?
   des objets d'art?
4. Quels sont les peintres que vous aimez? Et les sculpteurs? Et les danseurs? Et les musiciens?
5. Quelles ont été vos activités artistiques au cours des douze derniers mois? Avez-vous . . .

   visité un musée ou une exposition?
   assisté à un concert?
   visité des monuments historiques, des châteaux, et des cathédrales?
   assisté à un spectacle de ballet?
   écouté des disques ou des émissions de musique classique?
   regardé des films artistiques?
   assisté à un spectacle de *son et lumière*   sound and light display

⚜ # L'emploi de *si* dans la phrase conditionnelle

Présentation

As already noted, sentences with *si* clauses in the present can be followed by a result clause that uses the present, the future, or the imperative.

>Si vous êtes fatigué, vous pouvez vous reposer.
>Si vous allez en Belgique, essayez de visiter le musée de Binche.
>Si vous visitez le musée, vous verrez des masques extraordinaires.

Sentences with the *si* clause in the imperfect and the result clause in the conditional indicate what would happen if certain conditions were met. Although several different tenses can be used in the "if" clause in similar English constructions, only the imperfect tense is used in French.

>Si Jean travaillait plus,   *If John worked more,*
>il réussirait mieux.   *If John were to work more,* } *he would do better.*

Note that in French either clause can come first.

>Si j'avais de l'argent, j'achèterais un tableau.
>Je prendrais ce dessin s'il était meilleur marché.
>Je suis sûr que ce serait beaucoup plus cher si c'était un tableau original.

Préparation

Substitution: (1) S'il faisait mauvais, *nous* resterions à la maison. je / vous / mes amis / Claire / tu. (2) Si *Jacques* travaillait plus, *il* aurait de meilleures notes. vous / nous / les étudiants / tu / je. (3) *Pierre* viendrait s'*il* avait le temps. vous / mes parents / nous / Hélène.

A. Interview. Un reporter a interviewé des Français et il leur a posé la question suivante: «Que feriez-vous si vous aviez plus d'argent?» Donnez leurs réponses.

Modèle   je / aller aux États-Unis → **J'irais aux États-Unis si j'avais plus d'argent.**

1. je / prendre de longues vacances
2. Paul et sa femme / acheter une maison à la campagne
3. ma femme / prendre sa retraite
4. nous / faire un voyage au Canada
5. Pierre / acheter un tableau
6. Jean et moi, nous / mettre de l'argent à la banque
7. je / en donner une partie aux autres
8. nous / aller à Tahiti

B. Si c'était possible . . . Serge Lefèvre est un jeune artiste parisien qui étudie à l'École des Beaux-Arts. Il parle des choses qu'il aimerait faire.

Modèle   prendre des leçons de sculpture → **Si je pouvais, je prendrais des leçons de sculpture.**

1. faire des études en Italie
2. vendre quelques tableaux
3. aller voir toutes les expositions
4. étudier la peinture japonaise
5. travailler avec d'autres artistes
6. demander conseil à un grand artiste
7. suivre des cours de musique
8. apprendre à mieux dessiner

C. Ce n'est pas compliqué . . . Roland veut toujours savoir ce qui arriverait si. . . . Donnez les réponses de ses amis.

> **Modèle**   Que feriez-vous si vos amis étaient ici? (aller au musée) → **Si nos amis étaient ici, nous irions au musée.**

1. Qu'est-ce que nous ferions s'il y avait un agent? (conduire plus lentement)
2. Qu'est-ce que vous feriez si le professeur vous demandait des explications? (trouver une excuse)
3. Qu'est-ce que Jacques ferait s'il avait mal aux dents? (aller chez le dentiste)
4. Qu'est-ce qu'il ferait s'il n'avait pas de voiture? (marcher à pied)
5. Qu'est-ce que tu dirais si on te donnait mille francs? (dire merci)

Communication

A. Que feriez-vous? Que feriez-vous si vous étiez dans les situations suivantes? Complétez les phrases selon vos préférences.

1. S'il n'y avait pas de cours aujourd'hui . . .
2. Si je voulais devenir peintre . . .
3. Si j'avais besoin d'une nouvelle voiture . . .
4. Si je pouvais être une autre personne . . .
5. Si j'avais soixante ans . . .
6. Si j'étais millionnaire . . .
7. Si j'habitais dans un autre pays . . .
8. Si je pouvais choisir les programmes qu'on montre à la télé . . .

B. Mettez-vous à leur place. Comment serait votre vie si vous étiez un(e) étudiant(e) français(e)? Utilisez les suggestions suivantes pour parler de votre vie.

> **Exemple**   Si j'étais un étudiant français, je ferais mes études à l'université de Grenoble.

Have students put themselves in the place of a French-Canadian student.

Suggestions: vos études, votre appartement ou votre chambre, vos amis, votre famille, vos activités habituelles, vos loisirs, vos obligations, votre ville, etc.

C. Changez de rôle. Que feriez-vous si vous étiez à la place des personnes suivantes?

1. le professeur
2. un artiste
3. le président des États-Unis
4. le président de votre université
5. une vedette de cinéma
6. le directeur d'un musée

Follow-up: Add other professions and have students respond.

Les verbes *connaître* et *savoir*

Présentation

The irregular verbs **connaître** and **savoir** both correspond to the English verb *to know;* however, they cannot be used interchangeably.

connaître		savoir	
je **connais**	nous **connaissons**	je sais	nous savons
tu **connais**	vous **connaissez**	tu sais	vous savez
il/elle/on **connaît**	ils/elles **connaissent**	il/elle/on sait	ils/elles savent
passé composé: j'ai connu		passé composé: j'ai su	
futur: je connaîtrai		futur: je saurai	

Suggestion: Point out that the circumflex occurs only before the letter **t** in the forms of **connaître**.

A. **Connaître** is used in the sense of *to be familiar with* or *to be acquainted with.* It is always used with a direct object (e.g., people, places, etc.).

Je connais un artiste célèbre.
Est-ce que vous connaissez le vieux Lyon?
À cette époque-là, je connaissais bien Madame Bertrand.
Je n'ai pas connu mon grand-père.
Si nous passons six mois à Paris, nous connaîtrons bien la ville.

> **Faire la connaissance de** is another frequently used expression meaning *to meet* or *to become acquainted with.*

Est-ce que vous avez fait la connaissance de mon cousin?
J'ai fait sa connaissance à Paris.

B. **Savoir** is used in the sense of *to know facts* or *to know how.* It can be used with a direct object, a clause, an infinitive, or by itself.

Savez-vous la date de mon anniversaire?
Est-ce que tu sais qui est Chagall? Non, je ne sais pas qui c'est.
Il sait s'habiller avec élégance.
Nous savions qu'ils ne viendraient pas.   Point out the pronunciation of *je ne sais pas* in fast speech: [ʃepa].
Je ne saurai jamais toutes les réponses.

C. In the **passé composé**, **savoir** and **connaître** have idiomatic meanings.

J'ai su qu'ils étaient en Belgique.	*I learned that they were in Belgium.*
Comment est-ce que tu l'as su?	*How did you find it out?*
Elle l'a connu à Dijon.	*She met him (made his acquaintance) in Dijon.*

D. The following verbs are conjugated like **connaître**:

reconnaître *to recognize*   Je l'ai reconnu(e) tout de suite.
disparaître *to disappear*   Il y a un tableau qui a disparu.
paraître *to appear, to seem, to look*   Vous paraissez fatigué(e).

Suggestion: Point out that **il paraît que** *(it seems* or *I've heard that)* is used to relate hearsay. One uses, however, **on dirait** instead of **il paraît** in expressions such as **On dirait qu'il va pleuvoir.**

Préparation

Substitution: (1) Je connais cette danseuse. vous / mes parents / le professeur / nous / tu. (2) Je sais la réponse. tu / vous / les étudiants / mon ami / nous. (3) Je connaissais bien les Dupont à cette époque-là. nos parents / tu / nous / Anne / vous. (4) Je ne savais pas cela. vous / ces étudiants / nous / on.

Quelqu'un qui sait toujours tout. Jean-Paul Saitout est une de ces personnes qui sait tout et qui connaît tout le monde. C'est un véritable expert sur tous les sujets. Utilisez les indications données pour formuler ses réactions aux différents sujets mentionnés.

Modèles   la réponse → **Bien sûr, je sais la réponse.**
                Pierre → **Bien sûr, je connais Pierre.**

1. les dates de l'exposition
2. ce musée
3. les parents de Julien
4. dessiner
5. nager
6. un bon restaurant
7. Marseille
8. l'adresse de Michelle
9. le numéro de téléphone de Françoise
10. ce sculpteur

Communication

A. Savoir n'est pas connaître. Utilisez les suggestions suivantes pour poser des questions aux autres étudiants de votre classe au sujet de ce qu'ils savent et des gens ou des endroits qu'il connaissent.

    Exemples   des artistes → **Est-ce que tu connais des artistes?**
                       jouer à la pétanque → **Est-ce que tu sais jouer à la pétanque?**

1. peindre
2. les différents quartiers de votre ville
3. où on peut acheter de jolies reproductions
4. tes voisins
5. un danseur
6. faire du ski nautique
7. parler chinois
8. quels cours tu vas suivre le trimestre prochain
9. ?

Put different cues (e.g., **peindre; les différents quartiers de votre ville,** etc.) on individual note cards. Students circulate asking other students questions using the cues on their cards. They write down student answers to use in large-group sharing of information (e.g., **Michelle sait peindre, mais Roger ne sait pas peindre.**).

B. Je donne ma langue au chat. Posez des questions aux autres étudiants pour découvrir s'ils connaissent les mêmes personnes que vous ou s'ils savent les mêmes choses. S'ils n'arrivent pas à répondre, ils peuvent «donner leur langue au chat» *(give up).*

Have students answer each other's questions.

    Exemples   Est-ce que vous savez qui a sculpté la Statue de Liberté?

 # Les pronoms démonstratifs

Présentation

Demonstrative pronouns can replace nouns. They reflect the number and gender of the nouns they replace.

Les pronoms démonstratifs			
	Masculine	*Feminine*	
Singular	celui	celle	*the one, this one, that one*
Plural	ceux	celles	*the ones, these, those*

Demonstrative pronouns cannot stand alone.

A. Demonstrative pronouns can be followed by prepositional phrases.

À mon avis, les meilleures peintures sont celles des impressionnistes.

In my opinion, the best paintings are those of the impressionists.

Il prend l'avion pour Strasbourg, et moi, je prends celui pour Lyon.

He's taking the plane for Strasbourg, and I'm taking the one for Lyon.

Les vêtements de Monoprix sont moins chers que ceux des Galeries Lafayette.

Monoprix's clothes are less expensive than those of Galeries Lafayette.

The preposition **de** used with a demonstrative pronoun frequently indicates possession.

Cet appareil photo est très bon marché mais celui d'Anne est meilleur marché.

This camera is very cheap, but Anne's is cheaper.

À qui est cette affiche? C'est celle de Jacques.

Whose poster is this? It's Jack's.

Est-ce que tu as vu les nouveaux manteaux de Christian Dior? Oui, mais j'aime mieux ceux d'Yves Saint-Laurent.

Did you see Dior's new coats? Yes, but I prefer those of Yves Saint-Laurent.

B. Demonstrative pronouns can be followed by relative pronouns.

Quel tableau voulez-vous? Je préfère celui qui coûte le moins cher.

Which painting do you want? I prefer the one that costs the least.

Je préfère cette affiche à celle que Paul a achetée.

I prefer this poster to the one that Paul bought.

Ces gravures et celles qu'on a exposées l'année passée sont très belles.

These prints and the ones that were shown last year are very beautiful.

Ceux qui arriveront les premiers au musée attendront les autres.

Those (the people) who arrive first at the museum will wait for the others.

C. Demonstrative pronouns can be used with the suffixes **-ci** and **-là**.

Je ne sais pas quel dessin choisir. Celui-ci est moins cher, mais celui-là est plus joli.

I don't know which drawing to choose. This one is less expensive, but that one is prettier.

You may wish to tell students that **-ci** generally refers to the nearer item and **-là** to the more distant item.

D. Ceci *(this)* and **cela** *(that)* and the more informal **ça** *(that)* are used to refer to ideas or unspecified things rather than to specifically named items. Thus, they do not indicate gender and number.

Ceci va vous surprendre. *This is going to surprise you.*
Je ne comprends pas cela. *I don't understand that.*
Ça, c'est formidable! *That's great!*

Ça ne veut rien dire.　　　　*That doesn't mean anything.*
Ça alors!　　　　　　　　　*Really! (You've got to be kidding!)*

Transformation: Modèle: C'est la manteau de Jacques. → **C'est celui de Jacques.** (1) C'est la cravate du professeur. (2) Ce sont les chaussures de Guy. (3) Ce sont les étudiants de notre classe. (4) Ce sont les vêtements des enfants. (5) C'est la voiture de papa. (6) C'est la mode de l'année passée. (7) C'est le train pour Madrid . (8) C'est l'avion pour Tokyo.

Préparation

A. Contradictions. Jeannette et Paul ont des goûts très différents. Chaque fois que Jeannette donne son opinion sur quelque chose, Paul est de l'opinion opposée.

Modèle　　Cette reproduction est très jolie. → **Ah non, celle-ci est beaucoup plus jolie.**

1. Cette exposition est très bien organisée.
2. Ce peintre est très célèbre.
3. Ces tableaux sont bien faits.
4. Ces photos sont très belles.
5. Cet article est passionnant.
6. Cette affiche est amusante.
7. Cette danseuse a beaucoup de talent.
8. Ce château est très beau.

B. La nostalgie du bon vieux temps. Il y a des gens—même des personnes assez jeunes—qui pensent toujours que le passé était bien plus agréable que le présent. Honoré Regret est une de ces personnes. Reconstituez les phrases qu'il a prononcées.

Modèles　　Je n'aime pas ma nouvelle maison. (la maison où nous habitions autrefois) → **J'aimais mieux celle où nous habitions autrefois.**
Je n'aime pas ma nouvelle maison. (la maison de mes parents) → **J'aimais mieux celle de mes parents.**

Follow-up: Have students react to comments of Honoré Regret (Moi, je n'aime pas la mode d'il y a dix ans. Je préfère celle d'aujourd'hui, etc.)

1. Je n'aime pas la musique qu'on entend à la radio. (la musique qu'on entendait autrefois)
2. Je n'aime pas les vêtements d'aujourd'hui. (les vêtements qu'on portait quand j'étais jeune)
3. Je n'aime pas les jeux qu'on joue aujourd'hui. (les jeux de mon enfance)
4. Je n'aime pas les cours que je suis ce trimestre. (les cours que je suivais le trimestre passé)
5. Je n'aime pas mes professeurs. (les professeurs que j'avais au lycée)
6. Je n'aime pas la mode d'aujourd'hui. (la mode d'il y a dix ans)
7. Je n'aime pas ma nouvelle chambre. (la chambre où j'habitais l'année dernière)
8. Je n'aime pas les derniers tableaux de Picasso. (les tableaux de la période bleue)
9. Je n'aime pas mon nouveau camarade de chambre. (le camarade de chambre que j'avais l'année dernière)

Communication

A. Choix. Qu'est-ce que vous allez choisir dans chacune des situations suivantes? Utilisez un pronom démonstratif dans chacune de vos réponses.

Exemple Chaque comédien(ne) a son propre humour. Quel type d'humour préférez-vous? → **Je préfère celui de W. C. Fields.**

Option: Ask questions and have students answer, using options as a guide. Have students comment on their choices.

1. Chaque comédien(ne) a son propre humour. Quel type d'humour préférez-vous?
   a. l'humour de Woody Allen
   b. l'humour de Lily Tomlin
   c. l'humour d'Eddie Murphy
   d. ?

2. Quel(le) camarade de chambre allez-vous choisir?
   a. un garçon (une fille) qui est calme et sérieux(-euse), mais pas très amusant(e)
   b. un(e) autre qui adore s'amuser et inviter des amis mais qui ne travaille que rarement
   c. un(e) autre qui travaille tous les jours jusqu'à quatre heures du matin
   d. ?

3. Vous cherchez un appartement. Quel type d'appartement allez-vous choisir?
   a. un appartement très joli et très moderne, mais qui est très petit
   b. un appartement grand et confortable mais qui coûte assez cher
   c. un appartement confortable et bien situé, mais où on n'accepte pas les animaux
   d. ?

4. Vous êtes invité(e) à aller dîner dans un restaurant. Quel restaurant allez-vous choisir?
   a. un restaurant où on sert de la cuisine française
   b. un restaurant où la cuisine est assez médiocre mais l'ambiance est agréable
   c. un restaurant où on mange très bien mais le décor est assez ordinaire
   d. ?

5. Vous avez de la chance. Vous êtes invité(e) à quatre surprise-parties différentes le même soir. À quelle surprise-partie allez-vous aller?
   a. une où il y a toujours de bonnes choses à boire et à manger
   b. une où vous pouvez rencontrer des gens intéressants mais où vous ne connaissez aucun des invités
   c. une où vous êtes sûr(e) de retrouver tous vos amis
   d. ?

6. Vous avez décidé d'aller au cinéma. Quel film allez-vous choisir?
   a. un film qui promet beaucoup de suspense et d'aventure
   b. un film où vous êtes sûr(e) de vous amuser
   c. un film que personne ne connaît mais qui semble avoir un sujet très intéressant
   d. ?

7. Vous allez suivre un cours de français et vous avez le choix entre plusieurs professeurs. Quel type de professeur est-ce que vous allez choisir?
   a. un professeur qui sait rendre une classe intéressante
   b. un professeur qui donne de bonnes notes à tout le monde
   c. un professeur qui demande très peu de travail de ses étudiants
   d. ?

B. **Préférences.** Répondez aux questions suivantes.

1. Quels romans préférez-vous? Les romans d'aventure ou ceux de science-fiction?
2. Quelles chansons françaises préférez-vous? Les chansons de Johnny Halliday ou celles d'Édith Piaf?
3. Quelle peinture aimez-vous le mieux? La peinture des impressionnistes ou celle des cubistes?
4. Quels types de musée préférez-vous? Ceux où il y a seulement des tableaux ou ceux où on peut voir toutes sortes d'objets d'art?
5. Préférez-vous les sculptures d'Auguste Rodin ou celles d'Henry Moore?

Ask a student to leave the room. During his/her absence, have students put some of their possessions on a table. When the student returns, have different members of the class ask him/her to identify these objects (**À qui est ce livre de chimie? C'est celui de Diane.**).

 ## Les pronoms possessifs

Présentation

Possessive pronouns are used to replace nouns and possessive adjectives. They therefore have the same number and gender as the nouns they replace.

Les pronoms possessifs				
Singular		*Plural*		
Masculine	*Feminine*	*Masculine*	*Feminine*	
le mien	la mienne	les miens	les miennes	*mine*
le tien	la tienne	les tiens	les tiennes	*yours*
le sien	la sienne	les siens	les siennes	*his, hers, its*
le nôtre	la nôtre	les nôtres	les nôtres	*ours*
le vôtre	la vôtre	les vôtres	les vôtres	*yours*
le leur	la leur	les leurs	les leurs	*theirs*

Suggestion: Point out the [o] in the **le nôtre, le vôtre**, and related forms.

Avez-vous apporté votre programme? Moi, j'ai apporté le mien.
Nous avons fait nos devoirs, mais Nadine n'a pas fait les siens.
Je vous raconterai mes secrets si vous me racontez les vôtres.
Nous avons encore notre vieille voiture, mais Marie a vendu la sienne.

A. It is important to remember that the pronoun agrees in number and gender with the noun possessed and not with the possessor.

la chambre de Paul   la sienne
le chien de Suzanne   le sien

B. When the possessive pronoun is preceded by **à** or **de,** the forms are contracted in the usual way.

Je ne suis pas très content de mon appareil photo, mais eux, ils sont très satisfaits du leur.
Je pense à mes problèmes et elle, elle pense aux siens.

Transformation: Modèle: Voilà ma maison. → **Voilà la mienne.** (1) Voilà mes suggestions. (2) Voilà mes chaussures. (3) Voilà ton livre. (4) Voilà ta cravate. (5) Voilà son appartement. (6) Voilà sa robe. (7) Voilà notre village. (8) Voilà nos stylos. (9) Voilà votre chambre. (10) Voici nos devoirs. (11) Voilà leur passeport. (12) Voilà leurs examens.

Préparation

A. Visite des châteaux de la Loire. Un groupe d'amis sont en train de visiter les châteaux de la Loire. Valérie veut savoir ce que les autres ont apporté.

Modèle   Qui a apporté son appareil photo? (moi) → **Moi, j'ai apporté le mien.**

1. Qui a apporté sa caméra? (Marc)
2. Qui a déjà acheté son billet d'entrée? (Laurent)
3. Qui a apporté un Guide Michelin? (nous)
4. Qui a apporté sa carte de la région? (toi)
5. Qui a déjà vu sa chambre d'hôtel? (moi)
6. Qui a déjà retenu une table au restaurant? (mes amis)
7. Qui a apporté des lunettes de soleil? (nous)

Point out to students that the **Guide Michelin (rouge)** contains information about hotels and restaurants in French towns, each accompanied by a rating (four-star, three-star, etc.), current prices, and description of available amenities. The Michelin **guide vert**, on the other hand, describes a particular region and suggests places of interest and possible itineraries.

B. Il ne faut pas se tromper! Les habitants d'une petite ville ont prêté leurs tableaux et autres objets d'art pour une exposition organisée par la ville. Maintenant il faut les rendre. Ce n'est pas facile.

Modèle   Est-ce que ce tableau est à Madame Sabatier? (Non, Monsieur Lejeune) → **Non, ce n'est pas le sien, c'est celui de Monsieur Lejeune.**

1. Est-ce que cette gravure est à vous? (non, Madame Verneuil)
2. Est-ce que ces dessins sont à toi, Élise? (non, mon frère)
3. Est-ce que cette petite gravure est à vos voisins? (non, Mademoiselle Pasteur)
4. Est-ce que ces affiches sont à vous? (non, Monsieur Girard)
5. Est-ce que ce tableau est à Monsieur Denis? (non, Madame Boivin)
6. Est-ce que cette sculpture est à Monsieur Dumas? (non, Monsieur Lambert)

Communication

A. Questions/interview. Répondez aux questions suivantes ou utilisez-les pour interviewer un(e) autre étudiant(e).

1. Beaucoup d'Américains ont des ancêtres qui viennent d'Europe. D'où viennent les tiens?
2. L'anniversaire de George Washington est le 22 février. Quand est celui de Lincoln? Et le tien? Et celui de ton (ta) meilleur(e) ami(e)?
3. Certaines personnes préfèrent les grosses voitures, d'autres les petites voitures. Comment est la tienne? Et celle de tes parents?
4. Beaucoup d'étudiants passent leurs vacances de printemps en Floride. Et toi, où passes-tu les tiennes? Et tes parents, où passent-ils les leurs? Et ton professeur, sais-tu où il passe les siennes?
5. À ton avis, les vins français sont-ils meilleurs que les nôtres?
6. Il y a des étudiants qui font toujours leurs devoirs à la dernière minute. Quand fais-tu les tiens?
7. À ton avis, est-ce que les voitures étrangères sont plus économiques que les nôtres?

B. Vous et moi. Choisissez un(e) autre étudiant(e) avec qui vous allez parler et utilisez les suggestions suivantes pour guider la conversation.

1. Dites-lui quelle est votre boisson préférée et demandez-lui quelle est la sienne.
2. Dites-lui quels sont vos peintres préférés et demandez-lui quels sont les siens.
3. Dites-lui quels sont vos écrivains préférés et demandez-lui quels sont les siens.
4. Dites-lui comment est décoré votre appartement et demandez-lui comment est décoré le sien.
5. Dites-lui quel est votre musée préféré et demandez-lui quel est le sien.
6. Dites-lui quand est votre anniversaire et demandez-lui quand est le sien.
7. Donnez-lui votre numéro de téléphone et demandez-lui quel est le sien.
8. Donnez-lui votre adresse et demandez-lui quelle est la sienne.

Follow-up: Have students report back their partners' preferences.

MUSÉE RODIN
77, rue de Varenne (7e). Mo Varenne
DESSINS
de
RODIN
Dante et Virgile aux enfers
T.L.J. (sauf mardi) 10 h-17 h 15
23 NOVEMBRE – 27 FÉVRIER

EXPOSITION
Huis clos pour monstres
Bacon. Peintures récentes. Galerie Maeght-Lelong, Paris, jusqu'à fin mars.

SYNTHÈSE

Comment va le cinéma français?

Si vous me demandiez comment va le cinéma français, je vous répondrais qu'il va très bien, merci. Bien sûr, vous me diriez qu'on ne va *plus guère* au cinéma, que les gens se contentent de regarder la télévision confortablement *installés* dans leur fauteuil, que le cinéma connaît depuis les années 60 une crise longue et difficile.

hardly anymore

settled.

Vous auriez en partie raison. Mais je vous *ferais remarquer* qu'on *tourne* plus de films en France qu'aux États-Unis et que quatre *milliards* de spectateurs par an, ce n'est pas si mal que ça.

would point out

make / billions

Vous me demanderiez alors où sont tous ces spectateurs et pourquoi les salles sont souvent *à moitié vides*. Je serais bien obligée de *reconnaître* qu'il y a de moins en moins de gens qui *fréquentent* les salles de cinéma. Mais cela ne veut pas dire que les Français ne s'intéressent plus au cinéma. S'ils ne s'y intéressaient pas, pourquoi y aurait-il 15 millions de téléspectateurs qui chaque dimanche soir s'installent devant leur télévision pour regarder un film? La vérité est que les Français vont au cinéma, qu'ils y vont souvent, et qu'ils aiment ça, mais la plupart préfèrent voir les films chez eux!

half / empty / admit

frequent, go often to

Voici leurs réponses aux questions qu'on leur a posées *au cours d*'un récent sondage.

during

L'entrée d'un cinéma parisien

1. Allez-vous au cinéma . . .

plusieurs fois par semaine?	2,2 %
une fois par semaine?	10,7
une fois par mois?	34
moins souvent?	51,3
sans réponse	1,7

2. Parmi les genres de films suivants, quels sont . . .

	ceux que vous préférez?	et ceux que vous détestez?
Les films comiques	40,3 %	5,2 %
Les films policiers	29,5	7,5
Les films de science-fiction	23,9	25,9
Les films d'aventure	23,9	1,8
Les comédies dramatiques	17,7	17,2
Les grands classiques	17	12,6
Les westerns	15,3	19,3
Les dessins animés	13,9	5
Les comédies musicales	13,6	21,8
Les films à grand spectacle	12,2	11,8
Les films historiques	11,7	10,8
Les films politiques	10,3	27,8
Les films X	2,6	46
sans réponse	0,8	

3. Préférez-vous voir les films étrangers . . .

en version originale avec *sous-titres*?	23 %	subtitles
en version française?	68,3	
pas de préférence	7,3	
sans réponse	1,4	

4. Comment choisissez-vous les films que vous allez voir? Qu'est-ce qui vous influence le plus dans vos choix?

Le sujet du film	48,7 %	
La vedette	39,3	
Les commentaires de vos amis	37,5	
Les critiques des journaux	24	
Les émissions à la télévision	16,8	
Le *metteur en scène*	15,1	director
L'affiche	13,4	
Le titre	10,1	
La proximité de la salle	9,7	
Les *prix* obtenus par le film	3,1	awards
sans raison	7,9	
sans réponse	2,8	

5. Quels sont vos acteurs et actrices préférés? Donnez trois noms.

Alain Delon
Jean-Paul Belmondo
Jean Gabin

6. Quels sont vos metteurs en scène préférés? Donnez trois noms.

> Claude Lelouche
> François Truffaut
> Frederico Fellini

Inspiré d'un article de L'*Express*.

Compréhension   Répondez aux questions suivantes selon les renseignements donnés dans le texte.

1. Est-ce que l'auteur pense que le cinéma français est en assez bonne santé ou qu'il est très malade?
2. Pourquoi y a-t-il des raisons de penser que le cinéma français est en difficulté?
3. Où est-ce qu'on tourne le plus de films chaque année, en France ou aux États-Unis?
4. Est-ce que les Français fréquentent beaucoup les salles de cinéma?
5. Comment font-ils pour voir les films qui les intéressent?
6. Qu'est-ce que beaucoup de Français font le dimanche soir?
7. Quel est le pourcentage de gens qui vont au cinéma au moins une fois par semaine?
8. Quel genre de film les Français préfèrent-ils?
9. Et quels sont les films qu'ils aiment le moins?
10. Est-ce qu'ils préfèrent voir les films étrangers en version française ou en version originale avec sous-titres?
11. Qu'est-ce qui les influence le plus dans leur choix d'un film?
12. Quels sont leurs acteurs et actrices préférés?

Have students use the responses of the French people surveyed to write a résumé of French film preferences (e.g., **La majorité des Français vont au cinéma moins d'une fois par mois.**).

NOTES CULTURELLES

Le cinéma français

La France a toujours joué un rôle important dans l'histoire du cinéma aussi appelé «le septième art». Cette histoire a commencé en 1895 quand Louis Lumière a présenté ses premières projections animées à une assemblée de 120 personnes. C'est seulement deux ans plus tard que Georges Méliès a construit le premier studio du monde et a commencé à inventer des truquages.° À partir de ce moment-là, la vogue du cinéma s'est répandue° dans le monde entier.

La qualité du cinéma français s'est imposée dès les années vingt grâce aux œuvres des cinéastes° comme Germaine Dulac, Abel Gance, Jacques Feyder et René Clair.

C'est encore en France qu'une nouvelle orientation a été donnée au cinéma à la fin des années cinquante par les metteurs en scène de la «nouvelle vague».° Leurs noms (Godard, Truffaut, Varda, Malle, Resnais, etc.) sont bien connus des cinéphiles° du monde entier, et leurs œuvres continuent à retenir l'attention du public informé aussi bien en France qu'à l'étranger.

---

truquages *special effects*   s'est répandue *spread*   cinéastes *film makers*

«nouvelle vague» *"New Wave"*   cinéphiles *film lovers*

Les Français moyens sont loin d'être tous des cinéphiles. Beaucoup vont au cinéma surtout pour se distraire, et un grand nombre d'entre eux préfèrent rester à la maison pour regarder la télévision. Mais il existe aussi un assez large public bien informé qui recherche° la qualité. Les ciné-clubs, groupés en sept fédérations nationales, contribuent beaucoup à éduquer le public et attirent chaque année cinq millions de spectateurs. Les critiques des films occupent une place importante dans les principales revues françaises et il existe plusieurs revues spécialisées telles que *Les Cahiers du cinéma.*

recherche *seeks*

Communication

A. Et vous, aimez-vous le cinéma? Répondez vous-même aux questions du sondage présentées dans la Synthèse. Ensuite, comparez vos réponses à celles des autres étudiants ou bien à celles des Français.

Have students choose the film that they consider to be the best film of the year. Individual choices and reasons will be presented to the class and a vote taken to decide on the choice of the class.

B. Connaissance de la culture française. Pouvez-vous répondre aux questions suivantes? Sinon, consultez les réponses à la fin du test.

Suggested for listening.

1. Parmi les trois architectes français suivants, quel est celui qui a dessiné les plans de la ville de Washington?
   a. Le Corbusier   b. Pierre L'Enfant   c. Le Nôtre
2. Parmi les peintres suivants, quel est celui qui est considéré comme le principal représentant de l'école impressionniste?
   a. Renoir   b. Delacroix   c. Buffet
3. C'est un musicien du début du vingtième siècle dont l'œuvre la plus connue est le *Boléro.* Qui est-ce?
   a. Pierre Boulez   b. Camille Saint-Saëns   c. Maurice Ravel
4. Auteur de la célèbre phrase «une rose est une rose, est une rose, est une rose», cette femme de lettres américaine a passé une grande partie de sa vie en France où elle a connu et encouragé les artistes de son temps. Qui est-ce?
   a. Mary Cassatt   b. Gertrude Stein   c. Virginia Woolf
5. Parmi les trois artistes suivants, quel est celui qui a peint le tableau intitulé *Guernica?*
   a. Édouard Manet   b. Paul Gauguin   c. Pablo Picasso
6. Cet auteur d'origine roumaine est un des principaux représentants du théâtre de l'absurde. Qui est-ce?
   a. Jean Cocteau   b. Jean Anouilh   c. Eugène Ionesco
7. Il est généralement considéré comme un des plus grands poètes de l'époque romantique. Qui est-ce?
   a. Victor Hugo   b. La Fontaine   c. Ronsard
8. Parmi les trois villes suivantes, quelle est celle où il y a chaque année un festival d'art dramatique qui attire des jeunes du monde entier?
   a. Avignon   b. Cannes   c. Strasbourg
9. Un des trois peintres suivants a décoré l'Opéra de Paris et celui de New York. Qui est-ce?
   a. Matisse   b. Chagall   c. Van Gogh
10. Auteur de nombreux livres, cette femme a aussi écrit des scénarios de films et dirigé elle-même ses propres films. Qui est-ce?
    a. Simone de Beauvoir   b. Marguerite Duras   c. Georges Sand

New cognate vocabulary used in this activity is not intended to be active.

Réponses: 1. b; 2. a; 3. c; 4. b; 5. c; 6. c; 7. a; 8. a; 9. b; 10. b.

C. Votre culture. Chaque pays et même chaque génération a sa propre culture. Pensez aux artistes et aux œuvres que les gens de votre génération
connaissent et apprécient et composez un petit test culturel que vous
présenterez au reste de la classe (ou à votre professeur).

D. Place à l'imagination. Donnez libre cours *(free range)* à votre imagination
et composez des phrases sur le thème «si j'étais . . . ». Inspirez-vous des
suggestions suivantes.

> Students can be asked to create (individually or in small groups) single-line responses to the different suggestions. These suggestions can also be used for small-group or whole-class composition of longer ''prose poems.''

Exemple   Si j'étais un tableau, je ne voudrais pas rester toujours à la
même place sur un mur.

Si j'étais . . .

1. un tableau	5. un personnage de roman	9. le ciel
2. une statue	6. une chanson	10. une saison
3. une affiche	7. une fleur	11. un masque
4. un(e) sorcier(-ière)	8. la mer	12. ?

VOCABULAIRE

noms

le **billet d'entrée**   *entrance ticket*
la **centaine**   *approximately one hundred*
le **défilé**   *parade*
le **déguisement**   *costume*
le **dieu**   *god*
l'**endroit** (m)   *place*
l'**esprit** (m)   *spirit, mind*
le **fauteuil**   *armchair, seat (theater)*
la **gravure**   *sketch, print*
les **mauvais esprits** (m)   *evil spirits*
le **metteur en scène**   *director*
le **milliard**   *billion*
le **peintre**   *painter*
la **peinture**   *painting*
le **prix**   *award, prize*
la **sorcière**   *witch* (le **sorcier** = *warlock*)
le **spectacle**   *show*
le **sous-titre**   *subtitle*
le **tableau**   *painting*

verbes

s'asseoir   *to sit*
assister à   *to attend, to be present at*
bavarder   *to chat*
connaître   *to know, to be familiar with, to be
   acquainted with*
dessiner   *to draw*
disparaître   *to disappear*
faire la connaissance de   *to meet*

fêter   *to celebrate*
fréquenter   *to frequent, to go often*
paraître   *to appear, to seem, to look*
peindre   *to paint*
protéger   *to protect*
reconnaître   *to recognize, to admit*
remarquer   *to notice, to observe*
remercier   *to thank*
savoir   *to know, to know how*
tourner   *to make (a movie)*

adjectifs

éblouissant(e)   *dazzling*
étranger, étrangère   *foreign*
installé(e)   *settled*
vide   *empty*
vivant(e)   *alive*

adverbes

à moitié   *half*
ne . . . guère   *hardly, scarcely*

divers

les pronoms démonstratifs (voir pp. 333–334)

les pronoms possessifs (voir p. 337)

au cours de   *during, in the course of*
car   *because, for*
son et lumière   *sound and light display*
une fois pour toutes   *once and for all*

Vive la musique!

INTRODUCTION

La *folie* de la musique

Monsieur Clément est en retard parce qu'il a *manqué* son bus. Il entre dans la salle et s'installe discrètement dans le demi-cercle d'hommes et de femmes déjà *assis*. Il *enlève* sa cravate, la roule et la met dans sa poche. Il change de *lunettes* et cherche dans sa *serviette*. Il en sort un petit livre. Il trouve la *bonne* page. Il *remplit* ses poumons et se met à chanter avec les soixante-neuf autres membres de la *chorale*. Il oublie qu'il est comptable, qu'il est fatigué de sa journée de travail, qu'il a des soucis . . . *Il n'y a plus qu'*un ténor qui se donne au plaisir de chanter.

À la même heure, dans une autre ville, c'est Jo Berlioz (avec un nom comme ça, on est bien obligé d'aimer la musique), un *retraité* qui quitte sa maison pour aller à la *répétition* du *cercle philharmonique*. Il met son béret, prend son vélo, et *en avant* la musique!

Monsieur Clément et Monsieur Berlioz ne sont pas des cas isolés. Le nombre de gens qui appartiennent à une chorale ou à un cercle philharmonique a triplé en sept ans. Partout les gens (*y compris* les jeunes) s'enthousiasment pour la musique, non seulement la chanson populaire mais aussi la musique classique et l'opéra.

On *avait coutûme de* dire que le Français *moyen* ne s'intéresse qu'à la pétanque, à la *belote* et à la bonne cuisine. Serait-il en train de redécouvrir la musique?

Extrait et adapté d'un article de *L'Express*.

madness, craze

missed

seated / takes off
glasses / briefcase
right / fills
choir

All that remains is . . .
Have students note that the pronunciation of the **ch** in **chorale** and **chœur** is [k].
retired man
rehearsal / music club
forward

including

was in the habit of / average
a card game
Point out that Hector Berlioz (1803–1869) is a famous composer known for works such as *La damnation de Faust* and *La symphonie fantastique*.

Compréhension   Répondez aux questions suivantes selon les renseignements donnés dans le texte.

1. Qu'est-ce que Monsieur Clément va faire ce soir après son travail?
2. Pourquoi est-ce qu'il est en retard?
3. Combien de chanteurs y a-t-il dans sa chorale?
4. Qu'est-ce que la musique lui apporte?
5. Quelle est la profession de Monsieur Berlioz?
6. À quel groupe musical appartient-il?
7. Quel moyen de transport utilise-t-il pour aller à la répétition?
8. D'après le texte diriez-vous que l'intérêt pour la musique classique est en train de diminuer ou en train d'augmenter en France?
9. Pourquoi ce phénomène est-il assez surprenant?

NOTES CULTURELLES

La Musique Française

La musique est un langage qui n'a pas de frontières° et souvent on connaît et on apprécie certaines œuvres sans les associer avec un pays particulier. Un certain nombre de musiciens et compositeurs français ont leur place parmi les grands noms de la musique et sont bien connus du public américain. Par exemple, le *Boléro* de Maurice Ravel (1875–1937) et *L'après-midi d'un faune* de Claude Debussy (1862–1918) sont des classiques de l'impressionnisme qu'on retrouve au programme de bien des concerts. À l'époque classique on pourrait nommer François Couperin (1668–1733) et Jean-Philippe Rameau (1683–1764). Hector Berlioz (1803–1869, *La symphonie fantastique*) et Léo Delibes (1836–1891, *Coppélia*) ont leur place parmi les romantiques du 19ᵉ siècle. À l'époque moderne, le Groupe des Six, fondé° en 1918

et parmi lesquels° figuraient Francis Poulenc, Darius Milhaud, et Arthur Honegger, un suisse—ainsi que° des compositeurs comme Olivier Messaien, Erik Satie et plus récemment Pierre Boulez—ont beaucoup contribué à l'évolution de la musique classique moderne.

Les amateurs d'opéra ont probablement eu l'occasion d'entendre *Carmen*, *Les pêcheurs de perles* ou *L'arlésienne* de Georges Bizet (1838–1875) ou un opéra de Charles Gounod (1818–1893) tel que° *Faust* ou *Mireille*. Même le jazz, dont les origines sont typiquement américaines, occupe une place de première importance dans la vie musicale française. Au jazz américain s'ajoute° le jazz européen que des musiciens comme Stéphane Grapelli et Jean-Luc Ponty ont beaucoup contribué à développer.

frontières *borders between countries*   fondé *founded*
lesquels *whom*   ainsi que *as well as*   tel que *such as*
s'ajoute *is added*

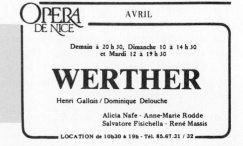

Et vous?

A. Jouez-vous d'un instrument de musique? Indiquez si vous jouez ou si vous ne jouez pas des instruments de musique suivants . . .

1. de la guitare

2. du violon

3. du piano

4. de la guitare électrique

5. de la trompette

6. du tambour

7. du trombone

8. de la clarinette
9. de la flûte

10. du saxophone

11. du violoncelle

12. du banjo

Point out that electronic synthesizer is **un synthétiseur (un synthé)** and **faire du synthétiseur** means *to play an electronic synthesizer.*

B. Vos préférences musicales. Avez-vous les mêmes préférences musicales que les autres étudiants de votre classe? Pour le savoir, répondez aux questions suivantes.

Exemple   Mon premier choix, c'est la musique classique.

1. Quel genre de musique aimez-vous? Classez dans l'ordre de vos préférences ces différents genres de musique.

You may ask one student to tabulate student answers.

—la musique classique
—le jazz
—le rock
—la musique folklorique
—les *chansons* en langue étrangère

—l'opéra
—la musique «country western»
—la musique populaire
—?

song

2. Quels sont vos chanteurs et chanteuses préférés? Et votre groupe musical préféré?
3. Avez-vous un *chef d'orchestre* préféré? Une symphonie préférée?

conductor
pieces
composer

4. Y a-t-il des *morceaux* de musiques que vous aimez particulièrement? Avez-vous un *compositeur* préféré?
5. Êtes-vous membre d'une chorale? D'un orchestre? D'un cercle philharmonique? D'un groupe musical? Étiez-vous membre d'un de ces groupes quand vous étiez au lycée?

Point out that the word for marching band is **la fanfare.** Although schools do not have bands, cities and various professional groups do.

Église Saint-Germain des Prés
(Métro Saint-Germain des Prés)

Mardi 2 Août 1983 à 21 heures

VIVALDI
LES QUATRE SAISONS
Concerto pour violon et violoncelle **Ph. NADAL,** Violoncelle

rock|jazz|folk
traditionnel
isques

Dans un café-théâtre à Paris

C. Où écoutez vous de la musique? Êtes-vous content(e) d'écouter vos disques ou la radio chez vous ou bien est-ce que . . .

—*vous vous réunissez* entre amis pour écouter ou jouer de la musique?   get together
—vous allez au concert?
—vous allez dans des clubs ou dans des *boîtes de nuit*?   nightclubs
—vous allez à des concerts *en plein air*?   outdoor

⚜ Le participe présent et l'infinitif

Présentation

The present participle is used to indicate that an action taking place is closely related to the action of the main verb. It is equivalent to English forms ending in -*ing* such as *speaking, walking, finding, choosing.* In French the present participle always ends in **-ant.** It is formed by adding **-ant** to the stem of the present-tense **nous** form of the verb.

nous **parlons**	→ parl**ant**	nous **faisons**	→ fais**ant**	
nous **finissons**	→ finiss**ant**	nous **commençons**	→ commenç**ant**	
nous **attendons**	→ attend**ant**	nous **mangeons**	→ mange**ant**	

There are only three irregular present participles in French:

être → **étant**   savoir → **sachant**   avoir → **ayant**

Sachant cela, nous avons pris la décision de rester.
L'avion **arrivant** de Paris aura un retard de trente minutes.
Étant étudiant, je n'avais pas beaucoup d'argent.

A. The most common use of the present participle is after the preposition **en.** It is used to indicate:

1. That two actions are taking place at the same time. English equivalents to this use are *while* or *upon* plus the *-ing* form of the verb.

Nous écoutons des disques **en faisant** nos devoirs.	*We listen to records while doing our homework.*
En entrant, j'ai tout de suite remarqué qu'un des musiciens était absent.	*Upon entering (as I entered) I immediately noticed that one of the musicians was absent.*
Elle s'est cassé la jambe **en faisant** du ski.	*She broke her leg skiing.*

2. The manner in which an action is done or the means by which an end is achieved. This use of the present participle is equivalent to using *by*, *in*, or *through* plus the *-ing* form of an English verb. Sometimes no preposition is used in English.

C'est **en jouant** tous les jours qu'on apprend à bien jouer.	*It is by playing every day that one learns to play well.*
Plusieurs personnes ont traversé la rue **en courant.**	*Several people ran across the street.*
Je me détends **en écoutant** de la musique classique.	*I relax by listening to classical music.*

B. Present participles are occasionally used as adjectives. In this case, they agree with the noun modified.

Jouez les morceaux **suivants.**	*Play the following pieces.*
Les réactions du public sont **encourageantes.**	*The reactions of the public are encouraging.*
C'est un événement **intéressant.**	*That's an interesting event.*

C. When prepositions other than **en** are used with verb forms, the verb is always in the infinitive.

Venez me voir **avant de** partir.	*Come to see me before leaving.*
Lisez lentement **pour** bien **comprendre.**	*Read slowly in order to understand well.*
Ne décidez pas **sans réfléchir.**	*Don't decide without thinking.*

D. After the preposition **après**, the past infinitive must be used. It is composed of the infinitive **avoir** or être plus the past participle. Note that the past participle agrees with the subject when the verb is conjugated with être.

Après **avoir entendu** cette chanson à la radio, je suis allé(e) acheter le disque.	*After hearing this song on the radio, I went out to buy the record.*
Elle a fait la connaissance de Jean-Claude après **être revenue** d'Europe.	*She met Jean-Claude after having returned from Europe.*
Ils ont fait le marché après **s'être reposés**.	*They went shopping after having rested.*

Transformation: Modèle: Je regarde la télévision quand je mange. → Je regarde la télévision en mangeant. (1) quand je fais mes devoirs. (2) quand je m'habille. (3) quand j'étudie. (4) quand je lis le journal. (5) quand je prépare le dîner. (6) quand je finis mon dîner. Modèle: Je regarde la télévision quand je mange → Je regarde la télévision avant de manger. (Utilisez les phrases de l'exercice précédent.) **Modèle:** Je regarde la télévision quand je mange. → **Je regarde la télévision après avoir mangé.** (Utilisez les phrases de l'exercice précédent.)

Préparation

A. Nous sommes tous mélomanes. On peut facilement écouter de la musique en faisant autre chose. Quand les personnes suivantes écoutent-elles de la musique?

Modèle   moi / quand je fais mes devoirs → **Moi, j'écoute de la musique en faisant mes devoirs.**

Point out that **mélomane** means *music lover.*

1. nous / quand nous préparons le dîner
2. mon père / quand il lit son journal
3. moi / quand je m'habille
4. nous / quand nous prenons notre petit déjeuner
5. mes amis / quand ils font du jogging
6. toi / quand tu fais le ménage
7. moi / quand je reviens de mon travail
8. vous / quand vous conduisez
9. ma sœur / quand elle va à l'université
10. toi / quand tu finis ton travail

B. Ils ont toutes sortes d'excuses. Monsieur Lebrun veut savoir quand les différents membres de sa famille vont faire certaines choses. Qu'est-ce qu'ils répondent?

Modèle   Quand est-ce que tu vas faire la vaisselle? (Je veux d'abord me reposer un peu.) → **Je la ferai après m'être reposé(e) un peu.**

1. Quand est-ce que Pierre va faire le marché? (Il veut d'abord finir de se préparer.)
2. Quand est-ce que les enfants vont ranger leurs jouets? (Ils veulent d'abord finir leur jeu.)
3. Quand est-ce que Josette va faire la vaisselle? (Elle veut d'abord aller à la bibliothèque.)
4. Quand est-ce que tu vas commencer à préparer le dîner? (Je veux d'abord me laver les mains.)

5. Quand est-ce que vous allez laver la voiture? (Nous voulons d'abord nous reposer.)
6. Quand est-ce que tu vas prendre une décision? (Je veux d'abord parler avec René.)
7. Quand est-ce que Claude va aller à la boulangerie? (Il veut d'abord réparer son vélo.)
8. Quand est-ce que ton ami Raymond va se marier? (Il veut d'abord trouver un travail.)

C. Assez d'excuses. Madame Lebrun est fatiguée d'entendre des excuses. Qu'est-ce qu'elle dit?

Modèle   Faites la vaisselle. Vous écouterez vos disques après. →
            Faites la vaisselle avant d'écouter vos disques.

1. Rangez votre chambre. Vous jouerez après.
2. Finis tes devoirs. Tu iras à la piscine après.
3. Va à la boulangerie. Tu répareras ton vélo après.
4. Lavez la voiture. Vous vous reposerez après.
5. Aide-moi un peu. Tu sortiras après.
6. Apprends à conduire. Tu achèteras une voiture après.
7. Lavez-vous les mains. Vous mangerez après.
8. Brosse-toi les dents. Tu te coucheras après.

D. Différences. Certaines personnes préfèrent écouter de la musique en faisant autre chose. D'autres préfèrent finir leur travail d'abord pour pouvoir mieux se concentrer. D'autres encore sont trop impatientes pour attendre. Quand Laurent, Colette, Nadine et Paul écoutent-ils de la musique?

Modèles   faire mes devoirs → **Laurent écoute de la musique en**
                                    faisant ses devoirs.
                                    Colette écoute de la musique après
                                    avoir fait ses devoirs.
                                    Nadine et Paul écoutent de la musique
                                    avant de faire leurs devoirs.

1. lire le journal   5. faire la cuisine
2. aller à l'université   6. s'habiller
3. se préparer le matin   7. faire le ménage
4. manger   8. finir mes devoirs

This exercise can be done as shown in the **modèles**, or each series can be done separately.

RADIO
● L'Orchestre national de France, dirigé par Charles Dutoit avec, en soliste, Pascal Rogé (piano) dans un programme Magnard et Ravel, le 25, à 20 h 30   (F.-M.).

Communication

A. Pendant, avant ou après? Quelles sont les choses que vous aimez faire en même temps ou l'une après l'autre? Faites des phrases qui expriment vos préférences personnelles en utilisant les verbes de chacune des deux colonnes suivantes. Vous pouvez les associer dans l'ordre que vous préférez.

Options: Written/oral. Have students compare their sentences. Written preparation may be helpful.

Exemple   manger / regarder la télévision → **Je n'aime pas manger en regardant la télévision.** ou **Je préfère regarder la télévision après avoir mangé.** ou **La plupart du temps, je ne peux pas regarder la télévision avant de manger parce que je rentre trop tard.**

étudier	se promener
parler avec des amis	écouter la radio
lire le journal	sortir
réfléchir	rentrer à la maison
se détendre	prendre une décision
écouter des disques	passer un examen
boire quelque chose	faire mes devoirs
regarder la télévision	aller se coucher
dormir	manger
?	?

Options: (1) Written. (2) Oral—ask questions or adapt for directed dialogue. (3) Have students work in small groups and report back their partners' responses.

B. Est-ce que tu peux . . . ? Répondez aux questions suivantes ou utilisez-les pour interviewer un(e) autre étudiant(e).

1. Est-ce que tu peux faire tes devoirs en regardant la télévision?
2. Est-ce que tu peux aller en classe après avoir passé une nuit sans dormir?
3. Est-ce que tu peux répéter une phrase en français après l'avoir entendue seulement une fois?
4. En général, est-ce que tu peux finir tout ton travail avant de te coucher?
5. Est-ce que tu peux faire les exercices de grammaire avant de lire les explications?
6. Est-ce que tu peux expliquer dix fois la même chose sans te mettre en colère?
7. Est-ce que tu peux marcher droit après avoir bu toute une bouteille de vin?
8. Est-ce que tu peux traverser le campus la nuit sans avoir peur?

C. Moi, je . . . Complétez les phrases suivantes selon votre expérience personnelle.

Student responses can be elicited by asking **Quand avez-vous peur?** etc.

1. J'ai peur avant de . . .
2. J'ai mal à la tête après avoir . . .
3. Je suis content(e) après avoir . . .
4. Je lis les journaux pour . . .
5. Je suis prudent(e) avant de . . .
6. Je suis fatigué(e) après avoir . . .

L'emploi des prépositions après les verbes

Présentation

As you have already seen, some verbs are followed by the preposition **de**, others by **à**, and still others by no preposition at all. The use of prepositions with verbs you have already learned can be summarized as follows:

Suggestion: Remind students that they are already familiar with many of these verbs.

A. Verbs followed by an infinitive:

1. The following verbs take no preposition at all before an infinitive:

aimer	désirer	espérer	penser	préférer	venir
aller	détester	laisser	pouvoir	savoir	vouloir

Je voudrais être musicien.
Il préfère ne pas parler de ça.

2. The following verbs take **de** before an infinitive:

accepter	se dépêcher	persuader
s'arrêter	dire	permettre
choisir	essayer	promettre
décider	éviter	refuser
défendre	finir	regretter
demander	oublier	rêver

Il rêve de jouer dans un orchestre philharmonique.
Vous avez promis de vous dépêcher de finir votre travail.

Demander, dire, permettre, and **promettre** can also take an indirect object.

Nous avons promis à nos amis d'aller au concert avec eux.
Elle lui a demandé de chanter quelque chose.

3. The following verbs take **à** before an infinitive:

aider	commencer	se mettre
s'amuser	continuer	résister
apprendre	hésiter	réussir
arriver	inviter	tenir
avoir		

Elle s'est mise à chanter.
Nous avons appris à peindre.

Avoir, aider, and **inviter** usually take a direct object, which precedes the preposition.

Les jeunes ont beaucoup de choses à nous apprendre.
On a invité les étudiants à participer à la discussion.
Elle a aidé Pierre à apprendre ce morceau de musique.

B. Verbs followed by a noun:

1. Some verbs that take a preposition in English do not take one in French.

attendre *to wait for*	Nous attendons la sortie des artistes.
chercher *to look for*	Je cherche l'entrée.
demander *to ask for*	Il faut demander la permission.
écouter *to listen to*	Tu écoutes des disques?
regarder *to look at*	Elle regarde les affiches.

2. Some verbs that take a preposition in French do not take one in English.

assister à *to attend, be present at*	Est-ce que vous avez l'intention d'assister à ce concert?
changer de *to change*	Tu changes d'avis comme tu changes de chemise.
entrer dans *to enter*	Nous sommes entrés dans un café.
se marier avec *to marry*	Josette va se marier avec un ami d'enfance.
obéir à *to obey*	Obéissez à vos parents.
répondre à *to answer*	Est-ce que tu as répondu à sa lettre?
ressembler à *to resemble*	Elle ressemble à son père.
se souvenir de *to remember*	Te souviens-tu de la date du concert?
téléphoner à *to telephone*	Je vais téléphoner à ma mère.
jouer à *to play a sport*	Nous jouons souvent au tennis.
jouer de *to play a musical instrument*	Il joue de la clarinette.

3. Some verbs take different prepositions in French and in English.

s'intéresser à *to be interested in*	Ils s'intéressent à la musique.
s'occuper de *to be busy with*	Occupez-vous de vos propres problèmes.
participer à *to participate in*	Nous avons participé à la discussion.

Substitution: (1) Elle a oublié de venir. a refusé / a essayé / s'est depêchée / a décidé / a accepté. (2) Nous avons promis à Pierre d'aller au concert. permis / dit / demandé / promis. (3) Est-ce que tu continues à parler français? commences / hésites / apprends / réussis. (4) Il apprend à jouer du piano. rêve / veut / sait / essaie. (5) Il s'est arrêté de chanter. s'est mis / préférait / a décidé / voulait / a hésité / a continué.

Préparation

A. Le nouveau chef d'orchestre. Françoise s'est présentée comme candidate pour un poste de chef d'orchestre. Voici pourquoi on l'a choisie.

Modèle   s'intéresser vraiment / musique → **Elle s'intéresse vraiment à la musique.**

1. promettre / faire beaucoup de changements
2. savoir / écouter
3. jouer / plusieurs instruments
4. écouter / les conseils des autres
5. répondre / nos besoins
6. accepter / commencer tout de suite
7. ne pas hésiter / dire ce qu'elle pense
8. chercher / un poste comme celui-ci
9. connaître / beaucoup de musiciens
10. vouloir / habiter dans cette région

B. **C'est dommage mais . . .** Un des musiciens de l'orchestre a été renvoyé *(fired)*. Voici les raisons.

Modèle   rêver / devenir célèbre → **Il rêvait de devenir célèbre.**

1. vouloir / être mieux payé
2. refuser / faire comme tout le monde
3. oublier souvent / venir aux répétitions
4. se dépêcher / partir après les répétitions
5. ne pas écouter / les conseils du chef d'orchestre
6. ne pas pouvoir / jouer un morceau sans se tromper
7. promettre toujours / faire mieux
8. essayer toujours / être le centre d'attention
9. commencer / embêter tout le monde
10. ne pas répondre / nos besoins

C. **Interview.** Un reporter interviewe un des membres d'un groupe de rock. Donnez les réponses du chanteur.

Modèle   Est-ce que votre groupe va jouer à Paris? (non, mais nous rêvons . . .) → **Non, mais nous rêvons de jouer à Paris.**

1. Est-ce que Mireille joue de la guitare aussi? (non, mais elle apprend . . .)
2. Est-ce que les gens s'intéressent à votre musique? (oui, ils commencent . . .)
3. Est-ce que les musiciens viennent à toutes les répétitions? (quelquefois, ils oublient . . .)
4. Est-ce que vous voudriez partir à l'étranger? (oui, mais nous hésitons . . .)
5. Est-ce que David va rester avec votre groupe? (oui, il a décidé . . .)
6. Est-ce que votre groupe a beaucoup de succès en province? (oui, il continue . . .)
7. Est-ce que vous chantez quelquefois en anglais? (oui, quelquefois, je m'amuse . . .)

Communication

Vous et la musique. Utilisez les verbes suivants pour formuler des questions que vous poserez à un(e) autre étudiant(e) au sujet de la musique.

Exemples   apprendre → **Est-ce que tu as appris à jouer d'un instrument de musique quand tu étais plus jeune? Est-ce que tu aimerais apprendre à jouer de la guitare?**

1. rêver
2. aimer
3. apprendre
4. essayer
5. écouter
6. réussir
7. préférer
8. aller
9. décider
10. refuser
11. se souvenir
12. ?

⚜   # Les pronoms relatifs

Suggestion: Point out that unlike interrogatives, **qui** and **que** can refer to both persons and objects.

Présentation

Relative pronouns are used to connect two clauses, a main clause and a dependent clause. They are never omitted in French, whereas in English we may say either *There is the girl I met*, or *There is the girl that I met*.

A. Qui and **que** *(who, that, which)* are used to refer to both persons and things.

1. Qui is used when the relative pronoun is the subject of the dependent clause.

Voilà une étudiante. Elle parle espagnol. → Voilà une étudiante **qui** parle espagnol.

Les musiciens **qui** ont joué ce morceau étaient excellents.
Avez-vous lu le sondage **qui** a paru dans *L'Express?*

2. Que is used when the relative pronoun is the direct object in the dependent clause.

Où est le disque? J'ai acheté le disque. → Où est le disque **que** j'ai acheté?

Quel est le morceau de musique **que** vous préférez?
Voici les chanteuses **que** nous avons interviewées.

　　Note again that the past participles of verbs conjugated with **avoir** agree with preceding direct objects.

Suggestion: Point out that the antecedent of **dont** takes the definite article.

B. Dont *(of whom, of which, whose)* is used to replace **de** plus a noun. It can refer to people or to things.

Voici la liste. Nous avons besoin de cette liste. → Voice la liste **dont** nous avons besoin.

J'ai rencontré le compositeur **dont** vous m'avez parlé.
Ce sont les gens **dont** le fils est chef d'orchestre.

C. Ce qui, ce que *(what, that which)*, and **ce dont** *(that of which)* are indefinite relative pronouns. They refer to ideas that do not have number or gender.

1. Ce qui is used as the subject of the dependent clause.

Je ne comprends pas **ce qui** est arrivé.
Ce qui m'impressionne le plus, c'est la façon dont elle joue du piano.
Elle aime **ce qui** est beau.

2. Ce que is used as the direct object of the dependent clause.

Il dit toujours **ce qu'**il pense.
Nous ne savons pas **ce que** les autres vont faire.
Voici tout **ce que** nous avons pu savoir.

3. **Ce dont** is used as the object of a verb or verb phrase that is used with the preposition **de** (**parler de, avoir besoin de,** etc.).

Je sais **ce dont** tu as envie.
Nous ne savons pas **ce dont** il est capable.
Ce dont vous parlez est intéressant.
Dites-moi tout **ce dont** vous vous souvenez.

Ce qui and **ce que** are frequently used in answers to questions beginning with **qu'est-ce qui** and **qu'est-ce que.**

Qu'est-ce qui intéresse les jeunes?
Je ne sais pas **ce qui** les intéresse.

Qu'est-ce que tu penses de ce groupe?
Je préfère ne pas dire **ce que** j'en pense.

Ce qui, ce que, and **ce dont** are also used when suggesting to someone what he or she should say or ask.

Demandez à Alain **ce qu'il** a pensé de ce concert.
Expliquez-nous **ce que** vous avez l'intention de faire.
Dites-moi **ce dont** vous avez besoin.

Transformation: Modèle: J'ai lu les journaux. Les journaux sont sur la table → J'ai lu les journaux qui sont sur la table. (1) Nous avons regardé le programme. Il commence à neuf heures et demie. (2) Je connais une vieille dame. Elle joue du trombone. (3) Nous avons assisté à un concert. Il était très intéressant. Modèle: J'ai lu les journaux. Mon frère m'a apporté ces journaux. → J'ai lu les journaux que mon frère m'a apportés.

(1) J'ai perdu le disque. Vous m'avez donné ce disque. (2) Nous avons trouvé la revue. Vous cherchiez cette revue. (3) Avez-vous suivi les conseils? Je vous ai donné ces conseils. Modèle: J'ai lu les journaux. Vous m'avez parlé de ces journaux. → J'ai lu les journaux dont vous m'avez parlé. (1) J'ai acheté un disque. J'avais très envie de ce disque. (2) Voici la liste des livres. Vous avez besoin de ces livres. (3) Dites-nous les détails. Vous vous souvenez de ces détails. Modèle: Je connais des gens. Leur fils est diplomate. → Je connais des gens dont le fils est diplomate.

(1) Voici un musicien. Ses œuvres sont célèbres. (2) Voilà les Français. J'ai fait leur connaissance à Paris. (3) Je connais un homme. Sa maison date du dix-septième siècle.

Préparation

A. **Un amoureux bien malheureux.** Bruno n'a pas de chance. Il aime Natacha mais elle n'a pas les mêmes goûts que lui. Qu'est-ce qu'il dit?

Modèle   J'ai écrit des chansons. → **Elle n'aime pas les chansons que j'ai écrites.**

1. J'ai acheté des disques.
2. Je lui ai apporté des fleurs.
3. J'ai composé des poèmes.
4. Je lui ai donné un cadeau.
5. Je lui ai dit des mots doux.
6. J'ai pris des photos.
7. Je lui ai envoyé une carte.
8. J'ai acheté de nouveaux vêtements.

Option: Repeat having students use demonstrative pronouns in their answers (e.g., **J'ai écrit des chansons. Elle n'aime pas celles que j'ai écrites.**).

B. **Elle a bon goût.** Brigitte a répondu à un questionnaire au sujet de ses préférences dans différents domaines en donnant les indications suivantes. Dites ce qu'elle aime et ce qu'elle n'aime pas.

Modèles   les chanteurs / Ils ont quelque chose à dire. → **J'aime les chanteurs qui ont quelque chose à dire.**
les chanteurs / Ils imitent les chanteurs anglais. → **Je n'aime pas ceux qui imitent les chanteurs anglais.**

Les domaines	Traits positifs	Traits négatifs
1. les chanteurs	Ils ont quelque chose à dire.	Ils imitent les chanteurs anglais.
2. les hommes	Ils ont l'esprit ouvert.	Ils se croient supérieurs.
3. les femmes	Elles savent ce qu'elles veulent.	Elles ne sont jamais contentes.
4. les vêtements	Ils sont de bonne qualité.	Ils ne sont pas bien coupés.
5. les gens	Ils disent ce qu'ils pensent.	Ils parlent tout le temps.

C. J'ai suivi tes conseils. Véronique a suivi les conseils que son amie Berna-dette lui a donnés. Qu'est-ce qu'elle dit?

Modèle   écouter les disques → **J'ai écouté les disques dont tu m'as parlé.**

1. aller au concert
2. lire le livre
3. consulter le médecin
4. aller chez le dentiste
5. acheter le disque
6. assister au spectacle
7. regarder l'émission
8. voir l'exposition

D. Snobisme. Certaines personnes sont très fières de connaître, même indi-rectement, des gens célèbres. Qu'est-ce que les personnes suivantes disent?

Modèle   avoir des amis / leur fils est chef d'orchestre → **Nous avons des amis dont le fils est chef d'orchestre.**

1. connaître des gens / leur fille chante à l'Opéra de Paris
2. rencontrer un vieux monsieur / son petit-fils est au Conservatoire
3. parler avec un ami / sa femme connaissait Édith Piaf
4. voir un ami / son frère a acheté un château
5. avoir une amie / son cousin fait partie de l'Orchestre Philharmonique de Boston
6. rencontrer une personne / sa famille descend des Bourbon

E. On se prépare pour un récital. Alain pose toutes sortes de questions à Geneviève à propos du récital que leurs amis vont donner ce soir. Donnez les réponses de Geneviève en utilisant le pronom relatif approprié.

Modèle   Qu'est-ce que tu vas faire après le récital? → **Je ne sais pas ce que je vais faire.**

1. Qu'est-ce qui s'est passé à la dernière répétition?
2. Qu'est-ce qu'on va faire après?
3. De quoi Hélène a-t-elle envie?
4. Qui va t'accompagner ce soir?
5. Qu'est-ce que Jacques va servir comme boissons?
6. Qu'est-ce qu'ils vont jouer ce soir?
7. De quoi ont-ils parlé ce matin?
8. Qu'est-ce qui va arriver si Michelle est malade?
9. Qu'est-ce que tu vas porter ce soir?
10. Qui va jouer du violon ce soir?
11. De quoi le chef d'orchestre a-t-il besoin?
12. Qui peut m'accompagner ce soir?

Communication

A. Vos opinions. Indiquez les types de gens et de choses que vous appréciez et ceux que vous n'appréciez pas du tout.

Exemple   J'apprécie les cours qui sont intéressants même s'ils sont un peu difficiles. Je n'aime pas ceux que je suis obligé(e) de suivre.

1. les chansons
2. les hommes
3. les femmes
4. les chanteurs/chanteuses
5. les livres
6. les amis
7. les vêtements
8. les professeurs
9. les voitures
10. les cours

B. Descriptions. Seul(e) ou avec un groupe d'étudiants, décrivez un chanteur ou une chanteuse, un compositeur, une chanson, etc., que vous aimez particulièrement (ou que vous n'aimez pas). Utilisez autant de pronoms relatifs que possible dans votre description.

Exemple   C'est une chanson qui est très amusante et dont tout le monde parle.

Other categories such as sports, restaurants, the arts, etc., can also be used as the basis for individual or small-group descriptions.

 Lequel et ses dérivés

Présentation

The forms of **lequel** can function either as interrogative pronouns or as relative pronouns. In both cases they reflect the number and gender of the noun they replace.

lequel		
	Singular	*Plural*
Masculine	lequel	lesquels
Feminine	laquelle	lesquelles

A. As interrogative pronouns the forms of **lequel** mean *which one*. They always refer to a definite object or person already mentioned (or mentioned in the same sentence).

Avez-vous écouté des disques? Lesquels?	*Did you listen to some records? Which ones?*
Parmi les capitales d'Europe, laquelle est la plus agréable?	*Among the capitals of Europe, which one is the nicest?*
Renoir, Monet et Degas sont tous des peintres impressionnistes. Lequel des trois préférez-vous?	*Renoir, Monet, and Degas are all impressionist painters. Which of the three do you prefer?*

*Suggeston: Point out that **qui** can follow a preposition when referring to people.*

B. As relative pronouns the forms of **lequel** are used after prepositions to refer to persons or things.

La cathédrale dans laquelle nous sommes entrés était très belle.	*The cathedral that we entered was very beautiful.*
Montrez-moi la chanson sur laquelle vous êtes en train de travailler.	*Show me the song you're working on.*
Qui sont ces danseuses avec lesquelles vous venez de parler?	*Who are those dancers with whom you were just speaking?*

C. When used with the prepositions **à** and **de**, the forms of **lequel** combine with the prepositions in the same way as the definite article.

	lequel = auquel		lequel = duquel
à +	laquelle = à laquelle	de +	laquelle = de laquelle
	lesquels = auxquels		lesquels = desquels
	lesquelles = auxquelles		lesquelles = desquelles

C'est le château près duquel nous avons campé.

That's the castle near which we camped.

Est-ce que c'est le compositeur auquel vous pensiez?

Is that the composer you were thinking about?

Auxquels de ces auteurs vous intéressiez-vous le plus?

In which of these authors were you most interested?

Transformation: Modèles:—Quel livre avez-vous lu? → Lequel avez-vous lu?—À quel film est-elle allée? → Auquel est-elle allée? (1) Quelles expositions avez-vous visitées? (2) Quels poèmes a-t-il écrits? (3) Quels auteurs as-tu étudiés? (4) À quel musicien a-t-il parlé? (5) De quels disques a-t-il besoin? (6) Dans quelle ville avez-vous vu ce spectacle? (7) De quel instrument jouez-vous? (8) Pour quel compositeur avez-vous le plus d'admiration? (9) À quelles activités avez-vous participé?

Préparation

A. Il veut tout savoir. Rémi veut savoir tout ce que Nadine a fait d'intéressant pendant qu'il était en voyage. Chaque fois que Nadine mentionne quelque chose, il veut encore quelques détails. Quelles sont les questions de Rémi?

Modèles   J'ai acheté quelques nouveaux disques. → **Lesquels as-tu achetés?**

Je suis allée au restaurant? → **Auquel es-tu allée?**

1. Je suis allée à quelques concerts.
2. J'ai appris à jouer quelques nouveaux morceaux de musique.
3. Henri et moi, nous sommes allés à quelques expositions.
4. J'ai parlé avec des anciens amis du lycée.
5. On a parlé de toutes sortes de choses intéressantes.
6. Je suis allée à quelques spectacles avec Marie-Claire.
7. Je suis allée visiter quelques musées.
8. J'ai entendu quelques nouvelles chansons à la radio.

B. Je vais te montrer la ville. Une amie étrangère vient d'arriver à Paris. Jacques veut lui faire connaître la ville et ses amis. Qu'est-ce qu'il dit?

Modèle   Voilà un musée. Il y a beaucoup de peintures impressionnistes dans ce musée. **Voilà le musée dans lequel il y a beaucoup de peintures impressionistes.**

1. Voilà une église. Mes amis se sont mariés dans cette église.
2. Je te présente un ami. Je loue un appartement avec lui.
3. Voici un garage. J'ai acheté ma voiture dans ce garage.
4. As-tu aimé le concert? Je t'ai emmenée à ce concert.
5. Voici un architecte. Je travaille pour lui.
6. Voici le lycée. J'ai fait mes études dans ce lycée.
7. Connaissais-tu ce chanteur? Je t'ai présentée à ce chanteur.
8. Aimes-tu les magasins? Nous sommes allés dans ces magasins.

Communication

A. Questions/interview. Répondez aux questions suivantes ou utilisez-les pour interviewer un(e) autre étudiant(e).

1. Quels sont les chanteurs et chanteuses pour lesquels tu as la plus d'admiration?
2. Parmi les œuvres d'art que tu connais, laquelle préfères-tu?
3. Parmi les films que tu as vus récemment, lequel d'entre eux te paraît le plus intéressant? Pourquoi?
4. Auquel des héros—ou à laquelle des héroïnes—de la littérature moderne est-ce que tu t'identifies le plus?
5. Quels sont les objets (affiches, œuvres d'art, etc.) avec lesquels tu as décoré ta chambre?
6. Est-ce que tu as des amis d'enfance avec lesquels tu es resté(e) en contact?
7. Y en a-t-il auxquels tu écris régulièrement?
8. De quoi parlez-vous quand vous vous retrouvez?

Options: Use as whole-class or small-group activity. If used in small groups, have students summarize their partners' answers.

B. Si oui, lesquels . . . ? Utilisez les phrases suivantes pour formuler des questions que vous poserez à un(e) autre étudiant(e). Si la réponse à votre question est «oui», utilisez la forme appropriée de «lequel» pour demander plus de détails à votre partenaire.

Exemples   Est-ce que tu aimes les chansons de Barbara Mandrell?
Oui, j'aime bien ses chansons.
Ah, oui! Lesquelles?

Demandez lui. . .
1. s'il/si elle est allé(e) à un concert le mois passé.
2. s'il/si elle aime les chansons françaises.
3. s'il/si elle a l'habitude d'écouter des disques en étudiant.
4. s'il/si elle a un danseur préféré.
5. s'il /si elle aime les œuvres de Bach.
6. s'il/si elle a appris à jouer des morceaux de musique.
7. s'il/si elle a déjà entendu des chansons canadiennes françaises.
8. s'il/si elle connaît des chanteurs français.
9. s'il/si elle joue d'un instrument de musique.
10. ?

SYNTHÈSE

Édith Piaf

Édith Piaf

Suggestion: If possible, provide some general background information about Piaf.

Elle n'a pas été remplacée. Le public attend toujours une nouvelle Piaf. Beaucoup de chanteuses ont essayé de l'imiter mais elles n'ont pas réussi. C'est pourquoi les disques de Piaf continuent à avoir un grand succès. Même aujourd'hui, *longtemps* après sa mort, on éprouve une émotion *profonde* en écoutant sa belle *voix émouvante.* Pourquoi cette place privilégiée dans le cœur du public est-elle restée vide?

  Piaf était capable d'émouvoir et d'enthousiasmer le public parce qu'elle n'était pas un produit fabriqué. Ses colères commes ses tendresses, ses *haines* comme ses amours, ses chagrins comme ses joies sont les *témoins* de son authenticité. Elle était impulsive, c'est vrai, mais

a long time
deep / voice / moving

hatred, sorrow
testimonies, witnesses

elle était sincère. Et c'est cette sincérité qui a gagné l'affection et l'indulgence du public. La nature avait donné à Piaf une voix capable d'exprimer le sublime, le pathétique. Mais une voix n'est rien si elle n'a rien à dire, si elle n'est pas nourrie d'une sensibilité venant de l'expérience de la vie, si elle n'est pas l'objet d'un travail constant.

Ce sont là les principales raisons qui séparent Piaf des autres chanteuses. *Inconsciemment*, Piaf a divisé sa vie en deux actes. Dans le premier acte, elle *s'abandonnait* à ses sentiments, à ses excès. Après avoir accumulé les souvenirs et les expériences, elle les transformait en chansons. C'était le deuxième acte.

Piaf a chanté l'amour admirablement, mais elle l'a rarement connu. Elle a surtout connu les *déceptions*, la solitude et la maladie. Après une déception amoureuse, elle passait des semaines et des mois dans un état de dépression totale. Et puis, un jour, elle décidait de se remettre au travail.

Si les chansons de Piaf étaient émouvantes, c'est parce qu'elles exprimaient des expériences et des sentiments réels. Les compositeurs qui travaillaient pour elle composaient des chansons qui étaient le *reflet* de ces expériences.

La préparation d'un spectacle demandait beaucoup de temps. Quelquefois Piaf aimait la musique d'une chanson mais non le texte. Alors, elle demandait aux compositeurs de changer ce qu'elle n'aimait pas. Ils l'écoutaient parce que Piaf connaissait bien son public et elle *se trompait* rarement. Après avoir choisi les chansons, Piaf préparait son concert. Elle le préparait pendant deux ou trois mois en y travaillant dix à douze heures par jour.

Puis, le soir de la première arrivait et elle triomphait. Elle était heureuse de son succès. Mais jamais pour très longtemps. Après un certain temps, elle commençait à *s'ennuyer*. Elle était prête pour un nouvel amour et un nouveau chagrin. Une nouvelle *moisson* de chansons était en train de naître.

Extrait et adapté d'un article de *Marie-France*.

Compréhension Répondez aux questions suivantes selon les renseignements donnés dans le texte.

1. Qui était Édith Piaf?
2. En général, quelle est la réaction des gens en l'écoutant chanter?
3. Pourquoi le public aimait-il tant Piaf?
4. À votre avis, est-ce qu'il suffit d'avoir une jolie voix pour être une bonne chanteuse?
5. En quoi consistaient les deux actes qui se sont répétés bien des fois au cours de sa vie?
6. Est-ce que Piaf a eu une vie très heureuse? Expliquez votre réponse.
7. Pourquoi les chansons de Piaf étaient-elles particulièrement émouvantes?
8. Pourquoi les compositeurs suivaient-ils généralement les conseils de Piaf?
9. Est-ce que Piaf travaillait beaucoup?
10. Est-ce qu'elle pouvait être satisfaite de son succès pendant très longtemps?

Suggestion: Have students note word families (**chanson, chanter, chanteur, chanteuse,** etc.)

unconsciously
gave in to

disappointments

reflection

was wrong

to be bored
harvest, crop

NOTES CULTURELLES

Les préférences musicales des jeunes Français

Depuis l'arrivée du transistor, on peut entendre de la musique partout en France–dans les rues, dans les ascenseurs et même sur la plage. Les statistiques indiquent que plus de quatre-vingts pour cent des jeunes ont chez eux un poste de radio qu'ils peuvent écouter quand ils veulent. La musique préférée des jeunes est le rock ou la musique pop mais ils aiment aussi la musique folklorique des États-Unis et d'Amérique du Sud, les variétés françaises et étrangères, les chansons folkloriques françaises et la musique classique. Plus de trois millions de jeunes jouent d'un instrument de musique—surtout de la guitare, du piano, et des instruments à cordes° comme le violon.

cordes *string*

Communication

A. **Vous et la musique.** Répondez aux questions suivantes ou utilisez-les pour interviewer un(e) autre étudiant(e).

1. Quel genre de musique préférez-vous?
2. Quels chanteurs ou chanteuses préférez-vous? Pourquoi? Et quel groupe?
3. Allez-vous souvent au concert? Si oui, à quelles sortes de concerts?
4. Avez-vous étudié la musique? Où et avec qui?
5. Est-ce que vous jouez d'un instrument de musique?
6. Avez-vous déjà écrit des chansons?
7. Est-ce que vous écoutez souvent la radio? Si oui, à quels moments de la journée?
8. Quand vous écoutez la radio, quelles émissions choisissez-vous de préférence?
9. Quelles sont les chaînes que vous écoutez le plus souvent? Et celles que vous n'écoutez jamais? Pourquoi?
10. Aimez-vous regarder les spectacles de variétés à la télé?

B. **Connaissez-vous la musique?** Préparez des questions que vous poserez aux autres étudiants de votre classe ou à votre professeur pour savoir s'ils connaissent bien la musique et les musicien(ne)s?

Exemples   De quel instrument Van Cliburn joue-t-il?
Qui est Georges Brassens?
Quelle est la chanson la plus populaire en ce moment?
Comment s'appelle le groupe anglais qui a beaucoup influencé la musique des années soixante?

C. Une soirée musicale. Choisissez parmi les spectacles et concerts suivants ceux que vous aimeriez aller voir. Choisissez au moins cinq endroits qui seraient des choix possibles pour vous. Ensuite, avec un groupe d'étudiants, décidez (en respectant les préférences respectives des étudiants de votre groupe) où vous allez passer la soirée ensemble.

Exemple Moi, je voudrais aller écouter «Un soir de fête aux Antilles» parce que je ne connais pas du tout la musique créole et je voudrais bien avoir l'occasion d'en écouter un peu.

MUSIQUE

GENEVIEVE ET BERNARD PICAVET, pianos. Œuvres de Chopin, Brahms, Herz, Lefebure, Wely. 19h30. **Lucernaire Forum.** Pl : 20 et 30 F.
MARIANNE CLEMENT, flûte avec Raul Sanchez, guitare. Œuvres de Bach, Haendel. 17h45. **Conciergerie du Palais.** Pl : 30 F. Etud : 15 F.

SAINTE CHAPELLE
FESTIVAL DE MUSIQUE SACREE
9 CONCERTS
du 29 mars au 7 avril

Voir calendrier
Loc. sur place
Tous les jours (10h à 18h)   278.67.46
887.12.41

ENSEMBLE DE CORDES ET PERCUSSIONS. Avec Georges Schmitt, flûte de pan. Œuvres de Bach, Vivaldi. 21h. **Eglise Saint-Germain-des-Prés.** Pl : 20 à 50 F.
EAST RIDGE HIGH SCHOOL VARSITY CHORUS. 33 chanteurs et musiciens. Madrigaux et négro-spirituals. 16h. **Kiosque à musique du jardin du Luxembourg.** Entrée libre.
PREMIERE RENCONTRE INTERNATIONALE D'ORCHESTRES DE JEUNES. Dir. Alfred Loewenguth. Concerts symphoniques d'orchestres français et étrangers. De 10h à 18h. **Parc Floral de Vincennes.** Entrée libre.
LINETTE DALMASSO, chanteuse-accordéoniste dans « écologiste et c'est pas triste ». Dimanche 6 à 21h. **Point Virgule,** 7, rue Ste-Croix-de-la-Bretonnerie (Mᵒ Hôtel-de-Ville). Pl : 30 F. Etud : 25 F.

UN SOIR de FETE aux Antilles

LA CANNE A SUCRE

20h30: DINER au Rythme des ANTILLES avec le Trio Créole
22h30: Orchestre et Attractions
LA CANNE A SUCRE
4, rue St-Beuve - 222.23.25
F. Dim. et Lun.

CLUB DES POÈTES
JEAN-PIERRE ROSNAY
POEMES DITS, POEMES CHANTES
2 spect. 22h15 et 23h30 (f. dim. et lun.)
30, rue de BOURGOGNE - 705.06 03

LA LOUISIANE, 176, rue Montmartre. 236.58.98. Déj. Dîn. soupers. Jazz New-Orléans. En alternance : Maxime Saury, Christian Morin ou High Society Jazz Band.
RIVER BOP, 67, rue Saint-André-des-Arts (Mᵒ Saint-Michel). 325.93.71. Tls sf Dim et Lun. A 22h : Aldo Romano en quintette. Avec Philippe Petit, Dominique Bertram, Patrick Gauthier, Jean-Pierre Fouquev, Benoît Wideman.
CLUB SALSA LATINE (à la Talmouse), 1, rue Laplace (5ᵉ). Mᵒ Panthéon. 326.29.83. Tls de 21h30 à 2h mat. Orchestre tropical.

SLOW-CLUB
130, rue de Rivoli 233.84.30
LA CELEBRE CAVE DE JAZZ
T.l.j. 21h30 à 2h du matin
Du mardi au vendredi
CLAUDE LUTER
Le samedi **RENE FRANC**
et son orchestre
Fermé dimanche et lundi

D. En direct d'Amérique . . . Seul(e) ou avec un groupe d'étudiants, préparez une émission spéciale d'environ trois heures pour une station de
radio française. Le but de ce programme est de donner aux Français une
idée de ce qu'est la musique américaine. Préparez un programme aussi
varié que possible et avec un grand choix de chanteurs, de groupes et de
genres différents. Expliquez les choix que vous avez faits.

Exemple   7:00-7:30 Concert George Gershwin
De sept heures à sept heures et demie, nous allons présenter
quelques morceaux de George Gershwin. C'est un des
compositeurs américains les plus célèbres.

VOCABULAIRE

noms

les instruments de musique (voir p. 347)

d'autres noms

la **boîte de nuit**   *nightclub*
le **cercle philharmonique**   *music club*
la **chanson**   *song*
le **chanteur,** la **chanteuse**   *singer*
le **chef d'orchestre**   *conductor*
le **compositeur**   *composer*
la **déception**   *disappointment*
la **folie**   *madness, craze*
la **haine**   *hatred*
le **morceau**   *piece*
la **répétition**   *rehearsal*
la **serviette**   *briefcase (also napkin)*
le **spectacle**   *show*
la **voix**   *voice*

verbes

abandonner   *to give up*
s'abandonner à   *to give in to*
enlever   *to take off, to remove*

s'ennuyer   *to be bored*
s'enthousiasmer   *to be enthusiastic*
jouer de   *to play (a musical instrument)*
manquer   *to miss*
remplir   *to fill*
se réunir   *to get together*
se tromper   *to be wrong*

adjectifs

assis(e)   *seated*
émouvant(e)   *moving*
°**folklorique**
moyen, moyenne   *average*
profond(e)   *deep*

divers

les pronoms relatifs (voir pp. 356–357)

lequel *et ses dérivés* (voir pp. 359–360)
en avant   *forward! march on!*
en plein air   *outdoor*
y compris   *including*

CHAPITRE DIX-NEUF

19

Jugements, décisions et responsabilités

Un bureau de vote dans une petite localité

INTRODUCTION

Les jeunes et la politique

Quelle est l'attitude des jeunes *envers* la politique? Pour connaître leur opinion, *L'Express* a posé les questions suivantes aux jeunes Français de dix-sept à vingt et un ans, ceux qui viennent d'*atteindre* ou vont bientôt atteindre l'âge de voter.

toward

reached

1. L'âge de la majorité est maintenant à dix-huit ans. Qu'est-ce que cela représente pour vous? Parmi les réponses suivantes, choisissez les trois réponses qui vous semblent les plus exactes.

Le *droit* de voter	58,4 %	right
Le fait d'être maintenant responsable de *soi-même*	47,0	oneself
La responsabilité devant la *loi*	45,6	law
L'acquisition de droits nouveaux	31,1	
L'indépendance, le droit de faire ce qu'on veut	25,8	
La liberté d'expression	23,7	
L'*entrée* dans le monde des adultes	17,6	entrance
Cela ne représente aucun changement	13,2	

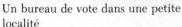

2. Vous intéressez-vous à la politique?

Beaucoup   7,9%
Assez   23,0
Un peu   42,0
Pas du tout   27,1

3. En ce qui concerne la politique, pensez-vous que vous êtes . . .

Très bien informé?   2,2%
Suffisamment informé?   23,9
Pas assez informé?   52,8
Pas du tout informé?   21,1

4. Est-ce que vous participez ou est-ce que vous avez déjà participé aux activités d'une organisation?

J'appartiens à une organisation de jeunes.   14,8%
Je suis membre d'un parti politique.   7,3
Je suis membre d'un *syndicat*.   6,6   union
Je suis membre d'un autre type d'organisation.   7,6

5. Est-ce que vous avez . . .

Participé à une *manifestation?*   54,0%   demonstration
Distribué des *tracts?*   26,1   leaflets
Participé à une *réunion* politique?   25,2   meeting
Mis des affiches?   14,3
Rien de tout cela   37,1

6. Si vous *deviez* participer à la création d'un mouvement politique,   were to
   quelles seraient vos principales suggestions pour son programme?

L'abolition du service militaire   64,0%
L'*égalité* à tous les *niveaux*   32,0   equality/levels
La réduction du chômage   28,0
La *lutte* contre l'inflation   22,8   fight, struggle
La liberté d'expression   20,2
De meilleures conditions de vie   14,0
L'environnement, l'écologie   10,3
Donner plus de possibilités aux jeunes   8,8
Améliorer les conditions de travail   8,5   to improve

7. Seriez-vous content s'il y avait d'autres événements comme la révolte des étudiants de mai 1968?

Je ne serais pas content.   40,6%
Je serais content.   32,7
Je ne sais pas.   26,7

8. Dans le cas où il y aurait des événements comme ceux de mai '68, que feriez-vous?

Je participerais aux manifestations.   55,4%
Je resterais chez moi.   18,1
Je m'opposerais aux manifestations.   2,9
Je ne sais pas ce que je ferais.   23,6

Point out that **les événements de mai '68** refers to the political, social, and educational upheaval that was initially started by French university students protesting against an outdated and impersonal university structure.

9. Pour quelles raisons un candidat *se présente*-t-il aux élections? Choi-   run for
sissez les deux raisons qui vous paraissent les plus importantes.

Pour servir son parti politique	51,9%
Pour se mettre au service du public	41,0
Pour changer la société	33,0
Par soif du pouvoir	28,0
À cause des avantages personnels	26,4
Pour devenir une *vedette*	6,7

out of

star

Have students answer survey questions and compare their answers with those of French young people.

Extrait et adapté d'un article de *L'Express* par Michel Labro.

Compréhension   Selon les renseignements donnés dans le texte, est-ce que les phrases suivantes sont vraies ou fausses? Corrigez le sens de la phrase s'il est faux.

1. *L'Express* a organisé ce sondage pour connaître l'opinion des gens qui vont prendre leur retraite.
2. Pour la plupart des jeunes Français, avoir dix-huit ans veut dire avoir le droit de voter.
3. Les jeunes Français ne semblent pas s'intéresser beaucoup à la politique.
4. La plupart d'entre eux sont très bien informés en ce qui concerne la politique.
5. La majorité des jeunes n'appartiennent à aucune organisation politique.
6. Beaucoup de jeunes ont déjà participé à des manifestations.
7. Les jeunes voudraient l'abolition du service militaire.
8. S'il y avait d'autres événements comme ceux du mai 1968, la plupart des jeunes resteraient chez eux.
9. Selon les jeunes, les candidats se présentent aux élections parce qu'ils veulent devenir des vedettes.

NOTES CULTURELLES

La vie politique

En France, le Président de la République est élu° au suffrage universel direct° pour un mandat° de sept ans. Il est chef de l'État et il nomme le premier ministre qui à son tour° est chargé de former le cabinet des ministres et de diriger la politique du gouvernement.

    Le Parlement, c'est-à-dire la branche législative du gouvernement, comprend deux assemblées: L'Assemblée nationale (aussi appelée la Chambre des députés) qui est composée de 490 députés élus au suffrage universel direct pour une durée° de cinq ans. Le Sénat qui comprend 306 sénateurs élus pour neuf ans par les conseillers généraux° et

les représentants des municipalités. Ces deux assemblées ont à peu près les mêmes pouvoirs.° L'Assemblée nationale siège° au palais Bourbon et le Sénat au palais du Luxembourg.

    Les principaux partis politiques de gauche à droite sont:

    —Le Parti communiste (P.C.). Dirigé par Georges Marchais.

    —Le Parti socialiste (P.S.). C'est le parti du Président François Mitterand.

    —L'Union pour la démocratie française (U.D.F.). C'est le parti de l'ancien Président Valéry Giscard D'Estaing.

    —Le Rassemblement pour la république (R.P.R.). Dirigé par Jacques Chirac.

élu *elected*   au suffrage universel direct *by popular vote*
mandat *term*   à son tour *in turn*   durée *period*
conseillers généraux *regional delegates*

pouvoirs *powers*   siège *meets*

Georges Marchais, chef du P.C.

Et vous?

A. Les devoirs et les responsabilités des citoyens. Quelle est votre opinion sur chacun des points suivants?

1. **Les lois:** Êtes-vous satisfait(e) des lois que nous avons dans ce pays? Y en a-t-il qu'il faudrait changer? Si oui, lesquelles et pourquoi?

2. **Le service militaire:** Êtes-vous pour ou contre le service militaire pour les hommes? Et pour les femmes? Que pensez-vous des objecteurs de conscience? Que pensez-vous des alternatives civiles au service militaire (comme le Corps de la Paix)?

3. **Les impôts:** Est-ce que nous payons trop ou pas assez d'*impôts*?   taxes
    À votre avis, est-ce que le gouvernement dépense pas assez ou trop d'argent pour . . .
    la défense du pays?
    l'éducation?
    l'entretien des routes et des bâtiments publics?
    le salaire des *fonctionnaires*?   government workers
    les services sociaux?
    la recherche?

4. **L'information:** Est-ce que *vous vous tenez au courant* de ce qui   keep up to date
    se passe . . .
    dans votre ville?   dans votre pays?
    dans votre état?   dans le monde?

Pendant le défilé de 14 juillet à Paris

5. **Le choix des représentants:** Savez-vous le nom de votre *maire*? De vos *conseillers municipaux*? De votre *député(e)*? De vos sénateurs? Est-ce que vous êtes content(e) d'eux? Aimeriez-vous occuper un de ces postes? Si oui, lequel et pourquoi?

mayor

city council members / congressman / congresswoman

B. **Sauriez-vous ce qu'il faut faire?** Quand on n'obéit pas aux lois et aux *règlements*, on risque d'avoir des *ennuis*. Mais pour obéir, il faut d'abord comprendre. Sauriez-vous ce qu'il faut faire si vous voyiez les inscriptions suivantes?

rules / problems

Have students think of signs that could be used in their classroom.

Point out to students that in France one must always yield the right of way to the person on the right unless otherwise indicated.

Parmi ces inscriptions, quelles sont celles qu'on peut voir . . .

sur une autoroute?	dans la rue?
sur une porte?	sur le mur d'un bâtiment?
dans une pièce?	dans un train ou dans un autobus?

Défense de stationner

no parking

Défense de fumer

no smoking

Poussez

push

Priorité à droite

yield to the vehicle on the right

Défense d'afficher

post no bills

Porte de secours

emergency exit

Il est <u>interdit</u> de marcher sur les pelouses

forbidden / lawns

Sens unique

one-way street

Prière de sonner avant d'entrer

please ring

Tirez

pull

Explain that **s.v.p.** is the abbreviation for **s'il vous plaît.**

Entrée interdite

Prière de ne pas déranger

please do not disturb

Frappez, s.v.p.

please knock

Chien méchant

beware of the dog (**méchant** = bad, mean, naughty)

Défense de parler au chauffeur

Stationnement réservé aux taxis

parking

Sortie obligatoire

this way out

Propriété privée

private

Le verbe *devoir*

Présentation

Devoir (*to have to, must, to be supposed to, should*) is an irregular verb

devoir	
je **dois**	nous **devons**
tu **dois**	vous **devez**
il/elle/on **doit**	ils/elles **doivent**
passé composé: j'ai dû	
futur: je devrai	

Because there is no exact English equivalent of the verb **devoir**, each of its tenses has a somewhat different English approximation.

A. The present tense of **devoir** is similar to the English *to have to, must,* or *to be supposed to* and is used to indicate:

1. Necessity or obligation:

Nous devons obéir aux lois.   *We must obey the laws.*
Je dois rentrer maintenant.   *I have to go home now.*

2. Probability or likelihood:

Il doit être trois heures.   *It must be (probably is) three o'clock.*

Vous devez être content de pouvoir voter maintenant.   *You must be happy to be able to vote now.*

3. Expectation:

Ils doivent partir aujourd'hui.   *They are supposed to leave today.*

B. The **passé composé** is similar to the English *had to* or *must have* and is used to indicate:

1. Necessity:

J'ai dû y retourner le jour suivant.   *I had to go back there the next day.*

2. Probability:

J'ai dû perdre mon passeport quand j'étais en Suisse.   *I must have lost (probably did lose) my passport when I was in Switzerland.*

C. The imperfect is similar to the English *was supposed to*, *was/were to*, or *must have*. It indicates:

1. Expectation:

Ils devaient annoncer les résultats des élections ce matin.

They were to (were supposed to) announce the election results this morning.

2. Probability:

Elle devait être très malheureuse.

She must have been (probably was) very unhappy.

D. The future tense is similar to *will have to* and indicates necessity.

Elle devra en acheter une autre.
Le gouvernement devra faire des réformes.

She will have to buy another one.
The government will have to make reforms.

E. The conditional tense is similar to *should* or *ought to* and is used to indicate:

1. Obligation:

Tu devrais voter. *You should vote.*

2. Probability:

Selon André, vous ne devriez pas avoir de difficultés.

According to André, you shouldn't have any difficulty.

F. In any tense, **devoir** plus a noun means *to owe*.

Je lui devais cinq dollars. *I owed him five dollars.*
Vous leur devez du respect. *You owe them respect.*

Substitution: (1) Je dois partir ce soir. vous / mes parents / tu / nous / je / mon ami. (2) Il devait jouer au tennis. je / François et Charles / nous / vous / tu. (3) Vous devriez apprendre l'allemand. nous / Raoul / tu / Annette et Lise.

Préparation

A. C'est la campagne électorale. Plusieurs étudiants ont décidé d'aider Madame Sauvigny dans sa campagne électorale. Ils parlent de ce qu'ils doivent faire aujourd'hui. Qu'est-ce qu'ils disent?

Modèle Valérie / aller à une réunion → **Valérie doit aller à une réunion.**

1. je / distribuer des tracts
2. nous / participer à une discussion
3. Pierre / rester chez lui pour étudier
4. Catherine / faire des recherches à la bibliothèque
5. tu / parler aux journalistes
6. les autres / mettre des affiches
7. vous / téléphoner aux gens que vous connaissez
8. nous / faire tout ce que nous pouvons

B. Résolutions. C'est le jour de l'an et Paulette et ses amis parlent des résolutions qu'ils devraient prendre. Reconstituez les phrases qu'ils ont prononcées.

Follow-up: Have students prepare resolutions for beginning of term (**Je devrais étudier plus sérieusement**, etc.)

Modèle je / me tenir au courant de ce qui se passe
Je devrais me tenir au courant de ce qui se passe.

1. nous / lire les journaux plus souvent
2. tu / être mieux informé
3. je / m'intéresser davantage à la politique
4. nous / aller à la bibliothèque plus souvent
5. je / mettre de l'argent à la banque
6. Paul / chercher du travail
7. tu / écrire plus souvent à tes parents
8. on / prendre le temps de se détendre

C. Aide bilingue. René accompagne un homme politique américain qui fait une tournée diplomatique au Québec. René doit traduire ce qu'il dit.

1. I am supposed to give a lecture tomorrow morning.
2. We should work together to solve our problems.
3. The President was supposed to call me this morning.
4. The others must be in Montreal now.
5. You must have been happy to learn the news.
6. We must keep up to date.
7. I owe you an explanation.
8. You should be interested in politics.

Communication

A. Parlons politique. Quelle est votre opinion sur les questions suivantes?

1. Qu'est-ce qu'un(e) candidat(e) doit faire pour gagner une élection?
2. Est-ce que les candidat(e)s devraient toujours dire la vérité?
3. Est-ce qu'ils/elles devraient répondre à toutes les questions des journalistes?
4. Qu'est-ce que le gouvernement devrait faire pour résoudre les principaux problèmes de notre pays?
5. Qu'est-ce que les citoyens devraient faire pour aider le pays à résoudre ces problèmes?
6. À votre avis, quels sont les principaux devoirs et responsabilités d'un citoyen?
7. Est-ce qu'on devrait changer certaines lois ou certaines institutions? Si oui, lesquelles?
8. Si vous deviez participer à la création d'un nouveau parti politique— ou d'un groupe d'action politique ou civique—quelles seraient vos priorités?

Options: Ask as questions or adapt for directed dialogue.

B. Trouvez quelqu'un qui . . . Trouvez des gens dans votre classe qui sont dans les situations suivantes.

1. quelqu'un qui a dû travailler toute la nuit pour se préparer au dernier examen de français
2. quelqu'un qui devrait aller à la bibliothèque plus souvent
3. quelqu'un qui devrait boire moins de bière
4. quelqu'un qui devrait être plus sérieux(-euse)
5. quelqu'un qui devait écrire une composition la semaine dernière mais qui ne l'a pas fait

6. quelqu'un qui ne doit rien à personne
7. quelqu'un qui a dû venir à l'université à pied ce matin parce que sa voiture ne marchait pas, ou parce qu'il(elle) a manqué l'autobus

⚜ Les verbes *falloir* et *valoir mieux*

Présentation

Falloir *(to be necessary, must, to have to)* and **valoir mieux** *(to be preferable, to be better)* are irregular verbs that occur only in the third-person singular impersonal forms. They are used to express obligations and value judgments.

	falloir	*valoir mieux*
Présent	il faut	il vaut mieux
Passé composé	il a fallu	il a mieux valu
Imparfait	il fallait	il valait mieux
Futur	il faudra	il vaudra mieux
Conditionnel	il faudrait	il vaudrait mieux

Pourquoi faut-il voter?

Si vous voulez être politicien, il faudra être mieux informé.

Qu'est-ce qu'il fallait faire pour réussir?

Il vaut mieux rester chez soi.

Dans ce cas-là, il vaudrait mieux attendre jusqu'à demain.

Why is it necessary to vote?

If you want to be a politician, you will have to (it will be necessary to) be better informed.

What was it necessary to do to succeed?

It is better to stay at home.

In that case, it would be better to wait until tomorrow.

A. Although **il faut** can mean *it is necessary* in the affirmative, **il ne faut pas** does *not* mean *it is not necessary*; it means *must not*. To convey the meaning *it is not necessary*, the expression **il n'est pas nécessaire de** is used.

Il faut travailler dur pour gagner une élection.

Il ne faut pas perdre du temps.

Il n'est pas nécessaire d'être parfait.

You have to work hard to win an election.

You must not waste any time.

You don't have to be perfect.

Il faut can be used with an indirect object followed by a noun. Its meaning in this case is usually *requires* or *takes*.

Il lui fallait de la patience.

Il nous a fallu trois heures pour répondre à ces lettres.

Il vous faudra beaucoup d'argent.

It required (he needed) patience.

It took us three hours to answer these letters.

You'll have to have (need) a lot of money.

B. **Valoir** by itself means *to be worth.* Although it can be conjugated in all persons, only the third-person forms (**vaut, valent**) are commonly used.

Ce dessin vaut cent francs.   *This sketch is worth a hundred francs.*
Ces tableaux ne valent rien.   *These paintings aren't worth anything.*

In addition to the expression **il vaut mieux** (*it is preferable*), **valoir** is also used in the idiomatic expression **valoir la peine** (*to be worth the trouble*).

Ça ne vaut pas la peine d'écouter   *It isn't worth the trouble to listen*
    ce candidat.   *to this candidate.*
Ça n'en vaut pas la peine.   *It's not worth it.*

Un vaurien is a good for nothing, a hood. **Un tiens vaut mieux que deux tu l'auras.** (*A bird in the hand is worth two in the bush.*)

Substitution: (1) Il vaudrait mieux vous spécialiser en sciences politiques / voter pour l'autre candidat / ne pas prendre une décision maintenant / être membre d'un parti politique / ne pas participer à cette manifestation. (2) Il me faudra beaucoup de temps pour décider. vous / nous / leur / lui / te. (3) Est-ce que ça vaut la peine de répondre à cette lettre? assister à cette conférence / visiter ce château / faire de la gymnastique / traduire ce passage.

Préparation

Qu'est-ce que je dois faire? Serge a parlé de ses problèmes à ses amis et il leur a demandé conseil. Qu'est-ce qu'ils ont répondu?

Modèle   Je suis découragé. (mais non, il ne faut pas) → **Mais non, il ne faut pas être découragé.**

1. Est-ce que je devrais participer à la manifestation? (non, ce n'est pas nécessaire)
2. Je pourrais rester chez moi. (oui, il vaudrait mieux)
3. Je ne vais rien dire à personne. (oui, il vaut mieux)
4. Je vais écouter les informations. (oui, il faudra)
5. Est-ce que je devrais aller à la réunion? (non, ça ne vaut pas la peine)
6. J'ai envie de tout abandonner. (non, il ne faut pas)
7. Je voudrais participer à la manifestation. (non, il ne faut pas)
8. Je vais essayer de changer. (oui, ça vaut la peine)

Options: (1) Written. (2) Oral—ask as questions (**Qu'est-ce qu'il faut faire pour réussir dans les études?**, etc.).

Communication

A. **Que faut-il faire ou ne pas faire?** Complétez les phrases suivantes en employant une ou plusieurs des expressions suivantes: **il faut, il ne faut pas, il n'est pas nécessaire de.**

Exemple   Pour réussir dans ses études . . . →
              Pour réussir dans ses études, il faut travailler régulièrement. ou
              Pour réussir dans ses études, il ne faut pas passer tout son temps dans les cafés. ou
              Pour réussir dans ses études, il n'est pas nécessaire d'être toujours d'accord avec ses professeurs.

1. Pour se tenir au courant de ce qui se passe dans le monde . . .
2. Pour être un leader politique . . .
3. Pour gagner une élection . . .
4. Pour réussir dans la vie . . .
5. Pour être heureux(-euse) . . .
6. Pour rester en bonne santé . . .
7. Pour voter intelligemment . . .

B. Qu'est-ce qu'il vaut mieux faire? À votre avis, que vaut-il mieux faire dans chacune des situations suivantes? Vous pouvez suggérer une autre solution ou une autre possibilité si vous le désirez.

Exemples　　continuer à produire des armes nucléaires ou s'arrêter d'en construire → **À mon avis, il vaut mieux arrêter la course aux armes nucléaires. C'est trop dangereux pour tout le monde.**
Moi, je crois qu'il vaut mieux continuer à en construire parce que nous en avons besoin pour la défense du pays.

1. continuer à construire des centrales nucléaires ou s'arrêter d'en construire
2. donner la priorité à la lutte contre la pollution ou à la lutte contre l'inflation
3. avoir des écoles bilingues pour ceux qui en ont besoin (ou qui préfèrent cela) ou enseigner seulement en anglais dans les écoles et les lycées américains
4. avoir des élections présidentielles tous les quatre ans ou les avoir tous les six ans
5. avoir des cours obligatoires dans les universités ou laisser aux étudiants la liberté de choisir leurs cours
6. encourager les étudiants à avoir une bonne culture générale ou les encourager à suivre un programme d'études qui les prépare à un métier ou à une profession

⚜ Le subjonctif des verbes réguliers

Présentation

The subjunctive must be learned as a new tense, though technically it is a different verb *mood*. It is rarely used in English, occurring usually in dependent clauses such as *I prefer that he be discreet*. The subjunctive mood is much more frequent in French. It generally occurs in **que** clauses that follow verbs or expressions indicating judgments, beliefs, emotions, or wishes.

The subjunctive of regular verbs (**-er, -ir, -re,** and verbs like **dormir**) is formed by adding the endings shown below to a stem that is found by dropping the **-ent** from the **ils/elles** form of the present tense (**parl-, finiss-, attend-, dorm-**).

Le subjonctif de parler		*Le subjonctif de* finir	
que je parle	nous parl**ions**	que je finisse	nous finiss**ions**
tu parles	vous parl**iez**	tu finisses	vous finiss**iez**
il/elle/on parle	ils/elles parl**ent**	il/elle/on finisse	ils/elles finiss**ent**

*Le subjonctif d'*attendre		*Le subjonctif de* dormir	
que j'attende	nous attend**ions**	que je dorme	nous dorm**ions**
tu attendes	vous attend**iez**	tu dormes	vous dorm**iez**
il/elle/on attende	ils/elles attend**ent**	il/elle/on dorme	ils/elles dorm**ent**

A. One of the most common uses of the subjunctive is after certain impersonal expressions. These expressions can be put in tenses other than the present as well as in the negative and interrogative forms. They are used to express:

Necessity or obligation
il faut que
il est nécessaire que

Uncertainty or impossibility
il est possible que
il est impossible que
il est rare que
il est peu probable que (*it is unlikely that*)
il semble que

Judgment
il vaut mieux que
il est préférable que
il est dommage que (*it is too bad that*)
il est bon que
il est juste que
il est naturel que
il est temps que

Suggestion: Point out that **il est probable** and **il paraît** take the indicative.

Il faut absolument que vous votiez.	*It is absolutely necessary that you vote.*
Il vaudrait mieux que le gouvernement établisse immédiatement son programme.	*It would be better for the government to establish its program immediately.*
Il serait préférable que tu répondes à sa lettre toi-même.	*It would be preferable that you answer his letter yourself.*
Il est peu probable que nous assistions à cette réunion.	*It's unlikely that we'll attend this meeting.*
Il était rare qu'il dorme plus de quatre heures par nuit.	*It was rare that he would sleep more than four hours a night.*

In conversational use of the expressions containing **être**, the **il est** is often replaced by **c'est:**

C'est dommage que ce candidat s'habille si mal.	*It's too bad that this candidate dresses so badly.*

B. Clauses in the subjunctive always include a specific subject. When the meaning is general and there is no specific subject, the impersonal expression is followed by an infinitive. Note the contrasts in the following sentences.

Il est impossible de gagner cette élection.	Il est impossible que je gagne cette élection.
Il serait bon de se reposer un peu.	Il serait bon que nous nous reposions un peu.
Il faut choisir.	Il faut que tu choisisses.

Il semble and **il est peu probable** cannot be followed by an infinitive. Note also that in all the expressions with **être** the infinitive is preceded by **de**.

Substitutions: (1) Il faut que je travaille. vous / Gérard / les étudiants / nous / tu. (2) Il est dommage que vous habitiez si loin. nous / Daniel / Marie et Jeannette / tu / je. (3) Il est possible que nous finissions avant midi. vous / je / Marc / André et Louise / tu. (4) Il vaudrait mieux que vous répondiez à cette question. tu / nous / je / Monsieur Leroi / les autres.

Préparation

A. Un étudiant en sciences politiques. Marcel parle de ce qu'il doit faire comme étudiant en sciences politiques. Qu'est-ce qu'il dit?

Modèle   parler avec les conseillers municipaux → **Il faut que nous parlions avec les conseillers municipaux.**

Have students note that the short form of **sciences politiques** is **sciences po.**

Repeat with **je** and **il.**

1. assister aux conférences
2. participer aux discussions
3. étudier beaucoup
4. passer nos examens de fin d'année
5. réussir à des examens
6. s'intéresser à la vie politique
7. poser des questions aux candidats
8. répondre à des questions difficiles
9. choisir un problème à étudier
10. présenter les résultats de nos recherches

B. Un candidat en difficulté. Il est presque certain que Maurice Sanveine ne gagnera pas aux prochaines élections. Un de ses amis lui donne quelques conseils. Qu'est-ce qu'il dit?

Modèle   il faut / regarder la situation en face → **Il faut que vous regardiez la situation en face.**

1. il est naturel / continuer à rêver
2. il est essentiel / réfléchir un peu
3. il n'est pas nécessaire / dépenser tant d'argent
4. il est peu probable / réussir à persuader le public
5. il est temps / abandonner votre campagne
6. il est important / penser à votre avenir
7. il vaudrait mieux / penser à autre chose
8. il est préférable / servir votre pays d'une autre façon

Communication

A. Décisions. La liste qui suit représente certaines habitudes, intentions ou préoccupations que vous pouvez avoir. Exprimez votre réaction envers chacune de ces suggestions en utilisant les expressions suivantes.

Exemples   finir mon travail → **Il faut que je finisse mon travail ce soir.** ou **Il est peu probable que je finisse mon travail ce soir.**

Il faut que je . . .
Il vaudrait mieux que je . . .
Il est temps que je . . .
Il est rare que je . . .
Il est peu probable que je . . .
Il n'est pas nécessaire que je . . .
Il est possible que je . . .

Suggestions: Payer mes dettes / essayer de me débrouiller seul(e) / répondre aux lettres qu'on m'a envoyées / vendre mes vieux livres / changer d'opinion / consacrer plus de temps à mes loisirs / me reposer / finir mon travail / sortir ce soir / me coucher tôt / choisir les cours que je suivrai le trimestre prochain

B. Que faire? À votre avis, que devrions-nous faire pour résoudre les problèmes suivants? Utilisez l'expression impersonnelle appropriée pour commencer votre phrase.

Exemples   changer l'âge de la retraite → **Il serait bon que nous changions l'âge de la retraite.**

Options: Written/oral. Have students discuss their choices with class or in small groups. Encourage them to add their own ideas.

arrêter l'inflation → **Il est temps que nous arrêtions l'inflation.**

1. changer l'âge de la retraite
2. arrêter l'inflation
3. encourager le développement des arts et de la culture
4. participer activement à la vie politique
5. créer de nouveaux emplois

6. limiter le nombre d'heures de travail
7. lutter contre la pollution
8. voter de nouveaux impôts
9. défendre les droits de tous les citoyens
10. ?

 ## Le subjonctif des verbes irréguliers

Présentation

Irregular verbs form the subjunctive in three different ways.

A. Some verbs that are irregular in other tenses are regular in the subjunctive; in other words, the subjunctive endings are added to the stem of the **ils/elles** form of the present tense.

Verb	Base form	Subjunctive form
conduire	ils **conduis**ent	que je conduise
connaître	ils **connaiss**ent	que je connaisse
dire	ils **dis**ent	que je dise
écrire	ils **écriv**ent	que j'écrive
courir	ils **cour**ent	que je coure
lire	ils **lis**ent	que je lise
ouvrir	ils **ouvr**ent	que j'ouvre
rire	ils **ri**ent	que je rie
suivre	ils **suiv**ent	que je suive

Il est temps que nous mettions fin à ce problème.
Il est rare que les gens conduisent à moins de 100 kmh.
Il serait bon que vous connaissiez mieux la situation.

B. The subjunctive of certain verbs is formed regularly in the **je, tu, il/elle/on,** and **ils/elles** forms. The stems of **nous** and **vous** forms are based on the **nous** form of the present tense. For instance, the subjunctive forms of **venir** are:

Le subjonctif de venir	
que je **vienne**	que nous **venions**
que tu **viennes**	que vous **veniez**
qu'il/elle/on **vienne**	qu'ils **viennent**

The subjunctive of verbs in this category (and others conjugated like them) is:

acheter	ils achètent	que j'achète
	nous achetons	que nous achetions
boire	ils boivent	que je boive
	nous buvons	que nous buvions
devoir	ils doivent	que je doive
	nous devons	que nous devions
prendre	ils prennent	que je prenne
	nous prenons	que nous prenions
venir	ils viennent	que je vienne
	nous venons	que nous venions
voir	ils voient	que je voie
	nous voyons	que nous voyions

Il est dommage que le gouvernement ne voie pas l'importance du problème.

Il vaudrait mieux que vous preniez une décision tout de suite.

C. The subjunctive of the following verbs is irregular.

1. Faire, pouvoir, and **savoir** each have a single stem for all the subjunctive forms.

Le subjonctif de faire		*Le subjonctif de* pouvoir	
que je **fasse**	que nous **fassions**	que je **puisse**	que nous **puissions**
que tu **fasses**	que vous **fassiez**	que tu **puisses**	que vous **puissiez**
qu'il/elle/on **fasse**	qu'ils/elles **fassent**	qu'il/elle/on **puisse**	qu'ils/elles **puissent**

Le subjonctif de savoir	
que je **sache**	que nous **sachions**
que tu **saches**	que vous **sachiez**
qu'il/elle/on **sache**	qu'ils/elles **sachent**

Il est temps que nous fassions quelque chose pour arrêter la pollution.

Il faut que vous sachiez ce qui se passe.

2. Aller and **vouloir** have two stems.

*Le subjonctif d'*aller		*Le subjonctif de* vouloir	
que j'**aille**	que nous **allions**	que je **veuille**	que nous **voulions**
que tu **ailles**	que vous **alliez**	que tu **veuilles**	que vous **vouliez**
qu'il/elle/on **aille**	qu'ils/elles **aillent**	qu'il/elle/on **veuille**	qu'ils/elles **veuillent**

Il faut que vous alliez voter.

Il est dommage que les gens ne veuillent rien faire.

3. **Être** and **avoir** are completely irregular.

Le subjonctif d'être		*Le subjonctif d'avoir*	
que je **sois**	que nous **soyons**	que j'**aie**	que nous **ayons**
que tu **sois**	que vous **soyez**	que tu **aies**	que vous **ayez**
qu'il/elle/on **soit**	qu'ils/elles **soient**	qu'il/elle/on **ait**	qu'ils/elles **aient**

Il faudrait que nous soyons plus prudents.
Il est peu probable qu'on ait les ressources suffisantes.

4. The subjunctive forms of **falloir** and **valoir** are **il faille** and **il vaille**.

Il est dommage qu'il faille partir.
Il est peu probable que ça en vaille la peine.

Préparation

A. Vous venez à la réunion? Armand essaie de persuader ses amis de venir à une réunion de son groupe d'action politique. Mais ils ont tous quelque chose d'autre à faire. Qu'est-ce qu'ils disent?

Modèle   Véronique / aller chez le dentiste → **Il faut que Véronique aille chez le dentiste.**

1. nous / écrire un rapport
2. Gérard / être de retour à cinq heures
3. je / aller voir ma grand-mère
4. vous / lire plusieurs articles
5. tu / conduire ta sœur à l'aéroport
6. je / prendre ma leçon de piano
7. Marcel et Robert / faire le marché

B. On parle de l'écologie. Les écologistes voudraient que les gens prennent davantage conscience de leurs responsabilités écologiques. Reconstituez certains des conseils qu'ils ont donnés au cours d'une discussion publique.

Modèle   Nous laissons mourir nos lacs et nos rivières. (il ne faut pas) → **Il ne faut pas que nous laissions mourir nos lacs et nos rivières.**

Follow-up: Form complete sentences and read as paragraph for listening practice.

1. Vous savez la vérité. (il est temps)
2. Tout le monde lit nos brochures. (il faut que)
3. Les gens suivent nos conseils. (il est important)
4. Vous conduisez plus lentement. (il faut que)
5. Vous achetez moins d'appareils électriques. (il est essentiel)
6. Nous faisons plus attention aux problèmes écologiques. (il est important)
7. Nous pouvons résoudre tous les problèmes immédiatement. (il ne semble pas)
8. Nous sommes obligés de changer nos habitudes de vie. (il est possible)
9. Les gens veulent faire quelque chose. (il est peu probable)
10. Nous avons un programme d'action. (il est temps)

52   En Bretagne, après la marée noire

Communication

A. Changeons de rôle. Vous êtes professeur. Dites à vos étudiants ce qu'il faut qu'ils fassent. Commencez chaque phrase par une des expressions suivantes: **il faut que, il est important que, il vaudrait mieux que,** etc.

Follow-up: Have students tell a roommate, teacher, etc., what he or she must do.

Exemple   étudier régulièrement → **Il est important que vous étudiiez régulièrement.**

1. remettre vos devoirs régulièrement
2. aller au laboratoire tous les jours
3. savoir les verbes irréguliers
4. venir en classe tous les jours
5. écrire une composition une fois par semaine
6. lire une centaine de pages chaque jour
7. pouvoir répondre aux questions
8. ?

B. Parents. Imaginez que vous avez un enfant. Expliquez-lui ce qu'il faut qu'il fasse.

Exemple   aller à l'école tous les jours → **Il faut que tu ailles à l'école tous les jours.**

1. apprendre à te discipliner toi-même
2. être plus poli
3. rentrer à la maison à huit heures
4. mettre la table pour le dîner
5. te laver derrière les oreilles
6. boire ton lait
7. avoir plus de patience avec ton petit frère
8. dire toujours la vérité
9. ?

C. Que devez-vous faire cette semaine? Indiquez ce que vous devez faire cette semaine. Commencez chaque phrase par **il faut.**

Exemples   **Il faut que j'aille chez le dentiste.**
Il faut que j'écrive des lettres.

D. À votre avis. À votre avis, quelles sont les responsabilités d'un bon citoyen? Comparez vos idées avec celles des autres étudiants.

Exemples   Il est important que tout le monde vote chaque fois qu'il y a une élection.
Il faudrait que tout le monde lise les journaux pour se tenir au courant de ce qui se passe.

SYNTHÈSE

Il faut sauver le lac Léman

«Quand j'avais treize ans, explique Paul Jacquier, maire d'un petit village sur la *rive* française du lac Léman, j'ai dû quitter l'école pour aider mon père qui était *pêcheur*. Je me souviens encore de l'odeur du matin sur le lac en été. L'air sentait bon, l'herbe fraîchement coupée. Quand j'avais soif, je buvais l'eau du lac. Il y avait alors douze familles de pêcheurs dans le village. Aujourd'hui il n'en reste plus que deux et personne n'aurait l'idée de boire l'eau du lac. Elle est bien trop polluée pour ça.»

bank
fisherman

Le lac Léman

Créé par des glaciers il y a cent vingt siècles, le plus grand lac d'Europe avait tranquillement *traversé* les âges. Vingt-cinq ans ont suffi à détruire cet *équilibre*. Le Léman est devenu un grand malade, même s'il offre* encore une impression de santé *grâce aux* belles montagnes qui *l'entourent*.

crossed
balance
thanks to
surround

Les pêcheurs et les scientifiques ont commencé à *s'apercevoir du* problème il y a une vingtaine d'années. Ils voulaient qu'on fasse quelque chose mais l'écologie n'était pas encore *à la mode* à cette époque-là. Il a donc fallu qu'ils prennent patience. En 1967 des chercheurs ont découvert une algue microscopique qui colore l'eau en rouge. Cette fois-ci il n'y avait plus de doute. Il fallait qu'on essaie de contrôler la pollution apportée aussi bien par les centres urbains que par les industries. On a dit aux industries et aux municipalités qu'elles devaient *nettoyer* leurs eaux *usées*.

notice

in fashion

clean up
used, waste

On se préoccupe aussi de la présence de mercure dans le lac. Heureusement cela n'a pas encore atteint un *niveau* critique et les gourmets peuvent continuer à manger les *fritures* du lac. Mais les pêcheurs remarquent que les meilleurs poissons deviennent de plus en plus rares. Ils ne veulent pas que ces *espèces* disparaissent. Pour les sauver il faudrait que les Suisses et les Français signent des *accords* pour limiter la pêche. Mais personne ne veut accepter une réglementation plus sévère que celle de son voisin.

level
fish fries

species
agreements
French fish fries consist of very small fish that are usually served in small restaurants near the rivers and lakes where the fish were caught.

«Nous sommes malades de voir le lac dans cet état, affirme Paul Jacquier. Mais ce n'est pas un problème que les municipalités locales peuvent *résoudre* seules. Il faut que les deux États *agissent* et qu'ils agissent vite.»

solve / act

Et les citoyens? Sont-ils prêts à agir? Leurs réponses aux questions d'un sondage montrent qu'ils se préoccupent sérieusement de ce problème.

***Offrir** is an irregular verb in the present tense (**j'offre, tu offres, il offre, nous offrons, vous offrez, ils offrent**) and the **passé composé** (**j'ai offert,** etc.). Verbs conjugated like **offrir** are: **couvrir** (*to cover*); **découvrir** (*to discover*); **ouvrir** (*to open*); and **souffrir** (*to suffer*).

Pollution des rivières, eau potable en DANGER!

ASSOCIATION QUEBECOISE DES TECHNIQUES DE L'EAU

LA MER DOIT VIVRE

À une manifestation antinucléaire

1. Pouvez-vous *classer* de l à 15, selon l'importance qu'ils ont pour vous, les problèmes de civilisation auxquels il faut que nous trouvions une solution?

rank

La pollution de l'air et de l'eau	40,0 %	
Les dangers de l'énergie nucléaire	25,0	
Le *gaspillage* de l'énergie	4,3	waste
La destruction du *milieu marin*	4,3	marine environment
L'extinction de certaines espèces animales	3,4	
Le *bruit*	3,0	noise
La présence de produits chimiques dans les aliments	3,0	
La destruction des *terres agricoles*	2,7	farmland
Le monopole des partis politiques	2,5	
Le pillage des ressources du *tiers monde*	2,4	third world
La centralisation politique et économique	2,3	
La prolifération du *béton* dans les villes	2,0	concrete
La tendance au gigantisme	2,0	
La prolifération des automobiles	2,0	
L'*isolement* des individus et l'absence de contacts personnels entre *voisins*	1,1	isolation neighbors

2. Les écologistes disent que si les sociétés industrielles continuent à se développer au rythme des trente dernières années, nous *courons** à   run
la catastrophe. Etes-vous d'accord avec cette analyse?

Oui   86%
Non   14

3. Selon vous, est-ce qu'il vaudrait mieux que nous abandonnions les technologies développées au cours des trente dernières années et que nous retournions aux méthodes du passé?
Oui   25,7%
Non   74,3

4. Pensez-vous qu'il soit possible de *concilier* le développement tech-   reconcile
nologique avec le respect de l'environnement et la satisfaction des besoins matériels et psychologiques des hommes?

Oui   89,8%
Non   10,2

5. Si les partis politiques n'acceptent pas les propositions et les *reven-*   demands
dications des écologistes, seriez-vous prêt à voter pour des candidats écologistes?

Oui   86,8%
Non   13,2

Extrait et adapté de plusieurs articles de *L'Express*.

Compréhension   Indiquez si les phrases suivantes sont vraies ou fausses. Si le sens de la phrase est faux, corrigez-le.

1. Monsieur Paul Jacquier est maire de la ville de Genève.
2. Il garde de bons souvenirs de son enfance.
3. À cette époque-là, le lac commençait déjà à être pollué.
4. De nos jours, on peut boire l'eau du lac sans aucun danger.
5. Les dernières vingt-cinq années ont eu plus d'effet sur le lac que les cent vingt siècles précédents.
6. Le lac Léman donne l'apparence d'être en bonne santé mais c'est une fausse impression.
7. C'est au début du siècle dernier qu'on a découvert l'algue microscopique qui colore l'eau en rouge.
8. On a demandé aux industries de nettoyer leurs eaux usées.
9. Les pêcheurs sont inquiets parce qu'ils ont peur que certaines espèces de poissons disparaissent.
10. Ils voudraient que le gouvernement suisse et le gouvernement français fassent quelque chose.
11. Selon les résultats du sondage, la pollution est le problème dont les Français se préoccupent le plus.
12. La plupart des Français pensent qu'il vaudrait mieux qu'on abandonne les technologies modernes et qu'on retourne aux méthodes du passé.

*Courir is an irregular verb. Its forms are: **je cours, tu cours, il/elle/on court, nous courons, vous courez, ils/elles courent**; passé composé: **j'ai couru**; futur: **je courrai**.

NOTES CULTURELLES

Le lac Léman

Le lac Léman forme une partie de la frontière naturelle entre la France et la Suisse. La rive° sud est française et la rive nord est suisse. Le Rhône, qui prend sa source en Suisse, traverse le lac Léman avant de continuer son cours entre les Alpes et le Jura et d'aller se jeter° dans la Mer Méditerranée. Évian, la principale ville française située sur le lac Léman, est une station thermale célèbre pour son eau minérale. Les principales villes suisses sont Lausanne et Genève. Genève est le siège° de plusieurs organisations internationales, et c'est là qu'ont lieu de nombreuses conférences internationales sur le désarmement, l'environnement et d'autres sujets d'intérêt mondial.

rive *bank, side*   se jeter *flow into*   siège *seat*

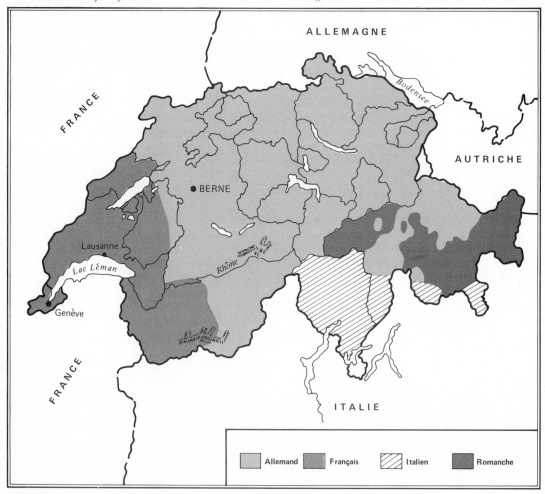

La Suisse linguistique

Communication

A. À votre avis. Répondez vous-même aux questions du sondage présenté dans l'article sur le lac Léman. Ensuite, comparez vos réponses avec celles des autres étudiants et celles des Français qui ont participé au sondage.

B. Pourriez-vous vous en passer? Si nous voulons résoudre le problème de la pollution, il faudra peut-être que nous changions notre style de vie et que nous nous passions de certaines choses auxquelles nous sommes habitués. Utilisez les catégories suivantes pour indiquer votre réaction dans chacun des cas présentés.

1—Je pourrais très facilement m'en passer.
2—Je pourrais m'en passer, s'il le fallait.
3—J'arriverais à m'en passer, mais avec beaucoup de difficulté.
4—Je ne pourrais absolument pas m'en passer.

_____ une télévision
_____ une radio
_____ une chaîne-stéréophonique
_____ une machine à laver
_____ une voiture
_____ une machine à laver la vaisselle

_____ un magnétophone
_____ un ordinateur
_____ des jeux électroniques
_____ avoir de l'eau chaude pour se laver
_____ avoir une maison bien chaude pendant l'hiver
_____ ?

C. La politique à l'université. Vous avez décidé de vous présenter comme candidat(e) pour le poste de président(e) d'une association d'étudiants. Quelles sont vos revendications et votre programme d'action? Qu'est-ce que vous allez demander à vos supporters de faire?

Exemple   Il est temps que l'administration comprenne que ça ne peut pas continuer comme ça.

D. Politique et humour. Nous avons trouvé dans un numéro de *Jeune Afrique* ces définitions des différents systèmes politiques. Dites si vous êtes d'accord ou non avec ces définitions. Si vous n'êtes pas d'accord, vous pouvez substituer vos propres définitions. (Quelques mots à savoir: **vache,** *cow;* **taureau,** *bull;* **tuer,** *to kill;* **jeter,** *to throw away;* **allonger,** *to stretch*)

> **Socialisme:** vous avez deux *vaches,* vous en donnez une à votre voisin.
> **Communisme:** vous avez deux vaches, le gouvernement vous les prend et vous donne du lait.
> **Fascisme:** vous avez deux vaches, le gouvernement vous les prend et vous vend du lait.
> **Nazisme:** vous avez deux vaches, le gouvernement vous les prend et vous envoie en prison.
> **Bureaucratie:** vous avez deux vaches, le gouvernement vous les prend, il *tue* la première et *jette* le lait produit par la seconde.
> **Capitalisme:** vous avez deux vaches, vous vendez la première et vous achetez un *taureau.*
> **Capitalisme** (suite): alors, une multinationale vous prend la vache et le taureau et vous vend du lait chaque fois plus *allongé* d'eau et chaque fois plus cher.
> **Socialisme démocratique:** vous avez deux vaches, vous en donnez une à votre voisin.
> —Et avec quoi achetez-vous le taureau?
> —Mais, le taureau, c'est votre voisin qui vous le donnera, parbleu! En échange de la vache!

Option: Have students create
definitions of similar terms—e.g.,
démocratie, justice.

VOCABULAIRE

noms

l'accord (m) *agreement*
le béton *concrete*
le bruit *noise*
le conseiller municipal *council member*
le député *congressman*
le droit *right*
l'égalité (f) *equality*
l'ennui (m) *problem*
l'entrée (f) *entrance*
l'équilibre (m) *balance*
l'espèce (f) *species*
le fonctionnaire *government worker*
le gaspillage *waste*
l'impôt (m) *tax*
l'isolement (m) *isolation*
la loi *law*
la lutte *fight, struggle*
le maire *mayor*
la manifestation *demonstration*
le niveau *level*
le pêcheur *fisherman*
la propriété *property*
la réunion *meeting*
la revendication *claim, demand*
la rive *bank*
la sortie *exit*
le syndicat *union*
le stationnement *parking*
le tiers monde *third world*
le tract *leaflet*
le voisin, la voisine *neighbor*

verbes

afficher *to post, to put up a sign*
agir *to act*
améliorer *to improve*

s'apercevoir *to notice*
atteindre *to reach*
concilier *to reconcile*
devoir *to have to, must, to be supposed to, to owe*
entourer *to surround*
frapper *to hit, to knock*
fumer *to smoke*
nettoyer *to clean, clean up*
pousser *to push*
résoudre *to resolve, to solve*
se présenter *to run (for office)*
stationner *to park*
se tenir au courant *to keep up to date*
tirer *to pull*
traverser *to cross*
valoir *to be worth*
valoir mieux *to be better*
°voter

adjectifs

interdit(e) *forbidden*
méchant(e) *bad, mean, naughty*
privé(e) *private*

divers

à la mode *in fashion*
défense de . . . *no . . . (it is prohibited to)*
ça ne vaut pas la peine de . . . *it's not worth the trouble to . . .*
envers *toward, in regard to*
grâce à *thanks to*
il est dommage que *it's too bad that*
il est peu probable que . . . *it's unlikely that . . .*
prière de . . . *please, kindly*
soi-même *oneself*

L'individu face à la société moderne

INTRODUCTION

La violence dans la société moderne

Il semble qu'en France, comme partout dans le monde, la violence soit en train de devenir un phénomène de la vie de tous les jours. Le gouvernement français a récemment *nommé* une commission pour étudier le problème de la violence en France. Son diagnostic est grave.

    Dans les usines, dans la rue, dans les conflits sociaux, dans les relations personnelles et sociales, *il existe* une agressivité nouvelle. Les insultes, la violence physique, le vandalisme font partie des *moyens* d'expression personnelle *tout comme* les *enlèvements* et les explosifs font partie de l'arsenal des terroristes. Cette violence vient souvent du besoin d'affirmer qu'on existe, du besoin d'être entendu dans un monde qu'on croit *sourd*. C'est quand il n'est plus possible de parler ni de comprendre qu'on a recours à la violence.

appointed, named

there exists

means

just as / kidnappings

deaf

La violence n'est pas une maladie nouvelle de notre société, mais il semble que nous soyons de moins en moins capables de tolérer le sentiment d'insécurité qu'elle provoque. Mais pourquoi cette panique? Et de quoi a-t-on peur?

Des jeunes d'abord. Trois personnes sur quatre pensent que les jeunes sont plus facilment *tentés* par la violence que les adultes. Et beaucoup de gens citent la délinquance des jeunes comme un problème majeur de notre société. Parmi les facteurs sociaux qui sont responsables de la délinquance juvénile on cite souvent la ville. Dans les villes de moins de 3000 habitants la délinquance des mineurs est de 2,2 pour cent. Dans celles de 50 000 à 100 000 habitants, elle est de 10,5 pour cent. Il semble aussi que la criminalité augmente avec la *hauteur* des *immeubles*. Dans les grandes villes les enfants sont non seulement condamnés à vivre dans la stérilité du béton, mais ils sont souvent exilés de leur propre maison. En effet, il est généralement interdit de laisser les enfants jouer dans les escaliers ou marcher sur les pelouses.

Souvent les enfants n'ont rien à faire et ils s'ennuient. «Ils devraient faire du sport, ça les occuperait», dit-on souvent. Oui, mais le sport est devenu, lui aussi, une activité très organisée et très compétitive. Il existe une obsession de la victoire et du succès qui contamine tous les aspects de la vie, même les loisirs. Et cette obsession du succès est peut-être, elle aussi, une forme de violence contre les individus . . . tout comme le *matraquage publicitaire* et la tyrannie de l'argent.

Il semble que toutes les restrictions imposées aux habitants des villes les rendent encore plus agressifs. Il suffit de conduire dans Paris à six heures du soir pour *s'en apercevoir*. Dans les grandes villes on tue, on *viole* et on vole plus que dans les petites villes. En France, par exemple, les 3/5 des crimes graves sont commis dans les sept grandes régions urbaines.

Pour lutter contre l'anonymité de la ville, certains membres de la commission ont proposé qu'on encourage les *camelots*, les artisans et les artistes de la rue. «Camelots, musiciens, chanteurs et mimes *méritent* de retrouver leur place dans la rue, disent-ils. Leur présence *rassure* et elle apporte une animation, une spontanéité et une joie dont les habitants des villes ont bien besoin.»

Extrait et adapté d'un article de *L'Express*.

Dans son coffre, le corps d'un voisin

tempted

Tué par son fils

height
buildings

Bébé disparu : aucune piste

being bombarded with
advertising

become aware of it
rapes

street vendors
deserve
is reassuring

Trois jeunes femmes assassinées

Compréhension   Selon les renseignements donnés dans le texte, est-ce que les phrases suivantes sont vraies ou fausses? Corrigez le sens de la phrase s'il est faux.

1. Le gouvernement a nommé une commission spéciale pour étudier le problème de la violence.
2. La commission ne pense pas que la violence soit un problème sérieux en France.
3. La plupart des gens pensent que les jeunes sont plus violents que les adultes.
4. Il y a moins de délinquance dans les grandes villes que dans les petites villes.
5. En France, les enfants peuvent jouer où ils veulent.
6. En général, il n'est pas permis de marcher sur les pelouses.
7. Les enfants s'ennuient parce qu'ils n'ont rien à faire.
8. La commission a suggéré qu'on encourage les artistes de la rue parce que leur présence rassurerait et amuserait les gens.

Follow-up: Have students compare with situation in the U.S.

NOTES CULTURELLES

«Une petite maison à la campagne»

La vie urbaine

L'article précédent ainsi qu'un° récent sondage d'opinion indique que la criminalité augmente et que les Français ont l'impression d'être moins en sécurité qu'autrefois. Mais quand on leur demande quelles mesures ils seraient prêts à prendre pour se protéger, on découvre que, contrairement aux Américains, très peu d'entre eux possèdent une arme à feu.° Ceux qui en ont une indiquent qu'ils hésiteraient beaucoup à l'utiliser pour se protéger.

Selon les sociologues, la violence est liée° à la densité de la population urbaine et aux tensions croissantes° qui en résultent. Pour échapper à ces tensions, de plus en plus de Français rêvent d'avoir une petite maison à la campagne pour y passer leurs vacances et leurs week-ends et peut-être pour y prendre leur retraite. Certains tournent même catégoriquement le dos à la société urbaine.

Ce sont cependant des exceptions. Malgré tous les problèmes de la vie urbaine, la ville continue à exercer un attrait considérable grâce aux° avantages qu'elle offre—diversité de l'emploi, divertissements,° style de vie. La tendance générale de la population française continue donc à être un mouvement de migration de la campagne vers les villes. Les sociologues appellent ce phénomène «l'exode rural».

ainsi qu'un *as well as*   arme à feu *firearm*   liée *linked*
croissantes *growing*   grâce aux *thanks to*
divertissements *entertainment*

Et vous?

The results of the original survey are included here for class discussion if desired.

Vous sentez-vous en sécurité? Les questions suivantes ont été posées aux Français pour savoir s'ils se sentaient en sécurité. Répondez vous-même à ces questions et comparez vos réponses à celles des autres étudiants.

1. Personnellement, vous sentez-vous plus, autant ou moins en sécurité qu'avant?
    —moins   67%
    —autant   26%
    —plus   4%
    —sans opinion 3%

2. Diriez-vous que la police fait bien son travail ou ne fait pas bien son travail?
    —Elle fait bien son travail.   57%
    —Elle ne fait pas bien son travail. 33%
    —sans opinion   10%

3. Si la police ne fait pas bien son travail, est-ce parce qu'elle est trop sévère ou parce qu'elle n'est pas assez sévère?
    —pas assez sévère   24%
    —trop sévère   3%
    —sans opinion   6%

4. Pour assurer votre sécurité possédez-vous . . .

	oui	non	
—un *fusil de chasse*?			hunting rifle
—un *chien de garde*?	23%	77%	watchdog
—une *matraque*?	21%	79%	club
—un *revolver*?	6%	94%	
—un *coffre-fort*?	6%	94%	safe
—un *signal d'alarme*?	3%	97%	
	1%	99%	

5. La justice distingue deux types de délinquance: la grande délinquance (crimes violents) et la petite délinquance (vandalisme et *vols*). Par quel type de délinquance pensez-vous être le plus menacé?   thefts (**voler** = *to steal*)
    —la grande délinquance   19%
    —la petite délinquance   44%
    —les deux également   23%
    —ni l'une ni l'autre   12%
    —sans opinion   2%

6. Il y a aujourd'hui une augmentation de la criminalité. Quelles sont, à votre avis, les deux raisons principales de ce phénomène?
    —Les gens n'ont plus le sens de l'autorité ou de la discipline. 44%
    —le chômage des jeunes 40%
    —les conditions de la vie moderne, spécialement dans les centres urbains 39% 28%
    —Il n'y a pas assez d'agents de police. 18% 15%
    —la libéralisation de la moralité 10%
    —les juges ne punissent pas assez sévèrement les *coupables*   guilty parties
    —la présence d'un grand nombre de travailleurs étrangers

7. Si votre sécurité était menacée, seriez-vous prêt(e) à avoir recours à la violence pour vous *défendre*?   defend
    —non   88%
    —oui   6%
    —sans opinion 6%

⚜ Les verbes *plaire* et *manquer*

Présentation

As you have already seen, **manquer** *(to miss)* can be used with a direct object (e.g., **manquer son train**—*to miss one's train*). **Manquer** can also mean "to miss" in the sense of being unhappy away from someone or something that is dear to you. The construction in this case is similar to that of the verb **plaire à** *(to be pleasing to, to be liked by)*, which is often used in place of **aimer**.

Notice the particular way these verbs are used and how the word order is the opposite of that of English:

Cette ville me plaît.	*I like this city.* (literally: this city is pleasing to me)
Cette voiture plaît à ma femme.	*My wife likes this car.* (literally: this car is pleasing to my wife).
Mes amis me manquent.	*I miss my friends.* (literally: my friends are lacking to me)

Although the verb **manquer** is a regular **-er** verb, **plaire** (and its opposite **déplaire**) are irregular verbs:

plaire	
je **plais**	nous **plaisons**
tu **plais**	vous **plaisez**
il/elle/on **plaît**	ils/elles **plaisent**
passé composé: j'ai plu	

Point out to students that **plaire** is most commonly used in the third-person singular and plural in the "to be pleasing to" construction.

Point out that **manquer** can also mean *to lack* or *not to be enough of* (e.g., **Il manque de tact; Nous manquons d'argent.**).

Est-ce que cette idée te plaît?	*Do you like this idea?*
Qu'est-ce qui te manque?	*What do you miss? (What do you need?)*
Est-ce que ça vous plairait d'aller faire un tour en ville?	*Would you like going for a walk in town?*
Qu'est-ce qui te manquerait le plus si tu devais habiter dans un pays étranger?	*What would you miss the most if you had to live in a foreign country?*
Pendant notre séjour aux États-Unis, le pain français nous a beaucoup manqué. Mais la vie américaine nous a beaucoup plu.	*During our stay in the United States, we missed French bread a lot. But we liked American life very much.*
Ce film ne m'a pas plu.	*I did not like this film.*
Nos amis ne lui plaisent pas.	*She/he does not like our friends.*

Se taire *(to keep quiet, to become silent)* is conjugated like **plaire** except that there is no circumflex in the **il/elle/on** form of the present tense.

Taisez-vous!	*Be quiet!*
Dites aux enfants de se taire.	*Tell the children to keep quiet.*
Il ne se tait jamais.	*He never keeps quiet.*

Substitution: (1) Ils ont manqué la classe. le train / l'autobus / une bonne occasion / l'avion. (2) Est-ce que vous lui avez manqué? tu / je / nous / ses amis.
Transformation: Marie aime le jazz → Le jazz lui plaît. (1) Sa sœur aime les tableaux de Gauguin. (2) Jean aime beaucoup les films italiens. (3) Nous aimons la marche à pied. (4) Est-ce que tu aimes tes cours? (5) Paul aimait son travail. (6) Vos amis ont aimé leur voyage. (7) Nous n'avons pas aimé ce concert. (8) Vous aimeriez ces disques. (9) Ils n'ont pas aimé ce livre.

Préparation

Dépaysement. Patrick a choisi de faire son service militaire dans la coopération. Il a été envoyé à l'Île de la Réunion où il travaille comme ingénieur agricole. Il parle de ce qu'il aime et de ce qui lui manque. Qu'est-ce qu'il dit?

> In France, as an alternative to traditional military service, one may *faire son service militaire dans la coopération*, i.e., by working as a technical adviser, teacher, etc., in a former colony with which France has retained close ties or in a developing country.

Modèle   sa nouvelle vie → **Ma nouvelle vie me plaît beaucoup.**

> Repeat with lui (e.g., **Sa nouvelle vie lui plaît beaucoup.**). Repeat in negative (e.g., **Sa nouvelle vie ne lui plaît pas beaucoup.**).

1. le climat
2. les plages
3. son travail
4. les gens avec qui il travaille
5. la cuisine créole
6. le mode de la vie

Modèle   la visite de l'île → **La visite de l'île m'a particulièrement plu.**

> Repeat with lui.

1. son premier Noël sous les Tropiques
2. le voyage qu'il a fait à l'Île Maurice
3. les contacts qu'il a eus avec les gens du pays
4. les promenades qu'il a faites à l'intérieur de l'Île
5. les maisons dans lesquelles il est entré
6. les gens qu'il a rencontrés

Modèle   son chien → **Mon chien me manque un peu.**

> Repeat with lui (**Son chien lui manque un peu.**). Repeat in passé composé (**Son chien lui a manqué un peu.**).

1. sa famille
2. ses amis de France
3. la cuisine de sa mère
4. sa voiture
5. son village
6. les repas en famille

Communication

A. Interview. Demandez à un(e) autre étudiant(e) son opinion sur les choses suivantes.

Exemple   la vie à l'université → **Est-ce que la vie à l'université te plaît?**

1. les cours qu'il/elle suit ce trimestre
2. ceux qu'il/elle a suivis le trimestre passé
3. les films qu'il/elle a vus récemment
4. le dernier livre qu'il/elle a lu
5. la cuisine française
6. l'idée de passer une année dans un pays étranger
7. la vie à la campagne
8. la vie dans une grande ville
9. ?

B. Votre vie à l'université. Qu'est-ce qui vous plaît? Qu'est-ce qui vous manque? Est-ce que la vie d'étudiant vous manquera quand vous quitterez l'université? Si oui, qu'est-ce qui vous manquera?

> **Exemple**   Mes cours et mes professeurs me plaisent assez, mais ma famille me manque beaucoup.

C. Les rêves ne coûtent pas cher. Imaginez que vous avez l'occasion de passer une année en France (ou à l'Île de la Réunion, si vous préférez!). À votre avis, qu'est-ce qui vous plairait? Qu'est-ce qui vous manquerait?

⚜ Le subjonctif avec les verbes de volition, d'émotion et de doute

Présentation

The subjunctive is used after certain verbs and expressions indicating that the action or condition of the second clause is not a definite fact. Thus, the use of the subjunctive is not always a question of rigid grammatical rules; it is partly a matter of the meaning or feeling the speaker wants to convey.

A. The subjunctive is always used following verbs or expressions of wanting or wishing (**vouloir, désirer, préférer, aimer mieux,** etc.).

> Other verbs in this category are **accepter** and **permettre**, which are generally used in the negative, and **vouloir bien**.

Je veux que vous soyez très prudent.	*I want you to be very careful.*
Elle ne veut pas que tu sortes seule le soir.	*She doesn't want you to go out alone at night.*
Nous voudrions qu'il y ait moins de violence à la télévision.	*We wish there were less violence on television.*
Jeannette et Daniel préfèrent que nous les accompagnions.	*Jeannette and Daniel prefer that we accompany them.*
J'aimerais mieux que vous ne marchiez pas sur la pelouse.	*I prefer that you not walk on the lawn.*
Il est préférable que vous finissiez vos devoirs immédiatement.	*It is preferable that you finish your homework immediately.*

B. The subjunctive is always used following verbs or expressions of emotion (**avoir peur, être content, regretter, être triste, être surpris,** etc.).

J'ai peur qu'il ait un accident.	*I'm afraid that he might have an accident.*
Il regrette que nous ne puissions pas y aller.	*He is sorry that we can't go.*
Tout le monde est content qu'il soit en prison.	*Everyone is happy that he is in prison.*
Les amis de Charles sont tristes qu'il ne leur écrive plus.	*Charles' friends are sad that he doesn't write to them anymore.*
Il est surpris que je ne veuille pas faire ça.	*He is surprised that I don't want to do that.*

C. The subjunctive is used following verbs or expressions of uncertainty or doubt.

Je doute qu'ils viennent.	*I doubt that they're coming.*
Je ne crois pas que tu le saches.	*I don't believe that you know it.*
Ne penses-tu pas que la situation soit grave?	*Don't you think the situation is serious?*
Je ne suis pas sûr qu'ils comprennent.	*I'm not sure they understand.*

Croire and **penser** are followed by the subjunctive only when used in the negative and interrogative—that is, when doubt is implied. Compare:

Je crois qu'il viendra.	Je ne crois pas qu'il vienne.
Tu penses qu'il y a trop de violence à la télévision.	Penses-tu qu'il y ait trop de violence à la télévision?

The verb **espérer** is never followed by the subjunctive.

Nous espérons que vous serez en sécurité.

D. The subjunctive is used only when the subject of the first clause is not the same as the subject of the second clause. When there is only one subject, an infinitive is used rather than the subjunctive. Compare the following sentences:

Suggestion: Point out that **croire** and **penser** can be followed by a second clause in which the subject is the same as the main clause.

Mon père veut que je finisse mes études.	Je veux finir mes études.
Elle est contente que nous partions.	Elle est contente de partir.

Substitution: (1) Je préfère que vous alliez à la banque maintenant. je veux / je ne crois pas / je doute / j'aimerais mieux / je regrette / je suis surpris. (2) Elle est triste que vous soyez malade. elle ne pense pas / elle n'est pas sûre / elle ne veut pas / elle est surprise. (3) Est-ce que vous regrettez que Lucien ne puisse pas venir? est-ce que vous êtes content / est-ce que vous êtes surpris / est-ce que vous avez peur / est-ce que vous êtes triste. (4) Nous croyons que les ouvriers feront grève. nous ne croyons pas / nous ne pensons pas / nous sommes certains / nous ne sommes pas sûrs / nous doutons / nous espérons / nous sommes surpris.

Préparation

A. Opinions. Paul Lefranc donne ses opinions sur la société actuelle. Reconstituez les phrases qu'il a prononcées.

Follow-up: Form complete sentences and read as paragraph for listening practice.

Modèle je crois / il y aura toujours des guerres → **Je crois qu'il y aura toujours des guerres.**

1. je suis content / on construit des centres de ré-éducation pour les criminels
2. je regrette / nous vendons des armes aux autres pays
3. je suis triste / certaines espèces sont en train de disparaître
4. je ne crois pas / on punit les criminels assez sévèrement
5. j'espère / le gouvernement prendra des mesures énergiques contre le terrorisme
6. je ne crois pas / nous pouvons résoudre tous nos problèmes

B. Est-ce que vous vous sentez en sécurité? Un reporter a demandé à différents groupes de Français de dire s'ils sont d'accord ou pas avec les phrases suivantes. Répondez selon les indications données.

Modèle   Les gens sont plus en sécurité aujourd'hui qu'autrefois. (je ne crois pas) → **Je ne crois pas que les gens soient plus en sécurité qu'autrefois.**

1. La police fait bien son travail. (nous ne sommes pas sûrs)
2. Il y a assez d'agents de police. (mes parents ne pensent pas)
3. Les gens ont peur de sortir seuls le soir. (c'est triste)
4. Les jeunes sont responsables de la violence. (je ne crois pas)
5. Les juges sont trop sévères. (nous pensons)
6. Il va y avoir des manifestations dans les rues. (nous croyons)
7. On ne peut pas se sentir en sécurité. (c'est dommage)
8. On ne pourra pas résoudre ce problème. (j'ai peur)

C. Différences d'opinion. Jean-Luc et ses parents ne sont pas toujours d'accord. Qu'est-ce qu'il dit?

Modèle   aller à l'université de Strasbourg / aller à l'université de Lille → **Moi, je voudrais aller à l'université de Strasbourg mais mes parents voudraient que j'aille à l'université de Lille.**

1. louer un appartement / habiter dans une résidence universitaire
2. acheter une moto / utiliser mon vieux vélo
3. apprendre à conduire / prendre des leçons de piano
4. inviter souvent mes amis / inviter mes amis seulement pendant les week-ends
5. faire des études de médecine / faire des études de droit
6. sortir tous les soirs / sortir moins souvent
7. choisir des cours intéressants / suivre des cours plus pratiques
8. m'amuser / être plus sérieux

Communication

A. Et vous? Et vous, avez-vous des différences d'opinion avec des personnes de votre entourage (amis, camarades de chambre, professeurs, etc.)? Si oui, lesquelles?

Exemple   Moi, je voudrais étudier la musique mais mes parents voudraient que j'étudie l'informatique.

B. Êtes-vous d'accord? Êtes-vous d'accord avec les opinions exprimées? Indiquez votre opinion en commençant la phrase avec *je crois, je suis sûr(e), je ne suis pas sûr(e)*, ou *je doute*, selon le cas.

Exemple   Les femmes sont aussi violentes que les hommes → **Je crois que les femmes sont aussi violentes que les hommes.** ou **Je ne crois pas que les femmes soient aussi violentes que les hommes.**

1. Les jeunes savent exactement ce qu'ils veulent dans la vie.
2. Les syndicats ouvriers ont trop d'influence.

Options: (1) Written. (2) Oral—read statements or ask as questions. Encourage students to explain their answers.

3. Les jeunes sont bien préparés pour la vie.
4. Les ouvriers font grève trop souvent.
5. Nous entrons dans une période de grande prospérité économique.
6. Les parents donnent trop de liberté à leurs enfants.
7. Les vieilles traditions sont en train de disparaître.
8. Les journalistes disent toujours la vérité.
9. On doit continuer à construire des centrales nucléaires.

C. Questions/interview. Répondez aux questions suivantes ou utilisez-les pour interviewer un(e) autre étudiant(e).   Suggested for class discussion.

1. Penses-tu que la violence soit un des principaux problèmes de notre société?
2. Crois-tu qu'il existe un rapport entre la violence à la télévision et la délinquance juvénile?
3. Penses-tu qu'on doive mettre les délinquants en prison?
4. Penses-tu qu'on puisse réhabiliter les criminels?
5. Penses-tu qu'on ait le droit de condamner quelqu'un à mort?
6. Voudrais-tu que les criminels soient punis plus sévèrement?
7. As-tu peur de traverser le campus le soir?
8. Penses-tu que les gens prennent assez de précautions pour se protéger contre les criminels?
9. Crois-tu qu'on doive interdire la possession de revolvers?

⚜   La forme passive

Présentation

A sentence in the passive voice is one in which the subject is acted upon: *A pedestrian was hit by a car.* This contrasts with a sentence in the active voice, in which case the subject performs the action: *A car hit a pedestrian.*

   The passive voice in French is formed by adding the past participle to the appropriate tense of **être.** The past participle agrees in number and gender with the subject.   Option: May be taught for recognition only.

Les magasins sont ouverts tous les jours.
L'Opéra de Paris a été construit entre 1862 et 1874.
Les résultats seront annoncés demain.
Il faut que ce travail soit fini avant midi.
Ils ont été séparés de leur famille.
Toutes les plantes ont été mangées par des insectes.

A. The tense of **être** in the passive construction is the same as the tense of the verb in the corresponding active form. Compare:

Active	Passive
On a arrêté le voleur.	Le voleur a été arrêté.
On arrêtera le voleur.	Le voleur sera arrêté.
On arrêterait le voleur.	Le voleur serait arrêté.
Il faut qu'on arrête le voleur.	Il faut que le voleur soit arrêté.

B. The passive voice is used less frequently in French than in English. When the agent (performer of the action) is known, French speakers often prefer to use the active voice instead of saying that an action has been completed by (**par**) an agent. Compare:

| **Passive** | **Active** |
| Le criminel a été arrêté par la police. | La police a arrêté le criminel. |

C. When there is no specific agent mentioned, French speakers often avoid the passive voice by using the impersonal pronouns **on** and **ils**. Compare:

Passive	**Active**	
Le criminel a été arrêté.	On a arrêté le criminel.	You may wish to point out that, in
	Ils ont arrêté le criminel.	contrast to **on**, **ils** generally refers to persons in authority.

The passive voice is very commonly used, however, in newspaper headlines, police reports, and other such documents.

D. Note that **dire** cannot be used in the passive voice: **On m'a dit que ton vélo a été volé** (*I was told that your bike was stolen.*).

Transformation: Modèle: Ma voiture a été volée → On a volé ma voiture. (1) La maison a été vendue. (2) Les cambrioleurs ont été arrêtés. (3) L'appartement ne sera pas loué. (4) De bons résultats ont été obtenus. (5) Aucune décision n'a été prise. Modèle: On a ouvert un nouveau magasin. → Un nouveau magasin a été ouvert. (1) On a volé ma bicyclette. (2) On a puni les enfants. (3) On a coupé les arbres. (4) On n'a jamais exploré cette région. (5) On a construit un nouvel aéroport.

Préparation

A. Au poste de police. Beaucoup de choses sont arrivées aujourd'hui. Qu'est-ce que les agents de police vont dire dans leur rapport?

Modèle   On a volé une voiture. → **Une voiture a été volée.**

1. On a arrêté les cambrioleurs.
2. On n'a jamais retrouvé le coupable.
3. On a volé les papiers de ce monsieur.
4. On a condamné le criminel à 15 ans de prison.
5. On a puni le coupable.
6. On a transporté la victime à l'hôpital.
7. On a cambriolé trois magasins.
8. On a prévenu le propriétaire.

B. Titres de journaux. Un rédacteur est en train de préparer les titres pour chacun des événements suivants. Aidez-le dans ce travail.

Modèle   Une compagnie américaine a acheté l'usine Grandjean. → **L'usine Grandjean a été achetée par une compagnie américaine.**

1. On a cambriolé l'appartement de la célèbre actrice Catherine Lenoir.
2. On a assassiné un diplomate étranger en visite officielle dans la capitale.
3. Des hommes habiteront sur la planète Mars en l'an 2050.
4. On va signer un accord entre les différents pays du Marché commun.
5. Le gouvernement a nommé une commission pour étudier le problème de la violence.
6. On a enlevé le fils du directeur d'une banque.

Communication

A. Vos débuts dans le journalisme. Maintenant c'est à vous de créer des titres de journaux au sujet d'événements réels ou imaginaires qui ont eu lieu dans votre ville ou dans votre université. Vous pouvez également créer des titres pour des événements historiques, réels ou imaginaires, passés ou futurs. Utilisez le passif dans vos titres.

Exemple   Le bureau d'un professeur a été occupé par des étudiants mécontents.

Suggested for individual or small-group writing.

B. Testez vos connaissance. Qui est responsable des découvertes et inventions suivantes?

Exemple   Qui a découvert le radium? → **Le radium a été découvert par Madame Curie.**

h   1. Qui a écrit «De la démocratie en Amérique»?

d   2. Qui a peint «Le Déjeuner sur l'herbe»?

e   3. Qui a sculpté la Statue de la Liberté?

i   4. Qui a découvert l'Amérique?

g   5. Qui a inventé le cinématographe?

c   6. Qui a découvert le radium?

j   7. Qui a fondé la ville de la Nouvelle-Orléans?

a   8. Qui a vendu la Louisiane aux États-Unis?

b   9. Qui a dessiné les plans de la ville de Washington?

f   10. Qui a aidé les Américains dans leur lutte pour leur indépendance?

a. Napoléon
b. L'Enfant
c. Madame Curie
d. Manet
e. Bartholdi
f. Lafayette
g. les frères Lumière
h. Alexis de Tocqueville
i. Christophe Colomb
j. Jean Baptiste Lemoyne

Les livres français aux Etats-Unis. Lesquels se vendent?

LA PRESENCE CULTURELLE FRANCAISE EN AMERIQUE

⚜ Autres emplois du subjonctif

Option: May be taught for recognition only.

Présentation

A. The subjunctive is used after certain conjunctions, the most important of which are:

à condition que *on the condition that*   jusqu'à ce que *until*
afin que *so that*   pour que *so that*
à moins que *unless*   pourvu que *provided that*
avant que *before*   sans que *without*
bien que *although*

Bien que la violence soit un problème, ce n'est pas le problème le plus important.
J'ai étudié la question afin que nous puissions prendre une décision.
Il sera condamné à moins qu'on puisse prouver son innocence.
Nous attendrons ici jusqu'à ce que Josette vienne.

Note that as with previous uses of the subjunctive, the subjects of both clauses must be different; otherwise, a preposition (**à condition de, afin de, avant, pour, sans**) and an infinitive would be used. Compare:

Je ferai cela **avant que vous partiez.**   Je ferai cela **avant de partir.**

Exceptions to this rule are **bien que, jusqu'à ce que**, and **pourvu que**, with which the subjects of both clauses may be the same.

Je vais continuer à travailler bien que j'aie envie de m'arrêter.
Nous chercherons jusqu'à ce que nous trouvions le coupable.

B. The subjunctive is used after a noun modified by a superlative or after **le seul, le dernier**, or **le premier** when judgment or uniqueness is implied.

C'est la personne la plus fascinante que je connaisse.
C'est le crime le plus horrible qui soit.
C'est le seul journal que je lise tous les jours.
C'est la seule chose que je ne puisse pas pardonner.
Tu es le meilleur ami qu'on puisse avoir.

C. The subjunctive is used after a noun or pronoun representing something or someone that is not yet identified or found.

Je cherche quelqu'un qui puisse faire ce travail.
Il me faut une auto qui soit très confortable.
Y a-t-il quelqu'un qui sache la réponse?
Il n'y a rien qui me plaise dans ce magasin.

Have students list those expressions requiring the subjunctive and those requiring the indicative.

Substitution: (1) *Je* continuerai jusqu'à ce que *je* réussisse. tu / vous / nous / cet étudiant. **(2)** *Nous* viendrons demain pourvu que *nous* ayons le temps. mes amis / vous / tu / je. **(3)** C'est le seul disque que nous ayons. le meilleur / le premier / le plus beau / le plus mauvais. **(4)** Il y a quelqu'un qui peut le faire. y a-t-il quelqu'un / il n'y a personne / je connais quelqu'un / je ne connais personne / c'est la seule personne.

Préparation

A. Projets. On ne peut pas toujours être sûr de ses projets. Qu'est-ce que Monsieur Humbert dit?

Modèle   Nous irons en Bretagne s'il ne pleut pas. → **Nous irons en Bretagne à moins qu'il pleuve.**

1. On voyagera en train s'il n'y a pas de grève.
2. Nous arriverons mardi si nous ne sommes pas retardés.
3. Ma femme ira voir sa tante si elle n'est pas trop fatiguée.
4. Les enfants viendront avec nous s'ils ne vont pas en colonie de vacances.
5. Nous ferons des promenades en bateau s'il ne fait pas mauvais.
6. On rentrera à Paris à la fin du mois si je ne peux rester plus longtemps.
7. Je serai obligé de rentrer si je ne réussis pas à persuader mon patron.

B. Opinions. Au cours d'une discussion entre amis, les opinions suivantes ont été exprimées. Utilisez les suggestions suivantes pour retrouver ce qui a été dit.

Modèle   Ils sont heureux. Ils sont pauvres. (bien que) → **Ils sont heureux bien qu'ils soient pauvres.**

1. Il faut prendre le temps de vivre. Il est trop tard. (avant que)
2. Les gens sont généreux. Ça ne leur coûte rien. (à condition que)
3. Il faut essayer. On réussit. (jusqu'à ce que)
4. Ce député a de bonnes idées. Il n'est pas très intelligent. (bien que)
5. On ne peut rien faire. Quelqu'un vous demande pourquoi. (sans que)
6. Il a dit ça. Tu te mets en colère. (pour que)

Communication

Nuances. L'utilisation du subjonctif et de certaines conjonctions peuvent vous permettre de nuancer vos pensées. Par exemple, au lieu de dire simplement *J'ai faim*, vous pouvez dire, *J'ai encore faim bien que je vienne de déjeuner*. Inspirez-vous de cet exemple pour compléter les phrases suivantes.   Suggested for writing.

1. L'année prochaine je _____ à moins que _____
2. Je ne peux pas _____ sans que quelqu'un _____
3. J'aimerais rencontrer quelqu'un qui _____
4. On peut toujours se débrouiller pourvu que _____
5. Je ne connais personne qui _____
6. Les professeurs sont indulgents pourvu que _____
7. La science et la technologie peuvent nous aider à condition que _____
8. Il faut trouver de nouvelles sources d'énergie pour que _____

SYNTHÈSE

Ceux qui ont dit non

Christian et Monique
Christian et Monique ont décidé de quitter la ville pour aller vivre à
la campagne.

«Il y a sept ans, raconte Christian, j'étais avocat et ma femme était
professeur. Nous avions un très joli appartement à Paris. Un jour, en
nous promenant dans la campagne, nous avons trouvé une vieille ferme
qui était *à vendre.* Nous l'avons achetée pour aller y passer les week-   for sale
ends. Pendant l'été nous avons commencé à la réparer avec l'aide de
quelques amis qui, eux aussi, *en avaient marre* des *embouteillages*   were fed up / traffic jams
parisiens. On était heureux ici, on a eu envie de rester et c'est ce qu'on
a fait.

Et puis aussi, ma femme et moi, nous voulions avoir des enfants,
mais nous ne voulions pas qu'ils grandissent dans l'atmosphère stérile
et *déprimante* d'une ville. Nous voulions qu'ils puissent grandir libres   depressing
et heureux, qu'ils apprennent en regardant vivre les gens et les *bêtes*   animals
autour d'eux. Nous voulions qu'ils sachent que le travail peut être un
plaisir si on aime ce qu'on fait. Ici, nous produisons presque tout ce
dont nous avons besoin et *au lieu de* vendre nos produits nous faisons   instead of
des échanges avec nos voisins. Nous redécouvrons la joie du travail et,
en même temps, la joie de vivre.»

Sylviane

Sylviane, elle, voudrait vivre dans une *communauté* urbaine.

 «Moi, dit-elle, je voudrais vivre dans une communauté, mais pas tout de suite. Je veux d'abord terminer mes études. Mes parents voudraient que je me marie, que j'aie des enfants et que j'aille habiter dans une banlieue tranquille. Mais ce genre de vie n'est pas pour moi. Je veux que ma vie serve à quelque chose.

 Personnellement, j'aimerais bien vivre à la campagne, mais je pense que c'est dans les villes que l'avenir du monde va être décidé. Je ne pense pas que nous ayons le droit d'abandonner ces décisions aux politiciens. Mais il est *également* important que nous apprenions à vivre et à lutter *ensemble*.»

commune

equally

together

Marie-Hélène

Marie-Hélène, elle, est fille de *cultivateurs*. Elle a quitté la ferme pour aller faire ses études en ville, mais maintenant, elle a décidé de revenir au village pour *prendre la succession de* son père.

 «Les gens ne croient pas que je puisse m'occuper d'une ferme parce que je suis une femme, dit-elle. Mais je suis en bonne santé et je n'ai pas peur de travailler dur. *D'ailleurs*, une femme peut conduire un tracteur tout aussi bien qu'un homme. Et puis, à la campagne, on a besoin de gens jeunes, enthousiastes et ouverts aux idées nouvelles. Mais dans la plupart des petits villages, surtout dans les régions où le *sol* n'est pas très riche, il n'y a que les vieux qui restent. Et les jeunes, eux, n'ont qu'une envie: quitter la ferme et aller vivre en ville où la vie es   s facile. Moi aussi, surtout avec les études que j'ai faites, je pourra   ir une bonne situation en ville, mais je doute que ma vie y soit plus heureuse ou plus utile qu'ici.

 Je ne regrette pourtant pas d'avoir fait des études. Le baccalauréat, *à quoi ça sert?* me direz-vous. Je crois que les choses que j'ai apprises à l'école pourront m'être utiles ici. Et même si elles ne sont pas directement utiles, je ne crois pas que ce soit une perte de temps. Il est toujours bon qu'une personne soit aussi *cultivée* que possible. Je crois que c'est surtout pour ça que mes parents voulaient que je fasse des études; pour ça et pour que j'aie la liberté de choisir ce que je voudrais vraiment. Ils ne voulaient pas m'influencer, mais maintenant ils sont bien contents que je revienne au village. Et moi aussi.»

farmers

to take over from

besides

soil

what good is it?

cultured, educated

Michel

Le père de Michel voulait que son fils fasse des études de droit et qu'il prenne ensuite sa succession à la tête de la compagnie qu'il *dirige*. Au début, Michel ne s'y est pas opposé, mais maintenant il a des doutes.

 «*J'ai fait mon droit* parce que mon père le voulait. Mais je ne suis pas sûr que ce soit ce que je veux vraiment. Je pourrais gagner beaucoup d'argent, c'est vrai, mais je ne suis pas sûr d'être *taillé* pour ce rôle. Le commerce m'ennuie. Ma véritable vocation, c'est l'*enseignement*. Je sais bien que c'est un travail difficile et mal payé, mais dans la vie, ce qui compte c'est de faire un métier qu'on aime. Mais j'ai peur que mes parents soient terriblement *déçus*. C'est *bête* d'ailleurs, parce que ma sœur, elle, s'intéresse aux *affaires* et je suis sûr qu'elle serait bien plus capable que moi de diriger une compagnie. Mais mon père ne veut pas *en entendre parler*. Il va falloir que nous essayions de le persuader.»

directs, runs

I studied law

cut out

teaching

disappointed / stupid

business

to hear about it

Compréhension   Répondez aux questions suivantes selon les renseignements donnés dans le texte.

1. Qu'est-ce que Christian et Monique faisaient avant d'aller vivre à la campagne?

2. Pourquoi ont-ils décidé de quitter Paris?

3. Qu'est ce qui leur plaît dans leur nouvelle vie?

4. Qu'est ce que les parents de Sylviane voulaient qu'elle fasse?

5. Et elle, que veut-elle faire de sa vie?

6. Pourquoi Marie-Hélène a-t-elle décidé de revenir à la ferme quand la plupart des autres jeunes quittent la campagne?

7. Pourquoi Marie-Hélène ne regrette-t-elle pas d'avoir fait des études?

8. Quel conflit existe-t-il entre les désirs de Michel et ceux de son père?

9. En quoi Michel et sa sœur sont-ils différents l'un de l'autre?

Option: Have students describe briefly one or several of the people presented.

NOTES CULTURELLES

Ceux qui ont dit non

Les Français pour qui l'individualisme est une vertu (bien qu'ils soient souvent assez conformistes dans leur vie de tous les jours) ont une admiration particulière pour ceux qui ont eu le courage de dire non. Que ce° soit dans le domaine des arts, de la politique ou de la science, il y a eu au cours des siècles des hommes et des femmes qui ont eu le courage de mettre en question les idées établies. Ainsi,° dans le domaine scientifique, la ténacité de Pasteur a ouvert la voie° à la biologie moderne. Dans le domaine artistique des peintres tels que° Cézanne et Matisse ont révolutionné notre sensibilité° artistique. À la

fin du siècle dernier, l'écrivain° Émile Zola s'est opposé à l'antisémitisme voilé° du gouvernement en prenant la défense de Dreyfus dans sa célèbre lettre intitulée «J'accuse . . . ».

Quelquefois ce sont les gens humbles et obscurs qui ont changé le cours de l'histoire. C'est le cas, par exemple, de la petite paysanne Jeanne d'Arc qui a su persuader le roi de lui confier° une armée pour aller défendre la France contre les Anglais. Plus récemment, il y a l'exemple des milliers de Français qui, pendant l'occupation allemande, ont répondu à l'appel du Général de Gaulle et ont lutté dans la Résistance, même quand tout semblait perdu.

que ce *whether it*   ainsi *thus*   voie *way*   tels que *such as*   sensibilité *sensitivity*

écrivain *writer*   voilé *veiled*   confier *give*

Communication

A. Choix et décisions

Options: Use for written composition or class discussion.

1. Que pensez-vous des décisions prises par chacune des personnes décrites dans «Ceux qui ont dit non»? Si vous vous trouviez dans les mêmes situations qu'eux, que feriez-vous?

2. Est-ce que vous préférez la vie à la ville ou la vie à la campagne? Quels sont les avantages et les inconvénients de l'une et de l'autre?

3. Est-ce que vous faites toujours ce qu'on vous demande ou est-ce que vous avez tendance à prendre vos propres décisions? Y a-t-il eu des

situations dans votre vie où vos désirs et ceux de quelqu'un d'autre étaient opposés? Décrivez brièvement une ou plusieurs de ces situations.

4. Connaissez-vous des gens qui ont dit non? (personnages historiques ou contemporains ou quelqu'un que vous connaissez personnellement) Qu'est-ce qu'ils ont fait?

B. **Vivent les différences!** Nous avons tous des opinions, des préférences et des valeurs différentes en ce qui concerne les petites choses aussi bien que les grandes. Quelles sont les vôtres? Complétez les phrases suivantes selon vos préférences et convictions personnelles.

Follow-up: Have students compare and contrast their opinions.

1. Je crois que . . .
2. Je ne pense pas que . . .
3. Je suis content(e) que . . .
4. Je regrette que . . .
5. Je voudrais que . . .
6. Je ne voudrais pas que . . .
7. J'ai peur que . . .
8. Je doute que . . .
9. J'espère que . . .

C. **Que faire?** Chacune des personnes suivantes se trouve devant un choix difficile. Que leur conseillez-vous?

Option: Use for listening.

1. Alain est étudiant en psychologie. Il a besoin d'étudier parce qu'il y a un examen important demain. Mais sa femme voudrait qu'ils aillent au cinéma ensemble. Elle travaille dans un hôpital et c'est la seule soirée libre qu'elle a cette semaine. Son fils, lui, voudrait qu'il répare son vélo. Et lui, il aimerait bien regarder un match de football à la télévision. À votre avis, que vaudrait-il mieux qu'il fasse?

2. Janine voudrait être architecte et pour y arriver il faudra qu'elle fasse encore cinq années d'études. Son fiancé Jérôme voudrait qu'ils se marient tout de suite et qu'ils aient des enfants. Que lui conseillez-vous?

3. Solange cherche du travail depuis plusieurs mois. Une compagnie située à cinq cents kilomètres de chez elle vient de lui téléphoner pour lui offrir un rendez-vous demain à dix heures. Le travail qu'on lui propose paraît très intéressant. Malheureusement, en ce moment sa sœur est à l'hôpital et Solange lui a promis de garder ses enfants âgés de deux et cinq ans pendant une semaine. Que doit-elle faire?

4. Christophe, un jeune Canadien de Toronto, voudrait faire des études de biologie marine et il pense que la meilleure université pour ce genre d'études est celle de Vancouver. D'un autre côté, il aimerait bien étudier dans une université de langue française et ses parents voudraient aussi qu'il ne soit pas trop loin de chez eux. À votre avis, que vaudrait-il mieux qu'il fasse?

5. Martine et Jean-Pierre sortent ensemble depuis plusieurs mois et ils s'aiment. Ils sont tous deux étudiants; lui a encore trois années d'études à faire et elle deux. Ils ont décidé de vivre ensemble, mais leurs parents ne pensent pas que ce soit une bonne idée de vivre ensemble sans être mariés. Le père de Martine est si opposé à cette idée qu'il menace de ne plus lui donner d'argent pour ses études. Que vaudrait-il mieux que Martine et Jean-Pierre fassent?

VOCABULAIRE

noms

les **affaires** (f)   *business*
la **bête**   *animal*
le **chien de garde**   *watchdog*
le **coffre-fort**   *safe*
la **communauté**   *commune*
° le **conflit**
le /la **coupable**   *guilty one*
le **cultivateur**   *farmer*
° la **délinquance**
l'**embouteillage** (m)   *traffic jam*
l'**enseignement** (m)   *teaching*
la **hauteur**   *height*
l'**immeuble** (m)   *building*
° l'**individu** (m)
le **moyen**   *means*
° la **spontanéité**
° le **vandalisme**
le **vol**   *theft*

verbes

s'apercevoir de   *to become aware of*
en avoir marre de   *to be fed up with*
° **contaminer**
défendre   *to defend*
déplaire   *to be displeasing to, to be disliked by*
diriger   *to direct, to run*
entendre parler de   *to hear about*
faire son droit   *to study law*
manquer   *to miss*
mériter   *to deserve*
nommer   *to appoint, to name*
plaire   *to be pleasing to, to be liked by*
rassurer   *to reassure*
se taire   *to keep quiet, to become silent*
tuer   *to kill*
violer   *to rape*

adjectifs

bête   *stupid*
° **condamné(e)**
cultivé(e)   *cultured, educated*
déçu(e)   *disappointed*
déprimant(e)   *depressing*
interdit(e)   *forbidden*
sourd(e)   *deaf*
taillé(e)   *cut out*
tenté(e)   *tempted*

adverbes

également   *equally*
ensemble   *together*

divers

conjonctions

à condition que   *on condition that*
afin que   *so that*
à moins que   *unless*
avant que   *before*
bien que   *although*
jusqu'à ce que   *until*
pour que   *so that*
pourvu que   *provided that*
sans que   *without*

d'autres expressions

à quoi ça sert?   *What good is it?*
à vendre   *for sale*
d'ailleurs   *besides*
il existe   *there exists*
tout comme   *just as*

21

À la recherche d'une identité

INTRODUCTION

Sur la *piste* des ancêtres

track, trail

—*Ça y est!* J'ai tué mon *arrière-grand-mère*!

That's it! / great-grandmother

—Et moi, j'arrive au 512!

Quelle joie pour les généalogistes amateurs d'employer le jargon des spécialistes. «Tuer un ancêtre», ça veut dire retrouver la date de sa mort. *Quant au chiffre* 512, il désigne la génération où nous avons 512

as for / number

411

ancêtres, c'est-à-dire la dixième génération. Et *puisqu*'on compte gé- | since
néralement trois générations par siècle, cela veut dire qu'on *est remonté* | has gone back to
à environ trois cent trente ans. C'est simple, n'est-ce pas?

Ce genre de dialogue s'entend de plus en plus à la sortie des salles
d'archives *départementales* et le nombre des généalogistes amateurs | departmental (France is divided into 95 **départements**.)
augmente de 20% par an. Pourquoi cet intérêt nouveau pour la gé-
néalogie?

«Autrefois, explique un des organisateurs d'un récent congrès international de généalogie, c'étaient seulement les aristocrates qui s'in-
téressaient à leur généalogie. C'était à la fois par *fierté* et pour profiter | pride
des avantages sociaux réservés aux nobles. Plus tard, au dix-neuvième
siècle, les *bourgeois* ont commencé à s'y intéresser aussi, pour essayer | members of the middle class
de trouver quelque ancêtre noble et ajouter une *particule* à leur nom. | *de* before a surname indicating nobility
C'était une généalogie de vanité.»

Aujourd'hui, il y a des gens de toutes les classes sociales qui
se passionnent pour la généalogie. Il y a pourtant encore bien des gens | are fascinated by
pour qui l'objectif plus ou moins *conscient* est de trouver parmi leurs | conscious
ancêtres quelque célébrité dont ils pourront être fiers d'être le descendant. Mais pour beaucoup de gens aussi, cet intérêt pour la généalogie
correspond à un besoin de retrouver leurs *racines*, leur place, leur iden- | roots
tité dans un monde caractérisé par le changement constant, la mobilité
professionnelle, l'insécurité sociale, la désintégration des familles et
l'isolement de l'individu. La généalogie offre une sorte de protection
contre toutes ces incertitudes. «Si nous ne savons pas où nous allons, au
moins nous savons d'où nous venons», disent les généalogistes. C'est
aussi une sorte d'affirmation de *soi*. Le succès du livre d'Alex Haley | oneself
intitulé *Racines*, qui raconte la saga d'un noir américain, reflète bien
le besoin d'établir et même de proclamer fièrement son identité ethnique, surtout pour les gens qui ont été si longtemps et si brutalement
coupés de leurs racines.

«Reconstruire son arbre généalogique n'offre *en soi* aucun intérêt, | in and of itself
dit Monsieur Roche, un des participants au congrès. Ce qui est passionnant, c'est de prendre un personnage, de reconstituer sa personnalité, de découvrir les événements qui ont influencé sa vie et de voir
comment il *a réagi* à ces événements.» Monsieur Roche a commencé à | reacted
s'intéresser à la généalogie il y a dix ans, après avoir acheté une vieille
ferme dans *le Jura*. Par curiosité, il a voulu connaître l'histoire de sa | mountainous region in eastern France / ended up by
maison et des gens qui habitaient là avant lui. Il *a fini par* écrire un
manuscrit de deux mille pages sur une famille qu'il ne connaissait même
pas. Ensuite, il s'est intéressé à sa propre famille et à celle de sa femme.

Ce n'est pas qu'en France qu'on essaie de retrouver la piste de ses
ancêtres. Les Québécois, eux aussi, se passionnent pour la généalogie.
Certains font même un voyage en France dans le seul but de venir
consulter les archives. L'institut généalogique Drouin de Montréal
possède 61 millions de *fiches* sur la population canadienne française. | file cards
Le grand *chic* est d'avoir au moins treize *trisaïeuls* nés dans «*la Belle* | fashion / great-great-grandparents / *i.e.*, Quebec Province / wool
Province». Cela donne droit à l'appellation de «Québécois pure *laine*».

Extrait et adapté d'articles de *L'Express* par Jacqueline Remy et Alain de Penanster.

Compréhension   Répondez aux questions suivantes selon les renseignements donnés dans le texte.

1. Que veut dire l'expression «tuer un ancêtre» pour un généalogiste?
2. Pourquoi un généalogiste est-il ravi «d'arriver au 512»?
3. Est-ce que l'intérêt pour la généalogie augmente ou diminue en France de nos jours?
4. Pourquoi est-ce qu'autrefois c'étaient seulement les nobles ou les bourgeois qui s'intéressaient à la généalogie?
5. Quelles sortes de gens s'intéressent maintenant à la généalogie?
6. Quelles sont les conditions sociales qui expliquent cet intérêt pour la généalogie?
7. De quoi le livre d'Alex Haley parle-t-il?
8. Qu'est-ce que Monsieur Roche trouve particulièrement intéressant dans la généalogie?
9. Quand et pourquoi a-t-il commencé à s'y intéresser?
10. Quel a été le résultat de ses recherches?
11. Comment un Québécois peut-il obtenir l'appellation de «Québécois pure laine»?

NOTES CULTURELLES

Le peuple français

Comparée à la population américaine, la population française paraît très homogène et très stable. Il n'est pas rare, en effet, qu'une famille ait vécu pendant plusieurs siècles dans le même village et même quelquefois dans la même maison.

On ne peut cependant° pas parler d'une «race» française car le peuple français est le résultat de l'assimilation de groupes ethniques très divers. En effet, la France étant située à la pointe occidentale de l'Europe, c'est là que les différentes migrations Est-Ouest se sont arrêtées. On peut donc dire que la France est le «melting pot» de l'Europe.

Aux temps préhistoriques, trois races différentes sont venues s'installer sur le sol français: (1) la race méditerranéenne composée de chasseurs et de nomades; (2) la race nordique dont les représentants sont grands et blonds; (3) la race alpine (les Celtes) composée surtout d'agriculteurs. Les Celtes qui se sont fixés sur le territoire français s'appelaient les Gaulois et leur pays, la Gaule.

Plus tard, d'autres invasions ont accentué encore la richesse ethnique et la variété de la population: les Romains au premier siècle

cependant *however*

avant J.-C.°; les Francs, d'origine germanique, arrivés au cinquième siècle et qui ont donné leur nom à la France; les Normands, d'orgine scandinave, au dixième siècle. Depuis un siècle, la France connaît de nouveau une importante immigration de travailleurs étrangers, surtout Nord-Africains et Italiens.

Parmi les noms «bien» français, on trouve donc de nombreaux noms d'origine étrangère. Les noms français les plus communs représentent des traits physiques (Legrand, Petit, Leroux, Leblanc); des traits psychologiques (Lesage, Lefranc); ou des noms de lieux (Laforêt, Dubourg, Fontaine, Deschamps, Dumont).

avant J.-C. (Jésus-Christ) *B.C.*

Et vous?

A. Proverbes et dictons. Bien que les proverbes et *dictons* fassent partie
de l'héritage culturel d'un peuple et bien qu'ils reflètent dans une
certaine mesure l'identité d'un peuple, beaucoup représentent aussi
une sorte de *sagesse* sans frontière.

    Pouvez-vous donner l'équivalent américain des proverbes sui-
vants ou en paraphraser le sens? Pouvez-vous les utiliser dans un
petit dialogue qui en illustre le sens?

sayings

wisdom

Quelques proverbes africains:
«Ne *repoussez* pas du pied la *pirogue* qui vous a aidé à traverser.»
«Si tu *élèves* un serpent, c'est sur toi-même qu'il apprendra à
mordre.»
«Tous ces *coqs* qui chantent, hier encore étaient des œufs.»

push away / canoe

raise

bite

roosters

Quelques proverbes français:
«Les absents ont toujours tort.»
«*Tel* père, tel fils.»
«Petit à petit, l'*oiseau* fait son *nid*.»

like (here), such

bird / nest

«Qui se ressemble, s'assemble.»
«Loin des yeux, loin du cœur.»
«Comme on fait son lit, on se couche.»
«Il n'y a que la vérité qui *blesse.*»   hurts
«Il n'y a que le premier pas qui coûte.»

B. Pensées et maximes. La Rochefoucauld, un écrivain français du 17e
siècle, est célèbre pour ses «*Maximes*» dans lesquelles il expose sans
indulgence nos petits et nos grands *défauts.* Beaucoup d'autres écri-   faults
vains ou autres personnages célèbres ont aussi exprimé leurs pensées
et leurs observations dans des phrases qui sont restées célèbres.

Indiquez si vous êtes d'accord avec ces pensées et maximes. Ensuite, écrivez vos propres maximes.

«L'*amour-propre* est le plus grand des flatteurs.»   self-esteem, vanity
«On ne donne rien si généreusement que ses conseils.»
«La *faiblesse* est plus opposée à la vertu que le vice.»   weakness
«*Il y va du* véritable amour comme de l'apparition des *esprits;* tout   it is the same with / ghosts
      le monde en parle, mais peu de gens en ont vu.»
«Nous aurions souvent honte de nos plus belles actions si le monde
      voyait tous les motifs qui les produisent.»
«*Quelque bien* qu'on dise de nous, on ne nous apprend rien de   whatever good
      nouveau.»
                    La Rochefoucauld, moraliste du 17e siècle

«Il faudrait essayer d'être heureux, ne serait-ce que pour donner
      l'exemple.»
                    Jacques Prévert, poète français, mort en 1977

«L'homme qui a le plus vécu n'est pas celui qui a compté le plus
      d'années, mais celui qui a le plus senti la vie.»
              Jean-Jacques Rousseau, philosophe français du 18e siècle

Proverbes & Dictons

**Brouillard qui ne tombe pas,
Donne après de l'eau en bas.**

**Hiver qui est par trop beau,
Nous promet été en eau.**

**Neige au blé est tel bénéfice
Qu'au vieillard la bonne pelisse**

Proverbes & Dictons

L'herbe cache et la pluie efface.

Nul pays n'a tout en partage.

Mieux vaut être désiré qu'importuné.

Epée de poltron n'a pas de pointe.

Les verbes *vivre*, *naître* et *mourir*

Présentation

Vivre *(to live)*, **naître** *(to be born)*, and **mourir** *(to die)* are irregular verbs.

vivre	
je **vis**	nous **vivons**
tu **vis**	vous **vivez**
il/elle/on **vit**	ils/elles **vivent**
passé composé: j'ai vécu	

En France les ouvriers vivent assez bien.
Molière a vécu au dix-septième siècle.
À cette époque-là, ils vivaient en Normandie.
Vive la liberté!

Note that **vivre** has a general meaning of *to be alive* or *to exist*, whereas **habiter** means only *to live or reside in or at a place*.

Option: Teach the present of **naître** for recognition only.

naître	
je **nais**	nous **naissons**
tu **nais**	vous **naissez**
il/elle/on **naît**	ils/elles **naissent**
passé composé: je suis né(e)	

Je suis né à Montréal.
Elle est née en 1959.
Un enfant qui naît de nos jours peut espérer vivre jusqu'à soixante-dix ans.

Most uses of **naître** are in the **passé composé**.

Option: Also introduce **mourir de soif, fatigue, chagrin, peur,** etc.

mourir	
je **meurs**	nous **mourons**
tu **meurs**	vous **mourez**
il/elle/on **meurt**	ils/elles **meurent**
passé composé: je suis mort(e)	
futur: je mourrai	

Je meurs de faim.
Il est mort l'année dernière.
Si je faisais cela, je mourrais de honte.

Substitution: (1) Je meurs de soif.   nous / cette pauvre plante / vous / les animaux. (2) En quelle année est-ce que vous êtes né?   tu / Georges et Michèle / votre père / le professeur. (3) À sa place, je serais mort de peur.   nous / vous / tu / les autres. (4) Nous vivons confortablement.   je / mon père / tu / nous / mes grands-parents / vous.

Préparation

Réunion de famille. Au cours d'une réunion de famille on parle des membres présents et passés de la famille. Reconstituez les phrases qui ont été prononcées.

Modèle   la petite Juliette / naître / en 1982 → **La petite Juliette est née en 1982.**

Follow-up: Form complete sentences and read as paragraph for listening practice.

1. Maman / naître / 1943
2. l'oncle Pierre et la tante Louise / naître / quelques années plus tard
3. Grand-papa / mourir / la même année
4. nos grands-parents / vivre / à l'étranger à cette époque-là
5. Grand-maman / vivre / jusqu'à l'âge de quatre-vingt-dix ans
6. mon cousin Henri et moi, nous / naître / le même jour
7. l'oncle André / mourir / pendant la guerre
8. nous / vivre / à Paris depuis notre mariage

Communication

A. Questions/interview. Répondez aux questions suivantes ou utilisez-les pour interviewer un(e) autre étudiant(e).

1. En quelle année est-ce que tu es né(e)?
2. Où est-ce que tu es né(e)?
3. Est-ce que tu as jamais vécu à l'étranger?
4. Où est-ce que tu vivais quand tu avais dix ans?
5. Est-ce que tu sais où tes ancêtres sont nés?
6. Jusqu'à quel âge est-ce que tu aimerais vivre?
7. Est-ce que tu aimerais vivre sur une autre planète si c'était possible?

Option: If used in small groups, have students report back their partners' answers.

B. Personnages célèbres. Utilisez les renseignements donnés dans le dictionnaire encyclopédique pour parler des personnages suivants.

Exemple   Rousseau (Jean-Jacques), philosophe français (1712–1778)
→ **Jean-Jacques Rousseau, philosophe français, est né en dix-sept cent douze et il est mort en dix-sept cent soixante-dix-huit.**

1. Sartre (Jean-Paul), philosophe et écrivain français (1905–1980)
2. Curie (Marie), physicienne française, née en Pologne (1867–1934)
3. Gaulle (Charles de), général et homme d'état français (1890–1970)
4. Camus (Albert), écrivain français (1913–1960)
5. Rodin (Auguste), sculpteur français (1840–1917)
6. Napoléon, empereur des Français (1769–1821)
7. Colette (Gabrielle), romancière française (1873–1954)
8. Racine (Jean), poète tragique français (1639–1699)
9. Hugo (Victor), écrivain français (1802–1885)
10. Sévigné (Madame de), auteur français (1626–1696)

Tell (or have students tell or find) the specific works or accomplishments for which these people are known. You may want to add other people to the list.

Le plus-que-parfait

Présentation

The **plus-que-parfait** (*pluperfect*, or *past perfect tense*) is used to indicate that one past action occurred before a second past action. The second past action is sometimes stated and sometimes simply understood: *I didn't know you **had finished** already; they **had not performed** yet.*

   The **plus-que-parfait** is formed by using the imperfect of **avoir** or **être** plus the past participle.

Le plus-que-parfait de *vendre*		Le plus-que-parfait de *partir*	
j'avais vendu	nous avions vendu	j'étais parti(e)	nous étions parti(e)s
tu avais vendu	vous aviez vendu	tu étais parti(e)	vous étiez parti(e)(s)
il/elle/on avait vendu	ils/elles avaient vendu	il/elle/on était parti(e)	ils/elles étaient parti(e)s

Elle avait déjà publié plusieurs albums quand elle est devenue célèbre.
Ils ont visité la Grèce l'été dernier parce qu'ils n'y étaient jamais allés avant.
C'était une personne que je n'avais jamais vue.
Êtes-vous allé(e) voir le film dont je vous avais parlé?
Je m'étais coupé le doigt en ouvrant une boîte.
Elle n'avait jamais pensé à se marier.
Nous n'avions jamais entendu parler de cet ancêtre.

Substitution: (1) Je n'avais jamais fait cela.   nous / vous / tu / on / nos amis. (2) Nous étions déjà arrivés.   vous / tu / les invités / mon journal. (3) Le jour précédent, je m'étais réveillé à dix heures.   tu / ma mère / nous / vous.

Préparation

A. Sur la piste des ancêtres. Philippe Laforêt, un «Cajun» de Louisiane, a retrouvé la trace d'un ancêtre canadien français, Jean-Baptiste Laforêt, qui avait vécu en Acadie avant d'être déporté en Louisiane par les autorités anglaises.

Modèle   Jean-Baptiste / naître en France → **Jean-Baptiste était né en France.**

1. il / vivre les premières années de sa vie en Normandie
2. il / venir au Canada quand il avait seize ans
3. il / s'installer en Acadie
4. il / apprendre le métier de boulanger
5. il / rencontrer Angèle sa future femme quelques années plus tard
6. Angèle / grandir en Acadie
7. ses parents / mourir quand elle avait douze ans
8. elle / s'occuper de ses petits frères et sœurs
9. elle / se débrouiller toute seule pour les élever
10. Jean-Baptiste et Angèle / se marier en 1750
11. ils / réussir à acheter une boutique
12. ils / devoir tout quitter quelques années plus tard

Nearly 6000 Acadians (French colonists who had settled in Acadia) were forced to flee to—or were deported to—Louisiana between 1765 and 1780 after Acadia was taken over by the British. Longfellow memorialized this tragic exodus in his long poem *Evangeline.* The Canadian singer Angèle Arsenault has also treated this episode in her song titled ''Évangéline.''

B. Une réunion de famille. À une réunion de famille les différents membres de la famille échangent des nouvelles et parlent de leur vie.

Modèle   Il a fait très froid l'hiver passé. (l'hiver précédent, assez beau) → **L'hiver précédent, il avait fait assez beau.**

1. L'été passé nous avons fait de l'alpinisme. (l'été précédent, du ski nautique)
2. Nous avons loué une petite maison. (l'été précédent, rester à l'hôtel)
3. L'année dernière mon fils a travaillé dans un restaurant. (avant ça, dans un hôpital)
4. Nous avons acheté notre bateau il y a deux ans. (l'année précédente, notre voiture)
5. L'année dernière ma fille a gagné le marathon. (l'année d'avant, une course cycliste)
6. Le trimestre passé j'ai suivi un cours de biologie (le trimestre précédent, un cours de chimie)
7. Cette saison, notre équipe a gagné trois matchs. (la saison précédente, six matchs)

Communication

Questions/interview. Répondez aux questions suivantes ou utilisez-les pour interviewer un(e) autre étudiant(e).

1. Est-ce que tu avais choisi ta future profession avant de commencer tes études à l'université?
2. Est-ce que tu avais déjà visité le campus avant de venir ici?
3. Est-ce que tu avais consulté d'autres personnes avant de prendre la décision de venir ici?
4. Est-ce que tu avais déjà rencontré d'autres étudiants de cette université avant de venir ici?
5. Est-ce que tu avais étudié le français avant de venir à l'université?
6. Est-ce que tu avais déjà étudié une autre langue avant de commencer l'étude du français?
7. Est-ce que tu avais déjà parlé avec ton professeur avant de commencer ce cours?
8. Est-ce que tu t'étais jamais intéressé(e) à la généalogie avant de lire ce chapitre?

Option: Have two students interview each other while class listens and takes notes. Then have listeners prepare an oral or written summary of the conversation.

Le conditionnel passé

Présentation

The **conditionnel passé** (*past conditional tense*) is used to describe a past hypothetical event or condition: *They **would have preferred** to stay*. It is composed of the conditional tense of **avoir** or **être** and the past participle.

Le conditionnel passé de *parler*		Le conditionnel passé d'*aller*	
j'aurais parlé	nous aurions parlé	je serais allé(e)	nous serions allé(e)s
tu aurais parlé	vous auriez parlé	tu serais allé(e)	vous seriez allé(e)(s)
il/elle/on aurait parlé	ils/elles auraient parlé	il/elle/on serait allé(e)	ils/elles seraient allé(e)s

À votre place, je n'aurais pas dit ça. — *If I were you, I wouldn't have said that.*

Dans ce cas-là, il aurait mieux valu que vous partiez. — *In that case, it would have been better for you to leave.*

Moi, je n'aurais jamais pu faire ça. — *I would never have been able to do that.*

Ils n'auraient pas dû se marier. — *They shouldn't have gotten married.*

Ils ont dit qu'ils auraient préféré venir un autre jour. — *They said they would have preferred to come another day.*

Substitutions: (1) Moi, j'aurais fait la même chose. les autres / Henri / vous / nous / tu. (2) À sa place, je serais venu plus tôt. nous / je / vous / tu / Micheline. (3) S'il avait fait beau, nous serions allés à la plage. je / Marie et moi / mes amis / vous. (4) Si nous avions vécu à cette époque-là, nous aurions été heureux. vous / je / mon père / tu / mes frères.

In French, as in English, the past conditional frequently occurs in sentences that contain a *si* clause. In such cases, the verb in the *si* clause is in the **plus-que-parfait** and the verb in the result clause in the **conditionnel passé.**

Option: Review si clauses.

S'il avait fait beau, nous serions allés à la plage.
Ça ne serait pas arrivé si tu avais fait attention.
Si vous aviez écouté, vous auriez compris.
Ils se seraient bien amusés s'ils étaient venus.

You may want to point out the difference between sentences such as **Ils ont dit qu'ils préféreraient venir un autre jour** and **Ils ont dit qu'ils auraient préféré venir un autre jour.** Both express the idea of the future in relation to the past, but the **conditionnel passé** implies that what they would have preferred to realize is impossible to realize.

Préparation

A. **À votre place.** Il y a toujours des gens qui pensent que leurs idées sont meilleures que celles des autres. Jean-Marie Dubourg est une de ces personnes et il n'a pas peur de dire ce que lui, il aurait fait s'il s'était trouvé dans la situation en question. Reconstituez les phrases qu'il a prononcées.

Modèle   prendre le train → **À votre place, j'aurais pris le train.**

Follow-up: Change to nous, il(s), elle(s), etc.

1. téléphoner à la police
2. me coucher plus tôt
3. venir à huit heures
4. m'arrêter immédiatement
5. réagir d'une autre façon
6. dire ce que je pensais
7. ne pas me mettre en colère
8. ne rien répondre

B. Si j'avais eu plus de temps. Un groupe d'Américains parlent de leurs voyages récents en France et chacun dit ce qu'il(elle) aurait fait s'ils avaient eu plus de temps. Reconstituez les phrases qu'ils ont prononcées.

Modèle   je / rendre visite à des amis   →   **Si j'avais eu plus de temps, j'aurais rendu visite à des amis.**

1. nous / rester plus longtemps à Paris
2. tu / aller à Chamonix
3. nous / visiter les châteaux de la Loire
4. vous / passer deux semaines en Provence
5. je / se promener le long de la Seine
6. Robert / faire du camping en Bretagne

Communication

A. Si . . . Imaginez ce qui se serait passé si les événements suivants avaient eu lieu.

Options: (1) Written. (2) Oral—ask as questions.

1. Si j'étais né(e) en France . . .
2. Si la Guerre Civile avait été gagnée par le Sud plutôt que par le Nord . . .
3. Si Christophe Colomb n'avait pas découvert l'Amérique . . .
4. Si on n'avait pas inventé l'automobile . . .
5. Si je n'avais pas décidé de faire mes études ici . . .
6. Si j'avais été totalement libre de choisir mes cours . . .
7. Si j'étais né(e) il y a deux cents ans . . .
8. Si les Indiens avaient été mieux traités par les pionniers . . .

B. Réactions. Nous avons tous des réactions différentes. Qu'est-ce que vous auriez fait si vous aviez été à la place des personnes décrites dans les paragraphes suivants?

Options: (1) Written. (2) Oral—have students compare reactions.

1. Paulette Dufour, une dame de soixante ans, se promenait dans la rue quand un jeune garçon lui a volé son sac. Elle a poursuivi le voleur, l'a attrapé et l'a emmené au poste de police. Et vous, qu'est-ce que vous auriez fait si vous aviez été à sa place?
2. Giselle avait besoin de faire réparer sa voiture. Elle a pris rendez-vous chez le mécanicien pour sept heures et demie. Elle y est arrivée à sept heures et demie précises. Elle a attendu pendant plus d'une heure sans que personne ne s'occupe d'elle. Furieuse, elle a finalement quitté le garage pour aller à son travail. Si vous aviez été dans la même situation, qu'est-ce que vous auriez fait?
3. Les Duroc conduisaient sur une petite route de campagne quand ils ont vu un chien blessé. Monsieur Duroc ne voulait pas s'arrêter mais Madame Duroc a insisté pour qu'ils aident la pauvre bête. Qu'est-ce que vous auriez fait à leur place?
4. Quand Monsieur et Madame Rochefort ont gagné vingt mille francs à la Loterie Nationale, ils ont mis tout cet argent à la banque. Si vous aviez gagné cet argent, qu'est-ce que vous auriez fait?
5. Robert vient de s'acheter une guitare. Il paie et le vendeur lui rend la monnaie. En sortant du magasin, il vérifie sa monnaie et il réalise que le vendeur lui a rendu cinquante francs de trop. «C'est mon jour de chance», pense-t-il. Qu'est-ce que vous auriez fait à sa place?

⚜ Les pronoms indéfinis

This presentation integrates indefinite pronouns, some of which have been used receptively already. Since this is basically a review section, it could be omitted if necessary.

Présentation

Indefinite pronouns can be used when there is no specific antecedent. The principal indefinite pronouns are:

A. Quelqu'un *(someone)*, **quelque chose** *(something)*, **quelque part** *(somewhere)*. These forms are considered masculine and are always singular.

Quelqu'un m'a téléphoné.
Avez-vous rencontré quelqu'un? Non, je n'ai rencontré personne.
J'ai entendu quelque chose dans la chambre.
Avez-vous quelque chose à boire? Non, nous n'avons rien à boire.

Note the negative counterpart of these pronouns: **quelqu'un** → **personne; quelque chose** → **rien** *(nothing)*; **quelque part** → **nulle part** *(nowhere)*.

When **quelqu'un** and **quelque chose** and their negative counterparts are modified by adjectives, the adjectives are preceded by **de** and are always masculine singular.

Nous avons fait la connaissance de quelqu'un d'intéressant.
Est-ce que vous avez découvert quelque chose de nouveau au sujet de vos ancêtres?
Il n'y a rien d'amusant à faire ici.

One of the most frequently used adjectives that can modify indefinite pronouns is **autre** *(else)*:

quelqu'un d'autre   *someone else*   personne d'autre   *no one else*
quelque chose d'autre   *something else*   rien d'autre   *nothing else*

Nous ne savons rien d'autre à leur sujet.
Connaissez-vous quelqu'un d'autre qui puisse le faire?

Note, however, that the word for *elsewhere* or *somewhere else* is **ailleurs.**

B. Quelques-uns, quelques-unes *(some, a few)* can refer to people or things:

Quelques-unes de ces vieilles maisons sont à vendre.
Il nous a présenté quelques-uns de ses cousins.

The pronoun **en** is used with **quelques-uns** and **quelques-unes** when they are direct objects.

Ils ont acheté quelques livres.   Ils en ont acheté quelques-uns.
Nous avons visité quelques-unes de ces villes.   Nous en avons visité quelques-unes.

C. Plusieurs *(several)*:

Plusieurs de mes ancêtres viennent de France.
Parmi les restaurants de cette ville, plusieurs sont excellents.

The partitive pronoun **en** is used when **plusieurs** is a direct object.

Elles ont gagné plusieurs matchs.	Elles en ont gagné plusieurs.
J'ai déjà entendu plusieurs de ces chansons.	J'en ai déjà entendu plusieurs.

D. Un(e) autre (*another one*), **d'autres** (*others*), **certain(e)s** (*certain ones, some*):

Un de mes ancêtres vient d'Afrique et un autre vient d'Espagne.
Certaines de ces lois sont injustes.
Certains se passionnent pour la généalogie, d'autres ne s'y intéressent pas du tout.

The pronoun **en** is used with **autre(s)** and **certain(e)s** when they are direct objects.

Je voudrais un autre sandwich.   Apportez-m'en un autre, s'il vous plaît.

E. Chacun, chacune (*each one*):

Chacun a le droit de faire ce qu'il veut.
Chacune de ces voitures a certains avantages.
J'ai écrit à chacun de mes amis, mais aucun n'a répondu.

Note that the negative counterpart of **chacun, chacune** is **aucun, aucune** (*none, not one*). **Aucun, aucune** also contrast with **plusieurs, quelques-uns, certains, tous**.

J'ai envoyé plusieurs lettres, mais je n'en ai reçu aucune.
Les ancêtres de ma femme étaient tous des aristocrates, mais aucun des miens n'était noble.

Transformation: Modèle: Nous avons étudié plusieurs documents. → Nous en avons étudié plusieurs. (1) Ils ont visité quelques châteaux. (2) Tu as écrit une autre lettre. (3) On va discuter quelques-uns de ces sujets. (4) Elle a visité plusieurs pays européens. Modèle: Est-ce que quelqu'un veut sortir? → Non, personne ne veut sortir. (1) Est-ce que quelque chose t'intéresse? (2) Certaines de ces lois sont-elles injustes? (3) Est-ce qu'il y a quelqu'un à la porte? (4) Avez-vous quelque chose d'autre à ajouter? (5) Est-ce que vous avez vu quelque chose d'amusant? (6) A-t-il compris quelque chose? (7) Est-ce que tu veux aller quelque part?

Préparation

A. La passion de la généalogie. Deux amis parlent de leurs recherches généalogiques et de ce qu'ils ont appris à propos de leurs ancêtres. Qu'est-ce qu'ils disent?

> **Modèle**   Est-ce que vous avez trouvé des documents qui étaient intéressants? (oui, quelques-uns) → **Oui, j'en ai trouvé quelques-uns.**

1. Est-ce que vous avez des ancêtres français? (oui, plusieurs)
2. Est-ce que vous avez des ancêtres célèbres? (non, aucun)
3. Est-ce que vous avez des parents qui habitent en Louisiane? (oui, quelques-uns)
4. Est-ce qu'il y a quelqu'un d'autre qui s'intéresse à l'histoire de votre famille? (non, personne)
5. Est-ce que vous avez trouvé quelque chose d'intéressant dans vos recherches? (non, rien)

B. Tout le monde n'est pas dans la même situation. Jean-Luc est de mauvaise humeur et il a l'impression que tout le monde est contre lui. Son amie Paulette, par contre, est de très bonne humeur et tout va bien pour elle. Donnez les réponses de Paulette.

Modèle   Je n'ai rencontré personne d'intéressant hier. → **Moi, j'ai rencontré quelqu'un d'intéressant.**

1. Je n'ai rien mangé de bon au restaurant universitaire.
2. Personne ne m'a téléphoné ce matin.
3. Je n'ai rien vu de nouveau.
4. Rien d'intéressant ne m'est arrivé hier.
5. Je n'ai rien acheté de nouveau en ville.
6. Je n'ai rien d'autre à te dire.
7. Je n'ai écrit aucune lettre cette semaine.
8. Aucun de mes amis n'est venu me voir.

Communication

Option: If used in small groups, encourage students to ask related questions.

Questions/interview. Répondez aux questions suivantes ou utilisez-les pour interviewer un(e) autre étudiant(e).

1. Est-ce que tu as téléphoné à quelqu'un hier soir? Est-ce que quelqu'un t'a téléphoné?
2. Est-ce que tu as fait quelque chose d'intéressant pendant le week-end?
3. Est-ce que quelques-uns de tes amis ont déjà voyagé en Europe? Si oui, quels pays ont-ils visités?
4. Est-ce que tu connais quelques-unes des chansons d'Édith Piaf? Si oui, lesquelles?
5. Est-ce que tu aimes travailler avec quelqu'un d'autre ou est-ce que tu préfères travailler seul(e)?
6. Est-ce que tu as fait la connaissance de quelqu'un d'intéressant récemment?
7. Est-ce que quelque chose d'amusant t'est arrivé cette semaine?
8. Est-ce que tu penses que certaines de nos lois soient injustes? Si oui, lesquelles?
9. Est-ce que tu connais bien chacun de tes professeurs?

SYNTHÈSE

Sources et racines: La terre et les ancêtres du peuple malgache
from Madagascar

Il n'y a pas de paysage typique de Madagascar. La seule généralisation qu'on puisse faire au sujet de l'aspect physique de cette île est que c'est un pays d'une extrême diversité. On y trouve des plateaux arides, des vallées vertes et fertiles, des forêts luxuriantes, des déserts, des plages tropicales, des *rizières* et des plantations de toutes sortes: café, canne à sucre, bananiers, *palmiers*, vanille, etc.

Suggestion: Point out that **la taille** applies to clothing; **la pointure** applies to shoes.

rice fields
palm trees

On peut observer une variété *tout* aussi grande dans le peuple malgache lui-même. Leur *teint* et leur *taille* varient selon leurs origines. Mais à cette diversité ethnique correspond une grande unité linguistique. Bien qu'il existe de nombreuses variantes dialectales, elles sont

just

complexion / size

toutes dérivées d'une langue commune. *Ainsi*, un Merina (habitant des plateaux du centre) et un Antandroy (habitant du sud de l'île) n'ont aucune difficulté à se comprendre, surtout si l'un et l'autre évitent d'*avaler* trop de syllabes. La langue malgache fait partie du groupe mélano-polynésien, mais elle a été enrichie d'éléments arabes ou bantous et aussi, plus récemment, de mots français et anglais qui ont été complètement malgachisés. Par exemple, les noms des jours de la semaine sont d'origine arabe (*alahady* pour dimanche), les noms des objets qu'on trouve dans une salle de classe sont anglais (*boky* pour livre, *penina* pour stylo, *tsaoka* pour craie) et certains produits alimentaires ont des noms d'origine française (*dibera* pour beurre, *dipaina* pour pain).

thus

swallow

En plus de l'unité apportée par une langue commune, la civilisation malgache possède un système de valeurs très cohérent. Le culte des ancêtres est *sans doute* le trait qui caractérise le plus cette unité des traditions culturelles. Partout dans le pays on trouve des *cimetières* qui sont de véritables villages pour les *morts*. On y trouve des *tombeaux* magnifiquement décorés, des jardins, des sculptures et des dessins racontant la vie des ancêtres qui y ont été *enterrés*. Les Malgaches n'ont pas peur de la mort, car elle est considérée simplement comme le passage d'une vie à l'autre. Bien que les coutumes varient avec les régions, dans tous les cas le rituel de la séparation entre morts et *vivants* doit être respecté. Les vivants, en particulier, doivent demander aux ancêtres déjà morts d'accepter dans leur société le nouveau mort; sinon, il risque d'*errer* éternellement et d'*embêter* les vivants au lieu de leur apporter ses conseils.

probably
cemeteries
dead / tombs

buried

living

to wander / bother

Un autre trait caractéristique de la culture malgache est l'importance de la *parole*. La parole malgache est un art et à l'occasion des mariages et des *enterrements* on fait venir des griots—c'est-à-dire, des professionnels de la parole. Dans certains cas, l'expression verbale remplace même la force physique. On raconte, par exemple, qu'au début du siècle dernier, une grande *bataille* de deux jours a opposé deux groupes rivaux; mais au lieu de *se battre* avec des armes, ils ont préféré se battre avec des mots.

spoken word
burials

battle
fight

La qualité d'un discours se reconnaît à la subtilité et à l'originalité des images et des allégories. Dans certaines régions on utilise même les hésitations et les silences pour «habiller» la parole. Les Français sont souvent désorientés par la complexité de la parole malgache; ils ne sont pas habitués non plus à penser dans une langue qui n'a ni *genre*, ni pluriel, ni verbe *être*!

The **griot** is not only a storyteller but also a poet, a musician, an historian, and a sorcerer who plays an important role in all the rituals of African life.

gender

Les images qui sont les plus utilisées par les orateurs viennent, bien entendu, des proverbes. Elles forment la base des discours. Pour que son discours soit plus riche et plus élégant encore, un orateur *citera* des séries entières de proverbes les uns après les autres et il le terminera par un petit poème, dont voici un exemple:

will quote

—Comment sont les *reproches*?
—Comme les vents, j'ai entendu leur nom. Mais je ne vois pas leurs *traits*.
—Comment sont les reproches?
—Ils sont comme le froid. On ne l'entend pas et il *engourdit*.

reproaches, criticism

features

makes you numb

Extrait et adapté d'un article de *Jeune Afrique*.

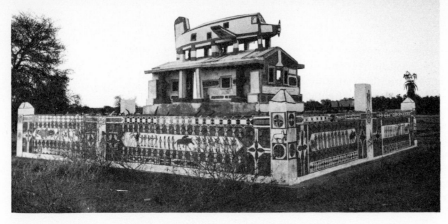

Dans un cimetière à
Madagascar

Compréhension   Complétez les phrases suivantes selon les renseignements
donnés dans le texte.

Option: Ask as questions.

1. On peut dire que Madagascar a un aspect physique très varié car . . .
2. Les habitants des différentes régions de Madagascar peuvent facilement
   se comprendre parce que . . .
3. Le malgache est une langue mélano-polynésienne, mais on y trouve aussi
   des mots . . .
4. La langue commune n'est pas le seul facteur d'unité; on trouve aussi dans
   la culture malgache . . .
5. Il est évident que le culte des morts a une place importante dans la culture
   malgache car . . .
6. La mort ne fait pas peur aux Malgaches car . . .
7. On peut voir que la parole est très importante dans la culture malgache
   car . . .
8. Les qualités principales d'un bon discours sont . . .

NOTES CULTURELLES

Le français moderne

Comme la langue malgache et toutes les
autres langues, le français est en constante
évolution. Les changements actuels sont
caractérisés surtout par la présence du
franglais—c'est-à-dire, l'utilisation de
nombreuses expressions et mots anglais tels
que *sexy*, le *tee-shirt*, un *job*—et par
l'influence du français familier.

Le français familier, la langue de la
conversation de tous les jours, diffère
considérablement de la langue écrite
soignée.° Ces différences se manifestent dans

la prononciation—on laisse tomber le *e* muet
aussi souvent que possible, disant, par
exemple, «jé pense», et on évite de faire des
liaisons: «ils sont entrés». Dans la syntaxe il y
a l'élision du *ne*: «c'est pas moi». L'ordre des
mots est souvent différent: «Dis, le frigo, il
marche pas, on dirait». Et dans le domaine
du vocabulaire on remarque l'emploi d'un
grand nombre d'abréviations—le frigo, la
télé, le prof—et un grand nombre de termes
plus ou moins argotiques—flic,° boulot,°
moche,° par exemple.

soigné *careful*

flic *policeman*   boulot *work*   moche *ugly*

426

Le français qu'on parle au Québec, excepté celui qu'on entend à la télévision et à la radio, possède certains traits caractéristiques qui le distinguent du français métropolitain.

Comme l'indique Victor Barbeau, auteur d'un livre sur ce sujet, «le français du Canada est dans une large mesure l'écho du français de la Renaissance», dont il tire° en particulier certains aspects de sa prononciation (par exemple, *è* prononcé *é*; roulement° des *r*; nasalité) et certains termes archaïques (par exemple, *char* pour *voiture*; *être gros d'argent* pour *être riche*; *bicher* pour *embrasser*). Il est aussi marqué fortement° par l'influence de l'anglais. On dit *cute* pour *mignon*; *le chèque* pour *l'addition*; *un date* pour *un rendez-vous*; *un big-shot* pour *une grosse légume* et *un billet de traffic* pour *une contravention*.

Les noms de lieux sont surtout français (Trois-Rivières, Lac St.-Jean) ou indiens (*Québec* veut dire «détroit»° et *Canada* veut dire «village»).

tire *draws* roulement *rolling*

fortement *strongly* détroit *strait*

Communication

A. Comment «habiller» la parole. Quand on ne connaît pas très bien une langue, on a souvent tendance à s'exprimer d'une façon un peu trop simple. Réfléchissez aux mots, expressions et constructions que vous pourriez utiliser pour enrichir les phrases suivantes.

Suggested for individual or small-group writing.

Exemple C'est un bon livre. → **Je viens de lire un livre qui m'a beaucoup impressionné(e). L'auteur a réussi à créer une œuvre qui est à la fois passionnante et intelligente.**

1. J'ai aimé ce film.
2. Paris est une très belle ville.
3. C'est un garçon charmant.
4. Ce vin n'est pas bon.
5. J'ai besoin d'une voiture.
6. Cet exercice est trop difficile.

B. L'art de la persuasion. Imaginez que vous êtes dans une ou plusieurs des situations suivantes. Préparez vos arguments pour persuader l'autre personne.

Options: (1) Have students present arguments and have class choose most convincing reason. (2) Assign roles and have students act out each situation.

1. Vous avez décidé de parler à votre patron(ne) pour lui demander une promotion ou une augmentation de salaire. Vous discutez avec lui (elle) pour lui expliquer que vous méritez cette promotion. Soyez persuasif(-ive).
2. Pendant les vacances de Noël vous aimeriez aller faire du ski avec des amis—ou passer quelques jours au soleil en Floride. Mais vos parents veulent que vous restiez à la maison pour passer la fête de Noël en famille. Essayez de les persuader.
3. Il n'y a chez vous qu'un seul poste de télévision. Vous avez envie de regarder un documentaire sur Madagascar mais votre ami(e) (frère, sœur, camarade de chambre) voudrait regarder un spectacle de variétés. Essayez de le (la) persuader de la valeur éducative et culturelle de votre choix.
4. Votre travail au cours du trimestre a été assez bon. Mais le jour de l'examen final vous avez été pris(e) de panique et vous avez tout oublié. Essayez de persuader votre professeur de ne pas compter votre examen final ou de vous donner une autre occasion de montrer ce que vous savez.

C. **Coutumes et légendes.** Chaque pays, chaque région, chaque groupe ethnique et même quelquefois chaque famille a ses propres coutumes et légendes. Essayez de raconter une de ces coutumes ou légendes.

D. **Le français familier.** Pouvez-vous deviner (*guess*) d'après le contexte le sens des mots en italique qui sont des mots du français familier?

1. Je viens d'acheter les *bouquins* dont j'ai besoin pour mon cours d'histoire. Ils étaient *vachement* chers: ça m'a coûté 150 *balles.* Maintenant je suis complètement *fauché* et mes parents ne m'enverront pas de *fric* avant la fin du mois.

2. Il faut que je fasse réparer ma *bagnole.* Il y a toutes sortes de *trucs* qui ne marchent pas dans le moteur. Heureusement, je connais un *mec* qui est mecanicien. C'est un de mes *copains.* Comme ça, ça me coûtera pas trop cher.

3. Je vais passer mon *bac* l'année prochaine. Il va falloir que je *bosse* dur parce que je ne suis pas très *calé* en *philo.* Après ça, je ne sais pas si j'irai à l'université ou si je chercherai du *boulot.* J'aimerais bien travailler dans une agence de voyage.

4. Moi, j'ai *rudement* faim; je n'ai rien *bouffé* depuis ce matin. Il n'y avait plus rien dans le *frigo.* Vous n'avez pas envie d'aller *bouffer* quelque chose avec moi? Il y a un petit restaurant *vachement chouette* tout près d'ici. On pourrait y aller tous ensemble. Je connais le patron; vous verrez; il est *sympa.*

bouquins = livres
vachement = très
balles = francs
fauché = sans argent
fric = argent
bagnole = voiture
trucs = choses
mec = homme, copains = amis
bac = baccalauréat
bosse = travaille, calé = fort, philo = philosophie
boulot = travail
rudement = très
bouffé = mangé
frigo = réfrigérateur
bouffer = manger
vachement chouette = très bien
sympa = sympathique

VOCABULAIRE

noms

l'amour-propre (m) *self-esteem, vanity*
° l'ancêtre (m)
l'arrière-grand-mère (f) *great-grandmother*
°la base
la bataille *battle*
le bourgeois, la bourgeoise *member of the middle class*
le chiffre *number*
le cimetière *cemetery*
°la complexité
le coq *rooster*
la craie *chalk*
le défaut *fault, failing*
°le descendant
le dicton *saying, maxim*
le discours *speech*
l'enterrement (m) *burial, funeral*
la faiblesse *weakness*
la fiche *file card, note card*
la fierté *pride*
°la généalogie
°la génération
le genre *gender*
la mort *death*
le mort *dead person*
le nid *nest*
l'oiseau (m) *bird*
le palmier *palm tree*
la parole *spoken word*
la piste *track, trace, trail*
la racine *root*
le reproche *reproach, criticism*
la sagesse *wisdom*
la taille *size*
le teint *complexion*
le tombeau *tomb*
le trait *feature*
les vivants *living persons*

verbes

avaler *to swallow*
se battre *to fight*
blesser *to hurt, to wound*
citer *to quote*
élever *to raise*
embêter *to bother, to annoy*
enterrer *to bury*
finir par *to end up by*
mordre *to bite*
mourir *to die*
naître *to be born*
se passionner pour *to be fascinated by*
réagir *to react*

adjectifs

blessé(e) *wounded*
conscient(e) *conscious*
°désorienté(e)
tel, telle *such*

adverbes

ainsi *thus, so*

divers

les pronoms indéfinis (voir pp. 422–423)

d'autres expressions
ça y est! *that's it!*
puisque *since*
quant à *as for*
sans doute *probably*
soi *oneself*

CHAPITRE VINGT-DEUX

Les Français et les Américains

22

Point out that **bandes dessinées** are commonly referred to as **les B.D.** in French, and that *le Nouvel Observateur*, like *l'Express*, is a weekly news magazine.

INTRODUCTION

Les Français vus par Claire Bretécher

Auteur de la bande dessinée intitulée «Les Frustrés», Claire Bretécher est une des *dessinatrices* les plus remarquables de notre époque. Pendant plusieurs années les Français ont pu lire chaque semaine ses bandes dessinées dans *le Nouvel Observateur*. Elle a aussi publié plusieurs albums qui ont été traduits en plusieurs langues.

    cartoonists (f)

Ses lecteurs les plus enthousiastes sont souvent ceux qu'elle ridiculise dans ses dessins: les *soi-disant* intellectuels, les libéraux, les femmes émancipées—*autrement dit*, les gens de son propre milieu. Elle donne à chacun l'occasion de rire de ses propres prétentions, de ses complexes et de ses *névroses*. «Mes dessins représentent des épisodes de la vie de tous les jours, dit-elle. J'observe et j'écoute les gens autour de moi, je me moque de mes propres problèmes».

    so-called

    in other words

    neuroses

    Suggestion: Mention that Bretécher cartoons have appeared in *Ms.* magazine.

Les personnages masculins des «Frustrés» sont des nouveaux riches *poseurs*, des intellectuels qui se prennent trop au sérieux, des chauvinistes condescendants, des *névrosés* de la vie moderne. Ses personnages féminins sont des femmes qui se croient émancipées mais ne le sont pas toujours, des femmes *parfois* vaines et irrationnelles, des féministes toujours prêtes à se battre pour leurs idées, des *ménagères opprimées*, des *femmes d'affaires* et des intellectuelles dissatisfaites.

    who put on airs, affected

    neurotics

    sometimes

    housewives / oppressed

    businesswomen

Dans ses bandes dessinées, Claire Bretécher se moque des femmes aussi bien que des hommes mais elle pense que les femmes apprécient ses dessins plus que les hommes. «Les femmes savent rire d'elles-mêmes, dit-elle. Les hommes se sentent blessés. Leur fierté est offensée». Claire Bretécher vient d'une famille de femmes fortes et, bien que mariée maintenant, elle a toujours pensé qu'il valait mieux rester *célibataire* plutôt que de se marier avec n'importe qui. Mais elle n'a pas beaucoup de patience avec les féministes non plus. «Il y a longtemps que j'ai *résolu* ces problèmes-là, dit-elle. Et puis, mon mari est un homme qui sait très bien qu'il ne faut pas compter sur moi pour faire le ménage, que mon argent est à moi et le sien est à lui et que je ne veux pas avoir d'enfants».

    single

    resolved

Elle a décidé de ne pas utiliser ses bandes dessinées pour exprimer ses idées féministes. «J'avais le choix, dit-elle. Je pouvais lutter pour les femmes, mais c'est fatigant et ça me limitait trop. Ou bien je pouvais oublier tout cela et m'adresser à tout le monde.» Voyant qu'elle n'est pas toujours *tendre* pour les femmes, certains hommes l'accusent de détester les femmes. «Ça, c'est idiot, explique-t-elle. Ils n'ont absolument rien compris et je suis fatiguée de tout leur expliquer.»

soft

En effet, Claire Bretécher s'identifie à ses propres personnages: la femme aux *hanches* trop grosses en train d'essayer des blue-jeans trop petits, la femme mariée qui boit un verre *en cachette* pendant la visite de sa *belle-mère*, la femme qui a peur de *vieillir* et la femme qui pense que personne ne l'aime ni ne la comprend. «Elles sont toutes moi», dit-elle.

hips
on the sly
mother-in-law / to age

You may wish to mention **beau-père, beau-frère,** and **belle-sœur.**

Avec la permission de Claire Bretécher.

UN HOMME SIMPLE

avoue *admit*

crevé *dead tired*
épuisant(e) *exhausting*

Compréhension Selon les renseignements donnés dans le texte, est-ce que les phrases suivantes sont vraies ou fausses? Si le sens de la phrase est faux, corrigez-le.

Option: Ask as questions.

1. Claire Bretécher est un personnage de bande dessinée qui est très populaire en France en ce moment.
2. La bande dessinée intitulée «Les Frustrés» était publiée chaque semaine dans le journal *Le Monde*.
3. Les situations qu'elle décrit représentent des faits qu'elle a observés dans la vie de tous les jours.
4. Elle se moque surtout des gens qui se prennent trop au sérieux.
5. Claire Bretécher se moque aussi bien des femmes que des hommes.
6. Claire Bretécher a l'intention de rester célibataire toute sa vie.
7. Claire Bretécher a décidé d'utiliser ses bandes dessinées pour faire connaître ses idées féministes.
8. Certains hommes pensent que Claire Bretécher déteste les femmes, mais ils se trompent.
9. Quand Claire Bretécher se moque des autres femmes, c'est un peu une façon de se moquer d'elle-même.

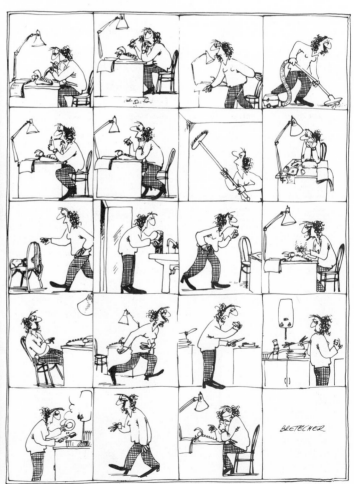

Claire Bretécher

NOTES CULTURELLES

La bande dessinée

Les aventures de Tintin, le jeune détective débrouillard,° ou celles d'Astérix, le petit Gaulois qui lutte contre les puissants° Romains, font partie du folklore national presque au même titre° que Napoléon et Victor Hugo. L'un et l'autre représentent la qualité de débrouillardise si chère aux

Français ainsi que cet esprit de rébellion et de défi° envers les autorités établies. Les bandes dessinées typiquement françaises ne sont pas les seules auxquelles les Français s'intéressent. Le *Journal de Mickey* et les mésaventures de Charlie Brown sont suivis avec intérêt par les amateurs de bandes dessinées de tous les âges.

débrouillard *resourceful*   puissants *powerful*   au même titre *in the same way*

défi *challenge*

Et vous?

Histoire sans paroles, ou . . . Est-ce qu'il faut que je vous fasse dessin? Même quand on est une grande dessinatrice comme Claire Bretécher, il y a des jours où l'inspiration ne vient pas. Et quand on est étudiant, ça doit bien arriver de temps en temps aussi. Alors, si c'est votre cas, inspirez-vous de ce dessin à gauche et du vocabulaire suggéré pour décrire une de vos confrontations avec la page blanche.

Vocabulaire supplémentaire

allumer une cigarette	*to light a cigarette*
enlever les toiles d'araignées	*to remove cobwebs*
faire une petite lessive dans le lavabo	*to do a little washing in the washbowl*
se faire une tasse de café	*to make oneself a cup of coffee*
une lampe de chevet	*bedside lamp*
une machine à écrire	*typewriter*
manquer d'inspiration	*to lack inspiration*
passer l'aspirateur	*to vacuum*
regarder / compter les mouches au plafond	*to watch / count the flies on the ceiling*
se ronger les ongles	*to bite one's fingernails*
taper à la machine	*to typewrite*

Le futur antérieur

Option: May be taught for recognition only.

Présentation

The future perfect tense is used to indicate that an action will have taken place prior to another future time (*We will have finished by noon.*) or prior to another future action (*They will have eaten when we get home.*). It is therefore used most frequently in clauses beginning with **quand** *(when)*, **lorsque** *(when)*, **aussitôt que** *(as soon as)*, or **dès que** *(as soon as)*. It is formed by using the future of **avoir** or **être** plus the past participle.

Remind students that although the meanings of **quand** and **lorsque** are essentially identical, **lorsque** is slightly more literary and that only **quand** can be used in questions.

Le futur antérieur de *parler*		Le futur antérieur d'*aller*	
j'aurai parlé	nous aurons parlé	je serai allé(e)	nous serons allé(e)s
tu auras parlé	vous aurez parlé	tu seras allé(e)	vous serez allé(e)(s)
il/elle/on aura parlé	ils/elles auront parlé	il/elle/on sera allé(e)	ils/elles seront allé(e)s

Est-ce que vous aurez fini ce travail avant la fin de la semaine?
Téléphone-moi aussitôt que tu seras rentré.
Nous nous mettrons à table dès que vous vous serez lavé les mains.
Elle vous téléphonera lorsqu'elle se sera reposée un peu de son voyage.

    Note that while in English one does not always use the future or future perfect tense after conjunctions like *when* or *as soon as*, in French the future or future perfect tense must be used to refer to future time. For example, **Je vous écrirai quand je serai rentré de vacances** might be expressed in English as *I'll write you when I return from vacation.*

Préparation

A. Il faudra attendre un peu. Madame Ronchamps doit souvent rappeler à sa famille qu'on ne peut pas toujours avoir ce qu'on veut immédiatement. Qu'est-ce qu'elle dit?

Modèle   Nous ne pouvons pas acheter une nouvelle voiture maintenant. Il faut d'abord que nous fassions des économies. → **Nous achèterons une nouvelle voiture quand nous aurons fait des économies.**

1. Tu ne peux pas sortir tout de suite. Il faut d'abord que tu finisses ton travail.
2. Tu ne peux pas aller jouer tout de suite. Il faut d'abord que tu fasses tes devoirs.
3. Je ne peux pas m'occuper de ça maintenant. Il faut d'abord que je prépare le dîner.
4. Vous ne pouvez pas commencer à manger tout de suite. Il faut d'abord que tes frères finissent de mettre la table.
5. Tu ne peux pas déjeuner tout de suite. Il faut d'abord que tu t'habilles.
6. Tu ne peux pas quitter la table maintenant. Il faut d'abord que tu boives ton lait.
7. Le plombier ne peut pas venir tout de suite. Il faut d'abord qu'il finisse un autre travail.
8. Nous ne pouvons pas jouer avec toi maintenant. Il faut d'abord que nous rentrions à la maison.

B. Ne remettez pas à demain ce que vous pouvez faire aujourd'hui. Marianne a toujours une excuse pour remettre à plus tard les choses qu'elle doit faire. Donnez l'équivalent français des phrases qu'elle a prononcées.

1. I'll do my homework when I've finished reading this magazine.   *Written preparation may be helpful.*
2. As soon as you return, we'll talk about that.
3. I'll write you as soon as I arrive in Paris.
4. I'll look for the recipe as soon as I've rested.
5. When I buy the book, I'll begin to study.
6. I'll go home when I finish my coffee.

Communication

Options: (1) Written. (2) Oral—ask questions or adapt for directed dialogue. (3) Have students work in small groups and report back their partners' responses.

Questions/interview. Répondez aux questions suivantes ou utilisez-les pour interviewer un(e) autre étudiant(e).

1. Lorsque tu auras fini tes études, est-ce que tu chercheras du travail ou est-ce que tu voyageras pendant quelque temps?
2. Quand tu seras rentré(e) chez toi ce soir, est-ce que tu te reposeras ou est-ce que tu auras encore du travail à faire?
3. Quand tu auras gagné un peu d'argent, est-ce que tu le dépenseras ou est-ce que tu le mettras à la banque?
4. Quand tu auras fini tout ton travail ce soir, est-ce que tu liras un bon livre ou est-ce que tu te coucheras tout de suite?
5. Lorsque tu auras quitté l'université, est-ce que tu y reviendras quelquefois, ou est-ce que tu n'y reviendras jamais?
6. Lorsque tu seras arrivé(e) à l'âge de la retraite, est-ce que tu continueras à travailler ou est-ce que tu prendras ta retraite?

 ## Le *faire* causatif

Présentation

The verb **faire** followed by an infinitive is used to indicate that the subject of a sentence is causing something to be done or having someone do something.

Nous faisons construire une maison.	*We're having a house built.*
Je ferai venir le médecin.	*I'll have the doctor come.*

A. The use of this pattern does not follow the usual pattern of verbs plus infinitive. The word order for causative **faire** is:

subject + **faire** + *infinitive* + *noun or noun phrase*

Elle fera redécorer son appartement.	*She'll have her apartment redecorated.*
Nous avons fait venir un spécialiste.	*We sent for a specialist.*
Le professeur fait beaucoup travailler ses élèves.	*The teacher makes his students work a lot.*
Faites entrer les visiteurs.	*Have the visitors come in.*
Ne faites pas attendre vos invités.	*Don't keep your guests waiting.*
Je vais faire réparer ma montre.	*I'm going to have my watch fixed.*

When a pronoun is used in place of the noun, the word order is *subject* + *object pronoun* + **faire** + *infinitive.*

Nous la ferons réparer.	*We'll have it fixed.*
Je les fais travailler.	*I make them work.*
Vous nous avez fait attendre longtemps.	*You kept us waiting a long time.*
Ne me faites pas rire.	*Don't make me laugh.*
Je vous inviterai quand j'aurai fait redécorer mon appartement.	*I will invite you when I have had my apartment redecorated.*

B. The verb **faire** can also be followed by a noun rather than an infinitive
in idiomatic expressions like **faire peur à** *(to scare)*, **faire mal à** *(to hurt)*,
and **faire confiance à** *(to trust)*. In this case the word order is *subject +*
faire *+ noun + indirect object.*

Ton chien fait peur à tout le monde.	*Your dog scares everybody.*
Il faut faire confiance à vos employés.	*You have to trust your employees.*

When the indirect object is replaced by a pronoun, it precedes **faire**,
except in the affirmative imperative.

Cette dent continue à me faire mal.	*That tooth still hurts me.*
Vous leur avez fait peur!	*You scared them!*
Ne me faites pas mal.	*Don't hurt me.*
Faites-moi confiance.	*Trust me.*

Préparation

Substitution: (1) Il fait attendre tout le monde. tu / cette dame / cet employé / vous / vos amis. (2) J'ai fait venir le médecin. entrer les visiteurs / réparer ma montre / laver la voiture / construire un garage. (3) Il ne fait confiance à personne. je / nous / le professeur / vous.

A. On ne peut pas tout faire soi-même. Au cours d'une soirée entre amis on
parle des projets des uns et des autres. Quelles réponses est-ce que différentes personnes ont données aux questions suivantes?

Modèle   Est-ce que Pierre a réparé sa moto lui-même? → **Non, il a
fait réparer sa moto.**

1. Est-ce que les Dupont ont construit leur maison eux-mêmes?
2. Est-ce que vous avez reconstruit votre arbre généalogique?
3. Est-ce que ton père lave sa voiture lui-même?
4. Est-ce que tu as fait ce pull toi-même?
5. Est-ce que Paul lavera ses vêtements lui-même quand tu seras partie?
6. Est-ce que vos parents vendront leur maison eux-mêmes?
7. Est-ce que vous allez repeindre le garage vous-même?

B. Une vieille maison à restaurer. Claude et Michelle viennent d'acheter une
vieille maison à la campagne. Ils sont en train de la faire restaurer.
Reconstituez les phrases qu'ils ont prononcées.

Modèle   nous / être en train de / faire redécorer / les
chambres → **Nous sommes en train de faire redécorer les
chambres.**

Follow-up: Form complete sentences and read as paragraph for listening practice.

1. avant de commencer / nous / faire venir architecte
2. il a fallu / nous / faire mettre l'électricité
3. le mois dernier / nous / faire vendre notre ancien appartement
4. en ce moment / nous / faire repeindre la salle à manger
5. les électriciens / nous / faire attendre longtemps
6. nous / avoir l'intention / faire construire un garage
7. il faudra / nous / faire refaire le mur du jardin
8. nous / faire venir des spécialistes / parce que / on / ne pas pouvoir / faire confiance aux ouvriers du village

Communication

Questions/interview. Répondez aux questions suivantes ou utilisez-les pour interviewer un(e) autre étudiant(e).

Options: Written/oral—small group interviews.

1. Est-ce que tu as envie de faire construire une maison ou de faire redécorer ton appartement?
2. Est-ce que tu laves ta voiture toi-même ou est-ce que tu la fais laver?
3. Est-ce que tu répares ta montre toi-même ou est-ce que tu la fais réparer?
4. Est-ce que tu aimes parler en classe ou est-ce que le professeur est obligé de te faire parler?
5. Est-ce que tu as tendance à faire confiance à tout le monde ou à ne faire confiance à personne?
6. Quelle est ta réaction quand on te fait attendre? Et toi, est-ce que tu fais souvent attendre tes amis?
7. À ton avis, est-ce que les professeurs font assez travailler les étudiants?
8. Qu'est-ce qui te fait peur?

 Le subjonctif passé

Présentation

The past subjunctive of all verbs is composed of the present subjunctive of **avoir** or **être** plus the past participle. It is used when the verb in the dependent clause represents a time period before the time of the verb in the independent clause.

Le subjonctif passé de *parler*		Le subjonctif passé d'*aller*	
que j'**aie parlé**	que nous **ayons parlé**	que je **sois allé(e)**	que nous **soyons allé(e)s**
que tu **aies parlé**	que vous **ayez parlé**	que tu **sois allé(e)**	que vous **soyez allé(e)(s)**
qu'il/elle/on **ait parlé**	qu'ils/elles **aient parlé**	qu'il/elle/on **soit allé(e)**	qu'ils/elles **soient allé(e)s**

Je regrette que vous ne soyez pas venu.

I'm sorry that you didn't come.

Je suis content qu'elles aient réussi.

I'm happy that they have succeeded.

Il est impossible qu'ils soient partis sans que nous l'ayons remarqué.

It's impossible that they left without our noticing it.

Substitutions: (1) C'est dommage que j'aie perdu. vous / Robert / tu / nous / les joueurs. (2) Je suis content que tu sois venu me voir. mes amis / vous / Claude / quelqu'un. (3) Je regrette que vous vous soyez mis en colère. nous / vous / Charlotte / les étudiants / tu. (4) C'est le meilleur livre que j'aie jamais lu. nous / tu / Colette / le professeur / mes amis.

Préparation

Réactions. Olivier donne son opinion sur ce qui est arrivé récemment à ses amis. Qu'est-ce qu'il dit?

Modèle   Pierre a réussi à tous ses examens. (je suis heureux) → **Je suis heureux que Pierre ait réussi à tous ses examens.**

1. Il a été accepté à Polytechnique. (je suis content)
2. Son cousin n'a pas été accepté. (j'ai peur)
3. André a décidé d'abandonner ses études. (je ne pense pas)
4. Tu as pu trouver du travail. (je suis ravi)
5. Nous nous sommes rencontrés il y a seulement six mois. (c'est incroyable)
6. Vous êtes partis trop tôt. (je regrette)
7. Tu n'es pas allé voir ce film. (j'espère)
8. Boris et François sont rentrés à quatre heures du matin. (je ne crois pas)
9. Ils se sont bien amusés. (je ne suis pas sûr)
10. Nous n'avons pas pu aider Monique. (c'est dommage)

Communication

Réactions. Exprimez vos réactions ou opinions vis-à-vis des événements suivants en utilisant des expressions telles que **je suis content(e) que, je regrette que, c'est dommage que,** etc.

Options: Written / oral. Have students prepare additional statements.

Exemple   Les Russes ont vendu l'Alaska aux États-Unis → **Je suis content(e) que les Russes aient vendu l'Alaska aux États-Unis.**

1. Alexander Graham Bell a inventé le téléphone.
2. On a inventé la bombe atomique.
3. On a construit beaucoup de centrales nucléaires.
4. On a ouvert beaucoup de restaurants «self-service».
5. On a dépensé beaucoup d'argent pour l'exploration de l'espace.
6. Les universités ont toujours accordé beaucoup d'importance aux sports.
7. Beaucoup de gens ont commencé à se préoccuper de la qualité de la vie.
8. Les colonies américaines se sont révoltées contre l'Angleterre.

BIENVENUE AU QUÉBEC
vivez
le français en famille!
AU COLLÈGE DE RIVIÈRE-DU-LOUP

⚜ Le verbe *recevoir*

Présentation

A. The verb **recevoir** is irregular:

recevoir	
je **reçois**	nous **recevons**
tu **reçois**	vous **recevez**
il/elle/on **reçoit**	ils/elles **reçoivent**

passé composé: j'ai **reçu**
futur: je **recevrai**
subjonctif: que je **reçoive**, que nous **recevions**

As-tu reçu des nouvelles de ton père?
Reçoivent-ils souvent des visites?
Je recevrai sûrement une lettre cette semaine.
Je doute qu'ils reçoivent souvent des visites.
Nous prendrons contact avec vous dès que nous aurons reçu votre lettre.
C'est la lettre la plus amusante que j'aie jamais reçue.

Décevoir (*to disappoint*) and **s'apercevoir de** (*to notice, to perceive*) are conjugated like **recevoir**.

Je ne voudrais pas vous décevoir.
Nous nous sommes aperçus immédiatement de notre erreur.
Cette conférence m'a beaucoup déçu(e).
Je suis déçu(e) que vous ne puissiez pas venir nous voir.

Option: **Décevoir** and **s'apercevoir** may be taught for recognition only.

B. Below are some items that are commonly used with **recevoir**:

du courrier (*mail*)	une carte postale
un colis (*a package*)	un mandat (*a money order*)
un cadeau (*a gift*)	une facture (*a bill*)
une lettre	des imprimés (*printed matter*)
un télégramme	

Substitutions: (1) Je reçois beaucoup de lettres. tu / mon camarade de chambre / vous / les gens célèbres / nous. (2) Il n'a pas encore reçu la lettre. je / nous / tu / vous. (3) Je me suis aperçu qu'elle ne disait rien. nous / vous / tout le monde / les autres / personne.

Préparation

A. Collectionneur de timbres. Richard collectionne les timbres. Il demande à ses amis s'ils reçoivent souvent du courrier avec des timbres intéressants.

Modèle Je / seulement des imprimés → **Je reçois seulement des imprimés.**

1. nous / quelquefois des lettres du Canada
2. tu / beaucoup de cartes postales
3. d'habitude / nous / rien d'intéressant
4. hier / je / un colis
5. mes parents / souvent des lettres du Japon
6. la semaine dernière / tu / un mandat
7. moi / seulement des factures

B. Lettre d'un prisonnier. Un prisonnier écrit à sa femme. Reconstituez les phrases qu'il a écrites.

Written preparation may be helpful.

Modèle   le gardien / me recevoir / demain / dans son bureau → **Le gardien me recevra demain dans son bureau.**

1. je / être très déçu / parce que / ne pas recevoir / visite / cette semaine
2. je / espérer / tu / recevoir / cette lettre / demain
3. je / être déçu/ tu / ne pas pouvoir / venir me voir
4. ce matin / je / s'apercevoir / absence d'un autre prisonnier
5. je / avoir peur / il / recevoir / punition sévère / si / on / le retrouver
6. à cause de cela / je / douter / nous / recevoir / permission de sortir dimanche

Communication

Questions/interview. Répondez aux questions suivantes ou utilisez-les pour interviewer un(e) autre étudiant(e).

Options: (1) Written. (2) Oral—ask questions or adapt for directed dialogue. (3) Have students work in small groups and report back their partners' responses.

1. Est-ce que tu reçois souvent des lettres? De qui?
2. Est-ce que tu as reçu des nouvelles de ta famille ou de tes amis récemment? Est-ce que tu es déçu(e) quand tu n'en reçois pas?
3. Est-ce que tu reçois des journaux étrangers? Lesquels?
4. Quelles revues américaines est-ce que tu reçois?
5. Est-ce que tu reçois souvent des amis? Quand tu les reçois, est-ce que tu préfères les inviter à dîner ou simplement leur offrir quelque chose à boire?
6. Est-ce que tu aimerais recevoir un étudiant étranger chez toi?
7. Qu'est-ce que tu ferais si tu recevais un étudiant étranger chez toi?
8. Quand est-ce que tu recevras ton diplôme? En quoi est-ce que tu te spécialises?
9. Qu'est-ce que tu aimerais recevoir pour ton anniversaire?

SYNTHÈSE

Les Français et les Américains

L'Express a interviewé Lawrence Wylie, professeur de civilisation française à Harvard et auteur de plusieurs livres sur les Français. Voici quelques-unes des conclusions auxquelles il est arrivé après avoir passé plusieurs années en France.

LE REPORTER   Vous vous intéressez beaucoup à la communication non verbale, au langage du corps et des gestes. Qu'avez-vous découvert en nous regardant vivre?

WYLIE   Beaucoup de choses. Parlons d'abord de l'aspect physique. Les Français peuvent reconnaître un Américain simplement à sa façon de marcher. Un Américain a besoin de plus d'*espace* qu'un Français. La *démarche* d'un Français est beaucoup plus contrôlée

space

way of walking

que celle d'un Américain. Le *buste* doit être droit, les *épaules* immobiles, les bras près du corps. D'ailleurs, ne dit-on pas toujours aux enfants «*Tiens-toi droit!*» «Ne *traîne* pas les pieds!»? Bien que votre *éducation* vous enseigne à ne pas faire de gestes, vous ne pouvez pas résister à en faire pour amplifier l'effet de la parole. Mais ce sont essentiellement des gestes des mains et de l'*avant-bras*. Les Français expriment beaucoup avec leur bouche, le plus souvent *arrondie*, *sans cesse* en mouvement: le *mépris* (Peuh!), le doute (Bof!), l'admiration (Au poil!).

upper body
shoulders
Stand up straight!
drag / upbringing

forearm
rounded / constantly
scorn

LE REPORTER   Quels sont, à votre avis, les principaux aspects de notre tempérament national?

WYLIE   Si vous m'aviez posé cette question il y a vingt-cinq ans, je vous aurais dit: l'attachement au passé. Les Français pensaient toujours au passé comme à une époque idéale. Aujourd'hui, je crois qu'ils vivent davantage dans le présent. Mais malgré tout, vous restez beaucoup plus tournés vers le passé que les Américains, pour lesquels seul le présent existe.

   Un autre trait fondamental de la culture française, à mon avis, est le besoin de définir. Les Français ont un besoin esthétique de définitions claires et rigoureuses. Cela vous conduit à créer des catégories rigides, des divisions, des subdivisions, des différentiations subtiles. Prenez par exemple l'enseignement de la géographie: vous partez du *tout*—   whole le monde—et vous le divisez en continents, à l'intérieur desquels vous étudiez successivement chacun des pays qui le composent. L'enfant américain, lui, fera des *études de cas:* comment vit un petit Argentin d'aujourd'hui, en quoi il ressemble à un petit Américain malgré les différences régionales.

		case studies

LE REPORTER   *En somme*, vous insistez sur les ressemblances; nous insistons sur les différences. — all things considered

WYLIE   Oui, moi, j'aime les généralisations. Mais dans une conversation avec des Français, il y a toujours quelqu'un pour me dire: «Je ne suis pas du tout de votre avis. Vous simplifiez beaucoup trop.»

LE REPORTER   Mais les Français adorent généraliser! Même sur des sujets qu'ils ne connaissent pas!

WYLIE   C'est vrai que les Français aiment bien avoir leur petite idée sur tout . . . Si on rencontre un médecin américain, il voudra toujours parler de médecine. Un médecin français vous parlera de musique, de littérature, de tout, *sauf* de médecine! — except

LE REPORTER   Parlez-nous de vos idées sur l'éducation des enfants français.

WYLIE   Je crois qu'il faut commencer par la famille. On a souvent dit que la famille était en train de se désintégrer. Je dirais exactement le contraire. Mais la différence est qu'elle repose aujourd'hui sur des *liens* — ties
plus affectifs, plus ouverts, moins autoritaires, mais *tout aussi* solides que dans le passé. Les familles — just as
françaises sont beaucoup plus *unies* que les familles — close
américaines. Vous ne verriez pas aux États-Unis des mères et des filles se promener *bras-dessus, bras-* — arm-in-arm
dessous. Ni des enfants qu'on tient par la main pour les conduire à l'école. Ni ces dimanches et ces vacances «en famille». Cette unité-là n'existe pas chez nous. Il y a en France un effort réel de compréhension des enfants *alors qu'*en Amérique on se contente généralement de — whereas
les traiter comme des *copains.* — friends, pals

Ce qui, *en revanche*, choque souvent les — on the other hand
Américains, c'est le côté négatif de l'éducation des petits Français. La base de l'éducation française, c'est le «non»: «Non, on ne fait pas cela. Non, c'est dangereux. Non, ce n'est pas comme ça que ça se fait!» On empêche l'enfant de faire des erreurs, d'apprendre par lui-même. Chez nous, c'est le contraire: l'enfant est encouragé, stimulé: «C'est bien! Continue!» L'enfant américain est plus *entreprenant.* En revanche, il — enterprising
dépend davantage des autres. La méthode française a, bien sûr, des avantages. Elle forme des enfants plus riches intérieurement, des personnalités plus fortes, qui ne comptent que sur elles-mêmes.

LE REPORTER   Est-ce vrai aussi pour les adultes?

WYLIE *Dans une certaine mesure.* Vous êtes habitués à vous   to a certain extent
protéger contre les autres. Vous *entourez* vos maisons   surround
d'un mur aussi haut que possible. Le soir, vous fermez
vos *volets.* Ça se voit même dans le langage. Quand on   shutters
demande à quelqu'un comment il va, il est fréquent
qu'il réponde: «Je me défends».

Vous, Français, vous vivez à l'intérieur d'un
système de cercles, chaque cercle étant entouré d'un
mur: le cercle de la personnalité, le cercle de la famille,
le cercle des amis, le cercle des *relations* du   acquaintances
travail . . .Cette importance du cercle se traduit dans
le langage. Le pronom «nous» s'applique à ceux qui
sont à l'intérieur du cercle; le «ils» s'applique à tous
ceux qui sont à l'extérieur. «Ils», c'est toujours
«l'ennemi»—c'est-à-dire, «les autres».

Ces cercles n'existent pas aux États-Unis. En
Amérique on change d'amis et de relations quand on
change de maison ou de travail. Prenez un cas typique:
Un Américain rencontre un Français qui vient d'arriver
aux États-Unis. Immédiatement, il l'invite à dîner chez
lui. Le Français pense: « Comme les Américains sont
ouverts et *accueillants*!» La semaine suivante, il reverra   welcoming
cet Américain qui ne le reconnaîtra peut-être pas. Ou il
verra cet Américain tous les jours pendant deux ans et
leurs relations resteront au même point. Les Français
ne comprennent pas ça. En France, il est difficile de
pénétrer dans un de ces cercles, mais une fois accepté,
c'est pour la vie!

Extrait et adapté d'un article de *L'Express.*

Compréhension Répondez aux questions suivantes, selon les renseignements
donnés dans le texte.

1. Selon Wylie, comment est-ce que les Français peuvent reconnaître un
   Américain dans la rue?
2. Selon Wylie, quels sont deux des principaux aspects du caractère français?
3. Qu'est-ce qui caractérise la conversation des Français? En quoi est-ce
   que les Américains sont différents?
4. Quels changements récents Wylie a-t-il observés dans la structure de la
   famille française?
5. Selon Wylie, les familles françaises sont plus unies que les familles américaines. Donnez quelques exemples de cette unité.
6. En quoi l'éducation d'un petit Français est-elle différente de celle d'un
   petit Américain?
7. Quels sont les avantages de chaque système d'éducation?
8. Selon Wylie, les Français ont tendance à se protéger contre les autres.
   Donnez quelques exemples de cette attitude.
9. Décrivez le système de cercles qui existe dans la société française.
10. Les Américains sont assez ouverts et accueillants dès qu'ils font la con-
    naissance de quelqu'un. En quoi les Français sont-ils différents?

NOTES CULTURELLES

Le caractère français

Selon le *Nouveau Guide France* (Guy Michaud et Georges Torrès;
Classiques Hachette) le caractère français a deux composantes principales:
le Français moyen qui est surtout un «sanguin» et le Parisien qui est
surtout un «nerveux».

Le Français moyen
Il est . . .

jovial: C'est le type du bon vivant°,
optimiste, amateur° de bon vin et de bonne
cuisine.

ingénieux°: Il a le sens pratique; il sait se
débrouiller. Il s'adapte facilement. Sa
présence d'esprit en fait un brillant
improvisateur.

sociable: Il est l'ami de tout le monde. Il se
sent bien en compagnie.

bon vivant *fun-loving* amateur *one who appreciates*
ingénieux *clever*

Le Parisien
Il est . . .

insouciant°: Son humeur est souvent
capricieuse et frivole. Il est assez bohème.

curieux: Ouvert à tout, il aime jouer et voir
jouer. Il paraît toujours pressé mais il aime
prendre son temps. Il aime suivre la mode ou
même la précéder.

moqueur: Il a l'esprit vif° et il est toujours
prêt à se moquer de° quelque chose—ou de
lui-même. Il aime les jeux de mots. En
France on dit encore que «le ridicule tue».

insouciant *carefree* vif *quick*   se moquer de *to make fun of*

Communication

A. Invitation à la discussion.

Suggested for written
composition or oral discussion.

1. À votre avis, quels sont les traits principaux du caractère américain?
2. Qu'est-ce que vous aimeriez changer dans la façon de vivre des Américains?
3. Quelles sont vos propres idées sur l'éducation des enfants?
4. Si un Français visitait les États-Unis pour la première fois, quelles observations pourrait-il faire au sujet du style de vie des Américains?

B. En fin de compte . . . En fin de compte (*everything considered*) quelles
sont vos raisons d'être satisfait(e) et quels sont vos regrets quand vous
pensez à la situation présente—ou passée—dans votre pays?

Exemples   En fin de compte, je suis bien content que mes grands-
parents aient choisi de venir vivre aux États-Unis.
Je regrette qu'on ait détruit tant de beaux paysages naturels
en construisant des autoroutes et des villes.

C. Tour d'horizon. Vous voulez laisser pour les générations futures un do-
cument qui décrive les principaux aspects de la vie contemporaine. Comment allez-vous la décrire? Pourriez-vous aussi décrire quelques aspects
de la vie en France ou dans d'autres pays francophones?

VOCABULAIRE

noms

l'araignée (f) *spider*
l'aspirateur (m) *vacuum cleaner*
la belle-mère *mother-in-law*
le cadeau *gift*
le colis *package*
le copain, la copine *friend, pal*
le courrier *mail*
le dessinateur, la dessinatrice *cartoonist*
l'éducation (f) *upbringing*
l'espace (m) *space*
la facture *bill*
la femme d'affaires *businesswoman*
les imprimés (m) *printed matter*
° la lampe
la lessive *wash, laundry*
° le lien *tie*
la machine à écrire *typewriter*
le mandat *money order*
la ménagère *housewife*
le mépris *scorn*
la mouche *fly*
la névrose *neurosis*
le plafond *ceiling*
le tout *whole*

verbes

s'apercevoir *to notice, to perceive*
avouer *to admit*
décevoir *to disappoint*
entourer *to surround*
faire confiance *to trust*
faire mal *to hurt*
faire peur *to scare*
recevoir *to receive*
résoudre *to resolve*

ronger *to gnaw*
taper *to type*
se tenir droit *to stand up straight*
traîner *to drag*
vieillir *to grow old*

adjectifs

accueillant(e) *welcoming, affable*
célibataire *single*
crevé(e) *dead tired*
entreprenant(e) *enterprising*
épuisant(e) *exhausting*
opprimé(e) *oppressed*
tendre *tender, soft*

adverbes

davantage *more, anymore*
dessous *below*
dessus *on top, above*
parfois *sometimes*
sans cesse *constantly*

divers

alors que *whereas*
autrement dit *in other words*
dans une certaine mesure *to a certain extent*
en cachette *on the sly*
en revanche *on the other hand*
en somme *all things considered*
sauf *except*
soi-disant *so-called*

Invitation à la lecture

You have now mastered most of the basic forms of the French language and are ready to enjoy literary works in their original form. In order to understand literature, other kinds of formal writing, and very formal speech, a knowledge of the **passé simple** is often necessary. The **passé simple** often replaces the more conversational **passé composé** in these types of writing. Thus, reading in French requires the recognition and understanding of the forms of the **passé simple**.

You may wish to suggest that students look at the full forms of irregular verbs, particularly **avoir** and **être**, in the tables in the Appendix.

Présentation

A. The forms of the **passé simple** for regular verbs are:

-er verbs, including aller	
je parlai	nous parlâmes
tu parlas	vous parlâtes
il/elle/on parla	ils/elles parlèrent

-re verbs	
je perdis	nous perdîmes
tu perdis	vous perdîtes
il/elle/on perdit	ils/elles perdirent

-ir verbs, including those like dormir	
je choisis	nous choisîmes
tu choisis	vous choisîtes
il/elle/on choisit	ils/elles choisirent

Un grand nombre de gens perdirent leur vie pendant la guerre.

Charles de Gaulle organisa la Résistance française.

Beaucoup de Français participèrent à la Résistance directement ou indirectement; d'autres choisirent la coopération ou le silence.

B. The following endings are added to the stems of irregular verbs: -s, -s, -t, -ˆmes, -ˆtes, -rent.

Verb	Stem	Verb	Stem	Verb	Stem	Verb	Stem	Verb	Stem
avoir	eu-	croire	cru-	faire	fi-	pouvoir	pu-	valoir	valu-
boire	bu-	devoir	du-	lire	lu-	prendre	pri-	venir	vin-
conduire	conduisi-	dire	di-	mettre	mi-	rire	ri-	vivre	vécu-
connaître	connu-	écrire	écrivi-	sourir	mouru-	savoir	su-	voir	vi-
courir	couru-	être	fu-	naître	naqui-	suivre	suivi-	vouloir	voulu-

Benjamin Franklin vécut à Paris pendant plusieurs années.

Lafayette se mit au service de la Révolution américaine.

Alexis de Tocqueville écrivit *De la démocratie en Amérique.*

Un grand nombre d'Acadiens qui furent exilés du Canada trouvèrent refuge en Louisiane.

Savez-vous quand eurent lieu les premiers Jeux Olympiques modernes?

Activités

A. Personnages et événements historiques. Les phrases suivantes décrivent certains personnes ou événements qui sont importants dans l'histoire de la France. Mettez les verbes au passé composé.

1. Madame Marie Curie obtint le prix Nobel de chimie en 1911.
2. Jacques Cartier découvrit le St.-Laurent.
3. La France envoya une armée commandée par le comte de Rochambeau pour aider le général Washington.
4. Les États-Unis achetèrent la Louisiane à Napoléon en 1803.
5. Marcel Proust écrivit *À la recherche du temps perdu.*
6. Les Anglais furent battus par les Américains à la bataille de Yorktown.
7. Henri IV établit la liberté de religion en France en 1598.
8. Après la défaite de Waterloo, Napoléon fut exilé à l'Île de Ste.-Hélène où il mourut.
9. Albert Camus, auteur du célèbre roman *La Peste*, naquit à Mondovi en Algérie.
10. Les Romains colonisèrent tout le sud de la France et firent construire des villes, des routes et des monuments.

B. Connaissez-vous l'histoire? Avec quel fait historique les personnages de la colonne à gauche sont-ils associés?

1. Ferdinand de Lesseps
2. Sarah Bernhardt
3. Antoine-Laurent de Lavoisier
4. Frédéric Bartholdi
5. Louis XIV
6. Auguste Rodin
7. Georges Bizet
8. Paul Gauguin
9. Jean-François Champollion
10. Claude-Joseph Rouget de Lisle
11. Claude Monet
12. Pierre de Coubertin

a. composa l'opéra intitulé *Carmen*
b. découvrit l'oxygène
c. sculpta la statue du *Penseur*
d. construisit le canal de Suez
e. sculpta la Statue de la Liberté
f. vécut une partie de sa vie à Tahiti
g. fut le rénovateur des Jeux Olympiques
h. fit construire le château de Versailles
i. devint la plus grande actrice de son temps
j. fut un des fondateurs de l'école impressionniste
k. traduisit les hiéroglyphes égyptiens
l. écrivit l'hymne national français

Follow-up: Ask students what each person listed did; have students respond in the **passé composé**.

If further controlled practice seems appropriate, workbook activities can be used. In addition, students can also be asked to find examples of the **passé simple** in the following readings and give the appropriate form of the **passé composé** and/or the meaning of these verbs.

Réponses: 1.d; 2.i; 3.b; 4.e; 5.h; 6.c; 7.a; 8.f; 9.k; 10.l; 11.j; 12.g

LECTURES

Présence française en Amérique du Nord

Il y a aujourd'hui plus de 130 millions de francophones. Le français est donc loin d'être une simple langue de culture littéraire comme on le croit souvent. Il est utilisé *à travers* le monde, non seulement par plusieurs peuples mais également par de nombreux organismes internationaux et diplomatiques. Ainsi, à l'UNESCO, les chefs de délégation qui s'expriment en français sont aussi nombreux que ceux qui s'expriment en anglais. Et aux Nations-Unies, une délégation sur trois utilise régulièrement le français. — throughout

Sur le continent américain, c'est le Québec qui constitue le cœur de la francophonie avec ses cinq millions de francophones et son *réseau* d'institutions politiques, économiques, sociales et culturelles. Les États-Unis eux-mêmes comptent plusieurs millions de gens qui sont d'origine canadienne française. — network

Bien que ce soit à New York que les Français *mirent pied à terre* pour la première fois en Amérique, c'est du Québec que partirent la plupart des explorateurs du Canada et des États-Unis. La ville de Québec elle-même fut fondée en 1608 par Samuel de Champlain. Mais avant de fonder le premier établissement permanent en Amérique, Champlain avait *parcouru* les *côtes* de la Nouvelle-Angleterre jusqu'à — set foot / traveled / coasts

Samuel de Champlain

la *Nouvelle-Écosse*. Il avait exploré ce qui est aujourd'hui Boston. C'est   Nova Scotia
lui aussi qui découvrit les montagnes du Vermont et le lac qui porte
maintenant son nom.

C'est du Québec aussi que Jean Brulé partit à la découverte du lac
Supérieur en 1628. Et à Red Banks dans le Wisconsin se trouve un
monument qui commémore la découverte du lac Michigan par Jean
Nicolet en 1634. Ce sont deux missionnaires canadiens, les pères Galinée
et Dollier de Casson qui établirent les premières cartes de l'Erie. Jolliet
et Marquette explorèrent le Mississippi jusqu'à l'Arkansas et un monument dans le Wyalusing State Park honore encore leur mémoire.
L'Ohio fut découvert par Cavelier de La Salle, dont la mémoire est
honorée à South Bend dans l'Indiana. C'est lui aussi qui explora le
Mississippi jusqu'à son *embouchure* et qui construisit le premier *navire*   mouth / ship
qui navigua sur les Grands Lacs.

On pourrait mentionner beaucoup d'autres explorateurs encore:
Daniel Duluth, dont une ville du Minnesota porte le nom; Jean-Baptiste
Lemoyne d'Iberville, qui fonda la Nouvelle-Orléans et qui traça les
plans du *Vieux Carré*; son frère Pierre, qui fonda les villes de Biloxi et   French Quarter
de Mobile et qui fut le premier colonisateur de la Louisiane. Il y eut
aussi Longueuil, qui explora le Tennessee et le Kentucky; Pierre Le-
sueur, qui découvrit la rivière Minnesota; les frères La Vérendrye, qui
explorèrent le Dakota, le Montana et le Wyoming où beaucoup de
localités portent encore des noms français; et beaucoup d'autres qu'il
serait trop long d'énumérer.

La colonisation du Nouveau Monde a donc été fortement marquée
par la présence française. Et on peut *se demander* ce que seraient les   wonder
États-Unis aujourd'hui si Napoléon n'avait pas vendu la Louisiane en
1803.

Extrait et adapté d'un discours prononcé par Gilles La Montagne, ancien maire de la ville de
Québec. Le texte a paru dans le *AATF National Bulletin*.

Compréhension Répondez aux questions suivantes selon les renseignements donnés dans le texte. Bien que le texte soit au passé simple, utilisez le passé composé dans vos réponses où il convient de l'utiliser.

1. Pourquoi peut-on dire que le français n'est pas seulement une langue de culture et qu'il garde une importance internationale?
2. Quel rôle le Québec joue-t-il en Amérique du Nord?
3. Est-ce qu'il y a beaucoup de gens d'origine française aux États-Unis?
4. Quel a été le point de départ de la plupart des explorateurs du Canada et des États-Unis?
5. Qui a fondé la ville de Québec et en quelle année?
6. Qui a découvert le lac Supérieur et en quelle année?
7. Pourquoi y a-t-il à South Bend un monument qui honore la mémoire de Cavelier de La Salle?
8. Quelle a été la contribution des deux frères Lemoyne d'Iberville?
9. Quelle partie des États-Unis les frères La Vérendrye ont-ils explorée?

Les Français et la Guerre d'Indépendance

L'influence française aux États-Unis ne se limite pas à celle des explorateurs et des pionniers. Une partie des principes démocratiques sur lesquels la nation américaine est fondée ont leur origine dans les idées que les philosophes français du dix-huitième siècle—Montesquieu, Rousseau, Voltaire, Diderot, d'Alembert et d'autres—avaient exprimées dans leurs écrits. Les idées des philosophes français furent ainsi mises en pratique aux États-Unis avant même que la Révolution française de 1789 puisse imposer ces mêmes principes sur le *sol* français.   soil

Au temps de la Guerre d'Indépendance, d'autre part, les Français apportèrent une aide à la fois économique et militaire aux treize colonies qui luttaient pour leur indépendance. Une des premières missions politiques de Benjamin Franklin fut d'obtenir l'aide financière de la France. Le Marquis de Lafayette de son côté, se passionna immédiatement pour la cause américaine, et après avoir équipé à ses propres *frais*   expenses un navire baptisté *La Victoire*, il vint se mettre au service de la révolution américaine.

Il faut dire *cependant* que l'aide de la France n'était pas uniquement   however motivée par la générosité et par l'amour de la liberté car le gouvernement français voyait là un moyen de combattre indirectement les Anglais. Il *cédait* aussi dans une certaine mesure à la pression de l'in-   gave in telligentsia française qui se passionnait pour les idées des philosophes et qui voyait dans la révolution américaine l'espoir d'une victoire des idées nouvelles.

Compréhension Selon les renseignements donnés dans le texte, comment la France a-t-elle aidé les États-Unis pendant la Guerre d'Indépendance et pourquoi est-elle venue à l'aide des Américains?

Réception en l'honneur de Benjamin Franklin à la Cour de France en 1778

Le lion et le rat

Il faut autant qu'on peut, obliger tout le monde:
On a souvent besoin d'un plus petit que soi.
De cette vérité deux fables *feront foi*,   will attest
    Tant la chose en *preuves* abonde.   proofs
    Entre les *pattes* d'un lion   paws
Un rat sortit de terre assez *à l'étourdie*.   dazed
Le roi des animaux, en cette occasion,
Montra ce qu'il était, et lui donna la vie.
    Ce *bienfait* ne fut pas perdu.   good deed
    Quelqu'un aurait-il jamais cru
    Qu'un lion d'un rat *eût affaire*?   had any need
Cependant il *advint* qu'*au sortir* des forêts   came to pass / at the exit
    Ce lion fut pris dans des *rêts*   nets
Dont ses *rugissements* ne le purent défaire.   roars
Sire Rat *accourut*, et fit tant par ses dents   came running
Qu'une *maille rongée* emporta tout l'ouvrage.   mesh / gnawed
    Patience et longueur de temps
    Font plus que force ni que rage.

Jean de La Fontaine (1621–1695)

Compréhension Répondez aux questions suivantes selon les renseignements
donnés dans la fable.

1. Quel conseil La Fontaine donne-t-il dans cette fable aux gens importants
   et puissants?
2. Quel conseil donne-t-il aux gens qui sont toujours pressés?
3. Qu'est-ce que le lion a fait quand le rat est apparu entre ses pattes?
4. Qu'est-ce qui est arrivé au lion quelque temps plus tard?
5. Qu'est-ce que le rat a fait pour l'aider?

Appendixes

International phonetic alphabet

Vowels

i	midi
u	nous
a	la
y	du
e	été
ɛ	mère
o	dos
ɔ	votre
ø	deux
œ	leur
ə	le
ɑ	pâte
ɛ̃	vin
õ	mon
ɑ̃	dans
œ̃	un

Consonants

p	petit
t	tête
k	quand
b	beau
d	danger
g	gare
f	fin
v	victoire
s	sa
z	zéro
m	maman
n	non
l	livre
ʃ	chien
ʒ	juge
ɲ	montagne
r	rêve

Semivowels

j	famille, métier, crayon
w	Louis, voici
ɥ	lui, depuis

Glossary of grammar terms

As you learn French, you may come across grammar terms in English with which you are not familiar. The following glossary is a reference list of grammar terms and definitions with examples. You will find that these terms are used in the grammar explanations of this and other textbooks. If the terms are unfamiliar to you, it will be helpful to refer to this list.

adjective a word used to modify, qualify, define, or specify a noun or noun equivalent (*intricate* design, *volcanic* ash, *medical* examination)
demonstrative adjective designates or points out a specific item (*this* area)
descriptive adjective provides description (*narrow* street)
interrogative adjective asks or questions (*Which* page?)
possessive adjective indicates possession (*our* house)
In French, the adjective form must agree with, or show the same gender and number as, the noun it modifies.

adverb a word used to qualify or modify a verb, adjective, another adverb, or some other modifying phrase or clause (soared *gracefully*, *rapidly* approaching train)

agreement the accordance of forms between subject and verb, in terms of person and number, or between tenses of verbs (The *bystander witnessed* the accident but *failed* to report it.)
In French, the form of the adjective must conform in gender and number with the modified noun or noun equivalent.

article one of several types of words used before a noun
definite article limits, defines, or specifies (*the* village)
indefinite article refers to a nonspecific member of a group or class (*a* village, *an* arrangement)
partitive article refers to an indefinite quantity of an item (*some* coffee, *any* tea). In French, the article takes different forms to indicate the gender and number of a noun.

auxiliary a verb or verb form used with other verbs to construct certain tenses, voices, or moods (He *is* leaving. She *has* arrived. You *must* listen.)

clause a group of words consisting of a subject and a predicate and functioning as part of a complex or compound sentence rather than a complete sentence
subordinate clause modifies and is dependent upon another clause (*Since the rain has stopped*, we can have a picnic.)
main clause is capable of standing independently as a complete sentence (If all goes well, *the plane will depart in twenty minutes.*)

cognate a word resembling a word in another language (*university* and *université* in French)

command *See* **mood** (**imperative**).

comparative   level of comparison used to show an increase or decrease of quantity or quality or to compare or show inequality between two items (*higher* prices, the *more* beautiful of the two mirrors, *less* diligently, *better* than)

comparison   modification of the form of an adjective or adverb to show change in the quantity or quality of an item or to show the relation between the items

conditional   a verb construction used in a contrary-to-fact statement consisting of a condition or an *if*-clause and a conclusion (If you had told me you were sick, *I would have offered* to help.)

conjugation   the set of forms a verb takes to indicate changes of person, number, tense, mood, and voice

conjunction   a word used to link or connect sentences or parts of sentences

contraction   an abbreviated or shortened form of a word or word group (*can't, we'll*)

gender   the classification of a word by sex. In English, almost all nouns are classified as masculine, feminine, or neuter according to the biological sex of the thing named; in French, however, a word is classified as feminine or masculine (there is no neuter classification) primarily on the basis of its linguistic form or derivation.

idiom   an expression that is grammatically or semantically unique to a particular language (*I caught a cold. Happy birthday.*)

indicative   *See* **mood.**

imperative   *See* **mood.**

infinitive   the basic form of the verb, and the one listed in dictionaries, with no indication of person or number; it is often used in verb constructions and as a verbal noun, usually with "to" in English or with **-er, ir,** or **-re** in French.

inversion   *See* **word order (inverted).**

mood   the form and construction a verb assumes to express the manner in which the action or state takes place.
imperative mood used to express commands (*Walk* to the park with me.)
indicative mood the form most frequently used, usually expressive of certainty and fact (My neighbor *walks* to the park every afternoon.)
subjunctive mood used in expression of possibility, doubt, or hypothetical situations (I wish he *were* here.)

noun   a word that names something and usually functions as a subject or an object (*lady, country, family*)

number   the form a word or phrase assumes to indicate singular or plural (*light/lights, mouse/mice, he has/they have*)
cardinal number used in counting or expressing quantity (*1, 23, 6,825*)
ordinal number refers to sequence (*second, fifteenth, thirty-first*)

object	a noun or noun equivalent **direct object** receives the action of the verb (The boy caught a *fish*.) **indirect object** affected by the action of the verb (Please do *me*, a favor.)
participle	a verb form used as an adjective or adverb and in forming tenses **past participle** relates to the past or a perfect tense and takes the appropriate ending (*written* proof, the door has been *locked*) **present participle** assumes the progressive "-ing" ending in English (*protesting* loudly; *seeing* them) In French, a participle used as an adjective or in an adjectival phrase must agree in gender and number with the modified noun or noun equivalent.
passive	*See* **voice (passive)**.
person	designated by the personal pronoun and/or by the verb form **first person** the speaker or writer (*I*, *we*) **second person** the person(s) addressed (*you*) In French, there are two forms of address: the familiar and the polite. **third person** the person or thing spoken about (*she*, *he*, *it*, *they*)
phrase	a word group that forms a unit of expression, often named after the part of speech it contains or forms
prefix	a letter or letter group added at the beginning of a word to alter the meaning (*non*committtal, *re*discover)
preposition	a connecting word used to indicate a spatial, temporal, causal, affective, directional, or some other relation between a noun or pronoun and the sentence or a portion of it (We waited *for* six hours. The article was written *by* a famous journalist.)
pronoun	a word used in place of a noun **demonstrative pronoun** refers to something previously mentioned in context (If you need hiking boots, I recommend *these*.) **indefinite pronoun** denotes a nonspecific class or item (*Nothing* has changed.) **interrogative pronoun** asks about a person or thing (*Whose* is this?) **object pronoun** functions as a direct, an indirect, or a prepositional object (Three persons saw *her*. Write *me* a letter. The flowers are for *you*.) **possessive pronoun** indicates possession (The blue car is *ours*.) **reflexive pronoun** refers back to the subject (They introduced *themselves*.) **subject pronoun** functions as the subject of a clause or sencence (*He* departed a while ago.)
reflexive construction	*See* **pronoun (reflexive)**.
sentence	a word group, or even a single word, that forms a meaningful complete expression **declarative sentence** states something and is followed by a period (*The museum contains many fine examples of folk art.*) **exclamatory sentence** exhibits force or passion and is followed by an exclamation point (*I want to be left alone!*)

interrogative sentence asks a question and is followed by a question mark (*Who are you?*)

subject   a noun or noun equivalent acting as the agent of the action or the person, place, thing, or abstraction spoken about (*The fishermen* drew in their nets. *The nets* were filled with the day's catch.)

suffix   a letter or letter group added to the end of a word to alter the meaning or function (like*ness*, transport*ation*, joy*ous*, love*ly*)

superlative   level of comparison used to express the utmost or lowest level or to indicate the highest or lowest relation in comparing more than two items (*highest* prices, the *most* beautiful, *least* diligently)

tense   the form a verb takes to express the time of the action, state, or condition in relation to the time of speaking or writing
imparfait relates to an action that continued over a period of time in the past (It *was existing*. We *were learning*.)
futur antérieur relates to something that has not yet occurred but will have taken place and be complete by some future time (It *will have* existed. We *will have* learned.)
future tense relates to something that has not yet occurred (It *will* exist. We *will* learn.)
plus-que-parfait relates to an occurrence that began and ended before or by a past event or time spoken or written of (It *had existed*. We *had learned*.)
passé composé relates to an occurrence that began at some point in the past but was finished by the time of speaking or writing (It *has existed*. We *have learned*.)
passé simple relates to an occurrence that began and ended at some point in the remote past. This is a literary tense. (He *died* in 1705. The revolution *took place* in 1971.)
present tense relates to now, the time of speaking or writing, or to a general, timeless fact (It *exists*. We *learn*. Fish *swim*).
progressive tense relates an action that is, was, or will be in progress or continuance (It *is happening*. It *was happening*. It *will be happening*.)

a word that expresses action or a state or condition (*walk, be, feel*)

verb   **intransitive verb** no receiver is necessary. (The light shines.)
orthographic-changing verb undergoes spelling changes in conjugation (infinitive: buy; past indicative: *bought*)
transitive verb requires a receiver or an object to complete the predicate (He *kicks* the ball.)

the form a verb takes to indicate the relation between the expressed action or state and the subject
voice   **active voice** indicates that the subject is the agent of the action (The child *sleeps*. The professor *lectures*.)
passive voice indicates that the subject does not initiate the action but that the action is directed toward the subject (I *was contacted* by my attorney. The road *got slippery* from the rain.)

word order the sequence of words in a clause or sentence

inverted word order an element other than the subject appears first (*If the weather permits*, we plan to vacation in the country. *Please* be on time. *Have* you met my parents?)

Regular Verbs

<table>
<tr>
<td rowspan="2">Infinitif
Participes</td>
<td colspan="5" align="center">Indicatif</td>
</tr>
<tr>
<td>Présent</td>
<td>Imparfait</td>
<td>Passé
composé</td>
<td>Passé
simple</td>
<td>Plus-que-
parfait</td>
</tr>
<tr>
<td>parler
parlant
parlé</td>
<td>parle
parles
parle
parlons
parlez
parlent</td>
<td>parlais
parlais
parlait
parlions
parliez
parlaient</td>
<td>ai parlé
as parlé
a parlé
avons parlé
avez parlé
ont parlé</td>
<td>parlai
parlas
parla
parlâmes
parlâtes
parlèrent</td>
<td>avais parlé
avais parlé
avait parlé
avions parlé
aviez parlé
avaient parlé</td>
</tr>
<tr>
<td>finir
finissant
fini</td>
<td>finis
finis
finit
finissons
finissez
finissent</td>
<td>finissais
finissais
finissait
finissions
finissiez
finissaient</td>
<td>ai fini
as fini
a fini
avons fini
avez fini
ont fini</td>
<td>finis
finis
finit
finîmes
finîtes
finirent</td>
<td>avais fini
avais fini
avait fini
avions fini
aviez fini
avaient fini</td>
</tr>
<tr>
<td>rendre
rendant
rendu</td>
<td>rends
rends
rend
rendons
rendez
rendent</td>
<td>rendais
rendais
rendait
rendions
rendiez
rendaient</td>
<td>ai rendu
as rendu
a rendu
avons rendu
avez rendu
ont rendu</td>
<td>rendis
rendis
rendit
rendîmes
rendîtes
rendirent</td>
<td>avais rendu
avais rendu
avait rendu
avions rendu
aviez rendu
avaient rendu</td>
</tr>
<tr>
<td>partir (dormir,
  s'endormir, mentir,
  sentir, servir, sortir)
partant
parti</td>
<td>pars
pars
part
partons
partez
partent</td>
<td>partais
partais
partait
partions
partiez
partaient</td>
<td>suis parti(e)
es parti(e)
est parti(e)
sommes parti(e)s
êtes parti(e)(s)
sont parti(e)s</td>
<td>partis
partis
partit
partîmes
partîtes
partirent</td>
<td>étais parti(e)
étais parti(e)
était parti(e)
étions parti(e)s
étiez parti(e)(s)
étaient parti(e)s</td>
</tr>
</table>

	Futur antérieur	Conditionnel		Impératif	Subjonctif	
Futur	**Futur antérieur**	**Présent**	**Passé**		**Présent**	**Passé composé du subjonctif**
parlerai	aurai parlé	parlerais	aurais parlé		parle	aie parlé
parleras	auras parlé	parlerais	aurais parlé	parle	parles	aies parlé
parlera	aura parlé	parlerait	aurait parlé		parle	ait parlé
parlerons	aurons parlé	parlerions	aurions parlé	parlons	parlions	ayons parlé
parlerez	aurez parlé	parleriez	auriez parlé	parlez	parliez	ayez parlé
parleront	auront parlé	parleraient	auraient parlé		parlent	aient parlé
finirai	aurai fini	finirais	aurais fini		finisse	aie fini
finiras	auras fini	finirais	aurais fini	finis	finisses	aies fini
finira	aura fini	finirait	aurait fini		finisse	ait fini
finirons	aurons fini	finirions	aurions fini	finissons	finissions	ayons fini
finirez	aurez fini	finiriez	auriez fini	finissez	finissiez	ayez fini
finiront	auront fini	finiraient	auraient fini		finissent	aient fini
rendrai	aurai rendu	rendrais	aurais rendu		rende	aie rendu
rendras	auras rendu	rendrais	aurais rendu	rends	rendes	aies rendu
rendra	aura rendu	rendrait	aurait rendu		rende	ait rendu
rendrons	aurons rendu	rendrions	aurions rendu	rendons	rendions	ayons rendu
rendrez	aurez rendu	rendriez	auriez rendu	rendez	rendiez	ayez rendu
rendront	auront rendu	rendraient	auraient rendu		rendent	aient rendu
partirai	serai parti(e)	partirais	serais parti(e)		parte	sois parti(e)
partiras	seras parti(e)	partirais	serais parti(e)	pars	partes	sois parti(e)
partira	sera parti(e)	partirait	serait parti(e)		parte	soit parti(e)
partirons	serons parti(e)s	partirions	serions parti(e)s	partons	partions	soyons parti(e)s
partirez	serez parti(e)(s)	partiriez	seriez parti(e)(s)	partez	partiez	soyez parti(e)(s)
partiront	seront parti(e)s	partiraient	seraient parti(e)s		partent	soient parti(e)s

Spelling-Changing Verbs

Infinitif Participes				Indicatif	
	Présent	Imparfait	Passé composé	Passé simple	Plus-que-parfait
acheter (lever, **mener,** **promener)** achetant acheté	achète achètes achète achetons achetez achètent	achetais achetais achetait achetions achetiez achetaient	ai acheté as acheté a acheté avons acheté avez acheté ont acheté	achetai achetas acheta achetâmes achetâtes achetèrent	avais acheté avais acheté avait acheté avions acheté aviez acheté avaient acheté
préférer (considérer, **espérer, exagérer,** **inquiéter, répéter)** préférant préféré	préfère préfères préfère préférons préférez préfèrent	préférais préférais préférait préférions préfériez préféraient	ai préféré as préféré a préféré avons préféré avez préféré ont préféré	préférai préféras préféra préférâmes préférâtes préférèrent	avais préféré avais préféré avait préféré avions préféré aviez préféré avaient préféré
manger (arranger, **changer, corriger,** **déranger, diriger,** **encourager, nager)** mangeant mangé	mange manges mange mangeons mangez mangent	mangeais mangeais mangeait mangions mangiez mangeaient	ai mangé as mangé a mangé avons mangé avez mangé ont mangé	mangeai mangeas mangea mangeâmes mangeâtes mangèrent	avais mangé avais mangé avait mangé avions mangé aviez mangé avaient mangé
payer (envoyer, **essayer,** **renvoyer)** payant payé	paie paies paie payons payez paient	payais payais payait payions payiez payaient	ai payé as payé a payé avons payé avez payé ont payé	payai payas paya payâmes payâtes payèrent	avais payé avais payé avait payé avions payé aviez payé avaient payé
commencer commençant commencé	commence commences commence commençons commencez commencent	commençais commençais commençait commencions commenciez commençaient	ai commencé as commencé a commencé avons commencé avez commencé ont commencé	commençai commenças commença commençâmes commençâtes commencèrent	avais commencé avais commencé avait commencé avions commencé aviez commencé avaient commencé
appeler (rappeler) appelant appelé	appelle appelles appelle appelons appelez appellent	appelais appelais appelait appelions appeliez appelaient	ai appelé as appelé a appelé avons appelé avez appelé ont appelé	appelai appelas appela appelâmes appelâtes appelèrent	avais appelé avais appelé avait appelé avions appelé aviez appelé avaient appelé

		Conditionnel		Impératif	Subjonctif	
Futur	Futur antérieur	Présent	Passé		Présent	Passé composé du subjonctif
achèterai	aurai acheté	achèterais	aurais acheté		achète	aie acheté
achèteras	auras acheté	achèterais	aurais acheté	achète	achètes	aies acheté
achètera	aura acheté	achèterait	aurait acheté		achète	ait acheté
achèterons	aurons acheté	achèterions	aurions acheté	achetons	achetions	ayons acheté
achèterez	aurez acheté	achèteriez	auriez acheté	achetez	achetiez	ayez acheté
achèteront	auront acheté	achèteraient	auraient acheté		achètent	aient acheté
préférerai	aurai préféré	préférerais	aurais préféré		préfère	aie préféré
préféreras	auras préféré	préférerais	aurais préféré	préfère	préfères	aies préféré
préférera	aura préféré	préférerait	aurait préféré		préfère	ait préféré
préférerons	aurons préféré	préférerions	aurions préféré	préférons	préférions	ayons préféré
préférerez	aurez préféré	préféreriez	auriez préféré	préférez	préfériez	ayez préféré
préféreront	auront préféré	préféreraient	auraient préféré		préfèrent	aient préféré
mangerai	aurai mangé	mangerais	aurais mangé		mange	aie mangé
mangeras	auras mangé	mangerais	aurais mangé	mange	manges	aies mangé
mangera	aura mangé	mangerait	aurait mangé		mange	ait mangé
mangerons	aurons mangé	mangerions	aurions mangé	mangeons	mangions	ayons mangé
mangerez	aurez mangé	mangeriez	auriez mangé	mangez	mangiez	ayez mangé
mangeront	auront mangé	mangeraient	auraient mangé		mangent	aient mangé
paierai	aurai payé	paierais	aurais payé		paie	aie payé
paieras	auras payé	paierais	aurais payé	paie	paies	aies payé
paiera	aura payé	paierait	aurait payé		paie	ait payé
paierons	aurons payé	paierions	aurions payé	payons	payions	ayons payé
paierez	aurez payé	paieriez	auriez payé	payez	payiez	ayez payé
paieront	auront payé	paieraient	auraient payé		paient	aient payé
commencerai	aurai commencé	commencerais	aurais commencé		commence	aie commencé
commenceras	auras commencé	commencerais	aurais commencé	commence	commences	aies commencé
commencera	aura commencé	commencerait	aurait commencé		commence	ait commencé
commencerons	aurons commencé	commencerions	aurions commencé	commençons	commencions	ayons commencé
commencerez	aurez commencé	commenceriez	auriez commencé	commencez	commenciez	ayez commencé
commenceront	auront commencé	commenceraient	auraient commencé		commencent	aient commencé
appellerai	aurai appelé	appellerais	aurais appelé		appelle	aie appelé
appelleras	auras appelé	appellerais	aurais appelé	appelle	appelles	aies appelé
appellera	aura appelé	appellerait	aurait appelé		appelle	ait appelé
appellerons	aurons appelé	appellerions	aurions appelé	appelons	appelions	ayons appelé
appellerez	aurez appelé	appelleriez	auriez appelé	appelez	appeliez	ayez appelé
appelleront	auront appelé	appelleront	auraient appelé		appellent	aient appelé

Auxiliary Verbs

Infinitif Participes					
			Indicatif		
	Présent	Imparfait	Passé composé	Passé simple	Plus-que-parfait
être	suis	étais	ai été	fus	avais été
étant	es	étais	as été	fus	avais été
été	est	était	a été	fut	avait été
	sommes	étions	avons été	fûmes	avions été
	êtes	étiez	avez été	fûtes	aviez été
	sont	étaient	ont été	furent	avaient été
avoir	ai	avais	ai eu	eus	avais eu
ayant	as	avais	as eu	eus	avais eu
eu	a	avait	a eu	eut	avait eu
	avons	avions	avons eu	eûmes	avions eu
	avez	aviez	avez eu	eûtes	aviez eu
	ont	avaient	ont eu	eurent	avaient eu

		Conditionnel		Impératif		Subjonctif	
Futur	Futur antérieur	Présent	Passé			Présent	Passé composé du subjonctif
serai	aurai été	serais	aurais été			sois	aie été
seras	auras été	serais	aurais été	sois		sois	aies été
sera	aura été	serait	aurait été			soit	ait été
serons	aurons été	serions	aurions été	soyons		soyons	ayons été
serez	aurez été	seriez	auriez été	soyez		soyez	ayez été
seront	auront été	seraient	auraient été			soient	aient été
aurai	aurai eu	aurais	aurais eu			aie	aie eu
auras	auras eu	aurais	aurais eu	aie		aies	aies eu
aura	aura eu	aurait	aurait eu			ait	ait eu
aurons	aurons eu	aurions	aurions eu	ayons		ayons	ayons eu
aurez	aurez eu	auriez	auriez eu	ayez		ayez	ayez eu
auront	auront eu	auraient	auraient eu			aient	aient eu

Irregular Verbs

Each verb in this list is conjugated like the model indicated by number. See the table of irregular verbs for the models.

admettre 11   construire 13   disparaître 4   reconduire 3   souffrir 14
(s')apercevoir 19   couvrir 15   inscrire 8   redire 7   surprendre 18
apprendre 18   décevoir 19   introduire 3   relire 12   se taire 16
attendre 18   découvrir 15   paraître 4   remettre 11   tenir 24
commettre 11   décrire 8   prévoir 25   revenir 24   traduire 3
comprendre 18   devenir 24   promettre 11   revoir 25   taire 16

Infinitif / Participes	Indicatif				
	Présent	Imparfait	Passé composé	Passé simple	Plus-que-parfait
1	vais	allais	suis allé(e)	allai	étais allé(e)
	vas	allais	es allé(e)	allas	étais allé(e)
aller	va	allait	est allé(e)	alla	était allé(e)
allant	allons	allions	sommes allé(e)s	allâmes	étions allé(e)s
allé	allez	alliez	êtes allé(e)(s)	allâtes	étiez allé(e)(s)
	vont	allaient	sont allé(e)s	allèrent	étaient allé(e)s
2	bois	buvais	ai bu	bus	avais bu
	bois	buvais	as bu	bus	avais bu
boire	boit	buvait	a bu	but	avait bu
buvant	buvons	buvions	avons bu	bûmes	avions bu
bu	buvez	buviez	avez bu	bûtes	aviez bu
	boivent	buvaient	ont bu	burent	avaient bu
3	conduis	conduisais	ai conduit	conduisis	avais conduit
	conduis	conduisais	as conduit	conduisis	avais conduit
conduire	conduit	conduisait	a conduit	conduisit	avait conduit
conduisant	conduisons	conduisions	avons conduit	conduisîmes	avions conduit
conduit	conduisez	conduisiez	avez conduit	conduisîtes	aviez conduit
	conduisent	conduisaient	ont conduit	conduisirent	avaient conduit
4	connais	connaissais	ai connu	connus	avais connu
	connais	connaissais	as connu	connus	avais connu
connaître	connaît	connaissait	a connu	connut	avait connu
connaissant	connaissons	connaissions	avons connu	connûmes	avions connu
connu	connaissez	connaissiez	avez connu	connûtes	aviez connu
	connaissent	connaissaient	ont connu	connurent	avaient connu
5	crois	croyais	ai cru	crus	avais cru
	crois	croyais	as cru	crus	avais cru
croire	croit	croyait	a cru	crut	avait cru
croyant	croyons	croyions	avons cru	crûmes	avions cru
cru	croyez	croyiez	avez cru	crûtes	aviez cru
	croient	croyaient	ont cru	crurent	avaient cru
6	dois	devais	ai dû	dus	avais dû
	dois	devais	as dû	dus	avais dû
devoir	doit	devait	a dû	dut	avait dû
devant	devons	devions	avons dû	dûmes	avions dû
dû	devez	deviez	avez dû	dûtes	aviez dû
	doivent	devaient	ont dû	durent	avaient dû

| | | Conditionnel | | Impératif | Subjonctif | |
Futur	Futur antérieur	Présent	Passé		Présent	Passé composé du subjonctif
irai	serai allé(e)	irais	serais allé(e)		aille	sois allé(e)
iras	seras allé(e)	irais	serais allé(e)	va	ailles	sois allé(e)
ira	sera allé(e)	irait	serait allé(e)		aille	soit allé(e)
irons	serons allé(e)s	irions	serions allé(e)s	allons	allions	soyons allé(e)s
irez	serez allé(e)(s)	iriez	seriez allé(e)(s)	allez	alliez	soyez allé(e)(s)
iront	seront allé(e)s	iraient	seraient allé(e)s		aillent	soient allé(e)s
boirai	aurai bu	boirais	aurais bu		boive	aie bu
boiras	auras bu	boirais	aurais bu	bois	boives	aies bu
boira	aura bu	boirait	aurait bu		boive	ait bu
boirons	aurons bu	boirions	aurions bu	buvons	buvions	ayons bu
boirez	aurez bu	boiriez	auriez bu	buvez	buviez	ayez bu
boiront	auront bu	boiraient	auraient bu		boivent	aient bu
conduirai	aurai conduit	conduirais	aurais conduit		conduise	aie conduit
conduiras	auras conduit	conduirais	aurais conduit	conduis	conduises	aies conduit
conduira	aura conduit	conduirait	aurait conduit		conduise	ait conduit
conduirons	aurons conduit	conduirions	aurions conduit	conduisons	conduisions	ayons conduit
conduirez	aurez conduit	conduiriez	auriez conduit	conduisez	conduisiez	ayez conduit
conduiront	auront conduit	conduiraient	auraient conduit		conduisent	aient conduit
connaîtrai	aurai connu	connaîtrais	aurais connu		connaisse	aie connu
connaîtras	auras connu	connaîtrais	aurais connu	connais	connaisses	aies connu
connaîtra	aura connu	connaîtrait	aurait connu		connaisse	ait connu
connaîtrons	aurons connu	connaîtrions	aurions connu	connaissons	connaissions	ayons connu
connaîtrez	aurez connu	connaîtriez	auriez connu	connaissez	connaissiez	ayez connu
connaîtront	auront connu	connaîtraient	auraient connu		connaissent	aient connu
croirai	aurai cru	croirais	aurais cru		croie	aie cru
croiras	auras cru	croirais	aurais cru	crois	croies	aies cru
croira	aura cru	croirait	aurait cru		croie	ait cru
croirons	aurons cru	croirions	aurions cru	croyons	croyions	ayons cru
croirez	aurez cru	croiriez	auriez cru	croyez	croyiez	ayez cru
croiront	auront cru	croiraient	auraient cru		croient	aient cru
devrai	aurai dû	devrais	aurais dû		doive	aie dû
devras	auras dû	devrais	aurais dû	dois	doives	aies dû
devra	aura dû	devrait	aurait dû		doive	ait dû
devrons	aurons dû	devrions	aurions dû	devons	devions	ayons dû
devrez	aurez dû	devriez	auriez dû	devez	deviez	ayez dû
devront	auront dû	devraient	auraient dû		doivent	aient dû

Indicatif

	Présent	Imparfait	Passé composé	Passé simple	Plus-que-parfait
7	dis	disais	ai dit	dis	avais dit
	dis	disais	as dit	dis	avais dit
dire	dit	disait	a dit	dit	avait dit
disant	disons	disions	avons dit	dîmes	avions dit
dit	dites	disiez	avez dit	dîtes	aviez dit
	disent	disaient	ont dit	dirent	avaient dit
8	écris	écrivais	ai écrit	écrivis	avais écrit
	écris	écrivais	as écrit	écrivis	avais écrit
écrire	écrit	écrivait	a écrit	écrivit	avait écrit
écrivant	écrivons	écrivions	avons écrit	écrivîmes	avions écrit
écrit	écrivez	écriviez	avez écrit	écrivîtes	aviez écrit
	écrivent	écrivaient	ont écrit	écrivirent	avaient écrit
9	fais	faisais	ai fait	fis	avais fait
	fais	faisais	as fait	fis	avais fait
faire	fait	faisait	a fait	fit	avait fait
faisant	faisons	faisions	avons fait	fîmes	avions fait
fait	faites	faisiez	avez fait	fîtes	aviez fait
	font	faisaient	ont fait	firent	avaient fait
10	lis	lisais	ai lu	lus	avais lu
	lis	lisais	as lu	lus	avais lu
lire	lit	lisait	a lu	lut	avait lu
lisant	lisons	lisions	avons lu	lûmes	avions lu
lu	lisez	lisiez	avez lu	lûtes	aviez lu
	lisent	lisaient	ont lu	lurent	avaient lu
11	mets	mettais	ai mis	mis	avais mis
	mets	mettais	as mis	mis	avais mis
mettre	met	mettait	a mis	mit	avait mis
mettant	mettons	mettions	avons mis	mîmes	avions mis
mis	mettez	mettiez	avez mis	mîtes	aviez mis
	mettent	mettaient	ont mis	mirent	avaient mis
12	meurs	mourais	suis mort(e)	mourus	étais mort(e)
	meurs	mourais	es mort(e)	mourus	étais mort(e)
mourir	meurt	mourait	est mort(e)	mourut	était mort(e)
mourant	mourons	mourions	sommes mort(e)s	mourûmes	étions mort(e)s
mort	mourez	mouriez	êtes mort(e)(s)	mourûtes	étiez mort(e)(s)
	meurent	mouraient	sont mort(e)s	moururent	étaient mort(e)s

	Futur antérieur	Conditionnel		Impératif	Subjonctif	
Futur		Présent	Passé		Présent	Passé composé du subjonctif
dirai	aurai dit	dirais	aurais dit		dise	aie dit
diras	auras dit	dirais	aurais dit	dis	dises	aies dit
dira	aura dit	dirait	aurait dit		dise	ait dit
dirons	aurons dit	dirions	aurions dit	disons	disions	ayons dit
direz	aurez dit	diriez	auriez dit	dites	disiez	ayez dit
diront	auront dit	diraient	auraient dit		disent	aient dit
écrirai	aurai écrit	écrirais	aurais écrit		écrive	aie écrit
écriras	auras écrit	écrirais	aurais écrit	écris	écrives	aies écrit
écrira	aura écrit	écrirait	aurait écrit		écrive	ait écrit
écrirons	aurons écrit	écririons	aurions écrit	écrivons	écrivions	ayons écrit
écrirez	aurez écrit	écririez	auriez écrit	écrivez	écriviez	ayez écrit
écriront	auront écrit	écriraient	auraient écrit		écrivent	aient écrit
ferai	aurai fait	ferais	aurais fait		fasse	aie fait
feras	auras fait	ferais	aurais fait	fais	fasses	aies fait
fera	aura fait	ferait	aurait fait		fasse	ait fait
ferons	aurons fait	ferions	aurions fait	faisons	fassions	ayons fait
ferez	aurez fait	feriez	auriez fait	faites	fassiez	ayez fait
feront	auront fait	feraient	auraient fait		fassent	aient fait
lirai	aurai lu	lirais	aurais lu		lise	aie lu
liras	auras lu	lirais	aurais lu	lis	lises	aies lu
lira	aura lu	lirait	aurait lu		lise	ait lu
lirons	aurons lu	lirions	aurions lu	lisons	lisions	ayons lu
lirez	aurez lu	liriez	auriez lu	lisez	lisiez	ayez lu
liront	auront lu	liraient	auraient lu		lisent	aient lu
mettrai	aurai mis	mettrais	aurais mis		mette	aie mis
mettras	auras mis	mettrais	aurais mis	mets	mettes	aies mis
mettra	aura mis	mettrait	aurait mis		mette	ait mis
mettrons	aurons mis	mettrions	aurions mis	mettons	mettions	ayons mis
mettrez	aurez mis	mettriez	auriez mis	mettez	mettiez	ayez mis
mettront	auront mis	mettraient	auraient mis		mettent	aient mis
mourrai	serai mort(e)	mourrais	serais mort(e)		meure	sois mort(e)
mourras	seras mort(e)	mourrais	serais mort(e)	meurs	meures	sois mort(e)
mourra	sera mort(e)	mourrait	serait mort(e)		meure	soit mort(e)
mourrons	serons mort(e)s	mourrions	serions mort(e)s	mourons	mourions	soyons mort(e)s
mourrez	serez mort(e)(s)	mourriez	seriez mort(e)(s)	mourez	mouriez	soyez mort(e)(s)
mourront	seront mort(e)s	mourraient	seraient mort(e)s		meurent	soient mort(e)s

Infinitif Participes	Présent	Imparfait	Passé composé	Passé simple	Plus-que-parfait
13	nais	naissais	suis né(e)	naquis	étais né(e)
	nais	naissais	es né(e)	naquis	étais né(e)
naître	naît	naissait	est né(e)	naquit	était né(e)
naissant	naissons	naissions	sommes né(e)s	naquîmes	étions né(e)s
né	naissez	naissiez	êtes né(e)(s)	naquîtes	étiez né(e)(s)
	naissent	naissaient	sont né(e)s	naquirent	étaient né(e)s
14	offre	offrais	ai offert	offris	avais offert
	offres	offrais	as offert	offris	avais offert
offrir	offre	offrait	a offert	offrit	avait offert
offrant	offrons	offrions	avons offert	offrîmes	avions offert
offert	offrez	offriez	avez offert	offrîtes	aviez offert
	offrent	offraient	ont offert	offrirent	avaient offert
15	ouvre	ouvrais	ai ouvert	ouvris	avais ouvert
	ouvres	ouvrais	as ouvert	ouvris	avais ouvert
ouvrir	ouvre	ouvrait	a ouvert	ouvrit	avait ouvert
ouvrant	ouvrons	ouvrions	avons ouvert	ouvrîmes	avions ouvert
ouvert	ouvrez	ouvriez	avez ouvert	ouvrîtes	aviez ouvert
	ouvrent	ouvraient	ont ouvert	ouvrirent	avaient ouvert
16	plais	plaisais	ai plu	plus	avais plu
	plais	plaisais	as plu	plus	avais plu
plaire	plaît	plaisait	a plu	plut	avait plu
plaisant	plaisons	plaisions	avons plu	plûmes	avions plu
plu	plaisez	plaisiez	avez plu	plûtes	aviez plu
	plaisent	plaisaient	ont plu	plurent	avaient plu
17	peux	pouvais	ai pu	pus	avais pu
	peux	pouvais	as pu	pus	avais pu
pouvoir	peut	pouvait	a pu	put	avait pu
pouvant	pouvons	pouvions	avons pu	pûmes	avions pu
pu	pouvez	pouviez	avez pu	pûtes	aviez pu
	peuvent	pouvaient	ont pu	purent	avaient pu
18	prends	prenais	ai pris	pris	avais pris
	prends	prenais	as pris	pris	avais pris
prendre	prend	prenait	a pris	prit	avait pris
prenant	prenons	prenions	avons pris	prîmes	avions pris
pris	prenez	preniez	avez pris	prîtes	aviez pris
	prennent	prenaient	ont pris	prirent	avaient pris

Indicatif

		Conditionnel		Impératif	Subjonctif	
Futur	Futur antérieur	Présent	Passé		Présent	Passé composé du subjonctif
naîtrai	serai né(e)	naîtrais	serais né(e)		naisse	sois né(e)
naîtras	seras né(e)	naîtrais	serais né(e)	nais	naisses	sois né(e)
naîtra	sera né(e)	naîtrait	serait né(e)		naisse	soit né(e)
naîtrons	serons né(e)s	naîtrions	serions né(e)s	naissons	naissions	soyons né(e)s
naîtrez	serez né(e)(s)	naîtriez	seriez né(e)(s)	naissez	naissiez	soyez né(e)(s)
naîtront	seront né(e)s	naîtraient	seraient né(e)s		naissent	soient né(e)s
offrirai	aurai offert	offrirais	aurais offert		offre	aie offert
offriras	auras offert	offrirais	aurais offert	offre	offres	aies offert
offrira	aura offert	offrirait	aurait offert		offre	ait offert
offrirons	aurons offert	offririons	aurions offert	offrons	offrions	ayons offert
offrirez	aurez offert	offririez	auriez offert	offrez	offriez	ayez offert
offriront	auront offert	offriraient	auraient offert		offrent	aient offert
ouvrirai	aurai ouvert	ouvrirais	aurais ouvert		ouvre	aie ouvert
ouvriras	auras ouvert	ouvrirais	aurais ouvert	ouvre	ouvres	aies ouvert
ouvrira	aura ouvert	ouvrirait	aurait ouvert		ouvre	ait ouvert
ouvrirons	aurons ouvert	ouvririons	aurions ouvert	ouvrons	ouvrions	ayons ouvert
ouvrirez	aurez ouvert	ouvririez	auriez ouvert	ouvrez	ouvriez	ayez ouvert
ouvriront	auront ouvert	ouvriraient	auraient ouvert		ouvrent	aient ouvert
plairai	aurai plu	plairais	aurais plu		plaise	aie plu
plairas	auras plu	plairais	aurais plu	plais	plaises	aies plu
plaira	aura plu	plairait	aurait plu		plaise	ait plu
plairons	aurons plu	plairions	aurions plu	plaisons	plaisions	ayons plu
plairez	aurez plu	plairiez	auriez plu	plaisez	plaisiez	ayez plu
plairont	auront plu	plairaient	auraient plu		plaisent	aient plu
pourrai	aurai pu	pourrais	aurais pu		puisse	aie pu
pourras	auras pu	pourrais	aurais pu	(pas d'impératif)	puisses	aies pu
pourra	aura pu	pourrait	aurait pu		puisse	ait pu
pourrons	aurons pu	pourrions	aurions pu		puissions	ayons pu
pourrez	aurez pu	pourriez	auriez pu		puissiez	ayez pu
pourront	auront pu	pourraient	auraient pu		puissent	aient pu
prendrai	aurai pris	prendrais	aurais pris		prenne	aie pris
prendras	auras pris	prendrais	aurais pris	prends	prennes	aies pris
prendra	aura pris	prendrait	aurait pris		prenne	ait pris
prendrons	aurons pris	prendrions	aurions pris	prenons	prenions	ayons pris
prendrez	aurez pris	prendriez	auriez pris	prenez	preniez	ayez pris
prendront	auront pris	prendraient	auraient pris		prennent	aient pris

Infinitif Participes	Présent	Imparfait	Passé composé	Passé simple	Plus-que-parfait
19	reçois	recevais	ai reçu	reçus	avais reçu
	reçois	recevais	as reçu	reçus	avais reçu
recevoir	reçoit	recevait	a reçu	reçut	avait reçu
recevant	recevons	recevions	avons reçu	reçûmes	avions reçu
reçu	recevez	receviez	avez reçu	reçûtes	aviez reçu
	reçoivent	recevaient	ont reçu	reçurent	avaient reçu
20	ris	riais	ai ri	ris	avais ri
	ris	riais	as ri	ris	avais ri
rire	rit	riait	a ri	rit	avait ri
riant	rions	riions	avons ri	rîmes	avions ri
ri	riez	riiez	avez ri	rîtes	aviez ri
	rient	riaient	ont ri	rirent	avaient ri
21	sais	savais	ai su	sus	avais su
	sais	savais	as su	sus	avais su
savoir	sait	savait	a su	sut	avait su
sachant	savons	savions	avons su	sûmes	avions su
su	savez	saviez	avez su	sûtes	aviez su
	savent	savaient	ont su	surent	avaient su
22	suis	suivais	ai suivi	suivis	avais suivi
	suis	suivais	as suivi	suivis	avais suivi
suivre	suit	suivait	a suivi	suivit	avait suivi
suivant	suivons	suivions	avons suivi	suivîmes	avions suivi
suivi	suivez	suiviez	avez suivi	suivîtes	aviez suivi
	suivent	suivaient	ont suivi	suivirent	avaient suivi
23	vaux	valais	ai valu	valus	avais valu
	vaux	valais	as valu	valus	avais valu
valoir	vaut	valait	a valu	valut	avait valu
valant	valons	valions	avons valu	valûmes	avions valu
valu	valez	valiez	avez valu	valûtes	aviez valu
	valent	valaient	ont valu	valurent	avaient valu
24	viens	venais	suis venu(e)	vins	étais venu(e)
	viens	venais	es venu(e)	vins	étais venu(e)
venir	vient	venait	est venu(e)	vint	était venu(e)
venant	venons	venions	sommes venu(e)s	vînmes	étions venu(e)s
venu	venez	veniez	êtes venu(e)(s)	vîntes	étiez venu(e)(s)
	viennent	venaient	sont venu(e)s	vinrent	étaient venu(e)s
25	vois	voyais	ai vu	vis	avais vu
	vois	voyais	as vu	vis	avais vu
voir	voit	voyait	a vu	vit	avait vu
voyant	voyons	voyions	avons vu	vîmes	avions vu
vu	voyez	voyiez	avez vu	vîtes	aviez vu
	voient	voyaient	ont vu	virent	avaient vu

		Conditionnel		**Impératif**	**Subjonctif**	
Futur	Futur antérieur	Présent	Passé		Présent	Passé composé du subjonctif
recevrai	aurai reçu	recevrais	aurais reçu		reçoive	aie reçu
recevras	auras reçu	recevrais	aurais reçu	reçois	reçoives	aies reçu
recevra	aura reçu	recevrait	aurait reçu		reçoive	ait reçu
recevrons	aurons reçu	recevrions	aurions reçu	recevons	recevions	ayons reçu
recevrez	aurez reçu	recevriez	auriez reçu	recevez	receviez	ayez reçu
recevront	auront reçu	recevraient	auraient reçu		reçoivent	aient reçu
rirai	aurai ri	rirais	aurais ri		rie	aie ri
riras	auras ri	rirais	aurais ri	ris	ries	aies ri
rira	aura ri	rirait	aurait ri		rie	ait ri
rirons	aurons ri	ririons	aurions ri	rions	riions	ayons ri
rirez	aurez ri	ririez	auriez ri	riez	riiez	ayez ri
riront	auront ri	riraient	auraient ri		rient	aient ri
saurai	aurai su	saurais	aurais su		sache	aie su
sauras	auras su	saurais	aurais su	sache	saches	aies su
saura	aura su	saurait	aurait su		sache	ait su
saurons	aurons su	saurions	aurions su	sachons	sachions	ayons su
saurez	aurez su	sauriez	auriez su	sachez	sachiez	ayez su
sauront	auront su	sauraient	auraient su		sachent	aient su
suivrai	aurai suivi	suivrais	aurais suivi		suive	aie suivi
suivras	auras suivi	suivrais	aurais suivi	suis	suives	aies suivi
suivra	aura suivi	suivrait	aurait suivi		suive	ait suivi
suivrons	aurons suivi	suivrions	aurions suivi	suivons	suivions	ayons suivi
suivrez	aurez suivi	suivriez	auriez suivi	suivez	suiviez	ayez suivi
suivront	auront suivi	suivraient	auraient suivi		suivent	aient suivi
vaudrai	aurai valu	vaudrais	aurais valu		vaille	aie valu
vaudras	auras valu	vaudrais	aurais valu	vaux	vailles	aies valu
vaudra	aura valu	vaudrait	aurait valu		vaille	ait valu
vaudrons	aurons valu	vaudrions	aurions valu	valons	valions	ayons valu
vaudrez	aurez valu	vaudriez	auriez valu	valez	valiez	ayez valu
vaudront	auront valu	vaudraient	auraient valu		vaillent	aient valu
viendrai	serai venu(e)	viendrais	serais venu(e)		vienne	sois venu(e)
viendras	seras venu(e)	viendrais	serais venu(e)	viens	viennes	sois venu(e)
viendra	sera venu(e)	viendrait	serait venu(e)		vienne	soit venu(e)
viendrons	serons venu(e)s	viendrions	serions venu(e)s	venons	venions	soyons venu(e)s
viendrez	serez venu(e)(s)	viendriez	seriez venu(e)(s)	venez	veniez	soyez venu(e)(s)
viendront	seront venu(e)s	viendraient	seraient venu(e)s		viennent	soient venu(e)s
verrai	aurai vu	verrais	aurais vu		voie	aie vu
verras	auras vu	verrais	aurais vu	vois	voies	aies vu
verra	aura vu	verrait	aurait vu		voie	ait vu
verrons	aurons vu	verrions	aurions vu	voyons	voyions	ayons vu
verrez	aurez vu	verriez	auriez vu	voyez	voyiez	ayez vu
verront	auront vu	verraient	auraient vu		voient	aient vu

Vocabulaire Français-Anglais

The vocabulary contains all words that appear in the **Introduction, Présentation, Préparation,** and **Synthèse** sections except articles, identical cognates, and vocabulary appearing in the **Notes culturelles** and the **Invitation à la lecture.** Irregular noun plurals are included, as are irregular feminine and plural forms of adjetives.

Abbreviations

adj	adjective	*m*	masculine
coll	colloquial	*pl*	plural
f	feminine	*pp*	past participle
irr	irregular	*s*	singular

A

à at, in, to; — **mon avis** in my opinion; — **cause de** because of; — **côté de** beside; — **droite** to the right; — **gauche** to the left; — **la fois** both, at the same time; — **genoux** on one's knees; — **moins que** unless; — **la télé** on TV; — **peu près** approximately, about

abandonner to abandon, give up; **s'— à** to give in to

abolir to abolish

absence *f* absence

absolu absolute

absolument absolutely

abusif, abusive abusive, harmful

accentuer to emphasize, accentuate

accepter to accept

accès *m* access

acclamer to cheer, acclaim

accompagner to accompany

accomplir to accomplish

accord *m* agreement; **être d'—** to agree

accorder to grant

accueillant hospitable

achat *m* purchase; **faire des —s** to go shopping

acheter to buy

acier *m* steel

acte *m* act

acteur *m*, **actrice** *f* actor, actress

actif, active active

activité *f* activity

actualités *f pl* news

actuel, actuelle present

addition *f* bill, addition

additionner to add

adepte *m* follower, initiate

adieu goodbye, farewell

admettre *irr* to admit

admirateur *m*, **admiratrice** *f* admirer

admirer to admire

adopter to adopt

adorer to like, adore

adresse *f* address

adulte *m* adult

adversaire *m* adversary, enemy

aérobique aerobic

aéroport *m* airport

affaires *f pl* business

affiche *f* poster, notice

afficher post, put up a sign; **défense d—** post no bills

affirmer to affirm

afin que in order that

africain African

Afrique *f* Africa

âge *m* age

âgé old

agence *f* agency, bureau; **— de voyage** travel agency

agent (de police) *m* police officer

agir to act

agréable pleasant, nice

agréablement pleasantly

agressivité *f* aggressiveness

agriculteur *m* farmer

agriculture *f* farming

aide *f* help

aider to help, aid

ailleurs elsewhere; **d'—** besides

aimer to like, love; **— mieux** to like better, prefer; **s'—** to like one another

ainsi thus, so

aisé well-to-do

ajouter to add

alcool *m* alcohol

Algérie *f* Algeria

algérien, algérienne Algerian

algue *f* algae

aliment *m* food, food product

alimentaire pertaining to food

alimentation *f* food, nourishment

Allemagne *f* Germany

allemand German

aller *irr* to go; **— à la pêche** to go fishing; **— à pied** to walk; **— bien** to be fine; **— chercher** to go get; **— en classe** to go to class

allumer to light

alors then; **— que** whereas

alpinisme *m* mountain climbing

alpiniste *m & f* mountain climber

amant *m* lover

amateur *m* enthusiast

ambitieux, ambitieuse ambitious

améliorer to improve

américain American

Amérique *f* America

amertume *f* bitterness

ami *m*, amie *f* friend; petit — boyfriend; petite —e girlfriend

amitié *f* friendship

amnésique *m* amnesiac

amour *m* love; — -propre self-esteem; vanity

amoureux, amoureuse pertaining to love

être amoureux to be in love

amplifier to amplify

amusant funny, amusing

amuser to amuse; s'—to have a good time

an *m* year; par — a year; le Nouvel — New Year's

analyse *f* analysis

ancêtre *m* ancestor

ancien, ancienne former, previous, old

anglais English

Angleterre *f* England

animal *m*, animaux *pl* animal

animateur *m*, animatrice *f* host of a TV show

animé lively, animated; les dessins —s cartoons

année *f* year

anniversaire *m* birthday

annoncer to announce

annuellement annually

anonymité *f* anonymity

anorak *m* ski jacket

anthropologie *f* anthropology

anxiété *f* anxiety

août *m* August

apercevoir *irr* to notice, see; s'— de to realize, notice

apéritif *m* before-dinner drink

appareil *m* machine; — -photo camera

apparemment apparently

apparition *f* apparition, appearance

appartement *m* apartment

appartenir to belong

appeler to call, name; s'— to be named

appliquer to apply

apporter to bring

apprécier to appreciate

apprendre *irr* to learn

approbation *f* approval

approprié appropriate

après after

après-midi *m* afternoon

arabe *m* Arab, Arabic

araignée *f* spider

arbre *m* tree; — généalogique family tree

architecture *f* architecture

argent *m* money; — de poche pocket money

arme *f* weapon

armée *f* army

arranger to suit, to be agreeable

arrêt *m* shop; — d'autobus bus stop

arrêter to stop, arrest; s'— to stop oneself

arrivée *f* arrival

arriver to arrive, happen

arrondi rounded, round

arrondissement *m* district, precinct (of Paris)

art *m* art; —s ménagers home economics

artère *f* artery

artichaut *n* artichoke

artificiel, artificielle artificial

artisan *m*, artisane *f* craftsman

artiste *m & f* artist

artistique artistic

ascenseur *m* elevator

Asie *f* Asia

aspect *m* look, appearance, aspect

aspirateur *m* vacuum cleaner

aspirine *f* aspirin

assassiner to assassinate, kill

s'asseoir *irr* to sit down

assez enough, rather; j'en ai — I've had it!

assiette *f* plate

assis seated

assister à to attend, to be present at

associé associated

assurer to assure, insure

astrologie *f* astrology

athlète *m & f* athlete

athlétisme *m* track and field

Atlantique *f* Atlantic

atmosphère *f* atmosphere

atomique atomic

attaché attached

atteindre *irr* to attain, reach

attendre *irr* to wait, to wait for

attention *f* attention; —! watch out! faire — to pay attention

attentivement carefully, attentively

attirer to attract

attraper to catch

attribuer to attribute

au to, at, in; — bas de at the bottom of; — contraire on the contrary; — cours de during; — début at the beginning; — -dessous de under; — -dessus de above; — lieu de instead of; — milieu de in the middle of; — moins at least; — revoir good-bye; — sérieux seriously; — sujet de about

auberge *f* inn; — de jeunesse youth hostel

aucun no, none

augmentation *f* increase

augmenter to increase

aujourd'hui today

aussi too, also; — . . . que as . . . as; — bien que as well as

aussitôt que as soon as

Australie *f* Australia

autant as much, as many; — que as much as

auteur *m* author

authenticité *f* authenticity

auto *f* car, auto

autobus *m* bus

autocar *m* bus

automne *m* autumn

automobiliste *m & f* driver

autoritaire authoritarian, strict

autorité *f* authority

autoroute *f* freeway

autour around

autre other, another; d' — part on the other hand

autrefois formerly

autrement otherwise; — dit in other words

Autriche *f* Austria

aux to, in, with; — États-Unis in, to the United States

avaler to swallow

avance: à l'— in advance; être en — to be early

avant (de) (que) before; en — forward! march on!

avantage *m* advantage

avant-bras *m* forearm

avec with

avenir *m* future

aventure *f* adventure

aventureux, aventureuse adventurous

avion *m* airplane; en — by plane; par — airmail

avis *m* opinion; à votre — in your opinion; changer d' — to change one's mind

avocat *m*, avocate *f* lawyer

avoir *irr* to have; — l'air to seem, appear; — 20 ans to be twenty; — besoin de to need; — de la chance to be lucky; — chaud to be warm; — envie de to feel like, want to; — faim to be hungry; — froid to be cold; — honte to be ashamed; — l'intention de to intend; — lieu to take place; — l'occasion to have the chance; — mal aux dents to have a toothache; — mal à la tête to have a headache; en — marre *coll* to be fed up; — peur to be afraid; — raison to be right; — rendez-vous to have a date or appointment; — soif to be thirsty; — sommeil to be sleepy; — tort to be wrong; — le vertige to be afraid of heights

avouer admit

avril *m* April

B

baccalauréat *m (coll le bac)* French high school diploma

bagarre *f* brawl

bagnole *f coll* car

baguette *f* long, thin loaf of French bread

bain *m* bath; la salle *f* de — bathroom; prendre un — de soleil to sunbathe; —s remous whirlpool; maillot *m* de — swimsuit

baiser *m* kiss

bal *m* dance, ball

balles *f pl coll* dough, francs

banane *f* banana

bananier *m* banana tree

bande *f* band, group; — dessinée comic strip

banlieue *f* suburb

banque *f* bank

baptême *m* baptism

bas *m* lower part; à — down with; au — de at the bottom of; là- — there, over there

bas *m pl* hose, stockings

base *f* basis, base

basé based

bataille *f* battle

bateau *m* bateaux *pl* boat, ship; par — by ship

battre to beat; se — to fight

bavarder to chat

beau, bel, belle, beaux, belles beautiful; il fait — the weather is nice; c'est bien — that's all well and good

beaucoup much, many, a lot

beau-père *m* father-in-law

beauté *f* beauty

bébé *m* baby

belge *m & f* Belgian

Belgique *f* Belgium

belle *f* beautiful

belle-fille *f* daughter-in-law

belle-mère *f* mother-in-law

belote *f* French card game

besoin *m* need; avoir — de to need

bête stupid

bête *f* beast, animal

béton *m* concrete

beurre *m* butter

bibliothèque *f* library

bicyclette *f* bicycle

bien well, very, quite; — sûr of course; eh — well, so; — entendu of course; — des many; — que although; — quelque — que whatever good that

bientôt soon; à — (see you) soon

bière *f* beer

bifteck *m* beefsteak

bijou *m* jewel

bijouterie *f* jewelry store

bilingue bilingual

billet *m* ticket, banknote; — d'entrée entrance ticket

biologie *f* biology

biscuit *m* cracker, cookie

bizarre weird, odd

blanc, blanche white

blessé hurt, wounded

blesser to hurt, wound

bleu blue

bœuf *m* beef, ox

boire *irr* to drink; — un pot (un verre, un coup) *coll* have a drink

boisson *f* drink

boîte *f* box, can; — de nuit nightclub

bombe *f* bomb

bon, bonne good; — marché cheap; la — page the right page; le — vieux temps the good old days

bonbon *m* candy

bonheur *m* happiness

bonjour hello, good day

bonsoir good evening

bord *m* edge; au — de la mer at the seashore; — de mer seashore

bosser *coll* to work hard

botte *f* boot

bouche *f* mouth

boucher *m* butcher

boucherie *f* butcher shop

bouffer *coll* to eat greedily, to gobble

boulangerie *f* bakery

boulot *m coll* work, job

bouquin *m coll* book

bourgeois *m* middle-class, bourgeois

bouteille *f* bottle

boutique *f* shop, store

bras *m* arm; —-dessus —-dessous arm in arm; avoir le — long to have connections

brasserie *f* brewery, tavern

Brésil *m* Brazil

brésilien, brésilienne Brazilian

Bretagne *f* Brittany, province in northwestern France

brièvement briefly

se brosser to brush

brousse *f* brush; bush

bruit *m* noise

brun brown

brutalement brutally, suddenly

Bruxelles Brussels

bruyant noisy

bulletin *m* bulletin; — **météorologique** weather report

bureau *m* office; — **de poste** post office; —**de tabac** tobacco shop

buste *m* upper body

but *m* aim, goal

C

ça (cela) that, it; — **y est!** That's it!

cacher to hide

cachette *f* hiding place; **en —** on the sly

cadeau *m* gift

cadre *m* business executive

café *m* coffee, café; — **au lait** coffee with milk; — **crème** coffee with cream; — **noir** black coffee

cahier *m* notebook

calculer to calculate; **une machine à —** adding machine

calé *coll* good; knowledgeable

Californie *f* California

calme calm

camarade *m & f* pal, friend; — **de chambre** *m & f* roommate

cambrioler to burglarize

cambrioleur *m* burglar

camelot *m* street vendor

caméra *f* movie camera

campagne *f* country, campaign

campement *m* campsite

camper to camp

camping *m* camping; **faire du —** to go camping

canadien, canadienne Canadian

canne à sucre *f* sugar cane

canot *m* canoe, boat

capacité *f* capacity, ability

capital *m* capital, property

capitale *f* capital (city)

capitalisme *m* capitalism

car for, because

caractère *m* character, personality

caractériser to characterize

caractéristique *f* characteristic

carême *m* Lent

carnaval *m* carnival

carnet *m* notebook

carotte *f* carrot

carte *f* card, map; — **postale** postcard; — **d'identité** identification card

cas *m* case

casser to break; — **les pieds** *coll* to bother, be a drag; **se —** to break; **se — la tête** *coll* to rack one's brain

catastrophe *m* catastrophy

catégorie *f* category

cathédrale *f* cathedral

catholique Catholic

cauchemar *m* nightmare

cause *f* cause; **à — de** because of

causerie *f* chat, talk show

ce it, that, he, she, they

ce, cet, cette this, that; **ces** these, those; **ce . . . -ci** this; **ce . . . -la** that

ce que (*object*) what, which

ce qui (*subject*) what, which

ceci this

céder to give in

cela that

célèbre famous

célébrer to celebrate

célébrité *f* celebrity

célibataire *m & f* bachelor, single woman

celui, celle the one; **ceux, celles** the ones

cendre *f* ash

cendrier *m* ashtray

cent hundred

centaine *f* around one hundred

centre *m* center

cependant however

cercle *m* circle, club; — **philharmonique** music club

cerise *f* cherry

ces *see* ce

cesse *f* cease; **sans cesse** constantly

cet *see* ce

cette *see* ce

ceux *see* celui

chacun each

chagrin *m* sorrow, sadness

chaîne *f* chain, channel; — **-stéréo** stereo

chaise *f* chair

chambre *f* bedroom; **camarade de —** roommate

chameau *m* camel

champion *m*, **championne** *f* champion

championnat *m* championship

chance *f* luck; **avoir de la —** to be lucky

changement *m* change

chanson *f* song

chanter to sing, celebrate

chanteur *m* **chanteuse** *f* singer

chapeau *m* hat

chapitre *m* chapter

chaque each

char *m* float, farm wagon

charcuterie *f* pork butcher shop

charmant charming, delightful

charme *m* charm

chasse *f* hunting

chasser to hunt

chat *m* cat

châtain brown (hair)

château *m* castle

chaud warm; **avoir —** to be warm, hot (*of persons*); **faire — ** to be warm, hot (*of weather*)

chauffeur *m* driver

chaussette *f* sock

chaussure *f* shoe

chauvinisme *m* chauvinism

chef *m* head, leader, chief, cook; — **d'orchestre** conductor

chemin *m* path, road; **demander son —** to ask one's way

chemise *f* shirt; — **de nuit** nightgown

chemisier *m* blouse

cher, chère dear, expensive

chercher to look for

chercheur *m* researcher

cheval *m* horse; **faire du —** to go horseback riding; **à —** on horseback

cheveux *m pl* hair

chez to (at) the house of, to (at) the place of business of

chic *m* fashionable

chien *m* dog; — **de garde** watchdog

chiffre *m* number

chimie *f* chemistry

chimique chemical

Chine *f* China

chinois Chinese

chirurgien *m* surgeon

chocolat *m* chocolate
choisir to choose
choix *m* choice
chômage *m* unemployment
chose *f* thing
chouette *coll* neat, cool
cidre *m* cider
ciel *m* sky; le — est couvert it's cloudy
cimetière *m* cemetery
cinéaste *m* film maker
cinéma *m* movies
cinq five
cinquante fifty
circonstance *f* circumstance
circuit *m* circuit, route
citer to quote, cite
civilisation *f* civilization
clair clear; bleu — light blue
clarinette *f* clarinet
classe *f* class; aller en — to go to class
classement *m* categorization
classique classical, classic
client *m* customer
climat *m* climate
cœur *m* heart
coffre-fort *m* safe
coin *m* corner; — du feu fireside
coïncidence *f* coincidence
colère *f* anger; se mettre en — to become angry
colis *m* package
collectif, collective collective
colline *f* hill
colonie *f* colony; — de vacances summer camp
colonisation *f* colonization
coloniser to colonize
colonne *f* column
colorer to color
combien how much, how many; — de temps how long
comédie *f* comedy
comédien *m*, comédienne *f* comedian
comité *m* committee
commandement *m* commandment
commander to order
comme like, as, as if; — dessert for dessert; tout — just as
commémorer to commemorate
commencer to begin

comment how
commentaire *m* comment
commerçant *m* small businessman, shopkeeper
commerce *m* business, trade
commettre *irr* to commit
commun common
communauté *f* community, commune
communiquer to communicate
communisme *m* Communism
compagnie *f* company
comptabilité *f* accounting
compétent competent
compétitif, compétitive competitive
complet *m* suit
complètement completely
complexité *f* complexity
compliqué complicated
comportement *m* behavior
composer to comprise, compose
compositeur *m* composer
composition *f* composition, term paper
compréhensif, compréhensive understnading
comprendre *irr* to understand
compris (*pp of* comprendre) understood, included; y — including
comptable *m* accountant
compte account; — rendu *m* report, review
compter to count
comte *m* count (*title*)
concentrer to concentrate
concerner to concern; en ce qui concerne concerning
concilier to reconcile
concours *m* contest, competition
condamner to condemn
condition *f* condition; à —que on the condition that
conditionnement *m* conditioning
conducteur *m* driver
conduire *irr* to drive; se — to behave; permis *m* de — driver's license
conférence *f* lecture, conference
confiance *f* confidence; faire — à to trust; avoir — en to trust
confier to entrust; se — à to confide in
confirmer to confirm

confiserie *f* candy store
confiture *f* jam
conflit *m* conflict
conformisme *m* conformity
conformiste conformist
confort *m* comfort
confortable comfortable
congrès *m* congress, conference
conjuger to conjugate
connaissance *f* acquaintance; —s knowledge; faire la — to meet
connaître *irr* to know, be acquainted with
connu (*pp of* connaitre) known
conquérant *m* conqueror
conquête *f* conquest
consacrer to devote, give
conscient conscious
conseil *m* council, advice
conseiller to advise
conseiller *m* adviser; — municipal town, city council member
conséquent: par — consequently
conservateur, conservatrice conservative
considéré considered
consommation *f* consumption, use
consommer to consume, use
constamment constantly
constituer to constitute
constructeur *m* builder
construire *irr* to build, construct
contaminer to contaminate
conte *m* story, tale
contemporain comtemporary
content happy
se contenter de to be happy, be content, be satisfied with
continuer to continue
contraire *m* opposite, contrary; au — on the contrary
contre against; par — on the other hand
contrôle *m* control
convertir to convert
copain *m*, copine *f* friend, pal
copie *f* copy
copier to copy
coq *m* rooster
corail *m* coral
corps *m* body; maillot *m* de — undershirt

correspondre to correspond
corriger to correct
corroborer to corroborate
corsage *m* blouse
côte *f* coast; **la Côte d'Azur** the French Riviera
côté *m* side, direction, way; **à — de** beside
cou *m* neck
se coucher to go to bed
couleur *f* color
coupable *m & f* guilty one
coupe *f* cup
couper to cut; **se —** to cut oneself
cour *f* court, courtyard
courageusement courageously
courageux, courageuse brave, courageous
courant; au — up to date
courir *irr* to run
courrier *m* mail
cours *m* class, course; **au — de** during, in the course of
course *f* race; **— à pied** foot race, running
court short
couscous *m* national dish of Algeria
couteau *m* knife
coûter to cost
coutume *f* custom, habit
couturier *m*, **couturière** *f* dressmaker, designer
couvert (*pp of* **couvrir**) covered; **le ciel est —** it's cloudy
couvrir *irr* to cover
craie *f* chalk
cravate *f* tie
crayon *m* pencil
créateur, créatrice creative
créativité *f* creativity
créer to create
crème *f* cream
créole creole
crevé dead tired, collapsed
cri *m* cry, shout
crier to shout, cry out
criminalité *f* crime
crise *f* crisis; **la — d'energie** energy crisis
critique *m* critic
critiquer to criticize
croire *irr* to believe, think
croisière *f* cruise; **— en voilier** sailboat cruise

cruel, cruelle cruel
cuiller or **cuillère** *f* spoon
cuisine *f* food, kitchen, cuisine; **faire la —** to cook
cuisinier *m*, **cuisinière** *f* cook
cuisse *f* thigh
cultivateur *m* farmer
cultivé educated, cultured
cultiver to cultivate
culturel, culturelle cultural
cure *f* **d'amaigrissement** weight-loss program
curé *m* parish priest
curieux, curieuse curious
curiosité *f* curiosity
cynique cynical

D

d'abord first (of all)
d'accord okay, agreed; **être —** to agree
dame *f* lady, woman
Danemark *m* Denmark
danger *m* danger; **être en —** to be in danger
dangereusement dangerously
dangereux, dangereuse dangerous
danois Danish
dans in, into, within
danse *f* dance
danser to dance
danseur, danseuse dancer
dauphin *m* dolphin
davantage more, anymore
de of, from, by, in; (as *partitive*) some, any
débarquer to land
débat *m* debate
débouché *m* job opening
se débrouiller to manage, get along
début *m* beginning; **au —** at the beginning
débutant beginner
décembre *m* December
déception *f* disappointment
décevoir *irr* to disappoint, to deceive
décision *f* decision; **prendre une —** to make a decision
décorateur *m*, **décoratrice** *f* decorator
décorer to decorate

décourager to discourage
découvert (*pp of* **découvrir**) discovered
découverte *f* discovery
découvrir *irr* to discover
décrire *irr* to describe
déçu (*pp of* **décevoir**) disappointed
défaite *f* defeat
défaut *m* fault, failing
défendre to forbid, defend
défense de . . . no . . . (it is prohibited)
défilé *m* parade
défiler to parade, march
définir to define
définitif, définitive final, definitive
définitivement definitely, finally
degré *m* degree
déguisement *m* disguise
déguiser to disguise
dehors outside
déjà already
déjeuner to eat lunch or breakfast
déjeuner *m* lunch; **petit —** breakfast
délicieux, délicieuse delicious
délinquance *f* delinquency
déluge *m* flood, deluge
demain tomorrow; **à —** see you tomorrow
demander to ask; **se —** to wonder
démarche *f* walk, bearing
déménagement *m* moving (residence)
demi half
demi *m* glass of draft beer
démocratie *f* democracy
démontrer to demonstrate
dent *f* tooth; **avoir mal aux —s** to have a toothache **se brosser les —s** to brush one's teeth
dentifrice *f* toothpaste
dentiste *m & f* dentist
déodorisant *m* deodorant
départ *m* departure, start
départemental pertaining to French *départements*
se dépêcher to hurry
dépendre to depend
dépenser to spend
dépenses *f pl* expenses
déplaire *irr* to displease, offend

déprimant depressing

depuis since, for, after, from; — quand since when, how long

député m, députée f congressman, congresswoman

déranger to disturb, bother

dernier, dernière last, most recent

derrière behind

des from, of; (as partitive) some, any

dès que as soon as

désagréable unpleasant

désastre m disaster

descendre to descend, go down, come down

désespoir m despair

désintégration f disintegration

désir m desire

désobéir to disobey

désorienté bewildered

desquels see lequel

dessin m drawing, sketch; — animé cartoon

dessinateur m, dessinatrice f draftsman, cartoonist

dessiner to draw, sketch; les bandes dessinées cartoons

dessous under; ci- — below

dessus above; au- — de prep over, above; ci- — adv above; bras- — bras-dessous arm in arm

destin m fate, destiny

se détacher move away

détaillé detailed

se détendre to relax

détente f relaxation

détester to hate

détruire irr to destroy

deux two

deuxième second

devant in front of, before

développé-couché m push-up

développement m development

développer to develop

devenir irr to become

devenu (pp of devenir) became

deviner to guess

devoir irr must, ought, have to

devoirs m pl homework

diagnostic m diagnosis

dialoguer to communicate

diamant m diamond

dictionnaire m dictionary

dicton m saying, maxim

diététique dietetic

Dieu m God

différent different

difficile hard, difficult

difficilement with difficulty

difficulté f difficulty

digérer to digest

digestif m after-dinner drink

dimanche m Sunday

diminuer to lessen, diminish

dîner m supper, dinner

dîner to dine, eat dinner

diplomatique diplomatic

diplôme m diploma, degree

diplômé having a degree, certified

dire irr to say, tell; c'est-à-dire that is to say; vouloir — to mean

directement directly

directeur, directrice director, head

dirigé directed, run

diriger to direct, guide

discours m speech

discret, discrète discreet

discuter to discuss

disparaître irr to disappear

disparu (pp of disparaître) disappeared

disque m record

dissatisfait dissatisfied

distingué distinguished

distraction f leisure-time activity, amusement, distraction

distribuer to pass out, distribute

divers different, various

diversité f diversity

diviser to divide

dix ten

dizaine f around ten

docteur m doctor

documentaire m documentary

doigt m finger

domaine m area, domain

dominer to dominate

dommage adv too bad

donc then, so, therefore

donner to give

dont whose, of whom, of which

dormir irr to sleep

dos m back; sac m à — backpack; à — de on the back of

doute m doubt; sans — probably

douter to doubt

douzaine f dozen

douze twelve

dramatique dramatic

drame m play, drama, story

drogue f drug, drugs

droit m right, law (profession); faire son — to study law

droit straight, right; tout — straight (ahead)

droite f right; à — to the right

du from, of; (as partitive) some, any

dû, due (pp of devoir) must, have to, due to

duquel m of which

dur hard; travailler — to work hard

durer to last

dynamique dynamic

dynastie f dynasty

E

eau f water

éblouissant dazzling

écaille f scale

échange m exchange

échec m failure

école f school

écologie f ecology

écologique ecological

économe economical, thrifty

économique economical

économiser to save

Écosse f Scotland; la Nouvelle — Nova Scotia

écouter to listen (to)

écran m screen

écrire irr to write

éditeur m editor

éducateur m, éducatrice f educator

éducatif, éducative educational

éducation f up-bringing, education

éduquer to educate

effet m effect; en — in fact, as a matter of fact

également equally

égalité f equality

église f church

Égypte f Egypt

égyptien, égyptienne Egyptian
eh bien well, so
élargir to broaden
électricien *m* electrician
électricité *f* electricity
électrique electric
électronique electronic
élégance *f* elegance
élégant elegant
élémentaire elementary
élève *m & f* pupil, student
élever to raise
éliminer to eliminate
elle she, it; her; elles *f pl* they,
    them; — même herself;
    —s-mêmes themselves
émancipé freed, emancipated
embêter to bother, annoy
embouchure *f* mouth of a river
embouteillage *m* traffic jam
embrasser to kiss, hug; s' — to
    kiss
émigrer to emigrate
émission *f* broadcast, program
emmener to take (along)
émouvant moving, touching
empêcher to prevent
empereur *m* emperor
s'empiler to pile up
emploi *m* job, work
employé *m*, employée *f*
    employee
employer to use
emporter to take along
emprisonner to imprison
emprunter to borrow
en of it, of them, some, any; in,
    into; — colère angry; — effet
    in fact; — face de across
    from; — tête ahead; — tout
    cas at any rate; — train de in
    the process of; — vacances on
    vacation; — ville downtown
enchère *f* bid; vente aux —s
    auction
encore still, yet, even; — une
    fois once again
encourageant encouraging
encourager to encourage
encyclopédie *f* encyclopedia
endroit *m* place, spot
énergie *f* energy
énergique energetic
enfance *f* childhood
enfant *m & f* child

enfin finally, at last, after all
engourdir to grow numb
enlèvement *m* kidnapping,
    abduction
enlever to take off, remove
ennui *m* problem, boredom
ennuyer to bore; s' — to be
ennuyeux, ennuyeuse boring
énorme enormous
enquête *f* survey
enquêteur *m*, enquêtrice *f*
    pollster
enregistré recorded
enrichir to enrich
enseignement *m* teaching
enseigner to teach
ensemble together
ensuite next, then
entendre to hear; — parler de
    to hear about; s'— to get
    along
entendu (*pp of* entendre) heard;
    bien —of course
enterrement *m* burial
enterrer to bury
enthousiasme *m* enthusiasm
s'enthousiasmer to be
    enthusiastic
enthousiaste enthusiastic
entier, entière entire, whole
entourer to surround
entrainer to carry away
entre between, among
entrée *f* entrance, entrée
entreprenant ambitious,
    enterprising
entreprise *f* business;
    administration *f* des —s
    business administration
entrer to enter
entretien *m* maintenance
entrevue *f* interview
envers toward, in regard to
envie *f* desire, envy; avoir — de
    to feel like, want to
environ about, around
envoyer to send
épaule *f* shoulder
épicerie *f* grocery store
épinards *m pl* spinach
époque *f* time, period; à cette
    — -là at that time, in those
    days
éprouver to feel
épuisant exhausting

équilibre *m* balance
équipe *f* team
équipement *m* equipment
érable *m* maple; eau *f* d'—
    maple sap
errer to wander
erreur *f* error, mistake
escalier *m* stairs; — de secours
    fire escape
espace *f* space
Espagne *f* Spain
espagnol Spanish
espèce *f* type, species
espérance *f* hope
espérer to hope
espionnage *m* électronique
    electronic surveillance
espoir *m* hope
esprit *m* mind, spirit; mauvais
    —s evil spirits
esquimau *m* Eskimo
essayer to try, try on
essence *f* gasoline
essentiel, essentielle essential
est *m* east
esthétique esthetic
estomac *m* stomach
et and
établir to establish, set up
établissement *m* establishment
étage *m* floor
étalé displayed
étape *f* stage
état *m* state; les États-Unis the
    United States
été *m* summer; en — in the
    summer
été (*pp of* être) been
éternellement eternally
éternité *f* eternity
ethnique ethnic
étiquette *f* label
étrange strange, odd
étranger, étrangère foreign,
    foreigner; à l'— abroad
être *irr* to be; — à to belong to
être *m* being
étude *f* study; faire des —s to
    study
étudiant *m* student
étudier to study
eu (*pp of* avoir) had
européen, européenne European
eux *m pl* (to) them; — -mêmes
    themselves

évaluer to evaluate
événement *m* event
évidemment evidently
éviter to avoid
évocatif, évocative evocative
évoluer to evolve
évoquer to evoke
exact exact, precise, right
exactement exactly
examen *m* test, exam
excepté except, with the exception of
exceptionnel, exceptionnelle exceptional
excès *m* excess
exemple *m* example; par —for example
exercer to do, practice; — un métier practice a trade
exercice *m* exercise
exil *m* exile
exister to exist; il existe there is/are
exotique exotic
expédition *f* expedition
expérience *f* experience, experiment
explication *f* explanation
expliquer to explain
explorateur *m* explorer
exploser to explode
explosif *m* explosive
exposé *m* oral report
exposition *f* exhibition, exhibit; — universelle World's Fair
expresso *m* espresso coffee
exprimer to express
extra-terrestre *m* extraterrestrial

F

fabrication *f* manufacture, construction
fabriquer to manufacture, make
face *f* face; en — de across; faire —à to face
facile easy
facilement easily
faciliter to facilitate
façon *f* way, manner; de toute — at any rate
facteur *m* factor
facture *f* bill
faible weak
faiblesse *f* weakness

faim *f* hunger; avoir — to be hungry
faire *irr* to do, make; — attention to pay attention; — beau (temps) to be fine weather; — du camping to camp; — confiance to trust; — la connaissance de to meet; — la cuisine to do the cooking; — face à to face; — grève to strike; — mal à to hurt; — le marché to do the shopping; — le ménage to do the housework; — partie to be a part, to belong; — peur à to frighten; — une promenade to take a walk; — remarquer to point out; — des rêves to dream; — du ski to ski; — du sport to participate in sports; — la vaisselle to do the dishes; — un voyage to take a trip; —du vent to be windy; ne t'en fais pas don't worry
fait *m* fact
falloir *irr* to be necessary
familial family
famille *f* family
fantaisie *f* fantasy, fancy, imagination
fantastique fantastic
fascinant fascinating
fataliste fatalist
fatigant tiring
fatigué tired
fatiguer to fatigue, tire
fauché *coll* broke
fauteuil armchair, seat (theater)
faux, fausse false, incorrect; vrai ou — true or false
faveur *f* favor; en — in favor
favori, favorite favorite
féministe feminist
féminité *f* femininity
femme *f* woman, wife
fenêtre *f* window
ferme *f* farm
fermer to close, shut
festivité *f* festivity
fête *f* festival, holiday
fêter to celebrate
feu *m* fire; le — rouge red light
feuilleton *m* soap opera, story
février *m* February

fiancé *m*, fiancée *f* fiancé, fiancée
fiche *f* file card, note card
fidèle faithful, loyal
fier, fière proud
fièrement proudly
fierté *f* pride
figuré figurative
fille *f* girl, daughter
film *m* film, movie; — policier detective film
fils *m* son
fin *f* end
finalement finally
financier, financière financial
finir to finish, end; — par to end up, finally
finlandais Finnish
Finlande *f* Finland
fleur *f* flower
fleuriste *m* florist
Floride *f* Florida
flûte *f* flute
foi *f* faith, belief
foie *m* liver
fois *f* time; à la —at the same time; encore une — again, once more; une — par jour once a day; une — pour toutes once and for all
folie *f* madness
folklorique popular, folk; les danses — folk dances
foncé dark
fonction *f* function, job
fonctionnaire *m* government worker
fonctionner to run, work, function
fondamental fundamental
fondateur *m* founder
fonder to found, establish
football *m* soccer; — américain football
force *f* force, strength
forcer to force, make, oblige
forêt *f* forest
formation *f* training, education
forme *f* form, kind, shape
formidable great, terrific
formule *f* formula
formuler to formulate
fort very, strong, loud
fou, folle crazy
fourchette *f* fork

frais *m pl* expenses
frais, fraîche fresh, cool; **il fait —** it's cool
franc *m* franc
français French
franchise *f* sincerity, frankness
francophone French-speaking
francophonie *f* countries or areas where French is spoken
frapper hit, knock
fréquemment frequently
fréquenter to frequent, go often
frère *m* brother
fric *m coll* money, dough
frigo *m coll* refrigerator
friture *f* fish fry
frivolité *f* frivolity
froid *m* cold; **avoir —** to be cold *(of persons)*; **faire —** to be cold *(of weather)*
fromage *m* cheese
frontière *f* border
frotter to rub; **se —** to rub
frustré frustrated
fumée *f* smoke
fumer to smoke
furieux, furieuse furious, mad
fusil *m* rifle, gun; **— de chasse** hunting rifle
futur *m* future

G

gagner to win, earn; **— sa vie** to earn one's living
galette *f* cookie, pancake
garagiste *m* mechanic, service-station owner
garçon *m* boy, waiter
garde: de — on duty
garder to keep, hold
gardien *m* watchman, guard
gare *f* railway station
gaspillage *m* waste
gâteau *m* cake
gauche *m* left; **à —** to the left
gazeux, gazeuse effervescent, carbonated
gendre *m* son-in-law
généalogie *f* genealogy
généalogique: arbre — family tree
généalogiste *m & f* genealogist
général general; **en —** in general, generally

généralement generally
généralisation *f* generalization
généraliser to generalize
génération *f* generation
générosité *f* generosity
Genève Geneva
genou *m* knee; **à —x** on one's knees
genre *m* kind, type, gender
gens *m & f pl* people, persons
gentil, gentille nice, kind
géographie *f* geography
géologie *f* geology
geste *m* gesture
gestion *f* business administration
glace *f* ice, ice cream
gorge *f* throat
gosse *m & f coll* kid, youngster
gourmand *m* person who likes to eat
goût *m* taste
gouvernement *m* government
gouvernemental, gouvernementaux *m pl* governmental
gouverner to govern, control
grâce à thanks to
graisser to grease
grammaire *m* grammar
grand big, large, great, important, tall
Grande Guerre *f* First World War
grandir to grow up
grand-mère *f* grandmother; **arrière- —** great-grandmother
grand-père *m* grandfather; **arrière- —** great-grandfather
grands-parents *m pl* grandparents
gratuit free
grave serious
gravure *f* sketch, print
grec, grecque Greek
Grèce *f* Greece
grève *f* strike; **faire —** to strike, go on strike
gris gray
gros, grosse large, big, fat
groupe *m* group
guerre *f* war; **la première — mondiale** the First World War
guider to guide, direct
guitare *f* guitar

gymnase *m* gymnasium
gymnastique *f* gymnastics; **faire de la —** to exercise

H

Words beginning with an aspirate **h** are indicated by an asterisk (*).

habiller to dress; **s'—** to get dressed
habitant *m* inhabitant
habiter to live, dwell, inhabit
habitude *f* habit, custom; **d'—** usually
habituellement habitually
habituer to accustom, be accustomed to
***haine** *f* hatred
***hanche** *f* hip
***handicappé** *m* **handicappée** *f* handicapped person
***haricot** *m* bean; **les —s verts** green beans
***hasard** *m* chance
***hausser** to raise, lift, shrug (shoulders)
***haut** high
***hauteur** *f* height
herbe *f* grass
héritage *m* heritage
***héros, héroïne** hero, heroine
hésitation *f* hesitation
hésiter to hesitate
heure *f* hour, time (of day), o'clock; **à l'—** on time; **de bonne —** early; **de l'—** by the hour, an hour; **une demi-—** a half hour; **vers dix —s** around 10 o'clock
heureusement fortunately, happily
heureux, heureuse happy
hier *m* yesterday; **— soir** last night, last evening
hiéroglyphes *m pl* hieroglyphics
hindou *m* Hindu
histoire *f* story, history
historique historical
hiver *m* winter
***Hollande** *f* Holland
***homard** *m* lobster
homme *m* man

***Hongrie** *f* Hungary
***hongrois** Hungarian
honnête honest
***honte** *f* shame; **avoir —** to be ashamed
hôpital *m* hospital
horaire *m* schedule
horizontalement horizontally
horoscope *m* horoscope
hors de outside
***hors-d'œuvre** *m pl* appetizer
hôtel *m* hotel
hôtesse *f* hostess; **— de l'air** flight attendant
***huit** eight
humain human
humeur *f* mood; **être de bonne (mauvaise) —** to be in a good (bad) mood
humour *m* humor
hydraulique hydraulic
hygiène *f* hygiene
humne *m* anthem
hypocrisie *f* hypocrisy
hypocrite hypocritical

I

ici here
idée *f* idea
identifier to identify
identité *f* identity; **carte** *f* **d'—** identification card; **papiers** *m pl* **d'—** identification papers
idiot idiotic
il he, it; **ils** *m pl* they; **il y a** there is (are); ago
île *f* island
illimité unlimited
illustre famous
illustrer to illustrate
image *f* picture, image
imaginaire imaginary
imaginer to imagine
imiter to copy, imitate
immédiatement immediately
immensité *f* immensity
immeuble *f* building, apartment building
impersonnel, impersonnelle impersonal
impôt *m* tax
impressionnant impressive
impressionner to impress

imprimés *m pl* printed matter
imprudent rash, not careful
impulsif, impulsive implusive
impulsivement impulsively
impur impure
incertitude *f* uncertainty
incliner: s'— to bow
inconsciemment unconsciously
inconvénient *m* disadvantage
Inde *f* India
indépendance *f* independence
indépendant independent
indien, indienne Indian
indiquer to indicate, show
indiscret, indiscrète indiscreet, nosy
indiscrétion *f* indiscretion
individu *m* individual
individualiste individualistic
individualité *f* individuality
individuel, individuelle individual
Indo-Chine *f* Indochina
industrie *f* industry
industriel, industrielle industrial
inégalité *f* inequality
inévitabilité *f* inevitability
inexplicable unexplainable
informaticien *m,* **informaticienne** *f* computer programmer
informatique *f* computer science
ingénieur *m* engineer
inhabituel, inhabituelle unhabitual, rare
injuste unfair, unjust
injustement unjustly
inquiet, inquiète uneasy, worried
inquiétude *f* worry
inscription *f* inscription, registration
inscrire *irr* to inscribe; **s'inscrire** to register
insecte *m* insect
insécurité *f* insecurity
inspection *f* inspection
inspiration *f* inspiration
inspirer to inspire
installé settled
institut *m* institute, institution
instituteur *m,* **institutrice** *f* elementary school teacher
instruction *f* education, instruction

insulte *f* insult
insulter to insult
intellectuel, intellectuelle intellectual
intellectuellement intellectually
intelligemment intelligently
interdire *irr* to prohibit, forbid
interdit *(pp of* **interdire)** forbidden
intéressant interesting
intéresser to interest; **s'— à** to be interested in
intérêt *m* interest
intérieur interior; **à l'—** inside
intérieurement inside, on the inside
interplanétaire interplanetary
interprétation *f* interpretation
interprète *m* interpreter
interroger to interrogate, ask
interviewer to interview
intimement intimately
intitulé intitled
intriguer to fascinate, intrigue
introduire *irr* to introduce
inutile useless
inventaire *m* inventory
inventer to invent
invité, invitée guest
inviter to invite
Irlande *f* Ireland
irrationnel, irrationnelle irrational
irrégulier, irrégulière irregular
irresponsable irresponsible
isolé isolated, deserted
isolement *m* isolation
Italie *f* Italy
italien, italienne Italian
italique: en — in italics
ivre drunk

J

jalousie *f* jealousy
jaloux, jalouse jealous
jamais never, ever; **ne . . . —** never
jambe *f* leg
jambon *m* ham
janvier *m* January
Japon *m* Japan
japonais Japanese
jardin *m* garden, backyard

jaune yellow
je I
jeu *m* game; les Jeux
  Olympiques the Olympic
  Games
jeudi *m* Thursday
jeune young; — fille *f* girl,
  young woman
jeunesse *f* youth; auberge *f* de
  — youth hostel
joie *f* joy
joli pretty
joue *f* cheek
jouer to play
jouet *m* toy
joueur *m*, joueuse *f* player
jour *m* day; deux fois par —
  twice a day; tous les —s every
  day; huit —s one week;
  quinze —s two weeks
journal *m*, journaux *pl*
  newspaper; — de mode
  fashion magazine
journalisme *m* journalism
journaliste *m & f* journalist
journée *f* day
judicieusement judiciously,
  wisely
juge *m* judge
juillet *m* July
juin *m* June
jupe *f* skirt
jupon *m* slip
Jura *m* mountainous region in
  eastern France
juridique judicial
jus *m* juice; — d'orange orange
  juice
jusquà as far as, until, up to;
  — ce que until
juste just, correct, right
justifier to justify

K

kilo (= kilogramme) *m* kilogram
kilométrage *m* distance traveled
  in kilometers
kilomètre *m* kilometer

L

la the; it, her
là there; — -bas (over) there; ce
  jour- — that day

laboratoire *m* laboratory
lac *m* lake
laid ugly
laine *f* wool
laisser to leave, let, allow
lait *m* milk
lampe *f* lamp; — de chevet
  bedside lamp
langage *m* language
langue *f* language, tongue
laquelle, *f* which one; lesquelles
  pl which ones
lavabo *m* washbowl
laver to wash; se — to wash
  (oneself); machine à —
  washing machine
le the; it, him
lèche-vitrine *m*; faire du — *coll*
  to windowshop
leçon *f* lesson
lecteur *m*, lectrice *f* reader
lecture *f* reading
légende *f* legend
légué given, bequeathed
légume *m* vegetable
lent slow
lentement slowly
lequel *m* which one; lesquels *pl*
  which ones
les the; them
lessive *f* washing; faire la — to
  do the washing
lettre *f* letter; l'étude des —s
  study of humanities
lever raise; se—get up
leur their; (to) them
liaison *f* relationship
libéral *m pl* libéraux liberal
libérer to liberate
liberté *f* freedom, liberty
librairie *f* bookstore
libre free
lien *m* tie
lieu *m* place; au — de instead
  of; avoir — to take place
ligne *f* line, figure
limite *f* limit; — de vitesse
  speed limit
linguistique linguistic
liqueur *m* liquor
lire *irr* to read
liste *f* list
litre *m* liter
littéraire literary
littérature *f* literature

livre *m* book
livre *f* pound
localité *f* locality, place
logement *m* lodging
loi *f* law
loin far; de — from a distance,
  a long way
loisir *m* leisure, spare-time
  activity
Londres *f* London
long, longue long; le — des rues
  along the streets
longtemps long, a long time
longueur *f* length
lorsque when
loterie *f* lottery
louer to rent
Louisiane *f* Louisiana
loup *m* wolf
lourd heavy
loyer *m* rent
lu (*pp of* lire) read
lui (to, for) him, (to, for) her;
  — -même himself
lumière *f* light
lundi *m* Monday
lunettes *f pl* glasses
lutte *f* wrestling, fight, struggle
lutter to fight, struggle
luxe *m* luxury
Luxembourg *m* Luxemburg
luxuriant luxurious, sumptuous
lycée *m* French secondary school
  equivalent to the American
  high school and junior
  college

M

ma my
machine *f* machine; — à
  calculer calculator; — à écrire
  typewriter; — à laver
  washing machine
magasin *m* store
magie *f* magic
magique magic
magnétophone *m* tape recorder
magnétoscope *m* videotape
  recorder
magnifique terrific, great,
  magnificent
magnifiquement magnificently
mai *m* May

maillot m **de bain** swimsuit; — **de corps** undershirt
main f hand
maintenant now
maire m mayor
mais but
maison f house; **à la** — at home
majestueux, majestueuse majestic
majeur major, of age
majorité f majority
mal m evil, wrong, pain; **avoir** — **aux dents** to have a toothache; **avoir** — **au dos** to have a backache; **avoir** — **à l'estomac** to have a stomach ache; **avoir** — **à la gorge** to have a sore throat; **avoir** — **à la tête** to have a headache
mal badly, poorly, ill
malade sick; **tomber** — to get sick
maladie f sickness, illness
malentendu m misunderstanding
malgache pertaining to Madagascar
malgré in spite of
malheur m misfortune
malheureusement unfortunately
malheureux, malheureuse unhappy, unfortunate
maman f mama, mom
mandat m mandate
manger to eat
manifestation f demonstration
manifester to demonstrate, show, protest
manœuvre m laborer
manquer to miss, lack; — **de tact** to lack tact
manteau m coat
manuel manual
manuscrit m manuscript
marchand m merchant
marchander to bargain
marche f walk, step; — **à pied** walking
marché m market; **bon** — cheap, inexpensive; **le Marché Commun** the Common Market
marcher to walk, run (of a machine)
mardi m Tuesday

mari m husband
mariage m marriage
marié married
se marier to marry
marin pertaining to the sea
marine f navy
Maroc m Morocco
marocain Moroccan
marquer to mark
marraine f godmother
marre: en avoir — coll to be fed up
marron brown
mars m March
martiniquais pertaining to Martinique
masque m mask
match m game; **le** — **de football** soccer game
matérialisme m materialism
matérialiste materialistic
matériel, matérielle material
maternel, maternelle maternal, mother
mathématiques f pl mathematics
matin m morning; **le** — in the morning
matraquage m bombardment, "hammering"
matraque f club
mauvais bad; **il fait** — the weather is bad
me (to) me, (to) myself
mec m coll guy
mécanicien m mechanic
mécanisme m working parts, mechanics
méchant bad, wicked, naughty
médecin m doctor
médecine f medicine (profession)
médical medical
médicament m medicine
meilleur best, better; — **marché** cheaper
membre m member
même same, even, very; **en** — **temps** at the same time; **moi-même** myself
mémoire f memory
menacer to threaten
ménage m household; **faire le** — to do the housework
ménager, ménagère pertaining to the household; **les tâches** housework

ménagère f housewife
mener to lead
mensonge m lie
mentionner to mention
mentir irr to lie
menton m chin
mépris m scorn
mer f sea; **au bord de la** — at the seashore
merci thank you
mercredi m Wednesday
mère f mother; **belle-** — mother-in-law, stepmother
mériter to earn, deserve
mes my
mesure f measure; **dans une certaine** — to a certain extent
mesurer to measure
météorologique meteorological, of weather; **le bulletin** — (la **météo**) weather report
méthode f method
méthodologie f methodology
métier m trade, business, profession
mètre m meter
métro m the subway; **station** f **de** — subway station
metteur en scène director
mettre irr to put, put on; — **pied à terre** to set foot, to land; — **la table** to set the table; **se** — **à** to begin to; **se** — **au travail** to start working; **se** — **en colère** to become angry
meubles m pl furniture
mexicain Mexican
Mexique m Mexico
micro-ordinateur m microcomputer, home computer
midi m noon; **le Midi (de la France)** the South (of France)
mien m, **mienne** f mine
mieux better, best; **aimer mieux** to prefer; **valoir mieux** to be better
milieu m middle, midst, environment; **au** — in the middle
militaire military
mille thousand
milliard m billion
millier m about a thousand
mineur m miner, minor

ministre *m* minister
minorité *f* minority
minuit *m* midnight
missionnaire *m* missionary
mobilité *f* mobility
mode *f* fashion; à la — in style
modéré moderate, reasonable
modérément moderately
moderne modern
modernisation *f* modernization
modeste modest
modifier to modify
moi me, I; — -même myself
moine *m* monk
moins less, minus; à — que
   unless; le — least; — de less
   than; au — at least; de — en
   — less and less; plus ou —
   more or less; deux heures —
   cinq five till two o'clock
mois *m* month
moisson *f* crop, harvest
moitié *f* half; à — half
moment *m* moment; à ce — -là
   at that moment, at that time;
   en ce — at this moment, now
mon my
monde *m* world, people; tout le
   — everybody; tiers — Third
   World nations
mondial world; la première
   guerre —e the First World War
monnaie *f* change, money;
   porte- — *m* change purse
monopole *m* monopoly
monotonie *f* monotony
monsieur *m* Mr., sir; messieurs
   pl gentlemen
monstre *m* monster
mont *m* mountain, mount
montagne *f* mountain
monter to go up, rise, bring up,
   get on, get in
montrer to show
se moquer de to make fun of
morceau *m* piece, bit
mordre to bite
mordu *m coll* fan, fanatic
mort *f* death
mort *(pp of* mourir) died, dead
mort *m*, morte *f* dead person
mosaique *m* mosaic
Moscou Moscow
mot *m* word; —s doux sweet
   nothings

moteur *m* motor
motiver to motivate
moto(cyclette) *f* motorcycle
se moucher to blow one's nose
mouche *f* fly
mouchoir *m* handkerchief
mourir *irr* to die
mouvement *m* movement
moyen, moyenne average
moyen *m* means, middle; — de
   transport means of
   transportation
mur *m* wall
musée *m* museum
musicien *m*, musicienne *f*
   musician
musique *f* music
mystère *m* mystery
mystérieux, mystérieuse
   mysterious

N

nager to swim
naïf, naïve naive
naissance *f* birth
naître *irr* to be born
natation *f* swimming
nationaliser to nationalize
nationalité *f* nationality
Nations-Unies *f pl* United
   Nations
naturel, naturelle natural
nautique: le ski— water-skiing
navet *m* turnip
navigateur, navigatrice
   navigator
navire *m* ship
ne no, not; — . . . aucun (e)
   not one; — . . . guère hardly,
   scarcely; — . . . jamais never;
   — . . . ni . . . ni neither . . .
   nor; — . . . pas not, no; —
   . . . plus no longer; — . . .
   personne nobody; — . . . que
   only, nothing but; — . . . rien
   nothing; n'est-ce pas? don't
   they? haven't you? isn't it?
né *(pp of* naître) born
nécessaire necessary
nécessité *f* necessity, need; par
   — out of necessity
négatif, négative negative
négliger to neglect
neige *f* snow

neiger to snow
Népal *m* Nepal
népalais pertaining to Nepal
nerveux, nerveuse nervous
nettoyer to clean
neuf nine
neuf, neuve new
neveu *m* nephew
névrose *f* neurosis
nez *m* nose
ni . . . ni neither . . . nor
nid *m* nest
nièce *f* niece
Nil *m* Nile
n'importe no matter; —
   comment in any way; — où
   anywhere; — quand any
   time; — qui anyone; — quoi
   anything
niveau *m* level
Noël *m* Christmas
noir black
nom *m* name
nombre *m* number
nombreux, nombreuse numerous
nommer to name
non no; — plus not . . . either,
   neither; mais — ! certainly
   not!
nord *m* North
Normandie *f* Normandy
Norvège *f* Norway
nos our
nostalgie *f* nostalgia
note *f* grade, note
noter to note, notice
notre our
nôtre *m & f* ours
nourrir to feed, nourish
nourriture *f* food
nous we, (to) us
nouveau, nouvel, nouvelle,
   nouveaux, nouvelles new; de
   — again
nouvelle *f* piece of news, short
   story
la Nouvelle-Orléans New
   Orleans
novembre *m* November
nuage *m* cloud
nuageux, nuageuse cloudy
nuancer to shade, vary
nucléaire nuclear
nuit *f* night; boîte de —
   nightclub

numérique numerical
numéro *m* number

O

obéir (à) to obey
objectif *m* objective
objet *m* object
obligatoire obligatory, required
obliger to oblige; **être obligé de
. . .** to be obliged to, have to
observe to observe, notice
obtenir *irr* to obtain, get
occasion *f* opportunity, chance;
d'— used, second-hand
occuper to occupy; **être occupé**
to be busy; **s'— de** to take
care of
octobre *m* October
odeur *f* smell, scent
odieux, odieuse odious
œil *m* **yeux** *pl* eye
œuf *m* egg
œuvre *f* (literary or art) work
officiel, officielle official
officier *m* officer
offrir *irr* to offer
oignon *m* onion
oiseau *m* bird
olympique Olympic; **les Jeux
Olympiques** the Olympic
Games
on one, somebody, we, they,
people
oncle *m* uncle
ongle *m* fingernail
onze eleven
opéra *m* opera
opposé opposite, opposed
opprimer to oppress
optimiste optimistic
orage *m* storm
orateur *m*, **oratrice** *f* orator
orchestre *m* band, orchestra
ordinaire ordinary
ordinateur *m* computer
ordre *m* order
oreille *f* ear
organisateur *m*, **organisatrice** *f*
organizer
organiser to organize
orgueil *m* pride, arrogance
orientation *f* orientation, training
originalité *f* originality
origine *f* origin

ou or; **— . . . —** either . . . or
où where
oublier to forget
ouest *m* West
oui yes; **mais —** of course
ouvert *(pp of* **ouvrir***)* open(ed)
ouvertement openly
ouverture *f* opening
ouvrier *m*, **ouvrière** *f* worker
ouvrir *irr* to open

P

page *f* page
pain *m* bread
pakistanais Pakistani
palais *m* palace
palmier *m* palm tree
pancarte *f* placard, sign
panique *f* panic
panneau *m* panel, board; **—
d'affichage** bulletin board
pantalon *m* pants
papier *m* paper; **—s d'identité**
identification papers
paquet *m* pack
par by, through; **— avion**
airmail, by plane;
— conséquent consequently;
— contre on the other hand;
— exemple for example;
— nécessité out of necessity;
— semaine a week
paradis *m* paradise, heaven
paraître *irr* to appear, seem
parapsychologie *f*
parapsychology
parc *m* park
parce que because
parcourir *irr* to travel through,
go over, peruse
parcouru *(pp of* **parcourir***)* gone
over, traveled
pardonner to pardon
parent *m* parent, relative
paresseux, paresseuse lazy
parfait perfect
parfaitement perfectly
parfois sometimes
parfum *m* perfume, scent
parfumerie *f* perfume (and other
beauty products) shop
parisien, parisienne Parisian
parler to speak, talk
parmi among

parole *f* word, speech
part *f* part; **autre —** somewhere
else; **d'une —** on one hand;
nulle — nowhere; **quelque —**
somewhere; **prendre —** to
take part
partager to share
partenaire *m & f* partner
parti *m* party; **un — politique** a
political party
participer to participate, take
part
particule *f* the **de** in a surname
denoting nobility
particulier, particulière
particular, special
particulièrement particularly
partie *f* part; **faire —** to be a
part; **en grande —** chiefly;
une surprise- — a party
partir to leave, depart
partout everywhere
paru *(pp of* **paraître***)* appeared
pas not, no; **ne . . . —** not, no;
— de . . . no; **— du tout** not
at all
pas *m* step
passé *m* past
passeport *m* passport
passer to spend, pass; **— un
examen** to take a test; **se —** to
happen, take place; **se — de**
to do without
passionnant thrilling, exciting
se passionner to be crazy over,
go in for, be fascinated by
passivité *f* passivity
pastis *m* anise-flavored liqueur
popular in the South of
France
pâté *m* paste; **— de maisons**
block (of buildings); **— de
foie gras** goose liver paste
paternel, paternelle paternal
pathétique pathetic, touching
patiemment patiently
patinage *m* skating; **— sur glace**
ice skating
pâtisserie *f* pastry, pastry shop
patron *m*, **patronne** *f* boss,
owner
pauvre poor, unfortunate
payer to pay, pay for
pays *m* country, area
paysage *m* scenery, landscape

peau *f* skin

pêche *f* peach, fishing; **aller à la — to go fishing**

pêcher to fish

pêcheur *m* fisherman

pédagogie *f* education, pedagogy

pédagogique pedagogical, pertaining to education

se peigner to comb (one's hair)

peindre *irr* to paint

peine *f* trouble, difficulty, sorrow

peintre *m* painter

peinture *f* painting, paint

pelouse *f* lawn

pendant during, for; **— que** while

pénétrer to penetrate

pensée *f* thought

penser to think; **— à** to think of (about); **— de** to have an opinion of

penseur *m* thinker

perdre to lose

père *m* father

période *f* period, time

périodique periodic

périodiquement periodically

périr to perish

permettre *irr* to allow, let, permit

permis *m* **de conduire** driver's license

personnage *m* character *(in literature)*

personnalité *f* personality

personne *f* person; **ne . . . —, — . . . ne** no one

personnel, personnelle personal

personnellement personally

persuader to persuade, convince

persuasif, persuasive persuasive

perte *f* loss

pessimiste pessimistic

peste *f* plague

pétanque *f* a type of outdoor bowling popular in southern France

petit small, little; **— déjeuner** breakfast; **— ami** boyfriend; **—e amie** girlfriend; **—s pois** peas

pétrole *m* oil, gas

peu little, a little, somewhat; **— à —** little by little; **— de** little,

few; **un —** a little; **être — probable** to be unlikely

peuple *m* people, nation

peur *f* fear; **avoir —** to be afraid; **faire —** to scare

peut-être perhaps

pharmacie *f* drugstore

pharmacien *m*, **pharmacienne** *f* pharmacist

phénomène *m* phenomenon

philosophe *m & f* philosopher

philosophie *f* philosophy

photographe *m* photographer

photographie *f* photography

photographier to photograph, take a pciture

phrase *f* sentence

physique *f* physics

physique physical

pianiste *m & f* pianist

pièce *f* piece, room; **— de théâtre** play

pied *m* foot; **à —** on foot

pilotage *m* flying

pilote *m* pilot, driver

piloter un avion to fly a plane

pique-nique *m* picnic; **faire un — to go on a picnic**

pirogue *f* canoe

piscine *f* swimming pool

piste *f* track, trace, trail

place *f* place, seat, (town) square; **à votre —** if I were you

plafond *m* ceiling

plage *f* beach

plaine *f* plain

plaire *irr* to please

plaisir *m* pleasure; **faire — à** to please

plaît: s'il vous — please

plan *m* plan, map

planète *f* planet

plante *f* plant

plat *m* dish; **mettre les pieds dans le —** *coll* to put one's foot in one's mouth

plein full; **en — air** outdoors

pleinement fully

pleurer to cry

pleuvoir *irr* to rain; **il pleut** it's raining

plombier *m* plumber

plu *(pp of* **plaire***)* pleased

plu *(pp of* **pleuvoir***)* rained

pluie *f* rain

plupart *f* most, majority

pluriel *m* plural

plus more, plus; **de —** besides, more; **de — en —** more and more; **en —** in addition, moreover; **il n'y a — que** all that is left is; **le —** (the) most; **ne . . . —** no longer, no more; **non —** not . . . either, neither; **ne — guère** hardly anymore; **— ou moins** more or less; **— que** more than

plusieurs several

plutôt rather; **— que** rather than

poche *f* pocket

poème *m* poem

poésie *f* poetry

poète *m* poet

poil *m* hair; **au —!** *coll* great, terrific

point *m* period; **— d'interrogation** question mark

poire *f* pear

pois: les petits — *m pl* peas

poisson *m* fish

poli polite

police *f* police; **agent de —** policeman; **poste de —** police station

policier, policière: un film — a detective film

poliment politely

politique *f* politics, political

polluer to pollute

Pologne *f* Poland

polonais Polish

polynésien, polynésienne Polynesian

pomme *f* apple; **— de terre** potato

populaire popular

popularité *f* popularity

porc *m* pork

porte *f* door

porter to wear, carry

portugais Portuguese

poser to place, put; **— une question** to ask a question

poseur, poseuse phony, snobbish

posséder to possess, own, have

possibilité *f* possibility, opportunity

postal postal; **une carte —e** postcard

poste *m* post, job; **— de télévision** television set; **— de police** police station

poste *f* mail, post office; **le bureau de —** post office

poulet *m* chicken

poumon *m* lung

pour for, in order to, on account of; **— que** in order that

pourcentage *m* percentage

pourquoi why

poursuivre *irr* to pursue, follow

pourtant however

pourvu que provided that

pousser to push

pouvoir *irr* to be able, can

pouvoir *m* power

pratique practical

pratique *f* practice

pratiquer to do, practice

précédent preceding

précéder to precede

précis precise, exact

précisément precisely

précoce precocious

prédire *irr* to foretell, predict

préférer to prefer

premier, première first; **— ministre** prime minister, premier

prendre *irr* to take; **— des décisions** to make decisions; **— le petit déjeuner** to eat breakfast; **— part** to participate, take part in; **— la succession de** to take over from

préoccuper to preoccupy; **se —** to be concerned with

préparer to prepare; **se —** to get ready

près near, close; **— de** near, close (to)

présentateur *m*, **présentatrice** *f* anchorman, anchorwoman

présenter to present, introduce; **se —** to run (for office)

presque almost, nearly

pressé in a hurry

prestigieux, prestigieuse prestigious

prêt ready

prêter to lend

prévenir *irr* to warn

prévoir *irr* to foresee

prière *f* prayer; **— de . . .** please (kindly) . . .

primitif, primitive primitive

principe *m* principle

printemps *m* spring

priorité *f* priority; **— à droite** yield to the right

pris *(pp of* **prendre***)* taken

prisonnier *m*, **prisonnière** *f* prisoner

privé private

prix *m* cost, prize, value

probabilité *f* probability

probable probable; **être peu —** to be unlikely

probablement probably

problème *m* problem

prochain next

proches *m pl* people close to you

proclamer to proclaim

produire *irr* to produce

produit *m* product

professeur *m* teacher, professor

professionnel, professionnelle professional

profiter de to profit from, take advantage

profond deep

programme *m* program, schedule

programmé computerized

progrès *m* progress

projet *m* project, plan

promenade *f* walk; **faire une — en voiture** to go for a ride

promener to walk (dog, etc.); **se — ** to take a walk

promettre *irr* to promise

promis *(pp of* **promettre***)* promised

pronom *m* pronoun

prononcer to pronounce, say

prononciation *f* pronunciation

propos: à — de about, concerning

proposer to propose, suggest

propre *adj* own, clean

propriétaire *m & f* owner

propriété *f* property

prospérité *f* prosperity

protéger to protect

prouver to prove

Provence *f* Provence (a province in southeastern France)

proverbe *m* proverb

provision *f* provision; **acheter les —s** to buy the groceries

provoquer to provoke, trigger

prudemment carefully, prudently

prudent careful, prudent

psychiatre *m* psychiatrist

psychiatrique psychiatric

psychologie *f* psychology

psychologique psychological

psychologue *m* psychologist

pu *(pp of* **pouvoir***)*

public, publique public

publicitaire *m & f* publicist

publicitaire: le matraquage — constant bombardment of advertising

publicité *f* advertising, publicity

publier to publish

puis then, afterwards, next

puissant powerful

pullover *or* **pull** *m* sweater

punir to punish

punition *f* punishment

pur pure

puritain puritanical

pyjama *m* pyjamas

pyramide *f* pyramid

Pyrénées *f pl* Pyrenees (mountains in southern France)

Q

qualité *f* quality

quand when; **— même** all the same

quant à as for

quantité *f* quantity

quarante forty

quart *m* fourth, quarter; **neuf heures et —** a quarter after nine; **neuf heures moins le —** a quarter of nine; **un — d'heure** a quarter of an hour

quartier *m* neighborhood

quatorze fourteen

quatre four

quatre-vingts eighty

que that, whom, which, what, than; **ce —** what, that which; **plus jeune — moi** younger

than I (am); **ne . . . —** only;
qu'est-ce — what
québécois pertaining to Quebec
quel, quelle what, which
quelque some, any, a few; **—
chose** something; **—s minutes**
a few minutes, **— part**
somewhere
quelquefois sometimes
quelqu'un somebody, anybody;
— d'autre someone else;
quelques-uns *m pl* **quelques-
unes** *f pl* some people, some
question *f* question; **poser une
—** to ask a question
qui who, whom, which, that;
— est-ce? who is it?
quinze fifteen
quitter to leave
quoi what, which; **à — ça sert?**
what good is it?
quotidien, quotidienne daily

R

racine *f* root
racisme *m* racism
raconter to tell
radio *f* radio
raffiné refined
raisin *m* grape
raison *f* reason; **avoir —** to be
right
raisonnable reasonable, sensible
randonnée *f* hike, trip
randonneur *m*, **randonneuse** *f*
hiker
ranger to put away, to put in order
rapide rapid
rappeler to recall; **se —** to
remember
rapport *m* relationship, rapport;
report
raquette *f* racquet
rarement rarely
se raser to shave
rassurer to reassure
ravi delighted
réagir to react
réaliser to realize, accomplish
réaliste realistic
réalité *f* reality; **en —** in reality
récemment recently
récent recent
recette *f* recipe

recevoir *irr* to receive, have guests
recherche *f* research; **faire des
—s** to do research
récif *m* reef
recommander to recommend
recommencer to begin again
reconnaître *irr* to recognize
reconnu (*pp of* **reconnaître**)
recognized
reconstituer to restore,
reconstitute
reconstruire *irr* to reconstruct
recours *m* recourse
reçu (*pp of* **recevoir**) received
redécorer to redecorate
redécouvrir *irr* to rediscover
redire *irr* to repeat
réduit reduced
réel, réelle real, authentic
réexaminer to reexamine
refaire *irr* to redo
se référer to refer
réfléchir to think, consider
reflet *m* reflection
refléter to reflect
réforme *f* reform
réfrigérateur *m* refrigerator
refuser to refuse
regarder to look at, watch
région *f* region
regretter to regret
régulièrement regularly
réhabiliter to rehabilitate
relations *f pl* acquaintances
religieux, religieuse religious
relire *irr* to reread
remarquable remarkable
remarquer to notice, observe
remède *m* remedy
remercier to thank
remettre *irr* to put back,
postpone, turn in; **se —** to
recover
remonter to go back, to date
back in time
remplacer to replace
remplir to fill
remuer to move
rencontre *f* meeting
rencontrer to meet by chance,
find; **se —** to meet
rendez-vous *m* date, meeting
rendre to render, return, make;
— visite to visit
renoncer to give up

rénovateur *m*, **rénovatrice** *f*
renovator
renseignements *m pl*
information
rentrer to return (home)
renvoyer to fire, dismiss
réorganiser to reorganize
réparer to repair
repas *m* meal
repasser to take again, iron
repeindre *irr* to repaint
répertoire *m* list, collection
répéter to repeat
répétition *f* repetition
répondre to answer
réponse *f* answer
reportage *m* reporting, report
reposer to put down; **se —** to
rest
repousser to push away
représentant *m* representative
repris (*pp of* **reprendre**) taken
again, started again
reproches *m pl* reproaches
république *f* republic
réputé famous, known; reputed
réseau *m* network
réserve *f* reservation
réservé reserved
résidence *f* residence; **—
universitaire** dormitory
résigné resigned
résister to resist
résoudre *irr* to resolve, solve
respecter to respect
respiration *f* breathing
respirer to breathe
responsabilité *f* responsibility
responsable responsible
ressemblance *f* resemblance
ressembler to resemble, look like
ressource *f* resource
restaurer to restore
reste *m* rest, remainder
rester to stay, remain
résultat *m* result
retard *m* tardiness, delay; **être
en —** to be late
retenir *irr* to retain, reserve
retour *m* return
retourner to return
retraite *m* retirement
retrouver to find again; meet by
appointment
réunion *f* meeting

se réunir to meet, get together
réussir to succeed; — à to pass (a test)
réussite *f* success
revanche: en — on the other hand
rêve *m* dream
se réveiller to wake, wake up
révéler to reveal
revendication *f* demand
revenir *irr* to come back, return
revenu *m* income
rêver to dream
revoir *irr* to see again; au — good-bye
révolte *f* revolt
se révolter to revolt, rebel
revue *f* magazine
rhume *m* cold
riche rich
ridiculiser to turn to ridicule
rien nothing; ne . . . — nothing; ne . . . — du tout nothing at all; — de spécial nothing special
rigide rigid
rigoureusement strictly, rigorously
rigoureux, rigoureuse rigorous
rire to laugh; pour — as a joke
rire *m* laughter
risque *m* risk
risquer to risk
rituel *m* ritual
rivalité *f* rivalry
rive *f* bank (of a river)
rivière *f* river, stream
rizière *f* rice paddy
robe *f* dress
roi *m* king
rôle *m* role; jouer un — to play a role
romain Roman
roman *m* novel
romantique romantic
rond *m* smoke ring
ronger to gnaw; se — les ongles to bite one's nails
rose pink
roter to belch
rôti *m* roast
rôtisserie *f* roast meat shop
rouge red
rougir to blush
roumain Rumanian

Roumanie *f* Rumania
rouspéter *coll* to gripe
route *f* route, road
roux red (*of hair*)
rudement *coll* very
rue *f* street
russe Russian
Russie *f* Russia
rythme *m* rhythm

S

sa his, her, its, one's
sac *m* bag, purse; — à dos backpack
sacré sacred
Sacré-Cœur *m* church in Montmartre, Paris
sacrifier to sacrifice
sage well-behaved
sagesse *f* wisdom
saison *f* season
salade *f* salad
salaire *m* salary, pay; une augmentation de — a raise
salle *f* room; la — de bain bathroom; la — à manger dining room; la — de séjour living room; la — de classe classroom
salut *m* (*informal greeting*) hi!
salutation *f* greeting, salutation
samedi *m* Saturday
sandale *f* sandal
sans without; — cesse constantly; — doute probably; — que without
santé *f* health; en bonne — in good health; à votre — to your health
satisfaire to satisfy
satisfaisant satisfying
satisfait satisfied
saucisson *m* salami
sauf except
sauter to jump; ça saute aux yeux *coll* it's evident
sauvage wild
sauvegarder to save, protect
savoir *irr* to know, know how
sceptique skeptical
science *f* science; —s politiques political science; —s économiques economics
scientifique scientific; scientist

scintillant sparkling, scintillating
scolaire: l'année — the school year
scrupuleusement scrupulously
sculpteur, sculpteuse sculptor
se (to, for) himself, herself, itself, oneself, themselves, each other
séance *f* session; — de travaux pratiques lab session
secours *m:* au —! help! l'escalier de — fire stairs; la porte de — emergency exit
secrétaire *m & f* secretary
sécurité *f* security
seize sixteen
séjour *m* stay; salle *f* de — living room
sélectif, sélective selective
sélection *f* selection
selon according to
semaine *f* week; une fois par — once a week
semblable such (a), similar
sembler to seem, appear
semestre *m* semester
sénateur *m* senator
sens *m* sense, meaning; direction; — unique one-way (street)
sensationnel, sensationnelle sensational
sensibilité *f* sensitivity
sentier *m* path, trail
sentiment *m* feeling, sentiment
sentir *irr* to smell; feel; se — bien to feel good
séparer to separate
sept seven
septembre *m* September
série *f* series
sérieusement seriously
sérieux, sérieuse serious
serpent *m* snake
serveuse *f* waitress
serviette *f* napkin; *also* briefcase
servir *irr* to serve, to be used; se — to help oneself
ses his, her, its
seul alone, only; tout — all by himself
seulement only
sévère strict
sévèrement severely
sévérité *f* strictness, severity
sexe *m* sex

sexisme *m* sexism
sexiste sexist, chauvinist
shampooing *m* shampoo
short *m* shorts
si if, so, whether; yes
Sibérie *f* Siberia
siècle *m* century
sien *m*, sienne *f* his, hers
signaler to point out, report
signe *m* sign
signifier to signify, mean
simplement simply
simplifier to simplify
sincère sincere
sincèrement sincerely
sincérité *f* sincerity
sinon if not
situé situated
situer to locate, situate
ski *m* ski; le — nautique water-
    skiing
slip *m* underpants
snobisme *m* snobbery
sociabilité *f* sociability
société *f* society
sociologie *f* sociology
sœur *f* sister
soi oneself; en — in and of
    itself; -même oneself; —
    -disant so-called
soif *f* thirst; avoir — to be
    thirsty
soin *m* care
soir *m* evening; hier — last night
soirée *f* evening
soixante sixty
soixante-dix seventy
sol *m* ground, soil
solaire solar
soldat *m* soldier
solde *m* sale
soleil *m* sun; faire du — to be
    sunny; un bain de — sunbath
solidarité *f* solidarity
somme *f* sum; en — all in all, in
    short
sommeil *m* sleep; avoir — to be
    sleepy
sommet *m* top
somptueusement sumptuously,
    richly
somptueux, somptueuse sumptuous
son his, her, its
son *m* sound
sonate *f* sonata

sondage *m* poll
sonner to ring
sorcier *m*; sorcière *f* wizard,
    witch
sorte *f* kind, sort
sortie *f* exit
sortir *irr* to leave, go out, take
    out
souci *m* worry
souffrir *irr* to suffer
soulever des poids to lift weights
soulier *m* shoe
souligner to underline,
    emphasize
soupe *f* soup
souple flexible
sourcil *m* eyebrow
sourd deal
sourire *m* smile
sous under
sous-sol *m* basement
sous-titre *m* subtitle
soutien-gorge *m* bra
souvenir *m* memory,
    recollection, souvenir
se souvenir (de) *irr* to remember
souvent often, frequently
spacieux, spacieuse spacious
spécial special
spécialement especially
se spécialiser to specialize, major
spécialité *f* specialty
spécifique specific
spécifiquement specifically
spectacle *m* show; — de variétés
    variety show
spectateur *m* spectatrice *f*
    spectator
spontané spontaneous
spontanéité *f* spontaneity
sportif, sportive athletic,
    pertaining to sports
stabilité *f* stability
stade *m* stadium
stationnement *m* parking
stationner to park
stéréophonique stereophonic
stérilité *f* sterility
stimulant stimulating
stimuler to stimulate
stricte strict
stupide stupid
stylo *m* pen
su (*pp of* savoir) learned,
    discovered

subdivisé subdivided
substituer to substitute
subtilité *f* subtlety
subvention *f* subsidy
succès *m* success
succession *f* inheritance, estate
sucre *m* sugar; canne *f* à —
    sugar cane
sud *m* South
Suède *f* Sweden
suédois Swedish
suer to sweat
suffire *irr* to be enough
suffisament sufficiently, enough
suffisant sufficient
suggérer to suggest
Suisse *f* Switzerland
suisse Swiss
suite: tout de — immediately
suivant following, next
suivre *irr* to follow; — un
    régime to diet; — un cours to
    take a course
sujet *m* subject; à ce — on this
    subject; au —de about,
    concerning
supérieur superior, higher
supériorité *f* superiority
supermarché *m* supermarket
supersonique supersonic
sur on, upon, about; une
    personne — quatre one person
    out of four
sûr sure, certain; bien — of
    course
surboum *f* *coll* party
surgelé *m* frozen product
sûrement surely
surpopulation *f* overpopulation
surprendre *irr* to surprise
surprise-partie *f* party
surtout especially, above all
symbole *m* symbol
symbolique symbolic
sympathique (sympa *coll*) nice
symptôme *m* symptom
syndicat *m* union
système *m* system

T

ta your
tabac *m* tobacco; bureau de —
    tobacco shop

table *f* table; être à — to be at
the table; **mettre la** — to set
the table; **se mettre à** — to
start eating
tableau *m* picture, table
taille *f* size
taillé *coll* cut out
tailleur *m* woman's suit
se taire *irr* to keep silent
tambour *m* drum
tant so much, so many
tante *f* aunt
taper to type
tapis *m* carpet
tard late
tarte *f* pie
tas: un — **de** a lot of
tasse *f* cup
Tchécoslovaquie *f* Czechoslovakia
tchèque Czech
te (to, for) you, (to, for) yourself
technicien *m*, **technicienne** *f*
technician
technologie *f* technology
technologique technological
teint *m* complexion
tel, telle such
télé *f* TV
téléfilm *m* TV movie
télégramme *m* telegram
téléphoner to telephone
téléphonique pertaining to the
telephone
télévisé televised
tellement so, so much
témoignage *m* testimony
témoin *m* witness
température *f* temperature
temps *m* time; weather; tense;
de — **en** — from time to
time; **en même** — at the same
time; **je passe mon** — **à lire** I
spend (my) time reading; **tout**
le — always
tendance *f* tendency
tendre tender
tendresse *f* tenderness
tenir *irr* to keep, hold; — **à** to
be anxious, to care about; **se**
— **au courant** to keep up to
date; **se** — **droit** to stand up
straight
tente *f* tent
tenter to tempt
terme *m* term

terrain *m* field; — **de camping**
campground; — **de golf** golf
course
terre *f* land, earth; **pomme de**
— *f* potato; — **agricole**
farmland
terriblement terribly
tes your
tête *f* head; **ne vous cassez pas la**
— *coll* don't rack your brain
thaïlandais pertaining to
Thailand
thé *m* tea
théâtre *m* theater; **pièce** *f* **de** —
play
tien *m* **tienne** *f* yours
tiens hey, look
tiers *m* third (*fraction*)
timbre *m* stamp
timide shy
timidement timidly
tirer to pull; — **la langue** to
stick out one's tongue
titre *m* title
toi you
toile cloth; — **d'araignée**
spider's web
tolérer to tolerate
tomate *f* tomato
tombeau *m* tomb, tombstone
tomber to fall; — **malade** to get
sick; — **amoureux** to fall in
love
ton your
tonne *f* ton
tort *m* wrong; **avoir** — to be
wrong
tôt soon; **plus** — sooner
totalement totally
toucher to touch
toujours always, still, ever
tour *m* trip, turn; **faire un** — **en**
ville to take a trip around the
city
tour *f* tower
tourbillon *m* whirlwind
touriste *m & f* tourist
touristique tourist
tourner to turn; to make (*movie*)
tout quite, very; — **aussi** just as;
— **droit** straight ahead; —
d'un coup all of a sudden; —
à fait completely; **pas du** —
not at all; — **seul** all alone;
— **de suite** immediately

tout, toute, tous, toutes all,
every; **tous les jours** every
day; **en** — **cas** at any rate;
— **le monde** everyone
tout *m* whole
tracer to trace
tract *m* leaflet
traditionnel, traditionnelle
traditional
traduire *irr* to translate
train *m* train; **en** — **de** in the
act of, (be) busy
traîner to drag, pull
trait *m* feature
traiter to treat
tranche *f* slice
tranquille quiet
tranquillement quietly
transatlantique transatlantic
transitoire passing, transitory
transport *m* transportation;
moyen de — *m* means of
transportation
transporter to transport
travail *m* work
travailler to work
travaux *m pl* works
travers: à — across
traverser to cross
treize thirteen
trente thirty
très very
trésor *m* treasure
tribu *f* tribe
trimestre *m* quarter
triompher to triumph
trisaïeul *m* great-great-
grandfather; —**e** great-great-
grandmother
triste sad
tristesse *f* sadness
trois three
troisième third
se tromper to be wrong
trompette *f* trumpet
trop too; — **de** too much, too
many
trottoir *m* sidewalk
trouver to find; **se** — to be
located, be found
truc *m coll* whatchamacallit, trick
truffe *f* truffle
tu you
tuer to kill
Tunisie *f* Tunisia

Turquie *f* Turkey
typique typical
tyrannie *f* tyranny

U

un, une one, a, an
uni united, close
unité *f* unity
univers *m* universe
universel, universelle universal
universitaire pertaining to the
    university
université *f* university
urbain urban
usé used, waste, worn out
usine *f* factory
utile useful
utilisation *f* use
utiliser to use

V

vacances *f pl* vacation, holiday;
    une colonie de — summer
    camp; **bonnes —** have a good
    vacation; **être en —** to be on
    vacation; **partir en —** to go
    on vacation
vachement *coll* really, very
vaisselle *f:* **faire la —** to do the
    dishes
valeur *f* value
valise *f* suitcase
vallée *f* valley
valoir *irr* to be worth; **— mieux**
    to be better; **— la peine** to be
    worth the trouble
vanille *f* vanilla
vanité *f* vanity
vaniteux, vaniteuse vain,
    conceited
varier to vary
variété *f* variety
veau *m* veal, calf
vécu *(pp of vivre)* lived
vedette *f* star
végétarien, végétarienne
    vegetarian
végétation *f* vegetation
vélo *m* bike
vélomoteur *m* motorbike

velouté velvety
vendre to sell; **à —** for sale
vendredi *m* Friday
venir *irr* to come; **— de** just, to
    have just
vent *m* wind
vente *f* sale; **— aux enchères**
    auction
ventre *m* belly, abdomen
verbe *m* verb
vérifier to verify
véritable real, genuine
vérité *f* truth
verre *m* glass
vers toward; **— dix heures**
    around ten o'clock
vert green; **les haricots —s** green
    beans
verticalement vertically
vertige *m* dizziness
veste *f* jacket
vêtements *m pl* clothes
vétérinaire *m* veterinarian
viande *f* meat
victime *f* victim
victoire *f* victory
vide empty
vidéocassette *f* videocassette
vie *f* life, living; **en —** alive
vieillesse *f* old age
vieillir to grow old
vierge *f* virgin
vieux, vieil, vieille old
village *m* town, village
ville *f* city, town
vin *m* wine
vingt twenty
viol *m* rape
violemment violently
violer to rape
violon *m* violin
violoncelle *m* cello
vipère *f* poisonous snake
viril virile
vis-à-vis concerning
visite *f* visit; **faire une —** to visit
visiter to visit
visiteur *m*, **visiteuse** *f* visitor
vitamine *f* vitamin
vite quick, quickly
vitesse *f* speed

vitrine *f* store window
vivant alive, *m* living person
vivre *irr* to live; **vive** long live
vocabulaire *m* vocabulary
vogue *f* fashion
voici here is (are), there is (are)
voilà there is (are)
voir *irr* to see, look
voisin *m*, **voisine** *f* neighbor
voisin neighboring
voiture *f* car
voix *f* voice
vol *m* robbery, flight
volcanique volcanic
voler to rob, to fly
volet *m* shutter
voleur *m*, **voleuse** *f* thief
vos your
voter to vote
vôtre your
vôtre *m & f* yours
vouloir *irr* to wish, want
voulu *(pp of vouloir)* wished,
    wanted
vous you; **— -même(s)** yourself,
    yourselves
voyage *m* trip; **faire un —** take
    a trip
voyager to travel
vrai true
vraiment really, truly
vu *(pp of voir)* seen, saw
vue *f* sight

W

W.-C. *m pl* water closet, toilet

Y

y in it, at it, to it, there; **il — a**
    there is (are); ago
yeux *(m pl of œil)* eyes
Yougoslavie *f* Yugoslavia

Z

Zaïre *m* Zaire (the former
    Belgian Congo)
zaïrois pertaining to Zaire
zodiaque *m* zodiac
zut darn, damn

Vocabulaire Anglais-Français

The vocabulary contains a selection of words that might be helpful in completing the **Présentation** and the **Communication** exercises. In addition, certain useful categories of words can be found on the pages indicated below.

Abbreviations

adj	adjective	*n*	noun
adv	adverb	*obj*	object
dir	direct	*pl*	plural
f	feminine	*prep*	preposition
ind	indirect	*pron*	pronoun
inf	infinitive	*subj*	subjunctive
irr	irregular	*v*	verb
m	masculine		

A

a un, une
able: to be —, can pouvoir *irr*
about (approximately) environ; (*in expressions of time*) vers
abroad à l'étranger
accept accepter
accomplish accomplir
according to selon
acquainted: to be — connaître *irr*
across en face de
address adresse *f*
admire admirer
admit admettre
advice conseil *m*
afraid: to be — avoir peur
Africa Afrique *f*
after après
afternoon après-midi *m*
again de nouveau, encore

against contre
age âge *m*; **old —** vieillesse *f*
ago il y a
airplane avion *m*
all tout, toute, tous, toutes; **not at — ** ne . . . pas du tout
allow laisser, permettre
almost presque
alone seul
already déjà
also aussi
although bien que (+ *subjunctive*), quoique (+ *subjunctive*)
always toujours, tout le temps
ambitious ambitieux, ambitieuse
among parmi
ancestor ancêtre *m*
and et
annoy embêter

another un autre, une autre
answer *v* répondre (à); *n* réponse *f*
anxious: be — tenir à
any du, de la, de l', des; quelque(s); en
(not) any more ne . . . plus
apartment appartement *m*; **— building** immeuble *m*
appreciate apprécier
April avril *m*
architect architecte *m*
are: there — il y a
around autour de
arrive arriver
artiste artiste *m & f*
as comme; **— much —** autant que; **— . . . —** aussi . . . que; **— soon —** aussitôt que; dès que

ashamed: be — avoir honte

ask demander (quelque chose à quelqu'un); **— a question** poser une question

assure assurer

at à; **— two o'clock** à deux heures; **— home** chez moi, chez vous, *etc.*; **— least** au moins; **— once** tout de suite; **— what time** à quelle heure

athletic sportif, sportive

attain atteindre *irr*

attend assiter à

attract attirer

author auteur *m*

authority autorité *f*

average moyen, moyenne

avoid éviter

B

backpack sac *m* — à dos

bad mauvais; **it's too —** il (c')est dommage; **the weather is —** il fait mauvais

badly mal

bank banque *f*

be être *irr*; **— able** pouvoir; **— afraid of** avoir peur (de); **— better** valoir mieux; **— sorry** regretter; **—worth** valoir

beach plage *f*

beat *v* battre

beautiful beau, bel, belle, beaux, belles

beauty beauté *f*

because parce que; **— of** à cause de

become devenir *irr*

bed: go to — se coucher

beer bière *f*

before *(time)* avant (+ *noun or pron*); avant de (*before inf*); avant que (+ *subj*); devant (*place*)

begin commencer (à), se mettre à

beginning commencement *m*, début *m*

behave se conduire *irr*

behavior comportement *m*

behind derrière

believe croire *irr*

belong appartenir *irr*; être à

beside à côté de

best *adj* meilleur; *adv* mieux

better *adj* meilleur; *adv* mieux; **be —** valoir mieux

between entre

bicycle bicyclette *f*, vélo *m*

big grand, gros

bilingual bilingue

bill addition *f*, facture *f*

billion milliard *m*

birthday anniversaire *m*

bitterness amertume *f*

blue bleu

blush rougir

body corps *m*

book livre *m*

bookstore librairie *f*

border frontière *f*

bore ennuyer; **be —d** s'ennuyer

boring ennuyeux, ennuyeuse

born né; **be —** naître

borrow emprunter

boss patron, patronne

bother déranger

bottle bouteille *f*, flacon *m*

boundary frontière *f*

boy garçon *m*

brave courageux, courageuse

break casser, se casser

breakfast petit déjeuner *m*; **eat —** prendre le petit déjeuner

bring apporter, conduire *irr*

Brittany Bretagne *f*

brother frère *m*

brush se brosser

budget budget *m*

build construire *irr*

builder constructeur *m*

burglar cambrioleur *m*

bus autobus *m*, autocar *m*; **— stop** arrêt d'autobus

business affaires *f pl*, commerce *m*, enterprise *f*; **—man (woman)** homme *m* d'affaires, femme *f* d'affaires

but mais

butter beurre *m*

buy acheter

by par, de

C

café café *m*

call appeler *irr*; **be —ed** s'appeler

camera appareil-photo *m*; **movie —** caméra *f*

campground terrain *m* de camping

camping camping *m*, **go —** faire du camping

campus campus *m*

can (be able) pouvoir *irr*

Canada Canada *m*

capital capitale *f*

car auto *f*, voiture *f*

card carte *f*; **play —s** jouer aux cartes

care: take — of s'occuper de

careful prudent

carry porter

castle château *m*

cat chat *m*

Catholic catholique

celebrate célébrer, fêter

century siècle *m*

chair chaise *f*

chalk craie *f*

chance occasion *f*, hasard *m*

change *v* changer; **— one's mind** changer d'avis

cheap bon marché

child enfant *m & f*

choice choix *m*

choose choisir

Christmas Noël *m*

church église *f*

cider cidre *m*

city ville *f*

class classe *f* **to go to —** aller en classe

classroom salle de classe *f*

clean *v* nettoyer, ranger; *adj* propre

climate climat *m*

close fermer

clothes vêtements *m pl*

cloudy nuageux, nuageuse; **it's —** le ciel est couvert

cold froid; **(illness)** rhume *m*; **be — (person)** avoir froid; **be — (weather)** faire froid

come venir *irr*; **— back** revenir *irr*, rentrer

commune communauté *f*

competent compétent

complicated compliqué

computer ordinateur *m*; **micro-, home —** micro-ordinateur; **— programmer** informaticien *m*,

informaticienne *f*; — **science** informatique *f*
concerned: be — with se préoccuper de
concerning sur, en ce qui concerne
conflict conflit *m*
congressman (woman) député *m*
construct construire *irr*
continue continuer (à)
cooking cuisine *f*
cool frais, fraîche; **it is —** (*weather*) il fait frais
correct corriger
cost coûter
council member conseiller *m* municipal
count compter
country pays *m*, campagne *f*
course (*in school*) cours *m*; (*of a meal*) plat *m*; **take a —** suivre un cours
cousin cousin *m*, cousine *f*
cream crème *f*
create créer
crisis crise *f*
criticize critiquer
cross *v* traverser
cup tasse *f*
curious curieux, curieuse
cut couper, (**oneself**) se couper

D

dance *v* danser
daughter fille *f*
day jour *m*, journée *f*; **every —** tous les jours
deal (a great deal) beaucoup
decide décider (de)
decision décision *f*; **make a —** prendre une décision
deep profond
defend défendre
demonstrate manifester
describe décrire *irr*
deserve mériter
desk bureau *m*
despair désespoir *m*
destroy détruire *irr*
detective story roman policier *m*
die mourir *irr*
different différent
difficult difficile

dine dîner
disadvantage inconvénient *m*
disappear disparaître *irr*
disappoint décevoir *irr*
disappointment déception *f*
discover découvrir *irr*
discovery découverte *f*
discuss discuter, parler (de)
dish plat *m*, assiette *f*
do faire *irr*; — **without** se passer de; — **the cooking** faire la cuisine; — **the dishes** faire la vaisselle; — **the housework** faire le ménage
dog chien *m*
dollar dollar *m*
door porte *f*
dormitory résidence *f* universitaire dortoir *m*
doubt *v* douter
dream *v* rêver; *n* rêve *m*
dress *v* s'habiller; *n* robe *f*
drink *v* boire *irr*; *n* boisson *f*
drive conduire *irr*
driver chauffeur *m*
during pendant

E

each chaque
ear oreille *f*
earlier plus tôt
early de bonne heure, tôt
earn gagner
east est *m*
easy facile
eat manger
economical économe, économique
education formation *f*, instruction *f*, éducation *f*
either non plus, ou
electronic électronique; — **surveillance** espionnage *m* électronique
employee employé *m*, employée *f*
end fin *f*
enormous énorme
enough assez
enter entrer (dans)
equality égalité
especially surtout
Europe Europe *f*
evening soir *m*
every chaque, tout; — **day** tous les jours

everyone tout le monde
everywhere partout
examination examen *m*; **pass an —** réussir à un examen; **take an —** passer un examen
except sauf, excepté
exercise *n* devoir *m*, exercice *m*
exhibit exposition *f*
expensive cher, chère
explain expliquer
explanation explication *f*
express exprimer

F

factory usine *f*
fail échouer; — **an examination** échouer à un examen
failure échec *m*
fall tomber; — **in love** tomber amoureux; — **ill** tomber malade
family famille *f*
famous célèbre
far loin; — **from** loin de
farmer agriculteur *m*, cultivateur *m*
fascinating fascinant
favorite préféré
fear *v* avoir peur (de)
feel sentir *irr* éprouver; — **like** avoir envie (de); — **good** se sentir bien
few peu (de + *noun*); **a —** quelques
fifty cinquante
fight *v* lutter, se battre; *n* lutte *f*
fill remplir
finally enfin
find trouver; — **out** découvrir
finish finir *irr*
first premier, première; — **of all** d'abord
five cinq
floor étage *m*
flower fleur *f*
follow suivre
for pour, depuis, pendant; car
forbid défendre
foreign étranger, étrangère
former ancien, ancienne
formerly autrefois
fortunately heureusement
free libre, *(cost)* gratuit

friend ami *m*, amie *f*; *coll* copain *m*, copine *f*
friendship amitié *f*
from de
front: in — of devant
full plein
funny amusant
furniture meubles *m pl*
future *n* avenir *m*; *adj* futur

G

game jeu *m*; *(sports)* match *m*
garden jardin *m*
geography géographie *f*
get (become) devenir *irr*; **(obtain)** obtenir *irr*; — **acquainted** connaître *irr*; — **along (manage)** se débrouiller; — **along (together)** s'entendre; — **angry** se mettre en colère; — **married** se marier; — **off (bus)** descendre; — **on (bus)** monter; — **up** se lever
gift cadeau *m*
girl fille *f*
give donner; — **out** distribuer; — **up** abandonner
glad content; heureux, heureuse
go aller *irr*; — **back** retourner; — **to bed** se coucher; — **home** rentrer; — **out** sortir; — **up** monter; — **down** descendre
goal but *m*
good bon, bonne; — **morning** bonjour
good-bye au revoir
government gouvernement *m*
grade note *f*
grammar grammaire *f*
great grand, célèbre; *coll* formidable
grow up grandir

H

half *adj* demi; *n* moitié *f*; — **hour** demi-heure *f*; — **past** et demi(e)
hand in remettre *irr*·
happen arriver, se passer
happiness bonheur *m*
happy content, heureux, heureuse
hate détester
hatred haine *f*

have avoir *irr*
he il; lui
he who celui qui
headache (have a headache) avoir mal à la tête
hear entendre; — **about** entendre parler de
heavy lourd
help *v* aider; *n* aide *f*
her *(dir obj)* la; *(ind obj)* lui; *(after prep)* elle; *(adj)* son, sa, ses
here ici
hers le sien, la sienne, *etc.*
hide cacher
high haut, élevé
him *(dir obj)* le; *(ind obj)* lui; *(after prep)* lui
his *(adj)* son, sa, ses; *(pron)* le sien, la sienne, *etc.*
historical historique
history histoire *f*
hold tenir *irr*
holiday fête *f*
home: at — à la maison, chez moi, chez toi, *etc.*
homework devoir *m*
honest honnête
hope *v* espérer
hospital hôpital *m*
hostel: youth — auberge de jeunesse *f*
hot chaud; **be —** *(person)* avoir chaud; **be —** *(weather)* faire chaud
hotel hôtel *m*
hour heure *f*
house maison *f*; **apartment —** immeuble *m*
how comment; — **long** depuis quand, depuis combien de temps; — **many,** — **much** combien (de); — **old is she?** quel âge a-t-elle?
however pourtant
hungry: be — avoir faim
hurry se dépêcher; **in a —** pressé
hurt faire mal à, blesser
husband mari *m*
hypocrisy hypocrisie *f*

I

I je, moi
ice, ice cream glace *f*

idea idée *f*
if si
immediately tout de suite, immédiatement
important important
impossible impossible
improve améliorer
in dans, en, à; — **front of** devant; — **back of** derrière
increase augmenter
independent indépendant
inhabit habiter
inhabitant habitant *m*
instead of au lieu de
intellectual intellectuel, intellectuelle
intelligent intelligent
intend avoir l'intention de
interest *n* intérêt *m*; *v* intéresser; **to be —ed** s'intéresser à
interesting intéressant
into dans, en; **go —** entrer dans
invent inventer
invite inviter
island île *f*
it *(subj)* il, elle, ce; *(dir obj)* le, la; — **is** *(+ weather expression)* il fait
its son, sa, ses

J

jealous jaloux, jalouse
job emploi *m*, poste *m*; *coll* boulot *m*
journalist journaliste *m & f*
just juste; **have —** venir de *(+ inf)*

K

kill tuer
kind sorte *f*, espèce *f*
know *(something)* savoir *irr*; **be acquainted with** *(someone or something)* connaître *irr*

L

laborer manœuvre *m*
lack manquer (de), avoir besoin (de)
lady dame *f*
lamp lampe *f*
language langue *f*, langage *m*
large grand

last dernier, dernière; passé; —
  night hier soir, cette nuit
late tard; **be** — être en retard
Latin latin *m*
laugh rire *irr*
law loi *f; (profession)* droit *m*
lawyer avocat *m*, avocate *f*
leaflet brochure *f*, tract *m*
learn apprendre (à) *irr*
leave *(something somewhere)*
  laisser; *(a place)* quitter,
  partir de, sortir de
left gauche *f;* **to the** — à gauche
less moins; — **and** — de moins
  en moins
lesson leçon *f*
let's verb stem + *-ons* ending
letter lettre *f*
liberty liberté *f*
library bibliothèque *f*
life vie *f*
like aimer, (se) aimer plaire
  bien, **feel** — avoir envie de
lip lèvre *f*
listen (to) écouter
literature littérature *f*
little *adj* petit; *adv* peu
live (dwell) habiter; **(exist)**
  vivre *irr*
living room salon *m*, salle de
  séjour *f*
located: be — être, se trouver,
  être situé
London Londres *m*
long long, longue; **how** —
  depuis quand; **no** —**er**
  ne . . . plus; — **time** longtemps
look for chercher
lose perdre
loss perte *f*
Louvre Louvre *m*
love aimer, adorer
luck chance *f*
lucky: be — avoir de la chance
lycée lycée *m*

M

magazine revue *f*, magazine *m*
magnificent magnifique
mail *n* courrier *m*
main principal: — **dish** entrée
majority plupart *f*
make faire *irr;* — **the**
  acquaintance of faire la
  connaissance de
man homme *m*

manage se débrouiller
many beaucoup (de); **how** —
  combien (de); **too** — trop (de)
map *(of country, state)* carte *f*
  (of city) plan *m*
marketing *(field of study)*
  marketing *m*
marriage mariage *m*
marry se marier (avec)
match *n* allumette *f*
mathematics mathématiques *f pl*
may pouvoir *irr*
mayor maire *m*
me me, moi
meal repas *m*
mean *v* vouloir dire; **be** — *adj*
  être méchant
medicine médicament *m*,
  (profession) médecine *f*
Mediterranean Méditerranée
meet faire la connaissance de;
  — **by appointment** retrouver;
  — **by chance** rencontrer; —
  together se réunir
memory souvenir *m*
menu carte *f*, menu *m*
method méthode *f*
middle milieu *m*
mild doux, douce
mine le mien, la mienne, *etc.*
miss *v* manquer
Miss mademoiselle *f; abbr* Mlle
modern moderne
money argent *m*
month mois *m;* **in the** — **of**
  August au mois d'août
more plus
morning matin *m*
most le plus; *(superlative* +
  adj.) le, la, les plus + *adj.;* la
  plupart de . . .
motorcycle motocyclette *f; coll*
  moto
mountain montagne *f*
movie cinéma *m*, film *m*
Mr. monsieur *m; abbr* M.
Mrs. madame *f; abbr* Mme
much beaucoup (de); **how** —
  combien (de); **too** — trop
  (de); **as** — autant de; **so** —
  tant de
museum musée *m*
music musique *f*
must devoir *irr;* falloir *irr;* être
  obligé de
my mon, ma, mes

N

name *n* nom *m; v* nommer;
  what's your —? comment
  vous appelez-vous?
nation nation *f* pays *m*
nationality nationalité *f*
natural naturel, naturelle
navy marine *f*
near près (de)
nearly presque
necessary nécessaire; **it is** — il
  faut, il est nécessaire
need *v* avoir besoin (de)
neighbor voisin *m*
neither . . . nor ne . . . ni . . .
  ni
nephew neveu *m*
never ne . . . jamais
new nouveau, nouvel, nouvelle,
  nouveaux, nouvelles; neuf,
  neuve
news: piece of — nouvelle *f;* —
  (in general) les nouvelles *f pl;*
  — *(on TV)* les actualités *f pl*,
  les informations *f pl*
newspaper journal *m*
next prochain
nice *(people)* sympathique;
  gentil, gentille; aimable;
  (things) agréable
night nuit *f;* —**club** boite de
  nuit *f;* **last** — hier soir
no non, pas (de), aucun, ne . . .
  aucun
no longer ne . . . plus
no more ne . . . plus
no one personne, ne . . .
noise bruit *m*
noisy bruyant
none aucun
noon midi *m*
north nord *m*
North America Amérique du
  Nord *f*
not ne . . .pas; — **at all** ne . . .
  pas du tout
notebook cahier *m*, carnet *m*
nothing rien, ne . . . rien
notice remarquer, observer,
  s'apercevoir
novel roman *m*
now maintenant
nuclear nucléaire
numerous nombreux,
  nombreuse

O

obey obéir (à)
obtain obtenir *irr*
occupy occuper
o'clock heure(s)
of de
offer offrir *irr*
office bureau *m;* **post —** bureau de poste *m*
often souvent, fréquemment
old vieux, vieil, vieille, âgé; ancien, ancienne; **How — are you** Quel âge avez-vous?; **I'm 21 years —** J'ai vingt et un ans; **— age** vieillesse *f;* **grow — vieillir**
on sur, à, dans; **— TV** à la télé; **— foot** à pied; **— time** à l'heure
once une fois; **at —** tout de suite
one un, une; *(indefinite pronoun)* on; **that —** celui-là; **this —** celui-ci
only *adj* seul; *adv* seulement; ne . . . que
open *v* ouvrir *irr; adj* ouvert
opera opéra *m*
opinion opinion *f,* avis *m;* **in your —** à votre avis
opportunity occasion *f*
orange orange *f*
order *v* commander, *conj* **in — that** pour que, afin que (+ *subj*); **in — to** pour, afin de (+ *inf*)
organization organisation *f*
other autre
ought, have to devoir *irr*
our notre, nos
ours le nôtre, la nôtre, les nôtres
owe devoir irr
own *v* posséder; *adj* propre
owner patron *m,* patronne *f;* propriétaire *m & f*

P

package *n* paquet *m,* colis *m*
painting tableau *m,* peinture *f*
palace palais *m,* château *m*
parent parent *m*
park parc *m*

part *n* partie *f;* **take — participer** (à); **to be a —** faire partie
party soirée *f,* surprise-partie *f;* **political —** parti *m*
pass: — a test réussir à un examen
past passé *m*
patience patience *f*
pay (for) payer *irr*
pen stylo *m*
pencil crayon *m*
people on; gens *m;* **many — beaucoup de gens**
percent pour cent
performance représentation *f*
perhaps peut-être
period époque *f*
permit permettre *irr*
person personne *f*
persuade persuader
philosophy philosophie *f*
picture tableau *m,* image *f*
place *n* endroit *m,* lieu *m;* **take — avoir lieu**
play: — an instrument jouer de; **— a sport** jouer à; **play** *n* pièce (de théâtre) *f*
please faire plaisir à, plaire
plumber plombier *m*
poem poème *m*
police officer agent (de police) *m*
polite poli
political politique
politics politique *f*
poor pauvre
popular populaire
possess posséder
possible possible
post office poste *f,* bureau de poste *m*
power pouvoir *m*
practical pratique
prefer préférer, aimer mieux
prepare préparer, se préparer (à)
present *adj* actuel, actuelle
president président *m*
pretty joli
prevent empêcher (de)
price prix *m*
prison prison *f*
problem problème *m,* ennui *m*
professional professionnel, professionnelle

program programme *m,* émission *f*
promise promettre *irr*
pronounce prononcer
psychiatrist psychiatre *m*
public public, publique
punish punir
put, put on mettre *irr*
Pyrenees Pyrénées *f pl*

Q

quality qualité *f*
quantity quantité *f*
quarter quartier *m,* trimestre; **— to** moins le quart; **— after** et quart
question *n* question *f; v* interroger; **ask a —** poser une question

R

radio radio *f*
railroad station gare *f*
rain *n* pluie *f; v* pleuvoir *irr*
raise lever, élever
rape *n* viol *m, v* violer
rapid rapide
rapidly rapidement, vite
rather plutôt
read lire *irr*
reading lecture *f*
realize se rendre compte (de), réaliser
receive recevoir *irr*
recently récemment
recipe recette *f*
recognize reconnaître *irr*
reconcile concilier
record disque *m*
refuse refuser
region région *f*
regret *n* regret *m; v* regretter
relative parent *m*
relax se détendre
remain rester
remember se souvenir (de) *irr*
repeat répéter
reply *n* réponse *f; v* répondre
representative représentant *m*
request demander
research recherches *f pl*
resemble ressembler (à)
resource ressource *f*

rest *n* (remainder) reste *m; v* se reposer
restaurant restaurant *m*
result *n* résultat *m*
retire prendre sa retraite
return (come back) revenir *irr;* (go back) retourner; (go home) rentrer; (give back) rendre; *n* retour *m*
rich riche
right *n* droit *m; (direction)* la droite; **to the —** à droite; **be — avoir raison**
river fleuve *m,* rivière *f*
Riviera Côte d'Azur *f*
room salle *f* bed— chambre *f;* **living —** salon *m,* salle de séjour *f*
roommate camarade de chambre *m & f*
run courir *irr; (function)* marcher; **— for office** se présenter
Russia Russie *f*
Russian russe

S

sad triste
salad salade *f*
salary salaire *m*
salesperson vendeur *m,* vendeuse *f*
same même
satisfied satisfait
save: — a person sauver; **— money** économiser
say dire *irr*
school école *f*
scientific scientifique
sculpture sculpture *f*
second second, deuxième
see voir *irr*
seem sembler, paraître, avoir l'air
sell vendre
send envoyer *irr*
sentence phrase *f*
serious sérieux, sérieuse
several plusieurs
she elle
shop *n* boutique; **tobacco —** bureau de tabac *m; v* faire le marché
should devoir *irr*
show montrer

sick malade; **—ness** maladie *f;* **to get —** tomber malade
sincere sincère
sister sœur *f*
sit down s'asseoir; **— —!** asseyez-vous!
ski ski *m;* **— jacket** anorak *m*
skyscraper gratte-ciel *m*
sleep dormir
sleepy: be — avoir sommeil
slowly lentement
small petit
smell sentir
smoke fumer
snake serpent *m*
snow *n* neige *f; v* neiger
so that pour que *(+ subj)*
soldier soldat *m*
solve résoudre *irr*
some du, de la, de l', des; quelque(s); *obj pron* en
something quelque chose (de)
sometimes quelquefois, parfois
soon tôt, bientôt; **as — as** dès que, aussitôt que
sorrow chagrin *m,* peine *f*
sorry: be — regretter
south sud; **— of France** le Midi
speak parler
special spécial
specialist spécialiste *m & f*
spend: — time passer; **— money** dépenser
sport sport *m;* **engage in —** faire du sport
stage étape *f*
stamp timbre *m*
star vedette *f*
state état *m*
station gare *f*
stay *n* séjour *m; v* rester
steak bifteck *m*
stereo chaine-stéréo *f*
still encore
stop (s')arrêter
store magasin *m*
story histoire *f;* conte *f;* **detective —** roman policier *m*
straight tout droit
street rue *f;* **in the —** dans la rue
strength force *f*
stress stress *m*
strict sévère
strike *n* grève *f; v* faire grève
strong fort

student étudiant, étudiante
study *n* étude *f; v* étudier
subject sujet *m;* **academic —** matière *f*
suburb banlieue *f*
subway métro *m;* **— station** station *f* de métro
succeed réussir
suit arranger
sun soleil *m*
sunny: to be — faire du soleil
sure sûr, certain
surprise surprendre *irr,* étonner
swim nager
system système *m*

T

table table *f;* **to set the —** mettre la table
take prendre; *(person)* emmener; *(thing)* emporter; **— a course** suivre un cours; **— a trip** faire un voyage; **— a walk** faire une promenade
talent talent *m*
talk parler
taxi taxi *m*
teach enseigner
teacher professeur *m*
team équipe *f*
telephone *n* téléphone *m; v* téléphoner
television télévision *f,* télé *f*
tell dire *irr;* raconter
tension tension *f*
terrific formidable
test examen *m,* interrogation *f*
text texte *m*
than que
thanks to grâce à
that *(adj)* ce, cet, cette, ces; *(pron)* celui, celle, ceux, celles; cela, ça; que, qui
the le, la, l', les
theater théâtre *m*
their leur, leurs
theirs le leur, la leur, *etc.*
them *(dir obj)* les; *(ind obj)* leur; *(after prep)* eux, elles
then puis, ensuite, alors
there là (-bas); **— is, are** il y a
therefore donc
these *(adj)* ces; *(pron)* ceux-ci, celles-ci

they ils, elles; eux, elles

thing chose *f*

think penser (à + *noun*);
réfléchir; croire *irr*; **what do
you — of that?** qu'est-ce que
vous pensez de cela?

thirsty: **be —** avoir soif

this *(adj)* ce, cet, cette; *(pron)*
celui-ci, celle-ci, ceci

those *(adj)* ces; *(pron)* ceux-là,
celles-là

ticket billet *m*, ticket *m*

time heure *f*, temps *m*, fois *f*,
époque *f*; **on —** à l'heure;
what — is it? quelle heure
est-il? **from — to —** de temps
en temps; **have a good —**
s'amuser; **at that —** à ce
moment-là, à cette époque-là

tired fatigué

to à, en; chez; **in order —** pour;
— the au, à l', à la, aux; **up
—** jusqu'à

tobacco shop bureau *m* de tabac

today aujourd'hui

together ensemble

tomorrow demain

too trop; **it's — bad** il (c')est
dommage; **— many, — much**
trop (de)

tourist touriste *m & f*

town ville *f*

train train *m*

travel *v* voyager

trip voyage *m*; **take a —** faire
un voyage

true vrai

trust faire confiance

truth vérité *f*

try essayer (de)

type genre *m*, espèce *f*, type *m*

U

uncle oncle *m*

under sous

understand comprendre *irr*

unemployment chômage *m*

unfair injuste

union syndicat *m*

university *n* université *f*, *adj*
universitaire

unless à moins que (+ *subj*)

unlikely peu probable

until jusqu'à ce que (+ *subj*)

us nous

use *n* utilisation *f*; *v* se servir
(de), utiliser

useful utile

usually d'habitude

V

vacation vacances *f pl*

vain vaniteux, vaniteuse

vegetables légumes *m pl*

verb verbe *m*

very très; **— much** beaucoup

violence violence *f*

visit *v (place)* visiter; *(person)*
faire une visite à, aller voir,
rendre visite à

vote *n* vote *m*, *v* voter

W

wait *v* attendre

wake up se réveiller

walk *v* se promener, marcher

wall mur *m*

want vouloir *irr*

war guerre *f*

warm chaud *m*; **be —** *(person)*
avoir chaud; *(weather)* faire
chaud

warn prévenir *irr*

wash laver, se laver

waste gaspillage *m*, gaspiller *m*

watch regarder

way façon *f*

we nous

wear porter

weather temps *m*

week semaine *f*

weekend week-end *m*

well bien; **I am —** je vais bien

west ouest *m*

what *(interrogative)* qu'est-ce
qui; que; qu'est-ce que; quoi;
quel, quelle; qu'est-ce que
c'est que; *(relative pron)* ce
que, ce qui

when quand

where où

which *(interrogative)* quel,
quelle; lequel, laquelle;
(relative pron) qui; **which one**
lequel, laquelle

while pendant que

who qui

whose dont

why pourquoi

wife femme *f*; **house—**
ménagère *f*

win gagner

windy: **it is—** il fait du vent

wisdom sagesse *f*

wish vouloir *irr*

with avec

without sans; **do —** se passer
de

woman femme *f*

word mot *m*; *(of song, spoken
word)* parole *f*

work *v* travailler; *n* travail *m*;
literary — œuvre, *f*

worker ouvrier *m*, ouvrière *f*

world monde *m*

worried inquiet, inquiète

worth: **be —** valoir

write écrire *irr*

writer écrivain *m*

wrong faux, fausse; **be —** avoir
tort, se tromper

Y

year an *m*, année *f*

yes oui

yesterday hier

yet encore

you vous, tu; *(dir or ind obj)* te,
vous; *(after prep)* toi, vous

young jeune

your votre, vos

yours le vôtre, la vôtre, *etc.*

youth jeunesse *f*

3 *(top left)*, The Image Works, Inc./Mark Antman. 3 *(top right)*, Monkmeyer Press Photo/Villota. 3 *(bottom left)*, Magnum Photos/Abbas. 3 *(bottom right)*, Magnum Photos/Richard Kavar. 10, Photo Researchers Inc./Helena Kolda. 11 *(top)*, Beryl Goldberg. 11 *(bottom)*, Art Resource/Yan Morvan. 12, The Image Works, Inc./Mark Antman. 15, Stock Boston/Mark Antman. 19, Stock Boston/Cary Wolinsky. 23, Beryl Goldberg. 24, The Image Works, Inc./Mark Antman. 25, Stock Boston/Owen Franken. 29, French Government Tourist Office. 30, Belgian National Tourist Office. 41, Stock Boston/Owen Franken. 45, Quebec Tourist Office. 46 *(top)*, The Image Works Inc./Mark Antman. 46 *(bottom)*, Stock Boston/Tyrone Hall. 47, Art Resource/Edward Jones. 53, Beryl Goldberg. 54, Monkmeyer Press Photo/Rogers. 57, Stock Boston/Mark Antman. 59, Stock Boston/Owen Franken. 65, 66, French Embassy Press & Information Division. 71 *(top and bottom)*, Dorka Raynor. 71 *(middle)*, French Embassy Press & Information Division. 71 *(bottom left)*, Monkmeyer Press Photo/Rogers. 73, Stock Boston/Cary Wolinsky. 79, Rapho/Photo Researchers/Goursat. 82, Photo Researchers Inc./Richard Frieman. 83, French West Indies Tourist Board. 88, DPI/Max Tortel. 89, Dorka Raynor. 91, The Image Works, Inc./Mark Antman. 93, Leo de Wys/R. Laird. 99, The Image Works, Inc./Mark Antman. 100 *(top)*, Monkmeyer Press Photo/Rogers. 100 *(bottom)*, Beryl Goldberg. 105, Robert Rapelye. 106, Beryl Goldberg. 113, Stock Boston/Owen Franken. 121 *(left)*, Monkmeyer Press Photo/Rogers. 121 *(right)*, Stock Boston/Owen Franken. 127, The Image Works, Inc./Mark Antman. 128 *(right)*, Magnum Photos/George Rodger. 137, The Image Works, Inc./Mark Antman. 141, Dorka Raynor. 143, Photo Researchers Inc./Frederick Ayer. 148 *(left and right)*, The Image Works, Inc./Mark Antman. 148 *(center)*, Photo Researchers Inc./Sabyie Weiss. 149 *(left and center)*, The Image Works, Inc./Mark Antman. 149 *(right)*, Beryl Goldberg. 153, Taurus Photos/Eric Kroll. 163, Beryl Goldberg. 167, Stock Boston/Owen Franken. 168, The Image Works, Inc./Mark Antman. 169, Stock Boston/Peter Menzel. 172, The Image Works, Inc./Mark Antman. 176, Stock Boston/Peter Menzel. 182, Stock Boston/Owen Franken. 190 *(left)*, Dorka Raynor. 190 *(right)*, Stock Boston/Owen Franken. 192 *(top)*, Magnum Photos/Marc Riboud. 192 *(bottom)*, Beryl Goldberg. 200, Monkmeyer Press Photo/Silberstein. 201, Monkmeyer Press Photo/Ruth Block. 210 *(top)*, Stock Boston/Cary Wolinsky. 210 *(bottom)*, Stock Boston/Owen Franken. 211, Stock Boston/Cary Wolinsky. 224 *(left)*, Stock Boston/Owen Franken. 224 *(right)*, The Image Works, Inc./Mark Antman. 227, Dorka Raynor. 229 *(bottom)*, The Image Works, Inc./Mark Antman. 229 *(others)*, Stock Boston/Owen Franken. 231, UPI. 244, Monkmeyer Press Photo/Rogers. 245, Stock Boston/Owen Franken. 249, Magnum Photos/René Burri. 250, 253, The Image Works, Inc./Mark Antman. 255, French Embassy Press & Information Division. 262, Monkmeyer Press Photo/Fujihira. 266, The Image Works, Inc./Mark Antman. 268, Monkmeyer Press Photo/Gisele Freund. 279, Contact Press/Christophe Gruner. 280, The Image Works/Mark Antman. 281, HRW/Russell Dian. 282, HRW/François Vikar. 284 *(top)*, Leo de Wys/S. Vidler. 284 *(bottom)*, Interphotothèque Documentation Française. 289, The Image Works, Inc./Mark Antman. 291, Beryl Goldberg. 297, HRW/Russell Dian. 301 *(top)*, The Image Works, Inc./Mark Antman. 301 *(bottom)*, Quebec Tourist Office. 302, Art Resource/Arthur Sirdofsky. 305, Dorka